D0948412

Fundamental Tax Reform

Fundamental Tax Reform

Issues, Choices, and
Implications

edited by
John W. Diamond and
George R. Zodrow

The MIT Press
Cambridge, Massachusetts
London, England

MIT Press books may be purchased at special quantity discounts for business or sales promotional use. For information, please e-mail special_sales@mitpress.mit.edu or write to Special Sales Department, The MIT Press, 55 Hayward Street, Cambridge, MA 02142.

This book was set in Palatino on 3B2 by Asco Typesetters, Hong Kong and was printed and bound in the United States of America.

Library of Congress Cataloging-in-Publication Data

Fundamental tax reform : issues, choices, and implications / edited by John W. Diamond and George R. Zodrow.
    p. cm.
Papers presented at a conference held at the James A. Baker III Institute for Public Policy at Rice University, in Apr. 2006.
Includes bibliographical references and index.
ISBN 978-0-262-04247-5 (hardcover : alk. paper) 1. Taxation—United States—
Congresses. 2. Corporations—Taxation—United States—Congresses. I. Diamond, John W. II. Zodrow, George R.
HJ2381.F857   2008
336.2′050973—dc22   2007018934

10 9 8 7 6 5 4 3 2 1

with special thanks to our parents, who have inspired us in so many ways
Jim Diamond and Lorice Pinney
and
Ada Czeslawa Zodrow and the memory of Leon Zodrow

Contents

Contributors

Henry J. Aaron
The Brookings Institution

James Alm
Georgia State University

Rosanne Altshuler
Rutgers University

Alan J. Auerbach
University of California, Berkeley

Charles L. Ballard
Michigan State University

Leonard E. Burman
Urban Institute

Robert S. Chirinko
University of Illinois at Chicago
and CESifo

John W. Diamond
Rice University

Robert D. Dietz
National Association of Home
Builders

Malcolm Gillis
Rice University

Roger H. Gordon
University of California, San
Diego

Jane G. Gravelle
Congressional Research Service

Harry Grubert
US Treasury Department

Timothy S. Gunning
Rice University

Arnold C. Harberger
University of California, Los
Angeles

Kevin A. Hassett
American Enterprise Institute

Thomas J. Kniesner
Syracuse University

Laurence J. Kotlikoff
Boston University

Edward J. McCaffery
University of Southern California
Law School

Peter Mieszkowski
Rice University

Pamela H. Moomau
Joint Committee on Taxation, US
Congress

Thomas S. Neubig
Ernst and Young LLP

Kathryn Newmark
American Enterprise Institute

James M. Poterba
Massachusetts Institute of
Technology

David Rapson
Boston University

Emmanuel Saez
University of California, Berkeley

Daniel Shaviro
New York University School of
Law

Robin Sickles
Rice University

Joel Slemrod
University of Michigan

Jeff Strnad
Stanford Law School

Alan D. Viard
American Enterprise Institute

George K. Yin
University of Virginia School of
Law

James P. Ziliak
University of Kentucky

George R. Zodrow
Rice University

List of Figures

List of Tables

Foreword by James A. Baker III

Thirty years ago, presidential candidate Jimmy Carter described the federal tax code as "a disgrace to the human race." As President Ford's campaign chairman in 1976, I didn't often find myself in agreement with then-Governor Carter. But when it came to the tax code, he was right. And, sad to say, he would still be right today.

Our federal tax system is unnecessarily complicated, making much of it incomprehensible to anyone but specialized accountants and attorneys. It is financially burdensome to the millions of tax payers who must comply with its byzantine provisions. It fails to reflect adequately the increasingly integrated nature of the modern global marketplace. It is crippled by special-interest loopholes that both drain revenue and undermine public respect for the law. And, perhaps most important, it is too often counterproductive in terms of promoting our vital national goals of higher investment and robust economic growth. In short, our current federal tax system is in acute need of repair and long overdue for a comprehensive overhaul.

This volume attempts to lay out in detail the economic issues that both drive and complicate the effort to reform our tax system. The various chapters discuss the range of subjects—from the behavioral response of individuals and business to taxes to the prospects for simplification under consumption tax—that shape the current academic debate on tax reform. Contributors very much represent a "who's who" among contemporary scholars of public finance. John Diamond and George Zodrow deserve great credit for organizing both this volume and the conference at which the papers were originally presented. The Baker Institute is indeed proud to have them at the helm of our Tax and Expenditure Policy Program.

But addressing the economic issues surrounding tax reform—though vital—will not be enough. Building a political consensus will also be critical. The experience of the Tax Reform Act of 1986 may be useful. As President Reagan's Secretary of the Treasury at the time, I was deeply involved in this effort from inception to enactment.

As passed into law, the tax reform act of 1986 lowered the top personal tax rate from 50 to 28 percent, reduced the number of brackets from 14 to 2, curbed or eliminated deductions and loopholes, and completely removed millions of low-income Americans from the tax rolls. Regrettably, this sweeping reform proved transitory, as subsequent decades saw marginal rates raised and some deductions and loopholes restored. Nonetheless, the Act *did* represent genuine reform of a system that had seemed impervious to fundamental change.

What are the lessons of our experience in 1986? Two loom large.

First, tax reform requires presidential leadership. President Reagan made tax reform a centerpiece of his second-term agenda. Throughout the long and difficult process leading to congressional passage, we at Treasury could count on the President's commitment to reform and his willingness to expend political capital to advance it.

Second, bipartisan support can be decisive. The easy majorities by which tax reform eventually passed the Congress in 1986 bear witness to its broad appeal across the political spectrum. We viewed influential Democrats such as House Ways and Means Chairman Dan Rostenkowski and Senate Finance Committee member Bill Bradley as full partners in our effort to overhaul the tax system.

I believe that the time is ripe again for reform. In late 2005 the President's Advisory Panel on Federal Tex Reform issued several alternative proposals that can serve as the basis for discussion of possible legislation. Volumes like this provide an important public service in delineating the economic rationale for reform. Not least, we should tackle tax reform *because it is the right thing to do.*

I cannot overemphasize this point. All of us—economists, policy makers, and concerned citizens alike—should keep our eyes on the prize: the creation of a simple, fair and pro-growth federal tax system that, in the words of the President Ford's Treasury Secretary, Bill Simon, "looks like someone designed it on purpose." The American taxpayer demands and deserves no less.

Baker was sixty-seventh Secretary of the Treasury and sixty-first Secretary of State. He is currently Honorary Chair of the James A. Baker III Institute for Public Policy at Rice University. This forward draws heavily on his remarks at a conference on Is It Time for Fundamental Tax Reform?: The Known, the Unknown, and the Unknowable *held at the James A. Baker III Institute of Public Policy, Rice University, April 27 and 28, 2006.*

Preface

Reform of the federal income tax system is a perennial policy item on the domestic policy agenda in the United States. Much attention in recent years has been devoted to proposals that are described as "fundamental tax reform," involving either widespread reforms of the existing income tax or its replacement with a new tax based on consumption, chosen from the wide range of consumption tax plans currently under discussion. However, the appropriate direction for such reform is uncertain, as suggested by the November 1, 2005, report of the President's Advisory Panel on Federal Tax Reform. The Advisory Panel recommended two options—a fairly comprehensive income tax and a hybrid income/consumption tax—and discussed at length a third consumption-based tax option. Given the considerable level of uncertainty about the appropriate direction for fundamental tax reform in the United States, an understanding of the complex issues involved in evaluating the many competing alternative tax reform proposals currently under discussion is essential to the sound formulation of public policy in the tax arena.

The papers in this volume reflect the efforts of some of our nation's foremost tax policy experts to advance this understanding. These experts initially presented their papers at an April 2006 conference held at the James A. Baker III Institute for Public Policy at Rice University. They carefully and thoroughly examine a wide variety of issues raised by the prospect of fundamental tax reform, and shed insights on the relative advantages and disadvantages of income and consumption taxation, as well as the many alternative ways of achieving a consumption tax reform.

This volume and the conference that preceded it would not have been possible without a very generous grant from the Alfred P. Sloan Foundation, and we are grateful to the Sloan Foundation, especially

Jesse Ausubel, both for its financial support and its help in planning the conference—including suggesting the "known, unknown and unknowable" theme that provided an organizing framework for this volume. We would also like to thank Baker Institute Director Edward Djerejian for his enthusiastic support of the conference and this volume, our colleagues at the Baker Institute Tax and Expenditure Policy Program, Peter Mieszkowski and Malcolm Gillis, for their wise counsel on numerous issues, and the Baker Institute staff, especially Katie Hamilton, Molly Hipp Hubbard, Damian Falcon, Sonja Fullbright, Nancy Granahan, Ryan Kirksey, Melissa Leuellen, Jason Lyons, Lisa McCaffety, Meredith Montgomery, and Fabian Salz for their assistance throughout the project. Finally, we would like to thank Pareen Bathia and Payton Odom, whose cheerful yet painstaking editorial assistance was essential to the preparation of this volume.

Introduction:
Is It Time for Fundamental
Tax Reform?

John W. Diamond and George
R. Zodrow

Reform of the federal income tax system is a perennial policy item on the domestic policy agenda in the United States, with much attention in recent years devoted to reforms that are described as fundamental restructurings of the existing system (Zodrow and Mieszkowski 2002a). Two general directions are commonly suggested for such fundamental tax reform. The first would build on the successful Tax Reform Act of 1986, moving the tax system further in the direction of a broad-based, relatively low-rate tax on a comprehensive measure of real economic income. Many of these income-based tax reform proposals would include some form of integration of the corporate and individual income taxes to ensure that all income is taxed only once, with much recent attention devoted to plans that would accomplish this at the individual (rather than the business) level, as outlined by the US Treasury (2003). A second approach would introduce a new consumption-based tax to replace the current system, which is a hybrid tax that has both income tax and consumption tax elements. Potential consumption-based tax reforms include taxes on a comprehensive measure of labor compensation such as the Hall and Rabushka (1983, 1995) flat tax and the Bradford (2005) X-tax, taxes on individual cash flow such as the USA (unlimited savings allowance) plan advocated by Senators Sam Nunn and Pete Domenici, as well as transactions-based taxes such as a national retail sales tax or a value-added tax (see Gillis, Mieszkowski, and Zodrow 1996 for descriptions of various plans).

Widespread interest in tax reform led to the formation of the President's Advisory Panel on Federal Tax Reform, which issued its long awaited report in November 2005. Unfortunately, that report reflects very accurately the current status of the debate surrounding tax reform. Specifically, rather than making a single reform proposal, the panel offered two recommendations—a relatively comprehensive

integrated income tax that it described as the simplified income tax
and a hybrid approach that it called the growth and investment
tax, which is largely a consumption tax system based on the Bradford
X-tax and supplemented by a flat low-rate individual level tax on capital income. In addition the panel discussed at considerable length a
pure consumption tax option, also based on the Bradford X-tax, which
it called the progressive consumption tax. This approach, however, did
not achieve the status of a recommendation as it did not receive the
requisite unanimous support.

Given the considerable level of uncertainty about the appropriate
direction for fundamental tax reform in the United States, an understanding of the many complex issues involved in evaluating the wide
range of competing tax reform proposals currently under discussion
is essential to the sound formulation of public policy in the tax arena.
The chapters in this volume reflect the efforts of some of our nation's
foremost tax policy experts to advance this understanding. In each
a wide variety of issues raised by the prospect of fundamental tax
reform are examined, including the relative advantages and disadvantages of income and consumption taxation as well as the many
alternative ways of achieving a consumption tax reform. Each of the
ten chapters that comprise this volume attempts to identify the most
critical issues in the fundamental tax reform debate, and to determine
whether the answers to these questions are known, unknown, or even
unknowable.

The chapters focus on four crucial aspects of fundamental tax reform
in the United States. First, two wide ranging overview chapters consider the general direction that such a change in the tax structure
should take—income or consumption tax reform. Alan Auerbach
begins by examining the strengths and weaknesses of the case for taxation based on consumption rather than income. He then constructs a
simple macroeconomic model to serve as a general framework for analyzing a wide range of specific issues raised by the panoply of current
reform proposals, including the many different forms of consumption
taxes.

Then Daniel Shaviro inquires whether the idealized proposals for
consumption tax reform that are the focus of current debates could
ever survive the political process. He argues that such a pure reform is
highly unlikely, discusses a wide variety of ways in which the pure
proposals might be modified, and concludes that such highly plausible
political adjustments would seriously impair the final product, reduc-

ing or eliminating the gains—especially in terms of simplicity in tax administration and compliance—that otherwise might be obtained from fundamental tax reform.

The next three chapters in the volume examine the effects of fundamental tax reform on businesses, especially their investment behavior. The current tax reform discussion in the United States and around the world differs to some extent from earlier debates on tax reform, in that much of the current interest in changing the tax structure focuses on improving the tax climate for business in order to stimulate additional saving, investment, employment, wages, and economic growth. In this regard Joel Slemrod inquires whether tax reform is good for business, and whether a tax reform that is good for business is also good for the nation. He reviews official positions of various business organizations and details how different businesses, depending on their characteristics in numerous dimensions, view various reforms quite differently—and differently from most academic economists. He concludes that fundamental tax reform will be possible only with significant support from the business community, and that although what is good for business is not necessarily also good for the country, for the most part tax policies that encourage businesses to invest and employ new workers are in the interest of the citizenry at large.

In order to understand the effects of fundamental tax reform on business, the nature of tax effects on investment decisions must be fully understood. Kevin Hassett and Kathryn Newmark examine in detail the evolution of academic thinking on this complex subject. They begin by reviewing various controversies that arose in the early literature on taxes and investment, and then turn to a wide-ranging discussion of recent theoretical and empirical research. They note that such work has been facilitated by the opportunity to examine the effects of recent significant changes in the US tax structure as well as tax changes in other countries prompted by international tax competition. After reviewing this work in considerable detail, they conclude that there has been some recent convergence in views regarding how taxes affect investment decisions.

The prospect of fundamental consumption tax reform in the United States has provoked considerable concern about the extent to which the transitional problems associated with such a reform would be extremely problematic. John Diamond and George Zodrow examine this issue within the context of a complex dynamic overlapping generations computable general equilibrium model of the US economy. They note that the dramatic changes in the treatment of business assets, including owner-occupied housing (in their model, housing owners are treated as businesses that provide housing services to themselves), associated with consumption tax reforms could, in principle, cause significant declines in business equity prices and home values. However, they also note that a wide variety of reform-induced factors, most of which are analyzed explicitly in their model, act to mitigate these declines. Their computer simulations suggest that in general, these declines are significantly smaller than often suggested; they also note that although much attention has been focused on potential declines in the values of owner-occupied housing, the potential for decline is most serious in the case of rental housing.

Third, given the ever-increasing importance of globalization, especially cross-country flows of both goods and mobile capital, no discussion of the effects of fundamental tax reform on business would be complete without careful consideration of international taxation issues, which are addressed in the next two chapters (Hassett and Newmark also touch briefly on international issues). Arnold Harberger focuses on the critical issue of the incidence of changes in the corporate income tax in a global economy. He argues that this question is best analyzed within the context of a four-sector (tradable and nontradable goods produced by both the corporate and the noncorporate sectors) general equilibrium model. Within that context he obtains a variety of incidence results, with his central conclusion being that domestic labor tends to bear the full burden—or more than the full burden (overshifting)—of the corporate income tax. In addition he argues that alternative results that suggest a larger burden on capital understate the degree of international capital mobility and the degree of substitutability between domestically produced goods and competing imports.

Harry Grubert and Rosanne Altshuler also examine the corporate income tax in a global economy but focus on an evaluation of potential reforms of the tax treatment of cross-border income flows. Specifically, they consider proposals for tax exemption of repatriated dividends (a territorial tax system) and a tax burden-neutral switch to a residence-based worldwide system under which foreign source income is taxed currently in the United States while corporate tax rates are reduced. They also discuss destination-based and origin-based consumption taxes. Their primary conclusion is that the burden-neutral worldwide tax system seems to offer greater efficiency gains among the two income tax options, particularly because of reduced incentives for income shifting across countries, which wastes resources and distorts effective tax rates on investment. They also argue that increasing international capital mobility makes greater reliance on the taxation of capital income at the individual level, rather than at the business level, substantially more attractive.

Finally, the last three chapters of the volume focus on the effects of fundamental tax reform on individual behavior. Thomas Kniesner and James Ziliak begin the discussion by reviewing the voluminous literature on individual behavioral responses to tax changes. Their focus is initially on work participation and effort, and they show that recent analyses that take into account life-cycle effects suggest labor supply is somewhat more responsive to tax factors than implied by most of the earlier literature. Kniesner and Ziliak then review the recent empirical literature on the effects of taxes on saving and on taxable income (including changes in the form of compensation, the nature of expenditures, and tax avoidance and evasion), and relate all of these results to two central issues critical to an understanding of the desirability of fundamental tax reform—the efficiency cost of taxation and the nature of an optimal personal income tax.

In a related study Laurence Kotlikoff and David Rapson focus on measuring the changes in the effective tax rates on labor supply and on savings that would arise from replacing the existing income tax with a specific consumption tax proposal—replacing both the federal income tax system and the Social Security payroll tax with a flat rate national retail sales tax coupled with a universal rebate and a significant reduction in government services, a plan termed the FairTax by its proponents. Kotlikoff and Rapson use a sophisticated computer program to calculate their effective tax rates, under the assumption that individuals smooth consumption over their life cycles. Their estimates indicate that the marginal effective tax rates on labor supply would in general be lower, and in many cases significantly lower, under the national retail sales tax than under the current income tax, while marginal effective tax rates on saving are significantly positive under the income tax but would be zero under their consumption tax option.

Finally, Edward McCaffery investigates the implications for fundamental tax reform of the relatively new field of behavioral economics, which examines the extent to which individual decision-making is inconsistent with the highly rational behavior commonly assumed in economic models. In particular, McCaffery focuses on the implications of individual myopia and lack of self-control. He argues against the popular conception that the insights of behavioral economics imply that saving should be promoted through ad hoc incentives under the existing income tax. Instead, he concludes that behavioral economics implies that ad hoc savings incentives are ineffective, and that the best approach is fundamental reform in the form of a postpaid consumption tax based on cash flow—a consumption tax that would allow a deduction for saving, tax all withdrawals from saving, include the proceeds of loans in the tax base, and allow deductions for repayment of both loan principal and interest.

Additional details on the central findings of these chapters are provided below.

Overviews of Economic and Political Issues

Alan Auerbach of the University of California, Berkeley, sets the stage for the rest of the discussions in the volume by providing a comprehensive overview of the case for fundamental tax reform, focusing on proposals based on taxing a measure of consumption rather than income. He begins with a review of the relative advantages and disadvantages of consumption-based and income-based tax systems. He argues that several strands of the recent academic literature generally support the position that consumption taxes are more efficient than income taxes, especially if individuals have a long planning horizon so that the distorted savings decisions attributable to capital income taxation are particularly costly. Auerbach notes several qualifications to the basic argument, some favoring capital income taxation and others favoring capital income subsidies, and concludes that consumption taxes are likely to be preferable to income taxes on efficiency grounds and may still be superior even if distributional concerns are taken into account.

Auerbach then examines the structure of alternative forms of consumption taxation within the context of a national income accounting model, focusing on a wide range of issues and carefully describing how different reform proposals that all fall under the consumption tax rubric may have dramatically different impacts in certain areas. He makes numerous observations and draws many conclusions from this analysis. For example, he notes that various proposals differ in their treatment of government purchases, including those of state and local governments, and that it is difficult even from a conceptual standpoint to define the correct treatment. He stresses that progressivity goals are much more easily achieved under the direct forms of consumption taxation, such as the Hall-Rabushka flat tax and the Bradford X-tax, than under indirect consumption taxes, such as a national retail sales tax or a value-added tax. He also describes how different forms of consumption taxes differ in the extent to which existing capital is subject to the new tax, creating a significant source of efficiency gains at the cost of raising potentially serious transitional issues. He argues that despite often-cited arguments to the contrary, the choice of an origin basis or a destination basis for a consumption tax should have minimal effects on the balance of trade, although it would have significant effects on asset values.

Auerbach also notes that different treatment of financial assets and liabilities under the various consumption tax options has important effects both during the transition period to the new system and in the long run, especially if our trading partners continue to use an income tax that creates new opportunities for international tax avoidance and evasion. He also describes various issues related to the timing of tax payments, the choice between taxation at the business or individual levels, which form of consumption taxation is most likely to have a positive impact on saving, especially in light of recent advances in behavioral economics that cast doubt on the far-sighted individual rationality assumed in conventional models of saving behavior, and numerous other issues.

Auerbach concludes that a consumption tax reform could yield many benefits, although the magnitudes of these benefits are difficult to measure given the current state of our knowledge. He argues that such a reform would yield efficiency gains by reducing or eliminating a wide variety of distortions, but that the size of the gains is uncertain, especially since the extent to which existing capital could be taxed is unclear. Moreover certain forms of consumption taxes can easily be made progressive, although they may be overly generous to those at the very top of the income distribution, especially in the absence of an effective estate tax. He notes that consumption taxes would not improve our trade balance or enhance our capacity to tax the underground economy. Finally, Auerbach concludes that even though fundamental tax reform may be impossible, incremental reforms in the right direction are an attractive alternative.

Daniel Shaviro of the New York University Law School reviews the literature on tax simplification under a consumption tax reform and extends it to consider the critical issue of how politics would affect the potential for simplification. He begins with a discussion of the most plausible scenarios that would lead to consumption tax reform. He argues that the two most likely scenarios would be either a bipartisan agreement or a Republican-led effort to enact a consumption tax. Shaviro dismisses two other scenarios as implausible. In particular, he considers a bidding war, similar to what occurred prior to the Economic Recovery Tax Act of 1981, to be implausible because of the long-term fiscal gap facing the United States, and a Democratic-led consumption tax reform as unlikely since most Democrats support income taxation.

Shaviro contends that a bipartisan agreement, similar to that underlying the enactment of the Tax Reform Act of 1986, could yield a progressive tax on wage earnings, such as the Bradford (2005) X-tax, but heavily modified to satisfy the need for political compromises. For example, Democrats might agree to exempt capital income from taxation in return for Republicans accepting a sufficiently progressive wage tax structure that would approximate the level of revenue and distributional features of the current income tax system. He comments, however, that such a compromise is unlikely to occur in the current political environment. Moreover he notes that to garner enough political support for a consumption-based reform, the bipartisan agreement would need to both lower tax rates for individuals and enlist a core group of supporters from the business community. He argues that to meet these requirements it is likely the reform would have to impose a one-time windfall loss on the owners of existing capital to raise revenue and allow for expensing of capital assets to enlist capital-intensive industries as allies.

Shaviro contends that the second plausible option is to move toward a consumption-based tax without explicitly repealing the current income tax following a Republican-led stealth process often referred to as the "five easy pieces" scenario. He outlines the five steps in this process as: reduce marginal rates, provide expensing for all business outlays, integrate the corporate and individual tax systems, significantly increase or eliminate contribution limits for pre-paid tax saving vehicles, and move the tax treatment of US business toward a territorial tax system by exempting the income of US companies earned abroad. Shaviro notes that the proponents of this approach have included an extraneous step because rate decreases have nothing to do with moving from an income to consumption-based tax system (outside of meeting revenue and distribution targets). At the same time this approach ignores important issues such as the appropriate tax treatment of interest payments or the elimination of politically popular deductions and income exclusions that must occur to achieve the simplicity and efficiency gains potentially attainable with consumption-based tax reforms.

Shaviro concludes that a consumption tax reform based on the "five easy pieces" approach would likely increase both the potential for tax planning and overall complexity. He notes that there is a lack of open deliberations regarding potential problems and solutions and a propensity for policy makers to avoid making controversial decisions that would have to be resolved for the tax system to work efficiently, such as the appropriate treatment of interest expense. Even with bipartisan agreement, Shaviro comments that an ambivalent attitude toward the efficient structure of a consumption-based tax system might lead to political compromises that create substantial complexities, such as the add-on layer of tax proposed by the President's Advisory Panel for Federal Tax Reform (2005). He concludes that even a bipartisan agreement would be unlikely to yield the simplification that is normally assumed in studies that ignore the effect of the political process on the end product of tax reform.

Business Issues

A critical aspect of any tax reform proposal is its effect on business. Three chapters in the volume examine the effects of alternative tax reforms on business behavior, especially with respect to domestic investment.

Joel Slemrod of the University of Michigan begins the discussion by asking whether fundamental tax reform, defined broadly to include traditional base-broadening, rate-lowering income tax reform as well as consumption tax reforms, is good for business and whether a tax reform that is favorable to business interests is also good for the nation as a whole.

To set the stage for his discussion, Slemrod describes business views on tax reform. He begins by summarizing the official positions of various business organizations, encompassing big business, small business, and special interest groups, on the desirability of tax reform. The positions vary considerably, but typically support general goals such as increasing tax simplicity, minimizing distortions of business decisions regarding investment and employment, lowering (or keeping constant) taxes on businesses, promoting international competitiveness, and providing transition rules to minimize the disruptions associated with tax changes. The official positions of big business seldom promote specific tax reform proposals, but several organizations representing small business are willing to support specific reform proposals, such as replacing the corporate income tax with a national retail sales tax or a tax on business transactions. Not surprisingly, organizations representing narrower special interest tend to support tax policies that promote those interests. Slemrod also notes that the role played by businesses in the passage of the Tax Reform Act of 1986 is instructive, as it highlights differences across various business sectors. For example, capital-intensive firms opposed the general thrust of the reform of lowering corporate tax rates by eliminating investment tax credits and accelerated depreciation, while the service and technology industries supported such a change. In addition various industries opposed provisions that were especially detrimental to their interests.

Slemrod notes that the positions that businesses take on tax reform focus on direct impacts on profitability holding before-tax profits constant, thus neglecting the general equilibrium feedback effects on output and input prices stressed by economists, especially in their evaluations of large scale reforms. He briefly reviews the theory of the incidence of the corporate income tax, stressing in particular the different ways that tax reforms affect new and existing capital and how these differences may cause the interests of shareholders, who are concerned about both old and new capital, to diverge from those of the rest of the population, which is concerned primarily with the tax treatment of new capital and its effects on saving, investment, labor productivity, and wages. He notes that this differential impact implies shareholders are likely to favor extensive transition rules to protect the value of their existing investments, while the rest of the population would favor immediate implementation without transition rules for efficiency-enhancing reforms.

Slemrod then considers a variety of additional issues. He stresses that the existing literature often overemphasizes the distinction between "business taxes" and other taxes. In economic terms, whether businesses remit the tax is unimportant—it is the ultimate economic incidence of the tax, or who bears the burden of the tax after all market adjustments occur, that is of primary importance. He also notes that although increased simplicity in the tax system is generally perceived to be desirable by business interests, it does not favor those businesses that profit from tax complexity (tax accountants and lawyers), including those that benefit from complexity by engaging in financial manipulations that reduce tax liability. Nevertheless, he notes that various studies indicate that the compliance costs of the US tax system are relatively high, and that many businesses favor provisions that would simplify the tax system, including imposing conformity between the definitions of income for tax and financial accounting purposes and establishing uniformity among the tax systems used by the states and the federal government.

Finally, he argues that most sector-specific concerns about the effects of fundamental tax reforms, such as those often expressed by the housing and retail sectors regarding the implementation of a consumption tax, may be exaggerated once all general equilibrium responses to the reform are taken into account.

Slemrod concludes that although business support would be critical to the passage of fundamental tax reform, it is not guaranteed because the effects of reform on businesses vary considerably and may be misinterpreted due to an overemphasis on the level of taxes "on" business relative to the effects of other taxes. In addition he notes that although what is good for business is not necessarily also good for the country, for the most part tax policies that encourage businesses to invest and employ new workers are in the interest of the citizenry at large.

Kevin Hassett and Kathryn Newmark of the American Enterprise Institute provide a thorough review of the recent literature on taxation and business behavior. They note that a number of recent tax reforms in the United States, as well as various reforms around the world prompted in part by increasing international tax competition, have provided many tax structure changes that have been used in empirical studies of investment behavior. After reviewing briefly the earlier literature on taxation and investment, they examine three areas that have been the focus of much recent research.

First, Hassett and Newmark observe that numerous recent papers have attempted to resolve the long-standing question of whether investment is significantly affected by economic fundamentals, especially the user cost of capital, as predicted by neoclassical theory. Although this proposition found little support in the early literature, more recent studies, which have stressed the importance of accurately measuring economic fundamentals as well as properly accounting for the costs of adjusting the capital stock, have consistently estimated significant effects of economic fundamentals on investment decisions while tending to minimize the importance of cash flow as a determinant of investment behavior. In addition several studies have clarified the nature of the costs of adjusting the capital stock, suggesting that the standard quadratic costs formulation may be inadequate, especially for large levels of investment.

Second, Hassett and Newmark examine various empirical analyses of the effects of recent tax reforms in the United States, which include reductions of individual tax rates on dividends and capital gains by the enactment of temporary "bonus depreciation" or partial expensing. They argue that these studies are generally consistent with the "new view" of the effects of dividend taxation, under which individual level dividend taxes have no effect on marginal investment decisions, as the benefit of deferral of dividend taxes offsets in present value terms all future taxes on investments financed with retained earnings. This in turn implies that the recent dividend tax cuts will have a positive effect on equity-financed investment only for new and emerging firms that tend to rely disproportionately on new share issues as a financing mechanism. In addition Hassett and Newmark argue that several recent studies of the temporary partial expensing provisions enacted in the United States indicate that they had a positive if not huge effect on the level of investment and that, in contrast to some pre-dictions, they resulted in little upward movement in the prices of capi-tal goods.

Finally, Hassett and Newmark briefly examine the effects of interna-tional tax systems on investment decisions, especially a foreign direct investment by large multinational firms. They note that virtually all recent studies conclude that source country taxes have a significant ef-fect on foreign direct investment, and that the magnitude of this effect appears to be increasing significantly over time. In addition they exam-ine the phenomenon of tax havens, noting that many multinationals aggressively use financial accounting manipulations, including transfer pricing, to ensure that a significant fraction of profits is located in tax havens or in other jurisdictions with relatively low tax rates. Hassett and Newmark also observe that an increasingly large fraction of in-vestment takes the form of investment in intangible goods. They argue that the extension of traditional analysis of the effects of taxation on in-vestment to account for investment in intangibles, as well as the effects of such investment on economic growth, is a critical area for future research.

Hassett and Newmark conclude that, although some of the effects of taxation on investment are still controversial, both theory and empiri-cal evidence suggest some convergence of different views. Specifically, this consensus tends to support the neoclassical model, especially the importance of the user cost of capital and the role of adjustment costs in understanding business behavior, a rehabilitation of the new view of the effects of dividend taxation, and the importance of international tax factors in modeling the behavior of US multinationals.

Some observers have argued that even if consumption-based fundamental tax reform is desirable from a long-run perspective, the transitional problems associated with implementation imply that it is politically infeasible. In particular, various researchers have argued that (1) the generous treatment of new investment under a consumption tax reform would result in a dramatic decline in the prices of existing business equity assets that face relatively high tax rates, and (2) the elimination of the preferential tax treatment of owner-occupied housing under the current income tax would result in significant declines in housing prices. John Diamond and George Zodrow examine these issues within the context of a large-scale dynamic overlapping generations computable general equilibrium model of the US economy. Their model has three production sectors—owner-occupied housing, rental housing, and a composite good sector that includes all nonhousing goods and services; homeowners are modeled as businesses that "produce" housing services which they then provide to themselves. The flat tax is the primary reform considered in their chapter on the grounds that it, as well as its variants (e.g., the X-tax), is among the most often-discussed consumption tax proposals, its enactment is believed to raise the most troublesome transitional issues among the various consumption-based tax reform options, and it is the main reform analyzed in existing studies of the effects of fundamental tax reform on housing values.

Diamond and Zodrow note that although a flat tax reform, in the absence of special transition rules, does create a tendency for declines in business equity asset prices and housing values, these tendencies are mitigated by many other reform-induced factors. These factors, all of which are considered explicitly in their model, include the costs of adjusting the existing capital stock in response to reform, reform-induced changes in after-tax rates of interest, the asset value effects of provisions for accelerated depreciation allowances under current law, and the efficiency gains obtained from eliminating distortions of saving and investment decisions and reducing distortions of the labor-leisure choices, as well as from improvements in the allocation of capital across business sectors.

The effects of a flat tax reform in the Diamond-Zodrow model are summarized as follows: The reform results in a long-run increase in GDP of nearly 5 percent, long-run increases in investment that range from about 2 percent in owner-occupied housing to between 15 and 17 percent in the other two production sectors, and a long-run increase in welfare of nearly 3 percent. However, these long-run gains do come at the expense of immediate one-time declines in the prices of business equity. These losses are greater than those predicted in some other recent simulation studies, but not nearly as large as those predicted by partial equilibrium models that ignore the various factors that tend to mitigate asset price declines in their general equilibrium model. The authors argue that these results suggest that special transition rules should be used with some caution, especially since they significantly reduce the long-run gains obtained from reform. Nevertheless, they stress that a reasonably strong case for transitional relief can be made for business assets with large amounts of remaining tax basis (book value that reflects deductions for depreciation not yet taken), especially in the rental housing sector. The Diamond-Zodrow analysis also suggests that the negative effects on house values of reducing the tax preferences for owner-occupied housing under a flat tax—equalizing the treatment of housing and other investment and eliminating housing-related deductions would be relatively small, once all general equilibrium effects are taken into account. Thus, although most discussion of transitional issues in the housing market has focused on owner-occupied housing, they emphasize that transitional problems, and thus the case for transition relief, is strongest in the rental housing sector.

Finally, Diamond and Zodrow note that the effects of the costs of adjusting the capital stock—at least if they are symmetric across production sectors—tend to cancel, as higher adjustment costs mitigate the fall in the value of business equity but exacerbate declines in the values of owner-occupied housing, in both cases by slowing down the reallocation of capital from owner-occupied housing to the other production sectors. Thus explicitly accounting for such differential asset price effects is essential to accurately estimating the welfare effects of fundamental tax reform.

International Business Issues

As noted above, the ever-increasing importance of globalization, especially cross-country flows of tradable goods and internationally mobile capital, implies that no discussion of the effects of fundamental tax reform on business would be complete without careful consideration of international tax issues.

Arnold Harberger of the University of California at Los Angeles examines the thorny question of determining tax incidence in a general equilibrium framework. He begins by noting that the lack of knowledge about how the receipts of a tax increase will be spent and the importance of accounting for other distortions that are present in the economy are critical to the determination of tax incidence. He argues that the assumption of demand neutrality—that the government spends tax receipts in the same manner individuals would have—breaks the problem up into manageable pieces. He notes that two potential paths are available to study tax incidence. The first is "pure incidence theory," which assumes demand neutrality and that no other distortions are present in the economy. The second is an analysis based on computable general equilibrium models—large-scale computer models that attempt to model the main features of the tax and expenditure system. He restricts his remarks to the first approach.

Harberger argues that neither an open nor a closed economy framework is always the best representation of the real world, but instead that different scenarios require that different modeling frameworks be used. He describes early analyses that obtained the surprising result that labor bears more than the full burden of the corporate income tax, which reversed closed economy results that indicated that capital bears the full burden of the tax. Harberger comments that it was not until he developed a four-sector general equilibrium model that he was comfortable with the notion that labor could more than fully bear the burden of the corporate income tax in an open economy. He notes that this approach led to an intuitive and communicable story of corporate tax incidence in an open economy.

Harberger designed his four-sector model to include manufacturing (corporate tradable), public utilities and transport (corporate nontradable), agriculture (noncorporate tradable) and services (noncorporate nontradable). He notes that the corporate tradable sector was the key sector because product prices for tradables and the rate of return to capital are fixed. Thus a change in the corporate tax rate must reduce the wage rate, which implies that labor bears at least the full burden of the corporate tax in the small open economy case. Taking into account interactions with the other three sectors, Harberger shows that labor bears more than the full burden of the corporate income tax, and, at the same time, foreign labor gains at the expense of foreign capital, and US consumers and landowners gain at the expense of US labor.

Next Harberger assumes that domestic and foreign manufactured goods are not homogeneous products, and thus not perfectly substitutable. He notes that in this case the decrease in wages is smaller because of an increase in prices in the manufacturing sector. However, labor still bears nearly the entire burden of the corporate income tax in this scenario. He also states that increases in prices in the corporate sector are unlikely to result in consumers bearing the full burden of the corporate income tax because substitution and scale effects imply a reallocation of capital to the nontradable sectors and the rest of the world. He notes that the results of Gravelle and Smetters (2006) indicating that labor bears very little of the burden of the corporate income tax are predicated on relatively low substitution parameters in the markets for capital and manufactured goods; he is much more comfortable with their results that are characterized by the highest substitutability of capital and manufactured goods.

Harberger concludes with a discussion of the potential for short-run, transitional, and dynamic analysis of the incidence of the corporate income tax. He suggests that transitional incidence analysis belongs in the category of the unknowable, but that dynamic incidence analysis is somewhat more tractable.

Harry Grubert of the US Treasury Department and Rosanne Altshuler of Rutgers University evaluate several recent proposals to reform the taxation of cross-border income and present new information on the burden of the current system. They begin by noting that efforts to reform the US corporate income tax are drawing more attention as a consequence of globalization, the increasing complexity associated with taxing cross-border corporate income, and the decline in corporate tax rates around the world. Grubert and Altshuler then highlight the main features of the current US corporate income tax, which taxes all repatriated and "foreign source" income after allowing for a limited credit for foreign taxes paid, and discuss some of the most important avoidance schemes that are used to reduce corporate taxes.

Grubert and Altshuler focus mainly on comparing two proposals to reform the tax treatment of cross-border income under the current income tax system, dividend exemption and burden neutral worldwide taxation. In addition they discuss the arguments related to the implementation of either a destination or origin-based consumption tax proposal. They evaluate each of the reform proposals relative to the current tax system on a number of important behavioral margins, such as the location of tangible and intangible capital, income repatriation, the location of income for tax purposes, financial decisions, incentives to export, incentives to lower foreign tax burdens, and host country tax treatment of US corporations.

Grubert and Altshuler note that dividend exemption would eliminate the burden associated with taxing repatriated corporate earnings, but that the allocation of expenses to exempt income and taxation of royalties would affect location decisions and the use of other tax avoidance schemes. They argue that dividend exemption would lead to a more efficient allocation of capital relative to the current system, but whether it would be simpler than the current system would depend on the specific details of the proposal.

Grubert and Altshuler explain that tax deferral is eliminated under burden-neutral worldwide taxation, and expense allocation rules are unnecessary because all foreign income is included in the tax base. They note that foreign tax credits would be maintained and assert that businesses with excess foreign tax credits would have an incentive to engage in tax planning. They stress that although this proposal would reduce the competitiveness of US corporations that operate abroad unless the corporate tax rate was reduced, domestic corporations would be more competitive. They calculate that a 28 percent corporate tax rate would be required to maintain the competitiveness of US corporations that operate abroad, and that at this rate 20 percent of active foreign source income would be earned by firms with excess foreign tax credits. They emphasize that increasing US competitiveness by lowering the corporate tax rate also increases the number of firms in an excess credit position, and thus reduces the benefit of reform.

Grubert and Altshuler conclude that burden-neutral worldwide taxation dominates the current system and the dividend exemption proposal. However, they stress that this conclusion depends on the number of businesses that maintain an excess foreign tax credit position and the response of foreign governments to changes in the US corporate tax rate. They admit that this proposal will create winners and losers, with the losers being those businesses with concentrated activity in low-tax areas.

Individual Issues

Although domestic and international business issues have taken center stage in recent discussions of fundamental tax reform, the effects of reform on individuals are still of paramount importance. The three chapters that form the final part of this volume examine these crucial issues.

In the opening chapter, Thomas Kniesner of Syracuse University and James Ziliak of the University of Kentucky review the voluminous empirical literature on the controversial issue of the extent of individual behavioral responses to tax changes. Kniesner and Ziliak begin by noting that an understanding of individual behavioral responses, especially in terms of labor supply, forms of compensation, and saving, is critical to an understanding of the economic effects of fundamental tax reforms and to the design of an "optimal" personal income tax. Moreover, because even the directions of such responses are typically ambiguous in theory, they can be discerned only with careful empirical analysis. They review the current state-of-the-art of such analyses, organizing their discussion around the standard life-cycle model of consumption with labor supply under uncertainty.

Kniesner and Ziliak highlight several general sets of results in their analysis. First, the empirical evidence on the responsiveness of male labor supply is mixed, largely due to estimation difficulties in the presence of complex budget sets. For example, although early work has suggested relatively large income effects on labor supply, subsequent research indicates that these effects, as well as compensated and uncompensated substitution effects, are relatively small. The most recent work, which is cast in a life-cycle context with uncertain wages and utilizes richer econometric specifications than earlier work, suggests a positive compensated labor supply elasticity slightly greater than 0.3 and an income effect slightly greater (in absolute value) than -0.5. This evidence implies a negative uncompensated wage elasticity—that is, male labor supply is backward bending—and also that leisure and consumption are substitutes.

Second, Kniesner and Ziliak observe that the most recent empirical analyses of the labor supply of women have separately estimated the effects of wage and tax changes on hours worked and labor force participation. Key issues in these analyses are accounting properly for the large fraction of women who do not participate in the labor market, the modeling of the extent of income pooling within the family, and calculating accurately the typically high marginal tax rates faced by the secondary earner within a family. The results of this literature suggest that the labor force participation elasticity may be relatively large (on the order of 1–2), and substantially exceeds the hours worked elasticity, which is typically estimated to be in the neighborhood of 0.7 or less, sometimes significantly less, especially for single women with no attachment to the welfare system. In addition several analyses indicate that labor supply elasticities for women are declining steadily over time, with some studies indicating that they are not statistically distinguishable from comparable elasticities among prime-age married men.

Third, Kniesner and Ziliak examine briefly an even more contentious issue—the responsiveness of saving to changes in taxes. They conclude that the literature on the responsiveness of saving to changes in after-tax returns is inconclusive, although most estimates suggest that the interest elasticity of saving is relatively low. In contrast, they note that wage elasticity of saving appears to be relatively high, on the order of one.

Fourth, the authors examine a currently hot topic, the elasticity of taxable income, which captures not only the traditional labor supply effects of taxes but a variety of additional responses, including changes in the form of compensation (e.g., taking more income in tax-deferred form or as nontaxable fringe benefits), changes in expenditures on tax-preferred activities (e.g., debt-financed housing purchases), and tax avoidance and evasion. They note that the range of estimates of the elasticity of taxable income is large (0–3), with more recent estimates toward the lower end of that range, in the neighborhood of 0.4 or lower, with most of the responsiveness of taxable income attributable to high-income taxpayers.

Finally, Kniesner and Ziliak stress that the behavioral parameters discussed above are important inputs into estimates of the efficiency cost of taxation and calculations of an "optimal" personal income tax. They illustrate these propositions by showing that the marginal welfare cost for labor income taxation in their model is on the order of 16 to 21 percent of revenues, and noting that a labor force participation elasticity in excess of one implies that a wage subsidy like the earned income tax credit is desirable—a result that does not obtain under the standard model where the labor supply response involves only hours worked. They conclude by noting that an optimal personal income tax must also consider the insurance benefits of progressive taxation.

The results presented by Kniesner and Ziliak demonstrate clearly that an understanding of the economic effects of any change in the tax structure requires accurate estimates of its effects on the marginal effective tax rates faced by individuals on labor force participation and effort and on saving. Laurence Kotlikoff and David Rapson conduct such an effective tax rate analysis for a specific consumption tax reform proposal—the replacement of the current federal income and payroll taxes with a national retail sales tax plan, referred to as the FairTax by its proponents. This proposed reform would apply a flat 23 percent rate, measured with respect to a tax base that includes the tax—that is, on a tax inclusive basis—to an extremely broad measure of consumption (although the consumption services from existing housing would not be taxed). In addition the proposal would provide for a universal tax rebate designed to ensure that poverty-level consumption for all households is tax free, indexation of Social Security benefits for any reform-induced inflation, and a significant reduction in government services so that the 23 percent rate would be fiscally sustainable.

Kotlikoff and Rapson use a highly sophisticated computer program to calculate average and marginal tax rates on labor supply and on saving under the current income tax and the proposed reform. This program calculates effective tax rates under the assumption that individuals act to smooth their consumption, which is assumed to be either constant or uniformly increasing over time. The program fully takes into account the details of the federal income and payroll tax systems and their interactions, as well as the effects of current tax changes on current and future income and payroll taxes and future social security benefits. Marginal effective tax rates on labor income are calculated by simulating the effects of a marginal increase in labor income under each system. The increase is assumed to be spent entirely on current consumption, with all future consumption held constant. Kotlikoff and Rapson define the marginal effective tax rate on labor income to be the ratio of the resulting increase in tax burden to the marginal increase in labor income. Similarly they calculate marginal effective tax rates on saving under the current income tax by comparing the increase in future consumption, uniformly distributed over all future years, attainable with a given reduction in current consumption, with and without the tax system. By comparison, the marginal effective tax rate on saving under their consumption tax reform is zero.

The results obtained by Kotlikoff and Rapson can be summarized as follows: First, they estimate that for a variety of different types of households the total effective federal marginal tax rates on labor supply under the current tax system are higher—and in many cases significantly higher—than under their proposed national retail sales tax reform in virtually all the scenarios they consider. In particular, marginal effective tax rates on labor income for some low- and middle-income households are nearly twice as large under the current income and payroll tax systems as they would be under the FairTax. Second, they estimate that marginal effective tax rates on the return to savings range from 22.6 to 54.2 percent under the current income and payroll tax system. By comparison, this rate is zero under a flat rate consumption tax plan. They argue that the reductions in marginal effective tax rates on labor supply and saving under a national retail sales tax would result in significant efficiency gains. Third, Kotlikoff and Rapson estimate that average remaining lifetime tax rates (taking into account the proposed reduction in government expenditures) would decline, and in many cases significantly, for all of the households they analyze. They stress that these reductions are progressive in the sense that low-income households experience a larger percentage reduction in their average tax rates than do higher income households. To some extent, this result obtains because low-income elderly households benefit both from the universal rebate under the FairTax plan and the indexation of Social Security benefits for the inflation attributable to the enactment of a national retail sales tax. A second factor contributing to the progressivity of a national retail sales tax is that it effectively taxes existing wealth (other than housing), since it causes consumer prices to increase roughly by the amount of the tax while asset prices remain constant. Kotlikoff and Rapson conclude that enactment of a consumption tax reform in the form of a flat rate national retail sales tax would simplify tax administration and compliance, and that the resulting favorable treatment of investment would stimulate foreign investment in the United States.

Finally, Edward J. McCaffery of the University of Southern California examines the implications for fundamental reform of the relatively new field of behavioral economics. Behavioral economics is about individual decision making, and its general argument is that individuals are not the rational agents commonly depicted in economic models. That is, contrary to the central assumption of rational dynamic optimization models, behavioral economics argues that individuals consistently make mistakes in their decision-making processes. In particular, in the behavioralist view, individuals are myopic rather than farsighted, lack self-control, act on limited information or misinformation, are extremely risk averse, and respond to commitment devices and the institutional features of saving plans in ways that are inconsistent with standard life-cycle optimization theory. McCaffery suggests that one must be careful in asserting that any behavior is irrational. For example, low saving by low-income individuals could reflect a realization that modestly higher savings could provide little financial cushion but would disqualify one for government aid programs in the event of a financial emergency.

Although McCaffery is sympathetic to applying the lessons of behavioral economics to analyses of fundamental tax reform, he argues against the most common current application, that behavioral economics implies that individual saving should be promoted through ad hoc incentives under the current income tax rather than the general savings incentive that occurs under a consumption tax. In his view, if individuals are irrational in the sense suggested by behavioral economics, then ad hoc savings incentives will be ineffective, and should be eliminated because they are complex, confusing, and costly.

McCaffery begins by challenging the traditional arguments for fundamental tax reform, including both base-broadening, rate-lowering income tax reform and replacing the income tax with a consumption tax. Both ideas have been floated for many years but have led to little in the way of fundamental reform. Because the US tax system is best characterized as a hybrid system that combines elements of both income and consumption taxation and thus is susceptible to avoidance techniques. For example, the "buy/borrow/die" scheme of investing in assets that yield only capital gains, borrowing against their appreciated value to finance consumption, and holding the assets (and the loans) until the gains avoid taxation at death that take advantage of the asymmetries caused by a hybrid structure. He argues that fundamental tax reform will not be achieved with marginal extensions of existing approaches, but only with a thorough rethinking of the theory of taxation, one that takes into account the insights of behavioral economics.

McCaffery argues that savings incentives under the income tax are unlikely to have significant effects on savings if individuals are rational life-cycle savers because rate of return effects are likely to be small, and high-income savers may already largely be avoiding or evading tax on the return to savings. He notes that saving incentives are likely to lead to arbitrage that lowers revenues without generating new saving (e.g., in the case of tax postpaid plans like traditional IRAs, which allow deductions for savings and tax all withdrawals).

In addition, however, McCaffery argues that savings incentives are unlikely to stimulate savings even if the results of the behavioral economics literature are valid. For example, tax prepaid plans (e.g., Roth

IRAs, which do not allow deductions for saving but exempt all capital income from tax) offer no immediate benefits to savers and thus are unlikely to stimulate savings by myopic individuals. Alternatively, because tax postpaid plans create arbitrage opportunities (drawing down existing savings to finance nominally "new" savings in the tax prepaid account), they generate new current funds that can fund more current consumption by myopic individuals.

McCaffery concludes that rather than relying on ad hoc saving incentives within an income tax, the United States should adopt a comprehensive progressive postpaid consumption tax (i.e., a system that allows unlimited and unrestricted traditional IRAs). He argues that such an approach would eliminate the arbitrage problems that plague savings incentives under the existing income tax and thus avoid their complexity, while providing a simple and uniform tax system that encourages saving—which could then be supplemented by private and public measures to increase savings as deemed necessary.

Conclusion

At one level one could argue that the case for fundamental tax reform of either the income tax or the consumption tax variety is inherently unknowable—that it is simply too difficult to determine definitively the consequences of such reforms in terms of its ultimate consequences for economic efficiency, equity, and simplicity. However, as is discussed in a narrower context in the contributions to this volume, such a conclusion appears to be unwarranted and indeed far too pessimistic. The current system effectively enshrines the status quo, which is plagued by a wide variety of serious problems. In examining the advantages and disadvantages of the current system relative to the various alternatives, each of the contributions to this volume significantly advances our knowledge of the economic effects of taxation, and thus represents an important step toward achieving fundamental tax reform.

I   Overviews

1 Tax Reform in the Twenty-first Century

Alan J. Auerbach

Over the next decade or so the United States may well undertake a major reform to make its tax system simpler, fairer, and more efficient. Both economic research and policy discussions have pointed in recent years to reforms that incorporate at least some elements of consumption taxation. But what constitutes a consumption tax, or entitles a system to be characterized as providing "consumption-tax treatment," is not so obvious. There are many characteristics that distinguish a consumption tax. Indeed the importance of different characteristics in delivering a tax system that is simpler, fairer, and more efficient is to a large extent what the chapters in this volume are about.

I will frame my discussion by going through the attributes of a consumption tax, considering the impact of the choices made in constructing different reform proposals. This is one place where the state of our knowledge comes into play, as on some issues our knowledge is considerable while on others more research is required. However, some decisions are of an unknowable nature, either because the necessary data are not available or because the circumstances we confront for the future go beyond our historical experience.

I begin nevertheless with a review of our state of knowledge on the fundamental issues relating to the choice between income and consumption taxation. Here, too, our thinking has evolved over the years, in part because of advances in economic theory and empirical evidence but also because of changes in the way we view the comparison. As with the choices among particular types of consumption tax, many important questions are still unanswered.

1.1   The Choice between Income and Consumption Taxes

1.1.1   Should Capital Income Be Taxed?

A consumption tax effectively exempts the return to saving from taxation, in a manner discussed more fully below. Thus the debate over whether a consumption tax would be more desirable than an income tax involves asking whether it is a good idea to tax capital income.

Through the years our perspective on whether a consumption tax would improve our tax system, in particular, whether it would make the tax system more efficient, has become considerably more sophisticated and has tended to favor consumption taxation. There are now several strands of the literature arguing that a consumption tax would be more efficient than an income tax. I will not attempt a detailed survey of this rich literature here; I will instead try to highlight some key results.[1]

The first line of analysis was to take the lifetime budget constraint in the two-period life-cycle model, observe that an income tax hits future consumption harder than current consumption, and inquire whether such differential taxation was consistent with basic optimal tax theory. Feldstein (1978) suggested that it was not and that an efficiency gain was available from adopting a consumption tax. His argument was based on the relative complementarity of current and future consumption with respect to leisure, a potentially knowable but difficult to estimate behavioral response. As the literature developed, however, the focus shifted to other behavioral responses.

One of the most frequently cited papers in this literature is that of Atkinson and Stiglitz (1976), who showed, under the assumption that preferences are weakly separable into consumption and leisure, that a progressive labor income tax is optimal by itself, namely that no variation in commodity taxes can improve social welfare. Although weak separability of preferences is not assured, it is a weaker restriction than equal complementarity with respect to leisure. Thus one could reasonably argue that while differential taxes on commodities might improve efficiency, the direction of improvement was not clear and was unlikely ever to be so. If one again interprets the different consumption goods as consumption in different periods, then the result may be seen as calling exclusively for a progressive tax on labor income or, in their model equivalently (because there are no initial assets and no transfers to other individuals), a progressive tax on lifetime consumption.

Even if the Atkinson-Stiglitz restriction on preferences is not satisfied, this violation does not necessarily imply that one would want to have higher taxes on future consumption than on current consumption, as would be effectively imposed by a capital income tax. A priori, a capital income subsidy is just as likely to be optimal as a capital income tax. In the Atkinson-Stiglitz framework, differential taxes on commodities can improve economic efficiency only if commodity demands differ among individuals even if after-tax income is held constant. Thus we would want to tax a good more heavily if, for a given level of after-tax labor income, it appeals more to higher ability individuals than to lower ability individuals. Is that the case for the future consumption on which capital income taxes would fall? Even if higher ability individuals have a propensity to save more, this does not imply that they would do so at lower income levels. Again, this is a potentially knowable variation in preferences, but a very hard one to estimate without making strong identifying assumptions to infer the potential behavior of some individuals from the observed behavior of others. Again, however, the shifting focus of economic theory has diverted attention somewhat from estimating these behavioral parameters.

A respite from the need for estimation comes from the literature extending the analysis to consider household decisions over longer horizons. Indeed, in the limit as the household's planning horizon becomes infinite, theory strengthens the case against any significant long-run tax on capital income. As shown by Judd (1985) and Chamley (1986) for a system with taxes on labor and capital income, the tax on capital income should converge to zero in the long run. Thus, if we ignore the distinction between consumption and wage taxes relating to the treatment of initial assets, the result calls for consumption tax treatment in the long run.

This conclusion is general in some respects. Unlike the conclusions of Feldstein and Atkinson and Stiglitz, it does not depend on individual preferences taking a particular form. The intuition is also very simple. For any given set of individual preferences, we might improve efficiency by taxing consumption in different periods at different rates. Taxing future consumption more heavily than current consumption could be achieved by taxing capital income. But it is implausible that we would want to tax consumption more and more heavily as we move into later and later periods, as would be the case if positive capital income taxes continued to apply. Thus at some point, regardless of the exact form of preferences, the capital income tax will have to converge to zero.

Although Judd and Chamley derived their results in simple representative agent models without ability differences or progressive taxation, their logic would apply just as well in the Atkinson-Stiglitz framework: even if weak separability failed to hold so that uniform taxation was not optimal, one wouldn't want to have arbitrarily large distortions facing consumption at distant future dates. The intuition associated with the Judd-Chamley result still resonates for long but finite horizons, in that a positive capital income tax in every year would still impose a very high effective tax rate on consumption, say, fifty years in the future.

Has theory given us a mandate for consumption taxes as the efficient solution to the optimal tax problem? Not yet. Aside from the usual restrictions that any modeling assumptions impose, there are particular problems in applying the Atkinson-Stiglitz result to the design of taxation over time. First, Atkinson and Stiglitz assume that each household has just one form of labor supply. Thus their result does not tell us how we should tax the labor supply of different household members, leaving the thorny issue of family taxation unaddressed. Putting aside how different members of a household should be treated at a given point in time, the assumption of a single type of labor also ignores the fact that there is labor income in different periods. Even if consumption were separable from all forms of leisure, there is no presumption that leisure at different dates should be subject to the same tax schedule. One might, for example, think that age-specific labor income tax schedules would make sense. Absent such taxes, we might choose to rely on capital income taxes as a proxy. For example, if we wished to tax the labor income of middle-aged individuals more heavily, then taxing capital income might indirectly do so, as this is the dominant group among savers.[2]

But, perhaps more important, applying a static analysis like that in the Atkinson-Stiglitz paper to behavior over time ignores the fact that we observe the labor supply and consumption decisions of early periods before those of later ones. Thus we might wish to implement a tax system in future periods that is conditioned on earlier decisions.[3] Considering such a dynamic model, Golosov et al. (2003) found that the Atkinson-Stiglitz result about uniform commodity taxation still applied across commodities *within* a given period but that a positive capital income tax was generally optimal. The intuition is that capital

income makes it more difficult for the government to impose a redistributive labor income tax because the cost to high ability individuals
of not working hard is reduced by their having access to additional
resources. Taxing capital income therefore weakens the self-selection
constraints that the government's tax system must satisfy, allowing
more scope for redistribution.

However, there are also arguments in favor of pushing capital income taxes below zero. If imperfectly competitive firms are restricting
production to levels at which price exceeds marginal cost, then to the
distortions of taxation we must add the additional noncompetitive
markup. Assuming that capital goods markets are among those in
which noncompetitive distortions exist, moreover, means that the departure from perfect competition will not simply distort consumption
by raising consumer prices, but will also discourage the use of capital
in production by raising capital goods prices.

This additional wedge in the capital goods market has two implications for policies that reduce capital income taxation, whether directly
or through a shift to consumption taxes. First, the efficiency gains will
be larger because the reduction is starting from a more distorted initial
equilibrium point. Second, the optimal capital income tax will be negative because even a zero capital income tax will leave the non-tax distortion of capital use in place.

Starting from an infinite horizon model in which the optimal long-
run capital income tax would be zero under perfect competition, and
using empirical parameter estimates of noncompetitive industrial
markups in the United States, Judd (1997) finds that the optimal capital income tax is negative in the long run. While the qualitative implications of this analysis are clear—the efficiency gains from eliminating
capital income taxes are bigger than otherwise estimated—the quantitative implications for other models, such as life-cycle simulation models, are not clear without further efforts at simulation modeling that
incorporate different types of imperfect competition. While the results
of such further analysis can be known, what is more difficult to know
is the extent to which tax policy should take the competitive environment as given. That is, if we are not currently pursuing an optimal policy with respect to regulation and antitrust enforcement, then should
tax policy be based on the current regulation and antitrust policy or a
more efficient one?

Thus, even though capital income taxes distort consumption more
and more over the infinite horizon, positive taxes on capital income

may be desirable if we seek to implement a plan for redistributive taxation, and negative taxes on capital income may be desirable to offset the effects of imperfect competition. On the other hand, one can scour the optimal taxation literature without finding a result suggesting that labor income and capital income should be treated equally by the tax system. This is hardly surprising, as there is no obvious intuition why such a result might make sense, leaving aside practical difficulties that arise in distinguishing capital income and labor income. It is no accident that the literature has focused on whether it is efficient for capital income taxes to be zero rather than on whether there should be equal taxes on capital income and labor income.

Even with all the complications in the literature, there has developed a strong theoretical basis for thinking that consumption taxes can be more efficient than income taxes. But theory typically fails to tell us what the optimal tax on capital income should be or how great the efficiency difference might be between an income tax and a consumption tax. Given the transition costs of moving from one tax system to another, and the imperfections of both the current system and any prospective version of the consumption tax, a small efficiency gain in moving to a consumption tax could easily be outweighed by the transition costs, so the move to a consumption tax would not be desirable even on the efficiency ground alone.

Can future research sharpen these predictions? Much of the work on dynamic optimal taxation is very recent. In time we are likely to gain a better idea of how large capital income tax wedges should be, at least in the very stylized models of the literature. These models typically have a simple structure with regard to individual decisions and assume considerable flexibility with respect to the choice of tax instruments, so they will continue to serve as a guide rather than as a source of estimates unless they incorporate considerably more realistic characterizations of individual and institutional behavior. But this is an important service, as the evolution of thinking about the comparison of income and consumption taxes to date demonstrates.

1.1.2 Bequests and Inheritances

There are many potential explanations for bequests, and they differ in how they would affect the previous analysis. A strong altruistic bequest motive, as in Barro (1974), turns the decisions of a life-cycle individual into the infinite horizon calculations of a dynasty, thereby increasing the deadweight loss from capital income taxation. At the other extreme, accidental bequests that occur because of incomplete annuity markets do not imply any extension of an individual's planning horizon. In between are models where there is some form of interest in the size of one's bequest, either because of a joy of giving or because the prospect of bequests can be used to elicit favorable behavior from one's potential heirs. While the empirical evidence strongly rejects the extreme version of Barro's predictions (Altonji et al. 1997), it is likely that observed bequests reflect a mixture of motives. Indeed this is Bernheim's (2002, p. 1196) conclusion based on a review of our knowledge from the empirical literature.

It is not clear how much the nature of the bequest motive matters for the choice between income and consumption taxes. As confirmed by simulations presented in Altig et al. (2001), even planned bequests, if they are motivated by the benefits of giving rather than the ultimate consumption of one's heirs, need have little impact on the desirability of consumption taxes. Moreover, as discussed above, the distortions of future consumption resulting from capital income taxation are already significant within the long-horizon life-cycle context, so the potential lengthening of the horizon beyond one's own lifetime doesn't make the efficiency argument for eliminating capital income taxes that much stronger.

Of course, the nature of the bequest motive matters considerably more as one considers the future of the estate tax or the possible role of inheritance taxes. A tax on unplanned bequests is a nondistortionary tax, whereas a tax on planned bequests is more akin to a capital income tax in its effects on saving behavior. Understanding the nature of the bequest motive, then, is very important to decisions about the role that transfer taxes should play in the tax system.

1.1.3 Eliminating Distortions in the Treatment of Assets and Liabilities

Tax reform discussion often relates not just to the overall level of capital income taxation but also to differential capital income taxation. Since Diamond and Mirrlees (1971) showed that efficient allocation of resources in production can be a desirable outcome even in the presence of other tax distortions, there has been a general sense that taxing different types of capital income at different rates reduces economic efficiency beyond the degree necessary to raise revenue for government spending and redistribution. Thus, we know that differential capital income taxation is a bad idea, at least under certain assumptions. Some take this as an additional argument in favor of consumption taxation, for taxing all capital income at a rate of zero is one method of implementing uniform capital income taxation.

Simulations suggest that the deadweight loss from differential capital income taxation is equivalent to raising overall capital income tax rates by several percentage points,[4] so removing these additional distortions would substantially increase the attractiveness of a consumption tax or some other method of eliminating capital income taxes. But to what extent does equalization of effective capital income tax rates require elimination of the income tax? Some (e.g., Hubbard 1997) have suggested thinking about reform of capital income taxation as consisting of two steps, the first of which involves eliminating differential capital income taxation and the second of which involves reducing this uniform capital income tax rate to zero. Whether this is a valid decomposition depends in part of political factors, particularly whether it is possible to eliminate the favorable treatment of certain assets, owner-occupied housing being a notable example, without adopting a major change in the tax base.

Analyzing the politics of tax reform is largely beyond this chapter's scope, but there is also a technical reason why a consumption tax might make it easier to eliminate differential capital income taxation: it is difficult to tax capital income uniformly when the income from any particular asset is difficult to measure. Measuring income from a depreciable asset requires measurement of depreciation, and taxing real income means adjusting measured income for inflation. If we make these corrections imperfectly, some differential taxation will remain under the income tax even if our objective is to provide uniform treatment.[5] Exempting capital income or adopting a consumption tax would each eliminate the need to measure capital income, and this would provide further scope for efficiency gains. How much of the existing differences in capital income taxes are due to such difficulties, rather than to willful distinctions in the treatment of different assets, has not been a focus of research, but is knowable if one is willing to put enough structure on the problem of measuring capital income. The most obvious differential in current law, though, is probably that between owner-occupied housing and other capital, a differential that clearly is not due primarily to the difficulty of measuring imputed rents.[6]

On the financial side of business activities, consumption taxes would eliminate existing distinctions between debt and equity and between dividends and capital gains. Again some of these differences are more difficult to eliminate under the income tax. For example, treating dividends and capital gains equally would require taxing capital gains effectively on accrual. The difficulties of doing so have been put forward as one reason for the current treatment, although these difficulties have been disputed (e.g., Shakow 1986), and alternatives suggested that do not require measuring accrued gains (Auerbach 1991; Bradford 1995; Auerbach and Bradford 2004). We know that taxing income as we do is likely to have an impact on financial decisions, given evidence from the literature that debt–equity ratios and dividend distribution policies depend on tax incentives.[7] But we do not have a clear sense of what the welfare gains would be from removing such tax distortions.

A problem in estimating the efficiency costs of financial distortions is that these distortions exist in an environment in which first-best behavior in the absence of tax distortions would be unlikely. With the existing agency problem due to the separation of ownership and control, tax-induced financial distortions could lessen deadweight loss, for example, by forcing entrenched managers to take on more debt and therefore to expend greater effort to stave off bankruptcy. With the determination of why firms pay dividends in the face of unfavorable tax treatment still not fully resolved, it is hard to know how removal of the tax penalty on dividend payments would change welfare. Under at least some interpretations of the "traditional" view of dividend taxation, reducing the tax on dividends will encourage dividend payment and reduce the equity cost of capital, in each case reducing a distortion. Under the "new" view, on the other hand, neither of these effects would be present; the dividend–capital gains tax differential would be capitalized for mature firms, and dividend tax cuts would amount to little more than lump-sum transfers to shareholders.

The potential gains from reducing or eliminating the distinction between debt and equity are therefore hard to quantify based on our present knowledge. Certainly the shift to a markedly different tax system would give us an opportunity to learn more from observed responses. But this information would not be available in advance.

1.1.4 How Large is the Capital Income Tax Wedge?

Calculations of the efficiency gains from eliminating the capital income tax wedge depend, of course, on this size of this wedge. If the before-tax rate of return to capital were high, a capital income tax could alter the price of future consumption substantially; if the before-tax rate of return were zero, on the other hand, a capital income tax at the same rate would collect no revenue and impose no distortions. Thus, although the theory might point toward elimination of capital income taxes, the potential efficiency gains depend critically on the size of the initial tax wedge.

The before-tax rate of return to capital in the US economy, as measured by capital income as a percentage of the capital stock, is quite high. For example, Feldstein, Poterba, and Dicks-Mireaux (1983) estimated that the US nonfinancial corporate capital stock had an average before-tax rate of return of 11.5 percent for the period 1948 to 1979. With the effective tax rates well above 50 percent estimated by the same authors, the implied tax wedge on capital income is sizable. On the other hand, the before-tax real interest rate on bonds such as Treasury securities has been much closer to zero over the years, rarely rising above a few percent regardless of the term of the bond or the method of calculating expected inflation. Even if the same high tax rates were applied, the tax wedge based on this lower rate of return would be much lower.

What is the right rate of return on which to base efficiency calculations? As argued by Gordon (1985) and developed by others in the literature (e.g., Kaplow 1994; Warren 1996; Weisbach 2004), often with particular reference to the consumption tax, the taxation of capital income in an efficient capital market should be evaluated relative to the safe rate of return. The remaining tax is a tax on the excess return to risk, which imposes no burden on the taxpayer and has no value to the government once an appropriate adjustment for risk is made. The logic is that (1) a tax on excess returns can be offset by investors by increasing their holdings of risky assets, leaving their after-tax budget set unaffected by the tax, (2) the riskiness of the government's revenue cannot be reduced by pooling because the private market has already accomplished all possible pooling, and (3) once the government transmits this risk back to the economy, the added "background" risk would offset the propensity for increased individual purchases of risky assets in response to the original taxation of excess risk. In the end the taxation of excess returns should leave the equilibrium unaffected.

If the safe rate of return is close to zero, then how large can the gains be from reducing the tax rate on this return to zero? Simulation results, such as in Auerbach and Kotlikoff (1987) and in subsequent papers using the Auerbach-Kotlikoff model, are based on a calibration technique that treats the entire rate of return to capital as normal returns to deferring consumption rather than as compensation for risk. It is difficult to know the extent to which such results might overstate the efficiency gains from adopting a consumption tax because there is no simple way of extending the model to one that incorporates aggregate risk, in which the risky and safe rates of return are determined in equilibrium and the risk premium changes as the tax system and equilibrium change. To get some idea of the potential magnitudes involved, in Auerbach (2006) I consider a simpler experiment, in which the economy's capital intensity is held constant but the initial rate of return to capital is taken to be substantially lower than in the standard simulation results in the literature. The new results suggest that the efficiency gains from adopting a consumption tax are very sensitive to the assumed level of the before tax interest rate: reducing the assumed before-tax interest rate by 60 percent reduces the estimated efficiency gain from adopting a consumption tax by more than 90 percent. This result is only suggestive, since it is not based on a model that explicitly incorporates risk and portfolio equilibrium. Further analysis is possible, and hence the results of such analysis potentially knowable, but the technical issues involved in simulating a general equilibrium model with aggregate risk are considerable.

It is also important to remember that capital income taxes are not simply symmetric proportional taxes on capital income. If they were, then the effective tax rate on capital income would not vary with the division of the observed rate of return between the safe rate of return and the excess return to risk-taking. But the tax system is much more complicated, and several factors suggest that as we take risk into account and recognize that the safe rate of return is lower than the observed return to capital, our estimated effective tax rate on that safe rate of return will be higher.

First, asymmetries in the tax system increase the tax burden on risky assets, a point understood since the work of Domar and Musgrave (1944). That is, the tax burden on the excess return is not zero, so for risky assets this must be added to the burden that the capital income tax imposes on the safe rate of return. Second, because depreciation schedules are not based on actual, ex post economic depreciation, the effective tax rate, even under a symmetric tax system, will vary with the safe discount rate and the extent to which depreciation itself is risky. As shown in the Auerbach (2006), reducing the assumed discount rate and taking risky depreciation into account will both tend to increase our estimate of the effective tax rate on investment. Moreover, for a given inflation rate and hence a given tax on the inflationary component of returns, a lower real return will translate into a higher overall effective tax rate.

Thus the rate of return relevant in calculating the intertemporal distortion may be lower than has been assumed in simulation models, but the tax rate applicable to that lower rate of return is likely to be higher. How much higher is difficult to know; the tax rate depends on an asset's riskiness, the extent to which the firm is able to offset one asset's losses with another asset's gains, and how tax asymmetries interact with adjustments for risk. There have been some attempts in the literature to adjust effective tax rates separately for tax asymmetries and risk (e.g. Auerbach 1983b), but these calculations are more illustrative than comprehensive. The magnitudes of these adjustments are at this point more knowable than known.

1.1.5 Summary: Income Taxation versus Consumption Taxation

Consumption taxes may be superior to income taxes, even when distributional considerations are taken into account. The gains may be greater still if the differential tax treatment of capital income present under the existing tax system is at least partially unavoidable under the income tax, or if the use of capital is distorted in the absence of taxation. But there may also be incentive reasons to maintain capital income taxes, and the significance of the capital income tax wedge may be substantially overstated by calculations based on observed before-tax rates of return. These conclusions, tentative and in conflict as they are, reflect the advances of recent decades in our thinking about the choice of tax base. We can learn more from future research. But conclusions based on rather abstract characterizations of income and consumption taxes cannot be applied to the evaluation of concrete reform proposals without considering further details of their design and implementation.

1.2   Attributes of Consumption Taxes

To characterize a consumption tax, let us start with one version of the national income identity relating the product and income sides of gross national product (GNP),

$$GNP = C + I + G + X - M + R^f = W + R + R^f, \qquad (1.1)$$

where C is consumption, I is gross domestic investment, G is government spending, X is exports, M is imports, W is wage income, R is domestic gross capital income, and R^f is net foreign income (i.e., foreign income of domestic residents less domestic income of foreign residents).[8] The standard method for imposing consumption taxes, as under the VAT, is to start on the income side, taxing all factor returns but then forgiving taxes on sales that do not represent consumption, in particular,

$$C = W + R - I - G - X + M \qquad (1.2)$$

so that sales for investment and export are free of tax while tax is imposed on imports.

1.2.1   Government Purchases

If the tax base is meant to be private consumption, then government purchases should also be excluded from the tax base. An equivalent treatment would be for the government budget to be adjusted to offset the taxation of government purchases, for there would be no change in the quantities of goods and services purchased by the government. But the government budget may not adjust, particularly if the federal government taxes the purchases of state and local governments and makes insufficient compensating transfers to these lower level governments. In this event, taxing government purchases would reduce the real budgets of state and local governments.

A relevant question here is how state and local governments would respond to the federal tax on their activities. We have some knowledge from the literature on the responses of subnational governments to fiscal shocks (e.g., Poterba 1994) suggesting that both spending cuts and tax increases will result, if we think of a federal tax on state and local governments as a fiscal shock. But we lack evidence about the effects of a federal tax increase per se. Perhaps the closest we come is evidence on the responsiveness to the federal deductibility of state and local taxes, which is inconclusive about the effects on state and local spending (Feldstein and Metcalf 1987). But this evidence is from an environment in which subnational governments could shift among different revenue sources with different federal tax treatment, so we lack evidence on how such governments would behave if the federal tax were truly unavoidable. Without a natural experiment similar in character to the reform being contemplated, the likely responses of governments are unknowable, at least before a reform takes place.

The treatment of state and local governments would differ among different consumption tax proposals. Some versions of a national retail sales tax would include state and local purchases in the tax base (Gale 2005). While this inclusion would also be possible under a standard credit-invoice VAT, the most recent version of the VAT considered in the United States, in the report of the President's Tax Reform Panel (2005, p. 198), would have left state and local purchases out, as would the VAT included in Graetz's (2002) proposal to use the VAT to eliminate the income tax for taxpayers with income below $100,000. Versions based on the subtraction method VAT, however, including the Hall-Rabushka (1985) flat tax and the Bradford (1986) X-tax, would implicitly tax government purchases because these systems do not include any method for providing a tax rebate to government purchasers from private producers, and would also tax the wage component of goods and services directly produced by governments.

Whether taxing the activities of state and local governments would improve welfare is unknown and largely unknowable. Starting from the view that it is a good idea to tax government-provided goods and services at the same rate as those provided privately to households, political economy considerations and an evaluation of the spillovers from government activities can make deviations in either direction possibly desirable. But it will be a difficult task ever to know the "right" answer.

1.2.2   The Consumption Base

Having dealt with the issue of government purchases, I will leave them out of the remaining analysis of the national income identity, starting instead from expression (1.2'):

$$C = W + R - I - X + M. \tag{1.2'}$$

It is useful to introduce another identity, the international accounts identity, which requires that the current and capital accounts balance:[9]

$$(X - M + R^f) + (-I^f) = 0, \tag{1.3}$$

where I^f is net foreign investment. Combining (1.2′) and (1.3) yields

$$C = W + (R - I) + (R^f - I^f), \tag{1.4}$$

which emphasizes that a consumption tax can also be conceived as a tax on wages plus taxes on the net cash flows (gross income less gross investment) from domestic and foreign activities.

The simplest manner in which "consumption" taxes do not tax consumption is by omitting certain elements of consumption from the tax base. It is common for credit-invoice VATs to "zero-rate" certain commodities with the objective of achieving more progressive taxation. It has been known for some time that the extent of redistribution possible through such variation in consumption tax rates is limited and distortionary, simply because it is difficult to distinguish enough between the rich and the poor based on their commodity bundles (e.g., Sah 1983).

It is a puzzle why the variation in consumption tax rates remains in tax systems that have preferable mechanisms for effecting redistribution, but as a result the relative difficulty of implementing differential commodity taxation under other types of consumption tax—for example, under the subtraction method VAT that forms the basis of the flat tax and the X-tax—has been seen as an advantage of these systems. More complex deviations from consumption taxation occur through the exclusion of certain elements of the components of consumption labeled $(R - I) + (R^f - I^f)$ in (1.4).

1.2.3   Treatment of Existing Capital

For an investment made today at zero present value, the future additions to R or R^f are equal in present value to the cost of today's investment added to I or I^f. Thus, with tax rates constant over time, the decision of whether to include or exclude the components $(R - I)$ and $(R^f - I^f)$ has no impact on the present value of government revenues, nor does it have any impact on the incentive to undertake marginal investments, since the effective tax rate on such investments is zero under both approaches. For some assets, notably owner-occupied housing and other consumer durables, it is difficult to impose a tax on the elements of $(R - I)$ because this requires the taxation of imputed rental income. That is, we observe the investment flows as components of I, but we do not observe all the components of R, just subsequent asset sales, not the flow of imputed rental income during the period of ownership. Hence virtually all consumption tax proposals must exclude these components. Under the VAT this would amount to taxing sales of new housing rather than the subsequent imputed rent.

But, with the net cash flows excluded from marginal new investments that have a present value of zero, there are remaining components of the cash flows $(R - I) + (R^f - I^f)$ for which the present value is not zero: the normal returns (including recovery of principal) from earlier investments and supernormal economic rents. Taxes on such sources of income can possibly enhance economic efficiency by reducing the burden of distortionary taxes.

Studies like those of Judd (1985) and Chamley (1986), which find that the capital income tax should converge to zero in the long run, also prescribe very high capital income taxes in the short run. In the limit, as the time period of positive capital income taxation shortens and the capital income tax rate rises, such a pattern of capital income taxation has effects approaching an immediate capital levy, with virtually no distortionary impact on subsequent behavior.

In detailed simulation analysis based on an overlapping life-cycle model, Auerbach and Kotlikoff (1987) find that a shift from an income tax to a consumption tax would increase economic efficiency, while a shift to a wage tax would reduce economic efficiency. Both a consumption tax and a wage tax would remove the distortion facing intertemporal consumption decisions, a change for which the literature would lead us to expect an efficiency gain. But a consumption tax would impose a capital levy, replacing the tax on income from existing assets with a tax on their principal as well. By eliminating capital income taxes that those accumulating wealth had expected to pay, adoption of a wage tax in a sense provides a capital bonus, which has the opposite impact of a capital levy on efficiency. Thus, as the simulations confirm, it is possible for a shift to wage taxation to reduce economic efficiency even as it removes the intertemporal distortion of consumption decisions.

These simulation results do not tell us what portion of the efficiency gains results from eliminating intertemporal consumption distortions, because the simulations combine this change with a change in the treatment of existing assets. But the fact that the treatment of existing assets can determine whether the overall efficiency gain is positive or negative suggests that the choice of transition provisions is critical. It also suggests that for this empirically based model, the efficiency gains from eliminating the intertemporal distortion of saving are not so large as to be decisive about whether to forsake the current tax system.

Implicit capital levies vary across consumption tax proposals, in part because the proposals vary in their transparency in regard to the presence of a levy. For the household-based consumed income tax, which most closely resembles the current tax system in its treatment of household income, a capital levy would take the form of an elimination of the tax basis of existing assets—a very transparent change. This has led those who designed the USA tax system, a 1990s version of the consumed income tax, to attempt a very complicated mechanism for providing transition relief that had various unintended and undesirable side effects (Ginsburg 1995). At the other extreme is the national retail sales tax; a popular current version, the FairTax, would provide no such relief. The flat tax and the X-tax do not include transition relief as part of their basic design, but such relief has been discussed in connection with the two proposals. As one would expect from comparing the results for transitions to a consumption tax and to a wage tax, providing transition relief under a flat tax or a USA tax substantially reduces the efficiency gains from adopting a consumption tax, in some simulations essentially eliminating any such gains (Auerbach 1996).

We know then that capital levies can be quantitatively important in evaluating possible tax reforms. We also know, however, that the efficiency effects depend on the degree to which capital levies can be adopted without being expected. Auerbach and Kotlikoff (1987) find that delaying implementation of a transition from income to consumption taxation reduces and can more than fully eliminate the efficiency gain by inducing a consumption spurt among those facing the capital levy. One capital levy might also increase expectations of another in the future, again working against the incentive to save.

What we don't know is how expectations are formed regarding capital levies, and how strong the motive of government is to engage in opportunistic tax policy changes. Policy changes don't involve explicit capital levies but implicit ones. This potentially weakens both anticipations and announcement effects. Consider, for example, a policy of increasing the corporate tax rate while introducing an investment tax credit that keeps the same effective tax rate on new investment. Although this policy is equivalent to a one-time capital levy, the equivalence is not transparent, so anticipation that such a policy is coming might have less of a negative impact on investment than anticipation of an explicit capital levy. Likewise, whereas a simple capital levy might strongly increase expectations of another, adoption of the credit cum tax rate increase may be less likely to trigger expectations of a repeat, which would involve a further increase in the credit and a further tax rate increase. This argument is even stronger in the case of shifting to a consumption tax. Would replacing the income tax with a consumption tax lead us to expect an increase in the consumption tax combined with an income subsidy?

Thus, if capital levies appear as by-products of legislation rather than as their central purpose, they may not have the same negative consequences for efficiency as some might fear. In principle, one could learn more about the effects of capital levies by examining the behavioral responses leading up to and following tax reforms, to gain a sense of what the expectations of agents were. But this task is econometrically very challenging, given that capital levies are embedded in broader policy changes that have additional incentive effects.

As to how opportunistic governments are likely to be, there seems little evidence that the imposition of capital levies is viewed consciously as a policy tool, at least in the United States. Of course, some arguments have favored using investment incentives instead of corporate tax rate cuts because the former have "more bang for the buck," the bang coming from excluding existing assets from tax benefits. On the other hand, the most significant piece of tax legislation in decades, the Tax Reform Act of 1986, included large implicit capital bonuses by simultaneously eliminating the investment tax credit and reducing the corporate tax rate (Auerbach 1989a).[10]

1.2.4 Origin versus Destination Basis

One particular element of the consumption tax base about which there has been considerable debate outside the economics profession is the flows from net foreign assets $(R^f - I^f)$. Under a standard destination-based value-added tax, these would be included indirectly through the border tax adjustments on imports and exports, since the current and capital accounts balance. The destination basis has been seen by some as providing a major competitive benefit for the United States if it adopts a standard VAT. But some taxes, notably the Hall-Rabushka flat tax, can be imposed on an origin basis and hence impose no special treatment on the cash flows associated with cross-border investments.

From the analogy with other types of investments, it should be evident that the choice between an origin basis and a destination basis has no impact on the incentives for inbound or outbound investment, just on asset values and the present value of government revenues.[11] Because there is no impact on cross-border investments, trade flows are not affected, provided that an immediate adjustment of exchange rates occurs. That is, assuming no differences between the two tax systems in terms of domestic or foreign price levels, a switch from an origin-based VAT to a destination-based VAT should lead to a currency appreciation for the adopting country that should just offset the incipient advantage of exporters and disadvantage of importers under the destination-based system.

The equivalence of destination-based and origin-based taxes is not exact because of the different treatment of net cash flows under the two systems. As discussed, a destination-based tax would expand the tax base by the present value of returns associated with a country's net foreign asset position. For the United States today, the net foreign asset position is negative, so the destination-based tax would tend to reduce revenues in present value, to the extent that rates of return on US and foreign assets are equal.[12] To the extent that a country's net asset position is close to zero, this would make little difference in terms of tax revenues. But there could still be a big difference in terms of the impact on asset values, even with a zero net international investment position, because the valuation effects would apply to gross asset positions. The cash flows of all US-owned assets held abroad would be hit by the cash-flow tax included in the destination-based VAT, and those of foreign-owned assets held in the United States would be subsidized. The fact that the taxes would be collected on traded commodities rather than on the capital flows is irrelevant, since the exchange rate adjustment would shift the incidence of the taxes onto the asset holders.[13]

As an example of the size of the potential asset revaluations associated with border adjustments, consider the case of the United States at the end of 2004, when, according to the Bureau of Economic Analysis, foreign-owned assets in the United States totaled $11.5 trillion and US-owned assets abroad were $9.1 trillion.[14] The border adjustment of a domestic VAT at a rate, say, of 30 percent, would require a 30 percent depreciation of foreign currencies relative to the dollar—a $2.7 trillion loss for US holders of foreign assets, and a gain of $4.9 ($11.5/ 0.7 – $11.5) trillion for foreign asset holders, relative to a 30 percent VAT with no border adjustment.

As in the discussion of capital levies above, it seems unlikely that asset revaluations that result from the decision to impose a border adjustment would have any significant effects on expectations of subsequent government policy. Border adjustments cannot be introduced to a tax system more than once.

1.2.5   Treatment of Financial Assets and Liabilities

As discussed above, a consumption tax would eliminate the differential tax treatment on the "sources" and "uses" sides of the capital market, imposing a zero tax on capital income regardless of the type of investment and regardless of the source of funds. But there are still distinctions of a more subtle variety among different approaches to consumption taxation. These distinctions may affect the relative attractiveness of the different approaches.

Following expression (1.4), a tax on consumption requires that gross private income be taxed and that gross investment purchases be deductible or in some other manner effectively excluded from the tax base. Except to the extent that they represent holding of foreign assets, financial positions do not show up in expression (1.4) because they net out. That is, we can also write expression (1.4) as

$$C = W + (R - I) + (R^f - I^f) + (F - J), \tag{1.4$'$}$$

where F is net flows from financial assets and J is net purchases of financial assets, and these both equal zero in the economy as a whole.

Note that as in the case of net foreign assets, the F and J each being zero in the aggregate does not imply the absence of wealth effects from a decision to tax the component flows; it simply means that these wealth effects cancel. Imposing a cash-flow tax on all financial assets and liabilities places a tax on the returns to all existing financial assets and presents a subsidy of equal magnitude to those with financial liabilities. This effect would occur even if F and J were not included explicitly in the tax base, if the price level rose and the financial assets and liabilities were not indexed to the price level. Some have argued that the adoption of a VAT or a retail sales tax would raise the price level by the extent of the tax, that such a price increase would simulate the imposition of a cash-flow tax on net financial assets. It follows, of course, that including financial flows in the tax base *and* having the price level rise by the extent of the tax would effectively impose the cash-flow tax on net asset positions twice. What would actually happen to the price level is largely a matter of how monetary policy reacts to tax reform.

Leaving aside these distributional effects of including financial flows in the cash-flow tax base, these flows would not equal zero if we consider only the flows of the private sector, for then the net cash flows between the private sector and the government would be included in the tax base. Taxing the cash flows to the private sector would have the effect of adding the present value of flows from existing government debt to the tax base; once again nominal assets would be hit twice if the price level rose, in this case raising the present value of tax collections twice because the tax applies to a positive net asset position.

Another variation in the taxation of financial flows would be to impose a cash-flow tax on flows of the business sector. Flows within the business sector would, again, cancel out in terms of revenue, assuming all businesses are subject to the same tax rate, but flows between the business sector and the household sector would not cancel out. Because the business sector is a net debtor to the household sector, this tax would have the effect of reducing the cash-flow tax base by the present value of interest on net existing liabilities, absent any special transition provisions. Such a variant of the cash-flow tax was described by the Meade Committee (Institute for Fiscal Studies 1978) as an "$R + F$" base cash-flow tax.

An administrative advantage of the $R + F$ base is that it eases the task of taxing the income generated by the financial services sector. Recall that the objective of the consumption tax is to include all capital income components of GNP, R, in the tax base. But some components of capital income may be disguised as interest payments. Including all elements of $R + F$ in the tax base obviates the need to identify components of F that should instead be included in R. Thus an $R + F$ base VAT applied to a financial services company would automatically tax interest-rate spreads that compensate the company for the services it renders. Another advantage of the $R + F$ base is that it would eliminate the incentives of an integrated company offering both real and financial services to shift profits from real to financial activities.

Unfortunately, as it eliminates one distinction, the $R + F$ base introduces another. As the Meade Committee (Institute for Fiscal Studies 1978, ch. 12) observed, the transactions of the business sector are related by an identity that, using our notation, can be written as

$$(R - I) + (F - J) + S = 0, \tag{1.5}$$

where S equals net inflows to the firms from sales of corporate shares and dividend payments (i.e., the net flows to firms from their shareholders). Under an R base tax that ignores financial transactions between the business and household sectors, both $(F - J)$ and S are omitted from the tax base. Thus transactions between a firm's creditors and shareholders are treated identically. Just as new share issues and dividends are excluded from the tax base, so are borrowing and interest payments. But once $(F - J)$ is included in the tax base, transactions with creditors are subject to a cash-flow tax—with taxes on borrowing and deductions for interest expense and repayment of principal— while transactions with shareholders are ignored.

How serious a problem is created by this distinction in how the sources of funds are treated under the $R + F$ base depends on the extent to which firms can manipulate payments between debt and equity, for example, by issuing debt and equity to the same party and overstating deductible interest payments while understating nondeductible dividends. The problem is similar to that under the R base of shifts on the output side between the firm's real and financial activities, so the decision of whether to group financial flows with the firm's transactions with its customers or with the firm's transactions with its shareholders depends in part on where the problem of manipulation is greater.

In practice, the standard credit-invoice value added tax approach follows the R base rather than the $R + F$ base. Financial services are either left out or dealt with through some alternative mechanism that attempts to get at the value added in the financial services sector.[15] This requires drawing a line between real and financial companies. The same R base approach characterizes the flat tax and the X-tax, which are variants of the VAT. The natural approach for household based taxes like the USA tax, on the other hand, is to cover both real and financial assets. On the other hand, many variants are conceivable. For example, McLure and Zodrow (1996) advocate implementing a cash-flow tax with an $R + F$ base at the *business* level (with a yield exemption at the household level). Their arguments for both the $R + F$ base over the R base and the cash-flow tax over the yield exemption approach include those presented here, but they suggest that it makes sense to impose the tax at the business level, to target potential tax avoidance behavior most directly, and to shift the costs of compliance away from less sophisticated household taxpayers.

The distinction between the R and $R + F$ bases has an analogy to the comparative treatment of real and financial flows under the income tax. The standard income tax follows what essentially is an $R + F$ approach, in that the income from both real and financial activities is included in the tax base and expenses from financial activities are deducted. As is true under a consumption tax, this removes the distinction on the receipts side but retains it with respect to flows between the firm and the holders of its assets. However, one prominent proposal, the comprehensive business income tax (CBIT) laid out by the US Treasury (1992), would shift the taxation of businesses to an R base approach, removing the tax on interest income and the deduction for interest paid. Again, as under a consumption tax, this would eliminate the distinction between debt and equity but introduce a distinction between real and financial activities of the firm. To maintain consistency in the treatment of debt and equity, the CBIT would also treat the income flows equally at the individual level, in this case by not taxing any such flows. As with the R base consumption tax, the issue of how to deal with financial enterprises arises under the CBIT as well. One could also contemplate an $R + F$-based CBIT, which would tax firms on financial and real income and provide them with a deduction for interest payments. But this would reduce the effective tax rate to zero for debt-financed investment and hence would require some sort of compensating tax at the debt-holder level.[16]

1.2.6   Timing of Tax Payments

Aside from their differences in the treatment of rents and normal returns to existing assets, the cash-flow and tax-exempt approaches to consumption taxation also differ with respect to the timing of tax collections. While the tax-exempt treatment simply imposes no taxes, cash-flow treatment arrives at the same zero present value through deductions and taxes at different dates that offset each other.

This dependence on offsetting tax effects at different dates means that when tax rates vary over time, the cash-flow tax no longer imposes a zero effective tax rate on capital accumulation. Indeed the effective tax rates could be very positive or negative if large tax rate changes occur over short periods, given that gross investment is fully deductible in one year and gross returns are fully subject to taxation in others. This led Bradford (1998b) among others to suggest replacing the immediate deduction of investment with the procedure of carrying the basis of investment forward with interest and taking depreciation deductions in accordance with the timing of economic depreciation. While these deductions would have the same present value as immediate expensing with tax rates constant, their timing would eliminate the distortion of investment decisions: marginal investments would face a zero effective tax rate regardless of the path of tax rates, as only supernormal rents would be subject to taxation in any period.

This "basis with interest" approach thus combines the insulation from tax rate changes and the timing of revenues of the tax exemption approach with the taxation of rents present under the cash-flow tax. However, this compromise has a major drawback relative to the simple cash-flow tax (and to tax exemption) of requiring that investors keep track of asset bases and calculate depreciation allowances over time.[17]

As discussed above, not having to measure capital income has been viewed as a benefit of a consumption tax based on cash flows. Indeed, rather than attempting to make a cash-flow tax look more like an income tax, Auerbach and Bradford (2004) adopt the opposite approach of considering how to make an income tax look more like a cash-flow tax. They developed a method of using the cash-flow tax with rising tax rates over time to simulate an income tax, suggesting that the advantages of eliminating basis outweigh the disadvantage of susceptibility to time-varying tax rates, particularly with financial innovation in that the identification of specific assets is made more difficult. Another instance of using the simplicity of cash-flow taxation in an income tax context is the Auerbach and Jorgenson (1980) proposal to provide immediate expensing of the discounted present value of depreciation allowances, thereby obviating the need to adjust allowances annually for inflation.

Thus, in terms of timing, a consumption tax can be made to look more like an income tax, and also an income tax to look more like a consumption tax. Moving in either direction has its costs and benefits, and the balance between the two is not clear. In any event, the "basis with interest" approach to consumption taxation has not become widely featured among consumption tax proposals.

1.2.7   Individual versus Business Taxation

Consumption taxes can be imposed either at the business level or at the individual level. The working of the business-level VAT has already been discussed. A consumed income tax starts with the individual income base from which is subtracted net saving. If saving is measured consistently with income, then all income that is not saved is consumed, so the result is a consumption tax. Similarly one can adopt a mixed approach, as under the flat tax or the X-tax, that starts with a VAT and shifts the taxation of wages from the business to the individual level. While the location of tax collection is irrelevant at some abstract level, it is likely have some real effects in practice.

First, the business–household borderline is not clear, and some income-producing activities might be included in the household sector under a business-level consumption tax. For example, how would a household's speculative holding of land be treated?

Second, progressive taxation based on an individual's circumstances can, realistically, only be applied to taxes at the individual level. Hence the flat tax and the X-tax transfer the wage component of the tax base to households in order to apply progressive rate schedules to that base.

Third, the difference in statutory incidence can also affect the measured price level. A value-added tax, or a retail sales tax, added to factor incomes can have a higher measured price level than if the same tax were collected from individual consumers through a consumed income tax. Although this difference simply reflects a convention in how the price level is measured—including indirect taxes but excluding direct taxes—it can have real effects to the extent that the price level matters, for example, for the indexation of transfer payments and the distribution of gains and losses between debtors and creditors. The price level also matters to the extent that wages are sticky, through either explicit rigidities due to contract and minimum wage provisions or other sources of sluggish adjustment.

Fourth, market prices of assets will differ according to the level at which taxes are collected. In comparing the impact on market values of a VAT and a consumed income tax, it is helpful to consider the treatment of traditional IRAs under current law. The securities inside an IRA have one market value, but this is not the after-tax value of the IRA to its owner (i.e., what the holder of the IRA could sell the account for if the future tax liability due on withdrawals was transferred along with the asset). If all investments were through IRAs, as effectively would be the case under an individual level consumption tax, the after-tax value of the existing IRA to the investor would fully capitalize these deferred taxes. Then a new IRA composed of the same portfolio of securities would face no taxes in present value under a system with constant tax rates over time.[18] If the taxes were payable not by individuals holding the IRAs, but instead by the firms issuing the securities held in the IRAs, the market values of the securities would already reflect the deferred taxes. There would be no difference in the after-tax value of the securities to investors, but the market values would adjust to offset the shift in statutory incidence of the tax from investors to firms.[19]

Because market values under economically equivalent consumption taxes can vary significantly, the impact on market values of adopting a consumption tax depends very much on how the tax is imposed, even if the ultimate economic impact of the tax does not. Consider a shift from the current US tax system to a consumption tax. As discussed above, a consumption tax without transition relief incorporates a form of capital levy in its tax on rents and the normal returns to existing assets. This capital levy would cause the after-tax values of assets to fall. An offsetting effect on asset values comes from an increase in asset demand because of a shift to the more favorable treatment of new investment. Still it is likely that the after-tax values of existing assets to investors would fall.[20] But the *market* values of the assets could rise if some taxes were shifted from the business level to the individual level. Given that the depreciation provisions of the current US corporate income tax favor new assets over existing assets, the values of corporate shares should capitalize this difference, simulating the impact of partial cash flow taxation.[21] Going to full cash-flow taxation, but shifting the entire tax to the individual level (e.g., by replacing the current corporate and personal income taxes with a consumed income tax), would lower the after-tax values of these assets to investors but *raise* their market values, since the taxes on asset sales would be due *after* the assets were sold.

Finally, some have argued that indirect consumption taxes are a more effective method of collecting taxes from individuals who do not report income or pay tax under the income tax. The logic is that these individuals who currently pay no tax would be hit by sales tax or VAT on their purchases. Presumably this supposed benefit of indirect consumption taxes would not apply to a household-level consumed income tax, for the tax evader would be no more likely to file a tax return than before. But the underlying logic is flawed, as the following discussion illustrates.

1.2.8   Activities outside the Tax System

In a simple world without intermediate inputs or investment, where income equals consumption, it is easy to see the flaw in the previous logic. Imagine that there are two sectors, sector 1 that is covered by the tax system and sector 2 that is not covered. Under the income tax, sector 1 pays taxes while sector 2 does not. Under an indirect consumption tax, sector 1 again pays taxes while sector 2 does not. Thus there has been no change in the tax base, and hence no possible reason for any change in tax incidence.

A somewhat more sophisticated analysis that takes intermediate inputs into account doesn't change the basic story. Suppose now that the first sector produces both investment goods and consumption goods, that the investment goods serve as capital in both sectors, and that both sectors are competitive, so that price equals marginal cost. Then, under an income tax, the costs of production and hence prices in the covered and uncovered sectors will be, respectively,

$$p_1 = \frac{w}{1-t}l_1 + p_1\frac{r}{1-t}k_1, \tag{1.6a}$$

$$p_2 = wl_2 + p_1rk_2, \tag{1.6b}$$

where w and r are the required after-tax returns to labor and capital, t is the income tax rate, and l_i and k_i and unit labor and capital requirements in each sector. Under an indirect consumption tax at rate τ, the effective tax rate on capital income becomes zero in the covered sector, so these expressions become

$$p_1 = \frac{w}{1-\tau}l_1 + p_1rk_1, \tag{1.7a}$$

$$p_2 = wl_2 + p_1rk_2. \tag{1.7b}$$

Because we are assuming that the tax change is revenue-neutral in present value, τ must be enough higher than t to make up for the revenue lost by setting the effective tax rate on capital to zero. Since only sector 1 is subject to taxation, this equal-revenue requirement implies that for given values of w and r, the solution for p_1 in expressions (1.6a) and (1.7a) must be the same, hence also the solutions for p_2 in (1.6b) and (1.7b). Thus, with no change in w and r, there will be no change in the relative production costs or prices of the commodities produced by the covered and uncovered sectors. However, the reduction in the cost of capital relative to labor in sector 1 will encourage a shift from labor to capital in production, and this increased demand for capital relative to labor will raise r relative to w. As discussed further in Hines (2004), this change will raise relative costs in whichever sector is more capital intensive, quite plausibly the covered sector.

Thus the shift to an indirect consumption tax like a VAT or a retail sales tax may actually encourage the expansion of activity in the uncovered sector, rather than contracting it. This leaves aside differences among approaches in their ease of enforcement. Some have seen a particular weakness in the retail sales tax approach, which provides less of a paper trail than the credit-invoice VAT and relies solely on final sellers for collection (President's Advisory Panel on Tax Reform 2005, pp. 217–18).

1.2.9   A Hybrid Tax System as a Partial Consumption Tax

The US tax system is frequently referred to as a hybrid system with elements of income taxation and consumption taxation because a considerable share of household assets is held in some sort of tax-sheltered account. Most of these accounts (the tax-exempt Roth IRA being the primary exception) are treated the way saving would be treated under a consumed income tax, with deductible contributions and taxable withdrawals. Most of the tax-sheltered accounts are associated with retirement saving, but there are now also vehicles that allow households to shelter saving for education (Section 529 plans) and medical expenses (health saving accounts).

It is frequently asserted that the current system is like a combination of an income tax and a consumption tax, with lower but not zero taxes on capital income. However, there are a number of significant differences between the current system—an income tax with some tax-sheltered saving—and a combined income-consumption tax, such as would be accomplished by having a broad-based, low-rate income tax along with, say, an add-on VAT. First, contributions to tax-sheltered accounts are capped, so that most high-income households will face the full rate of income tax at the margin even if a large share of their assets are in tax-sheltered accounts. Second, contributions to accounts can come from previously accumulated wealth, so that the capital levy associated with the consumption tax is completely absent. Finally, the full deductibility of interest combined with reduced taxation of capital income encourages borrowing to invest in tax favored assets rather than saving.[22]

Under standard economic analysis, the hybrid system would seem to be considerably inferior to a true combination of income and consumption taxes, since it may substantially reduce tax collections without reducing marginal tax rates on saving commensurately. But there is considerable thought that some deviations from standard economic analysis are needed to explain various aspects of observed saving behavior. These deviations could potentially influence several aspects of tax system design.

Should Capital Income Be Taxed?
With many individuals possibly saving too little for retirement,[23] one might think that lower taxes on capital income would provide even larger welfare gains than under standard assumptions, by encouraging people to overcome obstacles to saving. But this conclusion depends on the nature of the savings problem. Encouraging saving might be ineffective if individuals anticipate that additional saving will simply be squandered by a future self. Depending on the nature of the departure from standard rational choice assumptions, one might actually wish to tax capital income (Bernheim and Rangel 2005).

Tax Exempt or Deductible Accounts?
Under standard assumptions both approaches provide a zero effective tax rate on saving when tax rates are constant over time. But given evidence that contributions to deductible IRAs were greater among households with additional tax due on April 15 (Feenberg and Skinner 1989), there is some possibility that the immediate deduction is more salient than the eventual tax exemption.

Flexible or Restricted?
The current practice of earmarking tax-sheltered accounts for different purposes (retirement, education, medical expenses, etc.) is inconsistent with the implications of standard models, since it artificially restricts the flexibility of individuals who save. But some models of how individuals deal with self-control problems suggest that maintaining

such an artificial separation helps to "lock" funds away from temptation through a form of "mental accounting." (Shefrin and Thaler 1988).

Our knowledge about the extent to which contributions to tax-sheltered retirement accounts constitutes new saving is still imperfect.[24] But the possibility that substantial new saving is occurring even when individuals could fund the accounts by transferring assets seems very much at odds with the predictions of standard models of intertemporal choice. This possible existence of new saving may also relate to mental accounting behavior, with individuals imposing barriers on themselves against transferring assets from one type of account to another.

Nor would another type of restriction, on withdrawals from accounts, arise from standard assumptions. However, such restrictions are welfare-improving in models with time inconsistent preferences, in which individuals wish to bind their "future selves" from behaving in a profligate manner (Laibson 1997).

Default in or Out?
With full information about their options for saving, rational households would not seem likely to be affected by the default options of employer-sponsored retirement saving plans. But experimental evidence suggests that default options can exert a very strong influence on the level and pattern of contributions beyond the short run (Madrian and Shea 2001). Our knowledge on this point is clear enough that the President's Advisory Panel on Federal Tax Reform (2005, pp. 118–19) structured its Save at Work plans to have various "autosave" features aimed at increasing the saving of passive employees, including automatic enrollment, automatic growth in contribution percentages, and automatic rollover into another tax deferred plan upon changing employers.

Summary
Saving behavior may not conform to the predictions of standard models, and these deviations have potentially important implications for tax system design. But the nature of the deviations is also important. For example, the consumption tax's broad-based incentive to save may not lead to more saving than the welter of current saving schemes if mental accounts play a role in encouraging saving. On the other hand, the confusion that such schemes causes may blunt their potential benefits if imperfect information is a significant cause of undersaving.

Research in the behavioral economics of saving is still ongoing, so the state of our knowledge is likely to improve. But research to date suggests that alternative behavioral explanations for observed saving behavior may have different implications for policy. Our ability to advance our knowledge may depend literally on looking inside people's heads at their brain activity, as some very recent research in "neuroeconomics" has attempted to do.

1.2.10   Tax Progressivity

A common concern about adopting a consumption tax is that it would be less progressive than the income tax. This depends, of course, on the type of consumption tax involved and how one evaluates progressivity. The flat tax, for example, through its very high zero-bracket amount, can be viewed as progressive at the bottom of the income distribution, that is, when comparing those at the bottom to those in the middle. But it is less progressive at the top. This is one of the motivations of the proposal by Graetz (2002), namely to implement a VAT and eliminate the income tax for those with incomes below $100,000 but retain the income tax (at a lower rate) for incomes above $100,000.

However, other approaches based solely on consumption taxes appear to be successful at replicating the current distribution of the income tax burden. In their simulations Altig et al. (2001) find that in the long run the distributional effects of a switch from the income tax to the X-tax would be quite neutral, with very similar percentage increases in lifetime welfare for all lifetime income classes, with the slight differences among the groups favoring those with lower lifetime income. A similar conclusion was reached by the President's Tax Reform Panel in its report (p. 175) evaluating the Growth and Income Tax plan, which combines an X-tax with a 15 percent individual tax on interest, dividends, and capital gains.

Yet there remains skepticism that a consumption tax can be progressive enough to impose the same burden on those at the top as the current income tax. One way to interpret this concern is that it is about those at the very top, well within the highest 2 percent that formed the top group in the analysis of Altig et al. (2001). It is conceivable that the percentage welfare gains under the X-tax would have been higher for the very highest lifetime income groups had Altig et al. (2001) broken down their highest group into still smaller groups.

Another source of concern about those at the top may relate to bequests, which are very concentrated. In the presence of bequests, the form of consumption taxation and the nature of the bequest motive matter for calculations of progressivity. The simulations of Altig et al. (2001) included a realistic level and pattern of bequests, modeled as resulting from a "utility of bequests" motive. But they also found that the long-run welfare consequences, including the roughly equal percentage welfare gains by lifetime income groups, were not significantly affected by whether the bequest motive was present.

This finding may seem surprising, given the concentration of bequests among the wealthy. The likely explanation is that Altig et al. (2001) analyzed the X-tax whose nonwage portion is collected at the business level. As discussed above, this means that the tax is capitalized into the value of assets.[25] Thus it hits all eventual uses of wealth, not just lifetime consumption but also bequests. Under a personal consumption tax like the consumed income tax, on the other hand, the same treatment of bequests would require taxing bequests as consumption instead of taxing them upon eventual consumption by heirs. But (assuming tax rates to be constant over time) this shift in the timing of taxation would have no impact on heirs' consumption and hence no impact on the lifetime welfare of donors unless the utility of bequests was based on gross bequests, rather than on the level of consumption that bequests could finance.

Long-run comparisons of tax system progressivity do not take into account the incidence of transition provisions. Aside from its potential efficiency benefits, the capital levy component of some consumption tax schemes could be quite progressive. This would be even more the case to the extent that the assets are inherited, given the concentration of bequests and inheritances. And, as discussed above, the desirability of transfer taxes, be they on estates, inheritances, or gifts, depends very much on the nature of the bequest motive. If the estate tax is a relatively efficient tax instrument and can be maintained even as the income tax is replaced by a consumption tax, then a much greater consensus in favor of tax reform is possible.[26]

1.3 What Don't We Know, and When Will We Know It?

The benefits of a large-scale tax reform that shifts from the current tax system to some form of consumption taxation are enumerable but difficult to measure, given the state of our knowledge.

There are efficiency gains from reducing the capital income tax wedge, but the size of these gains is very uncertain, given technical issues associated with their estimation and the nature of behavioral deviations from standard modeling assumptions. There may also be gains in transition from the taxation of existing wealth, but their size and existence depends on the extent to which transition policy is anticipated and alters individual expectations and is politically feasible. Consumption taxes can sharply reduce the distortions of financial and investment decisions, but we do not know the extent to which these distortions can be eliminated simply through measures adopted within the context of the current tax system. Realistic consumption taxes can be progressive, but we don't know whether this is true at the very top of the income distribution. And estate taxes may occupy a key role in a progressive, efficient tax system, but this depends on the relative strengths of different bequest motives.

We do know not to adopt a consumption tax in order to improve our trade balance or our ability to tax underground activities. We also know that our existing knowledge must be continually recalibrated to a moving target. As financial innovation blurs the distinction between real and financial activities, for example, the benefits of a system that is unaffected by this distinction are likely to grow.

Adopting large tax reform is likely to enhance our knowledge about a lot of things. But taking a range of smaller steps in the right direction certainly looks attractive as an alternative, particularly when the benefits do not hinge on plucking strong assumptions from our bag of uncertainty.

Discussion

Henry J. Aaron

The title of this volume asks: Is it time for fundamental tax reform? Alan Auerbach's answer, as I read it, is: "Not yet," at least if the term "fundamental" implies replacement of the current system with a consumption tax. Furthermore, if action is to be based on clear evidence, "not yet" means "not for a long, long time." True to the canons of journal article authors and grant applicants, Alan says more research is needed to make the case for fundamental reform—a *lot* of research, ranging in difficulty from very hard to nearly impossible. And, please note Alan's chosen title—Tax Reform *in the twenty-first Century*. Between now and the twenty-second century, however, a lengthy menu of quite desirable and urgent modifications in the current tax system remains before us.

Whether or not Alan agrees with my characterization of his argument, let me explain why I think I am accurate and why Alan is right to urge that we put the campaign to replace the income tax with a consumption tax on hold.

Let's start with the standard model of rational decision makers operating in a world of frictionless capital markets. The alleged advantages of switching from an income to a consumption tax rest on a few considerations: the difference between how the two taxes treat the riskless return to new investments; how the tax system treats consumption out of old capital—that is, transition rules; and how behavior, especially saving, changes when tax rules change.

Whether the welfare gain from changing the taxation of riskless gains is large or small depends in part on the size of the riskless return. Some say that return is small—as little as half a percent a year. Others

The views expressed here are my own and do not necessarily reflect those of the trustees, officers, or other staff of the Brookings Institution.

say it is larger—perhaps 2 to 3 percent a year. But no one says that it is the full long-run total real return of 6 to 8 percent. If the riskless return is at the lower range, the efficiency gains are probably small.

The choices made regarding transition rules are likely to have larger welfare effects than will changes in the taxation of the riskless return. Fully taxing consumption from old capital—that is, expropriating income tax basis—is that *rara avis* of public finance, a lump-sum tax, that distorts nothing and therefore raises welfare by supplanting distortionary taxes. That *avis* becomes a lot less *rara*—and more distortionary—if people think it might happen again—but never mind.

Completely exempting consumption from old capital is, on the other hand, a lump-sum subsidy that reduces overall welfare, whether or not repeated. Leaving behavioral effects aside, therefore, the sign of the efficiency gains or losses of a switch to consumption taxation may well depend more on transition rules than on the treatment of the riskless rate of return. Were the legislators who enact the consumption tax ever in the future to go even a little bit wobbly on transition rules, a welfare loss is entirely possible. (I choose the word "wobbly" out of respect for the host of the conference at which the chapters in this volume were first presented, the Baker Institute; it was Margaret Thatcher who warned James Baker's boss, George H. W. Bush, during the first Iraq war, "Don't go wobbly on me, George." But I digress.)

Well, what about behavioral effects? In the frictionless, rational world the switch to a consumption tax is likely to boost saving. How much, alas, is close to a guess. And it is not hard to imagine that if the riskless return is as low as some consumption tax advocates argue, and if elasticities of saving with respect to the interest rate are small, the change in consumption may be minuscule.

Behavior may respond differently from that inferred from the standard model. If any of the bounds on rationality to which behavioral economics has lately drawn attention are significant, then a shift to consumption taxation could reduce rather than increase saving. For example, as Auerbach notes, "sheltered" savings vehicles no longer make sense in a consumption tax world. If Congress does away with them and if defaults matter, then the shift to consumption taxation can easily lower saving rather than raise it.

Well, what about simplification? The complexity of the current income tax derives from two broad sets of considerations. For most taxpayers the greatest concern is the proliferation of deductions, credits, allowances, and exclusions. It is they that increase demand for filing

cabinets, promote sales of computer software, and make tax preparation services a growth industry. It is they that enable Congress to influence private behavior and resource allocation without adding to
government employment or public expenditures.

The key point is that the motivation for many of these provisions has
little or nothing to do with the decision to tax or not to tax capital income. If one wants to promote home ownership, historic preservation,
hybrid cars, research and development outlays, and charitable gifts
without hiring government employees or raising appropriations, all
one needs is a *personal* tax, not a *personal income* tax. The solution to
this sort of complexity is the old tax reformer's agenda—base broadening and rate reduction.

Congress implemented much of this agenda in 1986. It has, alas,
spent the succeeding two decades atoning for that good deed. *What* to
do now is clear. *Why* replacement of the income tax with a consumption tax will increase congressional and executive willingness to do it
is not.

The second source of complexity—the one that directly matters little
to most filers but a lot to economists, lawyers, and accountants—
relates to the difficulties of measuring capital income. A switch to a tax
that does not tax capital income from one that does would seem to
hold out great promise of avoiding the problems associated with
measurement of capital income—once one has gotten by a transition
period.

The meaning of the word "transition" has been folded, spindled, and
mutilated of late. Take social security privatization, for example. In that
context, transition refers to an extremely long period. If relief is given
to owners of old capital, transition rules would require two tax systems
to operate in parallel, possibly for a very long time. Transitions are
complicated. Even if the new system is simpler than the old, it is far
from clear that there will be net simplification.

But would the new system *ever* be simpler? Maybe—but maybe not,
according to an excellent paper Joseph Bankman and Michael Schler
prepared for a recent conference on capital income taxation organized
jointly by the Urban Institute and the Brookings Institution. As Bankman and Schler point out, a consumption tax of any variety is still
open to fraud. Opportunities still exist to shift income from taxable to
exempt filers. Misstatement of prices in related party transactions can
still significantly influence cumulative tax burdens. If investment is
expensed, one either tolerates large tax rebates or must carry losses

forward with interest. Neither arrangement is simple. Transactions between filers with profits and others with losses will give ample opportunity to change the timing or amount of tax. The opportunities to delay tax will be many, and who among us is prepared to say that the probability of future tax holidays or moratoriums is zero? Clever tax planners will almost certainly find loopholes that no legislator can fully anticipate. Bankman and Schler agreed that swapping consumption for income taxation would extinguish some sheltering and avoidance opportunities and open others. They disagreed whether a resulting consumption tax regime would be simpler than the current income tax regime. I think that they would agree that a switch would be a bonanza for the current generation of tax lawyers and accountants. On my reading of the Bankman-Schler exchange, whether either the income or consumption tax wins the simplicity contest, it does so, at best, on points and by a split decision.

Gene Steuerle has pointed out that replacing the income tax with a consumption tax would not simplify lives of the tens of millions of individuals who are subject to benefit reduction rates under cash or in-kind transfer programs and the state and federal governments that enforce those benefit reduction rates. Benefit reduction rates have to be based on income not consumption. Those who receive and administer current transfer programs would have to cope with two personal "tax" regimes, not just one. Gene is bewildered that others do not recognize the force of this point. So, I confess, do I.

If the United States shifted to consumption taxation, complexity would also increase for every business that carries out operations both in the United States and in countries that stick with income taxation. They would have to cope with two tax regimes...well, actually, one more than now, as companies with extensive foreign operations already have to cope with source and destination income taxes and the host of other cross-national differences in tax rules.

Alan sketches a quite daunting research agenda. It includes not only extensions and improvements to the sorts of models in the development of which he has been a pioneer. It also extends to modifications in the underlying assumptions regarding how households and businesses make decisions. Such modifications seem important because so many households engage in behavior that seems inconsistent with far-sighted rationality and plausible parameter values. But, as many have pointed out, once one drops rationality assumptions, what does one put it their place?

I would like to emphasize an additional issue that seems to me to be particularly important in the current fiscal context. The impact of tax rules on individual behavior depends critically on people's expectations regarding the durability of tax rules. Modelers typically assume that people act as if statutory rules will remain in effect forever. That assumption is clearly wrong in two senses.

First, the laws currently in existence are unsustainable. Current tax rates and expenditure policies are mutually inconsistent. Either or both must eventually change. If people *are* as smart and as farsighted as standard models postulate, the rational actors must build such changes into their plans. But which changes? The number of ways that expenditure and tax policies can be changed to make them mutually consistent is infinite. I know of no plausible theory or empirical research to guide expectations on how *inconsistent* policies will be reconciled. Models that postulate constant policies are unlikely to represent accurately the behavior of fully rational people who know policies must change. If people are *not* as smart or as farsighted as standard models assume, then one should model actual decision processes to approximate actual behavioral responses.

Second, even when expenditure and tax policies have been mutually consistent, people know that Congress has changed the rules. Would it not be prudent for them to entertain the possibility that Congress will do so again? To assume that people are so rational and intelligent that they can whip off solutions to the dynamic optimization problems that very bright economists must use computers to solve, but are so blind that they think Congress is on autopilot raises a wee problem of internal inconsistency.

To understand how tax policies influence decisions, one needs to model expectations regarding legislative change. I know of no plausible theory or empirical research to guide expectations on how *consistent* policies will evolve. Alternatively, if modelers cannot settle on one set of expectations, perhaps economic actors cannot do so either. How should economic actors respond to policy changes that they rationally expect to occur but cannot predict? My own intuition is that this sort of uncertainty causes people to have much shorter decision horizons than economic models typically assume. But my real point is that this issue is too important to ignore.

For all of these reasons it is not time for fundamental tax reform, if "fundamental" is defined as replacing the current personal tax base with a different one or as replacing personal taxes with a tax on value added or retail sales. But it is time for fundamental reform in two other senses.

The first is that a lengthy menu of pretty far-reaching incremental modifications to the personal income tax could make filing simpler for most filers and reduce tax-induced distortions. This menu would include many of the items listed in the report of the president's tax reform panel, including the simplification of exemptions, standard deductions, and the earned income credit; putting a floor under charitable contributions; capping the exclusion of employer financed health insurance; and consolidation of rules regarding tax-sheltered retirement income. To these I would add the proposal to move aggressively to institute return-free tax payment for as many filers as possible and a proposal advanced years ago by Joe Pechman to cap personal interest deductions at the amount of reported capital income.

But the most fundamental tax reform is the most obvious. Within the next two decades the United States will need more revenue, probably half again as much as the current federal tax system generates. On January 27, 1996, President Clinton declared that "The era of big government is over." The next president may not come right out and say it, but the era of big tax cuts is over. In fact the era of tax increases is upon us. It is time now for economists to talk about how best to *raise* revenue. Next to the rather small effects from the changes likely to emerge from any politically plausible tax reform, the effects of required revenue increases will be huge. The menu will probably include increases in personal income tax rates. But income tax revenues probably cannot be increased enough to pay for the politically irreducible core of publicly financed services and benefits without causing unacceptable distortions in resource allocation and sharply boosting incentives to avoid and evade. We should, by all means, do as much as we can to improve the income tax. But it will almost certainly be necessary also to institute a broad-based indirect consumption tax, a value-added tax.

So here is my suggestion for another conference on fundamental tax reform—how should the United States go about raising sufficient revenue to pay for national defense, support basic health care for the elderly, disabled, and poor, and cover the cost of the rest of what most members of both political parties and the American people insist that government must do. That conference would, I believe, do much more for public welfare than further consideration of root-and-branch modifications that may increase or decrease efficiency and tax simplification, but not much.

Discussion

James M. Poterba

Auerbach provides a comprehensive guide to the economic effects of income and consumption taxation. His discussion can be divided into two parts, each of which makes an important contribution. The first is a careful exposition of the theoretical and empirical economic issues that arise in comparing income and consumption taxes. The second is a clear presentation of consumption tax design, with a summary of settled issues as well as a list of unresolved questions. Each part is best-of-breed, and this chapter is the most up-to-date introduction to these issues that I have seen. In the first part Auerbach is careful to point out that while a number of theoretical studies suggest that it may be optimal to set the capital income tax rate to zero, these studies are based on assumptions that warrant caution in interpreting the conclusions. In the second part he notes that some, but by no means all, of the consumption tax design issues have been the subject of prior analysis. While public finance economists have reached agreement on some potential design issues, others remain unresolved. Some of these issues, such as the treatment of financial institutions and the design of transition rules for the depreciable basis of existing assets, represent important challenges that warrant further study.

The first part of the chapter, which discusses what we know about the optimal tax treatment of capital income and the economic effects of different capital tax regimes, provides clear evidence of rapid intellectual progress in the last two decades. It is instructive to compare the knowledge base in 1986, when deliberations that led to the 1986 Tax Reform Act were taking place, with that today. The last two decades have witnessed the careful analysis of the transition from an income tax to a consumption tax in life-cycle general equilibrium models, the finding that in some classes of infinite horizon models the optimal steady-state capital income tax rate is zero, and many advances in the measurement of key behavioral parameters. To be sure, much remains to be learned. High on the priority list is evaluating the empirical significance of recent theoretical advances that highlight the impact of capital income taxation on the self-selection constraints that affect taxpayers' choices with regard to labor supply and other determinants of taxable income, and refining our estimates of the asset-price effects and short-run incidence of fundamental tax reforms. The last twenty years suggests optimism with regard to the pace of future advances in our understanding of these key issues.

The second part of the chapter focuses on consumption tax design. There are many different types of consumption tax. Some have been widely implemented—the value-added tax and the retail sales tax are leading examples. Other types, such as the X-tax developed by David Bradford and the US Treasury staff in the mid-1970s and the savings-exempt income tax that has been proposed periodically in the United States, have not been tried in practice. There remain important unresolved issues with regard to some aspects of these consumption tax models, and the record of intellectual progress here is less impressive than that with regard to conceptual issues. This is probably due to a combination of the fundamental difficulty of the underlying issues, the limited payoff to academic economists from working on detailed policy design issues, and the relative lack of policy attention to fundamental tax reform during the last two decades. Many important issues remain to be addressed before some consumption tax models will be ready for implementation.

This chapter offers a discussant much to admire and relatively little to disagree with. It is careful, balanced, and encyclopedic. My comments will therefore expand on two issues: the role of taxes on old capital in evaluating the efficiency gains from replacing an income tax with a consumption tax, and the role of tax-deferred saving accounts and other specialized vehicles in hybrid tax structures that embody some components of an income tax and some of a consumption tax. In each of these areas I will build on a general theme from this chapter: details are critically important in fundamental tax reform. Small design issues can have a significant impact on the efficiency effects and on the incidence of policy changes.

Let me first address the tax treatment of existing assets as part of a transition from an income tax to a consumption tax. One of the central advances of the last two decades is our enhanced understanding of the central role of transitional arrangements in determining the efficiency consequences of replacing an income tax with a consumption tax. Simulation results in Altig et al. (2001) and other studies demonstrate that replacing an income tax with a consumption tax results in substantial efficiency gains in the absence of transition relief, which means that "old capital" is taxed at the time of the policy switch. It has long been recognized that some of the efficiency gain associated with moving from an income tax to a consumption tax is due to the high transitional tax burden on old capital. Such a burden can be due, for example, to eliminating the taxable basis on assets that had not been fully depreciated under the income tax. The key insight of recent simulation models, however, is that when an income tax is replaced with a consumption tax and the reform includes generous transition relief provisions, it is possible for the resulting policy change to *reduce* economic efficiency. This implies that steady-state analysis is not a completely satisfactory guide when analyzing the welfare gain or loss associated with a reform, and it dictates careful analysis of transition relief provisions.

The efficiency consequences of providing transition relief are not the sole concern that is likely to emerge in practical tax reform debates. Equity issues are also central to the discussion of the structure of reform. It is unlikely that fundamental reform will result in taxes at the same rate on the holders of all existing assets. Rather, investors in some asset categories will probably face greater tax burdens than those in other categories. Such an outcome will appear unfair to many analysts. Why should two investors who were identical two days ago, one of whom purchased an asset that will face a high transitional tax burden while the other purchased an asset with a low tax burden, be treated in different ways? Particularly when it is relatively easy to document the change in effective tax burdens for different types of investors, equity concerns may prove important in discussions of tax reform. The desire to avoid unequal treatment of investors who at some ex ante period were identical may be a further constraint on the taxation of existing assets.

It is not clear whether the representative democratic political system in the United States and many other nations would ever enact a consumption tax reform with very limited transition relief. Not only does the political process respond to the interests and concerns of those with existing assets, but conceptual concerns about the chilling effect of a one-time "taking" from existing asset holders on incentives for *future* investors might deter policy makers from adopting such reforms. The problem of policy reform and the associated winners and losers, not just in the tax setting but in other contexts, has long been of interest to legal scholars. Shaviro (2000) offers a useful introduction to these issues.

Levying taxes on existing asset holders is not impossible, however, and one can find several examples of tax reforms that were associated with high transitional tax burdens for some asset holders. In the Tax Reform Act of 1986, for example, rules on the use of passive losses were tightened and some investors who had undertaken projects that they expected to generate substantial tax benefits were denied those benefits. The effective tax burden on the associated assets was increased as a result of the tax reform. Another example is provided by the United Kingdom's elimination of the tax deduction for mortgage interest payments. This set of reforms, which occurred gradually over nearly a decade, raised the effective tax burden on owner-occupiers. The reform was gradual, and initial deductions were subject to limits so relatively few households faced large increases in tax burdens. Substantial reduction in the US tax provisions that provide favorable treatment for owner occupied housing, either by taxing the imputed rent on owner-occupied housing or by disallowing a greater share of mortgage interest deductions, would probably meet with greater political opposition.

It is possible that more dramatic changes in the tax system make it easier to tax existing assets. For example, if a retail sales tax or a value-added tax were adopted as a replacement for the current corporate income tax, owners of existing assets who had remaining basis under the corporate income tax might find it more difficult to argue for some type of relief than if the existing corporate income tax were modified to allow for expensing. The question of how best to design reforms so that transition relief does not swamp the steady-state efficiency gains is one that deserves both academic and policy discussion.

Let me now consider a second issue raised in the chapter: the role of "hybrid" tax structures that embody some elements of income taxation, such as a household-level tax on capital income, as well as some elements of consumption taxation, such as saving accounts that are targeted for specific functions. One insight that bears emphasis is that exempting household-level capital income from taxation, while preserving a tax deduction for interest payments, is *not* a step toward a consumption tax system. Such a structure encourages tax arbitrage of a simple form: households borrow and invest the proceeds, thereby earning an after-tax return that exceeds the before-tax return available on their investments. The extent to which households engage in such tax arbitrage remains an unsettled empirical question, and my own research suggests that through most of the income distribution the extent of such tax arbitrage is limited. It is nevertheless important to emphasize that as a matter of tax design, a system with such arbitrage opportunities is unattractive. This simple observation raises a more general point: hybrid tax systems that combine some elements of income taxation with some elements of consumption taxation may lead to a tax *system* that is less attractive than either a pure income tax or a pure consumption tax. This represents a warning to proponents of piecemeal tax reform: adding some components of consumption taxation to the current hybrid structure does not guarantee achieving part of the efficiency gains that are associated with full consumption tax reform.

One of the most active research areas in applied public finance in recent years has been explicitly focused on the economic effects of tax-deferred saving accounts such as 401(k) plans and IRAs. This research raises questions about the models of consumer behavior that underlie the optimizing life-cycle models and infinite horizon models that are the workhorses of theoretical public finance. Household saving decisions appear to depend, to a remarkable degree, on the way saving choices are framed and on aspects of program design, such as whether the workplace saving default is "on" or "off," that neoclassical economic theory suggests should have no impact on intertemporal allocations. The active research program on the interface of economics and psychology has documented the impact of various behavioral cues on saving decisions, but it has not yet led to revision of theoretical models that can be used to address broad issues such as the efficiency gains of replacing an income tax with a consumption tax.

It is difficult to predict where this research will lead, but one can speculate both about the research program in behavioral economics and about its ultimate impact on research in public finance. It is possible that we will discover that for at least some households, framing the issues associated with tax policy, including the way taxes change a household's perceived returns to investment and saving, may be important factors in determining the behavioral response to the tax system. This possibility raises a host of new empirical and conceptual questions that bear on the ongoing tax reform debate. Are the set of households for whom framing issues matters quantitatively important, either as a share of all households or as a share of all investors? Does the behavior of these households have a significant effect on asset values, and on the equilibrium price signals that govern resource allocation? At a conceptual level, models in which framing affects choices may require a reformulation of the welfare analysis of tax reform. When minor changes in the decision-making environment can affect decisions about saving and life-cycle planning, we may need to revisit the welfare calculations that emerge from traditional life-cycle models. These issues, and others, suggest that there remains a great deal to learn about the economic analysis of tax reform.

Notes

I am grateful to George Zodrow, Henry Aaron, James Poterba, and the conference participants for comments on an earlier draft.

1. For a good recent survey of much of this literature, see Zodrow (2005).

2. Indeed Erosa and Gervais (2002) find in simulations of a life-cycle model that capital income taxes should be positive, although lower than labor income taxes if labor income taxes cannot vary by age.

3. This is distinct from problem of time consistency that arises in the design of policy over time where the government has an incentive to deviate from a previously announced policy, for example, to announce a capital income subsidy, but instead implements a capital income tax once capital has been accumulated. Even under a time consistent policy that is known in advance to taxpayers, the government may wish to condition one date's tax provisions on taxpayer behavior at earlier dates.

4. Auerbach (1989b) estimated, for example, that it would take a nearly 9 percentage point increase in the average tax rate on nonresidential capital to offset the welfare gain from shifting to uniform nonresidential taxation.

5. Measuring inflation inaccurately is not simply a matter of imposing the wrong tax rate on capital income but also of imposing tax rates that vary across assets, since the correction for inflation depends on the asset's depreciation rate.

6. There are certainly arguments that home ownership generates positive externalities and should therefore receive favorable tax treatment. But if it is ownership per se that generates the externality, the corrective tax would take the form of a subsidy to ownership and not also to incremental housing purchases.

7. See Auerbach (2002) for a recent review of the evidence.

8. The notation used for net foreign income reflects that fact that virtually all such income is capital income.

9. For simplicity, expression (1.3) omits international transfer payments from the current account balance. Such transfer payments include government and private foreign aid as well as tax payments to foreign governments.

10. There was an extended discussion of recapturing some of this windfall gain at the time, including a concrete proposal put forward by the Treasury prior to enactment, but in the end no such recapture was implemented. See Zodrow (1988).

11. See Auerbach (1997) for further discussion.

12. Net income from abroad, R^f, remained positive through 2005 for the United States, even though the US net international investment position had been negative for several years. This indicates that US assets abroad have been earning a higher rate of return than foreign assets in the United States. However, with the increasingly negative US international investment position, net income from abroad still is trending downward, virtually hitting zero in 2005 and falling below zero in the final quarter of that year.

13. The incidence of these taxes and subsidies does not require full adjustment of the nominal exchange rate. For example, if the domestic price level rose to offset the border adjustment in reaction to the shift from origin to destination basis, no change in the exchange rate would be necessary to maintain equilibrium, but domestic assets would rise in nominal value and hence still appreciate in units of the foreign currency. US-held foreign assets would have their real values reduced when deflated by the US price level.

14. See *http://www.bea.gov/bea/newsrelarchive/2005/intinv04_fax.pdf.*

15. See Ebrill et al. (2001, pp. 94–98) for further discussion of some alternative methods.

16. This issue does not arise under the $R + F$ base consumption tax, since including financial flows in the tax base adds not just an interest deduction but also an inclusion of borrowing, and hence leaves the effective tax rate unaffected.

17. Note, however, that the problem of imperfect measurement of depreciation is less of a problem here than under an income tax because depreciation allowances taken too early or late are adjusted by the rate of interest. Thus the error is only one of timing; there is no impact on the present value of the deductions.

18. The story is more complicated under the current system in which IRAs provide a higher rate of return than fully taxed assets. If the alternative investment is subject to income taxes but not subject to taxes on withdrawal, then there are offsetting effects on the value of the IRA, the relative impact of deferred taxes declining with respect to the length of the holding period as the advantage of tax-free investment grows. See Poterba (2004b) for further discussion.

19. The same distinction will apply to the domestic prices of foreign assets. Recall that under a VAT, border adjustments will cause the home currency to appreciate against foreign currencies in proportion to the border adjustment. As border adjustments effectively apply cash flow taxation to net foreign investment, this reduction in the domestic value of existing foreign assets is analogous to the reduction in value of domestic assets under a VAT. Under a consumed income tax, extending cash flow treatment to the purchases and sales of foreign assets would impose the same tax treatment as would border adjustments under a VAT, but would not induce a change in the exchange rate. Investors would be in the same after-tax positions under both systems, but the taxes would be collected at the company level and hence capitalized under the border-adjusted VAT.

20. See the simulations in Auerbach (1996) or Altig et al. (2001).

21. See, for example, Auerbach (1983b).

22. One might argue that the borrowed funds still must come from somewhere and therefore require additional saving on someone's part, but even this is not necessarily true because the funds can come from one's own sheltered investments. For example, an individual's pension fund saving can be used to purchase that same individual's new interest-deductible mortgage. In this example there would be no net saving, as the increased borrowing would exactly equal the increased pension assets.

23. The size of this undersaving problem remains unclear. One recent study (Scholz et al. 2004) argues that less than 20 percent of households save too little for retirement, and that the extent of undersaving among such households is generally small.

24. See Bernheim (2002) for a recent review of the literature.

25. Altig et al. (2001, tab. 4) find that the long-run value of Tobin's q, the ratio of market value to capital, is reduced by 12 percent by the X-tax.

26. For example, Aaron and Galper (1985) propose adopting a progressive consumed income tax but treating bequests as consumption and hence taxable.

2

Simplifying Assumptions: How Might the Politics of Consumption Tax Reform Affect (Impair) the End Product?

Daniel Shaviro

One big advantage of consumption taxation that its advocates, myself included, have claimed is simplification. A consumption tax would be a great deal less complicated technically than the present income tax, for example, requiring far fewer pages of tax statutes and regulations. More important, however, advocates of consumption taxation claim that its enactment would lead to a significant reduction in the resources devoted to tax planning, compliance, and administration, reflecting reduced opportunities to affect one's tax burden by engaging in purely tax-motivated transactions, or by choosing between economically equivalent tax characterizations of one's activities. This difference has been attributed, moreover, to eliminating structural features of the federal income tax, such as the realization requirement, rather than to the possible advantages of starting fresh with fewer barnacles than the current system has accumulated.

No responsible advocate of these views has doubted that serious compliance and interpretive issues would remain, such as cracking down on fraud and distinguishing between personal and business expenditures. The thought has been, however, that eliminating realization and related timing issues is bound to make things a lot better. The simplicity gains seem larger still if one takes the view that certain structural features of the current system, such as the two-level corporate tax and the debt-equity distinction, would be easiest to eliminate in a change of systems even though they are not intrinsic to an income tax.

However compelling one finds this line of argument, it cannot be deemed fully persuasive until one has looked carefully at the weak spots and pressure points that an actual consumption tax would likely have. Fortunately, the tax policy literature has recently started to do this (Weisbach 2000, 2003; Bankman and Schler 2005). The conclusion that seems to be emerging is that a well-designed consumption tax, while likely to involve significantly greater tax planning and compliance issues than its advocates might have expected or hoped for, would nonetheless probably be simpler than the current income tax.

This conclusion, although important if accepted, still does not put the tax simplification issue to rest. It reflects comparing to our actual income tax a conceptually pure consumption tax, with only limited departures from the ideal other than for administrative reasons. Perhaps one could design an income tax featuring only administrative compromises that would be simpler than the consumption tax that Congress had been subjecting to its dark arts for the past ninety-odd years.

Given this problem, my aim in this chapter is to take the consumption tax literature on simplification a step further, by adding politics to the picture. How would simplification be affected by changes to the proposed models that would be adopted in the course of actually enacting a consumption tax? For example, to what extent would tax shelters, even insofar as they would have been eliminated under the pure models, remain a problem by reason of politically induced changes in the design?

This inquiry necessarily involves stepping deep into the speculative wilderness. As Harold Wilson once said, a week is a long time in politics. Predicting what might happen in coming years is beyond anyone's powers. What is more, since I personally am skeptical about the prospects for replacement of the current income tax by a consumption tax, the issue has overtones for me of the Monty Python inquiry, "What if Queen Victoria could fly?"

The inquiry becomes a bit more tractable, however, if one emphasizes two particular questions. The first is what sorts of political scenarios would be most likely to lead to a major consumption-based tax reform. The second is what sorts of powerful political interests would likely need to be accommodated in the course of enactment.

I analyze these questions in section 2.1, where I select two main scenarios to examine. The first is a bipartisan process, like that underlying the enactment of the Tax Reform Act of 1986, that yields a progressive consumption tax based on David Bradford's X-tax model, but as heavily modified by the need for political compromises. The second is a Republican-led stealth process of moving toward consumption tax treatment of saving and investment without explicitly abandoning the current income tax.

Section 2.1 also discusses the main political and policy interests that might need to be accommodated in a major consumption-based reform. Section 2.2 discusses the possible implications for the stealth reform scenario of political factors, and section 2.3 does the same for the bipartisan X-tax scenario. Section 2.4 offers a brief conclusion.

2.1   The Possible Politics of Consumption-Based Tax Reform

2.1.1   Choosing Plausible Scenarios

Consumption-based tax reform cannot just appear one day, like the Ten Commandments in the biblical tale. There would have to be a particular way in which it happened, including a specific political process that ended in its enactment.

The problem of how it could happen may initially seem more open-ended than I believe it really is. With relatively fixed institutions, including not only Congress and the presidency but also political parties and interest groups, the process that leads to major tax legislation tends to involve one or another of a finite set of recognizable scenarios. In 1981, for example, enactment of the Economic Recovery Tax Act (ERTA) resulted from a Reagan administration campaign proposal followed by a bidding war between the two parties' congressional leaderships. By contrast, the Tax Reform Act of 1986 emerged out of cooperation, albeit conflictual at times, between the Reagan administration, the Democratic leadership of the House, and a relatively independent Republican leadership in the Senate, helped along by an array of retail-level concessions to particular members or interests that was needed because the leaders lacked the clout simply to impose their will. In 2001 and 2003 a Republican administration with tight parliamentary-style control of both houses of Congress was able to push through pretty much the legislation it wanted, subject to some congressional redesign and scaling back in 2003 especially. Each of these different scenarios ended up affecting the final content of the legislation.

Obviously it is impossible to say with any confidence how, if it came to pass at all, consumption-based tax reform would end up being enacted. National politics is a huge chaos system in which not only the inputs, but their relationship to the outputs, resist prediction. The specific scenario that would prevail, if any did, is fundamentally unknowable in advance. Still, the bold at heart can venture to identify the scenarios that they consider most likely.

Looking at the types of scenarios that have prevailed in recent tax legislation, a bidding war can be ruled out on the view that, in light of the long-term US fiscal gap, the consumption-style reform would need to be at least roughly revenue neutral over the official estimating period. Proponents therefore could not easily bid for support from one group without taking money from another group—hardly a recipe for bidding wars, which thrive on positive-sum games so far as the represented interests are concerned.

A bipartisan process after the manner of the 1986 tax reform would require that key Democrats embrace switching to consumption taxation in exchange for Republicans accepting sufficient progressivity. The rise of proposals, such as David Bradford's X-tax, that could largely match the progressivity of the current system makes this technically feasible, while leaving open the question of whether it is politically feasible. A process led at all levels by Republicans also seems possible, given their current control of Congress and the executive branch, along with widespread Republican interest in consumption taxation. A purely Democratic-led consumption-based reform is implausible given Democrats' support for income taxation. We have therefore two main scenarios to consider: a bipartisan bargain and a Republican-led exercise that is relatively top-down in parliamentary fashion.

2.1.2   Scenario 1: Bipartisan Consumption Tax Reform

The bipartisan bargain in 1986 relied on broadening the base and lowering marginal rates, in a manner that was estimated (under official conventions) to be revenue neutral and distributionally neutral over a five-year period. The analogous bargain that one might expect in the event of a bipartisan consumption-style reform seems fairly straightforward: the Democrats would agree to exempt capital income in exchange for the Republicans' accepting sufficiently graduated rates to bring about approximate revenue and distributional neutrality within the estimating period. This scenario raises three immediate questions, however. Under what circumstances might the parties agree to it? What other political prerequisites might need to be satisfied? And what model for consumption-based reform would the parties adopt?

A Bipartisan Bargain?

In today's hyperpartisan political environment, a 1986-style agreement between Republicans and Democrats to pursue consumption-based tax reform seems impossibly remote. Not only are the parties currently averse to cooperating on controversial matters, but the basis for a deal does not exist. For one thing, the unsettled revenue picture that results from the scheduled expiration of the 2001 tax cuts means that the parties lack a common baseline for setting revenue and distributional targets. For another, there has been no indication that Democrats' potential enthusiasm for such reform is any greater than for modifying Social Security to use individual accounts.

If things were to change, however, the parties' internal dynamics offer a basis for predicting how they would change. Both parties can be described as having, broadly speaking, two main factions or orientations in fiscal matters: one that is closer to the views of activists in the party "base," and one that is more centrist. Among Republicans, while the anti-tax "base" has been ascendant since George W. Bush took office, and to a lesser degree since the "Contract with America" congressional campaign of 1994, the more deficit-averse centrists often controlled tax policy between 1982 and 1990, and they are not entirely extinct at least in the Senate. The centrists might regain some influence if the anti-tax wing were blamed for one or more national political defeats.

Among Democrats, the battle between the more liberal supporters of traditional party themes and the more centrist Democratic Leadership Council types has been ongoing for many years. President Clinton showed how a deft practitioner of the latter approach can grasp and thereby neutralize seemingly Republican themes, as when he embraced the death penalty, called for making abortion rare albeit still legal, and participated in ending "welfare as we know it." A Democrat seeking national prominence in coming years via the Clinton strategy would have good reason to consider seriously progressive consumption taxation, and indeed to embrace it as a forward-looking "third way" if its political salability seemed good enough (which I admittedly doubt it would).

The party-level prerequisites for a bipartisan embrace of major consumption-based reform therefore seem clear. Centrist Democrats and Republicans would need to have gained sufficient traction to lead their parties towards a deal that could stick despite dissent from the left and right wings. This, in turn, would presumably have to follow a series of Democratic victories that fell short of reversing Republicans' current dominance and indicated that the parties had no good alternative to working together.

Other Political Prerequisites

The 1986 experience helps point us to other political prerequisites that might need to be satisfied, even if not in exactly the same way this time around. For one, the 1986 Act offered the public a sweetener along with the bitter medicine of repealing various tax preferences, by significantly lowering marginal rates. In 2005 the Tax Reform Panel appointed by President Bush attempted to reap a similar political benefit from proposing repeal of the alternative minimum tax (AMT), but found that this was not a good enough sweetener given that the AMT has not yet become as widely applicable as experts anticipate it will.

Perhaps AMT repeal would make more of an impression once it has begun to apply very widely. Or perhaps a revenue-conscious trade-in of the AMT, at least in part for higher rates, would be needed for tax reform once again to offer a sufficiently tolerable trade-off of gain for pain. Of course, for rate reduction to be possible in the context of moving to a progressive consumption tax without excessive revenue loss, the accompanying revenue gains would have to more than offset the impact of removing the intertemporal burden of the income tax on investment and saving. Imposing transition losses on existing wealth might need to be part of the story for this to be politically feasible.

Rate reduction and other direct benefits from reform may be needed politically for more than simply making the reform package palatable to the general public. Since interest group opposition to base-broadening is inevitable, reform proponents might need not just to buy off the most powerful opponents but also to have some real supporters. In 1986 service industries took this role, since they benefited from the rate reduction and were not adversely affected by the hit on capital-intensive industries from repealing the investment tax credit and slowing down tax depreciation. For a move to consumption taxation, the capital-intensive industries seem the more logical ally, especially if the AMT trade-in had involved moving cost recovery in more of an income tax direction. Rate reduction would make the shift an even better deal for these industries, while also creating a possible basis for support from others that were not losing industry-specific preferences.

One important change in the economic landscape since 1986 arguably makes this less likely to happen. The rise of investment in intangibles, which generally can be expensed under present law, would appear to weaken the political hand of those seeking to universalize expensing in lieu of lower marginal rates. Still, if we are to assume that a major consumption-based reform actually occurs (my assigned premise in this paper), industries that invest in physical capital look like natural interest group allies.

Again, I am not arguing that any of this is likely to happen. My aim, rather, is to offer a plausible scenario for how it would happen if it did.

Choice of a Progressive Consumption Tax Model

A crucial question, under the scenario of bipartisan consumption-based reform, is what model the parties would adopt. Two main alternatives have emerged in the tax reform literature of the last few decades. The first is a cash-flow tax on individuals, such as those discussed in Kaldor (1958), Andrews (1974), and in the Treasury Blueprints Study (Bradford et al. 1984). Under this approach, at least in its pure form, individuals, as opposed to businesses, would generally be the only parties designated as taxpayers. They would file tax returns as under present law, but with unlimited savings account deductions and—importantly—inclusion of borrowing.

The second is a two-tier consumption tax, such as the Hall-Rabushka flat tax or the Bradford X-tax. Under this approach both businesses and individuals would make tax payments to the government. The tax system would at least roughly resemble a value-added tax (VAT) such as those in widespread use around the world, modified to make wages deductible by businesses and includable by the individual recipients. Progressivity would be achieved through the rate structure applied to individuals' wages.

David Bradford, who played a central role in developing both approaches, devoted the design efforts of his later years exclusively to the X-tax. In conversation, he explained this as motivated by his belief that the X-tax was not only simpler (since individuals' borrowing and investments would not need to be tracked) but politically more feasible given the optics of classifying businesses as taxpayers rather than as nontaxpayers.

The subsequent example of the 2005 Tax Reform Panel, which proposed an X-tax but with an appended, if ill-fitting, 15 percent tax on individuals' investment income, helps dramatize the political dilemma that consumption tax advocates face. So long as people conceive of businesses and their owners as distinct persons, taxing business income at the individual level prompts the complaint that one is exempting "business," while doing so at the business level prompts concern about the owners of financial interests in businesses ("coupon-clippers," in old-fashioned parlance) who are not being directly taxed. This dilemma is potentially bad news not just for consumption taxation, but even for corporate integration under the income tax.

From the standpoint of the X-tax, the possible (whether or not sufficiently salient) responses are not limited to pointing out that taxing a business is a lot like taxing its owners. In addition one could make the point that the entire wage tax component of the X-tax is simply a device for delivering wage subsidies to the extent of people's wage income below the top bracket. If people accept that coupon-clippers pay a retail sales tax or VAT when they consume, one would like to think that they could recognize that making a revenue-neutral shift from such a tax to an X-tax actually *increases* the tax burden on coupon-clippers, since a higher business rate presumably is necessary to pay for the wage subsidy.

While opinions may reasonably differ regarding which of the two structures is more politically feasible, two considerations apart from the business level tax arguably support considering the X-tax the more likely tax reform vehicle. First, it has received significantly more attention in the last few years than cash-flow prototypes, as in the Tax Reform Panel's modified X-tax proposal. Second, the need expressly to include borrowing as taxable in a workable cash-flow tax strikes me as a political Achilles heel. "Expressly" is the key word here, as no one seems to worry about the fact that retail sales taxes and VATs effectively include borrowing by applying to consumer purchases whether debt-financed or not.

Experts may regard it as obvious that, if saving is deducted, dissaving should be included. The public, however, may not agree, given that loan proceeds, unlike wages, are not "income" in ordinary usage. Thus consider the USA tax, prominently proposed by Senators Sam Nunn and Pete Domenici in 1995, to which I will refer intermittently on the view that it represents an effort by politically savvy people to design a feasible consumption-based reform. While similar to a cash-flow tax at the individual level, albeit with a business level tax as well, the USA tax did not include loan proceeds as income. This was one reason among others why experts swiftly concluded that it was unworkable (e.g., see Kaplow 1995; Warren 1995). Given the likely political importance of being able to demonstrate basic workability, cash-flow consumption taxes may face an insoluble political dilemma, in the form of "damned if you do and damned if you don't," with respect to their treatment of loan proceeds generally.

I therefore adopt as my bipartisan scenario the enactment of something based on the X-tax, albeit as modified by passing through the congressional meat grinder in a process that involves a need to court or at least mollify politically powerful interest groups.

2.1.3   Scenario 2: Republican-Led Consumption Tax Reform

It is no secret that many of the Republicans most hostile to the current income tax would like nothing better than to replace it with a national retail sales tax (NRST), perhaps accompanied by some sort of rebate to ease the sting of its lacking a zero bracket for low-income individuals. In my admittedly subjective judgment, however, this is not a political scenario to take seriously. An NRST, in addition to being regarded by many experts as unworkable and likely to require an unattractively high nominal rate, strikes me as no easier to sell to the general public than Social Security privatization. Its evident regressivity (relative to current law) once in place may be disqualifying despite its one-time transition hit on existing wealth upon enactment.

The flat tax is a second Republicans-only possibility, but this as well has proved a hard sell politically. The X-tax would presumably be too progressive to appeal to Republicans in a process that they led unilaterally. What is more, any sort of fundamental tax reform that looks too dramatically new is hard to accomplish with only one party on board, given the likelihood of voter unease (and angry losers if the enactment is anywhere near revenue neutral) that the opposition party might be all too eager to stoke.

How to proceed in a Republican-dominated consumption-based reform would therefore be a puzzle if the process had to be overt. Recognizing the political problems with this course, however, many Republicans have already been calling for what they acknowledge is a stealth approach to consumption-based reform. Under the "five easy pieces" scenario (Christian and Robbins 2002), a de facto switch to a consumption tax would involve five steps, all of them already advanced by recent Republican-led legislation:

1. Reduce marginal rates (a step that I will ignore, important though it is to the Republicans' anti-tax wing, as it has nothing to do with the choice of tax base).

2. Provide expensing for all business outlays.

3. Adopt corporate integration.

4. Significantly increase or eliminate the deductible contribution limits for Roth-style IRA saving.

5. Move toward a territorial rather than a worldwide system of taxing US businesses, by exempting export and other foreign trade income of US companies.

Leading conservative activists have eagerly embraced this idea. Thus Stephen Moore, the president of the Club for Growth, urges consumption-based tax reform in "three or four or five easy pieces." Likewise the ubiquitous Grover Norquist emphasizes the need for stealth in any consumption-based reform, in order to blunt Democratic political attacks (Andrews and Kirkpatrick 2004).

The proponents of "five easy pieces" have not addressed borrowing, such as by limiting the politically popular home mortgage interest deduction. Indeed they have not suggested any tax changes to offset the revenue loss from the proposed steps. The proposal that marginal rates be reduced alongside the other changes would seem to refute any notion that the exercise is meant to be revenue neutral. The anti-tax, "starve the beast" philosophy of leading proponents, who generally come from the Republicans' currently ascendant anti-tax wing, suggests limiting tax increases to targets with more potential appeal to the base, such as state and local income tax deductions. They might also seek to "pay" for revenue-losing reform by simply shifting other projected revenues forward, such as by requiring or encouraging conversion of traditional IRAs into Roth IRAs. Finally, the centrists, who might be expected to care more about the new system's effective functioning, might offer little protest if they remain submerged politically.

Even without this exact pattern, stealth by its nature is likely to affect the end product. A one-party process in which public discussion and debate are kept to a minimum eliminates the dynamic whereby multiple players must refine their proposals in the course of their competition, negotiation, and efforts at persuasion. Like other Republican legislative efforts of the last few years, the enactment process would presumably be run by a handful of party insiders and lobbyists with limited interest in making the tax system work well, and less willingness to seek or even permit outside feedback. The improvements and corrections that one might expect either from an open process or from one run by experts might therefore be considerably less likely than in the more open, bipartisan X-tax scenario.

2.1.4   Other Possible Scenarios

Other consumption-based reform scenarios cannot be ruled out. However, only one has attracted enough recent attention to merit brief discussion here. This is Michael Graetz's proposal to adopt a straight VAT while raising the exemption amount (e.g., to $100,000) in the present income tax or alternative minimum tax.

I personally am skeptical about the Graetz proposal's political prospects, although then again I am skeptical about my two proposed scenarios as well. From a Republican standpoint, it adds a VAT without slaying the income tax, creating the possibility that the income tax exemption amount would start creeping downward again. From a Democratic standpoint, the difficulty of adjusting for the varying personal and household circumstances of families below the exemption amount suggests that the Graetz plan would raise significant low-end equity concerns. Without individual returns, it becomes difficult to provide rate graduation or adjust for household circumstances (e.g., the number of children) at lower income levels. Graetz's suggestion that employers might handle such adjustments has been challenged as administratively unrealistic (Greenstein and Lav 2005), and might also be unwelcome to companies that do not want to take on the extra burden.

More to the point, however, given that all of the possibilities face political obstacles, I would argue that the Graetz proposal does not really belong in a discussion of the possible simplification gains from a consumption-based reform. While Graetz touts the simplification that would result from relieving individuals with income below the threshold from needing to file annual tax returns, his plan offers less promise of simplifying business taxation and that of wealthy individuals, which is where the really significant amounts of money are spent on tax planning and compliance.

A scenario that I find more plausible than any discussed thus far, but that likewise lies outside the scope of this chapter, would involve enacting a VAT not as in the Graetz plan, for tax reform purposes, but to fund Social Security and Medicare benefits at a point when they were in imminent fiscal danger. Simply adding a new tax, however, clearly does not result in simplification.

Significant inflation might also end up being part of the political system's response to the fiscal gap. In addition to devaluing existing national debt, inflation could make it politically easier to raise income tax revenues and cut real Social Security benefits, if indexing to inflation in these two systems were reduced or eliminated. Likewise inflation could ease the slowing of Medicare growth if reimbursement rates for medical procedures were allowed to decline in real terms. The inflationary "cure" might require forcing the hand of the Federal Reserve Board, but Congress has the power to exert such pressure. The main significance of the inflationary scenario for consumption-based reform is that it might increase capital-intensive industries' support for expensing, as inflation reduced the value of unindexed income tax depreciation deductions. Again, however, this scenario, while potentially more realistic than those I examine in this chapter, lies outside the scope of an inquiry into how politics would affect a major consumption-based reform.

2.1.5 *Significance of the Fiscal Gap for Consumption-Based Reform*

The United States currently faces an enormous long-term fiscal gap, suggesting that tax increases are highly likely down the road (Kotlikoff and Burns 2004; Shaviro 2006). One feature that addressing the fiscal gap and overtly engaging in major tax reform have in common is that both are likely to be politically wrenching and controversial. Engaging in just one at a time would be difficult enough (even if, in the case of addressing the fiscal gap, it proves unavoidable). In my view, doing the two of them together would be even harder. It has often been said that major tax reform cannot raise revenue if it is to be politically feasible, and indeed that it has much better chances if it loses revenue, given that losers from tax changes tend to complain more strenuously than winners rejoice. In the case of the officially revenue-neutral 1986 reform, individuals as a group nominally gained, with the consequent revenue loss being offset by a tax increase on corporations that had murkier incidence and that came at a time when corporations' political stock was unusually low due to the flood of contemporary news accounts of highly profitable companies that had paid little or no tax.

Consumption-based reform would therefore likely take place under the shadow of a fiscal gap that was likely to require significant revenue increases soon. This might be important, even if scrupulously ignored in the enactment process, due to its possible effects on planning and on the credibility of legislative commitments under the reform.

2.1.6   Important Political Interests That Might Affect the End Product of Consumption-Based Reform

A comprehensive consumption tax with household filing would already be more complicated than a straight VAT, albeit for good reason given the adjustments it would permit for household circumstances. The process of complicating adjustment is unlikely to end there, however. Reflecting both arguments on the merits and raw political power, a whole host of further departures from the simplest consumption-based model would be likely. Accordingly, in this section I catalog some of the main areas where additional complexities, whether merited or not, would likely be demanded by important interests and/or policy considerations.

Homeownership
Few tax benefits in the existing income tax are more entrenched politically than those pertaining to homeownership. The true starting point for preferentiality is the exclusion of imputed rental income. Taking this as given, however, the main tax benefits are the itemized deduction for home mortgage interest and real property taxes, along with the exclusion for up to $500,000 of gain on the sale of a home. Of these benefits the home mortgage interest deduction appears to be the most politically sacrosanct. Thus the USA tax would have retained it, although the Tax Reform Panel proposed curtailing it in certain respects.

Charities
Deductions for charitable contributions likewise stand on strong political ground, as shown by their retention under the USA tax and in the Tax Reform Panel's plans. The special rule permitting donors to deduct the value, rather than just the basis, of appreciated property that they donate may be less strongly rooted, although it has defenders. The USA tax, but not the Tax Reform Panel, would have eliminated it.

There also is good reason to expect that the tax-exempt status of charitable organizations would generally be continued. However, the existence under present law of a tax on charities' unrelated business taxable income (UBTI) suggests the possibility that Congress might want to continue limiting the exemption to what it regarded as core charitable activities.

State and Local Governments
Under the administratively simplest consumption tax models, state and local governments would absorb a number of unfavorable changes. First, they would take a significant indirect hit if the current itemized deduction for various state and local taxes (such as income taxes) was eliminated. The Tax Reform Panel proposed disallowing as well state and local taxes paid by businesses.

Second, if interest income was generally tax exempt, the state and local government issuers of municipal bonds that yield tax-exempt interest would seemingly lose their competitive advantage. However, if rival issuers lost their interest deductions, the overall effect would be a wash in cases where the business borrower and the lender were in the same marginal rate bracket.[1] Given that municipal bonds are mainly sold to investors with relatively high marginal tax rates, this point casts considerable doubt on the claim that municipal bond issuers would lose a current advantage. On balance, their business competitors might be the ones who lose ground with respect to borrowing, since the businesses would no longer be able to deduct the interest expense associated with payments to tax-indifferent counterparties.

This analysis shows, contrary to conventional belief, that state and local governments would not lose a competitive advantage with respect to borrowing as such. Under present law the municipal bond preference merely preserves the advantage of being tax exempt even in cases where one uses debt financing. The reason governments might lose ground is that businesses competing with them for capital, whether or not through borrowing, would face a lower effective tax rate on their investments. Thus increased capital might flow to the business sector, potentially drawing from the tax-exempt sector as well as from abroad and from increased national saving.

Nonetheless, it would not be surprising if complaints focus on the loss of competitive advantage from municipal bonds' tax exemption, as determined by looking purely at taxation of the holder. The USA tax preserved the comparative status of municipal bond interest by making it better than exempt. The mechanism was permitting taxpayers who have deducted the cost of purchasing the bonds to include only repayments of principal, while excluding interest receipts. Even if this type of proposal lost out due to its peculiar optics, the underlying complaint might conceivably encourage other concessions.

A final, arguably less serious, complaint that state and local governments might make would pertain to the loss of their present ability to "piggyback" on federal tax returns when levying income taxes. It might be easy enough, however, for them to piggyback on the new federal consumption tax instead.

Pensions and Other Retirement-Related Financial Products

Under a standard neoclassical view of rational optimizers making saving decisions to maximize their expected utility over time, one probably would not expect eliminating the special status of tax-favored retirement plans, by excluding *all* returns to saving, to reduce retirement saving. Economists increasingly recognize, however, that saving behavior often does not seem consistent with rational optimization. For example, it appears to be strongly affected by the choice of default rule (e.g., whether one must opt in or opt out of participating in an employer pension plan), even if participants can easily change the default.

A consumption tax, depending on its structure, might undermine the degree of non–incentive-related encouragement of retirement saving that results under present law simply from having official ceilings on deductible contributions to retirement plans. Accordingly policy makers might conclude that something needed to be done to induce retirement saving after the policy change—whether through incentives (e.g., affirmatively subsidizing retirement saving) or through default rules and other steering or jawboning devices.

Financial Service Businesses

The taxation of financial service businesses can be a big problem under a consumption tax, because payment for the services may be embedded in financial instruments that some consumption tax models, such as the X-tax, generally ignore. The resulting effective exclusion of financial services from the consumption tax base would create an inefficient tax preference for these services relative to other consumption.

A similar problem exists under the current income tax, where financial institutions embed service fees in the interest rates they pay, thus giving consumers an implicit deduction. A consumption tax may make the problem both larger and more overt, however. Accordingly, unless restrained by the political power of such institutions, one might expect a greater effort to address the issue of exempt services than there has been under the existing income tax.

Traditional Capital-Intensive Businesses versus Service Businesses versus Businesses Using Intangible Capital
As noted above, consumption-based reform clearly has the greatest potential appeal to businesses that make extensive use of physical capital that, under the current income tax, gets depreciation rather than expensing. Potentially aiding the pro-consumption tax industries is their presence in states, such as Ohio and Michigan, that tend to be closely contested "battlegrounds" in presidential elections. Unions in these industries might add their support, although service businesses and those using intangibles might line up on the other side.

Health Insurance and Healthcare
The exclusion of employer-provided health care is one of the costliest tax benefits under the current income tax. Presumably repealing it would be politically difficult under the current system. Shifting to a consumption tax, even one with a very different structure, might not greatly change the political considerations.

The biggest policy problem with the exclusion, which is its encouraging over-insurance as a way of making routine health-care expenditures implicitly deductible, could be handled either by repealing or capping it, or by making all healthcare expenditures deductible. While the Tax Reform Panel proposed capping the exclusion, the approach of increasing medical deductions might have greater political appeal, albeit subject to concern about the revenue effects. In 2003 Congress added a new deduction for contributions to individual health savings accounts, and some experts have recently called for making medical expenses generally deductible (e.g., see Cogan, Hubbard, and Kessler 2004). It therefore seems possible that favorable treatment, either for health insurance or for health-care expenditures generally, would continue after the enactment of consumption-based reform.

The Elderly
In the transition, a consumption-based reform would likely increase tax burdens for the current elderly, although this would depend on the type of consumption tax adopted and on the mechanics of the tran-

sition. Given seniors' well-known political power, this raises obvious issues of political feasibility. It suggests that the reform might have to be linked to policies seniors favor, such as sustaining current law Social Security and Medicare benefits, supporting the view that an add-on VAT is politically more likely than consumption-based reform of the income tax.

Education
Present law contains a plethora of distinct tax benefits for educational expenses such as college tuition. While having so many makes little sense, the underlying issue of whether to provide tax benefits for education is independent of the choice between income and consumption taxation. The USA tax contained a limited tuition deduction, while the Tax Reform Panel offered the opportunity to make tax-free use of an IRA-style saving account to fund education expenses.

Oil and Gas Companies
Few industries have the political clout of oil and gas, which seems to fare well in a variety of political environments, ranging from the 1986 Act to energy policy under the George W. Bush administration. While a conceptually pure consumption tax would not offer special benefits to the oil and gas industry (leaving open the question of whether the benefits would simply migrate to other areas in federal law), one might not want to bet against their being found in any consumption tax that Congress actually enacted.

Often, under the existing income tax, benefits to particular industries involve timing. For example, a favored industry might be permitted to expense capital outlays. This tool for providing tax benefits would be eliminated if capital outlays generally were expensed. This does not mean, however, that the quest for special tax benefits would cease. Oil and gas companies would have plenty of options regarding the proposed structure of continuing tax preferences. For example, under the VAT-style business component of the X-tax, they might seek lower tax rates, like those applying to particular industries or items under various European VATs. Or, as under the old income tax rules for percentage depletion, they might seek to deduct more than 100 percent of their costs. Another alternative would be tax credits, such as the old investment tax credit, in addition to (or instead of a portion of) the expensing deduction. Yet another possibility would be expensing plus exclusion on the income side, as under the USA tax proposal for municipal bonds.

Other Special Industry Rules

While the power of the oil and gas industry is a given, other industries likewise invest enormous resources in lobbying Congress. Even if it is difficult to predict which industries would do best under a newly enacted consumption tax, it seems almost inevitable that a large number, with strong political connections, would seek favored treatment with some hope of success.

Necessities Such as Food and Rent

Retail sales taxes in the United States are notoriously less than comprehensive. Among other gaps, they often exclude consumer items that are considered necessities, such as food purchased for home preparation. The idea, presumably, is to increase the progressivity of the given tax instrument, notwithstanding that higher earners may typically spend higher absolute amounts on the excluded items. Under a national consumption tax, even with an individual-level component that permitted the achievement of progressivity, one cannot rule out the possibility that similar motivations would prevail.

For this to happen, optics presumably would have to play an important role. After all, under the present income tax no one has seriously suggested, so far as I know, that the food industry bear a reduced tax rate on the ground that food is a necessity. With a VAT-type structure, however, it is conceivable that retail sales tax-style reasoning would have greater political appeal than it appears to have under the income tax. The difference might lie in the application of folk notions of incidence, which seem to involve automatically assuming that a business-level income tax, as a "direct" tax, is borne by the company earning the income, while any consumption taxes that qualify as "indirect" are assumed to be borne by the consumer.[2]

2.2 "Five Easy Pieces"–Style Consumption-Based Reform

The "five easy pieces" plan to move toward consumption taxation by stealth has only four pieces that relate to the tax base, given that marginal rates are not a tax base issue. In this section, I examine each of the four pieces, considering both their possible design and how they might interact with the rest of the current tax system.

2.2.1   Expensing for All Business Outlays

Expensing for all business outlays, whether capital or ordinary by the light of income tax accounting, is routine and familiar in a consumption tax environment. As part of "five easy pieces" in the current legal, fiscal, and political environment, however, it can create, exacerbate, or unexpectedly fail to solve a number of significant problems.

Expensing within an Income Tax
There are major differences between expensing in a thoroughgoing consumption tax and expensing as a feature of the current income tax. Perhaps the most important difference is that the income tax neither requires loan proceeds to be treated as income nor generally disallows interest deductions claimed by businesses. The income tax treatment of interest can interact with expensing to make debt-financed investments better than exempt (i.e., subsidized, and thus potentially profitable after-tax even if they are economic losers before tax). In addition it can promote a host of tax-motivated transactions.

As an illustration, suppose that the interest rate, and the before-tax return on all assets, is 10 percent, while the tax rate is 40 percent. Under these circumstances, I can acquire a machine that costs $100, lasts for exactly a year, and yields $110. Without debt financing, and ignoring loss limits for the moment, I expense the $100 outlay this year, leading to a $40 reduction in tax liability, and I pay $44 of tax next year. This is the tax-exempt result that one expects under a consumption tax, since the up-front present value of my net tax payment is zero.

Now, however, suppose that I borrow the entire $100 for one year, at a 10 percent interest rate, from a tax-indifferent party. My before-tax cash flow is zero in both years (receive and invest $100, receive and repay $110). For income tax purposes, however, I deduct $100 in year 1 but then include only a net $100, rather than $110, in year 2 (since I can deduct the $10 interest payment). The result is that I effectively get to borrow $40 from the US Treasury for a year at a zero interest rate.

If the lender were paying tax at 40 percent, the problem would be eliminated. Since the lender would include the $10 interest payment in year 2, we would simply have shifted the overall before-tax positive return of $10 from myself to the lender, reflecting that it is the party that supplies the capital and thus gets the ordinary return. In a real world situation, however, this may not happen. As Edward Kleinbard (2005a,

p. 4) has noted, "the capital markets include large numbers of tax-able and tax-indifferent issuers and investors, and those markets are supremely efficient at pairing issuers and investors in ways that maximize their collective returns, and minimize revenues to the fisc." A shift to expensing might actually increase the number of tax-indifferent players, by increasing (especially in the early years when pre-effective date assets were still being depreciated) the number of taxpayers with losses that they could not use.

These problems already exist under present law, where debt is used to shift taxable income to the tax-indifferent sector, and where debt-financed accelerated depreciation involves a lesser version of the same mismatch between taxable investors' income and loss sides. Moreover it might not be a huge problem if tax-indifferent parties were limited to US persons, such as tax-exempts, loss companies, and taxpayers subject to mark-to-market taxation (who are tax indifferent so far as engaging in taxable transactions is concerned). However, with potentially unlimited foreign tax parties that are outside the US tax system, the revenue problems would be a lot more serious. A shift to expensing that was unaccompanied by newly addressing the tax arbitrage between consumption tax-style cost recovery and income tax-style treatment of debt would make things worse, and thus tend to increase tax planning responses.

Expensing and Loss Nonrefundability

In the present income tax, net losses are not refundable. That is, they may be used to offset other taxable income but do not generate net refunds from the government. In addition to discouraging risky investment, nonrefundability creates an incentive to shift tax losses from taxpayers who cannot use them to those who can. Nonrefundability thereby generates significant transaction costs, as "taxpayers attempt end-runs around the loss restriction rules, and the law responds with yet more complex rules and doctrines" (Bankman and Schler 2005, pp. 22–23). Even if expensing did not permanently increase the frequency of losses, it surely would do so in the transition period if taxpayers combined expensing of new assets with continued depreciation of older ones.

The history of the Economic Recovery Tax Act of 1981 offers a handy primer on the possible playout. Recognizing that many taxpayers would be unable to use the swifter depreciation deductions that the Act was providing, Congress enacted the safe harbor leasing rules, under which tax-motivated leasing transactions could be effective even if they lacked economic significance. Taxpayers responded by engaging in a large volume of leasing transactions that clearly amounted to little more than the sale of depreciation deductions, leading to a public outcry (and the repeal of safe harbor leasing), even though permitting such transactions had been exactly the point. Similar issues could be expected to arise if expensing is adopted today or in the future under the current income tax.

Leasing transactions are only one possible transactional response to heightened taxpayer problems with nonrefundability. A second common response is loss trafficking, or attempting to purchase and use the favorable tax attributes of loss companies, subject to statutory restriction. Or two companies can merge, when they would not otherwise have done so, because they anticipate that one will have net income while the other will have tax losses.[3]

Expensing and a More Level Playing Field for Business Investment
One clear advantage of expensing, relative to the array of cost recovery rules in the current income tax, is that it eliminates inter-asset distortions by creating the same effective tax rate (in principle, zero on the risk-free return to waiting) for all assets. Thus, even if one otherwise preferred income taxation to consumption taxation, one might conceivably view the difference as outweighed by the advantages of a uniform rule.

Unfortunately, a shift to expensing would not necessarily reduce inter-asset distortions for long. Lobbyists might soon go to work seeking results for their industries that were better than expensing even without regard to the use of debt. As noted above, the possibilities include special rates, expensing plus additional deductions in subsequent years, the use of credits, and expensing plus exclusion on the income side.

Perhaps it is unfair to blame the shift to expensing for subsequent departures from its use. The reason for mentioning the problem here is that one of its apparent advantages over the income tax's current range of cost recovery rules—its providing a salient uniform approach to cost recovery—might help less politically than many now expect. Indeed the fact that five easy pieces would likely be done in a political environment involving the use of stealth, and dominated by business interests, does little for one's confidence that uniform expensing would endure.

Expensing and the Prospect of Future Tax Increases
A final problem that could be associated with the shift to expensing concerns the fiscal gap. As shown by the well-known Cary Brown theorem, expensing is equivalent to yield exemption for the normal rate of return where tax rates are constant over time. If tax rates are, on average, expected to be constant but could randomly rise or fall, expensing yields the same expected tax rate (i.e., zero) as yield exemption, but subject to symmetric risk. However, where tax rates are more likely to rise than fall, as suggested by the fiscal gap, investments that are expensed have a positive expected tax rate. So the presumed consumption tax policy aim of avoiding the discouragement of saving and investment relative to immediate consumption may not be accomplished here (although for reasons unrelated to the retention in other respects of an income tax).

Arguably the more deferred the expected payout from an investment, the more likely it is that higher tax rates will have set in by the time the payout is realized. Accordingly an expectation of higher future tax rates may give rise to inter-asset distortions even with uniform expensing.

These considerations become all the more important as rising tax rates become more proximate and more predictable. The effective date for a higher tax rate generally is no earlier than the beginning of the calendar year when the change in rate was proposed, although it may be predictable in advance. Taxpayers would be expected to respond by accelerating income recognition and deferring the recognition of losses.

2.2.2 Corporate Integration

Corporate integration could be accomplished in a number of different ways. The plans that have recently been proposed in the United States under the current income tax (which are only a subset of the broader set of possibilities) include the following:

1. Exclusion of dividends from recipients' income, without any change in the tax treatment of corporate interest payouts. This was the approach taken in the Bush administration's corporate integration proposal of 2003, with the further proviso that the exclusion generally would be limited to distributions of previously taxed corporate income.

2. Exclusion of both dividends and corporate interest from recipients' income, with interest as well as dividends being nondeductible at the corporate level. This was the approach taken in the comprehensive business income tax (CBIT) that the US Treasury proposed in 1992.

3. Deductibility by corporations of a cost of capital allowance (COCA), generally without regard to actual payouts or the tax character of particular financial instruments, with accompanying automatic inclusions by the instruments' holders. This is the business enterprise income tax (BEIT) recently proposed by Edward Kleinbard (2005b).

4. Allowing shareholders, when including dividends in their taxable income, to claim a tax credit for what is deemed their allocable share of corporate-level taxes paid.

The complexity and tax planning issues that would arise in the aftermath of corporate integration would largely depend on the model that was followed, as well as on the details of its implementation. Since exploring all of the leading models could easily require an entire shelf of books, I will limit my commentary to what clearly seems the most prominent proposal today (as well as the one that would require the least change to current law). This is the Bush administration's proposal from 2003, under which dividends are excludable from shareholders' income. Congress partly adopted it in 2003, deleting the requirement of previous corporate-level taxation of the distributed income and making the tax rate for dividends 15 percent rather than zero.

Further reducing the tax rate on dividends to zero would potentially revive consideration of conditioning exemption on previous corporate-level taxation of the distributed income. However, there is good reason to suspect that this requirement would not be imposed. Even leaving aside any disinclination by proponents to limit the benefit, the proposed requirement attracted substantial criticism in 2003, on two main grounds. The first complaint concerned its complexity, since keeping track of whether distributions were out of income that had been taxed at the corporate level was by no means simple. The second complaint was that the requirement would unduly reduce the value of corporate tax preferences, by causing Congressionally intended corporate-level tax minimization to come, in some instances, at the price of shareholder-level taxability. These complaints might well carry the day even with a 0 percent rather than a 15 percent shareholder-level dividend tax.

With or without a previously taxed-income requirement, corporate integration would do nothing to address what Kleinbard (2005a, p. 3) calls the "primal flaw" in the current rules for taxing business income. Sophisticated financial engineers can, to a considerable degree, give a corporate financial instrument whatever tax characterization they like while also, and independently, creating whatever set of economic relationships between the investors they like. The consequence is a free pass (leaving aside the significant transaction costs) to give debt instruments to tax-indifferent parties and equity to taxpayers, with the consequence that the debt-financed portion of corporate investment may escape taxation at any level even in the absence of corporate tax preferences. Moreover, if "debt" and "equity" are merely labels that need not have associated economic characteristics, the notion in the economics literature that corporate "debt shields" are limited in practice by the associated default risk ceases to hold.

Putting it in terms of famous economic models of the corporate income tax, the Modigliani-Miller (1961) account of the trade-off between tax savings and bankruptcy risk has declining validity if financial engineers are ever more skillful at separating tax labels from economic substance. By contrast, the Miller equilibrium (from Miller 1977), in which the ratio of debt to equity depends on the ratio of capital from persons paying less than the corporate marginal rate (including tax-indifferent parties) to capital from persons paying more, would be expected to have increasing validity, as the tax labels borne by instruments become ever more elective and unrelated to the underlying economic relationships.

In this brave new world of a functioning Miller equilibrium, distortions resulting from the tax-induced holding of debt or equity would be eliminated insofar as the tax character of an interest in a corporation effectively became elective. There is, however, the implication that a significant portion of corporate income would never be taxed. Moreover, if shareholder-level capital gain remained taxable, further tax planning responses would arise, such as paying out dividends and then reinvesting the funds so as to eliminate the excess of value over basis.

2.2.3 Expanded Roth-Style Individual Retirement Accounts

Creating expanded tax-free saving accounts is a natural step to take in moving the current income tax in a consumption tax direction. This can be done in two ways. The first is to expand "traditional" individual retirement accounts (IRAs), under which contributions are expensed while withdrawals are fully taxed. The second is to expand Roth IRAs, under which contributions are nondeductible but withdrawals are tax-free. The George W. Bush administration and "five easy pieces" proponents have both favored Roth IRAs, for a reason that is easy to understand in terms of budgetary politics. Even though the two types of IRAs are equivalent over the long run if tax rates are constant, Roth IRAs result in lower near-term budget deficits, albeit in exchange for higher budget deficits down the road. Indeed one can even reduce short-term budget deficits in the short run, while worsening the fiscal gap over the long run, by offering taxpayers costly inducements to convert their traditional IRAs into Roth IRAs. This could be very tempting if "five easy pieces" proponents are eager to lower the short-term budgetary cost of their proposals and are not greatly concerned about effects on the long-term fiscal gap.

In principle, Roth IRAs are a perfectly reasonable consumption tax method, involving yield exemption rather than expensing. In an income tax environment, however, either type of IRA may end up creating a money machine for taxpayers that is unrelated to their net saving behavior. The basic idea is simply to finance one's IRA deposits through borrowing, taking care that the loan proceeds not be legally traceable to the accounts. This results in a tax arbitrage whereby one pays deductible interest while earning excludable returns. Indeed, if one can manage to be long and short on identical terms, one has what Steuerle (1985) calls a "pure tax arbitrage," having zero net effect on one's economic position. Such an arbitrage would not be self-limiting, in the manner, say, of debt-financed investment in housing, given the lack of any net effect on supply as compared to demand in the capital markets (since one is both long and short).

If one favors a consumption tax as a way of increasing net saving, debt-financed IRAs can be worse than not having IRAs at all, as they can increase current consumption through their income effect on the consumers to whom they offer a money machine. The problem is almost as bad if one favors a consumption tax to achieve neutrality in the timing of consumption. A taxpayer who reaches the IRA limits through debt-financed "saving" is subject to the income tax at the margin, thereby continuing the bias against saving.

Is this arbitrage scenario realistic, given that the current income tax law disallows deductions for consumer interest expense, along with any other interest expense that does not fall into an expressly allowable category? Perhaps the main ground for concluding that the scenario nonetheless is realistic is the deductibility of home mortgage interest. The Tax Reform Panel proposed reducing this tax benefit, but "five easy pieces" proponents who wanted to make their changes as anodyne as possible might not be inclined to follow suit. Moreover other sources of interest-deductible financing would likely be available to well-advised taxpayers as well. For example, business proprietors could presumably increase their business borrowing and use the extra free cash to fund IRA deposits. People who would otherwise have taxable net investment income could borrow enough to zero out this net income, while indirectly using the additional free cash in the same way. Thus while the consumer interest rule might impede taxpayer use of the arbitrage strategy for funding IRAs, it would by no means make the strategy untenable.

Perhaps the biggest problem with the tax arbitrage strategy, from an individual's tax planning standpoint, is that it assumes the congressional pledge not to tax future Roth IRA withdrawals is politically credible. Given the fiscal gap and pending entitlements funding crises, it is plausible that Congress will be desperate for revenue by the time that current workers are starting to live off the money in their retirement accounts. Only a few years ago, Congress imposed a tax on "excess" withdrawals from tax-free retirement accounts. While Congress swiftly repealed this provision, it was facing considerably less budgetary pressure than is likely in the future.

It would hardly be a triumph for the enactors of expanded Roth IRAs to escape tax arbitrage responses by not being credible to begin with. Either way, accordingly, the enactment would face problems that are not presented in a fiscally stable consumption tax environment.

2.2.4 Movement toward Territorial Taxation

In the international realm, a prominent recent description of the five easy pieces approach refers to "excluding export and other foreign trade income of American companies from tax in much the same way that other countries do in the world marketplace" (Christian and Robbins 2002). This appears to invite two possible interpretations. The first, closer to the words used, is that US companies would be taxed through a peculiar hybrid of the origin basis, used in all existing income tax systems, and the destination basis, typically used in VATs. Under the origin basis, income from sales to foreigners is included and deductions or cost recovery are allowed for business-related payments to foreigners. Under the destination basis, income from sales to foreigners is excluded and no deduction or cost recovery is allowed for payments to foreigners. Leaving aside administrative and transition issues, the two systems have identical incentive effects on cross-border trade (Shaviro 2004b, p. 93).

If five easy pieces allowed the exclusion of exports without changing the tax treatment of imports, it would create an inefficient subsidy for cross-border trade and would violate US treaty obligations relating to the World Trade Organization (WTO). In the recent past a much more limited export subsidy in the US income tax led to an adverse WTO finding, authorizing European complainants to levy retaliatory tariffs on US goods. Finally, its blending the "best" features (from a taxpayer's standpoint) of the origin and destination basis would invite abusive tax planning, such as repeatedly exporting and re-importing the same items in order to generate deductions without offsetting inclusions.

An alternative interpretation of the proposal, suggested by its reference to what other countries do, is that it would replace the current US international tax regime, involving worldwide taxation of US taxpayers subject to deferral of foreign subsidiaries' foreign source income, with a territorial system under which the United States would neither tax foreign source active business income of US companies nor allow deductions or credits with respect to such income, but would tax US-source income on exports. Various other countries have territorial systems (whereas none, presumably, combine origin and destination methods in the same tax base), and there is widespread academic support for, as well as opposition to, the idea of shifting to a territorial system.

At least if done properly, the shift would likely simplify the tax law on balance. For example, it would eliminate business planning to avoid the repatriation tax under present law, end the application of the highly complicated foreign tax credit regime to the exempted income, and reduce or eliminate the need for various other complex or manipulable rules, such as those for classifying foreign software income as between royalties, the sale of goods, and the sale of services (Grubert and Mutti 2001, pp. 10–12). On the other hand, shifting to a territorial system would strengthen the incentive to treat active business income as foreign source, such as through aggressive transfer pricing.

2.2.5   A Capital Gains Exclusion?

One last five easy pieces–style proposal is worth mentioning here, on the ground that it would be a strong candidate for adoption under a Republican-led stealth tax reform, even though it does not appear on the list set forth above. Proponents of a stealth consumption-style reform sometimes propose lowering the capital gains rate to zero (as in Norquist 2002). Presumably capital losses would be nondeductible.

Although the proposal is generally made across the board, one could imagine it being limited to shareholder capital gains on sales of corporate stock. This would be an obvious way to broaden corporate integration if one is not concerned about whether income has been taxed at the corporate level.[4] However, such a limitation would encourage taxpayers who were planning to sell appreciated assets to dump them into corporations and sell the stock. This in turn would presumably require the adoption of anti-abuse rules of some kind, to which there would then be tax planning responses, perhaps requiring a new generation of anti-abuse rules.

The intention, in any event, may be exempting capital gains across the board. This would simplify tax planning in one sense, by eliminating the issue of whether a given capital gain or loss has been realized. It would also call off the need to time one's taxable realizations for tax purposes, such as by waiting to the next tax year to take a gain, or by carefully pairing losses with gains to avoid net capital gain. In corporate taxation, exempting both dividends and capital gains from the sale of stock would eliminate the need to determine whether a given distribution to a shareholder was a true dividend or a taxable exchange. It also would eliminate the need to pay out dividends so that taxpayers would not have capital gains upon selling stock.

In various other respects, however, a capital gains exemption would be a boon for tax planning. In particular, it would increase the tax benefit from converting ordinary income into capital gain, and from arbitraging ordinary deductions against capital gain. These issues typically are prominent in tax planning and practice when the differential between the ordinary income and capital gains tax rates is significant. Again, the deductibility of interest expense, to the extent retained, might be critical to the arbitrage strategy.

2.2.6 *"Five Easy Pieces" Overall*

Even those who favor consumption taxation should seriously question whether the "five easy pieces" approach is likely to advance their objectives in an appealing way. If the pairing of income tax treatment of debt with consumption tax treatment of investments is permitted, and if corporate integration fails to address adequately the distinction under current law between debt and equity, the end product of the process might end up being quite bad.

The political economy of this sort of tax reform process should also excite great concern. If lobbyists run the process without visibility or informed debate, the safeguards that political competition can offer are lost. Recent congressional corruption scandals help to remind us how much the level of public scrutiny can affect substantive political outcomes.

The five easy pieces reform would also likely prove unstable politically. Not having been chosen by bipartisan consensus, it might prove highly vulnerable when Democrats were in a position to rewrite the tax laws. In addition the long-term fiscal gap, which it would be expected to increase even if budgetary game-playing muted the short-term impact on deficits, would inevitably make it ripe for revision.

2.3 Bipartisan X-Tax

The second consumption-based reform scenario that I examine has antecedents in tax reform processes (whether successful or abortive) from the past. In both 1977 and 1984, the US Treasury Department released studies of fundamental tax reform that considered both income and consumption-based alternatives. Likewise the Tax Reform Panel in 2005 offered two reform proposals with consumption tax features. Although consumption-based reform has not yet been identified in any such government-sponsored study as the preferred route, this might change in the future. In particular, suppose that a "new consensus of the experts" (Bradford 1998a) emerges in favor of progressive consumption taxation, and that Democratic leaders, perhaps in pursuit of Clintonian "triangulation," embrace it.

Were this to happen, and to involve the selection of the X-tax as the basic reform prototype, politics would affect the degree of simplification that was achieved in two main ways. First, it would affect the resolution of some of the basic structural issues that others, such as

Weisbach (2000, 2003) and Bankman and Schler (2005), have identified. Second, the political and policy interests that I identified in section 2.1, and perhaps others as well, would need to be considered and in some cases accommodated.

2.3.1 Politics and Some Basic Structural Choices in the X-Tax

Choice between Origin and Destination Basis
An initial design choice lies between use of the origin basis and the destination basis in cross-border business transactions. Again, under the former, which income taxes generally use, business payments for imports are deductible, while those received for exports are includable. Under the destination basis, typically used under VATs, payments made for imports and received for exports are disregarded.

Each of the two methods has its drawbacks. The origin basis requires transfer pricing for cross-border transactions between related parties. That is, if a US company buys from or sells to an overseas affiliate, the deemed price, while potentially economically irrelevant to the affiliated parties, may make a tax difference in the United States and abroad, leading to tax planning and costly litigation. The destination basis requires monitoring cross-border transactions to ensure that deductions are allowed only for purchases from domestic counterparties and that exclusions are limited to true exports. The destination basis also gives rise to what is known as the tourism problem, involving the difficulty of taxing US residents on their consumption while abroad.

The administrative choice between the two approaches is sometimes regarded as a close call, although aversion to transfer pricing induces many to prefer the destination basis. Weisbach (2000, 2003) argues emphatically for the destination basis, noting that game-playing under the origin basis is not limited to transfer pricing. For example, he describes opportunities to exploit the distinction that the X-tax draws between real transactions (which are taxed) and financial transactions (which are ignored) if the system, as under the origin basis, is "open," in the sense that a taxpayer has deductions or credits that need not be matched by the counterparty's inclusion (2003, pp. 217–18). In "closed" systems, by contrast, interbusiness transactions are ignored unless both the payer and the payee are taxpayers. The destination basis results in a closed system as to cross-border transactions.

Bankman and Schler (2005) provide illustrations suggesting that Weisbach is correct. They detail a number of scenarios in which taxpayers conceivably could attempt to game the X-tax system, such as by creating deductions or credits without offsetting income, or by shifting income to nontaxpayers. Under an open system, one might reasonably worry about whether all such transactions could sufficiently be prevented. Under a closed system, however, any transaction (other than paying wages that are taxable at less than the business rate) either is a wash—since both parties or neither will be subject to business tax consequences—or else creates net income as a sale to domestic consumers.

If we assume that Weisbach's argument for a closed system would win the general acceptance that I believe it deserves, the question becomes one of whether political considerations would impede its acceptance. Politically speaking, the following four main considerations come to mind:

1. Destination basis taxes are sometimes lauded by those seeking competitive trade advantages for the United States as "export subsidies" (since exports are tax free). Economists know better, recognizing that the origin and destination methods, once in place with constant tax rates, have identical incentive effects on cross-border trade. One way of explaining this point is to note that, over the long run, exports are effectively traded for imports. Thus, if you export an item tax free but then must pay tax on the import that you ultimately consume in exchange, your consumption has been taxed once, just as in the purely domestic case. However, the subsidy view is hard to allay among nonexperts, potentially favoring choice of the destination method among those who combine their lack of understanding of the economics with an eagerness to give US companies a competitive edge in international trade.

2. On the political debit side, some might object to the fact that US companies would be "escaping" tax on their receipt of money for their exports. While it would certainly be unreasonable to complain about this without acknowledging the flip side, their inability to deduct amounts paid for imports, one could imagine this becoming grounds for political controversy. A given company, for example, might have paid no net X-tax despite large net receipts from abroad in a given year. On the other hand, for the X-tax (or any other consumption tax) to be politically feasible to begin with, people would have to be willing to accept differences between net tax paid and the accounting income reported on financial statements. Moreover the view that this "tax

avoidance" reflected an export subsidy that was creating US jobs, although false, might at least create an offsetting talking point.

3. More reasonably on the debit side, since the United States is currently a net importer of capital, shifting to the destination basis would hand a net transition gain to foreign investors (Auerbach 1997, p. 145). Providers of foreign capital, having made US-deductible imports under the origin basis, would now inconsistently get the benefit of US-excludable exports under the destination basis.

4. Finally on the debit side, a destination-basis X-tax might be viewed as violating the General Agreement on Tariffs and Trade (GATT), which permits "export subsidies" (as it would classify the border adjustment, economics notwithstanding) only in the case of "indirect taxes." It also would violate dozens of bilateral tax treaties. While the distinction between direct and indirect taxes has little if any coherent economic content, the X-tax would probably be classified as a direct tax, unlike VATs, by reason of its treating wages as deductible by businesses and includable by workers.

Although some analysts regard this as a fatal objection to using the destination basis, Weisbach (2003, p. 218) argues that it simply means that the United States would need to seek a revision of the GATT. He notes that it is hard to see why anyone should object, given that the destination basis is not in fact an export subsidy. Moreover the allowability of destination basis VATs and wage subsidies when they are separated suggests that they ought to be permissible when combined.

Perhaps the more pertinent question for current purposes is whether any uncertainty about the needed GATT change would significantly discourage adoption of the destination basis. While this is hard to predict, my own view is that nationalistic pride would provide at least a partial counterweight to GATT-related anxiety. ("We can't let those foreigners tell us what to do! This is a matter of US sovereignty.") Given as well the political popularity of supposed export subsidies, I conclude that there are reasonable grounds for thinking that the destination basis would indeed prevail, assuming general expert agreement that it was preferable.

Dealing with Multiple Tax Rates
In the simplest comprehensive VAT, there are only two tax rates: the single positive rate that always applies to taxpayers and exemption for nontaxpayers such as foreign businesses and any domestic businesses

that are exempted under a special rule for small businesses. Assuming a closed system, all interbusiness cash flows in this simple world yield net tax revenue of zero. Thus, if both parties are taxpayers, the deduction or credit available to one is offset by the inclusion required of the other. If one or both parties are nontaxpayers, neither of these offsetting tax consequences arises. Only on sales to consumers does the system collect net revenue.

As soon as one introduces multiple tax rates, things become more complicated. For example, interbusiness transactions may have net tax consequences unless the buyer's deduction or credit is expressly based on the seller's liability. Relatedly, where particular commodities or types of businesses are supposed to bear special rates, one needs to coordinate the taxation of the various stages in the production process through the final retail stage so that it comes out "right" (however this is defined by the policy makers who created the special rates).

As Weisbach (2003, pp. 226–30) shows, further tax rate coordination issues arise if the production process involves companies that Congress has decided to give more than one tax rate. In addition suppose that (as is common in VATs) particular consumer goods, such as food or energy, get special tax rates that are supposed to apply throughout the production process. Questions then arise as to which of the receipts and outlays of a business that is involved with multiple types of products qualify for each rate.

For interbusiness transactions involving tax-favored (or disfavored) consumer goods, the net tax levied will come out "right" (i.e., as presumably intended) so long as (1) the applicable rate is levied on the final consumer sale and (2) at all prior stages the tax consequences of the inclusion and the offsetting deduction or credit are matched to ensure that they are the same. As under existing VATs, however, this can add significant complexity.

Loss Refundability
Absent concerns about fraud, a well-designed X-tax, like a typical VAT, would provide a net refund for the tax period to any business that had deductible or creditable outlays in excess of its includable receipts. Businesses would presumably be in a net refund position much more frequently under the X-tax than they are under existing VATs, given that they would be deducting or crediting wages in addition to interbusiness payments. With full refundability moreover businesses' incentive to overpay (or pretend to overpay) related parties,

such as owners' family members as a way of taking advantage of the lower rate brackets for wages, would continue indefinitely past the point of zeroing out current period net tax liability.

Whether justifiably (in light of the fraud problem) or not, full refundability seems unlikely as a political matter. The closest rule to full refundability that one could reasonably imagine is a carryover rule that permits refundable amounts to grow at a suitable interest rate. Even under this system, however, some businesses might be eager to circumvent the bar on refundability, whether due to the inadequacy of the interest rate being provided, or to being liquidity-constrained, or to the concern that they would never have net receipts against which the refunds could be used.

Absent full refundability or a sufficiently close equivalent, businesses would have incentives like those under present law to devise end runs around the loss limit. The central anti-tax planning idea of a closed system, that interbusiness transactions have zero net tax consequences, ceases to apply once some taxpayers have losses that they cannot use, making them tax indifferent at least in the short run. Wasteful transactions that shift tax losses to taxpayers with net income, and taxable income to taxpayers with net losses, potentially become profitable to the parties after-tax.

The tax planning responses could take a number of different forms. For example, a taxpayer in a loss posture might find taxable counterparties to buy and lease back its business property, generating an inclusion for the sale proceeds in the loss year, followed by offsetting deductions or credits for the rent payments in subsequent years (Bankman and Schler 2005). Or a loss taxpayer might make an installment sale of its property to a taxable counterparty, overstating the taxable inclusion of the loan principal and understating the disregarded interest payments.

Additionally nonrefundability would lead to clientele effects with regard to transactions between taxpayers on the one side and nontaxpayers (e.g., foreign businesses) on the other. Ordinarily business taxpayers should be indifferent between taxable and nontaxable counterparties (ignoring administrative burdens or delays in receiving rebates). To illustrate, suppose that the business tax rate is 30 percent. Taxpayers should be indifferent between (1) buying or selling with a taxable counterparty for $10 ($7 after-tax) and (2) doing the same at $7 with a nontaxpayer. If one has unusable net losses, however, one may be better off selling to taxpayers (so the income can soak up the losses) and buying from nontaxpayers (since the deduction or credit would not have full value).

Treatment of Small Businesses
European VATs typically exempt small businesses on the view that, say, a child's lemonade stand should not have to register as a business taxpayer. The key difference between treating something as a business for VAT purposes and treating the income it generates as taxable under a typical income tax arises from the fact that, under a closed system, businesses must register so that their counterparties will know how to treat the cash flows. This, presumably, is more demanding than simply filing an income tax return at the end of the year (which in any event is unnecessary for those who earn too little to owe any tax). Such considerations arguably support keeping very small, intermittent, or temporary businesses outside the system on the view that the compliance obligations would be too burdensome or unlikely to be well understood. The small businesses might also typically present burdensome audit and compliance issues in exchange for relatively little revenue—for example, involving the personal use of what ostensibly are business assets.

Under a closed system the small business exception should not be a problem with respect to interbusiness transactions, other than in relation to nonrefundability. Ignoring both sides of a transaction is just as symmetric as imposing a tax liability that is offset by an identical tax benefit. The problem lies rather in the nontaxation of the value-added component of a small business's operations, along with the possible difficulty of applying the graduated wage tax to workers in exempt small businesses.

Transition to the New System and Subsequent Rate Changes
Replacing the current income tax with a simple X-tax that used expensing would impose a wide range of transition gains and losses. Perhaps the most important one, however, is the effective wipeout of income tax basis that would result if the X-tax disregarded all unrecovered pre-enactment capital outlays.

David Bradford (1996b) used a hypothetical example involving tomato juice cans to explain the problem. Suppose a retailer bought tomato juice cans on December 31 for $10,000, and then sold them for the same amount on January 1. If the current income tax were in effect both years, the retailer would have no tax liability, as the outlay would be capitalized in the year it was made and allowed against the cash receipt the next year. If an X-tax using expensing were in effect both years, the taxpayer would get a deduction or credit in the first year that precisely offset (ignoring timing) the tax liability incurred in the second year. If, however, the tax system changed from the one to the other at midnight on New Year's Eve, with each system taking account only of cash flows occurring while it was in place, the taxpayer would never get the deduction, and thus would be taxed on its $10,000 gross receipt at the full consumption tax rate.

Some commentators laud the basis wipeout as equivalent to a lump-sum and hence nondistortionary wealth tax if no one either sees it coming or expects it to recur. I have elsewhere expressed skepticism about this scenario, noting that the change would not take place by surprise overnight and that it might affect subsequent expectations (Shaviro 2000). However, more germane for present purposes than the question of which of these two views is more correct is the question of whether a basis wipeout is likely, and how the approach to transition that Congress took would affect simplification and taxpayer behavior.

The concentrated and fairly visible losses to well-off taxpayers that would result from the basis wipeout seem unlikely, as a political matter, to be imposed. Thus it seems plausible that some form of transition relief would be provided. Yet, if we are operating under the assumption that an X-tax actually gets enacted, a transition hit may need to be politically tolerable after all, since otherwise the prospects for offering attractive rates would be dimmer.

Perhaps the simplest form of transition relief would involve permitting businesses immediately to deduct unrecovered basis at the new X-tax business rate, matching the tax rate on subsequent income arising from the capitalized expenditures. This would invite some game playing by taxpayers, such as disproportionately treating their loss assets as business assets that would generate deductions or credits in excess of any subsequent income. The up-front budgetary cost might make such a transition rule unlikely, however. It is hard to predict how Congress would resolve the dilemma of up-front budgetary cost versus demand for transition relief, although any resolution would likely be more complicated than a one-shot up-front basis recovery.

If transition were a one-time problem only, the issue would go away once it had been resolved in whatever fashion. Unfortunately, however, transition is an ongoing issue in an X-tax that uses expensing.

The broader category to which it belongs is rate changes. Newly enacting an X-tax changes its business rate from 0 percent to whatever positive rate Congress initially chooses. Similar transition issues arise anew each time Congress changes the rate in an X-tax in place. Thus, in terms of Bradford's tomato juice example, the taxpayer had transition losses because the X-tax rate was 0 percent on December 31 and the initial rate (e.g., 30 percent) on January 1. One would have exactly the same type of problem if the rate changed from 20 to 40 percent or (reversing the sign of the transition effect) from 40 to 20 percent.

David Bradford came to regard this problem as serious enough that he proposed modifying the X-tax design to use income tax-style accounting rather than expensing. Outlays that were expected to yield future income would be capitalized, with basis growing at a suitable interest rate so that the deferral of deductions would not reduce their present value relative to expensing.

The disadvantage to this approach is that it makes record-keeping more burdensome. It would require business taxpayers to keep records of basis, which would have to be increased by appropriate interest adjustments and reduced by allowable cost recovery. People might reasonably disagree about whether this is a big enough downside to overcome the advantages of Bradford's proposal. Computers would make compliance easier. Increased complexity might also, however, have the adverse side effect of inducing Congress to create a higher small business exemption.

Whether the Bradford proposal is meritorious on balance or not, its apparent and real complexity may make its adoption unlikely. Simplification would surely have to be a major part of the sales pitch that would lead to replacement of the current income tax. Retaining income tax–style accounting would cut directly against the sales pitch.

It therefore is worth asking what practical issues tax rate changes would bring up in an X-tax that used expensing. The basic tax planning response that one would expect is clear-cut. When tax rates were expected to increase, taxpayers would be eager to accelerate sales and defer outlays so that inclusions, but not deductions, would get the lower current rate. Expected tax rate declines would encourage the opposite response.

For interbusiness transactions between two taxpayers, the symmetry of a closed system would eliminate the net advantage of any such tax planning. Nonrefundability would complicate this, however, and uncertainty would create risk. In addition consumer transactions would not involve this symmetry, and thus would tend to migrate to low-rate years to the extent feasible.

Congress, in turn, might respond through the use of effective date rules such as those that are used at times under present law. For example, the new rate might, if enacted, be effective as of the date of its announcement or introduction. This might not be prohibitively burdensome from a compliance standpoint if business taxpayers were required to have (1) dated invoices for all of their interbusiness transactions and (2) daily records of their consumer sales. Once again, however, such requirements might strengthen the political case for setting the small business exemption higher.

Even early effective dates would not fully address taxpayer anticipation. A good example arose under the current income tax in 1992, when President Clinton was elected on a campaign platform calling for an increase in the top marginal rate. Some expressed outrage when the effective date turned out to be January 1, 1993, or before he took office but well after there was reason to believe a rate increase was coming. More generally, taxpayers will frequently have good grounds, even before a given legislative change is formally introduced, for anticipating that change in a particular direction is imminent.

Insofar as tax rates follow a kind of random walk, dependent on the vagaries of short-term politics, there would be no long-term systematic direction to the incentive effects of businesses anticipating rate changes. Instead, responses might await concrete information about the likely direction of the next turn in the road. However, the long-term fiscal gap supports a general expectation that over the long run marginal rates are likely to increase. With annual expensing this would amount to imposing an expected positive tax rate on saving and investment, by indicating that business receipts are likely to be taxed at a higher rate than that at which the underlying outlays are deducted or credited.

2.3.2 Important Political Interests in the Enactment Process

In the previous section politics figured only insofar as it would affect the basic structural choices that were made in implementing an X-tax. Analogizing the hypothetical process to the enactment of the Tax Reform Act of 1986, one might think of those choices as akin to the Treasury I stage, in which a basic, very ambitious tax reform plan was

designed that shaped the entire effort but that lacked most of the political concessions to particular interests, and to policy aims apart from
base-broadening-style tax reform that everyone knew would ultimately be necessary.

The analogy suggests that the end product of an X-tax enactment
might not look any more like a pure form of the tax than the 1986 Act
looked like Treasury I. From a simplification and tax planning standpoint, the question is to what degree this would compromise the entire
system, as opposed to simply creating discrete departures from the
pure structure. I address this question by looking at the important political interests identified in section 2.1.

Homeownership
It is difficult to believe that Congress would eliminate or even greatly
curtail the home mortgage interest deduction in the course of enacting
an X-tax. The most one could imagine it doing is adopting limitations
along the lines proposed by the Tax Reform Panel, which would have
(1) substantially lowered the ceiling on loan principal that generates
deductible interest and (2) converted the deduction into a percentage
credit that was below the top marginal rate.

If one believes that allowing the home mortgage interest deduction
is bad policy given the exclusion of homeowners' imputed rental income, retention of the tax benefit would be disappointing. From an X-
tax standpoint, however, the subsidy for homeownership is not the
only issue. The linkage of the tax benefit to borrowing raises a further
concern, given the arbitrage possibilities that are presented by the opportunity to combine borrowing deductibly with investing tax free.

Charities
The deduction for charitable contributions also seems likely to be
retained, or alternatively converted into a percentage credit. It also
might be made universally available, in contrast to present law, which
restricts it to itemizers. Such an expansion would likely receive significant political support from churches, whose contributors are thought
to be significantly affected by the current law restriction.

Eliminating the present rule under which charitable donors can deduct the full value, rather than simply the tax basis, of donated property is a longstanding tax reform cause that one might expect X-tax
proponents to favor (although the Tax Reform Panel proposed retaining the current rule). If the basis of donated property is easier to

establish than its value (which seems likely, other than for publicly traded property), the change would promote tax simplification. However, the change would be unwelcome to charities that significantly benefit from the current rule, such as universities and art museums.

On the deduction side only modest simplification, if any therefore seems likely. There might, however, be some planning and compliance simplification with respect to the charitable organizations themselves. For many decades such organizations have been among the tax-indifferent counterparties that taxpayers use in efforts to create untaxed income alongside deductible losses. Shifting to a closed system would eliminate this tax planning possibility. In addition the shift to a consumption tax would affect the need for certain rules that currently apply to charitable organizations, such as that imposing the unrelated business income tax (UBIT) on their debt-financed investment income.[5]

The UBIT might continue to apply to charities, since its rationale, whether one finds it convincing or not, arguably would survive the shift to a consumption tax.[6] Now, however, it presumably would take the form of requiring charities to register as taxable businesses with respect to the covered activities. Complications might arise if the Internal Revenue Service determined after the fact that a given business activity engaged in by a charity should have been registered as unrelated to the charity's exempt purpose.

State and Local Governments
Consumption-based tax reform is potentially adverse to the interests of state and local governments. First, although the issue is unrelated to the choice between income and consumption taxation, any major reform effort is likely to involve considering elimination of the itemized deduction for individuals' state and local tax payments. Thus both Treasury I in 1984 and the Tax Reform Panel in 2005 proposed repealing the deduction, and the Panel would also generally have repealed business deductions for state and local taxes. Repeal has significant political support from Republicans who want to curtail state and local government spending, and potentially to "red state" voters who realize that the repeal would result in a relative shift of tax liability to people in the "blue states." In addition, as noted by the Tax Reform Panel, the fact that the deduction is not allowed in the alternative minimum tax (AMT), which is applying to ever more individuals, means that the deduction is already being scaled back significantly.

On the other hand, both voters and government officials in relatively high-tax states, including prominent Republican governors, are likely to oppose repealing the deduction, even if the AMT induces them to accept a compromise. Moreover, given my premise that the X-tax would emerge from a bipartisan process, Democratic approval of the repeal would be needed as well and would be hard to secure given the importance of the issue to Democratic senators and members of Congress in states such as New York and California. One suspects therefore that at least something of the present law regular tax deduction will survive (whether as a deduction or a credit). It also is possible that any scaling back of the deduction would require political compensation to the state and local governments elsewhere in the design of the enacted X-tax.

Pensions and Other Retirement-Related Financial Products

Given the evidence that people's savings decisions are highly swayed by default rules concerning how much of their paychecks are set aside, it might be sufficient, under an X-tax, to create statutory rules establishing a suitable default. If affirmative incentives for a specified level of retirement saving were thought necessary, one possibility that has been discussed in the past would be to have the government supplement people's contributions to their special retirement accounts. The availability and amount of the government contribution could be inversely related to wages, although this would add an extra detail in X-tax filing and would effectively create additional marginal rates.

Financial Service Businesses

VATs typically exempt financial services businesses, yielding complicated line-drawing problems (Merrill and Adrion 1995), and giving an inefficient subsidy to the consumption services these businesses provide. Consider, for example, the common case of a finance company that is associated with a commonly owned active business (e.g., GMAC and General Motors). In the case of the X-tax the impetus to avoid exemption might be stronger, on the optical ground that the wage tax component makes the business-level tax look more like a tax on businesses rather than on consumers.

A solution would probably have to involve requiring financial service businesses, as appropriately defined, to register as such. How to define them is clearly a major problem. Once they were appropriately defined, one possible consequence of their special status would be inclusion of financial transactions rather than just real transactions in their tax bases. Thus all loan proceeds and insurance premiums, among other receipts, of a financial service business might be includable, while all of its loan and insurance outlays would be deductible or creditable. Financial service businesses would therefore be under straight cash flow accounting (Bradford 1996c).

Treating financial service businesses in this way would involve departing from the closed character of the X-tax system, since the financial firms' business counterparties would presumably still disregard financial transactions. This might create abuse potential. For example, in the event of a statutory rate increase, financial firms would profit after-tax from issuing financial instruments just before the effective date and settling the instruments through repayment just afterward. Likewise, if the tax rate was about to fall, they would benefit from making loans that generated deductions at the old higher rate, followed by counterparty repayment that they would include at the new lower rate. The fact that business counterparties were not reporting reciprocal inclusions and deductions on financial instruments would prevent these interbusiness transactions from being a wash overall. Various solutions have been suggested,[7] but they clearly require further development and exploration.

With constant tax rates, by contrast, full cash-flow taxation that was limited to financial firms might lead to overtaxation of the financial services that are provided at arm's length to other businesses. Suppose a financial firm embeds its service fee in the spread between the interest rates it charges and pays to business counterparties. While it would be taxed on the spread if using straight cash-flow accounting, the counterparties would not be deducting the spread if they were simply disregarding all cash flows from financial transactions. This could lead to inefficient underconsumption of financial services or the shifting of such services to be performed in-house.

The Tax Reform Panel proposed responding to this problem by having financial firms identify (for counterparty deduction) the service component of payments they received from business customers. It did not address the question of how this portion would be identified, given the parties' incentive to overstate it if the identification had no tax consequences for the financial firm. Obviously this is no trivial problem.

A final political issue posed by the tax treatment of financial service businesses concerns the political clout that various types of such businesses might exert. Thus, consider life insurance companies, which currently can provide tax-free investment income to the consumers who purchase their products. Universalizing the tax exemption for investment returns might prompt complaints about life insurance contracts' loss of relative advantage. Congress might conceivably respond by offering life insurance companies a tax break of some kind relative to the general application of cash flow taxation to financial businesses (if that was the approach generally taken). Or, like the USA tax with respect to municipal bonds, Congress might provide better-than-exempt treatment to consumers holding life insurance policies.

Traditional Capital-Intensive Businesses versus Service Businesses versus Businesses Using Intangible Capital
With only the first of these three groups being strongly motivated to support a shift to expensing, something to buy off the latter two groups might be necessary. In the 1986 Act, "rifleshot" transition rules favoring particular taxpayers were an important tool for buying off selected capital-intensive businesses. Perhaps some similarly targeted benefit could buy enough support from the other two groups to mute their collective opposition without costing too much revenue.

Health Insurance and Health Care
The importance of addressing overinsurance, whether by capping the exclusion on employer-provided benefits or making medical expenses generally deductible, has attracted increasing attention in recent years from tax policy and health-care experts. The Tax Reform Panel proposed capping the exclusion, a proposal that would likely attract powerful opposition if it were being seriously considered by Congress. The Cogan-Hubbard-Kessler approach of making all medical expenditures deductible would likely raise concerns about its revenue cost and about its conditioning the value of the tax benefit on one's marginal tax rate.[8]

    Even if we assume that addressing the incentive for overinsurance will be unavoidable at some point, it is not obvious that tax reform provides the best political occasion for doing so. An alternative approach, sparing tax reform the controversy but also denying it credit for the revenue gain from capping the exclusion, would be to do so in connection with addressing health-care issues more generally. For example, if Medicare reaches a crisis point at which funding increases or benefit cuts can no longer be postponed, simultaneously reducing the income tax exclusion could conceivably be grouped with any such changes under the rubric of a general "share the pain" approach.

The Elderly
Here the main issue is presumably mitigating or at least concealing the transition hit, or alternatively offering other benefits (e.g., delaying the effective date of entitlements reform) in a single legislative package.

Education
Given the plethora of distinct tax benefits for education in present law, it seems likely that any fresh start, whether or not involving consumption-based reform, could make things simpler. Percentage credits, proposed by the Tax Reform Panel in other settings but not here, would be one possible tool of choice.

Oil and Gas Companies
One of the main advantages sometimes attributed to shifting from an income tax to a consumption tax is that it would make inter-asset and interbusiness tax neutrality much easier to achieve. If everything is being expensed, one does not face the issue that arises under an income tax of differing departures from the rate of cost recovery that would be dictated by accurate income measurement.

The oil industry, given its notorious political clout, might provide an immediate test of this proposition. For cost recovery actually to be more neutral under a consumption tax than under the existing income tax, its being technically easier to achieve, while helpful, is not enough. One might also have to posit that providing treatment that was better than expensing would be a hard sell politically by reason of its arguably unfavorable optics. However, this would not necessarily be the case, given the variety of means (discussed earlier) that could be used to achieve better than exempt treatment.

Other Special Industry Rules
While few if any industries consistently match the political clout of oil and gas, many others might find themselves in a position to get better treatment than expensing. Consider, for example, the tax credits under current law for various energy-related outlays, research and experimentation expenditures, and rehabilitation expenditures. Even if the proponents of these items did not win special concessions at the time

when an X-tax was enacted, they or other proponents of special treatment for particular items could be expected to try again once the initial reform impulse had faded.

Necessities Such as Food and Rent
On a more optimistic note, although necessities such as food are often exempted or given lower rates in retail sales taxes and VATs, there may be reason to hope that this special treatment would not extend to an X-tax. For one thing, the treatment of wages in an X-tax provides an alternative vehicle for offering progressivity. For another, the optics would be different in an X-tax if people think of them as being paid at the business level by the business itself, rather than by consumers (presumably the standard popular view of a retail sales tax or VAT). Taxing rental payments for housing might also be feasible given the nominal imposition of the business portion of the X-tax, although an exemption for small businesses might cover small-scale operators in the field.

2.3.3   Other Structural Issues

Political considerations, in addition to motivating particular exceptions to a comprehensive consumption tax base, might also induce the adoption of broad structural features that would add complexity. Recent history suggests two possibilities in particular. The first is a 1986-style approach of limiting the deemed overuse of special tax benefits, as opposed to denying the benefits altogether. The second is an approach like that in the Tax Reform Panel's "Growth and Investment Tax Plan," where what was otherwise a consumption tax had as well a provision for taxing individuals' capital income to the extent not sheltered through tax-free saving accounts.

Limits on "Overusing" Tax Benefits
One of the most important structural features of the 1986 Act was its expanding the use of what I have called "selective limitations" on the deemed overuse of tax benefits (Shaviro 1989). These rules condition the allowability of a given tax benefit on its interplay with other items, often by preventing taxpayers from claiming an overall loss with respect to a given set of associated items. Examples from present law, several of which were introduced or expanded in 1986, include

nonrefundability, the alternative minimum tax, the passive loss rules, the investment interest limitation, the capital loss limitation, and the at-risk rules.

In the current income tax, such rules serve three distinct purposes. One is limiting the benefit one can immediately reap from outright cheating. A second is limiting the use of tax preferences that Congress deliberately enacted. A third is limiting taxpayers' ability to exploit the realization requirement, such as by selling loss assets while holding gain assets or borrowing against unrealized appreciation.

While the last of these three purposes would cease to be necessary under an X-tax, the first would remain, and it is a commonly cited reason for retaining nonrefundability (Bankman and Schler 2005). The second, limiting the use of deliberate tax preferences, would likewise remain if Congress departed sufficiently from giving the X-tax a comprehensive base. Thus one could (horrifyingly) imagine something like the AMT being imposed to limit tax benefits at the business and/or individual level.

Add-on Individual-Level Tax on Capital Income

A second set of possible politically induced structural issues is suggested by the decision of the Tax Reform Panel to complicate what was otherwise an X-tax proposal by adding a 15 percent tax on individuals' investment income, such as from interest, dividends, and capital gain. The apparent motivation, forestalling the criticism that wealthy investors were paying no tax (notwithstanding taxation at the business level), could potentially persuade Congress as well if it was enacting an X-tax through bipartisan compromise.

The complications that might result from the use of this approach include the following:

1. As under the Tax Reform Panel's plan, taxpayers would presumably be able to avoid the add-on capital income tax to the extent that they made use of tax-free saving accounts. Various complications associated with using the accounts might therefore arise, such as tracking distributions from the accounts to the extent that special rules limit their permissible use.

2. If some financial assets were exempt from the 15 percent tax, further tax planning would be required, such as not "wasting" one's exemptions by placing assets that yield tax-free income in a tax-free account.

3. If deductions were allowed against taxable financial income (as seems reasonable), items such as interest expense would need to be allocated or apportioned as between taxable and tax-free income. The line between personal and investment expenses, occasionally an issue under present law, would also have to be monitored.

4. Taxpayers would presumably try to avoid or at least defer the tax by holding assets at the business level. This might create a need for anti-abuse rules, like the accumulated earnings tax under present law. One might even need rules generally defining the working capital that a business is allowed to count as integral to its operations, given that the definition of a business would not be as entity-based as under present law.

2.3.4   *Public Assistance Benefits*

At present the earned income tax credit (EITC) is the only major program offering income support to the poor or near-poor that is formally integrated with the income tax. Other income support programs, such as Temporary Aid to Needy Families (TANF), Food Stamps, and Medicaid, rely on separate determinations of need. However, these programs generally use income in one way or another in determining eligibility and the amount of aid that one gets. (Earnings and assets also matter in particular programs.)

The EITC, by reason of its being administered through the income tax, is the only one of these programs that would be directly affected by enactment of an X-tax. For the other programs, however, a question would naturally arise as to whether they should change toward a consumption base as well. One argument for such a shift would be that the marginal burden of measuring income would be increased if not already necessary under the income tax. A second argument would be that if consumption or wages is the appropriate distributional measure for tax purposes, it should be considered as such more generally, including under the transfer programs. After all, the basic enterprise of measuring material well-being is the same in the tax and transfer systems.

Thus, under the X-tax, one could imagine wages being used to determine who should get TANF, Food Stamps, and Medicaid benefits. However, in the absence of complementary asset tests that do not fit well with a consumption tax philosophy, this would seem to mean that wealthy coupon-clippers should get the benefits. This, in turn, however, might alarm even the most stalwart consumption tax advocates.

How can a distributional measure that many prefer to income on the tax side seem less well-suited to the transfer side? The answer, I think, goes to the choice of time period for measuring how well-off one is. The core distributional argument for a consumption tax looks at lifetime income, which sets the budget line for lifetime consumption if one can borrow and lend freely between periods. However, we may want to help people who are poor in a given period even if they had resources in the past or expect to have resources (but cannot borrow against them) in the future. Thus consider an elderly retiree who has spent all of her lifetime earnings and is now destitute. Leaving aside the point that we can compel her to save through Social Security and Medicare, we may want to help her despite the resources she had in the past and the incentive problems associated with anticipating rescue.

2.3.5   Aftermath of Enacting an X-Tax

A final question concerns the effect of X-tax enactment on subsequent tax politics. One certainly would hope that a consensus bipartisan enactment would prove more stable than I have suggested the "five easy pieces" reform would be. But to what extent would the post-1986 history of gradually adding back special provisions repeat itself? After all, the enactment would swiftly become yesterday's news, of little interest to politicians who wanted to gain political credit for doing something today. Any optimism that this process could be averted might have to rest on some sort of partially exogenous change that resulted in the tax system's ceasing to be as much of a central political arena as it has been for the last few decades.

Such change has happened before. Tariffs, for example, no longer attract the level of constant political activity that they did for much of the nineteenth century and through the 1930s. Yet it is hard to see what would motivate the change this time around. Tariffs declined in importance as a revenue source with the rise of the income tax. They also had been blamed for the onset of the Great Depression, and may have lost ground politically due to the post–World War II rise of a larger export sector that was vulnerable to retaliation by other countries. Personal and business taxation, by contrast, would still be a crucial source of federal revenues rivaled only by payroll taxes.

Even if special interest activity became less of an ongoing factor in personal and business taxation, the activity might simply move elsewhere. This might be a relief for people who take particular interest in the tax system, but it would not necessarily mean that politically induced economic distortion and complexity were declining overall. An overall improvement would probably require a change in the basic political dynamics that apply at the national level and below, relating to policy transparency, political accountability, campaign financing, and other election dynamics such as the use of gerrymandering.

2.4   Conclusion

While there have been decades of academic debate regarding the relative theoretical merit of ideal income taxes and ideal consumption taxes, a major reason for favoring consumption-based reform has been dismay about the actual income tax that we observe. Its complexity, pervasive encouragement of socially wasteful tax planning, and susceptibility to creative avoidance schemes have prompted the hope that a consumption tax could do much better.

Depending on the particular path to consumption-based reform that Congress actually followed, these hopes might conceivably be realized to an extent. A reasonably well-designed consumption tax would avoid tax planning issues related to the realization requirement. In addition, while an income tax need not distinguish between debt and equity in the manner of the current system, consumption-based reform might aid politically in conforming their treatment. Finally, shifting to a destination-based consumption tax would permit the elimination of transfer pricing issues.

In other respects, however, reformers' simplification hopes might be disappointed. For example, despite the salience of expensing as a uniform cost recovery method, shifting to a consumption tax would not necessarily reduce Congress's inclination to use the tax system (or perhaps some other set of rules) to favor particular industries. Credits, exclusions, extra deductions, and special rates are all feasible routes to industry-specific tax favoritism. The use of special business rates, in the manner of various European VATs, would add a largely novel type of complexity to US federal tax practice and could undermine the administrative advantages of operating a closed system in which inter-business transactions were always a wash (nonrefundability aside). Finally, the likelihood of future tax increases by reason of the fiscal gap would cast a shadow over the system, subjecting long-term investment to a positive expected rate and inviting taxpayers to play timing games at the point when rate changes are more imminent.

The tax planning issues are likely to be a great deal worse in the event of a "five easy pieces"–style stealth reform. A process that relies on one party's tight legislative control and on concealing from the public the actual import of the policy changes does not inspire confidence for two distinct reasons. The first is the likely lack of open deliberation regarding possible problems with the changes and how they might be addressed. The second is the proponents' possible reluctance to make potentially controversial changes that would be needed for the system to work, such as addressing interest deductions and the arbitrage between consumption tax treatment of receipts and income tax treatment of outlays.

Even in the case of an open and bipartisan reform process, public ambivalence about the consumption tax norm could lead to political compromises that would create substantial complexity. One possibility is the use of 1986-style backup limitations on special tax benefits or dangers of abuse. Nonrefundability would already be one example of such a rule, and something like the current AMT is not out of the question either. A second possibility is the creation of an extra, even if low-rate and avoidable, tax on investment income in the manner of that in the 2005 Tax Reform Panel's GIT proposal.

"Tax simplification" is always an appealing slogan, in addition to being genuinely desirable. Once we get beyond slogans, however, simplification is a public good that few political actors value more than the opportunity to shift their own tax burdens to someone else. In our frequently corrupt political system, at once too responsive and not responsive enough, this greatly limits the actual tax simplification that one can ever realistically expect.

Discussion

James Alm

Over the years, I have worked on many tax reforms in Jamaica, Egypt, Colombia, the Russian Federation, Bangladesh, Indonesia, the Philippines, and several other countries (and US states). In all cases I have approached these reforms from the usual economics perspective of how does the current tax system achieve—or fail to achieve—the standard criteria of revenue adequacy, equity, and efficiency. The basic thrust of these reforms has often been similar, regardless of the specific circumstances of the country: expand the relevant tax bases and lower tax rates.

However, Daniel Shaviro takes an entirely different approach. Rather than examine the *economic* arguments for or against tax reform, Shaviro examines the *political* considerations that seem likely to affect and to influence—positively and negatively—the tax reform discussion. In particular, Shaviro focuses on three main issues:

• How would political pressure points affect the specifics of any consumption tax reform, especially the simplification that many advocates of consumption tax reform believe is one of its main advantages?

• What types of political scenarios would be most likely to lead to consumption tax reform, and what types of consumption taxation seem most likely to emerge?

• What types of political interests would need to be accommodated in the course of consumption tax reform?

Now this exercise is, of course, highly speculative. The answers to these questions are almost certain to be unknown and unknowable, in terms of the themes for this volume. Even so, this exercise is a fascinating one, and ultimately one that is also informative, sobering, and, in my view, profoundly depressing.

At the start, let me give my own summary of Shaviro's main conclusions. (Remember, this was written in summer 2006.)

First, it seems highly unlikely that the political circumstances will emerge that will allow any type of comprehensive tax reform, let alone a consumption-based tax reform.

Second, even so, the most likely current circumstances/options are two:

• A bipartisan process (à la the Tax Reform Act of 1986) led by centrist Democrats and Republicans that yields a progressive consumption tax (e.g., the Bradford X-tax)

• A Republican-led process pushed through with tight congressional control that moves by stealth toward a consumption tax (e.g., "five easy pieces").

But, *third*, even if the "perfect storm" of events actually occurred, the reform that would likely emerge from the political process would almost certainly not achieve any of the simplification goals advocates of consumption taxes believe are possible, for a variety of reasons. The specific reform options and issues are many, politics (and special interests) would hijack the process, and the most likely end result would be a complex, distorting, and unfair tax.

Now I should emphasize here that Shaviro (in the version of the chapter that I saw) gives a very comprehensive look at the main political interests, including such groups/issues as:

• Homeownership
• Charities
• State and local governments
• Pensions
• Financial service businesses
• Health insurance
• Education
• Oil and gas companies
• Necessities

I should also emphasize that Shaviro gives a very comprehensive look at many of the main choices and trade-offs that must be confronted in any tax reform:

- Fiscal gap
- Expensing
- Loss refundability
- Accounting choices (e.g., income versus consumption styles in accounting methods)
- Corporate integration
- Individual retirement accounts
- Origin versus destination basis taxation
- Capital gains
- Targeted tax benefits
- Small-business exemptions
- Transition issues
- Public assistance

These are wide-ranging lists of groups/issues. Even so there are, I think, some obvious omissions here. In terms of possible reform options, there is no discussion of the FairTax, a national retail sales tax that would replace the income and the payroll taxes. There is no discussion of the Hall-Rabushka flat tax. There is no discussion of the value-added tax (VAT), or of the combination of the VAT with a high-exemption individual income tax. In terms of political interests, there is little or no discussion of farmers, defense contractors, capital-intensive (and information-intensive) sectors, high-tech industries (including intellectual property issues), service industries, the elderly, unions, and intangibles, to name only a few candidates.

Despite these omissions the end result is a very plausible and convincing discussion of possible reform options, with an assessment of the likelihood of their passage. The scenarios are believable, well justified, and well reasoned. Again Shaviro's conclusion is that the most likely reform would not achieve any of the simplification goals advocates of consumption taxes believe are possible. Indeed, add politics to the mix, he argues, and the most likely end result would be a tax system that is not much of an improvement over the current system.

Recognizing the obvious qualifier that this exercise is highly speculative, let me give my own assessment of the known, the unknown, and the unknowable aspects of tax reform in the 2000s, an assessment that is somewhat different than Shaviro's.

First, I believe that the chances of any comprehensive reform—of any type—are remote. Why? The "perfect storm" surrounding (say) the Tax Reform Act of 1986 (TRA86) simply is not there:

• Unlike 1986, there is no consensus among the experts. Then most everyone agreed with cutting rates and expanding the base—and keeping an income base. Now there are many competing proposals with virtually no agreement.

• Unlike 1986, there are no obvious and easy selling points (e.g., reduce tax shelters, increase the corporate tax burden, lower marginal tax rates).

• Unlike 1986, there is not a political leader who seems able to generate political support for reform.

• Unlike 1986, the chances of bipartisan compromises in the current setting seem remote.

• Unlike 1986, the constraints imposed on any current reform process are likely to be far more severe and politically difficult (e.g., revenue neutrality, distributional neutrality, off-the-table items, open deliberations). Just ask those who served on the President's Advisory Panel on Tax Reform.

And even TRA86 was not, in the views of at least some observers, all that radical a tax reform.

At bottom, then, I remain very pessimistic that *any* tax comprehensive tax reform can be enacted in the current environment. Indeed I am becoming increasingly convinced that perhaps we now know too much. I am, of course, not suggesting that we, as public economics scholars, should not try to examine the many and disparate effects of tax reform (or, more broadly, the effects of any government policies)—these efforts will continue, as they should. However, I wonder whether (even compared to twenty years ago, with TRA86) our knowledge about the effects of any potential tax reforms paralyzes the political process.

When we (as academics) are better able to identity the many distributional and other effects of tax reform, we essentially mobilize the losers, and this means that the political process becomes immobilized because the losers from any potential change (no matter how small) lobby to prevent the change from occurring. And, as our research has advanced, we are better able to identify the losers (and the winners) from any changes (e.g., old capital). Of course, from an academic perspective, being able to identify the winners and the losers is obviously a plus, and I do not believe that we should ever abandon our efforts to examine and quantify these effects. However, from the broader public policy perspective, I am not so sure whether we are making things better or worse. In some sense, I believe that the case can be made that the big policy changes that have occurred over the years have been because of a broader perspective that, although there are losers and winners, the overall thrust of policy change is beneficial. When we are better able to identify the losers (and the winners), I believe that it often makes it harder to assemble the coalition necessary to pass the reforms.

Another way to make this same point (as suggested to me by James Poterba in private correspondence) is to note that we now have many more models and assumptions at our disposal, so that, if some group asks "Might we lose under this plan?" we are increasing the odds that we can find some model and some assumption under which this will be the case. Since the potential losers are the ones who will make the loudest noise, we may just be expanding the class of protesters.

In this regard it is worth asking whether there are lessons for the US tax reform discussions from other countries where tax reforms have actually occurred in the last several decades; that is, what are the conditions—political and economic—under which tax reform seems more likely, and what are the forms of tax reform that seem likely to emerge? I believe that the main known problems with tax systems that generate a demand for reform are that the tax system is excessively and unnecessarily complex, there are large distortions in behavior, and there are large and widespread horizontal and vertical inequities. These are often cited as the main reasons for reforming the US tax system. (There are, of course, other common problems: a narrow and shrinking tax base, large amounts of tax evasion and tax avoidance, widespread use of tax incentives, significant limitations in tax administration, an apparent—and largely undocumented—belief that taxes can be used to generate economic growth, a poor system of indirect taxation, and an outdated and ad hoc system.)

Similarly I believe that the known necessary (if not sufficient) conditions for a reform to be enacted are several. First, the tax system must be widely seen—by most all relevant players—as "broken." Second, there needs to be consensus on how to fix it. Third, there needs to be a strong "champion" who can generate political support for reform. (Especially in developing countries there often also needs to be an external party who can help "finance" the reform.) As I noted earlier, I am not convinced that any of these conditions are currently met in the United States.

Finally, I believe that the main known lessons from successful tax reforms around the world are several:

1. *Comprehensive reforms are often better than piecemeal reforms.* Now this goes somewhat against much conventional wisdom, and there are certainly risks that disaster can result when a system is shocked too much from a comprehensive reform. Even so, I believe that under many conditions comprehensive reform can work:

- Everyone recognizes that the system is broken.
- The government and the taxpayers need time to absorb the shock, and the time involved in the discussion of comprehensive reform often allows this.
- There is sufficient time for the tax administration to absorb the changes.

More generally, I think that the reasons for preferring comprehensive reform to piecemeal reform include such considerations as:

- Comprehensive reforms ensure that the separate pieces of the reform fit together so that the prices are "right."
- Comprehensive reforms ensure that everyone gains—and everyone loses—from some or another specific change, which increases the political likelihood of passage.
- Comprehensive reforms ensure that everyone recognizes that the system of taxation is "broken" and needs to be fixed.
- Comprehensive reforms ensure that the momentum of reform is maintained.
- Comprehensive reforms ensure that the gains (and losses) are large enough for taxpayers to actually see.

2. *The best time for comprehensive reform is—paradoxically—often in bad economic times.* This ensures that everyone's attention is focused and that everyone recognizes the necessity of tax reform.

3. *In many instances base broadening is consistent with equity* and *efficiency concerns.* For example, the elimination of tax preferences and more generally the broadening of the tax base can improve both vertical and horizontal equity by ensuring that the wealthy pay their "fair" share and that equals are treated equally. Base-broadening reforms also improve efficiency by reducing the incentives for income-shifting activities.

4. *Tax reforms must consider the specific circumstances of the country: there is no one-size-fits-all tax reform.* Now it is the case that most reforms have attempted to broaden the base and reduce the rates. Even so, the precise ways in which this is done certainly vary across the institutions, the traditions, the economic policies, and so on, of the specific country. These elements must be considered.

5. *Tax reforms must recognize and balance the trade-offs.* Any reform must balance adequacy considerations with efficiency considerations with equity considerations.

6. *Empirical analysis is often difficult, but crucial, for determining the details of any reform and in selling any reform.* Data are often problematic, even in the United States, and, as I emphasized earlier, quantifying the winners and losers can mobilize the political opposition. Even so, it is essential to try to quantify the effects of tax reforms. Such quantification is especially crucial in determining the distributional effects of tax reforms.

7. *The administrative dimension is important, but it is necessary first to get the policy "right" before dealing with administrative problems.* If the reform stops with administration, and leaves poor policy still in place, the result will still be poor policy.

8. *Tax reform should pay attention to the intergovernmental dimension.* Most often the reform effort focuses exclusively on the central government. However, fixing things at the central government while leaving in place poor tax policies at the subnational level will often compromise the goals of reform. In the US context, the impact of *federal* tax reform on *state and local* taxes is a crucial consideration, and one that is not typically given appropriate consideration.

9. *Reforms must consider implementation (and transition) issues, so keep things as simple as possible.* It has often been said that "tax administration is tax policy."

10. *There is much that we do not now—and cannot ever—know: the unknown and unknowable aspects of tax reform should keep us humble in any of our recommendations.*

I remain hopeful that all of these lessons—the known, the unknown, and the unknowable—might someday be applied in the United States.

Discussion

George K. Yin

It is a pleasure to contribute to this volume, which reminds me of why I decided to return to academe when I left the Joint Committee but also of what I miss most from my time at the Joint Committee—the opportunity to learn from very smart people grappling with difficult problems in a very sophisticated way.

In his analysis Dan Shaviro feeds various consumption tax reform proposals into the political meat grinder known as our legislative process, speculating about the effect likely political compromises will have on the end product of tax reform. He explains how the Bradford X-tax and a consumption tax proposal known as "five easy pieces" might be passed by the Congress, and forecasts the various changes to those proposals that might have to take place to accommodate political and other considerations in the course of passing those bills. His analysis adds an important new layer to some existing good work describing the difficult structural and administrative issues that certain consumption tax reform proposals will have to confront (McLure 1988; Weisbach 2000; Weisbach 2003; Shaviro 2004; Bankman and Schler 2005).

Dan is a very smart analyst, not just of law and economics but also of politics and the legislative process (Shaviro 1990), and I have very little to add to his many sharp and cogent observations and predictions. They are, as one would expect, not very encouraging. The prospect of political mutation (and possible mutilation) of any tax reform plan is surely a "known" upon which we can all agree. Like Dan, however, I don't think either one of his two main scenarios is that realistic from a political standpoint. Thus, rather than trying to second-guess some of his thoughts, I thought I would depress you in a different way by reviewing a broader set of policy options dictated by the current political situation. My comments are directed toward the opening theme of this volume, "Is It Time for Fundamental Tax Reform?" and clearly fall in the realm of the "unknown" category, if not also the "unknowable."[9]

When I put my political lens on, I simply cannot get the 800-pound gorilla out of my sight. I am referring, of course, to the budgetary situation mentioned by both Larry Kotlikoff and James Baker yesterday. Based on its baseline assumptions, the CBO estimates that growth over just the next ten years in Social Security, Medicare, and Medicaid will cost another 2 percent of GDP to about 11 percent of GDP total by 2016, with costs continuing to grow for many years beyond that point (CBO 2006, tab. 3-1). To put this amount in perspective, the entire defense budget and the entire discretionary nondefense budget are each estimated to be only about 3 percent of GDP by 2016. Thus, based on current trends, it is not difficult to envision a federal budget that will soon have to be devoted entirely to financing entitlement programs.

Unfortunately, we now have a similar problem on the tax front if one considers the expiring tax cuts as promises or liabilities incurred by the current Congress to be paid for in the future. The Joint Committee on Taxation and the CBO estimate that extension of all expiring tax cut items, including the reduced tax rates for dividends and capital gains, the higher AMT exemption amount known as the "AMT patch," and all of the other EGTRRA and JGTRRA tax cut provisions such as the reduced income tax rates, increased child credit, marriage penalty relief, and repeal of the estate and gift tax will cost about $3.3 trillion over the next ten years, inclusive of the additional debt service costs that would have to be incurred (CBO 2006, tab. 1-4). The cost of extending these cuts in 2016 alone will be about $600 billion, roughly 3 percent of the projected GDP.

Dan mentions in his chapter that a week is a long time in politics. Our current budget reality demonstrates how five years is an eternity. Five years ago many people had thoughts about tax reform, Social Security reform, health-care reform, tax simplification, and even paying off the national debt. Not any longer. It seems to me that if any of these reforms can even be attempted now, the nature of the reform will surely be colored by our new budget reality. Indeed, for the foreseeable future—which, by definition, is as far as this observer can see—the nation's entire domestic agenda will be dominated by concerns about the deficit and the long-term fiscal gap. Like others, I think of the upcoming period as a time of fiscal calamity (Auerbach, Gale, and Orszag 2006).

Some have suggested that the current situation is not that dissimilar to that of the mid-1980s. During that time of large budget deficits, President Reagan successfully diverted attention from the enactment of possible spending cuts and tax increases by pushing through a revenue-neutral tax reform proposal instead. But the analogy to the mid-1980s seems inapt to me. For one thing, we are now twenty years closer to the liabilities associated with the baby boomers' retirement, with that situation having been made worse by recent legislation. In addition, as noted, we now face similar challenges on the tax side. Thus I am not at all sure we can seriously think about a "revenue-neutral" tax reform any longer.

So let us assume that after taking whatever steps it can on the spending side, including entitlements, and using far too many budget and scoring gimmicks, Congress still finds itself in a budget pickle, as surely it will. What can we expect Congress to do on the tax side and with tax reform?

For one thing, Congress is not going to look at the consumption tax proposal known as "five easy pieces." Dan imagines the possibility of that proposal arising from a stealth effort supported only by Republicans, analogous to Republican-led tax efforts between 2001 and 2004. But tax *reform* is different from tax *cut* legislation; perhaps the single most defining characteristic of real tax reform is that it rubs many special interests the wrong way. The failure of Social Security reform in 2005 demonstrates the inability of one party to accomplish this on its own. More important, as Dan's analysis shows, "five easy pieces" doesn't work—it does not provide a blueprint of a coherent, alternative tax system. There are far too many loopholes. It would never be considered by a budget-conscious Congress.

Let us leave on the table for now Dan's other option—a Bradford X-tax—and add a few more. One would be enactment of a value-added tax, not, as some have suggested, as a replacement for part of the income or payroll tax but rather as a supplement to both. Another option would be the current income tax system but with higher rates. A third possibility would be leaving the minimum tax unindexed and letting it gradually subsume the regular income tax. And a final option would be a broadening of the current income tax base in an effort to minimize the amount tax rates would have to be raised. Let us speculate a little about which of these options is likely to be favored by liberal elites, conservative elites, and everyone else.

For liberal elites, I would think the supplemental VAT, the minimum tax, and the X-tax would all be rejected out of hand. Of the remaining choices, I would *hope* that liberal elites would prefer a broadening of the income tax base to higher income tax rates. Senator Wyden's bill (S. 1927), which is supported by Congressman Emanuel (Stamper 2005) and which seems to be about the only liberal version of tax reform in existence right now, modestly expands the income tax base while capping tax rates at 35 percent. It is not clear what further changes would be made to that bill if it had to be revenue neutral or revenue positive in our new budget-conscious world.

Conservative elites would probably immediately reject the supplemental VAT, the minimum tax, and the option of the current income tax system with higher rates. One might naturally think they would prefer the X-tax to the current income tax system with a more comprehensive base, but maybe not. A key question, it seems to me, is what the X-tax would end up looking like, including what type of rate structure it would have, in a revenue-starved world.

The Tax Reform Panel presented a revenue-neutral modified X-tax option with a top rate of 30 percent (President's Advisory Panel 2005). But there are several problems with that estimate. First, it assumes a tax base which, in Dan's judgment and in mine, is probably much more comprehensive than we are likely to see enacted. For example, the amount of base broadening assumed by the Panel is considerably greater than that accomplished by the Tax Reform Act of 1986, what many consider to be the high-water mark for tax reform efforts. Second, the Panel proposal includes an explicit 15 percent tax on household capital income. Although this provision is not consistent with the theoretical basis of the X-tax and would complicate it, it does help to lower the required business and household tax rates for the Panel's proposal and also offsets some of the pressure to make the proposed rate structure more progressive. Thus, if the 15 percent capital income tax were cut out of the Panel's proposal to make the option more coherent, the remaining tax system would have to have higher and more progressive rates than was projected by the Panel. Third, the Panel proposal is revenue neutral only relative to President Bush's world of permanent tax cuts, other new savings incentives, and termination of the AMT patch (President's Advisory Panel 2005; Burman and Gale 2005; Lazear and Poterba 2005). Relative to the real world where reform must produce some revenue above and beyond that provided by current law, the rates clearly would have to be higher still.

It might be helpful to compare tax rates under an X-tax and an income tax, assuming an equally comprehensive taxation of consumption under each. Because the X-tax would defer the taxation of income until the time of consumption, the resulting loss of tax revenue in the budget window would seem to force the X-tax to have higher rates. This effect would be offset to the extent old capital is taxed again under the X-tax but not under an income tax. My guess is that for both empirical and political reasons, the offset would not be large enough to cancel out the deferral effect. Thus the X-tax would have to have higher, perhaps significantly higher, rates than the income tax. For the same reasons concerns about distributional fairness would cause the X-tax to have a more steeply progressive rate structure than the income tax. The analysis of these issues might change if Congress were to focus on the long-term fiscal gap rather than the deficit, and consider a lifetime perspective rather than an annual or ten-year one, but I am skeptical that Congress will do that, setting aside the feasibility of doing so.

So the basic choice for conservative elites may be an income tax versus an X-tax with perhaps significantly higher and more progressive rates than the income tax. Add to this comparison the further likelihood—if only for reasons of perception (Ackerman and Altshuler 2006, p. 179)—that the X-tax will not be pure but will probably include some continued explicit taxation of capital income, and I would think the choice becomes fairly close. Finally, Dan points out that even a pure X-tax without any explicit taxation of capital would still distort the savings decision if tax rates increase in the future, as seems likely in our budget-conscious world.

What would be the preference of everyone else? We might hope that if the liberal and conservative elites could reach consensus, they would lead everyone else to the optimal choice. In my view, this is to some extent what happened in 1986, when most of the public was disinterested in, or openly hostile to, any major change in the tax law (Conlan, Wrightson, and Beam 1990, p. 242). Barring a repeat of that "Pollyannaish" scenario, the American people might opt for the current income tax system with higher tax rates. After all, asking them to accept (or maybe more to the point, asking our leaders to convince them of the necessity of) important changes to the tax base, which necessarily will create winners and losers *in addition to* an overall tax increase, may be simply too much to expect.

Finally, what is the most likely outcome? If, as seems likely, all of these choices are considered in an extremely contentious environment where the possibility of political stalemate is very high, the most likely outcome may be the minimum tax scenario because it would be the default. To me, this would be the most unfortunate outcome of all because of (1) the minimum tax's lack of indexing, which will mean we would return to the bad old days of automatic stealth tax increases that would be used in part to finance new pet projects created by the Congress; (2) the tax's distortive and unfair distinctions between married and single people, large and small families, and people in high-tax and low-tax states;[10] (3) its disproportionately adverse effect on the middle class; (4) its failure to reduce marginal tax rates to any significant extent when consideration is given to taxpayers whose exemption amount is phased out;[11] (5) its high compliance costs in forcing an increasing number of taxpayers to perform dual tax calculations for some number of years; and finally (6) the complete absence of any meaningful reform to simplify the law and make it more efficient and pro-growth.

The minimum tax has the reputation of a system with a broad base and low and flat tax rates, and some commentators argue that stumbling into the minimum tax wouldn't be all that bad; rather, it would reasonably resemble a desirable tax reform (Nelson 2006; Rauch 2006). I am afraid that those commentators need to take a closer look at the details of the minimum tax. As just noted, its rates are not particularly low or flat when the phaseout of the exemption amount is taken into account. In addition its base is neither broad nor sensible. By far the principal reasons taxpayers are affected by the minimum tax are its failure to permit a deduction for state and local taxes and personal exemptions, and its failure to index the exemption amount. Among other so-called base-broadeners, of which there are just a few, the only items of any significance are the required inclusion of tax-exempt interest income on certain private activity bonds and the disallowance of deductions for a portion of accelerated depreciation, miscellaneous itemized expenses, and interest on home equity loans. In addition nonrefundable personal credits like the educational credits are not permitted to reduce the amount of the minimum tax, although Congress has continually negated the application of this rule since 1998.[12]

Thus huge amounts of preferential income are unaffected by the minimum tax, including income exclusions for health insurance, other fringe benefits, inside buildup, interest on public-purpose bonds, untaxed Social Security and railroad retirement benefits, and retirement and other savings contributions; deductions for mortgage interest, charitable contributions (e.g., contributions of untaxed property appreciation), and most percentage depletion and intangible drilling costs; as well as the preferential rates for dividends and capital gains income and a host of smaller items (Joint Committee on Taxation 2005b, Joint Committee on Taxation 2006).[13] In short, allowing the minimum tax, at least as we know it today, gradually to subsume the income tax, a plan actually considered and rejected in the early plans leading up to the 1986 Tax Reform Act (McLure and Zodrow 1987, p. 39), would not be a viable way to achieve any sort of tax reform.[14]

My take-away from this possible, horrendous outcome is twofold. First, it highlights for me the critical importance of reformers of all stripes cooperating and reaching consensus regarding the proper direction for reform. Second, if reformers are unable to agree and something like the scenario I have described comes about, we might finally then have a tax system so outrageous as to trigger meaningful reform. But that reform would only occur in the long term, which I am afraid is small solace for most everyone concerned about tax reform today.

Notes

I am grateful for helpful comments offered by James Alm, Alan Auerbach, Joseph Bankman, Itai Grinberg, Edward Kleinbard, Michael Schler, David Weisbach, George Yin, the conference participants, and participants at a Tax Policy and Public Finance Workshop at UCLA Law School.

1. To illustrate, suppose the interest rate was 10 percent and that all taxpayers faced a 30 percent marginal rate. Municipal bonds would presumably pay 7 percent interest, giving them the same after-tax return as taxable bonds. The after-tax interest cost of issuing taxable bonds would also be 7 percent. If the tax rules were changed so that the interest on previously taxable bonds was neither includable nor deductible, their pre-tax rate presumably would change to 7 percent, but this would have no direct effect either on the supply side or on the demand side.

2. The General Agreement on Tariffs and Trade (GATT) distinguishes direct from indirect taxes (with "export subsidies" allowed only on the latter), on the view that the latter are "imposed on the product as opposed to the maker" (Westin 1997, p. 264n. 52).

3. For another example, when companies are going through bankruptcy proceedings, they may take great care to ensure that their favorable tax attributes will be affected as little as possible by reason of the noninclusion of their cancellation of indebtedness income. (Note that Section 108 cites exclusion in exchange for tax attribute reduction.)

4. The original Treasury corporate integration proposal in 2003 would have retained the capital gains on sales of corporate stock, but this reflected its concern about income that was untaxed at the corporate level. It offered increases in the basis of corporate stock to reflect inclusion in the shareholder's taxable income of undistributed dividends.

5. See Internal Revenue Code, Section 514.

6. The usual political rationale for the UBIT is that it protects taxable organizations against unfair competition. Under a consumption tax, the rationale might be that taxable organizations are unduly disfavored if consumer goods sold by their tax-exempt competitors are not taxable to consumers.

7. See, for example, Bradford 1996c (suggesting segregation of accounts from years to which different tax rates had applied, but noting that this approach might not be workable given the difficulty of "policing the segregation of different vintages").

8. The latter concern could be addressed by providing a percentage credit, rather than a deduction, for medical expenditures. The credit could also be made refundable so that its benefit would not be limited to the amount of one's positive tax liability.

9. Whether something is "unknowable" is a metaphysical question about which not enough is known. Thus "unknown" seems like the safest category in which to place my remarks.

10. Repeal of the state and local tax deduction may make sense in the context of a broad reform of the tax system but it seems like a fairly arbitrary feature of the existing AMT.

11. The $45,000 exemption amount for joint-filers ($58,000 in 2005 due to the "AMT patch") is gradually phased out for joint-filers with alternative minimum taxable income in excess of $150,000. The phase-out creates four different tax brackets of 26, 32.5, 35, and 28 percent. See Ackerman and Altshuler (2006, p. 170). The Tax Increase Prevention and Reconciliation Act of 2005, P.L. 109–222, which was signed into law in May 2006, increased the 2006 AMT exemption amount for joint-filers to $62,550 and thereby increased the range of alternative minimum taxable income that is subject to the 35 percent bracket.

12. P.L. 109–222 continues this treatment and permits nonrefundable personal credits to be used against the minimum tax in 2006.

13. Taxpayers who are in the AMT exemption amount phase-out range might have dividend or capital gain income taxed at higher than the regular maximum rate of 15 percent (Johnston 2006b), but there is no special denial of the preferential rate for such income in the AMT. See IRC, Section 55(b)(3).

14. One or more of the many undesirable features of the minimum tax might be changed, but then this option would soon become indistinguishable from the choice of a more comprehensive income tax base. Most people would presumably prefer the latter to the minimum tax scenario, but the minimum tax result may occur if Congress finds itself completely deadlocked in its tax and budget deliberations. Other criticisms of the minimum tax can be found in Burman and Weiner (2004) and Viard (2006).

II Business Issues

3

Is Tax Reform Good for Business? Is a Pro-business Tax Policy Good for America?

Joel Slemrod

3.1 What Does the Title Question Mean?

The questions posed in the title of this chapter are rife with ambiguity. The key concepts—what "tax reform" is, what "business" is, and what might be "good" for them—need some clarification. In this chapter I will interpret tax reform broadly. I will address both the kind of rate-reducing, base-broadening reform passed in 1986 and the more radical reforms of the tax system based on a consumption tax model, such as the flat tax, value-added tax, and retail sales tax. I will also discuss the implications of simplifying the tax process.

For the most part, I will interpret what is good for business to mean what is in the interest of the owners, or shareholders. This will depend on, inter alia, the profitability, and presumably the after-tax profitability, of ongoing businesses; I will often presume that this is reflected by the share price. Frequently I will have in mind what might be called "big" business, although I will say something about the differential impact on big versus not-so-big companies, and corporate versus noncorporate businesses.

"What's Good for America" in the title refers to the prosperity of Americans, where prosperity depends, other things equal, on GDP per capita, but also on the distribution of GDP per capita among the population, and may encompass things that Americans value but are not reflected in GDP, such as environmental quality, national security, and leisure time.

In 1953 Charles E. Wilson, president of General Motors, was nominated to be President Eisenhower's Secretary of Defense. During his confirmation hearing he was asked if in that position he would be able to make a decision adverse to the interests of General Motors. His answer suggested that no such conflict was likely to arise because, he said, "for years I [have] thought what was good for the country was good for General Motors and vice versa."

Taken at face value, Mr. Wilson was clearly wrong. Being good for General Motors, big business, or business owners is not the exclusive criterion by which tax reform or economic policy in general, should be evaluated. It is, though, a critical *instrument* for delivering prosperity. Loosely speaking, when businesses are profitable and rewarding their shareholders, they are also more likely to want to expand by investing and hiring more workers, which expands job opportunities, increases productivity, and puts upward pressure on real wages.

Sometimes the link between business prosperity and Americans' prosperity has an extra step. Higher business profitability raises stock prices, and a higher stock price makes equity-financed investment more attractive. But this link sometimes breaks down, as in the case of investment incentives that apply only to new investment. Even if these incentives make new investment more attractive, they can cause stock prices to decline because the stock price reflects not only the valuation of future investments but also the valuation of capital in place. Investment incentives imply that new capital can be obtained "at a discount," so the market value of "old" capital declines.

An extreme example exposes the disconnection between what is good for business and what is good for the country. A lump-sum transfer from government to businesses would raise their current profitability—and stock price—but would not be good public policy for at least two reasons. First of all, in a balanced-budget context, financing such a transfer would require raising distortionary taxes. Second, the transfer would raise distributional issues, given that business owners and shareholders are relatively affluent, and probably more affluent than the marginal taxpayers.[1]

A large literature addresses the effect of tax reform on the economy. In this chapter, I do not. In doing so, one would have to distinguish between the short term and the long term, and note that income gains can overstate welfare gains if part of the increased income comes at the expense of less leisure. One would have to be careful about whether the tax reform was revenue neutral and, if not, address whether deficits, and any accompanying increase in interest rates or inflation, are bad for the economy.

What I do address in this chapter is whether tax reform is likely to be good for business, and how the answer to that question relates to whether tax reform is good for the country's prosperity. It begins with what is, for economists, an unlikely place: inquiring about the policy positions of a sample of prominent business associations. Although public policy pronouncements are generally not couched as representing pure self-interest—indeed they generally emphasize the economy-wide benefits of their positions—one would have to be extraordinarily naïve not to think that perceived self-interest dominates the policy stances taken by business interests.

3.2   What Are Business Views about Tax Reform?

Business associations' public positions on tax reform are known. To the extent that these positions reflect the carefully considered self-interest of the member companies, these positions might provide some clues about what tax reforms are good for business.[2] In what follows, I review the stated positions of three sectors—big business, small business, and special interest groups—that might be particularly affected by tax reform as I have defined it.

3.2.1   Big Business

The National Association of Manufacturers (NAM), the country's largest industrial trade association that represents small and large manufacturers in every industrial sector, supports efforts to make the tax code fairer and simpler.[3] At a slightly less general level, it supports tax changes that

• Encourage savings and investment while minimizing the double taxation of corporate earnings,

• Include rules that permit US-based manufacturers to compete on a level playing field in the global marketplace,

• Recognize the important role of research and technology investment in US job growth and innovation,

• Strive to raise the required amount of revenue for the government without distorting a business's decision to invest capital and hire new workers,

• Include broad and strong transition rules that provide fair and equitable treatment for taxpayers who have committed substantial resources based on current law,

• Incorporate rules that make it easier for Treasury to administer the law and for taxpayers to comply with the law.

The NAM also supports two more specific tax reform initiatives: eliminating both the individual and corporate alternative minimum taxes, and ensuring that any proposed tax reform features no net increase in business taxes. Their guidelines imply, but do not explicitly support, other tax provisions such as a credit for research and development.

Several aspects of these tax reform guidelines are of interest. First of all, note the use of buzzwords such as "level playing field" and "fair and equitable treatment." More troubling is the line drawn with regard to "business taxes." As I will discuss later, this is a loosely defined term. I also note that the NAM supports lowering corporate taxes, but with regard to "business taxes," their objective is weaker—that they not be raised; I am, though, not exactly sure what noncorporate business taxes they have in mind when making this distinction. Being in favor of not "distorting a business's decision to invest capital" could be taken as support for a consumption tax, and extending this to not distorting business decisions to "hire new workers" might make sense for a limited set of taxes, but as a statement about all taxes it is patently unrealistic, as any tax triggered by labor income will distort the supply and demand for labor.

The Tax Executives Institute (TEI), the "preeminent" professional organization of business executives who are responsible for tax matters, advocates four principles that should guide the tax reform process:[4]

• Simplicity and administrability of the system.

• A US tax system that promotes rather than hinders the competitiveness of US businesses, defined as maintaining a low rate of corporate taxation and promoting incremental US business investment.

• A proper balance in the tax burden among sectors of the economy, and especially between the individual and business components.

• Keeping the ripple effect of tax reform on the states in the forefront of considerations.

I note the prominent allusion to perhaps the most ubiquitous tax policy buzzword of all, "competitiveness." This term does not have a clear meaning to economists, but TEI avoids any vagueness in its tax reform guidelines by defining it as a low rate of corporate taxation. TEI is also concerned that the tax system not stray from a proper balance between the individual and business components of tax, where, as with the NAM, exactly what is and is not a business tax is not spelled out.

The Fiscal Policy Task Force of the Business Roundtable, an association of chief executive officers of leading US corporations, advocates the following goals for tax reform:[5]

• Simplify the tax code for both individuals and corporations and thereby reduce compliance costs.

• Lower corporate income taxes.

• Reduce the cost of capital.

• Make all legitimate business expenses deductible.

• Eliminate aspects of the tax system that inhibit the competitiveness of US business operating abroad and hinder US-based companies to the advantage of their foreign counterparts.

• Do not raise net taxes on corporations, and have appropriate transition rules that do not produce "severe dislocations."

All three of these organizations emphasize the importance of not raising, and indeed reducing taxes, alternatively labeled as business taxes or corporate income taxes.

3.2.2   Small and Medium-Sized Business

The US Chamber of Commerce, which describes itself as the world's largest business federation representing more than 3 million businesses of all sizes, sectors, and regions, favors no particular alternative tax system proposal, although it supports moving toward a "simpler, fairer, and less burdensome" tax system. It does, though, endorse "end[ing] the current tax system's bias against saving and investment and reduc[ing] the system's administrative burdens and enormous compliance costs."[6]

Another small business association, the National Federation of Independent Business (NFIB), the largest advocacy organization representing small and independent businesses, supports making permanent the tax cuts passed in 2001 and 2003, which, it argues, would be especially helpful to the approximately 85 percent of small businesses that file tax returns as individuals and would provide small business owners with capital to reinvest and grow their businesses while creating stronger incentives for small business job creation. On long-term tax reform issues, NFIB says only that it supports simplifying the tax code for small business and increasing the expensing limit for small businesses.[7]

The National Small Business Association, whose primary mission is to "advocate state and federal policies that are beneficial to small business, the state, and the nation—and promote the growth of free enterprise," endorses the FairTax proposal for a national retail sales tax as a replacement for the individual federal income tax, the capital gains tax, all payroll taxes, corporate income taxes, the self-employment tax, and the estate and gift taxes.[8] This is a much more specific, and much more radical, tax reform position than any of the other business organizations whose publicly advocated policies I have investigated.

The American Business Conference (ABC), a coalition of chief executives of fast-growing, midsize American companies decries the corporate income tax as too complex, a drag on investment and therefore on productivity and overall economic growth, and unfair because it is a hidden tax.[9] It advocates abolishing the corporate tax and replacing it, after an appropriate transition period, with a tax on business transactions. This new tax should be completely integrated with the individual tax, apply to all (not just corporate) business transactions and, because it would be based on cash flow, would allow businesses to deduct immediately, rather than amortize over time, all new capital investment.

This sample of tax policy positions adopted by associations of small and medium-sized business associations suggest that they are less satisfied with incremental changes in the tax system, and more willing to entertain more radical tax policy surgery. However, it is difficult to discern whether that is representative of the views of their members, or mostly reflects something about the competitive political dynamic of these associations.

3.2.3   Special Interests

Many tax reform plans would eliminate or cut back on provisions that arguably provide preferential treatment to particular sectors. Not surprisingly, the tax reform positions of associations that represent some of these sectors tend to be more defensive.

For example, the National Association of Home Builders (NAHB) urges maintenance of tax incentives for housing, suggesting that they indicate the importance that housing carries in the federal agenda of priorities. It also advocates the adoption of certain law changes as a means of continuing federal support for housing while removing impediments that raise the cost of homes and home building. In addition any significant changes to the whole tax system must continue to recognize the importance of housing to the economy and to individual households' financial stability.[10]

The National Retail Federation (NRF), while applauding the report of the President's Advisory Panel on Federal Tax Reform as going a long way toward accomplishing needed tax simplification, objects to the provision in the panel's "Growth and Investment Tax Plan" option that would take away US retailers' ability to deduct the cost of imported goods.[11] Their views on a retail sales tax as a replacement for the income tax may be indicated by the fact that a study conducted in 2000 for the NRF by PricewaterhouseCoopers found that a national sales tax would result in a three-year decline in the economy, a four-year decline in employment, and an eight-year decline in consumer spending. In a letter to the editor, the NRF said that "many companies would be out of business before the benefits, if any, of this dangerous experiment with our nation's economy would be seen."[12]

The Grocery Manufacturers of America supports the simplified rate structure established by the Tax Reform Act of 1986, and opposes efforts to restore tax preferences that distort economic activity and eventually result in higher corporate rates. It opposes any increase in the corporate rates.[13]

The American Farm Bureau[14] supports replacing the current federal income tax system with a new tax code that encourages savings, investment, and entrepreneurship. The replacement system must be fair to agricultural producers and should meet the following objectives:

- Be revenue neutral so as not to produce a tax increase.
- Eliminate payroll taxes and self-employment taxes.
- End death taxes and capital gains taxes.
- Eliminate personal and corporate income taxes and the alternative minimum tax.
- Change the Constitution to prevent the reinstitution of the income tax.
- Require a two-thirds majority vote in Congress to raise taxes.

The National Farmers' Union supports a more progressive tax structure and opposes a flat tax.[15] It also advocates several incremental
changes to the existing income tax, such as a limited refundable federal
income tax credit equal to all or a percentage of the state and local real
estate taxes paid on farmland utilized for commercial production, tax-
free conversion of farm assets in exchange for investments in all categories available to the general public and other business entities, and an
investment tax credit for new and used equipment.

The National Association for the Self-Employed supports the simplification of the tax process on small business, and provisions "favorable
to the self-employed and micro-businesses."[16] The latter includes a permanent increase of the deductible percentage for business equipment
expensing, and an increase in the business meals deduction to at least
80 percent.

3.2.4   Business Role in the Tax Changes of the 1980s

Looking at the business role during the last wave of tax reform debate,
between 1981 and 1986, that culminated in the Tax Reform Act of 1986,
also reveals something about how business perceives its interest with
regard to tax policy.[17] Tax reduction was a major plank in the platform
of Ronald Reagan during the 1980 election, and after the election the
details of the tax cut package were sharply contested. Large cuts in
personal tax rates, phased in over three years, were the most visible
component. On the business side, legislative attention was focused on
the so-called 10-5-3 provision, which provided much faster depreciation for all assets but no reduction in the corporate tax rate structure.
In general, manufacturing interests supported the accelerated depreciation provisions, while small business interests preferred cuts in
individual and corporate rates. Other sectors, such as the timber and
securities industries as well as venture capitalists and high-tech, concentrated on securing cuts in the capital gains tax rate.

After the passage of the Economic Recovery Tax Act of 1981 (ERTA),
which featured significant, phased-in cuts in individual income tax
rates and accelerated deprecation for capital investment purchases,
concerns over projected deficits and recession led to the consideration
of retracting some of the ERTA provisions. This debate sharply divided
the business community, although eventually the National Association
of Manufacturers, the Business Roundtable, and the American Busi-

ness Conference said they would be willing to support some type of tax increase.

The legislative and political history leading up to the Tax Reform Act of 1986 (TRA86) has been widely chronicled, most vividly in Birnbaum and Murray (1987), so a detailed retelling is unnecessary. Although during the process many different tax plans were proposed and considered, most followed a "broaden the base, lower the rates" philosophy. As it applied to business taxation, this meant eliminating the investment tax credit, moving depreciation schedules back toward where they were pre-TRA86, and cutting back on some tax features that benefited only some sectors, while at the same time substantially cutting the corporate tax rate.

Business views toward the legislation that was to become TRA86 were split, largely on the fault line of the relative value (to the company's corporate tax liability) of reducing the corporate tax rate versus the cost of abandoning accelerated depreciation and the investment tax credit. Not surprisingly, capital-intensive industries, often in heavy manufacturing, tended to conclude that this trade-off did not benefit them.[18] High-tech and service industries tended to see this trade-off as favorable, although firms in the former industry coveted the R&D credit and the capital gains differential. The primary business sectors that opposed TRA86 were basic manufacturing and real estate. Other sectors opposed certain aspects of the bill; for example, many multinational companies opposed the bill's treatment of foreign-sector income, and the oil industry objected to the passive loss provisions. Real estate interests were opposed to the limitations on deductions for second homes and the passive loss rules, arguing that passive loss rules were necessary to build partnerships and keep rents low in low-income housing. Representatives of many small businesses, such as the National Association of Wholesaler-Distributors and the National Federation of Independent Business, were largely concerned with (and opposed to) any proposal to eliminate the initial lower rates in the graduated corporate rate schedule.

Soon after the May 1985 administration report, dubbed Treasury II, was announced, a group of companies formed the Tax Reform Action Coalition (TRAC), which eventually had 700 members. Its main objective was lower rates; although it did not formally oppose attempts to maintain special interest provisions, it discouraged its members from seeking them.[19]

Note that business provided some core support for the mid-1980s tax reform push even though the legislation that eventually emerged, the Tax Reform Act of 1986, achieved revenue neutrality by increasing corporate taxes and reducing individual income taxes. The reduction in individual income taxes was used as a selling point in a somewhat disingenuous manner, as descriptions of a "tax cut" for all typical families generally failed to account for the fact that the increased corporate taxes would, to a first approximation, reduce individuals' after-tax income just as surely as would an increase in personal income taxes, through a decline in pretax wages or returns to capital.

3.2.5   Reaction to the 2005 Tax Panel Report

In 2005, nearly two decades after TRA86 passed, the federal government had a brief flirtation with major tax reform. In January of that year, President Bush constituted the President's Advisory Panel on Federal Tax Reform, which in November issued a report entitled *Simple, Fair, and Pro-Growth: Proposals to Fix America's Tax System.* The report reviewed the case for a major overhaul of the federal income tax system, evaluated and reviewed several options, and presented in some detail two proposals: one a modified income tax and the other a consumption tax (the X-tax advocated by David Bradford 2005), supplemented (some would say diluted) by a tax on all capital income received by individuals at a flat 15 percent rate. Both proposals contained significant base-broadening aspects, most notably provisions to cut back on the value of the mortgage interest deduction, eliminate the deduction for state and local taxes paid and cap the exclusion for employer-provided health insurance.

The tax reform panel's report was not greeted with a political groundswell of support, to put it mildly. "Tax-Overhaul Blueprints Elicit Tepid Responses" is how the *Wall Street Journal* headlined its story on the report's release the next day. Key congressional Republicans received it noncommittally, with Senate Finance Chairman Charles Grassley of Iowa saying that certain ideas were "bound to be politically unpopular," and ranking Senate Finance Democrat Max Baucus lamenting that it "will not satisfy our hunger for reform and simplification." President Bush did not mention tax reform in his State of the Union address delivered in February 2006, and the issues it raised played no role in the 2006 congressional elections, nor so far in the policy discussions among the presidential candidates for the 2008 election.

Because it was immediately clear that the Panel's proposals had no political momentum, there was little public reaction from the business community despite the fact that the two proposals contained significant changes in how businesses were taxed; indeed, some of the most innovative proposals concerned business taxation. One such proposal would establish three categories of business, based on average annual cash receipts over the previous three years.[20] The Panel's modified income tax proposal would require all entities in the biggest size category (those with greater than $10 million of receipts) to be taxed at the entity level like corporations, regardless of whether or not they are legally corporations. Business entities with less than $10 million of receipts could elect to be taxed as corporations.

Furthermore small businesses (defined as those with less than $1 million in receipts) would benefit from a tax accounting system that is similar to their regular bookkeeping regimes. It would require small and medium-sized businesses to maintain designated bank accounts that apply only to business transactions, and require credit card issuers to report business transactions to the designated financial institution and to the IRS. Although clearly designed to improve compliance, this procedure would have implications for compliance costs. Medium-sized businesses would no longer have to keep track of basis and depreciation asset by asset but would instead use a set recovery percentage to the overall account balance for a given category of asset, promising compliance cost saving due to reduced record-keeping requirements.

3.3   Are They Right?

This brief review of the expressed positions of business representatives suggests that they evaluate tax changes, first and possibly foremost, by estimating whether their own companies' tax payments will go up or down, holding before-tax profits constant. Companies generally do not give first-order consideration to the extent to which tax reform will cause changes in, for example, the market prices of the products they sell or in the prices of the inputs they use, including the cost of labor. In other words, they ignore what economists would call general equilibrium impacts of tax changes, and do not think much about the ultimate incidence of tax changes on prices and profits.

This characterization is a plausible description of business views with regard to incremental changes to the current system, including the corporation income tax, but it is less plausible as an explanation for business views about wholesale tax changes, such as replacing all income taxes with a national retail sales tax. If it were, all businesses not in the retail sector would favor it as a replacement for corporation income tax, and all retail businesses would oppose it. (The latter is probably nearly true, but the former is definitely not.)

This discussion highlights a fascinating disconnect between how economists view the incidence of business taxes, and taxes in general, and how business interests, and most everyone other than economists, view these issues.

3.3.1   The Theory of Tax Incidence

There is a large and venerable literature in economics that attempts to assess who bears the burden of a given tax system. The correct answer depends on the economic model one uses to characterize the real economy. Although empirical analysis can, with varying degrees of confidence, rule out some modeling aspects and give credence to others, the true model and therefore the right answers are unknown. Although there is no clear consensus about the answers, there is a widely shared set of methodological assumptions in this literature.

The first is that the burden of taxes must be traced back to individuals. No student taking undergraduate public finance can get away with a statement like "the burden of tax X (or the X-tax!) falls on Exxon-Mobil." Perhaps some burden might fall on its shareholders, or on its workers, or on the purchasers of its products, but it is not meaningful, economists agree, to assign the burden to a company, even if it is a legal entity.

The second widely shared result is that the ultimate incidence of taxes depends entirely on what actions or states of the world trigger tax liability, and generally depends not at all on which related party—or what business entity—remits (writes the checks) the tax to the tax authority, or on who or what legal entity bears the legal liability for a tax. As I elaborate on below, this calls into question the very meaning of a "business tax."

Third, with a very few exceptions, economists' tax incidence models presume that all sectors are perfectly competitive with free entry; that is, they rule out both monopolies and oligopolistic market structures.

This assumption precludes the possibility that any business will persistently earn pure profits, where "pure" refers to profits over and above the return the capital and managerial resources could earn elsewhere; pure profits would attract entry, which would erode the profits until they disappeared. If the model builds in costs of adjusting to a new equilibrium when there are changes in the environment—including tax system changes—then (positive and negative) profits may be earned in the short run, but eventually the economy will return to a situation where no pure profits exist.

One of the most controversial questions in the theory of tax incidence is the incidence of the corporation income tax. Because many tax reform proposals move toward eliminating any distinction between corporate and noncorporate-source business income, the insights of this literature are particularly relevant to the topic at hand.

The modern literature begins with Harberger (1962), who pointed out that the corporation income tax applies only to some (i.e., corporate-source) income from some (i.e., equity) capital, and does not apply at all to activities outside the corporate sector, such as owner-occupied housing. Because, in the long run, capital is mobile across sectors (implying that the after-tax return must be the same everywhere), whatever burden is borne by capital owners will ultimately not depend on what sector their capital was originally invested in. Because the corporate and noncorporate sectors use capital and labor in different proportions, though, any tax-induced switch between corporate and noncorporate activity can have implications for the return to capital and labor. Harberger's calculations suggested that the burden of the corporation income tax would end up being borne almost entirely by owners of capital in the form of a lower after-tax return; therefore eliminating it would benefit those who own capital via a higher after-tax rate of return, while the wage rate would not be much affected.

Subsequent research, nicely summarized in Auerbach (2005), has clarified and differentiated how the system of taxing corporations affects corporate profitability, share prices, and the incentive to invest. First of all, the reallocation of real capital goods in response to changes in the tax structure takes time, so the after-tax return to real capital in the corporate sector does not immediately readjust to be equal to the after-tax return to capital used in other sectors. For example, if the corporate tax were to be reduced, there would be a period of time during which the after-tax return to corporate capital would exceed the after-tax return available elsewhere. The prospect of this positive differential—that gradually gets competed away as real capital moves toward the corporate sector and drives down its pretax rate of return and drives up the pretax rate for return of noncorporate investments—causes the market value of corporate shares to rise. Thus, even though in the long run corporate investments earn no higher (risk-adjusted) after-tax return than other investments, it is sensible for corporate interests to favor a reduction in corporate tax rates.

Another insight from the modern literature is that the distinction between a business as the owner of a set of assets and as an ongoing operation is critical for understanding the effect of taxation on, and the interest of business in, tax reform. This is because many tax reforms have differential effects on the value of existing capital assets and the value of newly purchased capital assets. As an example consider the impact of moving toward a tax system with more accelerated depreciation (in the extreme, toward immediate expensing) for newly purchased assets. That change will tend to increase the after-tax profitability of newly purchased assets, and therefore make investment more attractive. However, it will also make existing assets (that must, in the absence of transition rules, still be depreciated under the preexisting law) less valuable in comparison to comparable assets purchased once the new accelerated depreciation rules are in place. Whether any company's share price will rise or fall in the wake of this tax change depends on the relative importance of existing—sometimes called "old"—capital and the prospects of profitable future investment— "new" capital, as well as a wide variety of other factors.

For this reason there may be a divergence between the kind of tax reform that is good for business and the kind that is good for the economy, defined as in the broad interest of the citizenry. In terms of its impact on the economy, only the value of new capital matters, as a higher value makes new investments more attractive.[21] The shareholders' interests depend on both the effect on new capital and the effect on the old capital they own, and so this is a case where the interest of the business shareholders and the stewards of the economy are not identical.[22] The distinction between the share price impacts and the effect on the incentive to invest is especially important when the type of tax change being considered involves changes in depreciation schedules, or when unchanging depreciation schedules do not track actual economic depreciation of the capital goods. In either case, tax changes will affect old and new capital differentially.

Of course, the impact on old capital depends critically on the transition rules that apply to the existing capital. If rules were adopted so that, looking forward, old capital would not be disadvantaged relative to new capital, no capital losses would ensue. This, though, would be a large drain on the revenues collected, and would require higher tax rates to keep a reform revenue neutral. It would also eliminate a significant source of the purported efficiency gains from certain tax reforms—the lump-sum tax on the old capital. The interest of the economy looking forward and the owners of existing capital are in direct opposition on this issue.

This distinction is not only academic. Auerbach (1989a) examined the TRA86 and concluded that it increased corporate taxes at the margin of new investment, which caused a small decline in the value of competing existing assets but at the same time provided substantial windfalls to existing capital through the corporate tax rate reduction and repeal of the investment tax credit. His theoretical analysis suggested that TRA86 increased share prices without substantially increasing the incentive to invest and expand. Cutler's (1988) analysis of share price changes during important events in the legislative lead-up to TRA86 provided some support of this analysis; after accounting for changes in future cash flows, companies with greater shares of equipment in their capital stock benefited from the tax change, while companies with greater pre-reform investment rates suffered share declines. However, Cutler finds little evidence of a large market response to tax news.

The divergence between share price and the incentive to invest may also arise in the context of taxes that are triggered by dividend payments as opposed to being triggered by earnings. Under the "new" view of dividend taxes, for mature firms that can finance new investment with retained earnings, reductions in the former are capitalized into higher share prices but do not cause any reduction in the cost of capital. Lower taxes on dividends may, though, reduce the incentive to invest for new firms that need to raise equity to finance their expansion.

There are other reasons for a divergence between shareholder interests and incentives to invest and expand. If there are pure rents—returns that exceed normal returns to providers of capital—to the extent that these can be isolated and taxed, the burden will be borne by shareholders without affecting incentives to invest and expand. Rents of this sort can arise from decreasing returns to scale or from a monopoly position. A tax on monopoly profits will adversely affect the market value of the monopoly business but will not affect their incentives to invest. This reasoning may also apply to pure profits that arise in oligopolistic market structures, but here the issue is a bit more complicated.

Up to now I have been equating "business interests" with the shareholders, and ignoring any conflict between passive shareholders and either the founding entrepreneurs of a company or its professional management. But we know that their interests may diverge, and taxation may expose the fault lines between their interests. Compensation contracts offered to managers are structured with an eye on aligning the incentives of managers and shareholders, but this is never done perfectly. For the most part traditional incidence analysis does not address this issue, assessing burden through the effect on the return to capital, labor, and the relative prices of goods and services purchased.

These issues are especially important in trying to evaluate the impact of switching to a consumption tax on business value and future profitability. Some analyses have reached very stark conclusions, notably Gravelle (1995), who argued that a switch to a Hall-Rabushka flat tax would cause a stock market decline of at least 20 percent, and as much as 30 percent. Bradford (1996b) and Hall (1996) also suggested that the decline in stock market wealth would be significant. As already discussed, this result occurs in some simple models because, although the tax change reduces the marginal effective tax rate and increases the expected short-term profitability of new investment, it also drives down the price of existing assets (not benefiting from the reduced marginal effective tax rate) that must compete with the tax-favored new assets.

Lyon and Merrill (2001) suggest that the simple models that produce this conclusion leave out several factors that would mitigate the decline in stock market values, such as the presence of expensed intangible assets whose value would not be bid down by competition from new, expensible assets, and whose value would be enhanced if the consumption tax reform featured a lower statutory rate. The earlier analyses also often do not take account of the asset price effects of eliminating personal level taxes on dividends and capital gains that, as discussed above, may also offset any asset price decline that would otherwise occur. Lyon and Merrill conclude that the market decline would not be nearly as great as the earlier analyses suggest.

One additional uncertainty about the impact of eliminating the special taxation of corporate-source income is the fact that the business landscape has changed substantially since the 1960s when Harberger wrote his groundbreaking article. For one thing, since 1958 any corporation that has less than a small number (100 now, 75 before 2005, and 35 before 1996) of shareholders can elect to be taxed as an "S corporation," meaning that there is no entity-level tax and the corporation is taxed essentially like a partnership. Furthermore, since the 1997 "check-the-box" regulations, any business other than a public corporation, whether or not it is legally a corporation, can choose to be subject or not to the corporation tax. What this means is that except for publicly held corporations that cannot escape the corporation tax, the corporation tax is an option rather than an unavoidable consequence of incorporation. Businesses are more likely to choose to be subject to the corporation tax if the low rates of the graduated rate structure make it attractive.

All in all, there is considerable uncertainty about the impact—on share prices, investment, and profitability—of tax reforms that eliminate the current special treatment of corporate-source income, either under an income tax or a consumption tax. This suggests that the wariness of business interests as well as policy makers toward fundamental tax reform is, to some degree, warranted.

3.3.2   Business as Tax Collector

The public positions of business associations reveal that they are often adamant about cutting—or, certainly, not increasing—"business taxes." Clarifying the precise meaning of a "business tax," and distinguishing among remitting taxes to the government, having a statutory liability to pay tax, and bearing the burden of a tax is especially important because of the central role businesses play in the tax remittance and collection process.[23] The impetus behind the central role of business in tax remittance was most elegantly stated by Richard Bird, who wrote: "The key to effective taxation is information, and the key to information in the modern economy is the corporation. The corporation is thus the modern fiscal state's equivalent of the customs barrier at the border."[24] Collecting taxes from businesses makes use of the economies of scale for the tax authority obtained from dealing with a smaller number of larger tax-remitting units, many of which for other purposes have already developed sophisticated systems of record-keeping and accounting.

One measure of the central role of business in the US tax system is provided by Christensen, Cline, and Neubig (2001), who calculate that in 1999 businesses "paid, collected, and remitted" to all levels of government $231 billion of corporation income taxes, $1,088 billion of personal income tax withheld on behalf of their employees, and $641 billion of Social Security payroll taxes, including both the employer part and the (withheld) employee portion, and $654 billion of other taxes, for a total of $2,613 billion. This amounts to 83.8 percent of total taxes in 1999. Of the 83.8 percent, Christensen, Cline, and Neubig (2001) label 31.3 percent as "tax liability of business," 8.1 percent as the "business as tax collector," and 44.4 percent as "business as withholding agent." According to tax incidence theory these distinctions are, at a minimum, irrelevant and border on being meaningless.

The fact that in the previous paragraph the quoted word "remitted" is rendered in italics is meant to emphasize that it means only that a check is written to the IRS. It definitely does not indicate anything about bearing the burden of a tax. Remitting tax is not the same as bearing the burden of a tax, both because the tax burden can be shifted through the adjustment of market prices and because, in the case of businesses, it is not meaningful to say that businesses bear the burden of taxes. Moreover standard public finance theory holds that who or what entity remits tax or is legally liable for a tax, in the long run, will have no impact on either who bears the burden or the efficiency cost of raising revenue; only what triggers tax liability matters. For example, abstracting from administration and compliance issues, whether the retailer remits retail sales tax to the government or the customer remits it, in the long run the price received by the retailer will be the same and the price paid by the consumer will be the same.

This reasoning is critical to correctly understanding the impact of fundamental tax reform because many of the tax alternatives differ much more significantly in who remits tax than in what triggers tax liability. Thus focus on remittance or statutory liability can be seriously misleading about the ultimate impact.

The notion that businesses "collect" tax is especially nebulous. The phrase is used in many contexts, but most commonly in the context of retail sales taxes. For example, Christensen, Cline, and Neubig (2001, p. 497) assert that, for sales tax on final goods, businesses are responsible for "collecting and remitting" the tax, although the statutory liability lies with the consumer: "If the business does not collect the tax, the business still is responsible for remitting the tax liability." They contrast businesses collecting tax with businesses withholding tax by saying: "Unlike the tax collection responsibility, if an insufficient amount is withheld, the employee is responsible for paying the difference."

To see the problem with this term, consider a retail establishment that sets the before-tax prices it charges, and adds a 6 percent state sales tax to this price to all customers. This particular retail establishment, however, never bothers to remit the 6 percent of sales to the state tax authority. In what sense has it collected taxes? It may well have charged its customers more than it could have in the absence of the tax, but that is because (presumably) most other retailers remit the tax and thus must charge higher prices to maintain their profit margins.[25] In the interest of clarifying debates about taxation, I suggest that just as the phrase "businesses bear tax burdens" is discouraged by economists, we banish the phrase "businesses collect taxes." Business "withholding" has a clear meaning—it refers to cases where to some degree the locus of remittance responsibility differs from the locus of statutory responsibility. But business tax "collection" does not.

Christensen, Cline, and Neubig (2001, p. 503) say that "no study that we are aware of has examined the relationship of above-the-line taxes to pre-tax corporate profitability to test whether hidden non-income taxes reduce measured profitability." Although the theoretical analysis of incidence has certainly addressed how a wide range of taxes affects the return to capital, it is true that very little empirical analysis has been devoted to measuring the impact of taxes not ordinarily thought of as "business taxes" on the return to capital.

Distinguishing among the burden of taxes, the statutory responsibility for taxes, and the remittance responsibility is especially critical when evaluating tax changes that radically alter the last two, even if they do not alter the first. This is characteristic of radical tax alternatives. For example, a national retail sales tax would shift all the remittance responsibility onto retail businesses. The opposition to a RST by the leading retail business association suggests that they believe that this will be bad for that sector. The opposition is perhaps not only because of the hugely increased remittance responsibility but also because of the big increase in compliance costs (discussed below) that is likely to accompany the bearing of remittance responsibility, and the probable increase in tax noncompliance that will hurt the competitive position of compliant retail businesses, which will tend to be the larger, more visible, businesses.

Under a value added tax, which is equivalent to a RST absent remittance and statutory burden issues, the remittance responsibility is spread among all business sectors. One exception is businesses that export, since under the standard destination-based VAT system exports are "zero-rated" (i.e., untaxed, with tax paid on purchased inputs used to produce the exported goods refundable). The notion that this system provides a boon to a country's export sector is widespread. This is another example of the failure of general equilibrium reasoning to be accepted by noneconomists; economists widely believe that such a system (along with nondeductible imports) levied at a uniform rate on all final goods and services consumed domestically would be neutral toward trade flows, with the apparent immediate advantage afforded to exports offset by adjustments in exchange rates.

Because either an RST or a VAT would constitute a self-evidently radical change in the tax system, business representatives may be less likely to view the changes in their statutory liability as an indicator of how well they would fare under the tax reforms. The change in statutory tax liability is more likely to be used as a gauge of this in a contemplated switch to a Hall-Rabushka-style flat tax that, although actually closely akin to a VAT, retains the look of the current income tax because it has both a business tax with deductions for wages and salaries and a personal tax component.[26] Compared to the current corporation income tax, the flat tax business tax base substitutes immediate expensing of capital goods for depreciation and amortization, and also eliminates the deductibility of interest payments. To a first approximation, a corporation's business tax liability is more likely to increase the less investment intensive it is and the more leveraged it is.

The large potential changes are well illustrated by the two examples given in the latest edition of Hall and Rabushka's book explaining and advocating the flat tax.[27] In the first example, General Motors' 1993 corporate income tax liability would increase from $110 million to $2.72 billion under the flat tax, even though the rate of tax falls from 35 to 19 percent. The main reason for the increase, Hall and Rabushka say, is that General Motors had a large amount of debt, enough debt that they paid out $5.7 billion in interest in 1993, none of which would be deductible under the flat tax. In the second example, Intel's tax bill in 1993 would have fallen sharply, from $1.2 billion to 277 million. The large drop is, according to the authors, partly due to the lower rate of tax but also to the fact that in 1993 Intel had no debt at all (so the loss of interest deductibility would have no effect on their tax liability), and that Intel in that year was investing heavily in new plant and equipment.

3.3.3   Complexity and Compliance Costs

Favoring a simpler tax system, with lower compliance costs, is a nearly ubiquitous component of businesses' public positions on tax reform. It is, in addition, an objective, at least a stated objective, of all tax reform proposals. At first glance this appears to be an issue on which business interests and overall well-being, or prosperity, coincide. Certainly the compliance and administrative costs that accompany a complex tax system are deadweight losses to the economy.

There are reasons to think that these objectives do not always coincide. Certain sectors of the economy (accountants, lawyers, etc.) undoubtedly prosper because of complexity. More broadly, in some circumstances businesses may be able to profit from manipulating the labyrinthine aspects of taxation. One hears that there are business objections to the electronic transmission of corporate tax returns, pre-sumably because this would facilitate the IRS's auditing procedure. This leads to a more general consideration regarding the extent to which business favors an efficient tax system. Many conservatives do not, on the ground that an efficient tax system will lead to big (read "bigger than optimal") government. This recalls the late British econo-mist Joan Robinson's scathing characterization of protectionist trade policy as the equivalent of throwing rocks in one's own harbors.

Under the current system businesses bear costs from complying with the corporation income tax, and with the information reports required of pass-through entities including partnerships and S corporations. They also bear costs related to their role in helping to administer the in-come tax on individuals. They collect and pass along to the IRS infor-mation about their payments to employees, and withhold and remit tax on their employees' behalf. They do the same for miscellaneous payments to independent contractors.

Very little is known about the cost to businesses of complying with withholding and information reporting requirements. More is known about the compliance cost of the corporation income tax. According to Slemrod and Blumenthal (1996), for the biggest 1,500 or so companies in the United States, the average cost of compliance was $1.90 million in 1996. About 65 percent of the costs were for within-firm personnel, about 17 percent for within-firm nonpersonnel costs, and the rest, about 18 percent, were spent on outside assistance. About three-quarters of the cost can be attributed to the federal tax system, with about one-quarter for state and local tax requirements. Overall, the compliance costs for federal taxes only amounted to 2.7 percent of federal corporate tax revenues remitted by these firms; for both state and federal taxes, the ratio was 3.2 percent.

Slemrod and Venkatesh (2002) analyzed the compliance costs of businesses smaller than the biggest 1,500, focusing on businesses with at least $5 million in assets (or in the case of partnerships, those partnerships that have more than a certain number of partners). These businesses remitted $72.7 billion in taxes in 1999, not including any individual taxes owed by owners of pass-through entities. The survey results showed, for firms with $5 million or more in assets, average total compliance costs systematically increase with increasing firm size as measured by asset size. Firms in the $5 million to $10 million asset category had an average of about $35,000 in compliance costs; firms in the $10 million to $50 million category spent about $94,000 on average; firms with assets from $50 million to $100 million spent on average $150,000; firms ranging from $100 million to $250 million in asset size spent an average of $243,000; firms with $250 million to $1 billion in assets had an average of $426,000 in compliance costs; and firms with over $1 billion in assets incurred an average of $1,332,000 in compliance costs.

Slemrod and Venkatesh (2002) estimate that the total compliance costs for this sector in 1999 totaled between $21.0 billion and $22.3 billion, or between $23.0 and $24.4 billion in 2005 dollars. This represents a much higher (compared to the big business sector discussed above) fraction of corporate tax payments made by these companies, but this ratio is misleading on the high side because 60 percent of these companies are pass-through businesses such as partnerships and subchapter S corporations that do not themselves remit tax, although their owners pay tax on the income they generate. As a fraction of the tax paid by the non–pass-through entities and the *owners* of the pass-through entities, the percentage of compliance costs would certainly be significantly lower.

There is overwhelming evidence that although compliance costs are larger for larger companies, the ratio of compliance costs to any of several measures of size is lower for larger companies. Precisely understanding the ratio of size per se and compliance costs is difficult because larger firms also tend to have characteristics, such as multinationality, that tend to increase costs. Statistical analysis done by Slemrod and Blumenthal (1996) concluded that, holding constant other influences on compliance cost, a 10 percent increase in the size of a company is associated with an increase in compliance costs of between 4 and 6 percent. Put another way, a company that is 10 percent larger will, on average, have a ratio of cost to size that is 4 to 6 percent *lower*. Note, though, that we do not know how the ratio of compliance costs to tax liability changes with size.

That compliance costs scaled by assets, employment, or sales are lower for bigger companies is sometimes referred to as being "regressive," but this means something quite different than saying that a tax or a tax system generates a "regressive" distribution of tax burdens. For one thing, the size of a business bears little if any relationship to the income level of those individuals who might bear the burden of a tax nominally placed on the business. In addition one would need to trace the incidence of these costs to individuals before passing judgment on the distributional implications of these costs.

With some exceptions, compliance costs represent costs to society. The exceptions, where private costs differ from the social costs, are worth some attention. One concerns fines for noncompliance, which are certainly a private cost to the fined party but are a transfer from the private to the public sector rather than a social cost. Another example is when compliance costs are deductible from taxable income; in this case the private cost directly incurred by the taxpayer is less than the social cost programs, part of which is passed along to other taxpayers and/or beneficiaries of government programs.

A related issue arises because the survey-based estimates of compliance costs discussed here do not distinguish between involuntary costs that must be expended to comply with the law and discretionary costs that are incurred to avoid or evade taxes. Mills, Maydew, and Erickson (1998) show, for large companies, that greater compliance costs are associated with a lower effective tax rate, other things equal, suggesting that at least some of these costs represent tax planning and the like. To the extent that this happens, the compliance costs directly incurred by the business overstates the net private costs imposed by the tax system, since part of the compliance costs generate tax saving that is passed along through their negative effect on the government budget.

These surveys of compliance costs also provide a window into what aspects of tax reform businesses think would deliver the most simplification, or at least the largest reduction in compliance costs. As discussed in Slemrod and Blumenthal (1996), the largest businesses say that the biggest saving in compliance cost would result from conforming the tax and financial statement definition of income, estimated to lower compliance costs by 9.9 percent of the total. The second biggest saving, 6.9 percent, is estimated to come from establishing complete uniformity among states and between the states and the federal government. The overall saving is 24.8 percent, an average that varies fairly significantly across sectors. Not too surprisingly, the retail and wholesale trade sectors expect the lowest average saving, undoubtedly because the current system generates below-average compliance costs for firms in this sector. Based on the qualitative comments, discussed below, the relatively low estimate of potential compliance cost saving is probably due to skepticism concerning whether "fundamental" reform will, in reality, simplify tax compliance in their business, in particular, how it will affect the tax treatment of international transactions and financial operations.

An open-ended question about fundamental tax reform revealed quite a bit of skepticism about whether it would deliver considerable, or even positive, saving in compliance costs. The most often mentioned concern had to do with the transition period, with some respondents focusing on the complexity of the process and others on the potential for lost depreciation allowances, NOLs, and other tax benefits.[28] Many other respondents cautioned that any promised compliance cost saving would depend on the states' conforming to it, echoing the importance of this factor discussed above. Other concerns raised included whether a new tax system would end up as an add-on rather than a replacement for the income tax, and whether appropriate simplifying rules would be developed for international transactions, and for financial sector firms. A widespread opinion was that the compliance cost implications of radical reform are dwarfed by its other implications, both for the economy as a whole and for the tax liability of the responding firm.

Just as the burden of all taxes levied on business entities needs to be traced to individuals in their roles as customers, shareholders, workers, and the like, the burden of tax compliance costs initially borne by businesses must be so traced. The economic logic of how to do this tracing is the same, with the key question being what factors determine compliance costs. The preceding survey of the business compliance costs literature suggests that compliance costs depend, inter alia, on size (in a regressive way), sector, and multinationality. The dependence of costs on these aspects of business activity generates inefficient incentives, unless they mimic the true cost of enforcing taxes. For example, the relatively low compliance costs incurred by businesses in the retail sector would *inefficiently* attract firms into that sector unless it really is cheaper to collect taxes in this sector; in the latter case the relatively low compliance costs correctly reflect the fact that the true social cost of collecting taxes from this sector is relatively low. The same reasoning would apply to multinationality or size per se.

Sorting through the economics of this question is not easy, and the difficulties are nicely illustrated by the debate over "vendor discounts" in the retail sales tax. These discounts are offered by some states for the prompt remittance of the sales tax by retail establishments. These discounts are sometimes justified as compensation for the compliance costs incurred by the retailers. But if the discounts were just equal to a fraction of the tax liability, their effect would be identical to a statutory reduction in the tax rate, and the ultimate incidence of such a discount would be no different than that of a simple reduction in the rate. A similar issue applies to the "float" earned by firms in the tax remittance process, which refers to the interest they receive in the period between when the taxes are "collected" from consumers (in the case of a retail sales tax) or employees (in the case of withheld employee taxes) because they need not remit tax to the IRS immediately.

3.3.4   Business Tax Noncompliance

So far the focus of this chapter has been on what tax system is good for business and on what tax system is good for the economy as a whole. A separate, though related, question is what level and nature of enforcement is good from either perspective, for any given structure.

Although it is not particularly meaningful to say that businesses as entities bear tax burdens, it is meaningful to inquire as to the tax compliance behavior of business entities. With regard to one federal tax for which businesses are legally liable, the corporation income tax, it is known that the noncompliance rate is nontrivial.[29] The IRS has made corporation income tax gap estimates for tax year 2001, but not later, based on a rough projection from the 15- to 20-year-old Tax Compliance Measurement Program (TCMP) and other data, assuming that the compliance rates for each major component have not changed in the past two decades.[30] Corporate underreporting in 2001 was estimated to be $29.9 billion, of which corporations with over $10 million in assets make up $25.0 billion.[31] Compared to estimated 2001 tax year receipts paid voluntarily and in a timely fashion of $142.4 billion for corporate income tax collections, the overall underreporting rate (calculated as underreported tax divided by receipts plus underreported tax) is 17.4 percent. The estimated rate of noncompliance is starkly different for differently sized companies—13.9 percent for the bigger (greater than $5 million of assets) and 28.7 percent for smaller corporations. Little is known about noncompliance rates for businesses with less than $5 million in assets, although the pattern of higher noncompliance for smaller businesses is supported by the recent IRS estimate that self-employment income has a noncompliance rate of over 50 percent.

Note, however, that while the theory of corporation income tax incidence addresses a tax policy that applies generally to all corporations, a singular act of evasion does not, by definition, apply to all corporations. Although a policy that facilitates evasion for *all* corporations might attract entry and thereby be shifted to customers through lower prices and to capital or labor depending on the relative factor intensity in the corporate and noncorporate sectors, a successful act of evasion by one corporation will not be met by increased pressure from competitors. Thus the windfall gains to those companies that successfully play the tax lottery by acting aggressively probably accrue to the shareholders in their role as residual claimants, shared to some extent with the tax managers through incentivized compensation contracts.

If there are particular characteristics of corporations in certain sectors that facilitate evasion or abusive avoidance, such as the presence of corporate intangibles, the apparent gains that accrue to firms in these sectors via a lower effective tax rate will be partly eroded to the extent that competitors have similar characteristics and partly benefit some other constituency, including this sector's customers. The same argument applies to the incidence of increasing deterrence instruments, such as the penalties for detected evasion.

3.3.5   Sectoral Effects

Base-broadening tax reform will affect adversely those sectors that under the current system receive relatively preferential treatment.[32] Those sectors that do not will presumably be positively affected by the reduction in tax rates afforded by the revenue raised from base broadening. An oft-cited example of a potentially disfavored sector is owner-occupied housing. The impact would be similar to the Harberger analysis of intersectoral tax changes employed above to explain the impact of the corporate income tax. In the short run the newly disfavored sector will experience a decline in its after-tax return, earnings in the case of a business and service return net of taxes for owner-occupied housing; public companies will experience a reduced stock value and housing a decline in its market value.[33] The lower price means that investments in this sector are not as attractive as others. Over time the reduced investment will shrink the sector, which raises the before-tax rate of return. After a while, the sector has shrunk sufficiently so that its after-tax profitability is on a par with other sectors. Bruce and Holtz-Eakin (2001, p. 110) address this issue, and conclude that the price impacts on owner-occupied housing of even a fundamental reform of the federal income tax system would be "relatively modest," despite the dire view offered by many housing advocacy groups.

The same reasoning may apply to the consumption goods sector versus the capital goods sector in a switch to a consumption tax. Indeed some (observers and advocates) fear that switching to a retail sales tax would devastate the retail sector by causing retail spending to decline drastically. Some advocates of a consumption tax do so just because they view this—spun as an increase in saving rather than a decrease in spending—as a good thing. The prospect of a big drop in spending is almost surely overblown. Yes, the idea of having to add a 30 or so percent federal RST to every purchase is daunting, but not spending is not avoiding the tax—it is only postponing it to the day when the saved (or possibly bequeathed) money is spent. Estimates of the increase in the saving rate due to a move to a consumption tax amount to a fairly modest percentage decline in the amount of spending on consumption goods. In addition the pay-now-or-pay-later argument breaks down in the run-up to a switch to a consumption tax. If you know that tomorrow, but not today, there will be a big tax added to the purchase price of everything you buy, there is a substantial incentive to buy, and buy more, today.

The impact on other sectors thought to face losing their special tax status in a fundamental tax reform—such as the health insurance, non-profit, and financial sectors—has been widely studied, and studies of each are collected in Aaron and Gale (1996). To the extent that tax reform eliminates the reward to corporate tax sheltering, one could expect that business to shrink, as well.

3.4 Conclusions

Wide, if not unanimous, support for tax reform was critical to the passage of the Tax Reform Act of 1986, and such support will be just as critical in any future tax reform effort. But businesses often have an excessively narrow perspective regarding what is in their interest, placing a false distinction between what they see as taxes "on" business and other taxes. Moreover business is not monolithic, and tax reform will have differential impacts across sectors, size of business, and legal form.

From a policy perspective it is clear that what is good for business is not always the same as what is good for the country, both because business and share owners are just one (and a relatively affluent) constituency and because business owners have interests, such as the value of past investments, to protect. These distinctions should not distract us from the fact that for the most part, tax policies that induce businesses to invest in capital and hire workers, and to use their resources efficiently, are good for America, too.

Discussion

Robert D. Dietz

Joel Slemrod provides a useful and important overview of a number of economic issues that should be considered when analyzing the effects on business interests of any major tax policy change. Among the analytical issues Slemrod addresses are:

- Theory of business tax incidence
- Old versus new capital concerns
- New versus old views of dividend taxes
- Management versus passive ownership conflicts
- Entity choice considerations

For these issues Slemrod notes important research and links the general findings to the expected tax reform advocacy stances adopted by various business interests. He also cites specific business interests' and associations' positions with respect to tax policy.

Slemrod includes in his survey the analytical conclusion that "... the expressed positions of business representatives suggests that they evaluate tax changes, first and possibly foremost, by estimating whether their own companies' tax payments will go up or down, holding before-tax profits constant." He further states, "... [businesses] ignore what economists would call the general equilibrium impacts of tax changes, and do not think much about the ultimate incidence of tax changes on prices and profits." He uses this conclusion to explain why tax policies, from his point of view, that may benefit business interests in the long run are met with silence or opposed by such interests.

This conclusion mars an otherwise useful overview of business tax issues and their impact on the potential for tax reform. As I argue

The views expressed in this article do not necessarily reflect the views of the National Association of Home Builders or its members.

below, there are many reasons why the business community may be hostile to or unimpressed with various tax reform proposals. However, lack of consideration of general equilibrium effects is not a likely candidate.

Indeed this conclusion can be proved incorrect by noting that businesses, trade associations, and other political representatives of business interests often employ economists (including this author) and allocate resources to researching the potential impacts of minor and major tax policy proposals on not only after-tax profits, but also, and usually more important, on the changes these proposals will produce on the demand for and prices associated with their business product.

Business Tax Advocacy

Slemrod defines several classes of business, which he calls sectors, and notes their tax policies. For each of these sectors (big business, small and medium-sized businesses, and special interests) Slemrod identifies one or more trade associations. This is perhaps an imperfect classification of business interests because trade associations typically represent businesses of many sizes within a particular commercial sector.

For example, the membership of the National Association of Home Builders (NAHB) includes high production national builders, such as Centex, Lennar, and Pulte Homes, as well as local builders, who may only build one to four homes a year. As of 2006, NAHB had 235,000 members. One-third of these members are home builders and remodelers. The remaining members are associates working in the fields of housing finance and building products and services. The unifying philosophy of this group is a commitment to the importance of housing as a national priority.

This diverse range of membership produces challenges with respect to establishing positions on tax policy or any other government affairs. Many of the large home builders are organized as C corporations. However, some are privately owned partnerships. According to the 2002 Economic Census, 65 percent of the businesses in the residential building construction sector were organized as corporate entities. Of the rest, 27 percent were organized as sole proprietorships, 7 percent as partnerships, and 1 percent as other entities. Different entities, even within the same commercial sector, are likely to have different tax policy priorities.

To evaluate Slemrod's conclusion that business interests do not logically evaluate tax policy proposals, it is useful to consider how such organizations adopt policy. Again, using NAHB as an example, from NAHB's membership, 2,800 members are selected to serve on the association's board of directors.[34] The board of directors elects the association's senior officers and helps set the association's agenda through the consideration of specific policy resolutions. These resolutions originate from NAHB's various committees and councils. Once a policy is approved by the board of directors, NAHB's officers and professional staff in Washington provide analysis and action for these items in the media, on Capitol Hill, and within other government agencies.

While NAHB may be unusual with respect to the size of its board of directors, the point is that the consideration of policy is a deliberative one within the association. And in particular, the adoption of tax policy is not arrived at by examining last year's tax return and then tallying whether various tax proposals increase or decrease final tax liability. Interaction between association membership and professional staff, as well as consultation with outside economic research parties, produces analysis of major proposed changes in federal policy. A key aspect of this approach is to determine whether a given proposal will alter the fundamentals of the business sector associated with the trade association.

For example, NAHB worked with economists from consulting firms and academic institutions to examine the impacts of the 2005 President's Advisory Panel on Tax Reform proposals. This analysis was not limited to determining whether tax liability, holding profits constant, would increase or decrease. The primary focus of the research was to determine what effects the Panel's proposals would have on homeowners, residential investment, and housing prices, that is, the general equilibrium effects within the housing sector of the economy. This type of comprehensive analysis is also conducted for smaller tax policy changes.

Tax Policy Perspectives

If business interests consider the general equilibrium effects of tax reform, then what are the reasons for the business community's hostile or silent response to the Panel's tax reform proposals? Several more likely explanations are available.

Sector-Specific Impacts

As Slemrod notes, one explanation is that tax reform may result in changes that are harmful to specific sectors of the economy. For example, NAHB opposes any tax reform proposal that places at risk the following present-law provisions:

• Deductibility of mortgage interest payments
• Deductibility of home equity loan interest payments
• Deductibility of state and local property taxes paid
• Low-income housing tax credit

These tax policy positions reflect NAHB's mission to promote homeownership and access to affordable housing. Indeed President Bush instructed the 2005 Panel to craft tax policies that recognized the "importance of homeownership to society," which is consistent with an extensive social science literature demonstrating the social and private benefits of homeownership.[35]

NAHB strongly opposed the Panel's recommendations because the proposals significantly and negatively affected the tax policy commitment to homeownership and housing. Analysts may agree or disagree with both the purpose and methods of this policy, but it cannot be argued that the housing industry's perception that the Panel's recommendations represented a challenge to its interests was wrong. The Panel's recommendation would have reduced the value of the housing tax preferences in both the short run and long run for both home builders and homeowners. Other business sectors, such as the healthcare industry, had similar concerns.

Risk Aversion

A second factor that could motivate resistance to tax reform is risk aversion. While any tax reform effort may begin with a blueprint or roadmap document, such as the 2005 Panel report or the 1986 Treasury II document, it cannot be known with certainty how the process will evolve within Congress. Moreover, with respect to the general equilibrium consequences of a proposed tax policy change, there may be no agreement among experts as to what those effects are. As an example within the housing context, Bruce and Holtz-Eakin (1999) find that adoption of a flat tax would have modest effects on housing prices, while Capozza, Green, and Hendershott (1996) report significant declines in housing prices.

Risk aversion is a rational response to these uncertainties. Given the large number of moving parts that may lie within a comprehensive tax reform proposal, it may even be difficult for a business interest to determine the static tax liability effect, let alone the general equilibrium effect.

With respect to the types of tax policy changes (incremental or radical), Slemrod concludes that small and medium-sized business associations tend to support "radical tax policy surgery." In this case I believe he is confusing a preference by such groups to state general tax policy principles for a relative enthusiasm for comprehensive reform efforts. In general, risk aversion suggests that business interests are cautious concerning radical changes of tax rules.

Tax Policy-Making

If reluctance by business interests to embrace what some observers believe is a beneficial comprehensive tax reform proposal cannot be explained by sector specific factors or risk aversion, a final explanation may be at work. Business interests may have differing analytical beliefs about what constitutes "good" tax policy. It is probably fair to say that there is a rough majority within the tax economics community (e.g., members of the National Tax Association) in favor of a certain set of positive analytical methods and normative policy preferences. To the extent that business interests' tax preferences are at odds with the views of this majority, differing analytical approaches, rather than myopic tax calculations, may be the cause. An obvious example is whether to tax capital at all, which we can expect business interests (owners of capital) to oppose.

As another example, it is reasonable to expect that business interests, used to understanding gains from trade at the practical, everyday level, do not find the principles of dynamic scoring to be controversial. To the extent that tax reform is scored without macroeconomic effects, this methodology will certainly help shape the final set of policies, assuming that some budget constraint is used as a scoring target. It is fair to say that the support for dynamic scoring is stronger among business interests than it is among the tax economics community (although both support and recognition of its limits is certainly growing).

Similar to the issue of sector-specific impacts, business interests may also be more aware of regional or international business-related

consequences of tax reform. While there are exceptions, many economists who study federal tax issues are in general uninterested in such
spatial effects of tax policy. Consider the fact that spatial price differences (for which there is no accounting in the Internal Revenue Code)
overwhelm year to year temporal or inflation-related price differences
(for which there are many indexation measures). A household with
high income in a rural area may face relatively high income tax rates,
yet a household with the same income in a large metropolitan faces
the same rates but may be considered middling in income distribution
terms given local prices. International and regional concerns such as
these, which are respectively outside and within the federal tax system,
produce legitimate reasons for pause when considering tax policies
that affect competitiveness and after-tax profit for firms.

Another area where business interests may diverge from the majority of tax economists is with respect to externalities. The merits of
Pigovian tax polices are experiencing renewed attention among some
economists, yet many tax economists appear to be skeptical of such
policies.[36] From one perspective, this is understandable. With respect
to the income tax, tax economists are wary of divergences in operative
definitions of taxable income from comprehensive measures or real
economic income (Haig-Simons). However, as we teach undergraduate
economics students, tax policies may be an effective mechanism for
producing efficient social outcomes in the presence of market failures,
whether the externality is positive (e.g., technology diffusion, homeownership) or negative (e.g., pollution). Indeed, it was noted at a
May 2006 National Tax Association conference panel on health tax
preferences (in particular, discussing Antos 2006, Baicker, Dow, and
Wolfson 2006, and Furman 2006), that from the health economist's perspective, tax economists appear to be extremely reluctant to use tax
policy to accomplish any other objective than to raise revenue for the
government.[37]

Tax Reform and Simplification

A final reason for lack of business excitement for tax reform proposals
that some observers claim would benefit business interest is due to,
perhaps, one of the constants of nature: tax complexity. Tax reform is
often marketed as "tax simplification." Indeed the President's Panel
entitled their report "Simple, Fair and Pro-Growth." Who could oppose
such a plan? As usual, the devil is in the details. What appears in a pro-

posal to be simple inevitably becomes more complicated as anti-abuse provisions are added, as definitions are refined, as revenue consequences are considered, and so forth. Moreover in some cases the proposals appear to make the tax code more complicated.

For example, in the 2005 Panel proposal the mortgage interest deduction was transformed into a limited credit based on mortgage principal amounts. However, the Panel recognized that implementing this plan would be unfair to homebuyers who obtained mortgages under the present-law system. Hence the Panel included a slightly less unfair grandfathering mechanism that delayed full implementation of the proposal over a period of five years (an insubstantial length of time considering the length of the benchmark 30-year mortgage). Despite its good intentions the proposal increased the administrative burden for homebuyers (by creating two classes of mortgage interest payments according to debt thresholds), in addition to creating horizontal inequity for new homebuyers. Further the two classes of mortgage interest tax treatment created a disincentive for existing mortgage debt holders to sell a residence.

Any comprehensive tax reform effort is likely to involve complicated transition rules, but it is important to note two other sources of complexity that are not eliminated after a tax reform process. First, although much of the complexity in the tax code is rightly associated with anti-abuse provisions, sometimes these provisions have proved to be too broad, thereby incurring significant administrative costs associated with compliance. In other instances these costs have exceeded the social costs associated with the targeted abuse.[38] Another source of complexity in the tax code is the progressive nature of the present-law income tax. Rules that establish income phase-outs greatly increase complexity for taxpayers, and in particular, for sole proprietorships. Admittedly, tax preparation computer software offsets this burden, but unless the general national consensus for a progressive federal tax system changes, such administrative burdens will be present with or without tax reform.

Finally, tax reforms proposals that are less than entirely specified do not help business interests in adopting prudent policy positions. For example, the 2005 Panel recommendations called for an end to most tax credits. However, there was no definitive list published by the Panel as to what credits were to be eliminated. Further, given that some credits are allocated and claimed over multiple years (e.g., the New Markets Tax Credit and the Low Income Housing Tax Credit), there was no discussion as to how such programs would be treated. Moreover, from the aggregate perspective, the Panel did not produce a set of revenue estimates associated with the proposals that constituted each tax reform plan. We know that such estimates exist because the Panel reported that the proposals were approximately revenue neutral. Despite this the individual line items were not published. Certainly withholding this information interfered with the process of evaluating the merits of each proposal within the larger tax reform package.

Is Pro-Business Tax Policy Good for America?

With respect to Slemrod's second question concerning business-preferred tax policy and national interests, observers must certainly consider the usual measures of social welfare: gross domestic product, social amenities, income/wealth distribution, and economic risk. Slemrod indicates that tax policy that is good for business is not always what is best for the country, given the narrow interests of capital owners, who constitute just one segment of the national population.

However, it is worth considering the fact that because business interests must be sector-focused, they must take into account the general equilibrium consequences of tax proposals. Hence businesses must be aware of the effects of tax proposals on the demand side of their particular markets. So whether it be housing, education, transportation, or any other commercial sector, businesses are to a certain degree advocates for the consumers of their products. For example, NAHB supports the tax policy concerns of homeowners through its support of the mortgage interest deduction. This is due to the fact that home builders must be aware of the impacts of tax policy on homeowners and homebuyers. Consequently NAHB represents these groups when it conducts tax policy advocacy. This is not to suggest that the aggregation of business interests is a sufficient condition for determining welfare-maximizing tax policy, but it is certainly a necessary component to the larger public debate.

Conclusion

So what can we conclude regarding business interests and the prospects for tax reform? Given the concerns detailed earlier, one conclusion is that the nature of any tax reform process matters as much as the substance of the ideas under consideration.

Tax reform proposals in the future, from whatever source, must not read like reader-friendly versions of tax form instructions. This type of document is not surprising given the background of most tax analysts, who are accountants, lawyers, and economists with tax research and policy backgrounds. Such analysts are used to thinking within the interactive sphere of tax rules. However, it would be useful for economists, in particular, to encourage the inclusion of more discussion of the economic context and effects of tax policy in future reform proposals.

I agree that economists view the world differently, as Slemrod suggests. But I think that this difference is in sharper contrast with the views of tax lawyers than with the perspectives of business interests. Tax economists must be careful not think like tax lawyers, focusing on the theoretical principles of taxation. Rather, they should consider and report the intended and (more important) unintended effects of such proposals. Certainly no single set of point estimates can accompany such large packages, but this is not an excuse to fail to discuss what range of effects the research literature suggests would occur. Presently, think tanks and other institutions do a good job of producing this type of research. But this analysis is not present in official documents, so these studies have relatively lesser impact. At the very least, revenue estimates, when available, should accompany tax reform proposals.

Thus, if a tax reform plan includes a proposal to end the deduction for employer-provided health insurance, the proposal should discuss the economics of such a plan. What effect would this have on large and small businesses and their employees?

As another example, the Panel reported in its recommendations that less than 30 percent of taxpayers (including taxpayers residing in the same residence) benefited from the mortgage interest deduction during tax year 2002. While this may be a relevant statistic for taxpayer profile purposes, it is a misleading estimate for describing the economics associated with the tax benefit of the mortgage interest deduction. The economics of the demand for mortgage debt reveal it is a lifecycle-related event, whereby young households move from renting to owning (thereby acquiring a mortgage) and pay the principal of the debt over a period of years.[39] The Panel's limited benefit claim is similar to concluding that government programs for higher education are only of value to 6.7 percent of the US population (those currently attending college[40]), rather than for all beneficiaries of higher education over many years. A more meaningful statistic concerning the mortgage interest deduction is provided by a recent study from economists at the Congressional Budget Office who estimate that 94 percent of mortgage interest payments were deducted for tax year 2002.

Certainly discussions pertaining to the actual economics of these and other issues would help shape the debate surrounding any tax reform effort. In other words, if the question is on the merits of a tax reform proposal from the business and social welfare perspectives, the advocates of such reforms must also consider general equilibrium effects.

Discussion

Thomas S. Neubig

I appreciate the opportunity to comment on Joel Slemrod's discussion of whether a pro-business tax policy is good for America. I always find Joel's writings to be thought-provoking and insightful. Much of the tax reform discussion is on the effects on the general economy or on households, so Joel's contribution is refreshing in its focus on the motivations of business in the tax reform process. As Joel notes, despite a disconnect between the views of business and economists on good tax policy, "tax policies that induce businesses to invest in capital and hire workers, and to use their resources efficiently, are good for America, too."

My discussion of Joel's work will focus on his two key conclusions:

1. Businesses take "an excessively narrow perspective" of incremental tax reforms, by simply focusing on their own change in "business" tax liability, rather than the ultimate change in their shareholders' profitability from tax-induced changes in factor and product prices.

2. Businesses often will oppose tax reforms that may improve the overall economy if those reforms adversely affect the value of their past investments.

A Narrow View Focused on Their Own Tax Liability

Joel brings a new perspective to business tax issues by looking at published statements of business trade associations on tax policy to reveal their "carefully considered self-interest." He notes the multiplicity of buzzwords: "level playing field," "fair and equitable treatment," "competitiveness," and "business taxes." These are often a different way of

The views expressed are solely my own, and do not represent the views of Ernst & Young or any clients.

saying the public finance economists' buzzwords of "efficiency, fairness, and simplicity." However, he does report that large business associations emphasize the importance of reducing business taxes or corporate income taxes.

Although economists generally look at revealed preferences rather than verbal statements, especially those without binding budget constraints, Joel's review of current policy statements is consistent with reports of business behavior during the Tax Reform Act of 1986 debate. He notes that businesses were split largely on whether they benefited from the lower corporate tax rate (48 percent reduced to 34 percent) relative to the cost of slower depreciation and repeal of the investment tax credit.

Thus he concludes that businesses tend to have a narrow view of tax policy focused on their own business tax liability. Interestingly he also notes that many businesses supported the Tax Reform Act of 1986 even though corporate income taxes were estimated to increase by $121 billion over five years to pay for a corresponding decrease in personal income taxes. He highlights the "disingenuous manner" in which both the Treasury Department and the Joint Committee on Taxation presented distributional tables showing only reductions in household tax burdens by ignoring the corporate income tax increases. Perhaps politicians, and the general public, also have narrow perspectives on tax policy by focusing only on their own personal income tax liabilities, rather than the full general equilibrium effects on factor and product prices, which would include the effects of higher corporate income taxes.

The narrow business perspective (and also the narrow household perspective) have an important lesson for public finance specialists. Joel comments that current research leaves "considerable uncertainty about the impact—on share prices, investment, and profitability—of tax reforms that eliminate the current special treatment of corporate-source income, under either an income tax or a consumption tax." Thus businesses' own tax liability may be a reasonable, if flawed, first proxy for assessing the effects of proposed tax reforms in most instances, due to uncertainty about economic incidence.

If this is the case, then there is a question of which "business" taxes companies should use to evaluate the change in their liability. Joel is correct that a focus on the remittance or statutory liability can be seriously misleading about the ultimate incidence of a tax. However, I would point out that remittance or statutory liability has to be the initial starting point for an economic incidence analysis. Let me give two examples of how statutory tax liability can make a difference:

1. Although state and local sales taxes are typically referred to as retail sales taxes, over 40 percent of current sales taxes are estimated to fall on intermediate business inputs—business purchases of equipment and supplies (Cline et al. 2005). Thus what a naïve public finance economist might think is a destination tax borne largely by consumers has a significant origin-based tax element that is more likely borne by immobile factors (labor and landowners in the origin state with above-average sales taxes on business inputs), and thus distorts business location choices.

2. Although most sales taxes are remitted by retail establishments, to the extent that a seller doesn't collect the tax due to lack of nexus (or taxing authority) with the consumer's local jurisdiction, sales taxes have a use tax provision that then places the responsibility for the tax liability on the consumer. Since compliance rates under the sales tax are high for established retailers and extremely low for use tax by individual consumers, the remittance and statutory liability can have real economic effects for businesses. A local sales tax can place in-state retailers at a competitive disadvantage relative to out-of-state companies selling into the state without nexus, if the state doesn't enforce use tax liability. In this case a retail sales tax could be a burden on local retail owners and employees.

Besides real economic effects, information about business taxes can also have important insights for policy makers. In 2001 to 2003 there was considerable concern expressed by many public finance economists and state and local governments about the declining percentage of tax revenue from the state corporate income tax. Several studies by Bob Cline, Bill Fox, Andrew Phillips, and myself showed that property taxes paid by business are 4.4 times state corporate income taxes, and sales taxes on business inputs are 2.7 times state corporate income taxes (Cline et al. 2003, 2006). Business property taxes and sales tax on business inputs have to be estimated rather than simply pulled, as are state corporate income taxes, from government reports, but those measures of "business" taxes have been important to state and local policy makers understanding the relative lack of importance of the state corporate income tax compared to other location-specific, origin-based taxes that can affect companies' choice of location.

There is some recent evidence at the state level that the business community looks at more than just their own tax liability when considering more fundamental tax reforms. In both Ohio and Texas the business community has supported tax reforms designed to make the state more competitive, by replacing origin-based taxes with destination-based taxes. As with the Tax Reform Act of 1986 and recent federal changes that have focused on shareholder capital income taxation, businesses are supportive of tax policy changes that have positive economywide effects without necessarily lowering their own corporate tax liability.

Policy Economists' Search for a Free Lunch

Joel suggests that the treatment of existing capital and provisions for transitional relief are an example of where what's good for business diverges from what's good for the nation. He uses an example of a lump-sum subsidy to business that is good for business but bad for the economy. I agree with the example, but have trouble with the opposite example of lump-sum taxes. Economists are always looking for the holy grail of taxes with no economic distortions. They think they have found it with a lump-sum tax on old capital. I know very few companies or noneconomists who distinguish between old and new capital. Instead, they have a long-run view that new capital today will be old capital tomorrow, so the two should not be treated differently.

I address this issue in a recent article that tries to answer a question that came up after a discussion of the Advisory Panel's report among a large group of multinational tax directors (Neubig 2006). They asked "Why do Treasury economists seem to love the business cash-flow tax or expensing" compared to lowering the corporate income tax rate? In the article, I give seven reasons why most corporations prefer a lower marginal corporate tax rate to expensing of new capital investment.

Both Joel and I use the same notion of a disconnect between business and economists. In describing incidence theory, Joel observes: "This discussion highlights a fascinating *disconnect* between how economists view the incidence of business taxes, and taxes in general, and how business interests, and most everyone other than economists, views these issues." Similarly I note: "With economists and the business community differing so widely in their response to the Advisory Panel's expensing option, many observers are left wondering what caused the *disconnect*."

To explain the disconnect I will have to diverge from many of my academic colleagues and say that institutional details do matter in public policy. Some things that theoretical economists dismiss as unimportant or inconvenient for their theories are important to business. Let me give you two examples:

1. *The accounting treatment of profits and taxes.* Economic theory says investors pierce the corporate veil and ignore book profits and book taxes. Yet book taxes matter, if for no other reason than many corporate officers are compensated based on book results. Expensing accelerates tax deductions from future years into the first year, providing a significant cash-flow effect and reduction in the cost of capital, but expensing doesn't affect reported current taxes and profits, only deferred taxes, for book purposes. With expensing, public corporations would continue to have a high book effective tax rate on their current income, and would build up large deferred book tax liabilities.

In contrast, reducing the corporate marginal tax rate would immediately lower corporations' book effective tax rates, and increase their reported after-tax book profits. A lower corporate marginal tax rate would also immediately reduce corporations' deferred book tax liabilities and assets—a welcome development in an environment where two-thirds of the largest companies report deferred tax liabilities. However, the adverse financial reporting effects from a reduction in the effective tax rate for public corporations with deferred tax assets will be a significant political hurdle to lower corporate tax rates. This was one of the reasons why the domestic manufacturing tax relief was structured as a deduction rather than a rate differential.

2. *Replacing the income tax with a consumption tax.* Many economists recommend this because the efficiency gains come principally from imposing tax on existing capital, assuming no transition relief is provided for undepreciated assets or the elderly's current savings. Many economists assume that such lump-sum taxes on existing capital are the proverbial "free good." They are not. If the government can impose lump-sum taxes once, they can do it again and again in the future. Once burned, businesses do remember. That is why businesses made clear in 2005 that they don't want to pay for individual tax cuts with business tax increases as they did in 1986. (Joel recognizes this in his note 22. Alan Auerbach emphasizes the expectation effect of future additional lump-sum taxes in chapter 1 of this volume.) Economists need to adjust their rational expectation models to include the likelihood of

adverse efficiency effects from lump-sum taxes. This will also help explain some of the political opposition to tax reforms without meaningful transition relief.

Conclusion

Joel, as usual, has a number of new insights that reflect an examination of the issues that goes beyond the narrow parochial view of most economists. However, I don't think businesses have a narrow view of their interests when they make a distinction between what they see as taxes "on" business and other taxes. Businesses do look at their own tax liability, and at their book tax liability as reported on their financial statements, but they also factor in how tax policy will affect their products, markets, and customers.

Joel has highlighted some key disconnects between academic economists' and the business community's views on tax policy. Many academic economists think they know what drives business decisions, but if they talked more to the business community, they would find out that business decision-making is knowable. Although the ultimate incidence of all taxes is unknowable with complete certainty, economic incidence studies of specific taxes need to start with what is known, which is who remits and has the statutory liability for each individual tax, since institutional details and constraints matter to the ultimate economic incidence.

Joel states that "for a policy perspective, it is clear that what is good for business is not always the same as what is good for the country," since businesses protect the value of past investments. I agree, but the economists' distinction between old capital and new capital is highly theoretical, and probably should be scrapped when we think about "tax policies that induce businesses to invest in capital and hire workers, and to use their resources efficiently." As an economist, I don't believe that lump-sum taxes on existing capital are the free lunch that many theoretical economists or proponents of consumption taxes do.

Notes

I am grateful to Tomislav Ladika for helpful research assistance and to Tom Neubig, Robert Dennis, Robert Dietz, George Zodrow, and conference participants for helpful comments on an early draft.

1. Although, as Hubbard (1998) notes, there are numerous empirical studies that have found that proxies for internal funds have explanatory power for investment, suggesting that the amount of taxes paid as well as the effect of the tax system on the marginal incentive to invest may depress investment. See Hassett and Newmark (chapter 4 of this volume) for a critique of this view. This finding is consistent with the fact that some firms face constraints in obtaining external financing.

2. I do not know of evidence that demonstrates how well these associations represent the heterogeneous views of their member businesses. However, if one is interested in how business views affect policy, it may be appropriate to focus on the views of the business' lobbying groups, who represent to the actors in the political process the consensus views of their members. Of course, these associations are also in some sense in competition with each other, so there is likely to be the same kind of political dynamic in which political parties compete for voters and, depending on the environment, may or may not compete for the median "voter." In addition, as the discussion of the Tax Reform Act of 1986 suggests, ad hoc alignments of businesses may form to lobby for a particular positions on some tax legislation, and may be as influential as the standing associations.

Moreover the publicly stated views of business lobby groups may not reflect some underlying concerns of businesses. For example, Neubig (2006) argues that public corporations consider the impact of tax legislation on their earnings as reported on financial statements, over and above the impact on their "true" after-tax income.

3. The source for the positions, and the claim of being the nation's largest, is *www .nam.org/s_nam/sec.asp?CID=202107&DID=232960.*

4. Source: *http://www.tei.org/Resource.phx/public/index.htx.*

5. Source: *http://www.businessroundtable.org/taskForces/taskforce/index.aspx? qs=14C5BF159FE.*

6. Source: *www.uschamber.com/issues/index/econtax/default.*

7. Source: *www.nfib.com/page/agendasummary.html* and *www.nfib.com/page/taxRelief.html.*

8. Source: *www.nsba.biz/content/87.shtml.*

9. Source: *http://www.americanbusinessconference.org.*

10. Source: *www.nahb.org/generic.aspx?sectionID=200&genericContentID=9224.*

11. *The Cincinnati Post* (OH), November 15, 2005.

12. *The Daily Oklahoman* (Oklahoma City, OK), October 19, 2005.

13. Source: *http://www.gmabrands.com/.*

14. Source: *www.fb.org/issues/backgrd/tax-reform06.301.doc.*

15. Source: *http://www.nfu.org.*

16. Source: *http://www.nase.org.*

17. The discussion of the business role in the tax debates of the 1980s draws heavily from Martin (1991). Evaluating business reaction to post-1986 tax bills that did not purport to be comprehensive tax reform could also provide insights about business' tax policy trade-offs, although the trade-offs are less clear when the tax change is not revenue neutral, especially when it is not revenue neutral with respect to the set of what are traditionally considered to be "business taxes." One particularly interesting episode is the cuts in dividend taxation that was part of the Jobs and Growth Reconciliation Tax Act of 2003.

The Business Roundtable had called for such a reduction in 2002, and supported the legislation that implemented this. The Chamber of Commerce and the National Small Business Association also praised this provision after it passed.

18. Writing about the Treasury Department's tax proposal of November, 1984, Paul Craig Roberts said that if it were implemented, the United States would be "deindustrialized within a decade." Although many of the details of the tax reform package changed between November 1984 and October 1986, the key aspect of the corporate tax reforms that Roberts criticized—the replacement of ACRS with slower depreciation and the abolition of the investment tax credit—remained. This episode is recounted in Slemrod (1990b).

19. Martin (1991, p. 195) argues that two related factors caused many business groups to support base-broadening, rate-lowering tax reform in 1986. One was the prominent 1984 study by Citizens for Tax Justice that apparently documented wide disparities in effective corporate tax rates, reframing the debate as an equity (among businesses) issue. Second, many business interests had bought into the focus on accelerated depreciation in 1981 thinking that it uniformly helped business. But beginning in 1982 the notion of disparities between different business sectors dawned on those left out, in part fueled by academic studies that argued that the cost of capital varied widely by sector and type of asset, largely due to the differential effect of accelerated depreciation.

20. As Shaviro (2005) points out, maintaining this distinction would probably require rules to prevent taxpayers from artificially separating their businesses into separate pieces, in cases where they preferred to be treated as small or medium-sized businesses, and rules delineating at what point a business is new rather than a continuation of a previous one.

21. The impact on old capital could matter for the attractiveness of new investment if it raises the perceived probability that, in the future, more tax changes will be implemented that affect the value of the new—by then old—capital.

22. Auerbach (2005, and elsewhere) stresses that the distinction between how tax changes affect asset values and how they affect asset returns has a critical generational component because the change in asset values matters most for older asset holders who have accumulated capital and have short planning horizons. In contrast, the change in the rate of return will matter more for younger individuals who have accumulated little wealth and have longer planning horizons.

23. One important aspect of this role is the information reports that businesses provide the IRS about their transactions that have tax implications for other businesses and individuals.

24. Bird (2002).

25. The situation is a bit more complicated in the case of regulated utilities, where rates are set by state regulators to cover all costs—including taxes—so as to provide a just and reasonable return. This has recently become a controversial issue, as utility companies have been using losses from other subsidiaries to reduce taxes owed, often to zero. This issue is explored in a recent *New York Times* article entitled "Many Utilities Collect for Taxes They Never Pay," whose language seems to violate my dictum in the text about never saying that businesses "collect" taxes (Johnston 2006a).

26. The flat tax is essentially a VAT where payments to labor are taken out of the business base (i.e., made deductible) and taxed at the same rate under the personal tax. Absent transitional effects and possible (but not inevitable) changes in remittance responsibility, this is not a substantive change.

27. Hall and Rabushka (1995).

28. The references to lost tax benefits show the difficulty that some respondents had in separating the change in compliance costs from the change in tax liability that reform would bring.

29. For small corporations, the IRS used TCMP data adjusted for underreporting unlikely to be detected by the TCMP. For medium-sized corporations, the gap was calculated by estimating, based on operational (i.e., non-TCMP) audits, how much tax revenue would have been generated if the IRS examined all these corporations' tax returns. Finally, for large corporations, because the IRS routinely examines a high percentage of these companies, examination results were used as the basis of estimates of the tax gap. This description is based on US General Accounting Office (1988). One potentially important problem with these data is that the examination reports do not distinguish between adjustments that change the *timing* of tax liability and adjustments that change the liability in a way that will not be offset in future years. For this reason it is difficult to know the present value of the recommended adjustments from IRS examinations.

30. The tax gap numbers are drawn from Internal Revenue Service (2004).

31. Underreporting is only one of the three components of the total tax gap, which is estimated to be $282.5 billion. The other two components are nonfiling and underpayment. There is no estimate for corporate nonfiling, and underpayment is a quite different issue.

32. Yet another issue is the differential effect of tax reform on US companies and foreign companies that do business in the United States, and the relative impact on multinational US companies versus purely domestic companies. This is especially germane because many tax reform proposals would make fundamental changes in the extent to which the tax system is based on a territorial or worldwide principle. See Hines (1996).

33. See Diamond and Zodrow, chapter 5 in this volume.

34. In practice, there are approximately 1,700 voting members with the remaining members serving as alternates. The board meets three times a year. At a given meeting, there are usually approximately 1,000 voting members in attendance.

35. For a review of the literature and methodological issues, see Dietz and Haurin (2003).

36. For example, consider Greg Mankiw's Pigou club, which supports higher taxes on carbon emissions and gas purchases (*http://gregmankiw.blogspot.com/2006/06/pigou-club .html*).

37. Hence the unfortunate use of terminology that a tax reduction "costs" money, when in fact the tax cut may reduce deadweight welfare loss.

38. For example, the new Section 4965 was drafted broadly and may affect unintended parties. Without regulatory correction, the provision, which was intended to prevent the use of certain tax shelters, may negatively affect business arrangements established to comply with other aspects of the income tax code.

39. According to the 2005 American Community Survey, 32 percent of all owner-occupiers own their homes with no mortgage debt (including home equity loans). These homeowners tend to be older and higher income than owner-occupiers with mortgage debt.

40. Source: 2005 US Census and 2005 Digest of Education Statistics.

4

Taxation and Business Behavior: A Review of the Recent Literature

Kevin A. Hassett and Kathryn Newmark

The study of the economics of investment has advanced at a rapid pace in recent years. A number of factors have aligned to stimulate an impressive explosion of work. In particular, theoretical advances in the study of adjustment costs have led to new specifications of empirical investment equations that have proved quite informative, and international tax competition prompted by increasing globalization coupled with several major tax changes in the United States have provided ample tax variable variation to facilitate empirical study.

The US tax changes have been especially interesting because they have allowed researchers to explore some of the more hotly contested questions in the previous literature. The three recent reforms were the Economic Growth and Tax Relief Reconciliation Act of 2001 (EGTRRA), the Job Creation and Worker Assistance Act of 2002 (JCWAA), and the Jobs and Growth Tax Relief Reconciliation Act of 2003 (JGTRRA). The second two reforms were perhaps the most important to investment researchers. JCWAA introduced a provision that temporarily allowed firms a bonus first-year depreciation deduction, also called temporary partial expensing, equal to 30 percent of the purchase price of qualified investments. JGTRRA increased this temporary bonus depreciation to 50 percent and lowered the marginal tax rate on dividends and realized capital gains to 15 percent.

Partial expensing, a version of accelerated depreciation, provided researchers with a shock to the user cost of capital. Since it was explicitly temporary, the response of firms might be particularly informative about the role of adjustment costs in determining investment behavior, one of the hotter areas of research prior to the reforms. In addition the surge in demand expected to precede expiration of partial expensing might have led to a surge in capital goods prices if, as suggested by Goolsbee (1998), such goods are characterized by inelastic supply.

For dividends, the effects of the tax changes depend crucially on the marginal source of finance for firms. Prior to the passage of the dividend tax reduction, the literature was still in a significant state of flux regarding the debate between the "new" and "traditional" views of dividend taxation, views that have strikingly different implications. Under the new view of dividend taxation developed in Auerbach (1979), Bradford (1981), and King (1977), the marginal source of finance for new investment projects is retained earnings. In this case the tax advantage of retentions precisely offsets the double taxation of subsequent dividends, and taxes on dividends have no impact on investment incentives. On the other hand, under the traditional view in which firms rely on new share issues as the marginal source of funds, the dividend tax raises the cost of capital. Evidence from Poterba and Summers (1985) suggests that the traditional view might best characterize the investment behavior of UK firms, but Auerbach and Hassett (2003) find evidence that the investment behavior of US firms is about evenly split between the two views. The recent dividend tax change has allowed scholars to shed new light on this debate.

This chapter proceeds as follows: The next section briefly reviews the literature as it stood approximately four years ago, drawing heavily on Hassett and Hubbard (2002). Section 4.2 discusses recent extensions of the literature, but does not necessarily focus on the recent tax policy changes. Section 4.3 discusses the recent dividend tax and partial expensing literature. Section 4.4 reviews developments in international taxation and investment behavior, and section 4.5 concludes.

4.1   The Early Literature

For many years empirical investment researchers had extreme difficulty explaining investment behavior, and the accelerator-based models that did appear to predict time series fluctuations well were usually not improved by the inclusion of tax policy variables or the cost of capital more generally. For example, Chirinko and Eisner (1983) and Chirinko (1987) find that tax variables have little effect on investment.

User cost approaches generally relied on the pioneering work of Hall and Jorgenson (1967). Hall and Jorgenson ignore adjustment or installation costs, and also assume that no time is necessary to plan or build additions to the capital stock, that there is no investment tax credit, and that firms and investors expect tax laws to remain unchanged.

Within this framework they show that maximization of the present discounted value of after-corporate-tax cash flow over an infinite horizon implies that the before-tax nominal value of the gross marginal product of capital today equals today's user cost of capital, C, or

$$C = pT\left[\rho + \delta - E\left(\frac{\Delta p}{p}\right)\right], \tag{4.1}$$

$$T = \frac{1 - \tau Z}{1 - \tau}. \tag{4.2}$$

In these two equations, p denotes the price of new capital goods, $E(\Delta p/p)$ the percentage change in the price of capital goods expected over the period, ρ the nominal after-tax cost of funds (debt plus equity), δ the rate of physical depreciation, τ the corporate income tax rate, Z the present value of depreciation allowances per dollar invested, and T summarizes the tax information relevant for our discussion. As noted by Auerbach (1983b), $\delta - E(\Delta p/p)$ is the expected *net* rate of decline of the asset's value or the rate of economic depreciation, that is, the rate of physical depreciation offset by the expected capital gain.

Loosely speaking, equation (4.1) implies that the firm's optimal value of the marginal product of capital must be sufficient to cover investors' required rate of return, economic depreciation, and taxes. Equation (4.2) implies that a higher corporate income tax rate boosts taxes on income generated by the new capital and hence the user cost of capital (assuming $Z < 1$). In addition a more favorable system of tax depreciation (i.e., a higher value of Z) lowers the tax term and hence the cost of capital.

While early work assumed no adjustment costs, this model was subsequently extended to allow for costly capital stock adjustment by Auerbach (1983b, 1989). Auerbach demonstrates that adjustment costs introduce future user costs of capital into current investment decisions, and current investment depends on a weighted average of current and future one-period user costs, where the weights depend on the level of adjustment costs. Higher adjustment costs imply a higher weight on future one-period user costs. In addition Hayashi (1982) and Summers (1981b) pursue an alternative formulation of the model that relates investment to a tax-adjusted version of Tobin's Q.

Empirical analyses of the resulting neoclassical Q models of investment behavior, however, produced implausibly high adjustment cost estimates, and aggregate investment models based on the user cost formulation did no better. In a key literature review Bernanke, Bohn, and Riess (1988) found that the best forecasting models were accelerator models that relied on output growth to predict investment. The time series correlation between aggregate investment and the user cost of capital and other fundamental variables was very weak. Researchers responded to these results by pursuing two alternative strategies. One branch of the literature set out to explore the extent to which financing constraints due to capital market imperfections could plausibly explain the large accelerator effects in the aggregate data. Another set out to see if measurement problems might explain the poor performance of more fundamentals-based models. Early work in both areas was quite fruitful.

4.1.1 Financing Constraints

If firms face financing constraints, they cannot always rely on outside sources to provide the funds necessary for investment. Plausible models of asymmetric information in credit markets can lead to such liquidity constraints. These models predict that a firm's internal funds, by the firm's ability to secure financing, determine investment with neoclassical fundamentals that include the user cost of capital having limited explanatory power. Consistent with this model, Fazzari et al. (1988) find that if firms face financial constraints, their investment shows greater sensitivity to cash flow. Later empirical work that produced an enormous number of derivative papers has generally supported, until recently, the finding that cash flow matters for investment (see Hubbard 1998 for a review).

4.1.2 Measurement Error

Another possible explanation for the weakness of the neoclassical models is that the fundamentals are mismeasured or endogenous. Early attempts to address this in a user cost model include Auerbach and Hassett (1991) and Cummins, Hassett, and Hubbard (1994). Both papers improve the measurement of the user costs and utilize panel data to explore the cross-sectional implications of tax reforms, finding much greater responsiveness of investment to the user cost than was evident in time series studies, and obtaining more plausible estimates of adjustment costs.

It is useful to review for a moment the intuition underlying the approaches used in these two studies. Over time demand-driven economic booms can lead to circumstances where output, investment, and the interest rate increase at the same time. In such a world, time series regressions can even show that investment and the interest rate are positively correlated. But tax reforms often affect different assets differently. By exploring the cross-sectional differences in the investment responses to tax reform, these authors find evidence that suggests the tax reforms had a significant impact.

Hassett and Hubbard (2002) review the subsequent voluminous literature that relies on panel data to identify user cost effects. They conclude that the consensus of the literature is that the elasticity of investment with respect to the user cost of capital is between -0.5 and -1.0. While there is still some dispute over the exact size of user cost effects—notably, Chirinko, Fazzari, and Meyer (1999) estimate an elasticity of approximately -0.25—their presence is no longer in question.

4.2   More Recent Findings

The apparent success of both bodies of literature in explaining investment behavior created some tension in the early years of this decade. Liquidity constraint models were, after all, developed to help explain why investment does not respond to neoclassical fundamentals. If neoclassical fundamentals are so important, then why should financing constraints matter too?

A growing body of literature tends to favor the neoclassical over the financing constraint explanation. In this section we review this literature and then discuss extensions to the investment model that have allowed for more general adjustment cost technologies.

4.2.1   Neoclassical Fundamentals or Cash Flow?

Cummins, Hassett, and Oliner (2006) provide an example of the type of result that is becoming widespread. They point out that past attempts to estimate Q-models typically used the stock market value of the firm for the numerator of Q. Since stock market values may fluctuate more than fundamentals, including the user cost of capital, do (as described in Shiller 1989, 2000), then this approach may introduce significant measurement error into Q. They construct a measure of Q that bases the numerator on a present value calculation derived from observable analyst expectations. Their Q is found to be highly significant, and suggests adjustment costs that are low and plausible, equal to a small fraction of the total cost of a machine. The results using the analyst-based Q imply that the elasticity of investment with respect to fundamentals is about unity, more than twice the elasticity calculated using the market-based Q. Interestingly they find that all explanatory power for liquidity variables disappears if the analyst-based Q measure is used. This is even true for the firms that are most likely to be subject to liquidity constraints, as measured by S&P bond ratings, debt-equity ratios, and sales.

But are the cash-flow results really attributable to measurement error? Erickson and Whited (2007) examine the extent of the measurement problem by quantifying the noisiness of different proxies for marginal q, or what they call "true q." In theory, true q is observable, since one can calculate the market value of assets and their replacement cost, but in practice, this calculation is difficult. Erickson and Whited find that on average, only about half of the variation in proxies for q is due to variation in true q, and even the best proxies explain little of the true variation. Moreover elaborate procedures for estimating q can decrease the sample size and introduce estimation bias. Erickson and Whited (2002) stress that the cash flow results depend on an unrealistically large correlation between estimated q measures and true q.

As an alternative to Cummins, Hassett, and Oliner (2006), Erickson and Whited (2000) develop a generalized method of moments (GMM) estimation strategy that uses information in higher order moments to deal with the problem of noisy measures of marginal q. The GMM models produce larger investment coefficients than the OLS models and have 1.4 to 2.5 times the explanatory power, suggesting that, once measurement error is eliminated, the q model describes investment well and user costs have a large effect on investment. Furthermore they show that if measurement error is corrected, cash flow does not matter. These results have generally been confirmed by others. For example, when Hennessy (2004) and Agca and Mozumdar (2005) use the Erickson-Whited GMM estimator, the coefficient on cash flow is greatly reduced compared to the OLS estimates, although it is still significant in some cases.

Bond and Cummins (2001) show also that using stock market valuations to estimate average q results in serious measurement error. Using the alternative measure based on security analysts' forecasts of future earnings for publicly traded US companies first employed by Cummins, Hassett, and Oliner (2006), they find that investment is quite responsive to changes in fundamentals. Their estimated elasticity is close to −1.0. Like Erickson and Whited (2000) they find that cash flow becomes insignificant when measurement error is corrected. Bond et al. (2004) reach similar conclusions using the GMM methodology with data for publicly traded UK companies. Desai and Goolsbee (2004) also reach the conclusion that in models with proper controls for measurement error, fundamentals significantly affect investment and cash flow does not. Taken together, these studies provide considerable support for the neoclassical model of investment.

An alternative literature has challenged the financing constraint model on different grounds. Even if cash-flow effects do not disappear in investment equations, recent theoretical advances suggest that they are not necessarily related to capital market imperfections (Gomes 2001; Alti 2003; Abel and Eberly 2004, 2005; and Cooper and Ejarque 2001, 2003). For example, Cooper and Ejarque show that market power, instead of market imperfections, can generate a cash-flow effect. Because these models relax one or more of the assumptions necessary for average q to be a sufficient statistic for investment, cash flow becomes an important signal of a firm's growth potential. It thus has a significant effect on investment, without capital market imperfections.

Another line of research shows that even in assuming that capital markets are not perfect, it does not necessarily follow that firms face financing constraints. Implicit in much of the financing constraint literature is the contention that the investment behavior of firms that are more constrained will show greater responsiveness to cash flow. Yet Kaplan and Zingales (1997) examine the financial reports of the constrained firms in Fazzari et al. (1988) and determine that the firms with the greatest cash-flow sensitivity were actually unconstrained. Fazzari et al. (2000) and Kaplan and Zingales (2000) exchange critiques on the subject, and other studies also try to reconcile the two views (see Cleary 1999; Boyle and Guthrie 2003; Allayannis and Mozumdar 2004; Moyen 2004).

In particular, Moyen finds that the result depends on the criteria used to identify financially constrained firms. If financially constrained firms are defined by a standard investment model, the regressions will actually produce a smaller coefficient on cash flow for financially constrained firms than unconstrained firms. Because cash flow proxies for a firm's income, a positive cash-flow shock leads to more investment

by both constrained and unconstrained firms, but because unconstrained firms also issue debt to finance investment, their investment–
cash–flow sensitivity is amplified. For similar reasons Hennessy and
Whited (2007) demonstrate that the sensitivity of investment to cash
flow decreases as the cost premium that firms pay for equity financing
falls. They also find that this sensitivity increases with another financing cost parameter, the magnitude of a firm's bankruptcy costs. In light
of these results it is difficult to conclude that evidence of differences in
cash-flow sensitivity necessarily indicate financing constraints.

In short, the literature questions the financing constraint model on
three grounds. First, once measurement error in q is properly controlled for, cash flow has a much smaller, even insignificant, effect on
investment. Second, any effect that cash flow does have is not necessarily caused by liquidity constraints. Third, even if financing constraints
do exist, the evidence does not support the key assumption of the
model that cash-flow sensitivity must increase as the degree of constraint increases.

On a related note, there is also strong evidence that tax policy affects
entrepreneurship, that is, investment by early stage firms. Carroll et al.
(2000, 2001) examine the effect of personal income taxes on existing
firms. They find a large, statistically significant negative effect on hiring and on firm growth as measured by gross receipts. Looking at the
effect of taxes on the decision to start a business, Cullen and Gordon
(2002) emphasize the role that taxes play via their effects on risk. Gentry and Hubbard (2004) find that both the level of the marginal tax rate
and the progressivity of income taxes have a substantial negative effect
on entrepreneurial entry.

4.2.2 Alternative Adjustment Costs

Researchers have also explored the possibility that the assumption of
convex costs of adjusting the capital stock made in early extensions
of neoclassical model is incorrect so that the relationship between user
costs and investment is not linear. If adjustment costs are nonconvex or
capital investments are irreversible, the observed response of investment to changes in user costs in these models would be dampened.
Microeconomic models that reconsider the assumption of convexity of
adjustment costs provide evidence of a significant nonlinear relationship between user cost and investment. The evidence suggests that

models that rely purely on linear relationships do a poor job of predicting the response of firms to future policy changes.

Looking at plant-level data, Cooper and Haltiwanger (2000) observe both periods of no investment and "bursts" of large investment activity. They find that the data are best described by a model that incorporates a mix of convex and nonconvex adjustment costs as well as irreversibility.

Abel and Eberly (2002) also compare the standard model of investment to models that relax the assumption that adjustment costs are convex. The alternative models allow for a more general "augmented adjustment cost" function that includes fixed, linear, and convex costs of changing the capital stock. They find nonlinearities, potentially arising from fixed costs, that are statistically and quantitatively significant and that the alternative models outperform the standard model in predicting investment.

Chirinko and Schaller (2001) point out that in the presence of irreversibility, firms effectively have higher discount rates because the marginal productivity of capital required to induce a firm to invest has to be greater than the user cost of capital. The difference between the discount rate and the risk-adjusted market interest rate is what they call the "irreversibility premium." Using panel data on Canadian firms, they find that as irreversibility models predict, firms with very low investment are most likely to be affected by irreversibility, and have discount rates that are 600 to 800 basis points higher than other firms. Low growth and limited resale markets are the most important factors causing very low investment firms to face a higher irreversibility premium. Providing further evidence for the importance of irreversible capital, Zhou (2000) shows that investment is more sensitive to values of Q greater than 1 than values less than 1.

In contrast, Abel and Eberly (2004) demonstrate that adjustment costs do not necessarily account for the small response of investment to changes in fundamentals that is typically found in the standard neoclassical models. In their stylized model, the coefficient on Q can still be small, even without adjustment costs, if Q is relatively large or cash flow is relatively small.

Barnett and Sakellaris (1998, 1999) explore the possibly nonlinear relationship between investment and Q. They find that allowing for nonlinearity significantly increases the coefficient on Q and also that investment responds much more to large Q values than to small Q

values, a sign that the investment-Q relationship is convex. They find that the costs of adjustment imply an installation cost of about 10 percent of the price of a new machine, a much smaller and more reasonable estimate than was implied in earlier Q research that incorporated quadratic adjustment costs but consistent with the more recent research of Auerbach and Hassett (1991) and Cummins, Hassett, and Hubbard (1994).

Taken together, this research suggests that the standard quadratic adjustment cost model heavily relied upon by public finance economists may be inadequate for policy analysis, especially in circumstances where tax changes are large. Detailed extensions of these papers that incorporate the richness of the tax code would be of great value.

4.3   Research on the Effects of Recent Tax Changes

In this section we address recent attempts to learn more from the last three tax reforms in the United States. The first section focuses on the literature on recent changes in dividend taxation, and the second looks at the more limited literature on partial expensing or bonus depreciation.

A simple look at the trend in equipment and software investment over time is suggestive. Figure 4.1 shows that investment fell from the beginning of 2001 until the beginning of 2002, when JCWAA was passed. Subsequently, investment held steady and then took off, starting in the second quarter of 2003 when JGTRRA was passed. Of course, much more careful analysis of the data is required before one should conclude anything from this pattern.

4.3.1   Dividend Taxes

According to the "traditional" view of dividend taxes, a firm's marginal source of funds is new equity issues—defined broadly to include, for example, reductions in share repurchases—and investment is responsive to dividend taxes. According to the "new" view, however, a firm's marginal source of funds is retained earnings and investment levels are unresponsive to changes in dividend taxes, and time invariant dividend taxes are capitalized into the value of the firm. Research on this topic provides mixed evidence on the relative importance of the two views, although the most recent studies that explore the response to JGTRRA tend to favor the new view.

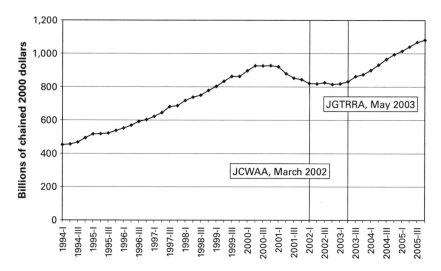

Figure 4.1
Gross private domestic investment: Software and equipment (source: National Income and Product Accounts, Bureau of Economic Analysis)

The user cost effects of JGTRRA are explored in Carroll, Hassett, and Mackie (2003). They show that under the traditional view, the tax changes reduced the marginal effective total tax rate by, under their baseline assumptions, about 4 percentage points, from 33.5 to 29.4 percent. Under the new view (and also accounting for the capital gains tax changes), the new law reduced the user cost from 29.6 to 27.7 percent.

The dividend tax reduction could, through these user cost changes, have a significant effect on investment. In addition, dividend payouts could respond, as could market value. A number of studies have investigated these possibilities.

Relying on a sample that predates the dividend change, Auerbach and Hassett (2003) examine investment financing directly and find considerable heterogeneity in their sample of firms, with capital market access an important factor in determining a firm's likelihood of issuing new shares. Under the new view, which posits that the marginal source of finance is retained earnings, the dividend is a residual and, they show, should be negatively correlated with investment and positively correlated with cash flow once one controls for Q. Under the old view, where the marginal source of finance is new share issues, such a correlation would not exist. They utilize this observation to test the validity of the two views and show that the responsiveness of dividends to cash flow and investment varies significantly across publicly traded US firms. They find that about half of firms seem to have dividend payout behavior consistent with the new view, whereas half appear to be more consistent with the traditional view.

Other studies have also implied that there are significantly more new view firms than might have been suggested in earlier work by Poterba and Summers (1985) that supported the traditional view. For example, Gentry, Kemsley, and Meyer (2003) exploit the unique tax characteristics of Real Estate Investment Trusts and find that dividend taxes are capitalized into share prices, lending support to the new view. Similarly Sialm (2005) uses time series data from 1917 to 2004 and also finds evidence of tax capitalization.

Through the user cost analysis just reviewed, Carroll, Hassett, and Mackie investigate the theoretical impact of dividend tax cuts on investment and find that the cuts reduced the overall cost of capital as well as differentials in user costs across industries. In a parallel piece, Poterba (2004a) prospectively calculated that JGTRRA would gradually increase the long-run level of dividends by 31 percent or $111 billion, a result that is consistent with the traditional view of dividend taxation. A similar increase under the new view might also be possible if the tax reduction is considered by firms to be temporary, as firms would choose to disgorge dividends during the low tax period.

Blouin, Raedy, and Shackelford (2004) find, for a small sample of firms, a statistically significant increase in both regular and special dividend payments following the tax cut. They argue, however, that the tax cut may not be causal. The economy was also improving at this time and investors were increasingly evaluating firms based on dividends, not earnings. Furthermore they find that greater ownership by individuals, the beneficiaries of the tax cut, did not make a company more likely to increase dividends.

Chetty and Saez (2005) document that after declining for over twenty years, the number of firms paying dividends began to increase after the 2003 tax change. The tax cut also encouraged dividend-paying firms to increase their payments, and as a result of these changes, total regular dividend payouts increased by 20 percent within six quarters. They estimate an elasticity of regular dividend payments with respect to the marginal tax rate on dividend income of -0.5, a finding that is robust to controls for a variety of firm characteristics. In contrast, Julio and Ikenberry (2004) find that the increase in dividend-paying firms began in late 2000, but Chetty and Saez (2005) argue that once changes in sample composition are controlled for, the increase did begin in 2003.

Brown, Liang, and Weisbenner (2004) argue that the increase in dividend payouts may have failed to increase total cash flows from firms to shareholders. They show that for many firms, share repurchases tended to decline at the same time. Chetty and Saez (2007) take issue with this interpretation, arguing that the Brown et al. comparison of pre- and post-reform dividend-paying firms is prone to selection bias. The pre-reform firms are an endogenously selected group that chose to pay dividends even before the tax change. Comparing the repurchasing behavior of the two groups of firms is similarly problematic because there is an upward trend in share repurchases among all firms over time. Controlling for the time trend, Chetty and Saez find that firms that initiated dividends after the tax change were actually less likely to have repurchased shares in the previous year, thus reversing the Brown et al. finding. They conclude that further research on share repurchases is necessary to determine the effect of the tax cuts on total payouts to shareholders following the dividend tax cut.

Auerbach and Hassett (2005b) examine the dividend response debate directly with an event study of the stock price response to news about the probability of dividend tax changes. They find that firms with higher dividend yields benefited more than other dividend-paying firms, which could support either the new or the traditional view depending on whether firms believe the tax cut is temporary. Lending support to the new view is additional evidence that non–dividend-paying firms and firms likely to issue new shares experienced a larger share price increase than other firms. This last point is driven by the fact that markets are forward-looking. A tax cut increases the future after-tax value of dividends, which increases the value of the firm today if it is expected that the firm will pay dividends in the future and that the tax cut will last into the future. Furthermore, if a firm is expected to issue new shares in the future, the present value of any future dividends is even greater and thus so is the increase in the value of the firm today.

They also explore whether similar effects could be observed during the 2004 presidential race. In 2004 Senator John Kerry vowed that he would let the dividend tax cut expire, whereas President Bush vowed its extension. Accordingly one might expect that the market would correlate the probability of a Kerry victory with expectations concerning future dividend tax rates. Auerbach and Hassett explore whether results consistent with the event study were also observable during the election by relating stock market outperformance to presidential futures. They find results that confirm the earlier event-study results, but also shed additional light on the dividend tax mechanism. In particular, under the new view, firms with high dividends should outperform when there is news about future dividend tax reductions because they will disgorge a higher percentage of their dividends in the low tax years. Under the traditional view, the lower dividend tax should lower the cost of capital disproportionately for high-dividend firms, giving them a value bonus that should increase with the permanence of the dividend tax cuts. The presidential future results suggest that the bonus to paying high dividends *declined* when the dividend taxes were more likely to be permanently low (i.e., when the probability of Kerry being elected declined), consistent with the new view.

Amromin, Harrison, and Sharpe (2005) interpret these results differently, arguing that the evidence supports the view that dividend taxes are irrelevant. In particular, they argue that share prices for non–dividend-paying firms, and for those likely to issue new shares, outperformed over the entire period, not just during the event days. In addition there was no relative outperformance of the US market relative to foreign markets during that period.

Auerbach and Hassett (2007) extend their earlier work and respond to Amromin et al. Their extension involves an analysis of options data around the 2004 election. When President Bush was elected, it likely conveyed a significant amount of information about the probability that dividend taxes would remain low in the future. Prior to the election, uncertainty about the outcome should have led to a high level of volatility, especially for the firms that should have been most influenced by dividend taxes. This would, they argue, be visible in options prices, which are especially sensitive to volatility. Consistent with this theory, they find that President Bush's re-election, and thus the greater certainty that the tax cuts would be extended, caused a greater decline in volatility for the firms most affected by dividend taxes in their earlier study.

In addition Auerbach and Hassett note that the standard errors for the aggregate runs reported in the Amromin et al. study are so large that they would be unable to detect the full theoretical effect of the dividend tax reductions even under the most aggressive assumptions, and even assuming that the entire effect occurred in one day.

Desai and Goolsbee (2004) also find support for the new view looking at the effect of the dividend tax cuts on investment. In their analysis of the 2003 dividend tax cuts, Desai and Goolsbee take a novel approach by using firm-level investment data to distinguish between the traditional and new views of dividend taxation. They determine that the investment behavior of their sample of firms is consistent with the new view; indeed, their estimates are quite close to those reported by Cummins, Hassett, and Oliner (2006).

To sum up, the dividend tax reduction led to a surge in share prices for firms that was a function of their dividend paying and share issuance behavior, and also to an increase in dividend payouts. The underlying pattern of the former change favors the new view, suggesting that the capital spending effects of the tax cut may be small, unless a surge in investment occurred for immature firms. The surge in dividend payouts would favor the traditional view if the dividend tax reduction were expected to be permanent by dividend-paying firms. If the tax reduction were expected to be temporary, new view firms would also be expected to accelerate their dividends.

4.3.2   Partial Expensing

President Bush signed the JCWAA in March 2002. The law provided a temporary increase in depreciation allowances, in the form of a 30 percent partial expensing provision for business spending on equipment and software. Recent work by Cohen, Hansen, and Hassett (2002) observes that the bonus depreciation lowered the user cost of capital. Since the previous law already allowed firms to accelerate depreciation, and since inflation was relatively low when the law was changed, the effects of the 30 percent expensing were relatively small if expected to be permanent. For example, for seven-year equipment, the effect on the user cost under their baseline assumptions would be a proportional reduction of only 2.5 percent. However, if firms expected the measure to expire, then there would be a strong incentive to pull investment forward in order to qualify for the extra credit. In that case the estimated user cost reduction was much larger, as much as 15 percent relative to the old law. In 2003 JGTRRA increased the bonus depreciation to 50 percent and extended its applicability by a few months. Clearly, a key a priori consideration regarding the effectiveness of these tax measures would be an understanding of the extent to which firms believed the measure would be permanent (in which case the 2.5 percent reduction would apply) or temporary (in which case the larger reduction would apply).

Desai and Goolsbee conclude that the combined tax reductions provided little stimulus to investment. Their argument is not based on an extensive inspection of investment after the tax change, but rather is an inference based on their results and a user cost analysis. They argue that the dividend tax reduction had little effect because of their result favoring the new view (described above), which neutralizes the effect of the dividend tax reduction. They also argue that the user cost effect of the expensing provisions was small, because firms were surprised by its expiration. But if firms knew that the tax cut would expire, then the effects are much larger; indeed, their model predicts almost a 20 percent increase in equipment investment in the expiration year under the most aggressive assumptions.

House and Shapiro (2006, p. 36) take the opposite approach, assuming that firms expected the expiration of the partial expensing provision, and explore the extent to which firms invested heavily in equipment before the expiration occurred. They find that investment increased the most for equipment with a longer recovery period, and that "bonus depreciation had a powerful effect on the composition of investment.... In spite of the sizeable effects on investment, the policy had only modest effects on aggregate employment and output."

As part of their investigation, House and Shapiro study the impact that temporarily higher investment demand should have on capital goods prices. Goolsbee (1998) argues that investment subsidies drive up the price of capital goods because they are inelastically supplied. House and Shapiro show that theoretically, in a closed economy, the price of capital goods should fully reflect the tax subsidy irrespective of the elasticity of supply. They find, however, that this effect is not visible in the data; indeed capital goods prices barely budged while demand was surging because of the credits.

This latter result is consistent with Hassett and Hubbard (1998), who find that the United States is a price taker in the world market for capital goods. Capital goods prices across countries tend to be highly correlated with one another and, at the same time, are uncorrelated with local factors such as tax credits. House and Shapiro argue that the price effects may not be visible in the US data because of internal adjustment costs. An interpretation more consistent with other evidence would be that the price of capital goods did not respond to the US surge in demand because it is set in the world market, and the US surge was not large enough to significantly influence world prices.

Summing up, there is evidence that investment surged prior to the expiration of the partial expensing provision, consistent with behavioral models that emphasize the role of economic fundamentals. In addition capital goods prices were little affected by the reform.

4.4   Recent Developments in the Study of International Taxation and Intangibles

4.4.1   Foreign Direct Investment

It has long been recognized that the US tax code can influence US foreign direct investment—that is, whether and how much US multinational firms choose to invest in their overseas divisions. Multinationals are taxed on income earned both at home and abroad, and can receive a tax credit for tax paid to foreign governments. Foreign income is taxed only upon repatriation to the United States, which gives firms an incentive to earn income in low-tax countries and let it grow tax free in the expectation that future US rates may be lower. The size of the foreign tax credit is limited to the size of firms' US tax liability, which discourages firms somewhat from locating in high-tax countries. The American Jobs Creation Act of 2004 made several changes to the tax treatment of foreign income, including a temporary tax reduction for dividend repatriations. Clausing (2007) argues that these changes make investment in low-tax countries even more desirable.

Clausing further points out that recent research indicates that taxes have a substantial impact on where and how much businesses choose to invest, with the elasticity of foreign investment with respect to taxes generally estimated to be greater than 1. Hines and Gordon (2002) report that studies using aggregate time series data generally estimate a tax elasticity of investment of -0.6, which indicates that a 10 percentage point reduction in the host country tax rate raises foreign direct investment by 6 percent. For studies relying on cross-sectional data, they report elasticities between -0.1 and -2.8, with studies of more recent time periods estimating larger elasticities.

De Mooij and Ederveen (2003) survey the literature on the tax responsiveness of foreign direct investment. They find that the median value of the tax rate elasticity is around -3.3. In 25 studies, the majority of the elasticities are negative, with the average value in a study ranging from -10.9 to $+1.3$. Study characteristics, particularly choice of data, are partly responsible for the considerable variation. Several studies find that the tax responsiveness of FDI has increased over time, likely due to increased globalization. Altshuler, Grubert, and Newlon (2001) find that the elasticity for US multinational corporations grew from -1.5 in 1984 to -2.8 in 1992, a statistically significant difference. Mutti (2003) also documents an increase in tax responsiveness from 1984 to 1992. Desai, Foley, and Hines (2002) suggest that the time trend may be due to the increasing ability of US multinationals to defer the US corporate tax via indirect ownership strategies. If US companies delay paying US taxes on their foreign profits, then foreign tax rates become a more important factor in their investment decisions. Desai, Foley, and Hines find that indirectly owned affiliates are indeed unusually sensitive to tax rate differences.

The downward pressure on corporate tax rates appears to be increasing sharply over time. Devereux, Lockwood, and Redoano (2004) document that nations appear to be engaged in a Nash tax competition, with empirical regularities in the tax data that are consistent with the game-theoretic model they develop. In particular, they argue that countries compete using two tools, the effective marginal tax rate and the statutory tax rate, and have well-defined and statistically significant reaction functions in both dimensions.

Desai, Foley, and Hines (2004) extend the tax responsiveness literature by looking at taxes other than corporate income taxes. They speculate that these "indirect" taxes may be particularly influential because many countries offer tax credits for corporate income taxes paid to foreign governments, but not for other kinds of taxes. They find that investment, as measured by assets, is about equally responsive to indirect taxes and corporate income taxes. A 10 percent higher indirect tax rate corresponds to 7.1 percent fewer assets, and a 10 percent higher corporate income tax rate results in 6.6 percent fewer assets. Both types of taxes are associated with lower output as well, but high income tax rates lower capital–labor ratios and profit rates, and high indirect tax rates do not.

A series of recent papers (Razin, Rubenstein, and Sadka 2004; Razin, Rubenstein, and Sadka 2005; Razin and Sadka 2006) looks at the effect of taxes specifically on bilateral FDI flows. The authors note that some pairs of OECD countries have no FDI flows between them, and to explain this, they develop a model that incorporates a fixed cost to setting up investment. FDI is therefore a two-step process: first, a decision whether to invest, and second, if investment will occur, how much to invest. Different factors may influence the two steps, and indeed, they find that the source country's tax rate mainly affects the selection step, while the destination country's tax rate mainly affects the magnitude of investment. They conclude that the explanation for the direction and magnitude of FDI flows is more complicated than simple tax rate differentials.

In summary, the recent literature suggests that foreign direct investment is sensitive to host country corporate income taxes. Moreover this sensitivity appears to be increasing significantly over time, presumably due to increasing international tax competition. In addition foreign direct investment is affected by indirect taxes. Finally, some recent research is refining models of the investment decision, separating tax effects on the decision to invest in a country from decisions regarding the level of investment once the source country is chosen.

4.4.2   Tax Avoidance: Tax Havens, Income Shifting, Transfer Pricing

International taxes may affect not only the location of investment, but also the location of income, as companies try to earn income in low-tax jurisdictions. "Tax havens" are small, low-tax countries where multinational corporations locate their profits, but typically not their actual business operations. Sullivan (2004a) notes that in 2001, US corporations located 30 percent of their foreign profits in subsidiaries in the top four tax havens, even though those countries accounted for only 5 percent of the productive capacity and 3 percent of the employment of all foreign subsidiaries. Hines (2004) provides similar evidence when he observes that tax havens have less than 1 percent of the world's population (outside the United States) and 2.3 percent of world GDP, but American firms locate 5.7 percent of their foreign employment and 8.4 percent of their foreign property, plants, and equipment in these countries. Sullivan (2004b) adds that tax-motivated profit shifting has accelerated over time: in 1999, the profits of foreign subsidiaries in tax havens were 42.5 percent of all foreign profits; by 2002 the tax haven profit share was nearly 60 percent.

Bartlesman and Beetsma (2003) show, however, that income shifting is not confined to tax havens. They find evidence that differences in corporate tax rates among OECD countries (excluding tax havens Ireland and Switzerland) result in substantial shifting. They estimate that if a country unilaterally raises its taxes, more than 65 percent of the additional revenue will be lost to income shifting—and this is a lower bound of the effect, since it comprises only income shifting due to changes in reported income and does not incorporate the possibility of income shifting via changes in capital structure.

One mechanism for income shifting is tax-motivated transfer pricing, the practice of multinational corporations of arranging intrafirm sales such that most of the profit is made in a low-tax country. As reviewed by Gordon and Hines (2002), most transfer pricing studies rely on indirect evidence, such as measures of profitability or tax liabilities, but there is also some direct evidence.

For example. looking at US pricing data for individual products, Swenson (2001) uses the variation in tariff rates and international corporate taxes over time to identify a strong responsiveness of import prices to tax incentives. Clausing (2003) analyzes monthly international trade prices for US companies and also finds strong direct evidence of tax-motivated transfer pricing. When a country's tax rate is 1 percent lower, the price of intrafirm exports to that country is 1.8 percent lower and the price of intrafirm exports from that country is 2.0 percent higher, consistent with a strategy of trying to earn profits in the location with the lowest taxes.

How big are the effects of all of this shifting? Engen and Hassett (2002) document that capital is mobile enough that there is an apparent Laffer curve in the international tax data. As can be seen in figure 4.2, countries with the largest tax rates generally have the lowest revenue from corporate taxes. This mobility apparently has a commensurate effect on wages. Hassett and Mathur (2006) show that in addition manufacturing wages appear to be highly responsive to capital tax rates, a sign that the flow of capital is significant enough to have a large impact on other fundamentals.

The international evidence of high elasticities that increase over time is an important amendment to the domestic literature. In the past the United States could have been appropriately modeled as a closed economy. Pressures from international tax competition, and increasingly mobile capital are likely key factors affecting the behavior of US firms at the present time.

In sum, empirical evidence suggests that many US multinationals engage in financial manipulations, particularly transfer pricing, designed to increase the share of their profits reported in tax havens and other countries with relatively low tax rates. Indeed, the responsiveness of US multinationals in this area may be sufficiently great that tax

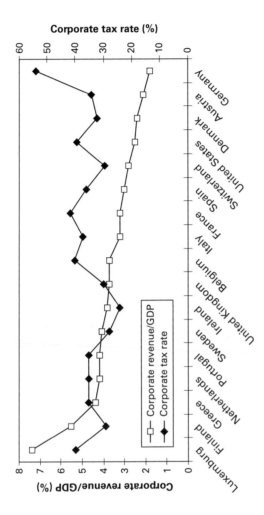

Figure 4.2
Corporate tax rates and corporate revenues in Europe and the United States in 2000 (source: Tax Database and Revenue Statistics, OECD 2002)

rate reductions will lead to revenue increases and significant effects on other variables, including wages.

4.4.3   Intangibles

Recent research suggests that an important source of investment has been overlooked in traditional measures. Corrado, Hulten, and Sichel (2006) point out that most intangibles investment, including R&D, software, and other computerized information, is usually excluded in published macroeconomic data. They estimate that $800 billion of intangibles investment was excluded in 2003, resulting in the exclusion of more than $3 trillion of business intangible capital stock. They further show that this discrepancy in the level of investment affects economic growth estimates. When intangible assets are included, the growth rate of output per hour increases by an estimated 10 to 20 percent, relative to a calculation that ignores intangibles. Moreover investment in intangibles has become more and more important over time. Beginning in the 1990s, the level of investment in intangibles exceeded the level of investment in tangibles, and in the 2000 to 2003 period, intangibles investment was greater than business fixed investment. Also in the 2000 to 2003 period, Corrado, Hulten, and Sichel's revised estimate of output is 12 percent higher than the published measure that excludes most intangibles investment; fifty years ago, the difference was only 5 percent.

Thus investment in intangible is becoming increasingly important over time. Moreover accurate measurement of this component of investment is essential to obtaining improved estimates of output and growth, and is a fertile ground for future research.

4.5   Conclusion

Recent tax reforms have provided researchers with new opportunities to investigate the responsiveness of investment to tax policy. The new literature suggests that the user cost of capital is statistically significant in investment equations, while deemphasizing liquidity as an explanation for the year-to-year variation in investment. The latter result, however, may simply reflect the fact that the most recent data do not include economic times that are harsh enough for liquidity constraints to be binding with a significant probability. The recent literature also suggests that relatively simple quadratic models of adjustment costs may be inadequate, especially for large changes in investment.

Several studies have also reexamined the longstanding debate between the new and traditional views of dividend taxation. In particular, given the user cost elasticities estimated in the recent literature and the user cost analysis of recent tax changes in the United States, one would not expect the recently enacted dividend tax reductions to lead to a surge in business fixed investment. This is because the new view of dividend taxation, which implies little marginal effect of dividend taxes on the user cost, appears to be favored by the latest research. The expiration of partial expensing has been found to have led to a significant but not outsized surge in capital spending with little effect on capital goods prices.

Finally, recent research suggests that tax factors are an important determinant of foreign direct investment, and that this dependence has been increasing over time. Also, while our understanding of the determinants of business fixed investment has advanced in recent years, it has ironically become increasingly less important in a growth accounting sense, as businesses now invest more in intangibles than they do in fixed capital. Our understanding of the determinants of intangible investment is significantly less developed, and an urgent focus of future research.

Discussion

Robert S. Chirinko

Applied economists crave variation. It allows researchers to cut through the difficult, sometimes intractable, identification problems that hamper estimation and inference. Substantial variation in the economic environment can shed light on the key parameters that impact policy analysis. For tax economists the last few years have been particularly fortuitous. Congress has enacted two important pieces of legislation that change incentives affecting business financial and real behavior and hence may prove very useful to applied researchers.[1]

Business spending on plant and equipment capital was stimulated by the Job Creation and Worker Assistance Act of 2002 (JCWAA/ 2002) that introduced partial expensing (or "bonus depreciation"). Specifically, JCWAA/2002 allowed 30 percent of capital costs to be expensed immediately and the balance deducted against taxable income according to pre–2002 depreciation schedules. The Jobs and Growth Tax Relief Reconciliation Act of 2003 (JGTRRA/2003) increased the partial expensing percentage from 30 to 50 percent. Both pieces of legislation lowered the user cost of capital and increased the incentive to invest. This incentive was particularly acute because the legislation was temporary at the time it was enacted.[2]

Firm financial decisions were also affected by the temporary lowering of the top marginal tax rates on dividends and capital gains to 15 percent in JGTRRA/2003. These changes affected the relative desirability of retaining and distributing funds, and thus they may generate insights into the relevance of the "traditional" and "new" views of dividend taxation.

While there are several noteworthy features in this survey by Kevin A. Hassett and Kathryn Newmark (hereafter H&N), perhaps the key contribution is that the authors update and expand the extensive survey of Hassett and Hubbard (2002) with the new empirical evidence generated in the wake of recent tax legislation. Following the template proposed by the editors of this volume, I will organize my comments on what is *known* and *unknown* concerning two topics covered by H&N (the user cost of capital and production function parameters) and a third timely topic relevant for understanding the effects of tax policies (corporate governance). I conclude with a discussion about what is *unknowable* and how this ongoing uncertainty should impact tax policy analysis.

User Cost of Capital

As with virtually all studies of tax incentives and business capital formation, H&N translate legislated tax policies into economic incentives with the user cost of capital introduced by Dale Jorgenson in 1963 and developed and expanded by, among others, Gravelle (1994), Hall and Jorgenson (1971), Jorgenson and Yun (2001), and King and Fullerton (1984). This concept is based on the equivalence between renting and owning a durable asset. With this insight, durable capital can be assigned a rental price that is easy to measure and analyze with the traditional tools of price theory.

While the general user cost framework is *known*, there appears to be a good deal of slippage between legislated tax polices and the specific variables entering the user cost. At least three *unknown* elements disrupt the construction of the user cost. First, the relevant marginal source of finance is uncertain. Capital expenditures can be financed from retained earnings (internal equity), debt, or new equity shares (external equity). Pecking order and trade-off theories of capital structure suggest that the marginal cost of finance differs among these three sources. For many firms, debt is the marginal source of finance, and in this case neither the corporate income tax (Stiglitz 1973) nor personal taxes on equity income affect capital formation.

Using an alternative formulation, many authors model finance costs as a weighted-average of debt and equity. In this case equity finance costs may be responsive to the personal tax changes in JGTRRA/2003 that decreased tax rates on dividends and capital gains. Under the traditional view of dividend taxation, these changes will decrease the user cost. By contrast, the new view predicts that the decrease in taxes will be capitalized into share prices and have no effect on capital formation. Which effect prevails depends on whether the marginal source of finance is from new equity issues (traditional view) or retained earnings (new view). Auerbach and Hassett (2003) find that firm behavior is evenly split between traditional and new views. H&N update these conclusions in light of the 2002 and 2003 tax acts and report that, on balance, the evidence favors the new view.

A second challenge to the user cost framework is presented by temporary tax incentives. The framework is suited for analyzing changes between steady-states and is not fully appropriate for studying the temporary tax changes enacted recently. How variables that reflect temporary tax stimuli should enter the user cost formula is far from clear. Moreover adjustment costs and other frictions weigh heavily on how quickly firms can respond to temporary incentives and, as noted by H&N, opinions vary widely about the importance of these frictions.

International taxation introduces a third set of complications. As discussed by H&N and by Altshuler and Grubert in this volume, tax havens, income shifting, and transfer pricing, inter alia, are used by firms in order to minimize tax payments. These actions undermine the usefulness of the user cost concept.

The implication of these and other unknowns is to induce measurement error in the user cost variable. When user cost measurement error takes a benign form as random fluctuations around a true value, the responsiveness of capital formation to tax policy and other stimuli are understated. However, more complicated forms of measurement error lead to ambiguous results concerning the impact on the estimated user cost coefficient. The quantitative importance of measurement error in the user cost remains largely unstudied. In one exception, Ballentine (1986) reports that only 8.1 percent of the dollar volume of corporate tax increases in the 1986 Tax Act (over a five-year period) is reflected in the variables entering the user cost of capital. Measurement error associated with the user cost of capital may be sizable.

Production Function Parameters

As with the concept of the user cost of capital, production functions describing long-run behavior are *known* by economists. Such functions include the Cobb-Douglas with its potentially restrictive assumption of an elasticity of substitution between capital and labor of unity, the more general constant elasticity of substitution (CES) production function that relaxes this constraint, and the class of flexible functional forms (e.g., the translog) that allows an ever more general pattern of substitution possibilities among factors of production. These production relations are important for tax policy analysis because of their central role in translating changes in tax incentives into changes in capital formation.

What remain *unknown* are the values of the parameters that characterize these production functions. Recovering substitution and scale parameters is a difficult task. With respect to capital taxation, the most frequent approach is to use investment data related to user cost and sales variables. Several factors mentioned by H&N—adjustment costs, financing constraints, Q and equity market misvaluations, and the slope of the supply curve of capital—make estimation of investment relations difficult, thus compromising the ability of investment models to deliver reliable estimates of relevant production function parameters.

More recent studies rely on micro data and econometric specifications to raise the signal-to-noise ratio in the variables entering the model.[3] Cummins, Hassett, and Hubbard (1994) take an innovative approach. They focus on those years in which there are sizable tax policy changes to mitigate concerns about endogeneity and measurement error (the latter discussed above with respect to the user cost). In their study, cross-sectional variation is key, and they report a substantial response of investment to the user cost. A second approach to mitigating the distorting effects of complex dynamics is pursued by Caballero, Engel, and Haltiwanger (1995). They exploit the innovative idea that distortions from short-run dynamics can be overcome by estimating production function parameters in a cointegrating equation that includes capital, output, and user cost variables. They report a substantial response of capital formation to the user cost; the elasticity of substitution between capital and labor is near unity. Lower estimates of the critical substitution elasticity are obtained by Chirinko, Fazzari, and Meyer (2007), who use long-run averages to estimate long-run variables (an approach based on spectral analysis). Their preferred estimate is about half as large as those reported by Cummins et al. and Caballero et al. Despite recent work with micro data, uncertainty remains about the value of key production function parameters.

Even if the micro parameters are *known* with a reasonable degree of certainty, their macro implications remain *unknown*. Consider the situation where several industries are characterized by zero substitution elasticities between capital and labor (i.e., Leontief fixed coefficients technologies). In the face of a stimulative tax policy, the aggregate capital stock may well change because of decreases in marginal costs and output prices that depend positively on the capital intensity of production. Thus economic activity may shift toward capital-intensive sectors, and the aggregate capital stock may respond to the tax policy. Aggregation questions received much attention in the macroeconomic growth literature in the 1960s and 1970s, though without a very constructive set of results (see the recent survey by Felipe and Fisher 2003). Those questions remain open and important.

Corporate Governance

As we were reminded by events in Houston (the trials of Kenneth Lay and Jeffrey Skilling) concurrent with the Baker Institute conference at which the papers in this volume were first presented, corporate governance problems pervade modern economies. Since the beginning of the twentieth century, new production technologies have necessitated large-scale operations to achieve minimum optimal scale and, in turn, have created the interrelated problems of obtaining substantial amounts of financial capital and employing the specialized talents of professional managers. The widely held public corporation arose as a solution to these problems. But it also resulted in the separation of beneficial ownership from corporate control and the emergence of important monitoring problems. Divergent incentives and asymmetric information between owners and managers give rise to governance problems (see Shleifer and Vishny 1997 for a survey). For example, the free cash-flow model of Jensen (1986) emphasizes how the different interests of managers and owners/shareholders leads managers to pursue projects that, when evaluated at the market discount rate used by shareholders, have negative net present value. As shown in Chirinko and Schaller (2004), the impact of agency problems can be assessed in terms of this wedge between effective and shareholders' discount rates. For firms most likely to be affected by Jensen agency problems, investment behavior appears to be guided by discount rates that are substantially lower than the market rate. The differential is between 350 and 400 basis points, thus lowering the user cost of capital guiding investment decisions.

While corporate governance problems are *known*, their impacts on tax policy evaluations remain largely *unknown*. Three cases are considered here. First, interpretations of the movement in the user cost in response to tax policy changes may be inaccurate in the presence of corporate governance problems. If the effective discount rate is less than the market discount rate and if this wedge is ignored in tax policy evaluations, then variations in the user cost will be understated and the implied elasticity with respect to capital formation overstated. Moreover the extent of these biases will vary across firms facing differing degrees of agency problems.

Second, as emphasized by H&N, whether firms are neoclassical or finance constrained has a major impact on tax policy evaluations. Tests that discriminate between the two models of firm behavior depend on variations in the discount rate (the bias mentioned above) or in cash flow. In the latter case agency problems create an important ambiguity. Is a positive response of investment to cash flow to be interpreted as a relaxation of finance constraints or as overinvestment driven by agency problems?

Third, the response of dividend decisions to taxes is important for discriminating between the traditional and new views of dividend taxation. However, dividends also play a role in attenuating agency problems by forcing misbehaving managers to release cash to shareholders. This additional role compromises tests of taxes and dividend behavior. The multiple ways in which governance problems can distort tax policy evaluations remain to be studied.

What Is Unknowable?

One can remain optimistic that future research will reduce, perhaps substantially, the number and extent of the unknowns discussed in these comments. However, despite best efforts, consensus values of key parameters and relations are likely to remain *unknowable*. Respectable disagreements by respectable researchers are likely to persist over ranges of parameters and modeling choices playing key roles in tax policy analysis.

The durability of this range of uncertainty has important implications for policy evaluations. Given the range of acceptable parameter estimates, definitive simulation results simply do not exist. Rather, tax policy analysis needs to be undertaken with a range of values.[4] The recently released study by the Office of Tax Policy Analysis, US Department of the Treasury (2006) is a splendid example of such sensitivity analysis. They report base case results for permanently extending several tax cuts initially enacted under EGTRRA/2001, JCWAA/2002, and JGTRRA/2003. Sensitivity analysis is then performed on two options for financing permanent tax cuts and on several key parameters—the intertemporal substitution elasticity for consumption and leisure, intratemporal substitution elasticity between leisure and consumption, the share of leisure in the time endowment, the rate of time preference, and the substitution elasticity between housing and nonhousing goods.

The Office of Tax Policy Analysis is to be applauded for bringing models on the research frontier to bear on policy evaluations and for undertaking sensitivity analysis. Unfortunately, one key parameter was not varied—the elasticity of substitution between capital and labor. As noted above, the range of estimates of this production function parameter remains wide. Moreover this substitution elasticity looms large in tax policy evaluations. For example, Engen, Gravelle, and Smetters (1997) simulate replacing a comprehensive income tax with a consumption tax, and report that, when the substitution elasticity is 1.0, net output would increase by 6.80 percent in the steady state. However, when this substitution elasticity is lowered to 0.50, the gain in welfare as measured by net output is only 3.80 percent. As reviewed in Chirinko (2002, tab 2), this substantial response of welfare improvements is repeated in other tax simulation models. Interestingly, the model conceptually closest to that used recently by the Treasury has a decline in welfare (due to the lower substitution elasticity) that is only 25 percent as large as that of Engen et al. All of this suggests the need for further investigation of the inner workings of these models by means of simulations.

Tax policy evaluations are sensitive to several underlying parameters and modeling choices. The range of reasonable models and parameter values is likely to remain wide. Given the durability of this range, techniques need to be developed for systematically quantifying model uncertainty. Such techniques might prove particularly useful in tax simulation models that, for the foreseeable future, will be shrouded by an important set of unknowables.

Discussion

Timothy S. Gunning

Hassett and Newmark provide a thorough literature review. They address a variety of developments in the economic literature on the determinants of investment behavior and link recent theoretical insights to subsequent empirical applications. One of their more significant contributions is their interpretation of the ongoing debate regarding whether adjustment costs are an important determinant of investment behavior and, if so, how to determine the nature of adjustment costs and their magnitudes. They also discuss recent work that provides empirical support for the often-maligned "new view" of the effects of dividend taxation, which concludes that dividend taxes have no incentive effects on investments financed with retained earnings.

Hassett and Newmark begin with a discussion of the path-breaking work of Hall and Jorgensen (1967), who showed that as long as investors expect tax laws to remain unchanged and there are no adjustment costs or investment tax credits, the maximization of the present discounted value of after-corporate-tax cash flow over an infinite horizon implies that the before-tax nominal value of the gross marginal product of capital today simply equals the current user cost of capital. They trace the literature to the more recent work of Auerbach (1983b, 1989a), which extended the analysis to allow for costly capital stock adjustment and showed that higher adjustment costs imply higher weights on future one-period user costs. They also note the seminal theoretical contributions of Hayashi (1982) and Summers (1981b), who integrated models of investment behavior in the presence of adjustment costs with models based on Tobin's Q-theory of investment. Hassett and Newmark observe that an early dilemma in this literature was that empirical implementations of these theories initially yielded estimates of adjustment costs that were implausibly high. However, more recently, Cummins, Hassett, and Hubbard (1994) obtained lower and thus more

plausible estimates by correcting for the measurement error attributable either to mismeasurement of macroeconomic fundamentals, such
as benchmark rates of interest and depreciation, or model misspecifica-
tion within the neoclassical framework. Hassett and Newmark also
discuss the well-known work of Bernanke, Bohn, and Riess (1988) that
described the evolution of "accelerator" models, which imply that investment growth is determined primarily by output growth. A useful
extension of the Hassett-Newmark chapter would be a more detailed
analysis of how these accelerator models compare to those constructed
in the early Q-theory literature, especially the contributions of Hayashi
(1982) and Summers (1981b).

Hassett and Newmark also thoroughly address the issue of whether
the standard neoclassical Q-theory model of investment behavior or
alternative models based on available cash flow better explain investment behavior. The authors support the view that the Q-theory
approach is far superior, as long as Q is accurately measured using
economic fundamentals rather than stock market value of the firm,
since the latter tends to have rapid fluctuations that lead to a great
deal of noise in estimation. From the standpoint of tractability, the
authors' approach is far more convenient than developing a dynamic
model that controls for time fluctuations or uses a more sophisticated
estimation technique that may compromise the number of degrees of
freedom. Nevertheless, it should be noted that while stock market fluctuations are econometrically inconvenient, they are a reflection of investment value. Bond and Cummins (2001) attempted to demonstrate
how the present discounted value of securities analysts' earnings forecasts can be used in a GMM (general method of moments) setting to
control for the source of measurement error, resulting in estimates on
the order of 0.03 to 0.10 for average Q. It appears that much of the debate can be reconciled by a method of moments approach. A standard
GMM approach has a history of increasing explanatory power and
does not rely on cash flows, as noted in Erickson and Whited (2000); it
would thus be appropriate to re-estimate Q based on a GMM approach.

Hassett and Newmark also highlight the work of Cooper and Ejarque (2001, 2003), who showed that market power is the source of cash-
flow effects rather than market imperfections. If it can be shown that
there are cash-flow effects in perfect markets, then it may be possible
that traditional market imperfections may not have much of an impact
on the measurement of Q. Furthermore, since the financing constraint

model has essentially presumed that market distortions are the source of the cash-flow effect rather than market power, it would be instructive to revisit the benchmark literature taking into account these recent advances in the literature.

Hassett and Newmark next review the voluminous literature on adjustment costs. Unfortunately, this literature has not fully reconciled past differences in estimation or parameter determination. While the literature has explored a broad array of potential inefficiencies and measurement problems, ranging from nonconvexity to investment irreversibility, it is still not obvious that the rudimentary assumptions and resulting model of Hall and Jorgensen (1967) are necessarily a poor depiction of the impact that the adjustment cost parameter has on economic inefficiencies. There seems to be little determination of what a reasonable value of the marginal adjustment cost parameter is, or what additional adjustment costs there are to consider. Hassett and Newmark note the possibility that early neoclassical model extensions did not model adjustment costs correctly. If that is the case, the examination of cash-flow effects and the choice of model estimation will not identify the source of adjustment cost distortion. While they briefly discuss a variety of alternative adjustment cost approaches, it would be highly instructive to develop further whether cash-flow effects are a driving force behind adjustment cost determination, or an ancillary result.

Hassett and Newmark also summarize the debate between the "new view" and "traditional view," and describe a body of research that has recently reopened the debate regarding which of these two views better describes the economic effects of dividend taxes. They conclude that empirical evidence suggests that the recent dividend tax reduction led to a surge in share prices for firms that pay relatively high dividends and that it also led to an increase in dividend payouts. It would be useful for these authors to investigate further whether these results favor the traditional view or the new view.

In summary, Hassett and Newmark provide an informative depiction of taxation and its effects on business investment behavior, including the impact of adjustment costs and the economic effects of dividend taxes. Their chapter gives an excellent and up-to-date review of this literature and will no doubt be a valuable guide to the theoretical and empirical literature on this crucial issue. Yet the chapter also illustrates the many questions that still confound researchers in this field. When calculating Q, should the estimation procedure be based on stock market values or fundamentals? How important are adjustment costs? What are the effects of alternative forms of adjustment costs and how important are adjustment costs in predicting the effects of tax policy changes? Does the empirical evidence on the recent dividend tax reductions support the new view or the traditional view? These questions are longstanding, but nevertheless still pressing, and are likely to engage researchers for many years to come. The comprehensive analysis of the investment literature presented by Hassett and Newmark will no doubt greatly illuminate many of the guideposts along the way.

Notes

1. The Economic Growth and Tax Relief Reconciliation Act of 2001 (EGTRRA/2001) was also enacted in recent years. However, unlike the other two pieces of legislation, EGTRRA/2001 did not directly affect business decisions.

2. The rate decreases were set to expire in 2008 but have been extended to 2010 in the Tax Increase Prevention and Reconciliation Act of 2005 (passed in July 2006).

3. See Chirinko (forthcoming) for a review of the estimates of substitution.

4. In his contribution to this volume, Harberger notes the need for assessments based on a range of parameter values with respect to the simulation results of Gravelle and Smetters (2001).

5 Consumption Tax Reform: Changes in Business Equity and Housing Prices

John W. Diamond and George R. Zodrow

Fundamental tax reform, often defined as replacing the income tax with some form of consumption-based taxation, has been discussed in both academic and policy circles in the United States for some time. The 2005 report of the President's Advisory Panel on Federal Income Tax Reform discussed a consumption-based tax—the Progressive Consumption Tax (PCT) option, modeled after the X-tax created by the late David Bradford (1986, 2005)—at length but ultimately decided against recommending this alternative.[1] Proponents of consumption-based reforms argue that they would generate a variety of benefits, and there is a voluminous literature examining the relative advantages and disadvantages of income and consumption taxes in terms of efficiency (especially with respect to reducing tax biases against saving and investment and promoting economic growth), horizontal and vertical equity (including views of vertical equity that take a lifetime rather than an annual perspective), and simplicity in administration and compliance.[2]

These familiar issues will not be revisited in this chapter. Rather, the focus of this study is on an analysis of two transitional issues that often arise in discussions of the feasibility of consumption tax reforms: (1) the potential reform-induced decline in the price of owner-occupied housing attributable to the enactment of a consumption tax that eliminates the preferential tax treatment of housing under the current income tax, and (2) the tendency of such a reform to impose a one-time windfall loss on the owners of existing business equity capital. These issues have played an important and controversial role in the tax reform debate. Some observers have argued that the prospect of large reform-induced windfall losses would create a huge impediment to the enactment of reform. In marked contrast, others have stressed that such losses create the potential for larger long-run efficiency gains from reform while simultaneously mitigating the distributional problems associated with the lower marginal tax rates at the top of the income distribution and the generous treatment of capital income that characterize a consumption tax. The flat tax is the primary reform considered in this chapter because it (as well as its variants such as the X-tax) is among the most often-discussed consumption tax proposals, its enactment is believed to raise the most troublesome transitional issues among the various consumption-based tax reform options, and it is the main reform analyzed in existing studies of the effects of fundamental reform on the housing values (Gravelle 1996; Capozza, Green, and Hendershott 1996).

An analysis of the transitional effects of implementing a flat tax provides an excellent example of the central theme of this volume—attempting to discern what is known, unknown, and unknowable about the desirability of enacting fundamental tax reform in the United States. Some might argue that the magnitudes of such transitional effects are inherently unknowable—that there is simply too much uncertainty regarding the appropriate modeling of economic behavior and the existing empirical estimates of key parameters that describe individual behaviors that are necessary to construct reasonable estimates of these effects, at least in the foreseeable future.[3] Although we recognize these difficulties, our own perspective is that it is preferable to view continuing efforts to model economic behavior as gradually moving us along a spectrum from the unknown to the known, even if the latter can never be fully attained. In particular, as economic models capture more elements of reality and empirical estimates of behavioral parameters are further refined, the range of what is unknown about the effects of fundamental tax reform, including its transitional effects, will be narrowed. The evolution over time of such analyses is a critical element in the policy making process. It is clear that if policy makers wait for definitive answers about what is known about the effects of fundamental tax reform, the status quo will simply be enshrined forever. However, enough is known about the problems of the existing income tax system that maintaining the status quo is not an attractive option. Accordingly movements along the spectrum from the unknown toward the known will clarify, and perhaps strengthen, the case for fundamental reform, and help to define which approach to reform is the most appropriate. Beyond that, it remains to be seen whether at some point it will be perceived by most observers that enough is known about the effects of fundamental tax reform to make it a reasonable and advisable course of action.

Part of this process is reflected in a wide variety of studies that have examined the effects of consumption tax reforms, some of which have considered transitional effects, and define what is currently known and unknown about these effects. For example, Auerbach (1996) and Altig, Auerbach, Kotlikoff, Smetters, and Walliser (2001)—hereafter AAKSW—use computable general equilibrium simulation models to compare the effects of revenue neutral moves from an income tax to several potential consumption-based tax systems, including estimates of the transitional effects of such a reform on asset prices. These models are significantly extended versions of the Auerbach-Kotlikoff (1987) model, and include 12 income groups within each of 55 age cohorts, a Social Security and Medicare system, an endogenous bequest motive, and various existing tax preferences under the income tax. However, these models are characterized by a single production sector and thus cannot be used to estimate reform-induced effects on housing values or other disaggregated asset price effects. In contrast, the model constructed by Fullerton and Rogers (1993)—hereafter FR—has many sectors including housing; however, the FR model is not well suited to the analysis of transitional issues because it calculates equilibria only once every five years after the enactment of reform and, by assuming myopic expectations, tends to systematically overstate transitional problems. Several other studies, including Capozza, Green, and Hendershott (1996)—hereafter CGH—Bruce and Holtz-Eakin (1999)—hereafter BHE—and Gravelle (1996), analyze the effects of consumption taxes on house values, but do so only in the context of partial equilibrium models.

The model constructed in this chapter is designed to expand what is known about the transitional effects of consumption tax reform, by examining the effects of the enactment of a flat tax on the prices of both housing and other capital assets in the context of a fully specified general equilibrium model. The analytical framework is a perfect foresight dynamic overlapping generations model with no uncertainty and three production sectors—a composite consumption good, owner-occupied housing and rental housing. Asset price effects—for both types of housing and for business equity—are calculated explicitly. Equilibria are calculated for every year after the enactment of a reform (which is assumed to be permanent) so that the transition path of the

economy can be observed in annual increments. However, unlike the
AAKSW and FR models, the model utilized in this chapter has not
yet been extended to include multiple income groups within each
generation.[4]

Our simulation results on the changes in business equity and housing prices associated with the enactment of a consumption-based flat
tax reform can be summarized as follows: The reform results in a long-
run increase in GDP of nearly 5 percent, long-run increases in investment that range from about 2 percent in owner-occupied housing to
between 15 and 17 percent in the other two production sectors, and a
long-run increase in welfare of nearly 3 percent. However, these gains
come at the expense of one-time windfall losses experienced by the
(primarily elderly) owners of business equity. These losses are greater
than those predicted in some other recent studies, but not nearly as
large as those predicted by partial equilibrium models that ignore a
wide variety of factors that tend to mitigate asset price declines in our
general equilibrium model. These results suggest special transition
rules should be used with caution, especially since they significantly
reduce the long-run gains obtained from reform. Nevertheless, a reasonably strong case for transitional relief can be made for business
assets with large amounts of remaining basis, especially in the rental
housing sector. Our analysis also suggests that the negative effects on
house values of reducing tax preferences for owner-occupied housing
under a flat tax would be relatively small once all general equilibrium
effects are taken into account. Finally, it is interesting to note that the
effects of adjustment costs—at least if they are symmetric across production sectors—tend to cancel, as higher adjustment costs mitigate
the fall in the value of business equity but exacerbate declines in the
values of owner-occupied housing, in both cases by slowing down
the reallocation of capital from owner-occupied housing to the other
production sectors. Thus explicitly accounting for such differential asset price effects is essential to accurately estimating the welfare effects
of fundamental tax reform.

The chapter is organized as follows: In section 5.1, we consider the
nature of the windfall tax on the owners of existing business equity
capital that tends to occur under a consumption tax, and in section 5.2,
we discuss the potential effects of a consumption-based tax reform on
the price of owner-occupied housing. In section 5.3, we outline the
model we use in the study (with details of the model and the calibration of the initial equilibrium provided in an appendix). In section 5.4,

we discuss the simulation results, and in section 5.5, we conclude and suggest directions for future research.

5.1   Effects on the Prices of Business Assets

Much of the concern about the transition from the current income tax to a consumption tax has focused on the potential one-time windfall loss imposed on the owners of existing capital assets (other than owner-occupied housing). For example, under the flat tax, allowing expensing is equivalent in present value to exempting from taxation the normal rate of return on all new investments. However, in the absence of transition rules under the flat tax, firms would not be allowed to deduct the remaining basis of existing assets, although the returns earned by such assets (and the proceeds of asset sales) would be included in the tax base. As a result the rate of return on existing assets would fall relative to the return on new investments, and arbitrage across new and existing assets would imply that the value of existing assets would fall; Gravelle (1996) constructs a simple model in which the decline is proportional to the rate of tax. Moreover, as long as the general price level remained unchanged under the flat tax, lenders would be insulated from this loss since the nominal value of outstanding bonds would be fixed; thus the entire reform-induced one-time windfall loss would be borne by business equity holders.[5] (Note that owners of owner-occupied housing would not be subject to this particular one-time tax; under both the existing income tax and the flat tax, owner-occupiers are neither taxed on the imputed rents from owner-occupied housing nor allowed expensing or depreciation deductions for housing purchases, and completely or largely escape the tax on capital gains from home sales.)

However, as described by Zodrow (2002), this analysis ignores a wide variety of other factors associated with the implementation of a flat tax that can affect existing business capital owners; most of these can be expected to reduce the one-time windfall tax on existing assets or offset its negative welfare effects. A partial list of these factors—all of which are considered in our model—includes (1) the costs of adjusting the capital stock, which would allow the owners of capital to earn above-normal returns on both existing assets and new investments during the period of transition to the new postreform equilibrium,[6] (2) a short-run (and perhaps a long-run) increase in the after-tax rate of interest, which would allow the owners of capital to earn a higher after-tax rate of return on existing assets and new investments, (3) the reduction under a lower rate flat tax of the expected tax on assets that were allowed accelerated depreciation allowances, including "bonus depreciation" and expensing of investments in research and development or advertising, under the current income tax,[7] and (4) the efficiency gains obtained from eliminating distortions of saving and investment decisions and reducing distortions of the labor–leisure choices, as well as from improvements in the allocation of capital across business sectors.[8]

Several studies have attempted to predict the net effect of some of these factors on asset values. For example, AAKSW find that the implementation of the flat tax reduces average asset values in the year of the reform by 3.6 percent when adjustment costs are considered, and by 10 percent in the absence of adjustment costs. Auerbach (1996) finds that implementing a flat tax would cause average asset values to decline initially by 5.7 percent without adjustment costs but to increase by 3 percent in the presence of adjustment costs. These findings suggest that the magnitude of the reform-induced windfall losses imposed on business equity assets are much smaller, and may even be fully offset, once the factors noted above are considered.

Note that these findings do not consider potentially important differences in reform-induced asset price changes across different types of assets. This is especially true for the case of owner-occupied housing, where the reform-induced asset price changes are fundamentally different than those for other assets. In addition capital reallocation across sectors coupled with adjustment costs play an important role in determining the asset price effects that arise when existing and new investments earn above normal rates of return during the transition to the postreform equilibrium.

5.2   Effects on the Price of Owner-Occupied Housing

A second contentious issue associated with implementing a consumption-based tax reform is its potentially negative effect on the price of owner-occupied housing. As noted previously, such a price decline is not a special case of the one-time reform-induced levy on business equity capital. Rather, this price decline is due to a reform-induced increase in the user cost of housing, as perceived by the owner-occupier, which arises primarily because (1) normal returns to business equity investments are effectively untaxed under the flat tax, making such investments relatively more attractive and raising the opportunity cost of equity-financed investment in owner-occupied housing, and (2) deductions for mortgage interest and property taxes are eliminated.[9] The increase in the user cost of owner-occupied housing that would occur under the flat tax would tend to reduce the demand for owner-occupied housing, which in turn would tend to result in a decline in the price of owner-occupied housing in the short run. In the long run the quantity of housing and the cost of housing would return to an equilibrium reflecting production costs, including the cost of land, and the absence of taxation.

Several analysts have commented on the impact of consumption tax reforms on housing prices, and the range of predicted effects is large. An analysis conducted by Data Resources Incorporated (Brinner et al. 1995) predicts that the present value of the loss of mortgage interest and property tax deductions alone would cause the aggregate value of owner-occupied housing to decline by 15 percent. CGH (1996) predict that implementing a flat tax would reduce owner-occupied housing prices by an average of 20 percent, assuming that interest rates fall by one percentage point. By comparison, Gravelle (1996) and BHE (1999) argue that both the short-run and the long-run effects of a flat tax on housing prices would be fairly small. Similarly Hall (1997) argues that implementation of the flat tax would result in a rather modest decline in the aggregate price of housing, assuming a two percentage point decline in the interest rate.

The case for large consumption tax reform-induced declines in housing prices is illustrated by CGH (1996). They estimate the reform-induced change in the price of owner-occupied housing using an asset market equilibrium model that incorporates a perfectly inelastic supply of residential land. Given this assumption, a change in the tax treatment of owner-occupied housing must be fully capitalized into the price of owner-occupied housing. Their model predicts that implementing the flat tax at a rate of 17 percent, with the before-tax rate of interest held constant, would reduce owner-occupied housing prices by an average of 29 percent. However, since they believe some reduction in interest rates is likely, they report that the average house price would decline by 20 (9) percent if the before-tax interest rate declines by 1 (2) percentage point(s).[10]

Other studies cast doubt on such large price declines, and shift the focus to the dynamic factors that would mitigate the effects of a consumption tax reform on the price of housing. For example, BHE (1999) employ a dynamic simulation model of the owner-occupied housing market that is capable of analyzing the partial equilibrium transition path of enacting a flat tax on the price of owner-occupied housing.[11] In their model, housing supply is modeled using a Cobb-Douglas production function that depends on inputs of structures and land, thus capturing the fact, stressed by CGH (1999, that the supply response of land is more inelastic than the supply response of structures. They assume an elasticity of supply for land equal to 0.2 and an elasticity of supply for structures equal to 0.8.[12] Their results indicate that the short-run impact of enacting a 17 percent flat tax, assuming the before-tax rate of interest is constant, would be a 10 percent increase in the nominal price of owner-occupied housing. This implies that the real price of owner-occupied housing would decline by roughly 6 percent. In the long run a smaller stock of capital would be employed in the production of owner-occupied housing and nominal housing prices would increase by 17 percent, leaving real housing prices unchanged. Most of the adjustment in this model occurs within ten years of the reform.[13]

Gravelle (1996) also finds that switching to a flat tax would likely have a small effect on the price of owner-occupied housing in the short run and a very small effect in the long run. She argues that several factors would mitigate the decline in the price of owner-occupied housing in the short run. These factors include reductions in new construction, the propensity for owners to temporarily remove existing houses from the market in response to temporary price declines, the conversion of owner-occupied houses to rental houses, and short-run technology and capacity constraints that limit profitable investment in other sectors.

Starting with a set of worst-case assumptions—the supply of housing is perfectly inelastic, housing demand is unit elastic, and the before-tax interest rate is constant—Gravelle finds that owner-occupied housing prices would fall by 22 percent. Modifying the assumptions to reflect the fact that the short-run supply of housing is not perfectly inelastic and that interest rates are likely to decline if a flat tax were implemented moderates the decline in the price of housing. If the elasticity of supply for owner-occupied housing is increased from zero to 0.5, the decline in housing prices is reduced from 22 to 13 percent. If the supply of housing is unit elastic and the interest rate falls by one percentage point, then the decline in the price of owner-occupied housing is reduced from 22 to 5 percent. Gravelle argues that in the long run the impact of a consumption tax reform on the price of owner-occupied housing is likely to be very small since the supply of housing is more elastic in the long run.

The housing component of the model used in this paper captures most of the important factors discussed by Brinner et al. (1995), CGH (1996), BHE (1999), and Gravelle (1996). The model explicitly accounts for changes in the level of new investment and the reallocation of the existing capital stock across the business and both owner-occupied and rental housing sectors, and examines the effects of the costs of adjusting the capital stock. In addition changes in consumer demands across rental and owner-occupied housing, including changes attributable to the elimination of deductibility of home mortgage interest and property taxes, as well as changes in demands for the composite good, are considered. It should be noted, however, that a weakness of the approach used in the model is that land is not modeled explicitly. Instead, the difficulties of converting land used initially for owner-occupied housing to other uses are captured indirectly by including the costs of adjusting the housing capital stock in the analysis. These costs are assumed to be symmetric—that is, to follow the same quadratic pattern for both declines and increases in investment, relative to the steady state level—and reflect the costs of reducing the level of new investment, reducing the level of replacement investment, converting owner-occupied housing to rental housing, and finally, if necessary, converting owner-occupied housing to production of the composite good.

5.3   Model Structure and Calibration

The distinguishing feature of the analytical approach used in this chapter is the treatment of owner-occupied and rental housing markets in the context of a dynamic overlapping-generations life-cycle computable general equilibrium model that explicitly calculates reform-induced changes in all asset values during the transition to a consumption tax reform. As noted previously, the model has three production sectors—owner-occupied housing, rental housing, and a composite good sector that includes all nonhousing goods and services. The time path of investment demands in all three sectors is modeled explicitly, in that we take into account capital stock adjustment costs. On the consumption side, we take into account the current tax advantage of owner-occupied housing relative to other assets in modeling the demands for the three goods. Thus our model allows for a fairly detailed description of the both the transitional and the long-run effects of implementing a consumption-based tax reform on the prices of housing and business assets, including both a composite good and rental housing. At the same time, however, our treatment of housing is less detailed than in some of the partial equilibrium studies noted above, since land is not considered and the model does not allow for multiple income groups within each generation. In this section we outline the basic structure of the model, which combines various features from similar and well-known models constructed by Auerbach and Kotlikoff (1987), Goulder and Summers (1989), Goulder (1989), Keuschnigg (1990), Fullerton and Rogers (1993) and Hayashi (1982). More detailed descriptions of the model and the calibration of the initial equilibrium are provided in the appendix, and the complete details are provided in Diamond and Zodrow (2005).

5.3.1   The Composite Good Production Sector

Firms in the composite good production sector produce output using a CES (constant elasticity of substitution) production function with capital and labor as inputs. Firms are assumed to choose the time path of investment to maximize the present value of firm profits or, equivalently, maximize firm value, net of all taxes and subject to quadratic costs of adjusting the capital stock. Total taxes in the composite good production sector include the corporate income tax or the business component of the flat tax and state and local property taxes. Each firm is assumed to maintain a fixed debt/asset ratio and pay out a constant fraction of earnings after taxes and depreciation in each period.

The model assumes individual-level arbitrage, which implies that the after-tax return to bonds must equal the after-tax return received by the shareholders of the firm. The value of the firm in the composite good sector equals the present value of all future net distributions to the owners of the firm.

5.3.2   The Owner-Occupied and Rental Housing Production Sectors

Housing is produced in the owner-occupied and rental housing production sectors where, following Goulder and Summers (1989) and Goulder (1989), rental housing is produced by noncorporate landlords and owner-occupied housing is produced by the owners. The technology used in the production of rental housing and owner-occupied housing is assumed to be identical—capital and labor combined in the same CES production function. Landlords and owner-occupiers are also are assumed to choose time paths of investment to maximize the equivalent of firm value, net of total taxes.

In the case of the rental housing sector the firm is modeled as a non-corporate firm, which implies that landlords are simply taxed at the individual level. In the owner-occupied housing sector the tax burden takes into account the facts that imputed rents are untaxed and maintenance expenditures are not deductible, while mortgage interest and property taxes are deductible. The optimal investment path is calculated as above.

5.3.3   Individual Behavior

On the individual side the model has a dynamic overlapping-generations framework with fifty-five generations alive at each point in time. There is a representative individual for each generation, who has an economic life span (which begins upon entry into the work force) of fifty-five years, with the first forty-five of those years spent working, and the last ten years spent in retirement. Individual tastes are identical so that differences in behavior across generations are due solely to differences in lifetime budget constraints. An individual accumulates assets from the time of "economic birth" that are used to finance both consumption over the life cycle, especially during the retirement period, and the making of bequests. The model follows Fullerton and Rogers (1993) in including a relatively primitive "target model" of bequests, with the real values of bequests assumed to be fixed and thus unaffected by changes in economic conditions, including changes in income.

The consumer is assumed to choose the time paths of consumption and leisure to maximize rest-of-life utility, which is a discounted sum of annual utilities, subject to a lifetime budget constraint that requires the present value of lifetime wealth including inheritances to equal the present value of lifetime consumption including bequests. Annual utility is assumed to be a CES function of consumption of an aggregate consumption good and leisure The aggregate consumption good is modeled as a CES function of the composite good and aggregate housing services (including a minimum purchase requirement for both goods), with aggregate housing services in turn modeled as CES function of owner-occupied and rental housing services. In addition the model includes a simple social security system, government purchases of the composite good, transfer payments, a hump-backed wage profile over the life cycle, a progressive tax on wage income, and constant average marginal tax rates applied to interest income, dividends, and capital gains.

5.4 Simulation Results

The reform simulated is the replacement of the federal income tax system (but not the payroll tax) with a revenue neutral Hall and Rabushka (1995) flat tax that applies a constant rate to a comprehensive measure of household labor incomes, with an exemption amount that is initially set at $20,000 per household,[14] and business real cash flow, which allows expensing of all nonfinancial business purchases and ignores financial flows and thus does not allow deductions for interest expense. The reform is assumed to be unanticipated and enacted immediately. Since adjustment costs are critical for analyzing transitional effects but there is uncertainty about the magnitude of these effects, simulation results are presented for the cases of no adjustment costs, intermediate adjustment costs, and high adjustment costs.[15] The assumption of a comprehensive flat tax base, which follows the admittedly highly optimistic Hall and Rabushka (1995) approach of assuming taxation of all fringe benefits, elimination of all deductions, and elimination of the Earned Income Tax Credit, implies that the required flat tax rate is relatively low—it ranges from 21.0 to 22.3 percent in the year of reform, depending on the level of adjustment costs, and gradually declines to a steady state value of 20.1 percent.[16] The following discussion begins with a summary of the macroeconomic effects of the enactment of such a flat tax on prices, output, investment, and the allocation of capital, and then examines the changes in business equity prices and housing prices that are the focus of the analysis, as well as the associated intergenerational redistributions.

5.4.1 Macroeconomic Effects on Prices, Output, Investment and Capital Allocation

Tables 5.1 through 5.3 show that the general time paths of the wage rate and interest rate are similar for all three levels of adjustment costs. In the year of enactment of the flat tax, the before-tax wage rate declines initially by 0.5 to 0.6 percent, as labor supply increases immediately by 1.8 to 2.0 percent, depending on the level of adjustment costs, while the capital stock is initially fixed. The increase in labor supply is a result of both an increase in the after-tax wage rate and an increase in the after-tax interest rate that causes individuals to substitute future consumption and leisure for current consumption and leisure.[17] Note that part of the increase in the wage rate and the resulting increase in labor supply is attributable to the reform-induced reallocation of capital from owner-occupied housing into the much more labor-intensive production of the composite good (discussed below), which stimulates the demand for labor. The wage rate then rises over time as increased saving leads to a higher capital–labor ratio. In the long-run steady state, the before-tax wage rate is 4.2 percent higher and the capital–labor ratio is 8.8 percent higher than in the initial steady state. The before-tax interest rate is 1.3 percentage points lower in the long-run steady state, with more than half of the decline occurring within ten years after reform. The after-tax interest rate initially increases by 0.9 to 1.6 percentage points, depending on the level of adjustment costs, and then declines steadily to a value 0.2 percentage points higher than in the initial steady state.

Gross domestic product (GDP) increases by 1.0 to 1.3 percent in the year of reform and by 4.9 percent in the long run. Even for the highest level of adjustment costs, most of the increase in GDP (4.2 percent) occurs within twenty years of the enactment of reform, as labor supply and aggregate investment increase and as capital is reallocated among the three production sectors. In the composite good sector, output is 1.4 to 1.5 percent larger in the year of reform and 5.2 percent larger in the long-run steady state. In the rental housing sector, output decreases by 0.0 to 1.4 percent in the year of reform, and increases by 1.2 percent in the long-run steady state. In the owner-occupied housing sector the change in output ranges from an increase of 0.1 percent to a decline of 1.5 percent in the year of reform, and is 3.6 percent larger in the long-run steady state.

Investment in the composite good sector increases by 11.4 to 44.6 percent in the year of reform, and then gradually falls to a level that is 16.9 percent higher than in the initial steady state. Investment in the rental housing sector increases by 18.9 to 52.8 percent in the year of reform and by 15.0 percent in the long-run steady state. Investment in owner-occupied housing decreases by 8.4 to 100.5 percent in the year of reform, and increases by 2.3 percent in the long-run steady state.[18] Investment in owner-occupied housing returns to its level in the initial steady state within three to eleven years after reform. These changes in investment imply a short-run increase in the savings rate of roughly 6.2 to 12.3 percent and a long-run increase in the savings rate of 8.4 percent.

The increase in investment in the composite good and rental housing sectors and the initial decline in investment in owner-occupied housing occur for two reasons. First, elimination of the tax on the normal rate of return to investment as well as the gradual decline in interest rates reduce the cost of capital and thus increase the optimal level of investment in the composite good and rental housing sectors relative to the initial steady state. Second, the reduction of the relative tax advantage of owner-occupied housing at the individual level due to the eliminated deductions for home mortgage interest and property taxes reduces demand for such housing and thus encourages a reallocation of capital from the owner-occupied housing sector to the composite good and rental housing sectors, and thus also increases investment in these sectors.

One of the economic benefits of fundamental tax reform is a more efficient allocation of capital across the housing and composite good sectors, but this naturally comes only with a reduction in investment in owner-occupied housing during a transition period following reform. The capital stocks in the composite good and rental housing sectors increase in every year after reform in relation to the initial steady state, and are 16.9 and 15.0 percent larger, respectively, in the long-run steady state. By comparison, in the owner-occupied housing sector, the stock of capital declines in relation to the initial steady state, as capital is reallocated from the owner-occupied housing to the rental housing and composite good sectors. Five years after the reform is enacted, the capital stock in the owner-occupied housing sector is 1.0 to 6.1 percent smaller than in the initial steady state, although it is 2.3 percent larger in the long-run steady state. In the long-run steady state, the share of the capital stock in the owner-occupied housing sector falls from 40.4 to 37.3 percent, while the share of composite good capital increases from 48.3 to 51.0 percent, and the share of rental housing capital increases modestly from 11.3 to 11.7 percent.

5.4.2   The Effects of Reform on Business Equity Prices and Housing Values

As noted previously, the transition to a consumption tax raises some interesting issues. Some observers have argued that in the absence of special transition rules, the windfall losses experienced by the owners of corporate equity and owner-occupied housing would be sufficiently large to make the enactment of a consumption tax reform politically infeasible. Others have countered that such windfall losses would be desirable because they would act to offset the reduction in progressivity associated with the flat tax, attributable to reducing the marginal tax rates on the wealthy and eliminating the taxation of the normal returns to capital. Yet others have concluded that these transitional problems are overstated, and that the enactment of a consumption tax reform would have little effect—or might even increase—the values of business assets and owner-occupied housing In this section, we examine the effect of a flat tax reform on asset values within the context of our model.

Table 5.1 shows the effects of implementing reform if adjustment costs are set approximately to zero and there are no transition rules. In this case the average value of equity in the composite good production sector (average Q) decreases by 16.5 percent in the year of reform, while the average value of equity in the rental housing sector (where remaining basis is relatively large) decreases by 29.9 percent. The effects of reform on the value of equity in the owner-occupied sector are much more modest, where home equity values initially fall by 2.9 percent which, with a debt–asset ratio of 0.35, is equivalent to a 1.9 percent decline in the total value of owner-occupied housing; equity values return to their initial levels by the fourth year after the reform.[19]

These windfall losses in the composite good and rental housing sectors are moderated when adjustment costs are added to the analysis, since the reallocation of capital to these sectors is slowed, allowing existing assets to earn above-normal returns during the transition. In the case of moderate adjustment costs, shown in table 5.2, the average value of equity in the composite good production sector falls by 10.4 percent in the year of reform, while the average value of equity in the rental housing sector falls by 26.3 percent. By comparison, adjustment costs—which are assumed to be symmetric across all sectors—slow down the reallocation of capital out of the owner-occupied housing sector, increasing windfall losses in that sector. This effect is magnified by higher interest rates during the transition. With moderate adjustment costs, the average value of equity in the owner-occupied housing sector initially falls by 4.2 percent, which is equivalent to a 2.7 percent decline in the total value of owner-occupied housing, and it now takes

Table 5.1
Base case simulation: No adjustment costs

Years after Enactment	0	1	2	4	6	10	20	50	100
Interest rate									
After-tax	0.3	1.4	1.6	1.3	1.0	0.6	0.3	0.2	0.2
Before-tax	−1.2	−0.1	0.2	−0.2	−0.5	−0.9	−1.2	−1.3	−1.3
Prices									
RH service	−1.4	−2.7	−4.1	−6.0	−7.2	−9.1	−11.2	−11.7	−11.7
OH service	−1.4	4.3	7.7	9.2	7.9	5.1	2.1	1.4	1.3
Wage rate	−0.5	0.8	1.7	2.6	3.0	3.5	4.1	4.2	4.2
Labor supply	1.8	1.9	2.0	2.1	2.1	2.0	1.8	1.8	1.8
Tax rates									
Flat tax	22.3	22.3	21.8	21.1	20.8	20.5	20.2	20.1	20.1
Payroll	7.1	7.0	6.9	6.8	6.8	6.8	6.8	6.7	6.7
Investment									
NH	44.6	35.4	27.6	19.8	17.9	17.7	17.1	17.0	16.9
RH	52.8	52.9	44.1	31.8	27.2	23.9	17.5	15.3	15.0
OH	−100.5	−55.0	−19.6	11.3	15.7	11.7	5.0	2.5	2.3
Capital stock									
NH	0.0	4.7	8.0	11.4	12.9	14.6	16.5	16.9	16.9
RH	0.0	2.0	4.0	6.7	8.5	11.0	14.1	14.9	15.0
OH	0.0	−3.9	−5.8	−6.1	−4.6	−1.9	1.4	2.2	2.3
Tobin's Q									
NH	−16.5	−19.9	−20.8	−20.4	−19.8	−19.2	−18.8	−18.7	−18.7
RH	−29.9	−31.4	−31.4	−30.4	−29.8	−29.4	−29.0	−28.9	−28.9
OH	−2.9	−2.4	−1.3	0.2	0.5	0.4	0.1	0.0	0.0
Firm value									
NH	−16.5	−16.1	−14.5	−11.3	−9.4	−7.4	−5.4	−4.9	−4.9
RH	−29.9	−30.0	−28.7	−25.8	−23.9	−21.6	−19.0	−18.4	−18.3
OH	−2.9	−6.2	−7.0	−5.9	−4.1	−1.5	1.5	2.2	2.3
Output									
GDP	1.0	2.2	3.1	4.0	4.3	4.5	4.8	4.9	4.9
NH	1.4	2.6	3.4	4.3	4.6	4.8	5.1	5.2	5.2
RH	−1.4	−0.8	−0.4	0.2	0.4	0.7	1.0	1.2	1.2
OH	−1.5	0.3	1.5	2.7	3.0	3.1	3.5	3.6	3.7

Table 5.2
Base case simulation: Moderate adjustment costs

Years after Enactment	0	1	2	4	6	10	20	50	100
Interest rate									
After-tax	0.2	1.0	1.3	1.2	1.0	0.7	0.3	0.2	0.2
Before-tax	−1.3	−0.5	−0.2	−0.3	−0.5	−0.8	−1.2	−1.3	−1.3
Prices									
RH service	−0.9	−1.8	−2.6	−4.2	−5.6	−7.8	−10.5	−11.6	−11.7
OH service	−0.9	1.2	3.0	5.1	5.8	5.4	2.9	1.5	1.3
Wage rate	−0.6	0.2	0.8	1.7	2.3	3.1	3.9	4.1	4.2
Labor supply	2.0	2.0	2.0	2.0	2.0	1.9	1.8	1.8	1.8
Tax rates									
Flat tax	21.4	21.7	21.6	21.3	21.0	20.6	20.2	20.1	20.1
Payroll	7.1	7.0	7.0	6.9	6.9	6.8	6.8	6.7	6.7
Investment									
NH	23.5	22.8	21.7	19.9	18.8	17.7	16.9	17.0	16.9
RH	32.1	33.6	33.1	30.5	27.9	24.2	18.0	15.4	15.0
OH	−33.6	−26.3	−18.2	−5.9	1.1	6.4	5.1	2.6	2.3
Capital stock									
NH	0.0	2.5	4.6	8.0	10.3	13.2	15.9	16.8	16.9
RH	0.0	1.2	2.5	4.7	6.6	9.5	13.2	14.8	15.0
OH	0.0	−1.3	−2.2	−3.2	−3.2	−2.2	0.6	2.1	2.3
Tobin's Q									
NH	−10.4	−13.8	−15.5	−17.0	−17.7	−18.2	−18.6	−18.6	−18.7
RH	−26.3	−27.9	−28.4	−28.4	−28.4	−28.4	−28.7	−28.9	−28.9
OH	−4.2	−4.0	−3.0	−1.0	0.2	1.0	0.6	0.1	0.0
Firm value									
NH	−10.4	−11.7	−11.6	−10.4	−9.2	−7.5	−5.7	−5.0	−4.9
RH	−26.3	−27.0	−26.6	−25.1	−23.6	−21.6	−19.3	−18.4	−18.3
OH	−4.2	−5.3	−5.2	−4.2	−3.1	−1.2	1.2	2.2	2.3
Output									
GDP	1.2	1.8	2.3	3.1	3.7	4.2	4.7	4.9	4.9
NH	1.5	2.1	2.6	3.4	3.9	4.5	5.0	5.2	5.2
RH	−0.9	−0.6	−0.3	0.2	0.5	0.7	1.1	1.2	1.2
OH	−0.9	−0.1	0.7	1.8	2.5	3.0	3.5	3.6	3.7

five years for the average value of equity in the owner-occupied housing sector returns to its initial value.

In the high adjustment costs case, shown in table 5.3, the above-normal returns earned during the transition imply that the average value of equity of firms in the composite good production sector only decreases by 0.1 percent in the year of reform, while the decline in the average value of equity in the rental firm sector is reduced to 19.9 percent. In this case, the average value of housing equity falls by 5.1 percent in the year of reform, which is equivalent to a 3.3 percent decline in the total value of owner-occupied housing.

Thus, our results suggest that implementing a flat tax would decrease the total value of owner-occupied housing by 1.9 to 3.3 percent in the year of reform, depending on the level of adjustment costs. In the year of reform, the before-tax interest rate falls by about 1.2 percentage points in our simulations. By comparison, allowing for a 2 percentage point decline in the before-tax rate of interest, CGH predict an average decline in the value of owner-occupied housing of 9 percent, three to four times the magnitude of our estimates.[20] Assuming no change in the before-tax rate of interest, BHE estimate that nominal house values would increase by 10 percent in the year of reform, which translates to a 5.9 percent decline in real house values given that the price level increases by 17 percent, still somewhat larger than those predicted by our model. Thus our estimates suggest that reform-induced declines in the prices of owner occupied housing would be modest, consistent with the conjectures of Hall (1997) and Gravelle (1996).[21] In addition we find that the period of transition would be roughly half as long as suggested by BHE. With moderate (high) adjustment costs, the decrease in the average value of owner-occupied housing dissipates within 7 (12) years of the reform, which is similar to the results with low- and high-supply elasticities presented by Bruce and Holtz-Eakin (1999). On the other hand, the declines in the values of rental housing are relatively large under all scenarios. This suggests that, even though most discussion of transitional issues in the housing market has focused on owner-occupied housing, the transitional problems and thus the case for transition relief is strongest in the rental housing sector.

5.4.3 Welfare Analysis

Figure 5.1 presents the intergenerational welfare effects of implementing the flat tax in the model, calculated as equivalent variations and

Table 5.3
Base case simulation: High adjustment costs

Years after Enactment	0	1	2	4	6	10	20	50	100
Interest rate									
After-tax	0.3	0.8	0.9	0.9	0.8	0.7	0.4	0.3	0.2
Before-tax	−1.2	−0.7	−0.6	−0.6	−0.6	−0.8	−1.1	−1.2	−1.3
Prices									
RH service	0.0	−0.6	−1.1	−2.1	−3.1	−4.8	−7.8	−10.9	−11.7
OH service	0.1	0.8	1.4	2.4	3.1	3.9	3.9	2.2	1.4
Wage rate	−0.6	−0.2	0.1	0.7	1.2	2.0	3.1	4.0	4.2
Labor supply	1.9	1.9	1.9	1.9	1.9	1.9	1.8	1.8	1.8
Tax rates									
Flat tax	21.0	21.3	21.3	21.2	21.0	20.8	20.4	20.2	20.1
Payroll	7.1	7.0	7.0	7.0	6.9	6.9	6.8	6.8	6.7
Investment									
NH	11.4	11.8	12.2	12.8	13.4	14.3	15.4	16.7	16.9
RH	18.9	19.1	19.2	19.2	19.0	18.7	17.1	15.5	15.0
OH	−8.4	−7.7	−6.7	−4.6	−3.0	−0.4	1.9	2.6	2.3
Capital stock									
NH	0.0	1.2	2.3	4.3	6.1	8.9	13.0	16.3	16.9
RH	0.0	0.7	1.4	2.8	4.0	6.1	10.0	13.9	14.9
OH	0.0	−0.3	−0.6	−1.0	−1.3	−1.4	−0.6	1.5	2.3
Tobin's Q									
NH	−0.1	−2.8	−4.6	−7.0	−8.9	−11.6	−15.6	−18.2	−18.6
RH	−19.9	−21.2	−21.9	−22.5	−23.1	−24.0	−26.1	−28.3	−28.9
OH	−5.1	−5.1	−4.5	−2.9	−1.6	0.2	1.5	0.7	0.0
Firm value									
NH	−0.1	−1.6	−2.4	−3.0	−3.3	−3.8	−4.6	−4.9	−4.9
RH	−19.9	−20.6	−20.7	−20.4	−20.0	−19.3	−18.7	−18.3	−18.3
OH	−5.1	−5.4	−5.0	−3.9	−2.8	−1.1	0.9	2.2	2.3
Output									
GDP	1.3	1.6	1.8	2.3	2.7	3.3	4.2	4.8	4.9
NH	1.5	1.7	2.0	2.5	2.9	3.5	4.4	5.1	5.2
RH	0.0	0.1	0.3	0.6	0.7	0.9	1.2	1.3	1.2
OH	0.1	0.5	0.8	1.4	1.9	2.5	3.4	3.7	3.7

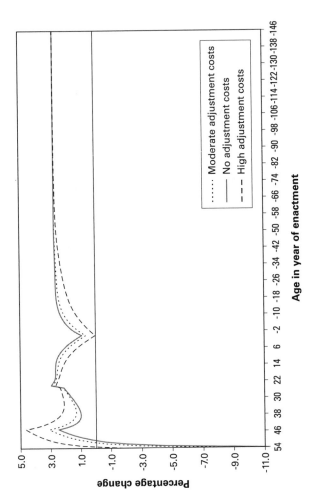

Figure 5.1
Equivalent variation for a flat tax reform

expressed as percentage changes of remaining lifetime utility, using a measure of lifetime resources including the value of leisure across all generations; these changes take into account all reform-induced welfare gains and losses considered in the model. The general pattern of welfare changes is similar under the varying levels of adjustment costs; however, the magnitudes and signs of the net welfare change vary considerably with the assumed level of adjustment costs for a particular generation. For example, the generation of age 54 in the year of enactment experiences a net welfare loss of 1.8 percent under the assumption of high adjustment costs and a net welfare loss of 11.3 percent with no adjustment costs. This reflects the fact that as the level of adjustment costs increases the one-time windfall tax on existing capital owners is potentially fully offset by above normal returns on new and existing investments. Note that for those who are retired at the time of reform (between the economic ages of 45 and 54), as the age in the year of enactment decreases, the net welfare gain increases. This occurs because the retired generations with longer life spans after reform receive inframarginal returns and a higher after-tax interest rate on their remaining financial wealth over a longer period of time.

The net welfare gains decline steadily for generations that are approximately within 7 to 12 years of retirement, depending on the levels of adjustment costs. This pattern of welfare gains is due primarily to two factors. First, replacing the federal income tax system with the flat tax raises the marginal tax rate of labor income for generations that are near retirement, since the wage profile has a "humped-back" shape and the income tax rates are structured in a progressive manner in the initial income tax steady state.[22] Second, the initial decrease in the wage rate tends to have a larger impact on older and middle-aged generations, since they have fewer years to benefit from the higher wage rates several years after reform, and during these years they are faced with the higher marginal tax rates on wage income near retirement. For this reason the welfare gains of younger individuals in the age range from 25 to 35 are larger the longer they have to benefit from higher wages and reductions in their marginal tax rates in their prime working years.

As discussed above, since the model assumes a "target" bequest, older generations are not allowed to pass on part of any windfall gains or losses to their heirs. Thus the generation of economic age 25 in the year of enactment experiences a discontinuous increase in net welfare since it is the first generation to receive an inheritance after reform and thus will benefit from the above-normal returns on business equity during the transition period. Generations older than age 25 would have received their inheritance before the reform and would suffer a welfare loss, since their inherited asset would be subject to the one time tax at the time of reform. The steady decline in the welfare gain for individuals younger than age 25 reflects the fact that these individuals would hold their inherited assets a shorter period of time over the transition period and would experience smaller welfare gains relative to older generations age 25 and younger. Net welfare continues to decline until the efficiency effects of reform begin to dominate other welfare effects. The discontinuity at age zero reflects the fact that generations born after reform can plan optimally over their entire life without any unexpected changes in the tax system. In the long-run steady state, the increase in net welfare is equal to 2.7 percent of remaining lifetime utility.

The relatively large net welfare gains (and smaller net welfare losses) in this study as compared to some of the other studies cited above are partially attributable to the increased efficiency gains that result from explicitly modeling the elimination of tax distortions of investment across the composite good, rental housing, and owner-occupied housing sectors. Furthermore, with higher levels of adjustment costs, the rate at which investment is reallocated across the three sectors tends to occur less rapidly. This leads to higher inframarginal returns and thus larger increases (smaller decreases) in the total real value of equity in the composite good and rental housing sectors. This study suggests that in this case these gains tend to almost completely offset the one-time tax on existing assets; at the same time, however, it must be noted that the relevance of these results are called into question by recent results that suggest adjustment costs to be significantly smaller than once believed (Hall 2004).

5.5 Conclusion

In this chapter we examined the transitional effects of implementing a specific type of consumption tax reform—a Hall-Rabushka flat tax—on the values of business equity and housing prices. Our analysis was conducted within the context of a dynamic overlapping-generations computable general equilibrium model that includes a corporate sector that produces a composite good as well as noncorporate rental and owner-occupied housing production sectors and allows for the costs of adjusting all capital stocks in response to the enactment of the reform.

Our results suggest that such a reform would potentially cause a one-time windfall loss to be experienced by the (primarily elderly) owners of existing business equity. However, the loss is smaller than predicted by partial equilibrium models, and is mitigated once the acceleration of deductions under the current tax system, general equilibrium effects on interest rates, reform-induced efficiency gains, and investment adjustment costs are considered. This suggests that special transition rules should be used with some caution, especially since they significantly reduce the long-run gains that can be attained from reform—a line of argument that is strengthened by the fact that several factors (noted above) that would mitigate transitional losses are not considered in our model but weakened by recent empirical evidence that suggests that adjustment costs are relatively small.

Nevertheless, the asset price declines at the time of reform are greater in our model than in some other studies such as Auerbach (1996) and AAKSW, presumably because of differences in estimates of remaining basis. It is clear that the estimate of remaining basis under the current tax system is the crucial piece of information in estimating the asset price declines associated with consumption tax reform. The amount of the undepreciated basis of depreciable assets under the current tax system is an issue that is knowable, although it is subject to some uncertainty because of a lack of data, and should be a focus of future research. Our welfare losses are far greater than those reported by Auerbach (1996) and AAKSW. This, however, is entirely attributed to the fact that our model assumes target bequests, so that elderly individuals experiencing an asset price decline must maintain a constant bequest and therefore experience very large declines in consumption.[23]

In general, the case for transition relief is strongest for business assets with large amounts of remaining basis which, in our model, is primarily the rental housing sector. At the same time our analysis suggests that the negative effects of reducing the tax preference for owner-occupied housing that exists under the current income tax system would be relatively small once all general equilibrium effects are taken into account. Thus our analysis suggests that reform-induced transitional problems in the housing market are significantly more severe for rental housing than for owner-occupied housing. It is also noteworthy that the effects of adjustment costs—at least if they are symmetric across production sectors—tend to cancel to some extent, as higher adjustment costs mitigate the fall in value of business equity but exacerbate declines in the values of owner-occupied housing, in both cases by slowing down the reallocation of capital from owner-occupied housing into rental housing and the corporate production sector. Thus explicitly accounting for these differential asset prices effects is essential to estimating accurately the potential welfare gains and losses associated with the enactment of consumption-based tax reforms.

Our analysis has been conducted within the framework of a single representative individual in each generation. An additional critical issue is the distribution of these welfare changes across lifetime income groups taking into account differences in investment patterns across income groups, especially since lower and middle income groups hold disproportionately large shares of their investment portfolios in owner-occupied housing relative to the upper income groups and the relative importance of tax-deferred assets varies across income groups. Another critical issue is the differential treatment during the transition of different types of capital as well as different business sectors. These topics are the focus of ongoing research.

In closing, we hope that our analysis has contributed to moving the understanding of the effects of fundamental tax reform modestly along the spectrum from the unknown to the known. It must be admitted that such analyses include simplifying assumptions about factors that are essentially unknowable. In particular, our analysis, like most others, assumes that any fundamental tax reform that is implemented would last forever. Past history, including the events following the enactment of the Tax Reform Act of 1986, clearly imply that such an assumption is highly optimistic. The potential for an unraveling of the effects of fundamental tax reform might be reduced by the introduction of supermajority requirements for adding preferences or raising tax rates or the reintroduction of "pay-as-you-go" budget rules (Bradford 2005; Auerbach and Hassett 2005a); moreover such provisions may be politically more palatable as part of a fundamental reform of the tax structure than under, for example, a more incremental reform of the existing income tax system. Nevertheless, the evolution of the tax system in future years is inherently unknowable, and the prospect of future tax "deforms" suggests that the potential gains from enacting fundamental tax reform may be overstated in analyses such as the one in this study.

More generally, the validity of analyses using overlapping generations computational general equilibrium analyses such as ours ranges somewhere between the unknown and the known. Such models have certainly gained wide acceptance in the economics profession and among policy makers, and some support for their use is provided by recent empirical analyses which suggest that sufficiently rich life-cycle models explain consumption and saving behavior reasonably well (Scholz, Seshadri, and Khitatrakun 2006). At the same time the behavioral assumptions underlying life-cycle models are strong, and often called into question by the relatively new behavioral economics literature discussed by McCaffery (chapter 10 in this volume).

In addition considerable uncertainty surrounds a wide variety of issues raised by such models, and there are many outstanding questions about (1) the parameter estimates used in simulations of these models, especially since some recent econometric estimates of several key parameters vary considerably from the conventional wisdom, (2) the saving behavior of the wealthy, especially the very wealthy who determine much of what happens to aggregate saving in the economy, and (3) the determinants of bequest behavior. Although many may debate whether the answers to these questions are unknown or known, they are in principle knowable—and their resolution will be the focus of much research as the debate on fundamental tax reform in the United States and elsewhere continues.

Appendix

In this appendix we provide a more detailed description of the model utilized in this chapter. A complete description is provided in Diamond and Zodrow (2005).

The Composite Good Production Sector

In each period s, firms in the composite good production sector produce output (X_s) using capital K_s^X and labor L_s^X, using a CES production function with an elasticity of substitution in production σ_X and a capital share parameter a_X. Firms are assumed to choose the time path of investment to maximize the present value of firm profits or, equivalently, maximize firm value V_X, net of all taxes. Total taxes in the composite good production sector in period s are

$$T_s^X = \tau_{bs}^X [p_s^X X_s - w_s L_s^X - f_{FT} I_s^X - \Phi_s^X I_s^X - f_{IT} i_s B_s^X - f_{IT} \delta_\tau^X K_{\tau s}^X]$$

$$+ (1 - \tau_{bs}^X) \tau_{ps}^X K_s^X,$$

where τ_{bs} is the tax rate on business income in the composite good sector, p_s^X is the price of the composite good, w_s is the wage rate, I_s^X is gross investment, Φ_s^X are (deductible) adjustment costs per unit of investment, i_s is the before-tax interest rate, B_s^X is total indebtedness, $\delta_{\tau s}^X$ is depreciation for tax purposes, $K_{\tau s}^X$ is the remaining tax basis of the capital stock, τ_{ps}^X is the property tax rate on both composite good sector and nonresidential capital, with property taxes assumed to be fully deductible against the business income tax, and f_{IT} (f_{FT}) is one under the income tax (flat tax) and zero otherwise.[24] Following Goulder and Summers (1989) and Cummins, Hassett, and Hubbard (1994), the adjustment cost function per unit of investment is assumed to be a quadratic function of gross investment per unit of capital

$$\Phi_s\left(\frac{I_s^X}{K_s^X}\right) = \frac{p_s^X(\beta^X/2)(I_s^X/K_s^X - \mu^X)^2}{I_s^X/K_s^X},$$

where β^X is the parameter that determines the level of adjustment costs and μ^X is set so that adjustment costs are zero in the steady state.

Assuming firms do not make any financial investments, total net cash receipts, including net new bonds issued B_s^X and net new shares issued VN_s^X, must either be used to finance new investments (including adjustment costs) or distributed to shareholders

$$[p_s^X X_s - w_s L_s^X - i_s B_s^X] - T_s^X + BN_s^X + VN_s^X = I_s^X(1 + \Phi_s^X) + DIV_s^X,$$

where DIV_s^X is the dividend payout in the composite good sector. Each firm is assumed to maintain a fixed debt/asset ratio b^X and pay out a constant fraction of earnings after taxes and depreciation in each period. This implies that new investments are financed with debt and new share issues if retained earnings do not supply enough equity to finance the desired level of investment.

The model assumes individual level arbitrage, which implies that the after-tax return to bonds must equal the after-tax return received by the shareholders of the firm, or

$$(1 - \tau_{bs}^X)i_s = \frac{(1 - \tau_{ds})DIV_s^X + (1 - \tau_{gs})(V_{s+1}^X - V_s^X - VN_s^X)}{V_s^X},$$

where τ_{is} is the average marginal personal income tax rate on interest income, τ_{ds} is the average marginal tax rate on dividends, τ_{gs} is the average effective annual accrual tax rate on capital gains

$(V_{s+1}^X - V_s^X - VN_s^X)$. Solving this expression for V_s^X, subject to the transversality condition requiring a finite value of the firm, yields

$$V_s^X = \sum_{u=s}^{\infty} \frac{[(1 - \tau_{du})/(1 - \tau_{gu})]DIV_u^X - VN_u^X}{\prod_{v=s}^{u}[1 + (1 - \tau_{iu})i_u/(1 - \tau_{gu})]}.$$

That is, the value of the firm in the composite good sector equals the present value of all future net distributions to the owners of the firm. The time path of investment that maximizes this expression in the presence of adjustment costs is

$$\frac{I_s^X}{K_s^X} = \frac{q_{s+1}^X - 1 + b^X + f_{FT}\Omega_s^X \tau_{bs} + f_{IT}Z_{s+1}^X}{p_s^X \beta^X (1 - \tau_{bs}\Omega_s^X)},$$

where q_{s+1}^X is shadow price of additional capital (commonly referred to as "marginal q," which equals the ratio of the market value of a marginal unit of capital to its replacement cost), Ω_s^X is a weighted average of the dividend and capital gains tax rates divided by one minus the capital gains tax rate, and Z_{s+1}^X is the tax savings from accelerated depreciation allowances on future investments.

The relationship between "marginal q" and "average q" (denoted as Q_s^X) is

$$q_s^X = \frac{V_s^X - X_s^X}{K_s^X} = Q_s^X - \frac{X_s^X}{K_s^X},$$

where X_s^X is the value of future depreciation deductions on the existing stock of capital used in the production of the composite good.

The Owner-Occupied and Rental Housing Production Sectors

Housing is produced in the owner-occupied and rental housing production sectors where, following Goulder and Summers (1989) and Goulder (1989), rental housing is produced by noncorporate landlords and owner-occupied housing is produced by the owners. The technology used in the production of rental housing (R_s) and owner-occupied housing (O_s) is assumed to be identical—capital and labor combined in a CES production function with an elasticity of substitution in production of σ_H and a capital share parameter of a_H.[25] Landlords and owner-occupiers are also are assumed to choose time paths of investment to maximize the equivalent of firm value, net of total taxes.

In the case of the rental housing sector, the firm is modeled as a non-corporate firm. This implies that landlords are taxed at the individual level, so total taxes paid are

$$T_s^R = \tau_{bs}^R [p_s^R R_s - w_s L_s^R - f_{FT} I_s^R - \Phi_s^R I_s^R - f_{IT} i_s B_s^R - m K_s^R - f_{IT} \delta_\tau^R K_{ts}^R]$$

$$+ (1 - \tau_{bs}^R) \tau_{ps}^R K_s^R,$$

where τ_{bs}^R is the average marginal tax rate applied to rental housing income,[26] m is annual maintenance expenditures per unit of rental housing capital, and the definitions of all other variables are analogous to those in the composite good production sector. Solving the cash flow equation in the rental housing sector for after-tax rents received by landlords S_s^R yields

$$S_s^R = p_s^R F_s^R(\cdot) - w_s L_s^R - i_s B_s^R - m K_s^R - T_s^R + B N_s^R + E_s^R - I_s^R (1 + \Phi_s^R),$$

where E_s^R is net new equity invested by landlords in the rental housing sector. Individual arbitrage in this case implies

$$(1 - \tau_{is}) i_s = \frac{S_s^R + (1 - \tau_{gs})(V_{s+1}^R - V_s^R - E_s^R)}{V_s^R},$$

which can be solved for the value of the rental housing firm

$$V_s^R = \sum_{u=s}^{\infty} \frac{[1/(1 - \tau_{gu})] S_s^R - E_s^R}{\prod_{v=s}^{u} [1 + (1 - \tau_{iu}) i_s / (1 - \tau_{gu})]}.$$

The time path of investment that maximizes this expression in the presence of adjustment costs is

$$\frac{I_s^R}{K_s^R} = \frac{q_{s+1}^R - \Omega_s^R + b^R \Omega_s^R + f_{FT} \Omega_s^R \tau_{bs}^R + f_{IT} Z_{s+1}^R}{p_s \Omega_s^R \beta^R (1 - \tau_{bs}^R)}.$$

The expression for relationship between "marginal q" and "average q" in the rental housing sector is analogous to that in the composite good sector.

By comparison, in the owner-occupied housing sector, since imputed rents are untaxed and maintenance expenditures are not deductible while mortgage interest and property taxes are deductible, total taxes are

$$T_s^O = -z_s \tau_{is} i_s B_s^O + (1 - z_s \tau_{is}) \tau_{ps}^O K_s^O,$$

where z_s is the fraction of individuals who are itemizers. The flow of (untaxed) imputed rents to owner-occupiers is

$$S_s^O = p_s^O F_s^O - w_s L_s^O - i_s B_s^O - T_s^O - m K_s^O + B N_s^O + E_s^O - I_s^O (1 + \Phi_s^O).$$

The expressions for individual-level arbitrage and firm value are analogous to those in the rental housing sector, and investment in the owner-occupied sector is

$$\frac{I_s^O}{K_s^O} = \frac{q_{s+1}^O - \Omega_s^O + b^O \Omega_s^O}{p_s \Omega_s^O \beta^O}.$$

The expression for relationship between "marginal q" and "average q" in the owner-occupied housing sector is analogous to that in the composite good sector.

Individual Behavior

On the individual side, the model has a dynamic overlapping-generations framework with fifty-five generations alive at each point in time. There is a representative individual for each generation, who has an economic life span (which begins upon entry into the work force) of fifty-five years, with the first forty-five of those years spent working and the last ten spent in retirement. Individual tastes are identical so that differences in behavior across generations are due solely to differences in lifetime budget constraints. An individual accumulates assets from the time of "economic birth" that are used to finance both consumption over the life cycle, especially during the retirement period, and the making of bequests. The model follows Fullerton and Rogers (1993) in including a relatively primitive "target model" of bequests, with the real values of bequests assumed to be fixed and thus unaffected by changes in economic conditions, including changes in income. Inheritances are assumed to be received at the economic age of 25.

At any point in time s, the consumer maximizes rest-of-life utility LU_s subject to a lifetime budget constraint that requires the present value of lifetime wealth including inheritances to equal the present value of lifetime consumption including bequests. In particular, an individual of age a at time $s = t$ chooses the time path of consumption of an aggregate consumption good and leisure in each period s to maximize rest-of-life utility

$$LU_s = \frac{\sigma}{\sigma - 1} \sum_{s=t}^{t+54-a} \frac{U_s(a)^{(1-\frac{1}{\sigma})}}{(1+\rho)^{s-t}},$$

where σ is the intertemporal elasticity of substitution, ρ is the pure rate of time preference, and $U_s(a)$ is assumed to be a CES function of consumption of the aggregate consumption good and leisure in period s with an intratemporal elasticity of ε and a leisure share parameter of a_E. The aggregate consumption good is modeled as a CES function of the composite good and aggregate housing services (including a minimum purchase requirement for both goods), with aggregate housing services in turn modeled as CES function of owner-occupied and rental housing services. In addition, as described in detail in Diamond and Zodrow (2005), the model includes exogenous population and technology growth rates, a simple social security system, government purchases of the composite good, transfer payments, a hump-backed wage profile over the life cycle, a progressive tax on wage income, and constant average marginal tax rates applied to interest income, dividends, and capital gains.

Parameter Values and Calibration

The parameter values shown in table 5.4 are chosen so that in the year of reform the initial income tax equilibrium closely resembles the prevailing features of the US economy in 2003. In addition a number of other parameter values are chosen to be consistent with empirical estimates and those used in other CGE studies, especially AAKSW (2001), Auerbach and Kotlikoff (1987), Auerbach (1996), and Fullerton and Rogers (1993).

The choice of the intertemporal elasticity of substitution (σ) determines the willingness of consumers to substitute consumption across periods in response to changes in the relative prices of consumption and thus plays a critical role in establishing the responsiveness of saving to the enactment of a consumption tax. This parameter is set equal to 0.35, reflecting a compromise between the value of 0.25 used by AAKSW and the value of 0.5 used by FR. This higher value can also be justified by the inclusion in the model of a "target" bequest motive and minimum required expenditures, which tend to reduce the magni-

Table 5.4
Utility function and technological parameter values

Symbol	Description	Value	Source
	Consumers		
ρ	Rate of time preference	0.004	AAKSW
σ	Intertemporal elasticity of substitution	0.35	AAKSW
ε	Intratemporal elasticity of substitution	0.6	FR
σ_{CH}	Elasticity of substitution for composite good and housing	0.5	—
σ_{RO}	Elasticity of substitution for rental and owner-occupied housing	0.8	—
α_E	Utility weight on leisure	0.3	—
α_C	Utility weight on composite consumption	0.72	—
α_G	Utility weight on composite good consumption	0.75	—
α_H	Utility weight on composite housing consumption	0.25	—
α_O	Utility weight on owner-occupied housing	0.78	—
α_R	Utility weight on rental housing	0.22	—
n	Population growth rate	0.01	AK, FR
	Technology		
g	Technological growth rate	0.01	AK, FR
α_1	Capital share in composite good production	0.25	—
α_2	Capital share in housing production	0.99	—
β_X	Composite good adjustment cost parameter	0,2,10	—
β_{rh}	Rental housing adjustment cost parameter	0,2,10	—
β_{oh}	Owner-occupied housing adjustment cost parameter	0,2,10	—
μ_X	Composite good adjustment cost parameter	0.1081	$\delta + 0.0201$
μ_h	Housing adjustment cost parameter	0.0391	$\delta_h + 0.0201$
ζ	Dividend payout ratio in the composite good sector	0.68	NIPA
b	Debt-to-capital ratio (in all three sectors)	0.35	FR
δ	Economic depreciation in the composite good sector	0.088	Jorgenson
δ_h	Economic depreciation in the housing sector	0.019	Jorgenson

tude of the saving responses in the model. The intratemporal elasticity of substitution (ε) determines consumer willingness to substitute between labor supply and leisure in response to changes in their relative prices and is thus critical in determining the labor supply response to a change in the after-tax wage. This parameter is set equal to 0.6.[27] The rate of time preference, ρ, is set equal to 0.004, consistent with AAKSW (2001).

The elasticities of substitution between the composite good and aggregate housing consumption (σ_{CH}) and between rental and owner housing (σ_{RO}) are chosen so that the values of the compensated own-price elasticities of owner and rental housing are both roughly -0.8 as reported in Rosen (1985).[28] The various weighting parameters in the production functions and utility function are set to replicate as closely as possible the actual pattern of aggregate production and consumption for the three goods in the model.

The initial steady-state values for the capital stocks, investment and consumption in each sector are calibrated to be consistent with data from the US Bureau of Economic Analysis (2004). The population growth rate and the technology growth rate are both assumed to be 1 percent. The size of adjustment costs and the extent to which the existing capital is discounted (relative to new investments) because of the existence of accelerated depreciation allowances and bonus depreciation are also important in determining the magnitude of asset price effects predicted by the model. The simulations are performed for three values of the adjustment cost parameter (β_X) in the composite good production sector: $\beta_X = 0$ as a benchmark case,[29] $\beta_X = 2$, following the estimates presented in Cummins, Hassett, and Hubbard (1994) and Shapiro (1986), and $\beta_X = 10$, following the earlier and considerably larger estimates presented in Summers (1981b). In the absence of data on the values of the adjustment cost parameters in the owner-occupied and rental housing sectors, these values are assumed to equal the values of the adjustment cost parameters in the composite good sector (although the values need not necessarily be equal). The model is calibrated so that in the initial equilibrium, the existence of accelerated depreciation allowances including bonus depreciation implies that undepreciated basis of capital in the composite good and rental sectors is equal to $8.3 trillion.[30]

The income tax system in the base case equilibrium raises $2,782 billion in total tax revenue; federal taxes raise $2,046 billion and state and local taxes raise $946 billion. The social security payroll tax raises $754 billion, which is assumed to equal the amount of social security benefits. The remaining federal taxes are raised by corporate and individual income taxes. The effective tax rate in the composite good sector is 26 percent, and the effective tax rate in the rental housing sector is 16.9 percent.[31] The income-weighted average marginal wage tax rate is equal to 25.2 percent and the average wage tax rate is 21.0 percent.[32] The tax rate on individual interest income is 14.7 percent, the tax rate on dividends is 12 percent, capital gains in the composite good and rental housing sectors are taxed at an effective annual accrual rate of 5

Table 5.5
Federal and state tax rates

Symbol	Description	Value
	Federal taxes	
τ_d	Dividend tax rate	0.106
τ_i	Interest income tax rate	0.081
τ_g	Composite good capital gains tax rate	0.04
τ_b	Effective composite good business tax rate	0.26
τ_{rs}	Effective rental housing tax rate	0.169
τ_{gr}	Rental housing capital gains tax rate	0.04
τ_{go}	Owner housing capital gains tax rate	0
τ_{wmarg}	Income-weighted marginal wage tax rate	0.252
τ_{wave}	Average wage tax rate	0.21
τ_s	Social security tax rate	0.1
	State taxes	
τ_c^{st}	Sales tax rate	0.075
τ_p^r	Housing property tax rate	0.0171
τ_p^{nr}	Composite good property tax rate	0.0081
τ_b^{st}	Average business tax rate	0.04
τ_w^{st}	Average wage tax rate	0.04

Table 5.6
Initial income tax steady-state values

	Composite good	Rental housing	Owner-occupied housing	Total
Output	10,107	400	1,227	11,734
Capital	12,069	2,813	10,107	24,989
Wages	7,690	8	25	7,724
Firm value	6,662	1,777	6,569	15,008
Investment	1,305	110	395	1,810
Earnings	1,943	—	—	1,943
Net services	—	105	383	488

percent, and capital gains in the owner-occupied housing sector are untaxed.[33] Federal government expenditures on goods and services are 79 percent of total federal revenues, and the remaining federal revenues are used to fund transfers. Government debt is set so that the debt to GDP ratio is 35 percent consistent with observed data, and this ratio is assumed to be constant at the same value in the steady state.

The state and local government sector raises $307 billion in property taxes, $222 billion in retail sales taxes (excluding excise taxes), $37 billion in business income taxes, and $380 billion in personal income taxes. The average property tax rate on capital in the composite good sector is 0.81 percent, and the average property tax rate on residential capital is 1.71 percent. The average state tax rate on personal and business income is set at 0.04 in order to raise state business revenues and state personal income tax revenues are consistent with data in US Bureau of Economic Analysis (2004). The state retail sales tax rate is set at 0.075, with the retail sales tax base assumed to include 56 percent of total nonhousing consumption.[34] It is assumed that state and local expenditures equal total state and local tax revenues. Table 5.5 presents initial values for the federal and state tax rates. Table 5.6 provides values for various variables in the initial steady-state equilibrium.

Discussion

Leonard E. Burman

This chapter captures many of the interesting dynamics of a transition from an income tax to a consumption tax or flat tax. The main finding is that after accounting for general equilibrium effects and adjustment costs, the transitional effects of the switch to a flat tax are significantly smaller than is typically assumed. Thus the shift to a consumption-type tax is less politically treacherous than is generally thought.

My focus is on the usefulness of the model as a guide to policy. I come at this as a skeptic of the efficiency gains that arise from such models. I believe that they are valuable because they develop rigorously the implications of a micro-theoretic model of individual and firm decision-making under various tax regimes, and clearly help move our understanding forward. Indeed this model produces several useful and plausible insights about the effect of tax reform on housing markets. The question, though, is how seriously policy makers should take its bottom line predictions.

To be clear, my comments reflect primarily on the limitations of what economists know about important questions—many discussed in this volume. While this chapter reflects a substantial intellectual achievement, the question is whether we've gotten to the point where we can reliably advise policy makers about the likely effects of tax reform. If the answer is no, a related question is what might be done to improve our level of confidence.

Effects on Housing Markets

One of the key concerns raised by critics of consumption taxation is that such a shift would slash the price of owner-occupied housing. The simple logic is that the substantial tax benefits for owner-occupied housing embodied in the income tax are capitalized into the value of homes and the land they are built upon. Taxing owner-occupied housing would thus diminish the value of homes by something close to the present value of the current law tax differential between homes and other investments.

In the Diamond-Zodrow model, however, owner-occupied housing prices fall, but only modestly. With high adjustment costs, capital moves slowly from the owner-occupied to the rental housing sector, which means the price adjustment is also slow.

The somewhat surprising result is that, in the short run, owners of rental capital suffer much larger capital losses than owners of owner-occupied housing. This seems counterintuitive in one sense: rental housing becomes a much more attractive investment when it becomes taxed the same as owner-occupied housing, so one would think that landlords would be better off. The problem is that, with no transition relief, owners of rental capital lose all of the depreciation deductions that they have yet to claim when the tax system replaces depreciation with expensing. Since rental housing is very long lived, a landlord could lose up to 31 years of deferred depreciation deductions. At the same time new investors in rental housing require lower rents to cover their costs when investment is expensed. The combination of lower rents and lost deductions makes existing landlords much worse off.

Other results of the model are more in line with the conventional wisdom (at least as held by consumption tax advocates). Almost everyone is better off than under the baseline scenario. Wages go up as do after-tax returns to capital. Young people work and save more. Only the current old lose out on a lifetime basis. They suffer from the implicit lump-sum tax on old capital and also because they would have benefited from lower marginal tax rates under the baseline progressive income tax. Under the new system they face higher average tax rates.

The authors conclude that adjustment costs moderate price responses, which reduces the need for transition relief and thus raises potential long-term efficiency gains. But another way to put it is that the efficiency gains from a model with no adjustment costs and no transition relief are vastly overstated, because either there are adjustment costs (which entail real economic costs) or there is a need for transition relief (which sacrifices the efficiency gains from the forgone lump-sum tax on old capital).

What's Known about These OLG Models?

The first thing that is obvious about these models is that nobody makes decisions this way. Jane Gravelle pointed out in her presidential speech to the National Tax Association how implausible it is that people would wake up and decide how hard to work today based on the opportunity cost of consumption in distant future time periods. The big intertemporal response in the Diamond-Zodrow model comes from people shifting leisure: in response to the tax reform, they reduce current consumption by a relatively small amount, but they increase their current labor supply, which implies a significant increase in saving. As a result future consumption and leisure increase substantially.

As noted in this volume, the key parameters—elasticities of substitution between goods and between current and future consumption, and the size of adjustment costs—are all highly uncertain. As a result the modeling of work and saving decisions—key elements of these models—is couched in uncertainty.

Moreover economists feel comfortable in positing that people respond to incentives, but that assumes that people understand the incentives. To assume that people are doing intertemporal substitution based on anything other than simple rules of thumb assumes a high level of individual rationality, more rationality than is plausible in most cases.

Even if people are perfectly rational, the decisions in this model rely on tax regimes remaining fixed in the future. Would even totally rational optimizing agents choose to work more now based on a projection of the tax regime and rates assumed to be in place 10, 20, or 30 years hence? For example, the optimal plan might be much different if consumption tax rates go up in the future, or there is an estate tax (and there is a bequest motive, which is absent in this model).

What's more, the main efficiency gain in this model comes from an implicit confiscation of wealth from the old. Real people may perceive that as a bad signal about future tax regimes with respect to savings.

But the bottom-line unknown is how important all these unknowns are to the robustness of the conclusions. All economic models are at best an approximation of reality, and this one is no different. However, that said, it is incumbent upon the authors to conduct more sensitivity tests to explore how robust or fragile the results are to the parameters that may be varied within the model. This does not resolve the issue of robustness with respect to features outside the model, such as the decision-making paradigm, but would serve as a minimum test of admissibility for policy making.

Other Limitations of the Model

This basic framework has many limitations, as does any overlapping generation model—or any computable general equilibrium model. It's not a criticism, but those limitations raise questions about the relevance of the results to policy.

First, the model assumes identical individuals. In the real world, incomes and preferences vary. This variation may be very important. For one thing, there are permanent differences in ability to earn income and inherited wealth, which could negate the strong conclusions about everyone benefiting from tax reform. (Diamond and Zodrow recognize this as an important limitation and are developing a model that will include heterogeneous agents.)

Second, the model assumes identical firms. In this model there is one representative firm in each industry. The three-sector model developed here is an improvement over the more prevalent two-sector models, but it still abstracts from an important source of heterogeneity, both in terms of the efficiency gains and the political costs of reform. In the real world, firms differ within an industry in terms of how old their capital stock is (and how much unused depreciation deductions they have), in their capital intensity, and other ways. To the extent that tax reform levels the playing field within an industry, the efficiency gains could be even larger than estimated here. However, the fact that some firms will be hit harder than others by the transition to a consumption tax has implications for the political feasibility of tax reform. Slemrod's survey (chapter 3 in this volume) illustrates this problem.

This model has no real bequest motive. People make a target level of bequest regardless of tax regime, which implies that the marginal utility of bequests is zero. This is an extreme assumption. Even with no utility of bequests, there would be some accidental bequests if there were precautionary savings, uncertain lifetimes, and no annuities market. With an explicit bequest motive, people would share some future consumption increases with their children. This would certainly alter the short-run conclusions, if not the long-term ones.

Another assumption is that the economy is closed, and all saving is subject to personal income tax. With elastically supplied foreign capital, the results could be much different (as Harberger and Gravelle discuss in chapter 6 of this volume).

There is no uncertainty. As Kniesner and Ziliak (chapter 8 in this volume) note, there is an insurance value of progressive taxation; with diminishing marginal utility of consumption and uncertain income, progressive tax rates can raise expected utility relative to flat tax rates (and even flat rate income or consumption taxes can increase utility relative to lump-sum taxes by reducing the variance of after-tax consumption). None of this is reflected in the model, meaning that the economic gain of switching from progressive income taxes to a flat tax or consumption tax is overstated.

There are doubtless many other margins where uncertainty matters. For example, people's desire to trade future consumption and leisure for current consumption and leisure would be altered if lifespan is uncertain (so the certainty equivalence of future consumption is lower).

The Value of Sensitivity Analysis

A number of sensitivity tests could be done that would help explain what is driving the results in the model, and which findings are particularly sensitive to assumptions. A key question is: What are the sources of the efficiency gains in the model? One component is simply income tax reform—eliminating progressive rates, deductions, and credits under the personal income tax and eliminating the corporate income tax. It would be straightforward and illuminating to measure that effect alone.

A second element is eliminating sectoral distortions between owner-occupied and rental housing and between housing and consumer goods. This effect could be measured by holding total capital and labor fixed and measuring the efficiency gains from leveling the playing field. This would show the gains from more efficiently allocating capital separate from the gains due to more saving and a larger capital stock.

An element in the allocational efficiency gains in the short run is the elasticity of substitution between owner-occupied and rental housing, which I think is probably too high. There are significant transaction costs to moving, especially for homeowners, and the short-run adjustment is likely to be much, much smaller than the long-run response. This could be modeled by setting the short-run elasticity of substitution much lower than the long-run elasticity, which is likely to be very high. Put differently, although the model reflects well adjustment costs on the supply side, there are likely to be significant adjustment costs on the demand side too, and they should be explored.

Finally, I'd like to see the results under much lower (and much higher) intertemporal elasticities to see how sensitive the conclusions are to that parameter.

Real-World Limitations

The biggest limitation to such theoretical exercises is that most people already face what is essentially a consumption tax regime because all of their saving is in IRAs, 401(k)s, pensions, and housing—all of which are untaxed—so presumably their work and saving decisions would not be altered much (except possibly due to changes in labor tax rates). I am hopeful that the authors will incorporate this fact when they develop the model with different income classes.

A second concern is that people may be making noneconomic life-cycle decisions about saving and consumption. In particular, they may save more when the only tax-preferred saving vehicle is an employer pension, with automatic payroll contribution, employer matching, and restrictions on withdrawals, than they would if all saving were tax free (and not subject to withdrawal restrictions). Employers would certainly have far less incentive to set up and maintain retirement plans if there were no special tax benefits and executives could do all the tax-free saving they want outside of pensions.

The model attempts to show that the need for transition relief will be much less than people think, but there will be demand for transition relief no matter what economic models show. Moreover, as the model demonstrates, those with lots of depreciation deductions to lose will be especially exercised (and for good reason).

Nonetheless, this model reflects a real contribution to the literature on the economic effects of transition to a consumption tax, and I look forward to seeing the extensions of the model that the authors plan.

Discussion

Alan D. Viard

This chapter makes a valuable contribution to the study of the transitional effects of tax reform. The authors conclude that declines in the value of existing capital will be relatively modest, with the exact impact depending on adjustment costs. This conclusion, which rebuts common, but unfounded, claims of large value declines, is solidly based on a careful modeling of the current tax system and the economy's response to tax reform.

Model Structure and Policy Experiment

The authors' model has the crucial building blocks required to examine the change in the market value of existing capital and the resulting impact on the aggregate utility of different cohorts; a general equilibrium methodology, rational expectations, a careful representation of the current tax system's key features, and separate analysis of owner-occupied housing and business capital. The last element is important because the two types of capital are affected differently by tax reform and because changes in their values have different political and distributional implications. The authors take an additional step forward by separating rental housing from other business capital, permitting recognition of the close substitutability between rental and owner-occupied housing.

Because the model is stylized, it is unavoidably restrictive along some dimensions. For example, it features perfect competition and exogenous debt–equity and payout ratios; it does not include uncertainty, heterogeneity within cohorts, or human capital. All of these simplifications seem acceptable for the purpose at hand. The closed-economy assumption is a little more troubling because it may rule out some important transitional effects. But, it is not easy to formulate an adequate alternative, given the formidable difficulties of modeling current international tax rules.

The authors examine a replacement of the current income tax system, including its uneven treatment of the three types of capital, with a Hall-Rabushka flat tax. This reform can be decomposed into three components:

• Consumption replaces income as the tax base. Accordingly the tax on interest income is repealed, along with the deduction for interest expense, including mortgage interest.

• Owner-occupied housing is taxed on a prepayment basis, with no deduction for home purchases and no taxation of net imputed rental income. Accordingly the property tax deduction is repealed.

• Progressivity is reduced by the flattening of the rate structure.

The authors study a pure textbook version of the flat tax that does not include transition relief, preferential treatment for owner-occupied housing, or limits on loss refundability. The reform is also assumed to be unanticipated. This policy experiment is a reasonable starting point, although I discuss below other experiments that also merit attention.

Results

I organize my discussion of Diamond and Zodrow's results around three key values that govern the effects of tax reform on the value of existing capital.[35] As will be seen, their model provides reasonable estimates, or ranges of estimates, for each of these values.

Three Key Values

The value of existing capital of type i in the income tax steady state, prior to the unanticipated reform, can be written as

$$V_y(i) = 1 - d_y(i).$$

In this equation the steady-state cost of producing and installing a unit of new capital of each type is normalized to unity. The expression $d_y(i)$ denotes the discount at which existing capital of type i is valued, under the income tax, relative to the cost of producing and installing a new unit of that capital. As discussed below, that discount reflects any deferred tax liabilities that arise from the timing features of the income tax.

The value of capital immediately after the unanticipated reform can be written as

$$V_{c,0}(i) = Q_{c,0}(i)[1 - d_c(i)].$$

The expression $Q_{c,0}(i)$ denotes the marginal cost of producing and installing a unit of new capital immediately after the reform. Although this cost returns to unity in the consumption tax steady state, it may diverge from unity during the transition. The expression $d_c(i)$ denotes the discount at which existing capital of type i is valued, under the consumption tax, relative to the cost of producing and installing a new unit of that capital. As discussed below, that discount reflects any deferred tax liabilities that arise from the timing features of the consumption tax.

The ratio of the two values is given by

$$\frac{V_{c,0}(i)}{V_y(i)} = Q_{c,0}(i) \frac{1 - d_c(i)}{1 - d_y(i)}.$$

It can be seen that the transitional impact of reform depends upon three values: the two deferred-tax discounts and the change in the marginal cost of producing and installing a unit of new capital. Existing capital suffers a greater loss if it faces larger deferred tax liabilities under the new consumption tax, if it has smaller deferred income tax liabilities that are forgiven by reform, and if reform initially reduces the cost of producing and installing new capital.

These expressions refer to the changes in the total value of capital. The proportional changes in the value of equity (the measures emphasized by the authors) are larger because firms and homeowners are leveraged and tax reform has little impact on the real value of their outstanding one-period-maturity debt. It should be noted that some tax reforms, such as the adoption of a retail sales tax or value-added tax, might prompt an increase in the consumer price level and a corresponding reduction in the real value of outstanding nominal debt. As the authors recognize, however, the adoption of a flat tax should leave the consumer price level unchanged.[36]

The authors' results imply that the deferred-income-tax discounts are zero for owner-occupied housing, 0.02 for rental housing, and 0.10 for nonhousing capital.[37] The deferred consumption tax discounts are, as explained below, zero for owner-occupied housing and 0.21 for both types of business capital. The results for the intermediate adjustment costs specification imply that $Q_{c,0}(i)$ equals 0.97 for owner-occupied housing, 1.04 for rental housing, and 1.08 for nonhousing capital.[38] The net result is a 3 percent decline in the value of owner-occupied housing, a 17 percent decline in the value of rental housing, and a 6 percent decline in the value of non-housing capital, with corresponding equity value declines of 4 percent, 26 percent, and 10 percent.

I now consider each of the key parameters in turn.

Deferred Tax Discounts: Largely Known

The deferred tax discounts are largely known because they depend upon the timing features of the two tax systems. If taxes are a uniform fraction of capital's net income over its lifetime, the discounts are zero because existing capital faces the same future tax burden as the new capital against which it competes in production. If taxes are a higher fraction of net income later in capital's lifetime, the discounts are, however, positive. In that case, existing capital carries a deferred tax liability, because it faces heavier future proportional tax burdens than newly produced capital. That liability depresses the value of existing capital relative to the cost of producing and installing new capital.

Because the flat tax examined by the authors is a pure textbook tax system, the relevant values of $d_c(i)$ are particularly easy to determine:

• Owner-occupied housing, which is taxed under the prepayment method, faces a zero deferred consumption tax discount. There is no deferred tax liability because no tax is levied at any time.[39]

• Both types of business capital, which receive standard consumption tax expensing treatment, face a deferred consumption tax discount equal to the consumption tax rate, which is 0.21 in the intermediate adjustment costs case.[40] Expensing imposes the same zero present-value tax as the prepayment method over the lifetime of capital, but the timing is different. Under expensing, the tax is negative when the capital is produced and positive thereafter, creating deferred tax liabilities.

If the current tax system were a pure textbook income tax, the value of $d_y(i)$ would be equally easy to determine. As Bradford (2000, pp. 319, 329n.15) notes, the deferred tax discount is zero under such a tax because taxes are a uniform fraction of net income over the lifetime of the capital asset. As the authors recognize, however, the current tax treatment of business capital differs from such a textbook tax by offering accelerated depreciation. Like expensing, accelerated depreciation reduces taxes early in capital's lifetime and increases it later, giving rise to deferred tax liabilities.

While the existence and rough magnitude of the deferred income tax discounts are known, their exact magnitudes are unknown. The authors' values—discounts of 2 percent for rental housing and 10 percent for nonhousing capital—depend on various assumptions. Two of the authors' assumptions, concerning dividend taxation and intangible capital, tend to understate the income-tax discount and thereby overstate transitional losses. One assumption, concerning bonus depreciation, tends to overstate the income-tax discount and thereby understate transitional losses.

First, the authors do not model the presence of intangible capital in the business sector. Since such capital is generally expensed by firms under current law, it faces a deferred income tax discount equal to the firm's tax rate. As Lyon and Merrill (2001) emphasize, the omission of intangible capital from analyses of tax reform understates the deferred income tax discount and overstates transitional losses.

Second, the authors adopt the traditional view of corporate dividend taxation, under which dividends are a constant share of net income and dividend taxes do not give rise to deferred liabilities. Under the Auerbach-Bradford-King "new" view, however, dividends are reduced by initial investment and increased by subsequent cash flow, with offsetting changes in capital gains. If the dividend tax rate exceeds the effective capital gains tax rate, a deferred income tax discount equal to the tax-rate difference then arises. To the extent that the new view is valid, the authors' use of the traditional view understates the deferred income tax discount for nonhousing capital.[41] But the importance of this point is diminished by the low dividend tax rate currently in effect and by uncertainty about the validity of the new view.

On the other hand, the authors model the tax system as including bonus depreciation (partial expensing), a source of substantial deferred tax liabilities. Although the tax system included this feature in 2003, the year that the authors take as their reference point, the provision expired at the end of 2004. Its inclusion overstates the deferred income tax discounts present in today's tax system.

Because of these and other issues the deferred income tax discounts cannot be pinned down with precision. On balance, the authors' model seems to provide reasonable estimates of their values.

Change in Cost of Producing and Installing New Capital: Less Well Known

In a world without adjustment costs, $Q_{c,0}(i)$ would necessarily equal one. The impact of tax reform on the value of capital, in both the short and long run, would then depend solely on the deferred tax discounts. The value of owner-occupied housing would remain at 1, the value of rental housing would fall from 0.98 to 0.79, and the value of nonhousing capital would fall from 0.90 to 0.79. These asset price responses would not depend on how reform altered each asset's effective tax rate or on the resulting changes in investors' demand for the assets; such demand changes would be manifested as instantaneous quantity responses rather than as price responses. Observation suggests, however, that adjustment costs of some type dampen the short-run quantity responses, causing part of the demand changes to appear in short-run price responses.[42]

The directions of the demand changes, and hence of the changes in $Q_{c,0}(i)$, are known. Because reform lowers the effective marginal tax rate on both types of business capital to zero, it increases the demand for these assets and pushes their values of $Q_{c,0}(i)$ above unity. In contrast, reform leaves the effective marginal tax rate on owner-occupied housing at its prior value of zero, diminishing its relative attractiveness and pushing its value of $Q_{c,0}(i)$ below unity.

The magnitudes of the changes in $Q_{c,0}(i)$ are, however, far from fully known. They depend on the strength of the demand changes for the different types of capital and also on the adjustment-cost mechanism that divides those demand changes between price and quantity responses. The authors showcase the latter uncertainty by varying the adjustment-cost parameter in their quadratic specification. With high adjustment costs, the changes in $Q_{c,0}(i)$ from unity are about twice as large as with intermediate costs; with low adjustment costs, they are about half as large.

Additional sources of variation could be explored. It may be useful to consider other types of adjustment costs. As Cooper and Haltiwanger (2006) discuss, some adjustment costs may not have the convexity implied by the quadratic assumption; in particular, there may be an important role for investment irreversibility. Also the demand changes are likely to be sensitive to the elasticities of substitution among the three sectors, so it would be helpful to consider variations in those parameters.

Although more sensitivity analysis would be useful, the authors examine a reasonable range of adjustment behavior and their results provide some indication of the range of plausible price responses.

Modest Decline in Value of Existing Capital

In summary, the authors find that all three types of capital decline in value, but that the declines are relatively modest. Their results arise from a well-grounded model that addresses the role of deferred tax discounts and adjustment costs and therefore offer a powerful rebuttal to claims that tax reform will cause large declines in asset values.

Some informal analyses of tax reform envision large declines in the value of owner-occupied housing, while other such analyses expect large declines in the value of business capital. Interestingly these conclusions arise from two equally extreme, and diametrically opposed, assumptions about adjustment costs. Those who see large declines in the value of owner-occupied housing assume fixed supply, which is equivalent to infinite adjustment costs. The authors show that the decline in home values is modest with finite adjustment costs, even if those costs are relatively large. Those who see large declines in the value of business capital assume zero adjustment costs (and also often overlook the deferred income tax liabilities that would be forgiven by tax reform). The authors show that the decline in the value of business capital is modest with positive adjustment costs, even if those costs are relatively small.

Modest Impact on Transitional Cohorts' Utility

The authors find only modest impacts on the utility of the early cohorts, reflecting the relatively small declines in the value of existing capital and the gains from higher after-tax rates of return after the reform.

The authors note one limitation of their model, a discontinuity in how tax reform affects those receiving bequests. Workers who received bequests immediately before the reform are harmed because the inherited assets decline in value. In contrast, workers who receive bequests immediately after the reform are unaffected by the reduction in the value of their parents' assets, due to the assumption that the parents do not respond by reducing the bequests that they leave. This discontinuity would disappear under a more realistic assumption of wealth-sensitive bequests. Nevertheless, the authors' approach is a clear improvement over pure life-cycle models that simply ignore bequests. The proper treatment of bequests is a challenging topic that should be a focus of future work.

Profits, Rents, and Risk

Diamond and Zodrow assume that there are no pure profits or rents in the economy. They suggest that this assumption may cause their model to overstate transitional losses. The argument is that reform might cause little or no reduction in the market value of future profits and rents. If so, the proportional reduction in the value of equity, which presumably includes a claim to these flows, would be even more modest than their results indicate.

This conclusion seems plausible. Profits and rents should fare better than capital during the transition and might actually rise in market value. Because these are not produced assets, they cannot be analyzed using the framework of this comment; it is instead necessary to directly compute the change in their after-tax present discounted value. Two factors would tend to increase this present value. By inducing an expansion of the capital stock, tax reform would probably increase before-tax profits and rents; with more capital, monopoly power should be more lucrative and land and other fixed assets should be more productive. Also firms face a lower tax rate under the flat tax than under the current system, further boosting after-tax profits and rents. An offsetting factor, though, is that future profits and rents would be discounted at a higher after-tax interest rate. In any case, the inclusion of profits and rents is a fruitful direction for further work.

Diamond and Zodrow also assume that there is no risk in the economy. In accord with their discussion of profits and rents, they suggest that omission of the returns to risk-taking may also cause their model to overstate transitional losses. Here, though, they are too apologetic. There is little reason to think that this omission biases their results.

In well-functioning capital markets, the after-tax ex ante market value of a future ex post risk premium is necessarily zero, for any level of risk aversion and any degree of uncertainty. If the income tax and the flat tax apply uniform tax rates to returns in all states of the world, the before-tax market value of the risk premium is also zero under each tax system. The omission of zero-market-value items clearly cannot distort calculations of changes in market value. Of course, the analysis must be modified if, due to limited loss refundability or other features, either or both tax systems apply different tax rates to returns in different states. Even then, though, it is hard to determine the direction or magnitude of any resulting impact on asset values.

Further Research

Because Diamond and Zodrow's model is well-suited to examine transitional questions, it should be used to study a wider range of policy experiments. It would be informative to consider tax reforms that included politically popular, perhaps inevitable, features such as transition relief, a continued preference for owner-occupied housing, and limited loss refundabililty.

It would also be useful to examine how other forms of consumption taxation, such as a graduated-rate Bradford X-tax, would affect the value of existing capital. The major relevant difference from the flat tax would probably be in the tax rate on business cash flow, which controls the deferred consumption tax discount. Relative to the flat tax, an equal-revenue X-tax would presumably put less of the tax burden on labor income and more of it on business cash flow. The higher business tax rate would induce a larger decline in the value of existing business capital.

Normative Question: Unknowable

One question that is unknowable, at least from the perspective of positive economics, is whether and to what extent existing capital *ought* to be taxed in conjunction with a move to consumption taxation. How should benefits and burdens be allocated across generations? Within each generation, is it fair to single out for tax those who saved in the past? If a capital levy is desirable, could or should it be imposed without a change in the prospective treatment of saving? Diamond and Zodrow's finding of modest declines in asset values undercuts arguments for sweeping transition relief, but the selection of an appropriate transition policy ultimately requires a resolution of these normative questions.

Transitional effects are an important aspect of fundamental tax reform. As research like that of Diamond and Zodrow increases our knowledge of these effects, policy makers will become better equipped to address the normative issues.

Notes

We have benefited from the comments of Len Burman and Alan Viard and the conference participants. The views expressed in this chapter are those of the authors and do not necessarily reflect those of the Baker Institute for Public Policy.

1. See Zodrow and McLure (2006) and the other analyses cited therein for discussions of the panel's report.

2. For example, see chapter 1 in this volume by Auerbach and the papers in Boskin (1996), Aaron and Gale (1996), Zodrow and Mieszkowski (2002b), and Aaron, Burman, and Steuerle (2007).

3. See Kotlikoff (1998), Gravelle (2006), and Diamond and Zodrow (2006) for recent discussions of the validity of using dynamic overlapping generations computable general equilibrium models of the type constructed in this chapter to analyze the effects of tax reforms, including discussions of the various assumptions made in such models (as noted by Burman in this volume).

4. In addition the model does not allow for different types of capital or endogenous growth, and thus cannot analyze the efficiency costs of differential taxation of different types of capital under the income tax, or any efficiency gains that might arise if reform-induced increases in investment increased the technological growth rate. Also, because the model assumes perfect certainty, the wage insurance properties of alternative tax systems cannot be analyzed. Finally, the current version of the model assumes a closed economy, and thus abstracts from international flows of capital and goods and services in response to the enactment of reform.

5. Since the flat tax is similar in structure to the current income tax in that taxes on wages are collected at the individual level so that wage contracts are expressed on a before-tax basis, most observers have argued that the implementation of this reform would not have much of an impact on the price level. Under these circumstances Gravelle (1996) argues that asset prices would fall by a factor equal to $t/(1 - b)$, where t is the tax rate under the flat tax and b is the debt–asset ratio.

6. We follow the conventional approach and assume that the costs of adjusting the capital stock are quadratic; for discussion of alternative approaches, see Hassett and Newmark (chapter 4 in this volume).

7. This point is stressed by Lyon and Merrill (1999).

8. The model tends to overstates transitional losses for two additional reasons. First, to the extent the "new view" of dividend taxation is accurate, the enactment of a consumption tax reform would benefit existing assets by removing individual level taxation of dividends that is capitalized into current asset prices; see Auerbach (1996). Because the model is based on the "traditional" view of dividend taxation, it does not capture this effect. One potential extension of the model is to allow some "traditional view" firms and some "new view" firms, consistent with the evidence presented in Auerbach and Hassett (2003). Second, as stressed by Hubbard (2002), the primary difference between income and consumption taxes is that only the latter exempts normal returns to capital; by comparison, above-normal returns and the returns to risk-taking are treated similarly under income and consumption taxes so that little change in the tax treatment of these components of the return to capital would result from reform. Since the model is characterized by perfect competition and certainty, it does not consider these factors In particular, as

discussed by Auerbach (chapter 1 in this volume), treating all of the return to capital as normal returns in the simulations of the effects of tax reform may significantly overstate the gains that could be achieved with a consumption tax reform..

9. The user cost of owner-occupied housing is defined as the sum of the opportunity cost of the homeowner's equity, the after-tax cost of mortgage interest, depreciation and maintenance expenditures, and (arguably) property tax payments.

10. They also note that housing price effects would vary widely across geographical areas, and that the largest price declines in percentage terms would occur for expensive urban homes that are typically owned by individuals with high marginal tax rates. Holtz-Eakin (1996) notes in his comments on the CGH paper that calculations with more recent data suggest much smaller price declines, for example, only 15 percent rather than 29 percent under a flat tax reform with no decline in interest rates.

11. BHE implicitly make the assumption that the Federal Reserve would accommodate the flat tax, which would imply that the price level—including the price of new and thus (in equilibrium) existing owner-occupied housing—would increase proportionally by the rate of the tax (this is an unusual assumption which we do not adopt in our analysis, see Diamond and Zodrow 1998). Note, however, that this one- time increase in the price of housing does not reflect a change in the real value of owner-occupied housing; rather, as described above, it reflects the fact that owner-occupied housing is not subject to the potential capital levy associated with the implementation of a consumption tax. Any decline in the real price of owner- occupied housing in the BHE (1999) model reflects the changes in consumer demand stressed by CGH (1996).

12. CGH (1998) argue that the large supply elasticities used in this study are responsible for the small impacts of reform on housing prices. They suggest that the structures elasticity might be on the order of 0.02 and the land elasticity could be even lower.

13. Somewhat surprisingly, this model yields a nominal short-run increase in the price of owner-occupied housing that is quite similar to the single-factor version of their model that ignores land. However, in the two-factor model the adjustment period is roughly twice as long as in the model that ignores land.

14. The exemption amount grows at the steady-state growth rate of the economy.

15. The simulation results are typically be presented as ranges for the range of adjustment costs noted above; unless otherwise noted, the first number corresponds to the value with high adjustment costs, and the second number corresponding to the value with no adjustment costs.

16. The associated payroll tax rate necessary to fund the pre-reform level of social security benefits is 9.5 percent in the year of reform and 9.2 percent in the long run equilibrium.

17. Note that the net-of-tax wage actually decreases for generations that are near the age of retirement at the time of reform. They have low wages because of the "humped-back" nature of their wage profile, and thus face higher marginal tax rates under the flat tax than under the progressive income tax rate structure in the initial equilibrium. This effect is far outweighed by the increase in the net-of-tax wage for all younger generations. In addition labor supply increases due to an income effect as the increase in the after-tax interest rate reduces the present value of future labor earnings.

18. Recall that this dramatic reduction in investment reflects not only the elimination of new and replacement investment in owner-occupied housing in the year of reform but

also the conversion of some owner-occupied housing to rental housing. The analysis assumes that such conversions would qualify for consumption tax treatment. Although such treatment is consistent with consumption tax treatment, it creates the potential for huge tax deferrals. Accordingly some proposals, including the progressive consumption tax option discussed by the recent presidential tax reform panel, limit expensing to assets purchased from other businesses. This would create a tax bias against conversions of owner-occupied housing, implying larger adjustment costs in the housing sector. However, only a very small level of adjustment costs is required in the model to limit disinvestment in the owner-occupied housing sector to declines in new and replacement investment.

19. In the long run, the value of average Q in the owner-occupied sector returns to its initial steady-state value because there are no business-level taxes in this sector. By comparison, the value of average Q in the other two sectors, which is adjusted for business tax factors, declines in the long run as a result of the more generous treatment of investment in these sectors under the flat tax.

20. With no change in the before-tax interest rate, CGH estimate a 29 percent decline in the value of owner-occupied housing.

21. Note, however, that these are average figures and thus do not capture the variation in housing price changes that would occur in different regions of the country; in particular, one would expect larger housing price declines in areas that have experienced recent rapid growth in housing prices and have homes that are owned predominantly by individuals in relatively high tax brackets.

22. For generations within seven years of retirement, implementing the flat tax actually raises the marginal tax rate on labor income due to the humped-back wage profile and the progressive income tax rates in the initial income tax steady state.

23. We are currently modifying the model to include a more realistic bequest motive.

24. That is, depreciation and interest expense are deductible under an income tax, while expensing is allowed under the flat tax with no interest deductions. The property tax on businesses is treated as a tax on capital rather than a benefit tax (Muthitacharoen and Zodrow 2006).

25. Thus the producer prices of rental and owner-occupied housing services are identical. However, rental and owner-occupied housing services are not perfect substitutes, so the mix of rental and owner-occupied housing services changes along the transition path to a new equilibrium.

26. The tax rate on rental housing income is a weighted average of the noncorporate tax rate on landlord profits and the corporate tax rate. The weight is determined by the share of rental housing produced in the corporate sector, which is equal to 10 percent.

27. The share parameter in the utility function is set so that the fraction of the endowment used for leisure and home production is 0.4, which, when coupled with an intratemporal elasticity of substitution of 0.6, implies that the aggregate labor supply elasticity is contained within the wide range of empirical estimates. This value is significantly lower than the value assumed in AAKSW (2001) and AK (1987) but yields an aggregate labor supply elasticity that is consistent with most of the empirical literature; it is inconsistent with the relatively large labor supply elasticities found in the recent work of Prescott (2005) and Davis and Henreckson (2005). Note, however, that this as-

sumption is conservative in that higher values of intratemporal elasticity of substitution would increase the beneficial effects of tax reform and reduce the potential for decline in housing values.

28. Estimates of housing demand elasticities span a wide range. DiPasquale and Wheaton (1994) report an estimated housing demand elasticity equal to −0.15, while Riddel (2004) reports an estimated housing price elasticity equal to −1.5.

29. To ensure convergence of the model, a positive value of the adjustment cost parameter is required; the results for the "no adjustment cost case" reflect a value of the adjustment cost parameter of 0.2. Note that the recent results of Hall (2004) suggest that adjustment costs for both capital and labor are quite small.

30. The $8.3 trillion figure is a nonpublished estimate provided by Joint Committee on Taxation.

31. See Auerbach (1996) and Gravelle (1994). The corporate share of the composite good sector is 61.5 percent, and the corporate share of the rental housing sector is 10 percent.

32. The value of the income weighted marginal wage tax rate is based on data presented in the report of the President's Advisory Panel on Federal Tax Reform (2005).

33. The effective annual accrual tax rate on capital gains in the owner-occupied housing sector is assumed to equal zero, since the Taxpayer Relief Act of 1997 exempted gains up to $250,000 on the sale of a house for single taxpayers and up to $500,000 for married taxpayers filing a joint return.

34. Note, however, that Ring (1999) estimates that on average roughly 40 percent of the state retail sales tax base is made up of business purchases. The taxation of business purchases under the state retail sales tax is ignored in this model, and thus the average state retail sales tax rate is overstated.

35. As discussed below, a different framework is required to analyze profits, rents, and risk, which are not included in the Diamond-Zodrow model.

36. Tax reforms alter the consumer price level only if they prompt the Federal Reserve to alter monetary policy. If the income tax were replaced by a sales tax or value-added tax, the statutory incidence of the labor tax wedge would move from households to firms, necessitating an immediate reduction in real wages to restore equilibrium. With an unchanged consumer price level, nominal wages would have to decline, a process that might be slow and difficult. To avoid this problem, the Fed might accommodate the tax by letting the consumer price level rise. But these concerns do not arise under a flat tax because the statutory incidence of the labor tax wedge remains on households. The Fed would therefore have no reason to engineer a change in the consumer price level.

37. For each type of capital, divide "firm value" by "capital," as listed in table 5.3, and add 0.35 (the debt parameter). The difference from 1 is the deferred income tax discount.

38. I obtained these values by multiplying the ratio of "firm value" to "capital" from table 5.3 by 1 minus the proportional decline in Tobin's Q (as listed in table 5.5), adding 0.35, and dividing by 1 minus the deferred consumption tax discount.

39. Under the flat tax, consumer durables and capital held by state and local governments and nonprofit organizations would also be taxed under the prepayment method and would also face a deferred consumption tax discount of zero. These assets are not included in the Diamond-Zodrow model.

40. The tax rate, and hence the deferred-consumption-tax discount, differs slightly across the three adjustment-cost specifications and over time.

41. This point does not apply to rental housing, which is treated as being in the non-corporate sector and therefore unaffected by dividend taxation.

42. Of course, the long-run price response still depends only on the timing characteristics of the tax systems. The 100-year percentage changes in Tobin's Q reported in tables 5.3 through 5.5 match the values computed with no adjustment costs, apart from differences due to the long-run tax rate differing slightly from 0.21.

III

International Business
Issues

6

Corporation Tax Incidence: Reflections on What Is Known, Unknown, and Unknowable

Arnold C. Harberger

Asked to comment on a topic as celestial as "the unknowable," I am inclined to deal with the most basic things first. Obviously the strictures imposed by a general equilibrium framework have to be counted among the most basic elements in the analysis of tax incidence—not just that of the corporation income tax, but of any tax whatsoever.

The problem, of course, lies in the fact that we cannot handle the incidence of a tax in a general equilibrium setting without knowing (or making assumptions about) *how the receipts of that tax are going to be spent,* and *what other distortions are deemed to be present in the economy.* Since there are millions of different ways in which the receipts of the tax might be spent, and millions of combinations of other distortions that might be present when the tax is imposed, increased, decreased or removed, it looks as if one can get "millions squared" different answers to the simple question, "What is the incidence of a single specific tax (or tax provision)?"

Economists have had to face this problem from the outset, but have not articulated it often enough or well enough for it to be clearly and widely recognized. To my mind, we cannot speak of *the* incidence of the corporation income tax in a way that somehow covers all of the "millions squared" possibilities of how the money will be spent or in the presence of the specific set of other distortions.

What we want is some way of saying, "this is the *essential* answer to the incidence question." And I believe we have found such a way. For incidence analysis this solution consists of assuming that the government spends its tax receipts in a fashion similar to the way that the people themselves would have spent the money. This assumption enables us to use a single set of demand functions, thus making the analysis simpler than it would be with any other way of handling government demand. For our convenience, let us call this the "demand neutrality" assumption.

The demand neutrality assumption allows us, at least in principle, to divide a real-world problem into modules. If we think of an increase in the corporation income tax, with the proceeds being spent on a new airport, we have an incidence module in which the government raises the money and spends it according to the "people's" demand function, and an expenditure-shifting module in which the government introduces its own airport-project demand function in place of the scaled-down version of the people's demand function that describes government demand under the assumption of demand neutrality. This possibility, of breaking the general equilibrium problem into an incidence module and an expenditure-shift module, is incredibly helpful. In particular, it enables us to conceive of such a thing as an *essential* answer to the incidence question.[1]

I would like readers to bear in mind that this *essential* answer to the incidence question is built on subtle foundations. I sometimes say that this answer lives more in economists' minds than in the real world. Well applied, it certainly has relevance for the real world, but certainly the real world will never replicate the mental experiments we make when we engage in our "professional" incidence analysis.

Economists are familiar with the havoc that preexisting distortions can wreak when we are analyzing the efficiency costs of taxation. The triangle of efficiency cost $(-1/2\ T_6 \Delta X_6)$ generated by imposing a new tax T_6 on good X_6 can be dwarfed by the induced efficiency cost or gain

$$\left[\sum_{j=1}^{5} T_j \left(\frac{\partial X_j}{\partial T_6} \right) \Delta T_6 \right]$$

that comes from the reactions in the markets for X_1 through X_5, all of them here assumed to have preexisting taxes or subsidies. Standard general equilibrium efficiency analysis tells us that T_6 always generates net efficiency costs in the absence of other distortions, but that in their presence it can bring either net benefits (e.g., a pollution tax or a tariff on a key input into the domestic production of an already protected final product) or enhanced net costs (e.g., a tax on wheat when corn, a substitute in both demand and supply, is already subsidized).

Something similar happens when the focus of our analysis is on incidence. In this case, the induced responses of commodities with existing taxes or subsidies simply generate an additional (or reduced) amount of tax, $[\sum T_j(\partial X_j/\partial T_6)\Delta T_6]$ the incidence of which we have to analyze. Thus, for example, when a new or increased corporation income tax causes capital to move from the corporate sector to the housing sector. It is, in principle, fully appropriate to include in an incidence analysis the additional property taxes and housing subsidies and other tax offsets that this move generates.

But this is not what we typically talk about on the subject of corporation tax incidence. Why? My answer is that the pattern of other taxes and subsidies is too time-and-place-specific for us to be able to carry on a reasonable discussion focused on the corporation income tax. To me, it is just like the question of how the government is going to spend the money that a tax generates. Just as there are a million ways that money can be spent, there are also a million patterns of other taxes and their rates, into which we could "insert" a corporation income tax of a particular configuration (e.g., striking all capital income, or just the returns to equity, integrated on dividends, on grossed-up-dividends, on after-tax corporate profits, or before-tax corporate profits, or not integrated at all with the personal income tax).

The reader should not infer that I am throwing in the towel with these remarks—that I am giving up in the face of a task that seems utterly hopeless. No, instead I am trying to emphasize that we simply *must* work with constructs that are artificial—in the sense of not being found in the real world—but useful in enabling us to think through problems that otherwise would be totally daunting.

On the whole, what the profession has done, is go down one of two roads. The first, "pure incidence theory," entails making the demand neutrality assumption plus that of "no other distortions." These assumptions give us a pretty pure module to work with, and also a pretty clear field on which to wage our intellectual battles. This is the road that most of our incidence literature has taken, and it is the one that I will try to stay on in the present chapter.

The second road is that of computable general equilibrium (CGE) analysis. Here it is possible to simulate the main skeleton of a real-world tax-expenditure system, and to see how the relative real incomes (or utilities) of different subgroups of the population would change if that system were altered in specific ways. For this road to be fruitful, the modeling and also the calibration to the actual tax-expenditure system of the country, must be of a very high professional quality. My impression is that most exercises of this type end up delving into the incidence of the entire tax (or tax-expenditure) system, and not into the incidence of particular elements of that system (e.g., the corpora-tion income tax, taken by itself). Not being myself a traveler on this second road, I will let these few remarks suffice.

As things stand, our main line of attack on the problem has been to build models with resource constraints, production and demand func-tions, and so forth, and to compare the results of running these models with no taxes at all, on the one hand, and with a corporation income tax, on the other. Personally I like this approach, which I think, if well executed, captures the essentials of economic behavior and economic structure, while allowing us to keep the analysis simple enough for us to understand how the machinery works. Making models more realis-tic by adding complications quickly gets us into situations where we either accept the model's answers on blind faith, or else remain skeptical about the results because we cannot internalize the mecha-nism that produced them. To be useful, then, our bare-bones skeleton has to be a very good one—capturing essential elements and leaving aside frills. It is perfectly reasonable that there should be discussion and debate among professionals as to how one can best represent an economy's most essential elements.

In all of this I am ready to classify as *known* the fact that economic behavior is well represented by things like demand and production functions, market equilibrium, and adding up—namely the bare bones of simple general equilibrium modeling. Similarly I would classify as *knowable* the key parameters of demand and production functions. These are knowable not down to decimals, but certainly as general orders of magnitude. I can "know" that the elasticity of substitution be-tween tradables and nontradables as composite commodities is well below unity, but that does not deny that many specific tradables will have quite good substitutes among the thousands of elements in the great basket that we call nontradables. Thus, if what I need for my modeling is the broad relation between tradables and nontradables (a relation that is modulated by the real exchange rate), and if what I am looking for is a rough order of magnitude, then I believe the relevant elasticity is *knowable*. But if what I need is great precision about this ag-gregate elasticity, or if I need to know a lot of component demand rela-tionships between specific tradables and specific nontradables, then I would, rather sadly, have to say that we are dipping our toes into the domain of the *unknowable*.

Where we *really* get into that domain, however, is when we consider the settings in which our scenarios will play. If the corporation income tax is raised or lowered, what will the money be spent on, or which expenditures will be cut, or which other taxes lowered or raised? And as we debate this issue in our seminars, how can we know the set of surrounding taxes and subsidies that will exist if and when our country (or some other country) decides to make a major shift in its rate of corporation tax? These are areas that I, for one, would want quite seriously to classify as *unknowable*.

6.1 Open or Closed Economy—A Matter of Scenarios

Too much paper and ink has been wasted on discussions that act as if, to be relevant, one must choose between an open- and a closed-economy model to represent the real world. This is not the right way to focus on the problem. Instead, it is much more meaningful to think of *scenarios*, or classes of disturbances that we want to analyze. In a nutshell, if one country (or a smallish subset of countries) decides to raise or lower its rate of corporation income tax, the appropriate model is one of an open economy. On the other hand, if all countries (or a set of big countries making up most of the world economy) choose to move their CIT rates in more-or-less parallel fashion, then the appropriate model is one of a closed economy.

I think that the big, world-level story of the past few decades, in which we have seen a pretty general worldwide reduction in corporate tax rates, is one for which the closed-economy model makes more sense than the open-economy one. However, that is not the main point that I would like to make. The main point is that both models are relevant, with the closed-economy model dealing with a *scenario* in which all countries impose (or raise or lower) a similar rate of corporation income tax together, and with the open-economy model dealing with the case where one country (or a small group of countries) does so alone, with the rest of the world standing pat. In this light, it makes no sense to ask economists to choose between the models. Which one to use depends on the type of problem we economists are trying to analyze.

6.2 Treating the Corporation Income Tax as a "Partial Factor Tax"

One tradition that I would like to follow in this chapter is that of treating the corporation income tax as a tax on the income from capital in a subsection of the economy known as the corporate sector. In a closed economy it would be a tax T_{kx} on the income from capital in X, the corporate sector, and not on that in Y, the noncorporate sector. In an open economy model, it would be a tax on the income from capital in A (the tradable-goods corporate sector, e.g., manufacturing) and in B (the nontradable-goods corporate sector, e.g., public utilities and transport). This tax would not affect the income from capital in C (the noncorporate tradable sector, e.g., agriculture) or in D (the noncorporate, nontradable sector, e.g., services). This classification comes pretty close to reality, if one thinks of the effective rate of CIT in a sector being that sector's corporate tax collections divided by that sector's total income from capital. By this measure the "corporate" sectoral rates T_{ka} and T_{kb} are typically *much* higher than the "noncorporate" sectoral rates T_{kc} and T_{kd}, sufficiently so that we can safely neglect the latter.[2]

Even with this simplification there is no reason why, in the real world, T_{ka} and T_{kb} should be the same, but for the purpose of getting a straightforward answer to the incidence question, we will consider them so.[3]

6.3 My Own Four-Sector Story

This story goes back to around 1970, to my public finance classes at the University of Chicago. I had been teaching the closed-economy model of incidence for more than a decade, and had just completed that exercise in this particular class. However, this class was different from its predecessors, in that its members had been exposed to the flowering of the monetary approach to the balance of payments (under Harry Johnson and Robert Mundell) and its related small-open-economy models of international trade. Hence it was quite natural for a couple of these students to rise in class with the question "How does this all work in the open economy?"

Being then perhaps faster on my feet than I am now, I quickly responded, "Let's find out," and moved directly to the equations of the closed-economy model.

Since the model had only two sectors, X (corporate) and Y (noncorporate), I really had only two options: make X tradable and Y nontradable, and vice versa. So then and there, in that classroom, we worked out the answers.

If Y is the tradable sector, its price-formation equation

$$dp_y = g_k dp_k + g_L dp_L \tag{6.1}$$

would be the relevant one (g_k and g_L are the shares of capital and labor in the production costs of Y). Standard open-economy assumptions would say that the small open economy would be a price-taker for tradables, and a price-taker in the world capital market. We would therefore impose $dp_y = dp_k = 0$, which would lead us to the conclusion that $dp_L = 0$. This in turn would mean that the price of the nontradable, corporate product (X) would rise to reflect the full amount of the tax:

$$dp_x = f_k(dp_k + T_{kx}) + f_L dp_L. \tag{6.2}$$

(Here f_k and f_L are the shares of the two factors in the production of X.) With dp_k and dp_L equal to zero, this yields $dp_x = f_k T_{ka}$. That is, "consumers" of the taxed sector's output would bear the tax. To allocate the tax to labor and capital, we would assume that they share the tax in accordance with their respective demands for X, labor bearing $\beta_{Lx} K_x T_{kx}$ and capital bearing $\beta_{kx} K_x T_{kx}$, the β's being the fractions in which product X ended up being bought by workers on the one hand and owners of capital on the other (with, of course, $\beta_{Lx} + \beta_{kx} = 1$).

This result was interesting in that it was identical to the result in the closed-economy case, where S_y, the elasticity of substitution between labor and capital in industry Y, was infinite. That case also led to no change in the relative prices of labor and capital in the Y industry, and (with p_L as the numeraire in that closed-economy case) to no change in p_y, and to $dp_x = f_k T_{kx}$.

We were surprised but did not dawdle over this result. Instead we went on to the case where X rather than Y was the tradable good. Inserting $dp_x = dp_k = 0$ into equation (6.2) we got

$$0 = f_k T_{kx} + f_L dp_L. \tag{6.3}$$

With all initial prices set equal to 1 (an innocuous assumption involving only the choice of units in which we measure products and factors), we have $f_k = K_x/X$ and $f_L = L_x/X$. Hence (6.3) resolves into

$$L_x dp_L = -K_x T_{kx}. \tag{6.3'}$$

This is a super-intuitive answer. For what it says is that if p_x cannot go up, and p_k cannot go down (owing to the international mobility of X and K), then the only way activity X can stay in business is for p_L to go down by enough to absorb (in industry X itself) the full weight of the tax paid by that industry.

But if p_L goes down in industry X, it must also go down in industry Y. So labor as a whole loses $K_x T_{kx}[(L_x + L_y)/L_x]$. That is, labor bears, in the first instance, $(L_x + L_y)/L_x$ times the burden of the tax.

Part of this burden will come back to laborers, of course, in their role as consumers of the now nontradable good Y. Its price will go down to reflect the loss sustained by workers in the Y industry, and this price reduction will redound as a benefit to labor and capital in their role as consumers. Hence labor will end up bearing $[L_x + L_y(1 - \beta_{Ly})]dp_L$, capital will gain $-\beta_{ky} L_y dp_L$, and the government will get tax revenue equal to $-L_x dp_L$. (Recall that dp_L is negative; see equation 6.3'.)

This result, then, said that not only would labor bear the burden of the tax in this open-economy scenario; it would bear significantly *more* than the full burden. When this result came out in class, we almost fell off our chairs. For in the closed-economy case we had studied an outcome in which capital would bear $[K_x + K_y(1 - \beta_{ky})]T_{kx}$, labor would gain $\beta_{Ly} K_y T_{kx}$, and the government would get $K_x T_{kx}$. This result emerged when S_x, the elasticity of substitution between labor and capital in the corporate sector, was infinite. Now, looking at the open-economy case, we got the mirror image of this result, but with labor rather than capital being the unlucky factor that ends up bearing more than the full burden of the tax.

So we ended up surprised, perhaps bemused, by the open-economy results, particularly the uncanny parallelism between what we now obtained in the open-economy case, and what we had previously gotten in the closed economy case—uncanny because what had earlier been the fate of owners of capital was now being visited upon the labor factor.

I was at least sufficiently attracted by this result that I kept showing it to my classes in the years following 1970. However, I never really *liked* it, in that I felt it was yielding important insights into how the corporation income tax might really work. This suit of clothes just did not seem to fit right on the customer.

I have no good excuse, other than always being busy and always struggling to fulfill duties and commitments, for why I did not right away seek a suit of clothes that fit better, but I did not. It was not until around 1980, when I was involved in guiding the PhD dissertation work of Arturo Fernandez Perez, that all of a sudden I experienced my personal "epiphany" on this subject. That came with the realization that what the problem called for was the four-sector model of manufacturing (A), public utilities and transport (B), agriculture (C), and services (D). This led to a straightforward, highly intuitive and easily communicated story of corporation tax incidence in the open economy.

The key sector in this story is the corporate tradable sector (manufacturing). For this sector, now A, the old story of X as the tradable sector still applies. The price of the product p_a cannot change, the return to capital p_k cannot change, so when the tax wedge T_{ka} is inserted in the price formation equation for A, we get $K_a T_{ka} = -L_a dp_L$. This determines the whole pattern of incidence and price formation throughout the economy.

In manufacturing, wages have to go down as shown; otherwise, we must go to a corner solution with zero output. And they must go down so as precisely to offset the added cost imposed by the tax wedge. Thus dp_L for the whole economy is determined in the manufacturing (corporate tradable) sector. The reduced wage causes p_d, the price level of services, to go down. The price level for agriculture cannot go down because it is determined internationally (for the small open economy). Here we introduced an important "trick," by allowing land to be a significant productive factor in agriculture, and by keeping reproducible capital (K) out of agriculture. With this simplification the lower wage results in increasing land rents, but of course with no change in the international price level of agriculture products. This leaves public utilities and transport, sector B, which we assume to be subject to the same partial tax on capital (T_{ka}) as sector A. Hence if the shares of capital and labor are the same in B as in A, the price of B will not change. It is more likely, however, that B will be significantly more capital intensive than A, in which case p_b will have to rise to reflect that portion of the (now greater) tax wedge in B that is not absorbed by the decline in p_L. Since product B is nontradable, there is no impediment to a rise in its price.

Once I had internalized this vision, I became willing to talk in public about open-economy tax incidence, and I felt no reluctance to peddle the notion, not just of labor tending to fully bear but more than that— to *more than fully bear* the burden of the corporation income tax. This would be even more certain in a small open economy than in a very big one, since in the big economy case some of the impact of the tax might be absorbed through a general worldwide fall in the rate of return to capital. And I pretty much hold to this judgment to this day, even after having experimented with various margins.

6.4   The Small Open Economy—A Price-Taker in the World Capital Market

Obviously one way in which one could get different results from those outlined above would be if the (net-of-tax) rate of return to capital would itself move as a consequence of a country's having (versus not having) a corporation income tax. We first try to deal with this case for the small open economy. The first step is to recognize that we have no reason to postulate that the world rate of return will be significantly different, with the small country having or not having a CIT. The tougher question is whether in the small country itself it is plausible that the rate of return would be different with the tax than without it. Here again I say no, but I recognize that the argument is much more subtle than the one above.

As a decades-long student of real exchange rate behavior in developing countries, I definitely reject the idea that such a country faces a completely flat supply curve of foreign funds to its market. The supply curve of funds has to be upward sloping, with respect to the real rate of return required. This may be thought of as being based on increasing degrees of perceived country risk, or on other forces. But the main point is that it depends on factors other than the presence or absence of a corporation income tax.

To make my point very clear, I want to model the small country as having no net borrowing from abroad in the absence of the CIT and no net borrowing in its presence. The movement of funds that takes place as a consequence of the imposition of a CIT in that country should, I think, be viewed as a movement of the country's residents' own funds out of the country (as the Argentines are said to have had, at times, as much as a year's GDP worth of money stashed away in Miami, New York, London, Paris, and other centers).

It is very important to realize that our standard comparative static modeling of the incidence of the CIT does not examine the transition during which a significant chunk of the preexisting capital stock (in the no CIT case) moves abroad as a consequence of the imposition of the CIT. Rather than look at this transition, the analysis looks at two steady-state equilibria—one without the CIT and with a larger capital stock invested in the country, the other with the CIT and with a smaller capital stock invested in the country. What I am saying is that the clearest, most natural assumption to make about these two steady-state equilibria is that in each of them trade is balanced.[4]

6.5   Capital Reallocations in the Large-Country Case

I have always thought of the United States as exemplifying the large-country case in almost any context. In the particular case we are treating here, this means that we should allow for a possible fall in the worldwide real return to capital, as a consequence of the imposition of a CIT in the United States Just as the rate of return will likely be driven down under a CIT in the closed-economy case, with capital shifting from the corporate to the noncorporate sector, in the open-economy case capital will also run away from the corporate sectors (A and B). But now it has two places to go—to the local noncorporate sectors (C and D), and to the capital markets of the rest of the world. One would naturally expect a smaller drop in the rate of return in the open-economy case than in the closed-economy case, simply because of the existence of an additional very large sponge (the rest of the world's capital market) to help absorb the capital that is being ejected from, in this case, the US corporate sector, as a consequence of the tax.

But again I would reject any notion that a US corporation income tax alone would cause a differential change in rates of after-tax return, here and abroad. For the big countries there is really just one world capital market. Billions of dollars daily cross both the Atlantic and the Pacific, seeking to gain as little as an eighth of a point of interest in covered interest arbitrage. If ever there was a market in which the law of one price could be said to be regularly and vigorously pursued by lots of economically potent and highly knowledgeable participants (the great international banks and financial houses), this is it. So yes, we can have p_k changing in this large-country, open-economy scenario, but not differentially.

Pursuing an approach like this a decade ago, I developed a simple example (Harberger 1995) that was "rigged" so that owners of capital, all over the world, would bear a direct burden (unadjusted for their role as consumers) that was precisely equal to what the US government (the model one, not the real one) got from a hypothetical corporation income tax levied only by the United States. In that numerical exercise the net-of-tax rate of return to capital (worldwide) dropped from 9 to 8 percent. Thus a 1 percentage point fall in the return to capital, all over the world, was assumed to create a loss to the owners of that capital, just equal to total CIT collections within the United States.

To complete this picture, we should note other gainers and losers. If capital as a whole bears the full burden, and US corporate capital bears only, say, 1/4 of it, the rest will be borne by capital abroad. This will be matched by a gain to labor abroad, and a loss to foreign landowners, who will now have to pay higher wages. In the United States, landowners will gain from lower wages, as will the consumers of services. Consumers will lose, however, as a consequence of higher prices in the (capital-intensive) public utilities and transport sector. Consumers of housing (worldwide) should gain as a result of the drop in the worldwide rate of return to capital.

But the assumed US tax rate on the earnings of corporate capital was 50 percent. This meant that in manufacturing, the "critical sector" (where the main action takes place), the gross-of-tax return would rise to 16 percent. Only 1/8 of the tax "wedge" of 8 percent was absorbed by owners of capital in that sector. The rest, with given prices of manufactured products, had to be borne by US labor. The wage of labor had to fall to the extent that US labor *in manufacturing* suffered a loss equal to 7/8 of CIT receipts *from the US manufacturing sector*. But if only 20 percent of US labor was engaged in manufacturing, then the loss suffered by all US labor would be 5 times as great, equal to 35/8 of CIT receipts in US manufacturing.

In this chapter, I will develop a similar scenario, adding extra details along the way. The first such detail is the assumption that the US stock of reproducible productive capital is divided 1/4, 1/4, and 1/2 between manufacturing, public utilities and transport, and services (including those from housing). This means that half of the CIT receipts come from the manufacturing sector, so labor ends up bearing a burden equal to 35/16 of total CIT receipts.

This and subsequent steps in the present exercise are illustrated in table 6.1. The first panel of this table focuses on the burdens borne by US capital. As already noted, capital in manufacturing bears 1/8 of the CIT receipts from manufacturing, which means 1/16 of total CIT receipts. The public utilities and transport sector has a capital stock equal to that of manufacturing, so its capital owners bear a cost of equal size. Since the services sector has twice the capital of manufacturing, its capital owners bear twice the burden of those in sector *A*. Taken together, the owners of US capital bear, as factor owners, a burden equal to 1/4 of total CIT receipts. The obvious inference is that foreign owners of capital bear a burden three times this large. This would have its reflection in a roughly equal gain to foreign workers. The underlined figure in the lower right corner of table 6.1 gives the key summary statistic of US capital's share of the burden.

Table 6.1
Illustrative incidence exercise: The US case

	Manufacturing	Public utilities	Agriculture	Services	Total
US reproducible capital income (% dist)	25	25	0	50	100
Share of sectoral CIT receipts borne by capital stock	1/8	1/8	—	—	—
Share of total CIT receipts borne by capital stock	1/16	1/16	—	1/8	—
US labor income (% dist)	20	10	6	64	100
Share of sectoral CIT receipts borne by labor stock	7/8	3.5/8	—	—	—
Share of total CIT receipts borne by labor stock	7/16	3.5/16	2.1/16	3.2 × 7/16	35/16
US consumer benefits					
Rising price of PUT (1/2–1/16–3.5/16)		−3.5/16			
Falling price of services				1/8	
From lower rate of return					
From lower wage				3.2 × 7/16	
Total consumer benefit		−3.5/16		1.525	1.306
Allocation of US consumer benefit (as fraction of total US CIT revenue)					
Allocated to capital	(0.30 × 1.306)				0.392
Allocated to labor	(0.68 × 1.306)				0.888
Allocated to landowners	(0.02 × 1.306)				0.026
Total incidence					
On US capital					0.250 − 0.392 = 0.142
On US landowners					−2.1/16 − 0.026 = −0.157
On US labor					35/16 − 0.888 = 1.30

Next we turn to US labor. The second panel of table 6.1 shows first, the assumed percentage distribution of US labor income. Second, we record the fact, already discussed, that labor *in manufacturing* has to absorb 7/8 of the CIT tax wedge *in manufacturing*. Since sector B has only half the labor force of sector A, but an equal capital stock, its labor bears a burden that is only half as big, relative to general CIT revenues. Line 3 of panel 2 expresses labor's losses as a fraction of total CIT revenues (from sectors A plus B). The easiest way to read this row is to start with the burden borne by labor in manufacturing, and project labor's losses in the other sectors according to their respective shares of labor earnings. Thus (3.5/16) equals 7/16 times 10/20 percent; (2.1/16) equals 7/16 times 6/20 percent; (3.2 × 7/16) equals 7/16 times 64/20 percent. When all these labor costs are added up, we get 35/16 as labor's burden (qua factor of production), expressed as a multiple of total CIT revenues.

The third panel of table 6.1 explores the effects of all this upon prices. Let me state explicitly that I am treating the world price of manufactures as the numéraire—by far the most convenient numéraire, as manufacturing is the sector where the real action takes place. Its world price being constant made it easy for us to do all the calculations thus far reported. The changes in factor prices that we have derived obviously have their effects on product prices, as does the fact that prices have to rise in the public utilities and transport sector stemming from a higher corporate tax per unit of product (because it is more capital intensive than manufacturing).

The third panel starts out with measures showing how much of the PUT tax wedge gets passed on to consumers. This sector pays half of total CIT revenues, of which 1/16 is absorbed by capital in the sector (panel 1) and 3.5/16 is absorbed by labor (panel 2). This leaves 3.5/16 to be absorbed by consumers through higher prices, as shown in panel 3.

Services sector prices fall, in our scenario, for two reasons—the reduction in capital's rate of return from 9 to 8 percent and the drop in labor's wage. We read off the first of these consumer benefits from capital's loss in sector D (panel 1) and the second from labor's loss in sector D (panel 2). These are recorded in the appropriate places in panel 3. The total service sector consumer benefit turns out to be over 1.5 times total CIT revenues. When reduced by the consumer loss in sector B, this becomes 1.306 times total CIT revenues.

In panel 4 of table 6.1 we allocate this consumer benefit among US factors of production—30 percent to capital, 2 percent to landowners, and 68 percent to labor. There follows the final calculation in which factor costs $(+)$ are offset by allocated consumer benefits $(-)$. The final reckoning is net benefits to US capital and to US landowners, each equal to about 15 percent of CIT revenues, together with a cost to US workers equal to 130 percent of those revenues.[5]

6.6   Differentiated Products in Manufacturing

Clearly, the most natural candidate for our next step of modification is the assumption that domestic and foreign manufactures are homogeneous products. Such an assumption is plausible for agriculture, fishing, and mining but certainly not for manufacturing. Hence in this section we will pursue the idea that some part of the tax wedge will be reflected in a rise in p_a relative to p_a^*, the external price level of manufactures. For simplicity, I will stick with the assumption that capital, worldwide, bears the full burden of the tax, so we will still have the rate of return falling from 9 to 8 percent as a consequence of the tax. We are again dealing with a wedge equal to 7/8 of CIT receipts from the manufacturing sector. Earlier we had all of this being reflected in reduced wage levels. Now, let us say only 4/8 is so reflected, with the remaining 3/8 representing a "new" burden on consumers of US manufactures. Table 6.2 presents this revised scenario.

The burden on capital as a factor remains in this scenario the same as before: US capital bears 1/4 of the burden; worldwide capital bears exactly the full burden. But now wages fall less because the prices of manufactured goods can (and do) rise. The specific reduction in wages embodied in table 6.2 is 4/7 the size of that in table 6.2. Hence the burden on labor as a factor ends up at 20/16 rather than 35/16 of total CIT revenues.

But in the final calculation, labor's burden does not fall quite so sharply. This is because labor suffers over 2/3 of the extra consumer cost, entailed in the rising price level of US manufactures. In the end, labor ends up with a total burden (as factor and as consumers) equal to 0.961 of CIT revenues, as compared with 1.306 in table 6.1. US capital shifts from being a beneficiary to the tune of some 14 percent of CIT receipts, to bearing a net (factor cum consumer) burden of about 12 percent of CIT revenues. The two factors—US labor and US capital—

Table 6.2
Illustrative incidence exercise: Differentiated manufactured products

	Manufacturing	Public utilities	Agriculture	Services	Total
US reproducible capital income (% dist)	25	25	0	50	100
Share of sectoral CIT receipts borne by capital stock	1/8	1/8	—	—	—
Share of total CIT receipts borne by capital stock	1/16	1/16	—	1/8	1/4
US labor income (% dist)	20	10	6	64	100
Share of sectoral CIT receipts borne by labor stock	4/8	2/8	—	—	—
Share of total CIT receipts borne by labor stock	4/16	2/16	1.2/16	$3.2 \times 4/16$	20/16
US consumer benefits					
Rising price of manufacture (8/16−1/16−4/16)		−3/16			
Rising price of PUT (8/16−1/16−2/16)		−5/16			
Falling price of services				1/8	
From lower rate of return				$3.2 \times 4/16$	
From lower wage		−8/16			
Total consumer benefit				0.925	0.425
Allocation of US consumer benefit (as fraction of total US CIT revenue)					
Allocated to capital	(0.30 × 0.425)				0.1275
Allocated to labor	(0.68 × 0.425)				0.289
Allocated to landowners	(0.02 × 0.425)				0.0085
Total incidence					
On US capital				0.250 − 0.1275 = 0.1175	
On US landowners				−1.2/16 − 0.0085 = −0.0835	
On US labor				20/16 − 0.289 = 0.961	

thus bear 108 percent of CIT receipts, with the extra 8 percent going to U.S. landowners in their combined factor/consumer roles.

I find these two scenarios to yield results that are close enough to each other to lead to reasonably robust conclusions. US labor bears "around" 100 percent of the burden of CIT, leaning above it as the passthrough of the tax to consumers of US manufactures gets smaller. Capital bears a small positive burden with passthrough, and gains a small positive benefit without the passthrough. Landowners pick up a benefit to offset the degree to which labor and capital together bear more than 100 percent of the burden.

Altogether, it seems that in any scenario fitting the general template of tables 6.1 and 6.2, US labor and US capital must together bear somewhat more than 100 percent of the burden in their combined factor/ consumer roles. Why? Because farmers seem bound to gain as long as there is any net consumer benefit. And if the net outcome for the farmers is positive, that extra burden must also fall on US labor and capital.

6.7   Why Not a Fuller Passthrough of the Tax via Rising Prices of US Manufactures?

This is an easy question to answer, but it requires opening a door that we have luckily been able to keep closed until now. The right way to look at the equilibria of tables 6.1 and 6.2 is to consider them as post-tax phenomena. What we call CIT revenues is the tax rate applied to $K'_a + K'_b$, the primes representing values in the with-tax situation.[6]

If we now assume no reduction in the rate of return and no reduction in US wage rates, we would have all the burden passed to US consumers, whether of manufactures or of PUT. To see what is wrong under this scenario, one must consider the incentives for capital to move out of the United States, and the incentives for foreign economies to absorb that capital. In both manufacturing and PUT, we would have a double incentive to use less capital—as product prices would have risen to reflect the tax, so scale would be lower because of reduced demand. Factor substitutions would additionally occur because the cost of capital would have risen (by the amount of the tax) relative to that of labor. This ejected capital would go to the services sector, and abroad. Furthermore the amount sent abroad must equal the amount foreign economies *want to accept* (according to their factor-demand relationships). The bottom line is that neither US services nor

foreign economies will demand these funds unless the equilibrium rate
of return goes down.

6.8 Note on the Paper by Gravelle and Smetters

This is an appropriate time to comment specifically on a recent paper
by Gravelle and Smetters (2001). Broadly speaking, I see this paper
almost as a natural extension of my 1995 paper, in that it employs
the same four-sector breakdown, treats the CIT as a partial factor tax
striking the earnings of capital in just two of those sectors, and
employs the "trick" of having land as an important factor (separate
from reproducible capital) in the agricultural sector. It goes well beyond my paper in introducing implicit parametric demand and production both at home and abroad. I can only applaud these additional
developments.[7]

I am troubled not at all by the modeling per se, but rather by the parameter values that are displayed in the tables. Let me say at the outset
that I am not particularly worried about Cobb-Douglas production
functions or about sectoral demands based on a Cobb-Douglas function. But if I were to modify these assumptions (implying substitution
elasticities of -1), my inclination would be to consider $-1/2$ as a first
alternative. (For big sectors like food, rises in sectoral prices lead to a
larger fraction of income being spent on the sector's goods. Among factors, a doubling of the cost of labor would in most cases lead to a larger
fraction of expenditures going to labor, and similarly for capital.)

My biggest objection, as already noted, concerns what the authors
call the portfolio-substitution or capital-substitution elasticities. This
represents the responsiveness of capital owners to differentials in rates
of return at home and abroad. At issue here is how one looks at the
international capital market. The authors cite Feldstein and Horioka
(1980), who highlight the high correlation between national rates of
saving and of investment. Nothing is wrong with their correlations,
but as I noted long ago (Harberger 1980), they refer to gross saving
and gross investment. Once the depreciation component that is mathematically common to both is eliminated, the resulting correlation between national rates of net saving and net investment is much lower.
But basically neither of these correlations is evidence of market imperfections. What is needed here is data on relative rates of return. I like to
think of the world capital markets as an interconnected hydraulic net-

work. One does not need perfect connections in all market segments in order to effectively equalize rates (among the major advanced-country markets); one only needs a sufficient number of active players in the markets where the pipes are fully open and where the flows are massive and highly responsive to small differentials. This is what I think I see in the world of covered interest arbitrage by major financial institutions; it is why I want to stick only with the highest of Gravelle and Smetters's portfolio elasticities.

The other elasticity that troubles me is the one between domestic and foreign manufactured products. My instinct is to think of pairwise comparisons—Ford versus Toyota, Philips versus Zenith, Exxon versus British Petroleum. What would happen, I ask, if one of these raised its prices by 50 to 100 percent vis-à-vis the other? My economist's bones tell me that such a phenomenon could not occur. Yet an elasticity of substitution of −3 implies an average own-price elasticity of −1.5, which in turn implies huge market power.[8]

Once I narrow down Gravelle and Smetters' tables to what I feel is a plausible range of parameters, I get domestic labor bearing between 38 and 71 percent of the burden, and domestic capital bearing between 36 and 55 percent of the burden with a presumption toward the 71/36 extreme. (See their table 2, rows 6 and 9.)

Compare this 71/36 extreme with my 96/12 result (my table 6.2). These could easily belong to the same family, and even more so when one considers that the Gravelle-Smetters measure includes excess burden while mine does not; also their measure probably includes the loss (from reduced rate of return) that US capital owners sustain on the capital that they shift abroad as a result of the tax. Thus I think our results are pretty close to one another, once somewhat comparable assumptions are imposed.

On other matters, I hope I can persuade Gravelle and Smetters to join my crusade for clarity of concept. Statements like "the original Harberger (1962) argument that the incidence is borne mainly by capital is now dead among academics" should be accompanied by the warning that if so, these academics have to understand that the choice between an open and a closed economy is a matter of *scenarios*, not of reality. I am sure that most academics would agree that the closed-economy result (that 100 percent borne by capital is in the middle, not at the extreme, of the plausible range of outcomes) is the one that would apply in the case of a general worldwide increase or reduction in the rate of corporation income taxation, and that the closed-economy model is the right one to use in this case. Likewise I hope that most academics would agree that the open-economy model is the right one to use if one country alone changes its CIT rate. And at the same time they should agree that the circumstances of these two scenarios are sufficiently different that there is no presumption that we can make generalizations about incidence that would apply equally well, regardless of whether a tax change was being implemented by one country alone or by all countries simultaneously. The key is to use an analytical framework that is appropriate for the scenario that one is exploring.

6.9   Notes on Short-Run, Transitional, and Dynamic Incidence

This is a good topic with which to conclude this chapter because it brings us sharply back to the opening theme, especially to the *unknown* and *unknowable* parts of that theme. To start with something relatively simple, let us take the topic of short-run incidence. Here the idea has always been that the owners or shareholders of an enterprise: (1) have holdings of a set of assets that represent fixed factors in the short run, and (2) are the residual claimants to the financial flows generated by that enterprise. These two characteristics in turn pretty much guarantee that they will initially bear the incidence of a new tax wedge.

But how long will this last? There is now a disequilibrium between the rate of return to capital in the taxed sectors, and that in the rest of the market. The capital stock will end up reallocated so as to once again equalize rates of return between the taxed and nontaxed sectors. As this happens, rates of return will presumably go down in the non-taxed sector and up in the taxed sector. Can we say anything about how long such a process will take? I think we can say very little. Adjustment will be faster, the higher the rate of depreciation in the taxed industry and the more readily saleable its capital assets. But adjustment will also be faster, the smaller is the size of the tax change in question. For with a tiny tax change, the needed adjustment of the capital stock might turn out to be possible almost instantaneously, and without any extra cost. In such a case we might jump to the long-run equilibrium solution in a single period, whereas with a big tax wedge, a slow depreciation rate, and "implanted" (unsaleable) capital assets, it might take ten years to reach the long-run solution.

All this makes me want to say that the details of such a transition process are pretty close to *unknowable*. We can build models of the usual kind, with parameters in orders of magnitude that we consider plausible, to get answers to the question of long-run incidence. But when we have to add dynamics to such a model, I don't think we can pin down the parameters of the dynamic process to a range that is narrow enough for us to learn much (if anything) from the exercise. I do not need a dynamic model to reach the judgment that rate-of-return equalization will not happen in one or two years (for a big tax wedge) but will probably have happened by ten or twelve years. Do I think that a research project could be designed that would convince me that yes, the adjustment will take place in four or five years, but almost certainly not take as long as six or seven years? No way!

Happily we can do somewhat better on dynamic incidence than on the transition problem, but even here it takes a strong assumption to get easy answers. That assumption is that the time path of the total relevant capital stock (within the total closed or open economy) is going to be the same, with or without the tax. Then we can say that once equilibrium is reached (i.e., once the transition is complete), we can think of a rolling equilibrium in a growing economy. In such a rolling equilibrium the net-of-tax returns in all sectors would be continuously "equalized" (with due adjustments for risk, etc.), and goods and factor markets would be continuously cleared. In short, our dynamic picture would be a set of images, each of which would come from our standard comparative-static model, only with a progressively larger capital stock and labor force, and a progressively more advanced technology, year-by-year as we modeled the passage of time.

I see no real problems with this; its only potential weakness seems to be the assumption that the time path of $\bar{K}_t$ is independent of the tax. This is an assumption that I personally find quite easy to live with. My own experience with high-real rates of return (up to 3 percent real per month on bank deposits, up to 20 percent real per year on Central Bank bonds) in Latin America leads me to the conclusion that ordinary people do not modify their consumption/saving decisions very significantly in response to higher yields. (This does not deny that the allocation of given savings among asset groups is responsive to differences in yield. It also, correctly for this purpose, defines savings in a national-income sense, excluding capital gains and losses on existing assets.) So with this assumption we can say we have a pretty good sense of what a rolling dynamic equilibrium looks like. Of course, this is just a modest extension of the results we have been getting from comparative-static models for half a century.

Once we release the assumption that the time path of the total capital stock is independent of the tax we are analyzing, all bets are off. Now everything depends on the dynamic mechanism by which total saving responds, which is something about which I neither see nor foresee any professional consensus for a long time to come.

Here I think our best bet is to make the most of what we know, and leave in limbo the remaining questions. To put some flesh on the bones of this argument, let me pose the question of the incidence of the corporation income tax in the United States. I am ready to assume that the time path of the world capital stock is independent of the time path of United States and other corporation tax rates. So for me the incidence problem seems manageable. But for someone else who isn't ready to go along with this key assumption, I would suggest posing the question the following way. Suppose that the world capital stock were frozen at today's level, and certain changes in one or more CIT rates were implemented. What would be the efficiency and incidence consequences, as this given capital stock is reallocated so as once again to "equalize" rates of return and to clear all markets? The answer to this question may not be the final answer to these people, but I think it would be a good start.

One could then ask them to project, for the future, a time path of $\bar{K}_t$ with no change in rates, and another for $\bar{K}_t$ with the changes we are analyzing. The easy case here would be one in which the equilibrium rate of growth was the same, with and without the tax changes, and in which, then, the time path of total capital with the tax changes ended up being year by year, a certain fraction of its time path without the tax changes. This would permit us to replicate the rolling equilibrium based on the assumption that $\bar{K}_t$ is independent, with an alternative rolling equilibrium in which the new $\bar{K}_t$ is simply β times the old one. Incidence for any period could then be derivable from our old, user-friendly, comparative-static models.

But in the end, the whole story of dynamic incidence depends on what we are prepared to assume about saving behavior. I'm afraid that whatever is assumed here is bound, for a long time to come, to have a huge Bayesian component. The idea that we will somehow stumble upon evidence that will lead to a general professional consensus regarding the responsiveness of saving to rates of return is, to me, just a dream.

6.10   Summary and Conclusions

1. The world never gives us a "clean" incidence scenario in which we can trace out the consequences of a tax change by simply following the data. I believe incidence exercises will always be "in our heads" as we insert tax changes into models that we think adequately represent the real world in its main relevant aspects.

2. If we want to answer an actual "real-world" question, we have to think of inserting "our" tax change into a setup in which we clearly specify how the proceeds are likely to be spent (or used to reduce other taxes), and what other distortions will be present as our incidence scenario is played out. It is clear that without such a specification the pattern of response could be almost anything—that is, would reasonably be called *unknowable*.

3. If we want to answer the standard "academic" question of what is *the* incidence of the corporation income tax, we have to think of creating clear scenarios in terms of which such a question makes sense. The traditional wisdom has been that we should insert "our" tax into a scenario with *no other distortions* and under an assumption of *demand neutrality*.

4. Even when we do this, we have to sharply distinguish between a *closed-economy scenario* (where all major countries insert, raise or lower a corporation income tax) and an *open-economy scenario* in which just one or only a few countries do so. Note that when speaking of the real world, I do not talk about a single country as being a closed economy. But the world as a whole, of course, is one.

5. I felt uncomfortable with my own analysis of the open-economy case until I came upon the notion of a four-sector model, with manufacturing, public utilities and transport, agriculture and services representing the four possible combinations of corporate/noncorporate and tradable/nontradable.

6. I make a major point of the wisdom of building models in which rates of return are "equalized" around the world. For a small economy, this means that its country's risk premium will be no different "with" or "without" its CIT. For a large modern economy like the United States, it means that any change in its rate of return (induced by its CIT) will be shared with the rest of the world.

7. This assumption, plus that of the small country being a price-taker in product markets for tradable goods, practically guarantees that labor

(in its role as a factor of production) will bear more than the full burden of the corporation income tax in a small country. In their roles as consumers, labor and capital would gain somewhat, but labor still would end up bearing more than the full CIT burden.

8. The example of table 6.1 shows labor bearing somewhat more than the full burden of the CIT in an economy that looks something like that of the United States, where at the same time the same full burden is also precisely borne (by design of the table) by the owners of capital throughout the world. There is no double-counting here. Foreign labor gains at the expense of foreign capital, and US consumers and land-owners gain at the expense of US labor.

9. Table 6.2 incorporates the realistic possibility that the country is not a complete price-taker for manufactured goods. It allows close to half of the burden of the CIT paid in that sector to be pushed forward to consumers of manufactured products. This changes the final incidence picture derived from table 6.1. Instead of labor ending up bearing (as factor and consumers) 130 percent of the burden of the CIT, it now ends up with 96 percent of the burden. Again, worldwide capital, by construction, bears 100 percent of the CIT burden.

10. No example is given with consumers of manufactures bearing the full weight of the CIT paid by that sector because I consider that extreme case to be unrealistic. Some important ejection of capital from the corporate sector is virtually inevitable. If there is any passthrough via higher prices to consumers, demand for capital will fall in both the tradable and nontradable corporate sectors, from both a scale effect and a substitution effect. This capital will have to be absorbed by the rest of the world plus the local nontradable sectors, entailing a fall in the rate of return to capital there.

11. In brief comments on the paper by Gravelle and Smetters, I have nothing but praise for their two-region, four-sector model as such, but have serious problems with two of their key parametric judgments. The most important of these concerns the workings of the international capital market. I find it quite implausible that relative real rates of return would change, as between, say, Europe and the United States, as a consequence of a change in the CIT of the United States. On the other problematic parameter, I believe that although product differentiation permits differential movements of manufactured goods prices between, say, the United States and Europe, a high degree of substitutability nonetheless prevails. All this leads to my feeling quite easy with the

results that they get under their highest assumptions regarding substitutability in the capital and manufactured-goods markets, but uneasy with their lower substitutability cases.

12. Unfortunately, Gravelle and Smetters's generalizations about their results focus on US capital bearing close to the full burden and US labor bearing little. These generalizations come from parts of their tables that assume relatively low substitutability in the capital and manufactured-goods markets.

13. On the subject of short-run and transitional incidence, I find the idea of the immediate impact being borne by the immediate residual claimants (equity owners) to be quite acceptable, but it doesn't teach us much. It by definition creates a capital-market disequilibrium which will presumably be resolved over time. I believe that the time path of this resolution (the transition) belongs in the class of the *unknowable*.

14. Dynamic incidence is somewhat more tractable. If one is ready to consider the time path of the total capital stock to be independent of the tax, dynamic incidence can be derived from a rolling equilibrium of the comparative-static model, with growing stocks of labor and capital and with steadily improving technology. With endogenous savings, a significant subclass of models would lead to an equilibrium "with" the CIT characterized by a given K/L ratio, and to an equilibrium "without" the CIT involving a lower K/L ratio. At any given point in time one would then solve the incidence problem by imposing a "with tax" equilibrium capital stock that was, say, β times that stock in the "without tax" situation.

If, however, we want dynamic results based on solid knowledge about people's saving behavior, I think we would have to use the term *unknown*, if not *unknowable*.

Discussion

Malcolm Gillis

The Harberger Model: Generations I through III, and Beyond

I take as my assignment the provision of historical perspective on this latest Harberger contribution on corporate tax incidence. I first interacted with Professor Harberger just two years after earning my PhD. Then, much of economics was still *unknown* to me. In the ensuing decades, I was privileged to learn from him in several overseas venues, including Colombia, Bolivia, and Indonesia. Because of that experience, whole new areas of economics became *known* to me. Over the course of his long career, he has transformed study and analysis not only in public finance but also in project evaluation, international economics, and economic development. He has been the economist most responsible for shrinking our zones of ignorance about incidence, inflation, and trade distortions. We know with some certainty that Al has mentored upward of two dozen finance and economy ministers plus hundreds of economics professors all over the world. But *unknowable* is the number of economists worldwide he has won over, through his example, to the practice of what he has always called "good economics." I would put that number somewhere in the tens of thousands. But the exact number will, of course, never be known. Practitioners of "good economics" the world over are content with this inexactitude, for, following Professor Harberger, they are well aware that, as for many things in economics, precision is ordinarily not possible at any price.

This most recent of his contributions on incidence contains, among other strengths, an eloquent plea for pursuing the *essence* of truly important questions in a world in which full and complete answers often cannot be bought except at prohibitive costs, in which case they are not *worth knowing*. Generation I of the Harberger model of corporate tax incidence (1962) demonstrates how the effects of the corporate tax play out in a two-sector closed economy, with capital mobile between sectors, under plausible parameter values. Generation II was, of course, his early 1970s work on the open-economy incidence model, while generation III, his four-sector model, appeared after 1980.

In all these cases he has remained squarely on message: we do well when we devise lean, spare incidence models enfolding the most salient and relevant aspects of the real world. The models may then be deployed for a limited number of well specified scenarios that are both significant and teachable, rather than upon *all possible* scenarios.

The first Harberger model—generation I—was truly pathbreaking. It awakened the economics profession to the theretofore unrecognized truth that for a closed economy, the longer-term incidence of the corporate tax was on all capital income in the taxing economy, not just capital employed in the corporate sector. Moreover, in this scenario, capital bears more than 100 percent of the tax. This result obtained under quite plausible assumptions for the relevant elasticities of product or factor substitution. However, the *efficiency* costs of the tax would vary greatly, according as the relevant elasticities are large or small. The Harberger conclusions soon displaced a competing view, based on some not-so-good econometrics, wherein the full burden of the tax was shifted forward to consumers in the form of higher product prices. That was generation I.

In those days few asked many questions about the effects of openness or capital mobility, as the profession as a whole tended to view US foreign trade as having relatively negligible share of the economy and, moreover, considered capital relatively immobile internationally. Professor Harberger and his students, however, were very much concerned both with openness and mobility of capital. This gave rise to Harberger's generation II in the early 1970s. From this model we learned that labor would overbear the *brunt* of the burden of the corporate tax. Labor ends up bearing much more than 100 percent of the tax burden even if we do not count excess burdens, or efficiency costs.

Over the next decade or so, the economics profession, or at least the public finance subset, largely came around to the view that long-held assumptions of international immobility of capital were counterfactual. When properly measured, the evidence of capital mobility across borders far outweighed that supporting immobility, then and now. So it was that with Harberger II, it became widely recognized that migrating capital would largely escape the tax burden. The conclusions of the Harberger generation I closed-economy model were by now inapplicable for all time. Or were they?

Here, just as many in the Federal Reserve System in the early years of the twenty-first century learned too much from nearly a decade of recent Japanese deflation, many economists learned too much from generation II of the Harberger incidence model. Why?

Beginning in the early 1980s, the pace of tax reform worldwide quickened notably, with many similarities in the various reform programs. (I note parenthetically that Professor Harberger had a hand, directly, as in Indonesia, or indirectly, as in the United States, in many of these programs.) In particular, governments in developed and developing countries moved away from steeply progressive rates of income tax adopted in the 1940s, 1950s, and 1960s. Notably, from 1984 through 1994, no less than 35 nations, from the United States to Indonesia, Ghana, and Mexico, enacted tax reforms involving much simplified taxes imposed at much lower, flatter rates. This movement enfolded capital taxes as well, including in virtually all reforming countries, corporate income taxes.

For this period the appropriate model for understanding incidence in the reforming countries was not Harberger generation II but Harberger generation I: the closed-economy model. As Professor Harberger has explained in numerous settings since then, when all countries—or even a few big ones—comprising most of the world economy select lower corporate tax rates in roughly parallel fashion over, say four to seven years, the appropriate model to use would not be the open-economy one where capital can successfully migrate away from the corporate tax burden.

Harberger III emerged around 1980, and has been successfully tweaked several times since. This latest member of the family of Harberger incidence models utilizes not two, but four sectors, thereby allowing richer conclusions than possible with the earlier generations.

The model is quite versatile. Suppose that one wishes to consider what might happen should a small open economy such as Chile reduce its rate of capital tax? The four-sector model is easily adoptable to *that* scenario. Alternatively, suppose that one is concerned about capital reallocation in the large country case, as when the United States increases or decreases corporate tax rates? Now, with differentiated products in the corporate manufacturing sector, we find both additional complexity but also more robust conclusions than possible with Harberger generation II. Capital bears a sizable fraction of the burden of a tax increase, prices of manufactured goods do rise, and labor's share is adversely affected, both on the income sources and the income uses side.

It is well worth noting that the three generations of the Harberger models for analyzing corporate tax incidence can be easily adapted to illuminate other important issues in economics generally and public finance in particular. For example, the open-economy versions can be utilized to assess the efficacy of subnational government incentives to attract capital investment. And although the focus of all Harberger incidence models is upon corporate tax incidence, they may also be usefully applied to the analysis of incidence of subsidies to either labor or capital.

Professor Harberger closes this contribution with timely reminders concerning the time path of adjustment when tax rates are changed. Totally in character, he places a high premium on essence and a low premium on the search for basically unknowable details. When the tax is changed, will the results work themselves out fully in two years, five, or ten? For a very small tax change in economies with rapid depreciation rates and few stranded (unsaleable) capital assets, the expected adjustments might be as short as a year. Contrarily, for a major tax change, in an economy with slow depreciation and many "stranded" assets, a decade-long transition might be required.

To sum up, one may say that the master mentor has struck yet again. To understand what Professor Harberger has meant all these years by the phrase "good economics," you could not do better than reading his chapter. I, for one, eagerly await generation IV of the Harberger family of incidence models.

Discussion

Jane G. Gravelle

Harberger's chapter addresses the question of whether domestic labor bears the burden of a corporate tax in an open economy. Its basic conclusion is that assuming other countries do not respond to a tax rate change, domestic labor "overbears" the burden of a corporate tax—that is, more than 100 percent of the burden falls on labor.

Harberger does suggest that if countries raise or lower their taxes in tandem with the United States, then the analysis reverts to the closed economy result, where, in general, labor bears none of the tax.

Most of this comment refers to the open-economy results and contrasts those results with the findings of Gravelle and Smetters (2006), who, using a four-sector model patterned after the Harberger model, find that labor bears little of the tax. There are four reasons for the differences between Harberger's results and our own: assumptions about capital–labor ratios, the allowance for imperfect product substitutability and imperfect capital mobility, the effect of debt finance, and the possibility, as suggested in Harberger's chapter, that a closed-economy model may be more appropriate.

Harberger's analysis assumes perfect mobility of capital and assumes that imports and domestic consumption of the corporate traded good are perfect substitutes. Even adopting those assumptions the Gravelle and Smetters (2006) results show a much lower burden on labor income, as shown in table 6.3. Harberger's analysis shows 130 percent of the burden falling on labor, with land rents and capital income rising; Gravelle and Smetters find only 70 percent of the burden falling on labor.

To understand these differences consider first the nominal effect on wages when the price of the traded good is the numeraire. In that

The views expressed in this comment do not necessarily reflect those of the Congressional Research Service.

Table 6.3
Distribution of tax burden: Perfect substitution case

Tax regime	Harberger	Gravelle and Smetters
Burden on labor	130%	71%
Burden on capital	−14%	36%
Burden on land	−16%	−1%

Sources: Harberger (chapter 6 in this volume), Gravelle and Smetters (2006).

case the burden on labor, labor times the change in wage, is $L_{dw} = [(L/L_1)(K_1/(K_1 + K_2)) - s(L/L_1)(K_1/K)] dt$, where L equals total labor, w equals the wage rate, K equals total capital, L_1 equals labor in the corporate tradable sector, K_1 equals capital in the corporate tradable sector, K_2 equals capital in the corporate nontradable sector, s equals the share of world capital, and t equals the tax rate.

The burden of the tax in this case will be very sensitive to factor intensities. As an illustration, let $s = 0$ (a small country case). In the Harberger model, the share of labor in the corporate tradable sector is one-fifth, and the capital stock in the corporate tradable sector is half the total corporate capital stock, leading to a $(5 \times 1/2)$ or 250 percent burden on labor. In the Gravelle and Smetters paper, the labor share is one-third, and the share of the corporate capital stock in the corporate tradable sector is 1/3, leading to a $(3 \times 1/3)$ or 100 percent burden on labor. The corporate tradable sector, primarily manufacturing is, according to our analysis, relatively labor intensive. The nontradable corporate sector, primarily utilities and transportation, is relatively capital intensive as is the nontradable noncorporate sector, which includes housing. (The agricultural sector is quite small.)

There are other factors that bring these numbers closer together. The second term, for example, which accounts for the large country effect, reduces the burden on labor to 219 percent for the Harberger model and 84 percent for the Gravelle and Smetters model. The other important differential, which reduces to Harberger burden to 130 percent but has a much more limited effect on the Gravelle and Smetters results, is the change in other prices in the economy. Because the nominal wage rate falls so much in the Harberger model, the noncorporate nontradable sector's price falls significantly. This price effect is very small in the Gravelle and Smetters model. The assumptions also vary in some other ways (e.g., existing foreign ownership of capital), but the principal reason for the differences between a real burden of 130 percent and one of 71 percent is the difference in factor intensities.

Table 6.4
Effect of imperfect substitution in portfolios and traded corporate product: Gravelle/Smetters

	Without produced capital		With produced capital and growth	
	Capital	Labor	Capital	Labor
Closed economy	100%	0%	100%	0%
Elasticities of 3	76%	18%	72%	21%
Perfect substitution	36%	71%	35%	73%

Source: Gravelle and Smetters (2006).

The second reason for the difference in conclusions about the burden of the tax is the use of product and portfolio substitution elasticities, which are set to infinity in the Harberger model. Gravelle and Smetters, who report sensitivity analysis with a variety of elasticity assumptions suggest that setting both these elasticities at around 3 (still a relatively high elasticity) is more consistent with the empirical evidence.

Table 6.4 shows some sample effects of elasticities in the Gravelle and Smetters model under two assumptions, one without produced capital goods (similar to the Harberger model) and one with produced capital goods and a steady-state growth rate of 2 percent. (Note that some of the burden can be exported). A third reason to believe that labor bears little of the burden in an open economy is the option of debt finance, combined with the typical features of corporate taxes, at least as imposed in the United States, which usually subsidize debt by allowing a deduction for nominal interest at the statutory tax rate, but taxing only the real return and often at a lower rate. Harberger argues in his chapter that billions of dollars cross the Atlantic to achieve a modest gain in interest rates. Yet the empirical evidence on foreign direct investment, the dominant form of equity investment, suggests elasticities on the order of 3 or less. These views could be reconciled if we view debt as far more mobile among countries, which seems reasonable. But if the corporate tax does not fall on debt finance, but rather subsidizes it, then it is possible for the corporate tax to induce an inflow rather than an outflow of capital, benefiting rather than penalizing labor.

The final reason that labor may bear little of the tax is that especially for the United States, it may be that a change in tax rates on our part induces a change in a similar direction abroad. If these changes were precisely the same, we would be back in the world of the closed economy of Harberger (1962). There is actually some evidence (Randolph 2005) that countries do change their tax rates in a similar fashion, and this evidence suggests a partial shift back to the closed economy.

In addition to this argument for considering, at least in part, the closed economy effects is that the analysis in both this chapter by Harberger and Gravelle and Smetters (2006) treats the corporate tax as a pure territorial or source based tax. If the tax were a residence based tax (only applying to earnings of US owners of capital), then the closed-economy case would be appropriate. There are some elements of residence based taxes in the US tax system: we defer rather than forgive tax on income invested abroad through foreign subsidiaries, and tax income (while allowing a foreign tax credit) when income is repatriated or earned through a branch.

On the whole, I think the evidence points in the direction of capital rather than domestic labor bearing most, perhaps all, or even more than 100 percent of the tax in an open economy. I think it still appropriate to assign that tax to capital income in preparing distributional analyses as is currently done by the Treasury Department and the Congressional Budget Office.

Notes

1. Economists have to make a similar assumption when dealing with the measurement of the efficiency costs (excess burdens) of taxation. Here the practice has been to use the convention of "lump-sum taxes and transfers" to keep individuals and households on their original set of demand functions. In this case module 1 would deal with the efficiency costs of the corporation income tax, with lump-sum taxes and transfers keeping the purchasing power of individuals and households the same as before, and module 2 would deal with the efficiency effects of taking away these lump-sum taxes and transfers and using the net proceeds to finance the airport project.

2. More elegantly, we could consider the average rate of CIT collections in C and D $(\bar{T}_{cd})$ as a general tax on the income of all capital, the incidence of which would fall exclusively on the income from capital, assuming that factor to be in fixed supply $(K_a + K_b + K_c + K_d = \bar{K})$. Then the partial factor taxes would be $(T_a - \bar{T}_{cd})$, $(T_b - \bar{T}_{cd})$, $(T_c - \bar{T}_{cd})$, and $(T_d - \bar{T}_{cd})$. We would neglect $(T_c - \bar{T}_{cd})$ and $(T_d - \bar{T}_{cd})$ as being small and averaging out to zero over the two nontradable sectors (C and D).

3. The main reason why T_{ka} and T_{kb} would differ in the real world would not be different official rates of tax on corporate profits, but rather different ratios of debt to equity, as between "manufacturing," on the one hand, and "public utilities plus transport," on the other. Typically the latter sector has significantly higher equilibrium debt–equity ratios, thus causing its "effective" rate of corporation income tax to be lower.

4. The alternative assumption is to treat the national income of the country as incorporating the return to the capital that its residents (the Argentines) shifted abroad as a conse-

quence of the tax. Under this assumption one has not balanced trade but balanced payments, with one piece of capital income shifting from domestic source to foreign sources as a consequence of the tax. The natural result of this would be an appreciation of the *equilibrium* (steady-state) real exchange rate as a consequence of the tax, making tradables (both corporate and noncorporate) relatively cheaper, and nontradables (both corporate and noncorporate) relatively more expensive. I do not believe that this would make for an important modification of the incidence conclusions that we get, based on balanced trade in both the before-tax and the after-tax equilibria. In any case, I see no basis for thinking that the equilibrium real rate of return on capital will be different, with or without the corporation income tax. The conclusion is that we should continue to treat the small open economy as a price-taker in the international capital market.

5. Our methodology does not include "excess burden" as a part of incidence. I always have liked the distinction between "burden" (an incidence problem) and "excess burden" (an efficiency problem). Mathematically "burden" can be treated (as I do here) as a first-order effect ($\sum F_j dp_j$, with F standing for factors), and "excess burden" as a second order effect, such as $\frac{1}{2}\sum_j dF_j dp_j$. Anyway, readers should realize that the measures of "burden" presented here are intended to exclude "excess burden."

6. A nuance concerning tables 6.1 and 6.2: since they are counting only the capital stock that remains in the United States in the presence of the tax, they leave out of account the reduction net yield (from 9 to 8 percent in my example) on the capital that relocated abroad in the presence of the tax. This would add somewhat to the burden on US capital owners, but it would qualify as a second-order effect, $dK_f dp_k$, where dK_f is US capital shifted abroad as a result of the tax.

7. In self-defense, however, I must say that there is nothing unrigorous about solutions to the incidence problem that are based on price-formation equations, at least so long as one is willing to employ the assumptions of competitive behavior plus production functions that are homogeneous of degree one. These assumptions are fully sufficient in the small-country case (the country being a price-taker in both the capital market and the markets for tradable goods). These assumptions do not go all the way in the cases where world rates of return change as a result of the tax, nor in the case where tradable products are differentiated. But they can be made to give simple and straightforward answers to scenarios in which specific changes in world rates of return, and specific degrees of passthrough of the CIT into manufactured goods prices are explored. This is what I do in the present chapter.

8. Consider two sets of goods A and B where outside substitutes are negligible. If the elasticity of substitution between A and B is γ_{ab}, let us write $d \log A - d \log B = \gamma_{ab}(d \log p_a - d \log p_b)$. Set $d \log p_b$ equal to zero, and you get $d \log A / d \log p_a - d \log B / d \log p_a = \gamma_{ab}$. Thus $\eta^*_{aa} - \eta^*_{ba} = \gamma_{ab}$. Similarly, setting $d \log p_a$ equal to zero gets $\eta^*_{bb} - \eta^*_{ab} = \gamma_{ab}$. Neglecting outside substitutes means relative quantities A/B respond only to the relative price p_A/p_B. This leads to $\eta^*_{bb} \equiv \eta^*_{ba}$ and $\eta^*_{aa} = -\eta^*_{ab}$. Substituting gets $\eta^*_{aa} + \eta^*_{bb} = \gamma_{ab}$; that is, the elasticity of substitution is the sum of the two own-price elasticities (asterisks represent substitution-effect-only elasticities.)

7 Corporate Taxes in the World Economy: Reforming the Taxation of Cross-border Income

Harry Grubert and Rosanne Altshuler

Globalization and the decline in corporate tax rates around the world have focused attention on the corporate tax in an international context. The current US system for taxing cross-border corporate income is very complex, induces inefficient behavioral responses, and leaves both companies and policy analysts dissatisfied. A number of proposals have been put forward to address this situation. For example, the President's Advisory Panel on Federal Tax Reform recommended two approaches for the taxation of cross-border income: adoption of a territorial tax system within the context of a simplified income tax and a destination-based cash-flow tax within the context of a consumption-tax prototype.[1] It is important to recognize that these proposals for reform of the current system and others that have been debated all have differing strengths and weaknesses. The goal of this chapter is to evaluate proposals for reform of the taxation of cross-border income within the constraints of current knowledge.

While we focus on the taxation of cross-border income, particularly direct investment, analyzing the cross-border issue cannot be isolated from the rest of the tax system. As we note, increased capital mobility justifies a change in the mix of corporate and personal taxation within a given revenue constraint. Lowering the corporate statutory rate within general base broadening and a shift of more of the taxation of capital to the personal level is consistent with an attractive option described below for the taxation of cross-border corporate income. International considerations also tilt the choice between lowering the corporate rate versus expensing toward a simple reduction in the corporate rate. A lower corporate rate reduces the incentives for shifting income out of the United States, which both loses revenue and magnifies the attractiveness of investing in low-tax locations.

One of the difficulties in evaluating reform proposals is that the models and estimates of behavioral elasticities required for judging an international tax system definitively are beyond the scope of current knowledge, and we cannot assume that they will ultimately be knowable. There is an extensive literature on the alternative principles that should guide the process, including capital export neutrality (CEN), capital import neutrality (CIN), and more recently, capital ownership neutrality (CON). However, none of these benchmarks is satisfactory because the argument supporting them usually takes place within very simple models. The necessity to examine all the important responses to a change in the tax on international corporate income such as the choice of where to exploit intangible assets like patents, the choice of where to locate income and expenses for tax purposes, and the choice between alternative types of financing in different locations, among other decision margins, makes it clear that no one-dimensional criterion is useful and that a complete evaluation of any reform proposal is probably not feasible.

Nevertheless, it is clear that progress can be made along a number of decision margins. For example, the resources companies devote to avoiding the tax on repatriating income is a waste and is rendered unnecessary under several reform proposals. Furthermore, while it is difficult to conclude where in the range between pure residence taxation under CEN and pure source taxation under CIN is optimal, it is probably true that tax burdens far out of the range, such as large (in absolute value) negative tax rates, on the one hand, and double taxation, on the other, do not represent good tax policy. The current system creates incentives for behavior that are inefficient under any criterion and these distortions are the main subject of this chapter.

The alternative international tax reforms we consider within an income tax rubric are dividend exemption, similar to the proposal made by the Tax Reform Panel, and a constant burden worldwide option in which there is no deferral privilege for active earnings retained abroad, no required allocations of expenses to foreign income, and a reduction in the US tax rate on foreign income so as to leave the overall residual US tax on foreign business income unchanged. This latter option is a variant of the international component of the system proposed by Edward Kleinbard (see Kleinbard 2005, 2006). On the consumption tax side we review the relative merits of destination- and origin-based systems. As a sidelight, we examine whether a destination-based *income* tax, which some analysts have proposed, is a policy that should seriously be considered. Finally, while we concentrate almost exclusively on the taxation of foreign source income, we do comment on how international considerations might alter the analysis of the reform of the corporate tax on domestic income.

While international taxation may seem complicated, there are in fact only a small number of moving parts. One question is whether a system imposes a US tax on repatriated income. Dividend exemption, for example, would eliminate any repatriation tax on active income earned abroad. Another question is whether the system provides an incentive for manipulating transfer prices. The worldwide system does not because all foreign income is taxed currently. The only qualification is the possibility of companies having excess foreign tax credits, which would continue to offer them incentives for income shifting. For this reason the frequency of excess credits will be an important consideration in evaluating the worldwide proposal. Furthermore this question of excess credits brings us to another important issue, which is the taxation of royalties and other intangible income. Under current law, most royalties, although deductible abroad, are exempt from US tax because of available excess foreign tax credits. But royalties are fully taxed under dividend exemption, for example.

Burden neutral worldwide taxation seems to dominate dividend exemption because it eliminates many more distortions in addition to repatriation behavior. These include transfer price planning, the shifting of the location of debt and the need to make expense allocations. The option would increase the effective tax rates on investment in low-tax countries while not increasing the average US tax rate on foreign source income. However, within the state of current knowledge, we cannot be certain that this improves the worldwide allocation of capital.

Finally, another advantage of the burden neutral option is that it has fewer components that are susceptible to pressure during the political process. Under dividend exemption the full taxation of royalties and the required allocation of expenses to exempt income are critical components. There would be predictable attempts to exempt royalties in addition to dividends, or tax them at a much lower rate, and to water down the expense allocation requirement. This would completely change the character of the option. In contrast, the burden neutral proposal has just one critical parameter, the corporate tax rate, and any attempt to lower it would be constrained by its necessary application to domestic income as well. Further any attempt to raise (or lower) the corporate rate would generate a national policy debate.

An important remaining issue is the basic tax rate on all corporate income and coordinating the foreign and domestic components. Estimates from the Treasury tax files suggest that the burden neutral option requires a tax rate on foreign income of about 28 percent. But revenue neutral base broadening on the domestic side would only bring the corporate rate down to about 32 percent.[2] In this chapter we consider the income tax options and consumption taxes separately. There could of course be a combination of the two, for example, a moderate VAT that would permit lower corporate and personal rates.

The obvious answer to the conundrum of coordinating foreign and domestic components within the income tax rubric is to shift more of the tax on capital to the personal level. In an open economy the corporate and personal tax systems cannot be considered separately. Increasing the tax on capital at the personal level while reducing the tax on broad-based corporate income to 28 percent would greatly enhance the competitiveness of the domestic operations of US corporations and also keep the average tax burden on their foreign operations unchanged. A lower US corporate tax burden would increase the attractiveness of investing in the United States by foreign companies. We do not have a full answer to how to make this shift. (Repealing the special lower tax rate on dividends enacted with the Jobs and Growth Tax Relief Reconciliation Act of 2003 (JGTRRA), for example, only buys about one-third to one-half of the reduction from 32 to 28 percent.) But the benefits of such a switch would seem to make the enquiry worthwhile.

Lowering the corporate rate on US domestic income would tend to reduce a behavioral distortion we do not emphasize in the chapter, the ultimate US saver's choice between investing in US and foreign companies. Corporate tax rates have been coming down around the world. A recent study by the Institute for Fiscal Studies indicates the average G7 tax rate went down by eight percentage points from 1996 to 2005. The European Union's core 15 members' average tax rate is now 30 percent.[3] Furthermore this decline is reflected in the tax burden of US manufacturing subsidiaries abroad. The 2002 Treasury tax files indicate that the average statutory tax rate abroad that they operate in is, weighted by their income, about 29 percent. Their effective tax rate on net income is only about 16 percent.

US shareholders have the opportunity for enjoying these lower foreign rates by investing directly in foreign companies. In this chapter we do not explore ambitious integration schemes such as full partnership taxation with the current inclusion of all corporate income at the individual shareholder level. This would achieve the goals of the corporate level schemes for the taxation of cross-border income that we do study. But, for one thing, this would require the look through to the ultimate earnings of the foreign corporations owned by US shareholders, which would be very impracticable. It also raises the question of how to tax foreign owners of US corporate income. Nevertheless, it appears better to move toward integration by lowering taxes at the corporate level because that brings the cross-border benefits.

Although the burden neutral worldwide option holds the overall US tax burden on foreign income equal to the current burden, we recognize that US companies that are mainly in low-tax locations may find that the resulting 28 percent rate puts them at a competitive disadvantage. Lowering the corporate rate even further may offset any impact on competitiveness but diminishes the benefits of the option relative to the current system by increasing the frequency and size of excess credits. An important unknown in an evaluation of the trade-off between a lower US corporate tax rate and the occurrence of excess credits is the reaction of foreign governments. If foreign governments were to follow suit and lower rates, fewer companies would find themselves with excess foreign tax credits.

The plan of the remainder of the chapter is as follows. We start with a brief description of the current US system along with data on the tax actually borne by different types of cross-border income such as dividends and royalties. This is followed by a short presentation of the reform options. The next section discusses important shortcomings of the standards that have been proposed for evaluating the efficiency of international tax systems. We then spell out the various behavioral margins that the international tax system acts upon and review the empirical evidence on how company behavior is affected along these decision margins. The penultimate section provides an evaluation of the alternative reform proposals. The final section offers some concluding thoughts on tax reform in an open economy.

Harry Grubert and Rosanne Altshuler

7.1 Current US System for Taxing International Income: What Income Does It Tax?

The United States imposes a tax on all repatriated foreign income, including not only dividends but also royalties, interest, and other foreign payments. Taxpayers can also identify certain income as "foreign source" even though it may have no connection with any US business activity abroad. Income from exports is an example. Under the current "sales source" rules, 50 percent of export sales income can be classified as foreign source.

Under the current system certain types of foreign income do not qualify for deferral and are instead taxed upon accrual under what are generally referred to as controlled foreign corporation (CFC) rules. These rules are part of the Subpart F provisions of the tax code. In general, these "anti-tax avoidance" provisions deny deferred taxation on foreign subsidiary income that is considered abusive or "tainted." Tainted income includes passive portfolio income and the payment of interest, dividends, and royalties from one CFC to a CFC in another jurisdiction.

Taxpayers receive a foreign tax credit against tentative US tax for foreign taxes paid on foreign source income, including a credit for the underlying foreign corporate tax linked to a dividend. However, this credit is limited to what the US tax would have been had the income been earned in the United States. The limitation on the credit prevents countries that are host to large amounts of US foreign activity from imposing exorbitant tax rates on the income generated from US companies and diverting revenues from the US Treasury. In fact the justification for the credit limitation has to do with the behavior of governments and not the behavior or burden of US taxpayers.

Two steps are important in the foreign tax credit limitation calculation. First, the foreign income is separated into baskets to restrict cross-crediting, namely credits flowing over from highly taxed income to shield income that has been lightly taxed. Before the 2004 American Jobs Creation Act (AJCA) the three significant income baskets were general nonfinancial active income, financial services income, and passive income. The AJCA effectively collapsed the baskets into two, active income and passive income. Within any basket, excess credits generated by one type of income (e.g., dividends) can flow over to other income in the basket (e.g., royalties) and shield that income from any residual US tax.

In the second step of the foreign tax credit limitation calculation, parent overhead expenses such as interest are allocated to each basket to calculate the net foreign income on which the credit can be claimed. This only affects companies if they cannot credit all the foreign taxes they have paid. If a company has excess credits, allocation of expenses to foreign income increases US tax by reducing allowable credits. If the company does not have excess credits, or is currently not repatriating income, the allocations have no effect on current US tax liability. Allocations of overhead expenses can be very large and play an important role in some of the reform options.

To illustrate these provisions, consider two companies A and B, each with a single investment abroad. Company A invests in a low-tax country with a statutory and effective tax rate of 10 percent while B invests in a country with a 40 percent tax rate. The US statutory rate is 35 percent. Company A and B each earn 100 abroad (under both US and foreign income concepts) and repatriate the entire amount. Assume first that there are no required allocations of parent overhead expense for the purpose of determining the foreign tax credit. If A repatriates all its income it has a tentative US tax of 35, but it receives a credit of 10 for foreign taxes paid, leaving a residual US tax of 25. Company B has paid 40 in US tax but only receives a credit of 35 on its 100 of (grossed-up) foreign income. It has excess credits of 5.

Now assume that each has to allocate 10 of parent interest to foreign income when calculating its foreign tax credit limitation. Therefore, while each still has the same amount of gross foreign income of 100, their foreign tax credit limitation is now 35 percent of the *net* foreign income of 90, or 31.5. This has no effect on company A because it has only paid foreign tax of 10. But B's US tax liability goes up by 3.5. It reports foreign income of 100 on its tax return but it only gets a credit of 31.5.

Finally, what if 10 of the 100 gross foreign income is in the form not of a dividend but a royalty deductible abroad? Nothing changes for A because its foreign tax drops to 9 but this is just offset by the higher residual US tax after the credit of 9. But company B is better off. B saves 4 of foreign tax because it pays 36 on taxable income in the foreign country of 90. The lower foreign tax has no effect on US tax because it can still only credit 31.5. So it has a net gain of 4 of reduced worldwide tax liability. In effect, the royalty is taxed nowhere because it is deductible abroad and shielded by available excess credits at home.

In 2000, tabulations of the Treasury tax files indicate that the US residual tax on corporate "foreign" income was $12.7 billion. Admittedly, this figure does not adequately convey the "true" effective tax burden on foreign income, in part because of the way "foreign income" is defined in US law. Some income produced in the United States can end up being classified as foreign and some produced abroad can be classified as domestic. Both positive and negative adjustments should in principle be made. The $12.7 billion is an overstatement of the true US tax burden on foreign income to the extent that income is shifted out of the United States and retained in a low-tax jurisdiction abroad. On the other hand, the $12.7 billion may be an understatement because in 2000 the interest allocations mandated under the US rules were overly strict, effectively classifying some foreign income as domestic and subject to full US tax. The added US tax on income misclassified as domestic should be added to the burden on foreign income.[4] The $12.7 billion measure also does not include "implicit" taxes, the costs companies bear to avoid the actual tax. An important example is the cost of avoiding the repatriation tax on dividends through various planning strategies. Each of these "unseen" positive and negative components (income shifting, allocations, tax planning costs) is an important consideration in comparing the reform options.

It is useful, nevertheless, to look inside the $12.7 billion of revenue to see the components of "foreign" income and how they are taxed. Understanding the current taxation of the different components of foreign income helps focus attention on the most important behavioral changes that result from the current system. One thing that is clear is that a relatively small amount of revenue is accounted for by dividends, at most 15 percent in 2000. Less than half of the tax revenues from foreign income in 2000—$5.6 billion—was derived from the general, active nonfinancial foreign tax credit basket, and only about $1.3 billion of that was from dividend repatriations. The remaining $4.3 billion was from royalties, interest received from subsidiaries and export income. $4.6 billion of US tax came from the financial services basket, and of that only about $0.3 billion was from dividends. The remainder was split about evenly between tax on the income of unincorporated foreign branches of US banks and interest received directly by US banks on foreign loans. Finally, $2.1 billion of revenue was obtained from the passive basket (and the remaining 0.4 billion from the other baskets). Most of this $2.1 billion is financial income earned by US controlled companies abroad that is taxed currently to the parent under the US anti-abuse rules.

Export income and, in particular, royalties in the active basket require further comment. A significant amount of each are now shielded from US tax because of excess credits originating from highly taxed dividends. In the case of royalties this creates a tax incentive to exploit intellectual property like a patent for a new computer chip abroad rather than in the United States, since the returns will escape US taxation. Similarly the shielding of export income is an export incentive for companies with excess foreign tax credits. As we will see, many of the reform proposals affect both of these decision margins.

Tax provisions affecting royalties and the income from intangible assets in general are of particular importance because they have become a significant source of foreign direct investment income. The exploitation of parent "know-how" is a very important motivation for foreign investment. Data published by the Department of Commerce indicate that royalties and license fees received by US companies in 2004 amounted to $52.6 billion (Survey of Current Business 2005). Total direct investment income not including royalty income but including deferred income amounted to $233.6 billion in 2004. Treasury tabulations for 2000 indicate that royalties received by US multinational companies (MNCs) amounted to $45.1 billion or more than 35 percent of total net repatriated nonfinancial foreign income, which is dominated by manufacturing. It is also of interest that these royalty payments only yielded additional taxes of $5.8 billion. Almost two-thirds were shielded by excess credits arising from dividends. Moreover recent work suggests that royalties represent less than half of the contribution that parent R&D makes to subsidiary income (see Mutti and Grubert 2006). The problems of estimating the "correct" arm's-length royalties and the prices of intangible intensive goods and services create opportunities for shifting income to low-tax locations. Accordingly the tax system can influence the choice between exploiting intellectual property at home or abroad and also the choice of which country is the best foreign location.

7.2   The Alternative Reform Options

This section briefly outlines the reform options we consider. The goal is to highlight how the simple elements of international taxation (e.g., whether and when there is a tax on active foreign income, whether expense allocation rules are imposed, and the treatment of royalties) that affect behavioral margins change across the options. Our analysis of the reform options follows our discussion of what is known about behavioral responses.

7.2.1 Dividend Exemption

Reforms suggested recently by the President's Advisory Panel on Federal Tax Reform (2005) and by the staff of the Joint Committee on Taxation (2005a) include dividend exemption proposals. These recommendations have generated increased interest in understanding the consequences of adopting a dividend exemption system for the United States. The basic features we consider are based on the dividend exemption system described in Grubert and Mutti (2001) and are similar to both recent proposals.

The starting point for the reform is the elimination of the repatriation tax applied to dividend income from foreign affiliates. This income would be exempt from US taxation, and the foreign tax credits associated with it would no longer play any role in the tax system. Income that is deductible abroad would be taxed in the United States so that all income is taxed once. Thus royalties and interest paid to the US parent, which are deductible expenses abroad, would be taxed at the US tax rate. As should be clear from the previous section, these are significant changes relative to the current system. Passive income would continue to be taxed on a current basis, and the current anti-tax avoidance provisions contained in Subpart F of the tax code would remain in place.

Any dividend exemption system adopted in the United States would be expected to be paired with rules that allocate parent overhead expenses, such as interest, to exempt income. (This would be an extension of the US tax principle that expenses related to exempt income be allocated to exempt income.) Expense allocations prevent companies from generating negative effective tax rates abroad by earning exempt income in a low-tax country while taking deductions in the United States. Under the dividend exemption scheme we consider, the amount of the parent company interest expense disallowed would be based on the relative size of gross domestic and foreign assets as under AJCA. This allocation scheme is often described as providing "worldwide fungibility" to companies. Parent R&D expenses would not be allocated and would thus be fully deductible at the US tax rate since royalties are fully taxed at the US tax rate.[5] As under present law other overhead expenses would also be subject to allocation rules.

Income from export sales would not be classified as active foreign income and would be fully taxable. Further, since excess credits no longer play any role in the system, the current "sales source" rules under which 50 percent of export income can be classified as foreign source is no longer relevant. As a result the export incentive provided to companies with excess credits under current law would be eliminated.

Based on the Grubert (2001) analysis of tax revenues under this dividend exemption scheme as well as the revenue estimate attached to the Joint Committee on Taxation option,[6] we expect that this reform would generate a small revenue gain at the current 35 percent corporate statutory tax rate.[7] While we make the assumption that this option imposes about the same average burden on foreign source income as current law for our analysis, we recognize that our estimate is not precise since it does not take into account the full range of possible behavioral responses.

7.2.2   Constant Burden Worldwide Taxation

The alternative reform we consider within the context of an income tax represents the other end of the spectrum with regard to active income earned abroad. Under constant burden worldwide taxation, deferral is eliminated. All foreign income is part of the worldwide base and is taxed immediately. Removing deferral from the code has the potential to remove all tax-planning incentives. Transfer prices would, potentially, be irrelevant at least to the extent that companies do not have excess foreign tax credits.[8]

Since all foreign income is in the worldwide taxable base, overhead expenses that support foreign investment should be deductible from the base. Following this logic, we pair this provision with the elimination of expense allocation rules. While this may violate the rules of correct income measurement, it has several major advantages as explained below. It decreases the frequency of excess credits and reduces the extent to which the corporate tax rate has to fall to keep average tax burdens on foreign source income unchanged. In addition, removing companies from the burden of having to allocate expenses would be a major simplification to current law.

The foreign tax credit would be maintained as would the foreign tax credit limitation.[9] As mentioned above, without a foreign tax credit limitation foreign governments would have an incentive to divert revenues from the US Treasury by raising rates on US investment. Importantly, firms with excess credits under the new regime would face tax-planning incentives. As a result understanding the frequency of excess credit positions is of critical importance.

This reform of the US tax system would reduce the competitiveness of US companies abroad if it were not paired with a reduction in rates. For this reason we pair worldwide taxation with a reduction in the tax rate on foreign source income that holds the current US tax burden on this income constant. The procedure used to estimate the rate is described in our analysis of the reform options. The estimate does not take into account any extra revenue that would end up in the worldwide tax base due to the reduction in tax planning costs associated with this reform. As discussed further in section 7.4, the burden neutral rate turns out to be approximately 28 percent. This revenue neutral rate is based on work with the Treasury tax files but should not be interpreted as an official Treasury estimate.

Our calculations based on the 2002 tax files suggest that companies with about 30 percent of total foreign source income would end up in excess credit at the burden neutral rate of 28 percent. The companies in excess credit are dominated by those in petroleum which are virtually all in excess credit as under current law. In contrast, only about 18 percent of the foreign income of manufacturing parents would be in excess credit. And we might expect the frequency of excess credits to fall as a result of the decline in foreign tax rates since 2002.

7.2.3 Destination-Based and Origin-Based Consumption Taxes

The tax reform debate often focuses on proposals to replace the current income tax system with a consumption tax. While there are a host of issues to consider, many of which are addressed in other chapters in this volume, our focus is on the international implications of a switch from income to consumption taxation.[10] For simplicity, we consider a consumption tax in the form of a VAT and ignore issues such as the taxation of financial institutions.

Consumption taxes can be imposed on either a destination basis or an origin basis. Under a destination base, sales to customers abroad (exports) are excluded while purchases from abroad (imports) are included. The tax base is the value added of domestic consumption wherever it is produced. An origin base, in contrast, would not impose a tax on goods produced outside of the United States. The tax base under this variant is domestic consumption plus net exports. As we will see, the different bases will have important implications for the behavioral margins.

The tax treatment of royalties from abroad, which can be thought of as representing payments on the export of an intangible asset, depends on the base. Under a destination base, royalties received from abroad would be exempt (and royalties paid to foreigners would not be deductible). In contrast, all royalties would be included in the tax base (and all royalty payments would be deductible), if the consumption tax were implemented using an origin base. Expense allocations do not arise under a consumption tax.

7.3   An Efficiency Criterion for Foreign Investment?

As we noted in the introduction, a definitive analysis of the relative merits of alternative reforms is difficult because it requires more complete models than have been presented, and furthermore relevant parameter estimates for a more fully articulated model are unlikely to be available anytime soon. Several standards have been proposed for optimal worldwide efficiency such as capital export neutrality (CEN), capital import neutrality (CIN), and capital ownership neutrality (CON), but each is based on a consideration of only a partial view of all the decision margins facing companies making cross-border investments.[11] For example, all focus on investment of tangible capital without considering the critical role of the location of intangible capital. Also none of them takes the opportunities for income shifting into account. As a result there is frequently not a very good mapping between efficiency criteria such as CEN or CIN that have been proposed and a particular reform alternative. For example, when the details of how a policy really works are examined, it becomes clear that dividend exemption, which appears to be a move toward CIN, is actually a move toward CEN (Grubert and Mutti 2001).

The usual standards that have been proposed such as CEN or CIN explicitly or implicitly make very special assumptions for which there is very little empirical evidence. One issue is the supply of capital available to US multinational companies. For example, CEN assumes that all investment by US companies comes from domestic saving, more correctly from a fixed pool of capital available to the US corporate sector.[12] CIN and CON seem to assume that capital is supplied at a fixed rate by the integrated world capital market, but that is only the start of the story. As mentioned above, all three ignore the presence of intangible assets and how they affect the relationship between investments in different locations, or how opportunities for income shifting under one system or another alter effective tax rates in different locations.

Therefore, even if we accept an integrated worldwide capital market that offers financing to companies on the same terms regardless of where they are based, that is not sufficient to choose the optimal policy. Consider a potential investment in a low-tax location. The question is what other investments in that or other locations it competes with. We can imagine various situations. One extreme example might be a locational intangible like a fast food trademark that requires that the company produce locally in order to supply its customers. In that case, all competitors compete in the same location and should bear the same (presumably local) tax burden. At the other extreme is a mobile intangible like the design of a computer chip that can be produced in various locations for the worldwide market. In that case, the competitors for the potential low-tax investment may be in high-tax locations including the United States.[13] CIN and CON implicitly assume the first case and CEN seems to lean toward the second where all foreign affiliate production substitutes for domestic US production. For example, CON fits the case of various bidders for an existing asset, like a pub in Ireland, with a given product and a circumscribed local market that will not be altered by the transaction. None of the standards proposed fits all cases and tax policy cannot feasibly be calibrated to have different rules for different cases.

Furthermore, even if we assume that the low-tax investment only has local competitors, CIN or CON may not be optimal because opportunities for income shifting can magnify the benefit of a low-tax location. The tax planning itself also wastes resources. For example, the investment might be financed by borrowing by a related party in a high-tax location, or the subsidiary may pay low royalties for a very valuable patent, creating very low or negative effective tax burdens. Being part of a multinational company may offer the subsidiary substantially lower tax burdens than purely local competitors.

Accordingly what reform within an income tax can hope to accomplish is to eliminate unnecessary waste and the possibility of extremely high or low tax burdens that are not justified under any standard. Then we can at least be sure that we are moving toward the optimum without overshooting it and running the risk of making things worse.

7.4   The Behavioral Margins Impacted by International Tax Systems

As we have stressed above, international tax systems can act on many behavioral margins in addition to the choice of location. The current tax system induces a number of behavioral responses that both waste resources and lead to inappropriate incentives to invest tangible and intangible capital in various locations. These include strategies to avoid the US repatriation tax on dividends, to shift debt from high-tax to low-tax locations, and to shift income to low-tax locations by distorting transfer prices or paying inadequate royalties. Besides directly wasting resources, these strategies can lead to inefficient choices between related party and arm's-length transactions and a distribution of tangible and intangible assets across locations that cannot be justified on any conceptual basis.

In our evaluation of the distortions that may be eliminated by some of the reform proposals, we focus on how the proposals affect the location of tangible capital, the location of intangible capital, the repatriation decision, financing decisions, income shifting, incentives to lower foreign tax burdens, export decisions, and host government decisions regarding the taxation of US companies. More is known about the distortion of behavior along some of these margins than others.[14] The remainder of this section reviews available evidence that is of relevance to our analysis of reform options.

7.4.1   Location of Tangible Capital

There is ample empirical evidence that the location of assets held in US multinational corporations is sensitive to variations in effective tax rates across foreign locations.[15] Less empirical work has focused on the role played by repatriation taxes in explaining the distribution of US corporate investment abroad. Grubert and Mutti (2001) and Altshuler and Grubert (2001) use the Treasury tax files to explore whether the location decisions of MNCs are sensitive to residual US taxes. These papers focus on the location of the real assets held abroad in US manufacturing subsidiaries.

Grubert and Mutti (2001) include measures of repatriation taxes in country-level asset location regressions and find that these taxes do not seem to affect the choice among investment locations abroad. They also present evidence on the relevance of repatriation taxes to location decisions derived from firm-level data that include information on the foreign tax credit position of parent corporations. If repatriation taxes play a significant role in a parent's decision making, a parent that expects to be in an excess foreign tax credit position should be more responsive to the local tax rate in the host country than a parent that expects to pay a residual US tax. However, the firm-level regressions fail to identify any impact of repatriation taxes on location decisions: parent companies in excess credit positions are no more sensitive to differences in host country tax rates than parents without excess credits.

Grubert and Mutti (2001) use the current excess credit position of the parent to measure prospective repatriation taxes. Altshuler and Grubert (2001) investigate whether alternative measures of expected credit positions will succeed in identifying an impact of repatriation taxes on location decisions. Most of their attempts to identify the tax sensitivity of firms who expect excess credits to shield any home country tax liability fail to find any excess responsiveness. Repatriation taxes do not seem to play a significant role in the location decisions of US multinationals. Altshuler and Grubert do find that firms with large carryforwards of tax credits seem to have more investment in low-tax countries; however, the size of the effect is not very significant.

7.4.2 Location of Intangible Capital

US direct investment abroad is strongly motivated by the exploitation of intangible assets like patents and trademarks. As discussed in the previous section, the ability to shield taxes on royalties and income shifting opportunities creates an incentive to exploit intangible assets abroad. Even though part of the return on intangibles is paid out in deductible royalties, the evidence suggests that the foreign subsidiary retains a significant portion, which means that a low-tax jurisdiction is a favorable potential location.

There is little empirical evidence on the impact of taxes on the location of intangible capital. Although the returns to intangible assets are not fully captured in royalties, these payments can be used as an indication of where intangible assets are being invested. Data in the Bureau of Economic Analysis (BEA) Benchmark Surveys of US Investment Abroad in 1994 and 1999 suggest that low-tax countries are becoming much more important destinations for US produced intangible assets (see Altshuler and Grubert 2004 for further discussion). Specifically, the share of total affiliate royalties accounted for by Ireland and Singapore doubled between 1994 and 1999. The share of total royalties paid by subsidiaries in these locations increased from 9.3 percent to 20.9 percent, and the share of royalties paid to the US parent increased from 8.4 percent to 19.6 percent. In 1999 royalties paid by Irish affiliates exceeded royalties paid by German or UK affiliates, and total royalties paid by Singapore affiliates were only 25 percent lower than royalties paid by Japanese affiliates.[16]

7.4.3   Repatriation Planning and the Associated Efficiency Loss

One important consideration in evaluating reform alternatives is the implicit costs companies incur in order to avoid repatriating income back to the United States. For example, companies can engage in various strategies that avoid repatriation but allow the parent to have use of the income retained abroad (Altshuler and Grubert 2002). The costs of these strategies include payments to tax planners, extra borrowing costs for the parent company, and so forth. All of the reform proposals we look at eliminate these efficiency losses, either by exempting dividends entirely or by taxing all subsidiary income currently, so it is of interest to know the magnitude of the benefits. The efficiency loss due to the repatriation tax has been estimated using repatriation equations both by Grubert and Mutti (2001) and by Desai, Foley, and Hines (2001). These papers used somewhat differing specifications but came to similar conclusions, that the implicit costs of retention are about 1 percent of total subsidiary before-tax income. Grubert and Mutti estimated that the costs of repatriation tax avoidance strategies were about 1.7 percent of income in locations with an effective tax rate below 10 percent.

But companies' response to the one-year moratorium on the US tax on dividend repatriations in the AJCA of 2004 may suggest that the estimated one percent cost is too low. Under the AJCA provision, companies could bring back accumulated earnings and for the portion above a historical average pay only 5.25 percent before proportionately scaled down credits. They apparently brought back hundreds of billions of dollars in response to this opportunity.[17] Could the implicit costs of deferral be 5 percent or more in low-tax locations?

We have taken another look at the evidence to see if the companies' response to AJCA is more understandable. In particular, we have looked at the impact of large potential accumulations by highly profitable companies as their repatriations change through time. The cost of deferring a given amount of current income presumably rises as the amount of accumulated retained earnings from the past increases. It is more expensive to use more complex strategies after the most obvious uses of retained earnings have been exploited. The regressions in table 7.1 in the appendix report the results of this analysis. We look at the level of current repatriations and how they depend on repatriation taxes and profitability and the interaction of profitability and subsidiary age, which indicate total potential accumulated retentions, with repatriation taxes. The issue is whether ignoring these considerations in the earlier specifications understated the responsiveness of dividends to the US repatriation tax, and thus underestimated the deadweight loss attributable to repressed repatriations.

The regressions in table 7.1 in the appendix thus compare two specifications for the repatriation equation, including one that allows for the possibility that larger accumulations over time reduce the negative effect of the repatriation tax. The data come from the Treasury tax files for 2002. The dependent variable in each case is the ratio of dividends to subsidiary sales. The "old" specification just has subsidiary age, profitability, and the interaction of current profitability with the US repatriation tax as independent variables. The "new" specification adds interaction terms, including the product of profitability and age and the added interaction of that potential accumulation variable with the tax rate and a measure of parent excess credit expectations.

The results do indicate that the repressing effect of the repatriation tax declines over time. In the new specification, the negative effect of the repatriation tax on dividends by a new subsidiary is much stronger than would be indicated by the coefficient in the old specification. But the negative effect of taxes completely disappears when the subsidiary is about 25 years old. The extent of the bias in the original specification depends on the age distribution of the subsidiaries in the original sample. However, when the age distribution of subsidiaries is considered, the "old" specification did not seem to understate the average responsiveness used to make the former efficiency loss estimate. Nevertheless, tax responsiveness in general may be underestimated because of standard errors-in-the-variables bias. The actual repatriation tax faced by each company is very difficult to estimate because of transitory perturbations. (We use the country average effective tax rate to identify the long run average residual US tax.) Accordingly, in view of the large repatriations after the AJCA one year provision, it may well be that we should attribute a higher cost to the current tax on repatriated income.

7.4.4   Income Shifting: Is It Getting Worse and Why Is It Bad?

Opportunities for cross-border shifting are an important feature of the current system. Placing debt in high-tax locations and transferring very valuable intangible assets to low-tax subsidiaries without adequate compensation in the form of royalties are probably the most important methods. There is some evidence on the extent to which firms use these two methods, shifting financial income and intangible income, to lower tax burdens. Interest stripping is likely the easiest way for firms to minimize worldwide tax payments. Altshuler and Grubert (2002) present evidence from the Treasury tax files that the financial structure of MNCs is influenced by local tax rates. In a regression with debt-to-asset ratios as a dependent variable, they show that CFC leverage is a highly significant negative function of local statutory tax rates. Further work with the Treasury tax files suggests that the location of intangible income and the allocation of debt among high- and low-tax countries seem to account for all of the observed differences in profitability across high- and low-statutory tax countries (see Grubert 2003).

As we will see, the proposals differ significantly in their impact on income shifting incentives. Dividend exemption eliminates the current incentive to transfer intangibles out of the United States if the company has excess credits but leaves other opportunities for income shifting in place, if anything stronger. Burden neutral worldwide taxation removes all incentives for income shifting by US companies abroad except for any possible role of continuing excess credit positions. As for the consumption tax alternatives, the destination-based tax has no incentives for income manipulation because the tax base is purely domestic consumption, but an origin-based tax preserves incentives for income shifting because the tax base is domestic consumption plus net exports.

Before proceeding, we should clarify just what the transfer pricing incentives are in the current system. It is sometimes convenient to think of the benefit of shifting a dollar of income from one country to another as simply the difference between the respective statutory tax rates, $t_1 - t_2$, but this must be modified because of the US foreign tax credit system. The marginal incentive to shift depends critically on whether the taxpayer has excess credits. For an excess limit taxpayer (a taxpayer without excess credits), the gain from lower income in the high-tax country is not $t_1 - t_{US}$, if t_1 is above the US tax rate, because the high-tax subsidiary would create a useable excess credit of $t_1 - t_{US}$ if it repatriated its income back to the parent. The tax on the foreign income is only at the US tax rate. Similarly the shift to the low-tax subsidiary has to consider the "implicit" cost of retaining income, including any possible future repatriation taxes. These were discussed in the preceding section. In any case, the gain is smaller than the simple tax differential.

If the parent is in an excess credit position, the benefit of shifting from one foreign country to another foreign country is the statutory tax differential because repatriation considerations, positive or negative, are irrelevant. But the benefit of shifting income in and out of the United States can be very different. For example, under the "sales source" rules, half of export income can be classified as foreign source. This means that for a company with excess credits, the tax rate on export income is in effect 17.5 percent because half of the income is shielded by credits. Accordingly the US company has an incentive to overprice exports if the foreign tax rate exceeds 17.5 percent, not 35 percent, because the excess credits can flow over to shield half of the export income.

The effect of excess credits on the incentives for deductible payments made by the subsidiary to the parent is particularly striking. The parent has an incentive to capitalize the subsidiary with loans rather than equity because the interest coming back will be free of US taxes but deductible against foreign tax abroad. More important is the case of royalties which are foreign source under US law. The MNC will gain from higher royalties from any foreign country with a positive tax rate because the royalties deductible abroad are exempt at home because of the available excess credits. (As noted elsewhere in the chapter, about two-thirds of royalties do not result in a US tax liability.) This obviously creates a strong incentive to exploit a mobile intangible asset abroad rather than at home when the worldwide market can conveniently be supplied from either location.

The costs of income shifting may have several sources. One is the cost of the services of lawyers and accountants who plan the transactions. Another is the risk of additional expenses if the transaction is challenged by tax authorities. The shifting costs may also include the greater use of related party transactions instead of arm's-length transactions because the related party transactions provide the opportunities for income shifting.

Income shifting has three significant effects. The first, and most obvious, effect is that companies save tax at the expense of high-tax countries. The second effect is that, as indicated above, the shifting also uses up real resources, including additional accounting and audit expenses and less than optimal financing structures. The third is that opportunities for income shifting alter the tax costs of investing in a particular location. The tax advantages of a low-tax investment are magnified because the investment can become the destination for income shifted from low-tax affiliates. At the same time the effective tax burden on high-tax investments can be lowered because some of the income generated is taxed at lower rates.

The evidence of income shifting, basically the strong relationship between profitability and local statutory tax rates, goes back a long way (Grubert and Mutti 1991, Hines and Rice 1994, among others). Altshuler and Grubert (2006), on the basis of a comparison of Treasury data for manufacturing subsidiaries in 1996 and 2000, indicate that income shifting has increased. For example, in identical regressions that used the ratio of before-tax earnings and profits to sales as the dependent variable, the coefficient for the host country statutory rate was −0.16 in 1996 and −0.26 in 2000. (An analysis of the 2002 files indicates a coefficient similar to 2000.) The −0.26 coefficient implies a profit ratio in a country with a 10 percent tax rate that is almost twice as large as one with a 40 percent statutory tax rate. It is important to note that this evidence only pertains to profitability differences among foreign countries. At this point in our knowledge, we do not know whether the high profits in low-tax countries constitute income shifted from another foreign country or income shifted from the United States.

The shifting equations and the 2002 Treasury Controlled Foreign Corporation (CFC) level files can be used to make rough estimates of the deadweight loss and the gain to the companies from income shifting. In fact, if the marginal (and average) costs of shifting are a linear function of the amount of income shifted, these will be equal in magnitude.[18] The data for manufacturing subsidiaries indicate that about 8 percent of total affiliate income ends up in low-tax countries because of income shifting. This quantity is found by finding the threshold statutory tax rate t_t so that the amount of income shifted out, calculated from the coefficient and the difference between the subsidiary's tax rate and t_t, is just equal to the amount shifted in, which is calculated symmetrically for subsidiaries with statutory tax rates below t_t. But because of planning costs, the high-tax subsidiaries would have kept more than 8 percent of total income in the absence of shifting. That is, some income is lost because of the expenses attributable to shifting. We assume that the costs of shifting are borne by the high-tax subsidiary and are deductible at its tax rate.

The linearity assumption, with its implication of equal costs and net gains, means that the tax saving from the income that ends up in low-tax subsidiaries should just be equal to twice the after-tax cost of the shift. That is, the companies' *net* gain from the shift is equal to the gross tax saving from the income shifted to the low-tax subsidiaries minus the after tax cost of the shift. The tax saving for the income that is shifted to low-tax subsidiaries is calculated from the difference in statutory tax rates between sending and receiving subsidiaries, each weighted by the amount of income shifted. On the basis of these assumptions, we conclude that the efficiency cost of shifting income is 1.7 percent of total before-tax income, which is equal to the companies' net gain.[19] This company gain is equal to the tax gain from the net income that gets shifted after costs, with the costs assumed deductible at the higher country rates. In this rough estimate the location of the affiliates is taken as given, and the available income is considered to be shifted after the locational choices have been made. The next step is to explore how the choice of location is distorted because of income-shifting opportunities.

7.4.5 Income Shifting and Effective Tax Rates

As discussed earlier, it is unlikely that we can know with any precision what the efficient burdens on foreign investment should be. Furthermore it is difficult to know how some of the policy options translate into effective tax rates. Under current law multinational companies can use various planning methods to lower their host country tax burdens far below the level paid by local companies. Most of the opportunities for income shifting will continue under dividend exemption.

An example of the difficulty in determining whether tax avoidance opportunities contribute to worldwide efficiency is provided by a simple technique that US companies use to lower tax burdens abroad. They inject equity into a tax haven finance subsidiary which lends the funds to an operating affiliate in another country. The interest is deductible from tax in the host country but can be retained as equity in the tax haven. This is "inside" debt so the MNC's outside credit status is not affected. It used to be difficult for MNCs to avail themselves of this device because of the anti-abuse rules in Subpart F, but the "check-the-box" regulations issued in 1997 greatly simplified the process and led to widespread use of these tax haven finance entities. It is not clear, however, whether their use is an improvement or deterioration in terms of worldwide efficiency. Conceivably they could improve efficiency because companies would switch from locations with low tax rates to those that have very high tax burdens in the absence of the interest stripping. This technique would no longer offer any benefits to the companies under burden neutral worldwide taxation because all income would be included currently in the US tax base. We assume that the corporate tax rate on foreign income will fall in order to keep the total residual tax the same, so that average competitiveness remains unchanged. But the pattern of tax burdens across countries may change and we cannot be absolutely sure that the new pattern improves efficiency.

But it is probably fair to say that negative tax rates on investment in some locations lead to wasteful investments, and this can easily happen under the current system in the case of production abroad with a large intangible component.[20] The negative tax rates occur because income is shifted from a high-tax location to a low-tax investment by aggressive transfer prices, or a deduction is taken in a high-tax location even though the item produces income in the low-tax jurisdiction. We can take investment in Ireland as an example. The Treasury 2002 files for CFCs in manufacturing indicate that before-tax profits in relation to sales are almost three times higher in Ireland, on average, than the group mean. These "excess" profits presumably reflect the fact that very valuable intellectual property is located in Ireland and the royalties paid back to the United States, while significant, do not fully reflect its contribution. (Parallel regressions for royalties and profits indicate that only about one-third of the contribution of the parent's R&D to CFC profits on average is paid back as royalties.)

We can use these data for Irish manufacturing to construct an example. As noted in Grubert (2004), the link between intangible and tangible investments can be modeled in several alternative ways, but let us make the simplest possible assumptions. Consider a plant producing a high-tech product that can be located either in Ireland or the United States. First, we assume that the Irish subsidiary can costlessly defer income indefinitely. Without the intellectual property, the plant would earn a "normal" before-tax return of 10, but it would earn 30 with the valuable patent. If the plant is located in Ireland instead of the United States, the company saves 4.5 on the excess return of 20, namely the 7 it would pay at the US tax rate less the 2.5 it would pay at the current Irish statutory rate of 12.5 percent. This far exceeds the simple 2.25 difference in tax burdens on the normal return. Even if the Irish plant were much less productive than the US plant, earning only 23 instead of 30, it would still be preferred. The effective tax on the investment in the Irish plant is the Irish tax of 1.25 on the 10 of income before shifting less the 4.5 saved on the shifted income, or a negative 3.25.

The advantages of a low-tax location would be preserved under dividend exemption but not under the constant overall burden worldwide system, which would maintain overall competitiveness abroad but not necessarily in low-tax jurisdictions. This might be disturbing to the "competitiveness" advocates of CIN or CON. In the context of the earlier discussion of alternative criteria for investment efficiency, intangible or excess returns should be distinguished from returns on "standard" capital. If the United States imposes higher tax burdens on the latter than their foreign competitors, capital can easily flow to the foreign companies who would make the investment instead. But valuable intangibles presumably have some unique features that can be much less easily replicated by foreign companies. One could, of course, think of models of strategic competition to capture rents of the kind that go back to Brander and Spencer (1985). These models do not seem to have offered very convincing reasons for export subsidies, and indeed the case of intangible assets is identical to the case of exports because it is simply the export of US created services. They are intellectual property that was created in the United States whose value has not been included in the US tax base. It is, in principle, possible that selective export subsidies would improve US welfare, but this would require information about market behavior which is unlikely to be available, apart from any World Trade Organization (WTO) concerns. The same argument would apply to exports of intellectual property.

7.5   Analysis of Alternative Reform Options

7.5.1   Dividend Exemption

Dividend exemption eliminates the burden of repatriation taxes. But the treatment of dividend remittances is only one element of this reform option. The rules allocating interest and other overhead expenses to exempt income that prevent companies from generating negative tax rates and the full taxation of royalties will affect both location and tax planning incentives. In fact, as we will see, all the margins we have considered will change under dividend exemption. And, depending on how it is designed, the system may not be any simpler than the current system.[21]

Start by considering how the incentive to invest in low-tax affiliates abroad changes under dividend exemption for companies that currently have excess credits. The parent faces no repatriation tax under either system. But under dividend exemption there are no excess credits to shield export income and royalty payments. The current "sales-source" rules that provide a tax benefit for export income for companies in excess credits would no longer have any impact. The taxation of the royalty stream eliminates the tax benefit to exploit intangibles overseas that exists under current law. This represents a dramatic change from current law. As we mentioned at the start of this chapter, almost two-thirds of US taxes on royalties are currently shielded by excess credits from dividends.

The effect of the interest expense allocation rules is the same under dividend exemption as it is for firms with excess credits under the current system. Both systems impose worldwide fungibility. The difference is that these rules would be relevant for all companies under dividend exemption while they are binding only for companies in excess credits now. Under worldwide fungibility, interest expense in the United States is allocated against foreign source income only if the debt-to-asset ratio on the books of foreign subsidiaries abroad is lower than the worldwide ratio. Because the allocation causes the company to lose a deduction for interest in the United States, this creates an incentive to reduce tax payments abroad by shifting deductions to high-tax countries until the amount of debt abroad reaches the worldwide ratio.

Now consider companies that are currently in excess limit positions. These companies no longer face any tax cost of repatriation and the associated deadweight loss vanishes. While the taxation of royalties does not change, the effect of the expense allocation rules is significantly different under dividend exemption. Companies in excess limit will no longer benefit from the ability to deduct expenses at the higher US rate while retaining low-tax income abroad. As a result companies will find it much more difficult to generate extremely low effective tax rates on investments abroad. Under dividend exemption companies formerly in excess limit positions will now have an incentive to shift debt abroad until the debt to asset ratio on the books of foreign subsidiaries equals the worldwide debt to asset ratio.

Altshuler and Grubert (2001) use effective tax rate calculations for typical investments in low-tax affiliates to quantify the burden of US taxes under the current system and dividend exemption.[22] The results are of interest because the dividend exemption regime they model is the same one we consider.[23] Based on data from the Commerce Department, the calculations assume that the typical investment abroad is comprised of 85 percent tangible assets and 15 percent intangible assets and is financed with a mix of debt (US and local) and equity. The effective tax rate is a weighted average of the rates faced by excess limit and excess credit companies. The weights are based on information from the Treasury tax files. The affiliate is located in a country with a statutory tax rate of seven percent which is assumed to equal the local effective tax rate on net equity (the host country allows for economic depreciation on tangible capital and grants no investment tax credit). The effective tax rate estimates include the estimated efficiency loss from deferred repatriations based on Grubert and Mutti (2001) and discussed above in section 7.3.

Using these parameters, Altshuler and Grubert (2001) calculate that the effective tax rate for a typical investment in a low-tax affiliate for US companies increases from about 5 percent under current law to about 9 percent under dividend exemption. For an investment in intangible assets, the effective tax rate increases from about 26 to 35 percent. These effective tax rate calculations do not take income shifting into account and, as a result, may overestimate the actual burdens companies will face in low-tax jurisdictions. The results of the effective tax rate analysis do suggest that, as Grubert and Mutti (2001) first pointed out, dividend exemption may move the US tax system closer to one that preserves CEN.

Under dividend exemption, many companies will have an incentive to engage in tax planning to try to undo the increase in the effective tax rate on intangible assets in low-tax locations. In particular, companies have an incentive to lower royalty payments and increase exempt equity income that can be repatriated tax free as dividends. Companies may underpay royalties by using inappropriate transfer prices or other devices. In fact the empirical analysis in Grubert (2001) suggests that a move to dividend exemption may lead to a significant decline in royalty payments.[24] As a result the incentive to exploit intangibles abroad, although reduced due to the full taxation of royalties, still exists under dividend exemption.

As this discussion has made clear, dividend exemption does not solve income-shifting problems. It simply removes the repatriation tax burden. However, relative to the current system, income shifting becomes more attractive under exemption only to the extent of the burden of the repatriation tax, which we think is small.

To sum up, dividend exemption removes the repatriation burden and may lead to a more efficient distribution of assets abroad by reducing opportunities to drive effective tax rates for investment abroad to extremely low levels through the low or zero tax on royalties and the frequent ability to deduct interest expense fully against domestic income. Although we do not know what efficiency criterion is optimal, it is safe to say that this outcome would be an improvement relative to the current system. However, the incentives for transfer pricing and understating royalties make it difficult to give a precise evaluation of the overall effect of dividend exemption on future tax burdens.

It should also be noted that dividend exemption gives foreign governments the incentive to lower taxes on US companies. This is one of the behavioral margins that should be considered in the evaluation of alternative reforms. Under the worldwide tax alternative, foreign governments do not have this incentive since firms will (for the most part) be in excess limit positions. If anything foreign governments would have the incentive to raise their taxes on US companies because it would have no effect on investment and would simply be offset by US credits.

7.5.2   Constant Burden Worldwide Taxation

Constant burden worldwide taxation seems to dominate both the current system and dividend exemption. However, as mentioned in the introduction, the attractiveness of the regime ultimately depends on the extent to which companies find themselves in excess credit positions. To fix ideas, start by assuming that no firms end up with excess credits. Consider the behavioral margins we have focused on under this new tax system. There is no efficiency loss associated with repatriating income back to the United States since all subsidiary income is taxed currently. There is no incentive to engage in income shifting: eliminating deferral removes the benefit of moving income offshore and from high-tax to low-tax locations through transfer pricing.[25] The benefits of offshore tax havens are no longer relevant. Effective tax rates for investment in tangible and intangible assets will not vary across locations.[26] Tax considerations will no longer affect financing decisions. Companies do not have to make expense allocations. The tax system is simpler and less wasteful.

Admittedly, eliminating parent overhead expense allocations seems to contradict the tax principle that foreign income should be measured correctly. But it would result in a great deal of simplification. Furthermore, retaining them would require a lower tax rate to keep the tax burden on foreign income unchanged and it would increase the frequency of excess credits. Requiring expense allocations would increase excess credits in the first instance, and they would increase even further as the tax rate drops to maintain burden neutrality. Because all worldwide income is included in the US tax base, the main policy issue from eliminating allocations is the mirror image of the excess credit issue. Foreign governments may have an incentive to raise taxes on US companies if they are in excess limit with no deferral privilege because there would be no risk of discouraging US investments.

Since foreign tax credits would be limited (for the same policy reasons as under current law), some firms could find themselves with excess foreign tax credits. The presence of excess credits creates tax benefits for engaging in tax planning. Shifting income out of the United States and to low-tax locations from high-tax locations is attractive if excess credits are available to shield the residual US tax. Low-tax locations are attractive for tangible and intangible assets when firms have excess credits as are planning techniques that lower foreign tax burdens. In short, knowing the burden-neutral rate and frequency of excess credits at that rate are essential to evaluating the attractiveness of this policy option. To be sure, the burden-neutral worldwide option increases effective tax rates on investment in low-tax countries while preserving overall competitiveness, but within the state of current knowledge we cannot be certain that this improves the efficiency of the worldwide allocation of capital.

The Burden-Neutral Tax Rate on Worldwide Foreign Income

The intent of lowering the rate is to keep the overall "competitiveness" of US operations abroad unchanged, although there would obviously be winners and losers across the group of MNCs. An important step in evaluating this option is finding what the corporate rate would have to be. The Treasury corporate tax files were therefore used to make a rough estimate of this "burden-neutral" rate. All subsidiary income is taxed, but first intercompany dividends have to be removed from income. Otherwise, the income would be counted twice, in both the paying and receiving subsidiary.

The calculation of the burden-neutral tax rate required, among other steps, the estimation of what foreign tax credits would accompany the newly included income. The difficult part of taking out dividends as they come up the tiers is knowing the taxes that come up with the dividends. Companies seem to include the taxes paid lower in the tier in the foreign taxes they report on the information return they file for each CFC with their tax returns, the Form 5471. Under current law, the parent receives a credit for these taxes when the income is finally repatriated.[27] Because of this problem of knowing which taxes are included with the dividend, the estimates are probably subject to substantial uncertainty.

As indicated earlier, the calculation left the taxation of domestic corporate income unchanged because we focus only on foreign income. (We ignore the pool of previously unrepatriated income that could be subjected to a small one-time tax under the reform option.)

Accordingly the burden-neutral rate based on "static" calculations is about 28 percent. (As noted above, this estimate is not intended to be and should not be interpreted as an official Treasury estimate.) We can expect both positive and negative behavioral responses. Companies would have less of an incentive to lower foreign taxes, which would lose US revenue because of the higher credits. On the other hand, companies might have less of an incentive to shift income out of the United States, which would lower foreign tax credits.

The previous discussion showed that it is important to estimate the frequency of excess credits in this new scheme. If a company has excess credits, it still has an incentive to shift income from the United States and other high-tax countries to low-tax countries. Any tax saving is not offset by increased US tax. Calculations from the Treasury tax files indicate that about 30 percent of active foreign source income would continue to be in excess credit at the 28 percent rate. This compares with 50 percent of total foreign income that is earned by companies in excess credit in 2002 under current law. The 30 percent of income in excess credit under the burden-neutral proposal is dominated by petroleum companies, which often pay very high taxes in producing countries.[28] Only 18 percent of the foreign income earned in manufacturing companies would be in excess credit.

Companies that operate mainly in low-tax locations abroad may find that the 28 percent rate puts them at a competitive disadvantage. Lowering the rate even further may offset any impact on competitiveness but at the same time will increase the frequency and size of excess credits. For example, lowering the tax rate from 28 to 20 percent would raise the manufacturing income in excess credit from 18 to 42 percent. With more firms in excess credit positions, the benefits of the reform relative to the current system are reduced. Evaluating the trade-off between a lower rate and the occurrence of excess credits is difficult because it depends on the extent to which foreign governments respond to the lower US rate, among other things.

The Balance of Corporate and Personal Taxation
If the corporate tax rate is reduced to 28 percent, the tax burden on domestic corporate income would go down substantially even with base broadening such as the elimination of accelerated depreciation. But changing the mix of corporate and personal taxation in this direction is the correct response to the increase in capital mobility worldwide. The corporate-personal split of a given combined tax on corporate income, which is largely irrelevant in a closed economy, can become very important as capital mobility increases. Let us abstract from the specific cross-border issues such as the income shifting we have been discussing and assume that corporate and personal taxation correspond completely to source and residence taxation. There are no repatriation taxes at the corporate level, and we rule out income shifting. If portfolio capital mobility increases, US individual shareholders find it easier to escape a burdensome US corporate tax by investing in foreign companies. As globalization increases, foreign companies may find it easier to base their operations in low-tax countries from which they can supply the US market. Lowering the corporate component of the tax on capital would offset these behavioral reactions and move in the direction of a more efficient tax system. The coordinated burden neutral scheme would increase the competitiveness of the domestic corporate sector while preserving the competitiveness of US companies abroad.

Admittedly, the 28 percent rate will create some big winners and losers even though it makes the companies as a group whole and they save a great deal in reduced planning costs. (The government also gains in lower enforcement costs.) The losers would be the companies who concentrate their activities in low-tax locations. One possibility is that some of the losers may "invert" (i.e. expatriate) by incorporating in a tax haven. This may be difficult for companies with valuable intangible assets because of the toll charge in US law. The Tax Reform Panel did recommend that the US rule specifying that the residence of a company depends purely on place of incorporation be expanded. In any case, this is a serious issue that we hope to explore more fully in future work.

Lowering the corporate rate to 28 percent while retaining the top personal rate of 35 percent might induce high-income taxpayers to shelter more of their income in corporations. But the remaining tax on dividends and capital gains would reduce the attractiveness of that strategy. If anything there seems to be the opposite incentive under current law.

7.5.3   Destination-Based and Origin-Based Consumption Taxes

The two consumption tax bases have different implications for some important behavioral margins.[29] As explained above in section 7.1, a destination-based tax is a tax on consumption in the United States. Exports are exempt from tax and imports are taxed. An origin-based tax has a slightly more complicated base: domestic consumption plus net exports. It is convenient to think of the origin-based tax as a prepayment system compared with the destination-based tax. As indicated before, under the origin base the tax is prepaid on the exports going out. Eventually a destination tax collects an equivalent amount of tax on the imports financed by additional exports *if* the value of additional exports equals the present value of the additional imports they finance. Thus the equivalence between the bases holds only when prospective investments abroad earn normal returns (a dollar invested abroad finances imports with a present value of a dollar).

Because imports and exports appear in the determination of the origin tax base, companies have an incentive to understate the value of exports and overstate imports. In contrast, the destination tax base is pure unrelated party consumption. Transfer price abuse can create above-normal returns that break the equivalence between the bases. Under the origin base the tax on exports works like a prepayment mechanism, which has the effect of exempting any above-normal returns from tax. Exports include royalties, which may be thought of as payments on the export of an intangible asset. The origin base therefore provides incentives to shift income to low-tax locations abroad through transfer pricing.

The destination base seems to dominate the origin base by removing important transfer pricing incentives. Up to this point, however, we have ignored the importance of the Internet and downloads by consumers of software and entertainment.[30] Under a destination-based tax there is an incentive to shop in the country with the lowest tax rate. This incentive is eliminated if boundaries can be monitored (except to the extent that both the shopping and the consumption are done abroad creating what is called the "tourism" problem). While it is possible to tackle this problem in the case of packages that can be checked at the border, it is particularly difficult (if not impossible?), however, to monitor the border when transactions take place over the Internet. Whether the revenue and efficiency loss associated with this cross-border shopping problem are large enough to make the transfer pricing problems of an origin-based tax attractive is an open question.[31]

A consumption tax eliminates the marginal tax on investment in the United States and would increase investment in the US business sector by both domestic and foreign companies. As Grubert and Newlon (1995) note, the effect on net capital inflows and the overall US capital stock is ambiguous because of the possible outflow of capital from the nonbusiness sector, particularly housing. If this causes a decrease in US interest rates, the outflow of investment in debt, which is highly mobile, might outweigh the inflow of equity into the business sector.

7.5.4 A Destination-Based Income Tax?

Some economists, notably Gary Hufbauer, have suggested that the US corporate tax be put on a destination basis, with a rebate for exports and a tax on imports.[32] Apart from WTO problems, this has obvious purely mechanical difficulties because the corporate tax only applies to part of the economy. It is not clear what tax would apply to imports by consumers or noncorporate entities. In addition, if companies could continue to enjoy the deferral of income abroad, the rebate on exports implies that they could invest before-tax income abroad in a low-tax location and effectively obtain consumption tax treatment. There would only be a tax when the investment was liquidated and used to finance imports.

But let us abstract from these problems by assuming the same income tax on all business entities and that all trade is through these entities. Furthermore income cannot be deferred abroad. (This would require very complicated rules.) Under these very extreme assumptions it appears that as in a consumption tax, the exclusion of exports from the tax base and the nondeductibility of imports from the tax base would not distort trade because the rebate on the export side just offsets the tax on the import side. Furthermore there would be benefits in reduced transfer pricing incentives because of the exclusion of exports and imports from the tax base.

There is one major remaining difficulty because of the fundamental difference between a consumption tax and an income tax. (This was pointed out to us by Dan Shaviro.) Unlike an income tax, a consumption tax does not require accruals and capitalizations. Therefore consider an exporter who gets a rebate on his export sales and uses the proceeds to buy a foreign machine that he brings back. He cannot get a deduction for the machine, but this may not be very damaging because the machine would have to be depreciated over its lifetime and the present value of these depreciation deductions may be small. In the extreme the machine could last forever. But by being able to buy it with before-tax dollars, he effectively gets expensing for the machine. This would be the right result under a consumption tax because all investment is expensed regardless of whether the machine is foreign or domestic. The rebate on exports in an income tax is, however, a clear incentive to buy foreign machines.

7.6   Conclusions

We have used the available evidence to evaluate two options for the reform of the taxation of cross-border corporate income. One option is the exemption of dividends from active business income abroad. The other is burden neutral worldwide taxation in which all of a US multinational company's worldwide income would be taxed currently, but the overall US burden on foreign direct investment income would remain unchanged by eliminating the allocation of parent overhead expenses to foreign income and lowering the basic corporate rate. The evaluation required looking at the various behavioral margins that the international tax system can have an impact on. These include the choice of repatriations, the location of business activity, particularly where intellectual property is exploited, and the location of income through the shifting of debt and the pricing of intercompany transactions.

Dividend exemption offers an efficiency gain by eliminating the need to avoid repatriations and the costs that entails. Furthermore it does not increase the attractiveness of low-tax locations compared to current law. The reasons are the full taxation of royalties, which are no longer shielded by excess credits arising from dividends, and the allocation of overhead expenses to exempt income, which would directly reduce deductions against domestic taxable income.

But the burden neutral worldwide option promises broader benefits. In particular, for most companies it will eliminate incentives for locating income in low-tax locations. Therefore a great deal of tax planning will become unnecessary and effective tax rates on investing in low-tax locations will not be affected by income-shifting opportunities. At the same time the companies are at a minimum made whole by the lower corporate rate and the elimination of expense allocations.

However, the burden neutral worldwide option requires a substantial cut in the corporate rate, to about 28 percent. Applying this rate to all corporate income would imply a reduction of the effective tax rate on domestic income, even with feasible base broadening. But we suggest that this might be accomplished, within a fixed revenue constraint, by shifting more of the taxation of corporate income to the personal level. That would in any case be an appropriate response to increased globalization. It would increase the attractiveness of the United States for investment by both foreign and domestic companies, and it would reduce the incentive for individual US shareholders to escape the impact of the US corporate tax by investing in lightly taxed foreign companies.

Appendix

Data Sources

The basic data source for the regressions reported in table 7.1 and the estimates reported in the chapter are the linked Forms 1120, 1118, and 5471 Treasury tax files for 2002 provided by the Statistics of Income Division of the Internal Revenue Service. The Form 1120 is the basic corporate return giving the parent's income and deductions. Corporations use Form 1118 to claim a foreign tax credit and report all repatriated income as well as deductions. Multinational companies file a

Table 7.1
Another look at repatriation equations: Simple specifications

	CFC dividends/sales	
	(1)	(2)
CFC earnings/Sales	0.293***	0.524***
	(0.044)	(0.057)
CFC earnings/Sales × Residual US tax	−0.697***	−1.92***
	(0.171)	(0.231)
CFC age	0.000	
	(0.001)	
CFC earnings/Sales × CFC age		−0.111***
		(0.018)
CFC earnings/Sales × CFC age × Residual US tax		0.740***
		(0.099)
CFC earnings/Sales × CFC age × Residual US tax × Parent excess credit expectations		−0.346
		(0.247)
Constant	0.004	0.007
	(0.004)	(0.003)
Adjusted R^2	0.10	0.19
Number of observations	752	752

Data source: 2002 Treasury tax files. See appendix for further details.
Notes: Standard errors in parentheses. The Treasury tax files and variables are described in the appendix. Observations are weighted by CFC sales. *** denote statistical significance at the one percent level. See appendix for description of variables.

Form 5471 for each of their controlled foreign corporations (CFCs). This form gives the CFC's income, foreign taxes paid and transactions with related parties including the parent. The statutory tax rates used in the calculation of the efficiency loss due to income shifting in section 7.3 are taken from Price Waterhouse (2002).

Description of Variables in Table 7.1

The coefficient estimates in table 7.1 are from regressions using CFC information from the Form 5471 and parent information from the Form 1118. The sample includes the manufacturing CFCs (with the addition of software companies) of nonfinancial parent companies. Only CFCs with positive earnings and profits (E&P) are included in the analysis. The observations are weighted by CFC sales. The dependent variable is the ratio of CFC dividends to sales. The "old" specification, described in the text and shown in column 1, includes measures of CFC profitability, CFC age, and the parent's dividend repatriation tax.

We control for profitability by including CFC E&P as a proportion of sales as an independent variable. CFC age is based on date of incorporation. The residual US tax is the tax price of dividend repatriations assuming the parent is in excess limit. The country's average effective tax rate is used to construct the residual tax and is calculated by dividing taxes paid by E&P before tax. As described in the text, the "new" specification shown in column 2 includes a measure of potential accumulated profits and the interaction between the accumulation variable and a measure of parent excess credit expectations. Our measure of potential accumulated profits is a simple interaction of current profitability, CFC E&P/sales, with CFC age. We measure parent excess credit expectations as the ratio of taxes paid on dividends to total dividends (both variables are from the 1118 form). The higher is this effective tax rate on dividends, the larger are potential credits, and the more likely the parent will find itself with excess credits in the current period *and* credit carryforwards that would prevent future dividend remittances from facing any repatriation tax.

Discussion

Charles L. Ballard

One of the themes of this volume is the distinction between the known, the unknown, and the unknowable. I thus begin with some things that are known, regarding the Grubert and Altshuler discussion on corporate taxes in the world economy.

1. The issues associated with the tax treatment of foreign-source income are extremely complex. In order to have a reasonably complete understanding of this area of public finance, one needs to know about excess credits, dividend-repatriation rules, sales-source rules, separate baskets, transfer pricing, interest stripping, and much, much more.

2. These issues have become increasingly important over time. Few trends in the world economy have been more important in recent decades than the rapid growth of international trade, international capital flows, and cross-border investment.

3. The third known thing flows from the first two. There is a great need for the economics profession to achieve a deeper understanding of these issues because of their complexity and importance. Thus it is appropriate, and even imperative, that a volume such as this one include a chapter dealing with cross-border issues.

4. Just as it is necessary to have a chapter on this subject, it is necessary for it to be written by top scholars in the field. We are fortunate to have this chapter by Harry Grubert and Rosanne Altshuler, who are both among a very elite group of the world's foremost experts in the area.

Many of the arcane rules in the tax code give rise to opportunities for tax planning and income shifting. As emphasized by Grubert and Altshuler, these tax laws have an effect on incentives across a very wide range of behavioral margins. One of the best services provided by Grubert and Altshuler is a review of the state of the profession's knowledge about behavioral responses with respect to several of these margins. These include the location of tangible capital, the location of intangible capital, dividend-repatriation planning, and income shifting. Although we know a few things about these responses, one of the main things we know is that there is a great deal we do not know. For example, we do not know the extent to which high profits in low-tax countries are the result of income shifted from other foreign countries or income shifted from the United States.

There are also some facts we think we know, although we have an incomplete understanding of *why* the facts are as they are. For example, investment choice across locations does not seem to be sensitive to repatriation taxes. Thus, plenty of research remains to be done. And yet policy makers cannot wait until economists have answered all of the relevant questions. The day when we know everything we need to know may never come, and if it ever does, it probably won't come any time soon. On that basis, mindful of the uncertainties, Grubert and Altshuler press forward to consider some policy proposals. They concentrate primarily on two proposals: dividend exemption and a burden-neutral system of worldwide taxation. The latter option would eliminate the privilege of deferral for active earnings retained abroad. I would have preferred to see a discussion of an even wider range of possible policies. Nevertheless, Grubert and Altshuler perform a valuable service with their in-depth analysis of these two policies.

Grubert and Altshuler argue persuasively in favor of burden-neutral worldwide taxation. Under this proposal, which taxes dividends but not royalties, firms would have an incentive to reclassify dividend income as royalties. Under the alternative proposal of dividend exemption, the incentive goes in the opposite direction: firms would have an incentive to reduce royalty payments, and to increase tax-free repatriations of dividends. The extent to which these shifts would occur is ultimately an empirical question. Hines (1995) and Grubert (2001) have found that royalty payments do indeed respond to tax prices. If either of these proposals is ultimately enacted, economists will be provided with rich new opportunities for research.

In my view, this chapter's arguments in favor of burden-neutral worldwide taxation are fairly persuasive. However, I do not know whether there is a consensus within the economics profession in favor of this type of proposal. Even if such a consensus does exist, it is not clear that the public can be persuaded. It is notoriously difficult to get

Congress to pass tax-reform legislation that both (1) maintains revenue and (2) enhances efficiency.

I must mention two other issues about which we have less knowledge than we would like to have. The first of these is the response of foreign governments to a major change in the US tax treatment of foreign-source income. This is especially difficult to predict, since it depends on political factors as much as on economic ones.

A second issue has to do with the value of the dollar. In much of the literature on the tax treatment of foreign-source income, it is assumed (often implicitly) that the world macroeconomy is in balance. That seems like a strong assumption in today's financial environment, in which the United States is borrowing several hundred billion dollars per year from abroad. No one knows for certain what this will do the value of the dollar, but it is unlikely that the longer term trend of the dollar is anything other than downward. The big question is whether the dollar's retreat will be orderly or precipitous. A sufficiently large shock to currency exchange rates has the potential to swamp some of the effects that we believe we know are caused by the tax treatment of foreign-source income.

Discussion

Roger H. Gordon

In past discussions of tax reform, international tax issues have often been relegated to a brief discussion at the end. I am delighted to see international tax issues take such a prominent position in this volume.

The existing tax treatment of the foreign-source income of US multinationals is very complicated, and generates complicated behavioral responses by firms, making tax reform discussion particularly appropriate. The US currently taxes the income of foreign subsidiaries of US firms only when this income is repatriated from abroad. A tax credit is then given for any taxes already paid abroad on this income, up to the US tax liabilities due.

Given the many ways that firms respond, Grubert and Altshuler (hereafter GA) document that the US in fact collects little tax revenue from US multinationals on their foreign-source income. In addition there is a large body of past academic work providing evidence that US multinationals also manage to avoid considerable US tax on the income generated from their US operations.

Given these problems generated by the existing US tax structure, it is more than appropriate to consider seriously the possibility of fundamental reform in the way the US treats the foreign-source income of US multinationals. The objective of GA is to assess four possible directions for reform

1. Shifting to a "territorial" system, in which earnings repatriated from foreign subsidiaries are not subject to domestic corporate tax.

2. Worldwide taxation of foreign-source income at accrual.

3. Destination-based corporate taxation.

4. Origin-based corporate taxation.

In keeping with the ground rules used by the President's Tax Reform Commission, GA focus on revenue neutral tax reforms. To compensate for any direct revenue effects of the proposed changes, they include as well in each reform specific changes in the US rules allocating income across location and/or a change in the US statutory corporate tax rate so as to leave forecasted tax revenue unaffected.

Two of these reforms (a "territorial" system and a destination-based tax) were the alternatives proposed by the President's Tax Reform Commission. The US Treasury during the first Bush administration proposed shifting to an origin-based tax system, a reform they designated a "comprehensive business income tax." As a result these three proposals merit particular scrutiny. The remaining proposal, as seen below, merits inclusion in the list since it probably corresponds more closely to the instincts of public finance economists.

Several of these alternative strategies for taxing foreign-source income are in use in other countries, providing evidence about the likely consequences of such reforms. For example, quite a few countries have a "territorial" system, including Canada, Germany, and France. New Zealand has recently shifted to worldwide taxation at accrual, providing some direct experience. The value-added tax in most countries makes use of a destination-based structure, providing substantial experience here.

That one of the authors worked on the President's Tax Reform Proposals, and the other is the in-house expert at the US Treasury provides yet further reason to pay particular attention to their assessments of these alternative policies. They are also among the key contributors to the existing academic literature examining how US multinationals respond to existing tax incentives.

To set the stage for its discussion of possible reforms, this chapter does a nice job of laying out the many distortions created by existing tax provisions, and the potentially large efficiency costs that result. For one, US firms appear to have been very successful in modifying their behavior to avoid most any domestic corporate taxes on the dividends they receive from their foreign subsidiaries. These strategies must involve at least some real costs, however; otherwise, firms would not have responded so dramatically to the one-time reduced tax rate on these repatriated dividends available in 2005.

Multinationals also seem to be very effective at shifting taxable income from high-tax-rate to low-tax-rate locations, in order to lessen their overall tax liabilities. Foreign-owned subsidiaries in the United States, for example, report very little taxable profits here. While the parent firms of US multinationals do report substantial taxable profits here, their foreign subsidiaries in low-taxed countries commonly report far higher profit rates, suggesting that substantial income has been shifted abroad. The empirical evidence suggests that the two main strategies used for shifting income to low-tax countries are the strategic use of debt and the strategic choice of location for patent ownership. In particular, the US parent of a multinational can reduce its domestic taxable income by borrowing from its subsidiaries located in low-taxed countries and paying royalties to these subsidiaries for use of patents owned by these subsidiaries, regardless of where the R&D was done.[33]

Such behavior also appears to be very responsive to tax provisions. The sixfold increase in dividend repatriations during 2005 in response to a temporary reduction in the tax rate on repatriated dividends is one recent and dramatic example. The academic literature provides much other evidence that taxes do affect firm behavior.

GA then argue that the past theoretical work does not provide clear guidance about how best to design the tax provisions affecting foreign-source income. The traditional guidelines they note are capital-export neutrality (CEN) requiring equal tax rates regardless of the country in which a multinational might invest, and capital-import neutrality (CIN) requiring equal tax rates on investment in a given country regardless of the home country of the investing firm.[34]

These criteria provide unclear guidance about directions for tax reform for a variety of reasons. To satisfy these guidelines simultaneously, not only must the US law tax profits equally regardless of location, but foreign tax laws must also be identical to the US tax law and tax-crediting provisions must ensure no compounding of taxes on cross-border investments. No US reforms alone can achieve this. It is not even clear that it is in the interest of the United States to do what it can to satisfy these criteria. Trade-offs among the criteria are inevitable, and there is no traditional approach for judging how to make these trade-offs. Furthermore, they argue, none of these theories take into account the key response by multinationals to existing tax distortions: income shifting.

While I very much agree with the authors that the criteria above provide little help in guiding discussion of possible tax reforms, I nonetheless think that the past theory can be useful in guiding such discussion. One important past result in Diamond and Mirrlees (1971), for example, is that the optimal tax system should maintain production efficiency even if it distorts factor supplies and perhaps consumption decisions. In a closed economy, production efficiency implies that individuals should face the same tax rate on their labor income regardless of the company they work for and the form of their compensation, and the same tax rate on their capital income regardless of the company they invest in and the type of security used in investing in the company.

Formally, individual h has indirect utility $V_h(w_h^n, r_h^n)$, where w_h^n is the best available net-of-tax wage rate and r_h^n is the best available net-of-tax rate of return to savings. The individual can work and invest in any firm. So we can characterize an individual's choice among jobs by $w_h^n = f(\{w_{hc}^f(1 - t_{cf})\})$ and her choice among investment options by $r_h^n = g(\{r_c^f(1 - \tau_{cf})\})$. Here t_{cf} represents the tax rate on the labor income w_{hc}^f individual h could potentially earn from company c when paid in form f (e.g., wages vs. stock options), while τ_{cf} represents the tax rate on capital income r_c^f from company c paid through a type of security f (e.g., stocks vs. bonds).

Diamond-Mirrlees then solve for the tax structure that maximizes a weighted sum of individual utility and government revenue: their result on production efficiency argues that the resulting optimal tax structure should have a "level playing field." That is, the same tax rate should be imposed on each potential source of labor income so that all of the t_{cf} are equal. Similarly the tax structure should not distort where or how individuals invest so that all of the τ_{cf} are equal as well.

This result directly generalizes to an open economy. Consider first a simplified setting where any activity abroad by a US resident occurs through the foreign subsidiaries of US multinationals. Ignore for the moment the complications created by existing tax-crediting arrangements, and assume that the United States can simply tax whatever income is left net of any foreign taxes.

An individual who is a resident of the United States can earn labor income abroad to the extent that her labor effort involves the creation of ideas that raise productivity elsewhere.[35] She can also earn a return on investments abroad undertaken by US multinationals. Formally, we reinterpret w_{hc}^f as the labor income reported for tax purposes in some country c (net of any local taxes) that takes the form f (e.g., royalty income vs. excess profits), where t_{cf} is the resulting effective US tax rate (in present value) on this income. Similarly r_c^f is the capital income reported in any country c (net of any resulting local taxes) that takes the form f, while τ_{cf} is the effective US tax rate on this income. The functions $f(.)$ and $g(.)$ now capture the opportunities the individual faces to shift taxable income across countries, and to defer repatriation (perhaps at a cost) in order to face a lower US tax rate.

As before, the Diamond-Mirrlees result on production efficiency argues that the optimal US tax structure should have a "level playing field," and so should impose the same US tax rates regardless of the country where the individual reports earning labor or capital income. Note that this conclusion follows regardless of the shape of the functions $f(.)$ and $g(.)$.

How would such a tax structure look in practice? For labor (royalty) income, there can be various approaches. One is to tax labor income of US residents at the US rate as it accrues in each country.[36] Another would be to tax all funds repatriated from abroad, whether in the form of dividends or capital gains.[37] Note that this latter approach roughly corresponds to the existing US tax treatment of repatriated dividends, and is directly analogous to the current US tax treatment of labor compensation that takes the form of contributions to a pension plan.

To replicate the tax treatment of domestic capital income for foreign-source capital income, the immediate approach would be to tax all capital income as it accrues each year at the US corporate rate, regardless of location. If the desired tax rates on capital and labor income are the same, then one approach would be to tax US multinationals on their worldwide income net of depreciation deductions at accrual.[38]

Note that these tax structures by design satisfy CEN. However, unless the tax rates abroad equal the US rates, they do not satisfy CIN. That is, local firms abroad face the local tax rate while US subsidiaries there face the US rate.

The framework above also has implications for how the United States should tax any foreign-owned subsidiaries located in the United States. While such taxes generate revenue just from foreign investors, US residents are still affected indirectly, since market-clearing wage rates and interest rates would need to change in order for the United States to remain an attractive place to do business. Standard results here suggest that the United States should tax the income from such FDI only to the extent that the United States, by doing so, can take advantage of its market power in world markets. If the United States were a price taker in world markets, then FDI in the United States should not be taxed. This implies, for example, that Honda or Toyota plants in the United States should face a very different corporate tax rate than do Ford, GM, or Chrysler. Of course, we almost always see equal tax rates on firms operating in the domestic economy, regardless of nationality, contrary to this forecast from the optimal tax models. I return to this issue below.

The framework above omits a variety of considerations that can have important implications for the optimal tax structure. For example, US activity abroad could generate information spillovers affecting the location of future economic activity and future tax revenue. Here, there is really only speculation and no hard evidence.

A key omitted complication, emphasized by GA, is tax-crediting arrangements. If foreign governments tax the earnings of US subsidiaries, then the firms receive a credit for these taxes against their US tax liabilities. If firms do not have excess credits under the policies above, then the behavior of firms would not be affected by this added complication.

However, the US government would now have an incentive to induce activity to relocate. If patents, for example, are located in the United States, then the United States receives all of the resulting tax revenue, whereas if the patents are located abroad then the United States receives only the residual tax revenue left net of any foreign tax credits. At the margin a firm may be indifferent between locating their patent in the United States or abroad, but US tax revenue is higher given the credit if the patent is located in the United States. To induce firms to relocate patents to the United States, one approach would be to impose a higher US tax rate on foreign-source income than on US source income.

Tax-crediting arrangements also complicate the choice of tax treatment for foreign-source capital income. If the United States were to lower slightly its tax rate on the foreign-source income of domestic multinationals, then US multinationals will shift more of their income abroad for tax purposes, even holding the allocation of capital unchanged. Since income in the United States is subject to the full US rate, while income reported abroad pays the United States only the taxes left net of any credits, this behavioral response is again an efficiency loss. Again, a higher US corporate tax rate on foreign-source income helps to lessen such income shifting. US multinationals could also shift some of their real investment abroad in response to the lower tax rate. If the United States is small relative to world capital markets, however, then the equilibrium domestic capital stock (and taxable domestic profits) should remain entirely unchanged—foreign investors will simply replace the US investors. With the same revenue collected from capital in the United States, but at least some residual tax revenue collected from the profits of US subsidiaries abroad, efficiency is increased by this cut in the tax rate on foreign-source income.[39] To take advantage of both effects, the United States can increase its statutory tax rate on foreign-source income to induce more income shifting into the United States, and in addition adjust depreciation provisions to improve investment incentives for US subsidiaries investing abroad.[40]

Given these benchmarks, what if anything can be added to the discussion in GA about the net efficiency effects of each of the four proposals they consider? While I find the theoretical discussion above helpful in considering what proposals could be appropriate, in the end the efficiency effects conceptually are straightforward to assess directly. Efficiency changes only to the extent that investors change behavior in response to a tax change. For a marginal tax change, investors must be effectively indifferent if they are willing to change behavior in response. Overall efficiency effects can then be judged simply by the implications of these behavioral responses for US government revenue. Efficiency increases to the extent US tax revenue rises due to the behavioral responses, and conversely. This in fact seems to be the criterion underlying the discussion in GA.

Consider then each of the proposals in turn. Exempting foreign-source dividends from domestic tax moves the tax system further from one that imposes a full tax on repatriated profits generated by ideas (patents) exploited abroad, and reduces the US tax rate on foreign-source capital income. While US tax revenue may increase a bit due to greater repatriations, it falls due to more income shifting abroad. GA I think rightly forecast small effects on net, given how little revenue is currently collected on repatriated dividends.

Worldwide taxation at accrual corresponds closely to the recommendations coming out of the above theory, at least those ignoring complications brought on by tax credits. In order to leave unchanged the tax revenue collected on foreign-source income, however, they propose reducing the statutory tax rate on this income to 28 percent. Unfortunately, this creates an incentive to shift patent ownership abroad, to avoid the higher domestic statutory tax rate. As discussed above, the pressures created by the tax credit seem to be to keep the statutory tax rate on foreign-source income high but to allow generous depreciation provisions for foreign-source income. This might be an alternative way to go to try to leave revenue unaffected. Another could be to reduce the overall corporate tax rate, and not just the rate that applies to foreign-source income.

Based on the theory above, a destination-based corporate tax should ensure that labor income is ultimately taxed by the United States at the same rate regardless of where ideas are used or where the resulting income is reported for tax purposes. As GA emphasize, this reform would imply no US taxes on capital income earned abroad, creating incentives for US firms to shift their assets abroad. As discussed above, some such incentive may be attractive as a result of its interaction with tax crediting arrangements. Whether this is the right size of such an incentive is hard to judge.

The final proposal they consider is an origin-based corporate tax. Under this tax, labor income earned abroad is untaxed, creating strong incentives to shift both real activity and income abroad. In addition capital income earned abroad is untaxed, again distorting the location of both real investment and taxable income.

All of these points are consistent with the thrust of their chapter. The theoretical model above, though, involves some implicit assumptions that merit further discussion. For one, the model above assumed that US residents invest abroad solely through US multinationals, so ignores any cross-border portfolio investment. In addition the model implicitly assumed that the parent firm of a multinational owned by US investors must be located in the United States.

What happens if either assumption does not in fact hold? If cross-border portfolio investment is feasible, then US residents can choose whether to invest abroad through US multinationals or instead through portfolio investment. If US multinationals are taxed at accrual on their foreign-source income, as occurs under GA's second proposal, but individuals face tax only at repatriation for any portfolio investments they undertake abroad, then a tax incentive is created for individuals to prefer portfolio investments. To avoid introducing such distortions, the underlying corporate profits earned on shares US individuals buy in foreign firms would also need to be subject to US corporate taxes at accrual. Under existing tax conventions, however, the United States is not in a position to impose corporate taxes based solely on portfolio holdings in a foreign firm, since by existing international conventions it does not have tax nexus.

There is at best very limited evidence to date on the extent to which cross-border portfolio investment is a readily available substitute for FDI by US multinationals.[41] Under a "territorial" tax system, corporate taxes are the same regardless of the ownership of a firm, while personal taxes should be the same whether a firm located abroad is owned through a US multinational or through direct purchase of shares. With a "territorial" system there are no tax distortions affecting therefore the choice between portfolio investment and FDI through a US multinational. The current US tax system approximates a "territorial" system, given how little tax revenue is collected on repatriated profits, so also introduces minimal distortions to portfolio investment against FDI.

While we are not in a position to learn anything about how responsive behavior is to a distortion between portfolio choice and FDI, that capital flight is such a problem in many other countries suggests the scale of the potential problem.

To what degree might firms owned by US investors respond to any of the reforms above by changing the country of location of the parent firms? While there have been a few well-publicized examples of US firms shifting abroad their tax home to avoid taxes at repatriation on their foreign-source income, we really have no evidence to date on how responsive behavior is to these incentives, simply because so little taxes are collected in practice on the repatriations by US firms. One explanation for why most all countries tax foreign-owned subsidiaries located in the country at the same corporate tax rate as domestic-owned firms, despite the forecasts from the model above that foreign-owned firms should be taxed much more lightly, is that domestic firms could easily change their "nationality" if tax incentives were nontrivial. For example, China has granted foreign-owned firms operating in China a lower corporate tax rate than that faced by domestic-owned firms. The apparent result is substantial investment by Chinese residents in Hong Kong firms that then invest the funds back in China, in the process qualifying for a more favorable corporate tax rate. The pressures have been sufficient that China is now considering eliminating these differential tax rates.

Among the proposals above, only the proposal to tax the worldwide profits of US multinationals at accrual introduces distortions affecting portfolio investments or the choice of "nationality" of firms operating in the United States. Our lack of information about how responsive either form of behavior might be to tax incentives introduces a serious question about the advisability of this particular reform. This represents the key "unknown" in the discussion above. With this qualification, I very much agree with their assessments of the four possible tax reforms.

Notes

We thank Gordon Wilson for providing very useful help with the Treasury tax files. We thank Charles Ballard, John Diamond, Geraldine Gerardi, Roger Gordon, Arnold Harberger, Edward Kleinbard, Charles Rossotti, and George Yin for helpful comments on a previous draft. Nothing in this chapter should be construed as reflecting the views and policy of the US Treasury Department.

1. See President's Advisory Panel on Federal Tax Reform (2005) for details.

2. The estimate assumes the repeal of the 9 percent deduction for domestic "production" income introduced in 2004.

3. The average tax rates include state and local taxes, which are very important in Germany and Japan among other countries. The Survey of Current Business indicates that US state corporate taxes were 3.2 percent of corporate income in 2004.

4. As indicated in the example above, this is only relevant for companies with excess credits.

5. No dividend exemption scheme in force in any other country that we are aware of imposes these allocation rules.

6. The dividend exemption option put forward by the Joint Committee on Taxation is estimated to raise $54.8 billion over fiscal years 2005 to 2014 (Joint Committee on Taxation 2005a).

7. Grubert (2001) points out that the revenue estimates depend critically on the specific features of the plan adopted. Potential behavioral responses by US companies can have a significant impact on revenues.

8. Transfer pricing rules would still be necessary for inbound companies.

9. One possible variation on this burden neutral scheme is to introduce a per country system for foreign tax credit limitations. This becomes more practical if deferral is eliminated because the problem of tracing intercompany payments up the tiers of subsidiaries disappears. Intercompany payments can be removed from the receiving subsidiaries' income, and only the company's own earnings from business transactions count. But this system, which would add complications, does not seem to have any obvious advantages compared to an overall system of credits. It is true that if the parent were in excess credit in an overall system, the per country limitation would eliminate the advantages of shifting income to a low-tax location. But the incentive to locate intangibles in a high-tax location would remain because the deductible royalties would drive down the country's average tax rate. (Presumably the royalties would be put in the country's basket. One could contemplate a per country, per item system but that would make it even more complicated.) Furthermore, if the parent were in excess limit in an overall system, the per country system could create excess credits where they did not exist before, with their attendant shifting incentives. Finally, instituting a per country system increases the tax on the companies, so the burden-neutral tax rate would have to be lower.

10. See chapters 1 and 2 by Auerbach and Shaviro in this volume.

11. The concepts of CEN and CIN, introduced by Richman (1963), have been widely discussed in the literature. The CON efficiency benchmark is introduced in Desai and Hines (2003). We concentrate on these standards which take worldwide efficiency as the goal. Some have proposed national welfare under the assumption that home governments can not obtain reciprocal concessions necessary to approximate worldwide efficiency.

12. In his comment on our paper, Roger Gordon assumes no portfolio mobility, which leads to conclusions equivalent to those reached under CEN.

13. See Grubert and Mutti (1995) for a discussion of the general second-best rule.

14. Hines (1997, 1999) and, most recently, Gordon and Hines (2002) review the literature on the impact of taxation on the activities of multinational companies. We refer to more recent evidence in this section and focus on empirical evidence that can be used to evaluate our options.

15. See, for example, Grubert and Mutti (1991, 2000), Hines and Rice (1994), Altshuler, Grubert, and Newlon (1998), and more recently, Altshuler and Grubert (2004).

16. Detailed data on royalty payments by subsidiaries from the 2004 BEA Benchmark Survey are not yet available. The US direct investment data published annually in the Survey of Current Business, however, does contain information on royalty payments from US affiliates to US parents. The story has not changed. Ireland and Singapore account for almost 20 percent of total royalties. Royalties from Irish affiliates remain larger than those from German and United Kingdom affiliates, and royalties from Singapore affiliates are still significant relative to those from Japanese affiliates (royalties paid from Singapore affiliates are about two-thirds as large as those paid by Japanese affiliates).

17. Data from the Federal Reserve Flow of Funds Accounts show a more than sixfold increase in the after-tax distributed profits of foreign subsidiaries between 2004 and 2005. Repatriated foreign profits in national income grew from $35 billion in 2004 to $217 billion in 2005 (Table F7, March 9, 2006).

18. We assume the marginal cost schedule is zero at the origin.

19. Note that we assume that shifting is between foreign affiliates and not into and out of the United States. Taking the possibility of shifting into and out of the United States into account would increase the deadweight loss.

20. The literature that studies the sources of income shifting and its implications for real investment is limited. Grubert and Slemrod (1998) investigate the link between income shifting and investment in one particular low-tax jurisdiction, Puerto Rico. Grubert (2003) estimates the implications of income shifting for real investment in low-tax locations as part of a larger study of the links between intangible income, intercompany transactions, income shifting, and location choice.

21. See Grubert and Mutti (2001) and Graetz and Oosterhuis (2002) for analyses of the simplification potential of dividend exemption systems.

22. The model is an extension of the one presented in Grubert and Mutti (2001).

23. The effective tax rate estimates in both Grubert and Mutti (2001) and Altshuler and Grubert (2001) assumed allocations to exempt income under worldwide fungibility.

24. Hines (1995) and Grubert (1998 and 2001) have found that royalty payments received by US multinationals are responsive to tax prices.

25. Transfer pricing rules would still of course be necessary for foreign companies operating in the United States.

26. There is some limited evidence that adopting the constant burden worldwide tax system would decrease the sensitivity of location decisions to differences in host country tax rates. The Tax Reform Act of 1986 (TRA86) provides an interesting case study. TRA86 added foreign tax credit baskets, making cross-crediting more difficult, and limited deferral on active financial income. Altshuler and Hubbard (2002) investigate the impact of local effective tax rates on the location of assets held by financial parents before and after TRA86. They find that the allocation of assets held in financial subsidiaries was more sensitive to taxes than the allocation of assets held in manufacturing subsidiaries prior to TRA86. Interestingly Altshuler and Hubbard find a drop in both the magnitude and significance of the effect of differences in host country tax rates on asset location choice after TRA86. In fact the authors find that host country taxes play no role in the allocation of assets held in financial subsidiaries after TRA86.

27. The inclusion of these taxes in the Treasury data may explain the large discrepancy in estimated average effective tax rates for holding company countries like the Netherlands depending on whether Treasury or Commerce Department data are examined.

28. The estimated excess credits in petroleum may be overstated because many of the companies may be choosing the safe harbor rule for the crediting of some very high petroleum taxes abroad. They can choose to credit these at the US rate, which would fall to 28 percent under the proposal.

29. Much of the material in this section is drawn from the comprehensive analysis of the international implications of consumption taxation that appears in Grubert and Newlon (1995).

30. Downloads are not a problem for business imports because they do not get a deduction. Under a subtraction method VAT companies would presumably only get a deduction if they bought from a registered taxable taxpayer. In an invoice-credit system they would have no credits against VAT liabilities.

31. David Bradford attempts to address this conflict by proposing a rather complex scheme that combines an origin base for cross-border shopping with a cash flow type of tax for business to eliminate transfer price abuse (see Bradford 2004).

32. For an early discussion of a destination-based income tax, see Carlson, Hufbauer, and Krauss (1976).

33. US tax law does restrict interest and R&D expense deductions by the US parent of a multinational, based on the fraction of the overall firms assets located in the United States.

34. They then add another criterion to this list, capital-ownership neutrality (CON), proposed recently by Desai and Hines (2003).

35. Payments could take the form of royalties. Alternatively, an entrepreneur could be paid for her ingenuity by receiving an above-normal return on shares she owns in foreign subsidiaries. GA focus on these choices, so where patents are located and where firms earning above normal profits choose to locate production.

36. To tax foreign-source labor income but not capital income, one approach is to allow expensing for any new capital investments.

37. To avoid taxes on capital income, one approach here would be to allow firms a deduction for equity investments by the US parent in a foreign subsidiary.

38. If desired tax rates on labor and capital income differ, then the depreciation rate can be adjusted to generate the desired capital-income tax rate while the statutory rate remains appropriate for any labor income.

39. The extra residual tax revenue may be larger if the US investment occurs in low-tax rather than in high-tax host countries.

40. Contrary to this recommendation, existing US law applies slower depreciation provisions for investments abroad than for investments in the United States.

41. See Gordon and Jun (1993) for some evidence.

IV

Individual Issues

8

Evidence of Tax-Induced Individual Behavioral Responses

Thomas J. Kniesner and James P. Ziliak

The Clinton revenue estimates are based on the fallacy that taxpayers will not change their behavior in response to a 37% jump in their marginal tax rates....

Martin Feldstein (1993)

Estimating the effects of income taxes on individual behaviors such as labor supply, compensation, saving, and taxable income have been focal points of economic research for several decades. Because income taxes account for nearly 80 percent of all federal revenues collected, their effects on individual behaviors and the attendant tax collections figure prominently in tax policy debates. For example, in 1993 the Clinton administration proposed increasing marginal tax rates by about one-third for the highest income Americans. In estimating how much revenue the tax increase would produce, they assumed hours worked by American taxpayers would change little and that tax collections would then rise by an amount directly proportional to the rate hike. Feldstein (1993) countered that the tax increase would substantially lower work effort by encouraging primary workers to reduce their hours of work and encouraging secondary workers in high-income households to leave the labor force, and that the tax increase would induce high-income workers to alter the form and timing of their compensation. Feldstein concluded that the combined negative behavioral responses of work effort and compensation would raise tax revenues much less than predicted, and that revenues might even fall. Whether because of or in spite of the Clinton tax policies, actual tax collections went well above both the administration's and Feldstein's forecasts in the late 1990s, re-emphasizing our limited understanding of the behavioral consequences of income taxes. We describe here what is known, knowable, and likely unknowable about the effects of income taxes on individual and household decisions.

Knowledge of the empirical consequences of income taxation on labor supply, consumption, and saving is of first-order importance not only to inform policy about the magnitudes of the possible behavioral and distributional consequences of fundamental tax reform, but also to inform policy on the direction of the response. Consider first the case of labor supply. Supporters of replacing current graduated marginal tax rates with a flat tax typically cite positive labor supply consequences of a flat tax. Economic theory does not provide a definitive answer on the effect of a flat tax on labor supply over much of the income distribution. The ambiguity is from possible offsetting substitution and income effects when the after-tax wage rate changes. Suppose moving to a flat tax lowers the marginal tax rate for the typical worker. Decreasing the marginal tax rate raises the price of leisure, inducing a substitution effect away from leisure and toward market work. Reducing the marginal tax rate also increases effective income so that the person generally wants more leisure and less work after the net wage rises. The total effect on labor supplied is ambiguous a priori due to offsetting income and substitution effects. Additional ex ante complexity of the effects of taxes on labor supply or other dimensions of individual behavior occurs if persons inaccurately perceive the tax system or are concerned with their economic situation relative to others (see the discussions by Saez and by Sickles in this volume), which is discussed comprehensively by McCaffery (see chapter 10 in this volume).

Consider too the effects on saving of a flat tax proposal. The lower marginal tax rate raises income available to save. It also raises the after-tax return to saving, which raises the relative price of current consumption and induces a substitution away from consumption. Simultaneously the lower tax rate causes an income effect toward consumption. The overall effect of tax reform on saving is also ambiguous.

Predictions of the behavioral effects of tax reform also become complicated to disentangle theoretically if one relaxes the common assumption of separability between consumption and labor supply decisions (Heckman 1974a). Empirical research is the key to determining whether tax policy will have its intended effects when consumption and labor supply interact in the person's utility function, particularly where the issue is the effect on the tax base or the efficiency cost of taxation with an eye toward a so-called optimal personal income tax.

We mainly organize our description of the individual and household behavioral effects of income taxes around a canonical life-cycle model of consumption and labor supply under uncertainty (Ziliak and Kniesner 2005). The general framework permits us to depict the two primary sets of parameters of interest for tax policy: (1) the parameters that govern intratemporal decisions that provide estimates of compensated, uncompensated, and nonlabor income elasticities of consumption and labor supply, and (2) the parameters that govern intertemporal decisions that provide estimates of the elasticity of substitution of consumption and labor supplied over time.

From the two-part conceptual framework we use as an organizational tool, we can discuss a number of configurations that yield estimating equations commonly found in the literature, such as static models of taxation and labor supply (Hausman 1981) and saving (Boskin 1978), as well as life-cycle models of taxation and consumption (Zeldes 1989) and labor supply (Ziliak and Kniesner 1999). We also demonstrate how nested inside our model of individual behavior are specifications found in the recent literature on the elasticity of taxable income (Giertz 2004). It is then straightforward to characterize exact measures of deadweight loss to facilitate discussion of the efficiency cost of distortionary taxation (Auerbach 1985). Our main goal is to leave the reader with a clear picture of what we know, what we do not know, and what we are unlikely to know about microeconometric estimates of taxation and labor supply, consumption, saving, and how generic tax reform proposals would affect economic well-being.

It is important to note that we focus on microeconometric estimates from US data involving cross-sectional and time series differences in the federal income tax. We are largely silent concerning possible estimates from macro country data (Davis and Henrekson 2004; Prescott 2004; Alesina, Glaeser, and Sacerdote 2005) or from data on idiosyncratic occupations (Camerer et al. 1997; Oettinger 1999; Farber 2005). Not only are the microeconometric estimates we discuss of interest on their own, but they are also commonly used (1) as inputs into partial equilibrium calculations of deadweight loss and optimal taxation and (2) as inputs into computable general equilibrium models of the economy as found in Altig et al. (2001) and by Diamond and Zodrow (chapter 5 in this volume).

In summary, economists know reasonably well the effects of personal income taxes on labor supply and taxable income, including quantity effects and the attendant excess burden implications. Existing estimates along with improvements in computing technology permit detailed numerical simulations of tax reform proposals, including point estimates and confidence intervals of likely effects. A key topic that is currently poorly known but could be knowable is the overall saving effects of personal income taxes. To examine saving more precisely, we would need more agreement on the appropriate life-cycle model to estimate, particularly, the form of future discounting, plus better data on total saving. What we are unlikely to know any time soon are the details of a comprehensive optimal personal income tax. A truly optimal tax system takes account of three avenues through which income taxes affect economic well-being: efficiency costs of collecting the tax (including administrative and compliance costs), social equity concerns regarding the distribution of net income, and consumption smoothing as income fluctuates due to events not insurable privately. In addition to having to examine the three dimensions simultaneously, there is the complication of whether families make group or unitary decisions and whether there are interfamily social interactions in behavior. It seems unlikely to us that economists will any time soon compute the quantitative properties of a comprehensive optimal tax structure.

8.1   What We Know about Taxes and Men

A result that has appeared regularly in traditional empirical research on male labor supply is that intratemporal uncompensated wage and intertemporal substitution effects are small and imprecisely estimated. There was little agreement on whether the estimated compensated wage effects were positive or if the Slutsky matrix conditions held empirically (Hausman 1981; Pencavel 1986; MaCurdy, Green, and Paarsch 1990; Triest 1990; Blundell and MaCurdy 1999). A positive compensated wage effect means that a revenue-neutral move to a flatter tax induces more hours worked and reduces deadweight loss, but a negative compensated wage effect produces outcomes opposite to those intended by proponents of tax reform.

Hausman (1981) estimated an uncompensated wage effect near zero, but a large negative income effect, resulting in a relatively large positive compensated wage effect. Triest (1990), using similar methods to Hausman but with data from a different year (1983 instead of 1975 in Hausman), was unable to reproduce Hausman's large income effect and thus concluded that both the uncompensated and compensated wage effects for men were near zero. MaCurdy et al. (1990), using more robust econometric techniques described below and the same year as Hausman, found, like Triest, no evidence of a large compensated wage effect. The lack of consensus on the magnitude and sign of compensated wage effects has muddied discussions of the welfare implications of a flatter tax structure.

A focal debate in the labor supply and tax literature has been on how to incorporate the economic nuances of the piecewise-linear budget constraint into model estimation. The groundbreaking work by Burtless and Hausman (1978) and Hausman (1981) applied a maximum likelihood procedure that rested on strong behavioral assumptions: that a worker has complete knowledge of all tax brackets ex ante, that the Slutsky condition is satisfied at all internal kink points of the budget constraint, and that the before-tax wage and nonwage income are exogenous to labor supply.

Before-tax wage exogeneity is unlikely because researchers have most often used average hourly earnings. If hours worked are measured with error, then so is average hourly earnings, which then becomes endogenous. MaCurdy, Green, and Paarsch (1990) noted that maximum likelihood models such as Hausman's force a nonnegative estimated wage effect and a nonpositive estimated income effect; that is, the piecewise-linear budget constraint models guarantee Slutsky integrability. Because of the econometric complexity and stringent ex ante restrictions that the maximum likelihood estimator used in the well-known and heavily cited papers of Hausman place on estimated labor supply parameters, MaCurdy et al. (1990) advocated an alternative instrumental-variables estimator.

The alternative instrumental variables approach first approximates the piecewise linear budget set with a smooth, continuously differentiable budget constraint and then instruments for the endogenous after-tax wage and virtual nonlinear income terms. Using the more flexible instrumental variables estimator, MaCurdy et al. (1990) find that male labor supply is largely unresponsive to the economic environment, including taxes.

Although there was an abundance of papers on the effects of taxes on labor supply in the 1970s and 1980s, empirical research on the joint effects of income taxes on labor supply and consumption/saving outcomes—both within and across periods—is virtually nonexistent. Much of the research on labor supply and taxation has been conducted with static models on cross-sectional data, and all previous empirical work on taxes and labor supply in a life-cycle setting maintains the assumption of additive separability between consumption and leisure (Blundell et al. 1998; Ziliak and Kniesner 1999). Existing research on consumption and taxation mostly examines how distortionary income taxation affects efforts to smooth consumption (Varian 1980; Strawczynski 1998; Auerbach and Feenberg 2000; Kniesner and Ziliak 2002b; Low and Maldoom 2004). Estimates of labor-supply tax effects in the context of a flexible framework also reveal saving effects, which are critical to more informed tax policy, especially if government agencies such as the Congressional Budget Office score tax revenue effects dynamically (Mankiw and Weinzierl 2006). In recent research (Ziliak and Kniesner 2005) we extended the labor supply and taxation literature by estimating a life-cycle model of consumption, saving, and labor supply under uncertainty with nonlinear wage income taxation that relaxes the standard assumption of strong separability in consumption and labor supply choices within periods.

8.1.1 Organizing Model

We use the model in Ziliak and Kniesner (2005) as an organizing vehicle for the remainder of the discussion of male labor supply. Consider a consumer choosing consumption/saving and labor supply in an environment of economic uncertainty. The uncertainty comes from unknown future paths of wages, prices, taxes, and interest rates. For tractability intertemporal preferences are taken as time separable, as are budgets. Intertemporal separability rules out consumption or labor supply habits, wherein current utility from consumption or labor supply depends on their history, and rules out budget nonseparabilities due to possible endogenous human capital (Shaw 1989; Imai and Keane 2004) or joint nonlinear taxation of wage and capital incomes (Blomquist 1985; Ziliak and Kniesner 1999), which in many cases enlarge the labor supply response so that the estimates we emphasize here are for the most part conservative. Most important, we enrich the empirical specification by introducing nonseparabilities in within-period preferences over consumption/saving and labor supplied, which makes them jointly determined.

   The familiar necessary condition for an equilibrium solution with consumption, saving and labor supply equates the marginal rate of substitution (*MRS*) of market hours for consumption to the after-tax wage rate, $\omega_t \equiv w_t(1 - \tau_t)$,

$$-\frac{U_{h,t}}{U_{C,t}} = \omega_t, \tag{8.1}$$

where C_t is composite nondurable consumption, h_t is annual hours of work, w_t is the gross hourly wage rate, $U_{C,t}$ is the first derivative of within-period utility with respect to consumption, $U_{h,t}$ is the first derivative of utility with respect to hours of work, and $\tau_t = \partial T_t(\cdot)/\partial h_t$ is the marginal tax rate. Given a parametric or nonparametric specification of preferences, cross-sectional data are sufficient to identify intratemporal preferences, which in turn reveal the familiar compensated and uncompensated wage elasticities of labor supply and common measures of the efficiency cost of income taxes and tax reforms.

The allocation of wealth over time is determined by the Euler condition

$$\lambda_A^t = \beta E_t[(1 + r_t)\lambda_A^{t+1}], \tag{8.2}$$

where $\lambda_A^{t+1} = \partial V^{t+1}/\partial A_{t+1}$ is the marginal utility of wealth, $\beta = 1/(1 + \rho)$ is the time discount rate, E_t is the expectations operator conditional on information available at time t, and r_t is a risk-free interest rate. Identifying intertemporal preferences requires data with a time dimension to estimate the allocation of wealth over time as governed by the Euler condition in (8.2).

A key parameter in life-cycle models of consumption/saving is the intertemporal substitution elasticity (*ISE*), which is the proportional change in consumption expenditure across periods necessary to keep the marginal utility of wealth constant given an anticipated one-percent change in relative consumption prices. Related is the Frisch (marginal utility of wealth constant) specific substitution elasticity between any two goods j and k

$$e_{jk}^F = e_{jk}^U + e_j e_k s_k \Phi, \tag{8.3}$$

where e_{jk}^F is the Frisch elasticity, e_{jk}^U is the compensated (cross) price elasticity, e_j and e_k are expenditure (income) elasticities, s_k is the share of good k in the household budget, and Φ is the *ISE* (Browning 2005). Under simple specifications where consumption is independent of the path of wages, $e_{jk}^F = e_j \Phi \approx e_{jk}^Y$, where e_{jk}^Y is the income-constant

Marshallian cross-price elasticity of demand. Because Φ, and in turn e_{jk}^F, are not generally identifiable with cross-sectional data, recovering lifetime preference parameters requires panel data (MaCurdy 1983) or cohort data (Blundell, Browning, Meghir 1994).

Our empirical strategy is a two-stage estimation method where in the first stage we estimate the intratemporal (*MRS*) equilibrium condition, $-U_{h,t}/U_{C,t} = \omega_t$, by specifying a direct translog functional form for within-period preferences that permits interdependent marginal utilities of consumption (saving) and labor supply. Demographics come into the model via the method of demographic translating, where the utility parameters are explicit functions of demographic characteristics. Given estimated within-period preference parameters, we construct the period-specific utility and marginal utility functions and assume a Box-Cox transformation governs the utility related functions to estimate the intertemporal preference parameters from equation (8.2). The intertemporal preference parameters in our model permit variation in risk aversion and the *ISE* according to time-varying demographic characteristics. In general, estimation of the *MRS* and the evolution of lifetime wealth are complicated, both because they are nonlinear in the parameters and because the regressors are endogenous (hours of work and leisure, consumption/saving, and wages in the *MRS* equation and both utility and marginal utility in the intertemporal wealth equation).

8.1.2 Data Issues

To identify the tax effects on work incentives and consumption/saving in Ziliak and Kniesner (2005), we used household-level data on male heads of household from the 1980 to 1999 waves of the Panel Study of Income Dynamics (1979–1998 calendar years).

Our data span multiple tax reforms in the United States: the Economic Recovery Tax Act of 1981, the Tax Reform Act of 1986, the Omnibus Reconciliation Tax Acts of 1990 and 1993, and the Taxpayer Relief Act of 1997. Together the tax reforms of 1981 and 1986 reduced marginal tax rates across the board, reduced the number of tax brackets from 16 to 4, and expanded the taxable income base. Although the tax reforms of the 1990s reversed the trend of the 1980s reforms by adding two new higher marginal tax rates on high-income Americans, the tax reforms of the 1990s also significantly expanded the earned income tax credit among low-income working families.

Focusing on prime-age male heads of household allowed us to ignore issues associated with labor force nonparticipation (discussed below in the context of female labor supply). When constructing annual taxable income we assume that married men filed joint tax returns and unmarried men filed as head of household. Adjusted gross income is the sum of labor earnings, cash transfers, and property income. To approximate the actual marginal tax rate facing the household, we included property income in AGI, inclusive of wife's earnings in cases where working men have working wives. For tractability we abstracted from the fact that an inclusive property income measure may generate interdependencies both within periods in spousal labor supply choices, and across periods in intertemporal labor supply, as discussed in Ziliak and Kniesner (1999).

8.1.3   Estimated Effects of Taxes on Consumption/Saving and Labor Supply

Table 8.1 presents the main results from Ziliak and Kniesner (2005) expressed in concepts most useful for labor-market and tax policy: namely income elasticity, compensated and uncompensated wage elasticities for within-period preferences, and the *ISE* and Frisch specific substitution elasticities for intertemporal preferences. Here we focus on labor supply and consumption effects. In a later section we translate

Table 8.1
Selected intratemporal and intertemporal elasticities

Real changes in	Consumption	Labor supply
After-tax income (Y_t) or wages (ω_t)		
Income elasticity	0.035	−0.517
	(0.015)	(0.078)
Compensated elasticity	0.086	0.328
	(0.014)	(0.064)
Uncompensated elasticity	0.232	−0.468
	(0.080)	(0.098)
Intertemporal substitution elasticity	−0.964	—
	(0.009)	
Frisch specific substitution elasticity	0.072	0.535
	(0.010)	(0.124)

Note: The elasticities, which are based on the parameter estimates in tables 1 and 2 of Ziliak and Kniesner (2005), are evaluated at the mean values of the functions. The standard errors are based on 1,000 bootstrap replications of the *MRS* and Euler equations.

our estimated effects of taxes into implications for the effects of tax policy on saving. In Ziliak and Kniesner (2005) we find that consumption and work hours are direct complements so that consumption and leisure are direct substitutes.

Evaluated at the sample means of hours, net wages, and nondurable consumption, the nonlabor (property) income elasticities for consumption and labor supply are 0.035 and −0.517, indicating that both consumption and leisure are normal goods. Note that the nonlabor income elasticity of consumption is not the same as the total income elasticity often reported in consumption studies. The corresponding utility-constant compensated wage elasticities of consumption and labor supply are 0.086 and 0.328.

Our estimated compensated wage elasticity of labor supply exceeds that typically reported in the literature and implies a sizable deadweight loss of taxation. Specifically, in a model based on linear preferences and additive separability between consumption and hours, we find a compensated wage elasticity about half that reported here. Below we discuss whether the difference is driven more by functional form differences than by the possibility of nonseparability between consumption and labor supply. Because of the sizable nonlabor income effect relative to the compensated wage effect, we find that the uncompensated wage elasticity of labor supply is negative. Male labor supply bends backward. Although the income elasticity of labor supply is large, it is in the range of previous estimates reported in the literature, as is the finding of backward-bending male labor supply (Blundell and MaCurdy 1999; Pencavel 1986). Important for estimates of the economic efficiency of the tax system is that we do find an upward-sloping compensated labor-supply supply function.

The estimate of the *ISE* at the means is about −1.0 for nondurable expenditures, which is consistent with strictly concave intertemporal preferences. Given the *ISE* and compensated wage elasticities, the Frisch-specific substitution elasticity of labor supply is 0.54. The parallel Frisch net wage elasticity of consumption is 0.072. Our basic estimates imply that consumption and leisure are substitutes within periods. Intertemporally the elasticities in table 8.1 confirm that with an anticipated increase in the real after-tax wage, hours of market work increase, leisure falls, and consumption rises. Collectively the elasticity estimates in table 8.1 indicate possible welfare gains from increased labor supply and consumption from revenue-neutral tax reforms that raise after-tax wages.

In Ziliak and Kniesner (2005) we also considered a number of specification checks on our base-case results in table 8.1. To avoid mixing stocks and flows, we primarily measure consumption as total nondurable consumption expenditures for the family. For completeness we also present estimates replacing imputed nondurable expenditures with food expenditures as the measure of consumption.

Food is the prevalent measure of expenditures used in consumption-based analyses in the PSID, though more by default than choice because food may be a poor proxy for the preferred nondurable consumption measure. The property income effect for food consumption is about 0.5; because the point elasticity involves multiplying the marginal effect by the ratio of property income to food consumption, the elasticity is also about 0.5 (average food spending is of comparable magnitude to average property income). Using food consumption leads to a significantly larger uncompensated wage elasticity of consumption. As in the case of nondurables, the Frisch-specific substitution elasticity is positive, reflecting that food consumption and leisure are substitutes. Indeed the coefficient on the food consumption–leisure interaction term is 15.14 with a standard error of 0.90, as compared to the base case estimate of 4.26 (0.43). The implications for labor supply elasticities in the case of food consumption are to cut the estimated property income elasticity in half and to cut the compensated wage elasticity by about two-thirds. Although the qualitative results remain unchanged when we switched from nondurable consumption to food consumption, the magnitudes clearly depend on the consumption measure.

A final robustness check we performed in Ziliak and Kniesner (2005) was to impose the common assumption of additivity between consumption and leisure to examine how important allowing for nonseparabilities in within-period preferences is for key parameters used in policy evaluation. Focusing on the labor supply results, and imposing separability between consumption and leisure, produces significantly larger nonlabor income, compensated wage, and Frisch wage elasticities of labor supply but a correspondingly smaller (in absolute value) uncompensated wage elasticity of labor supply.

The pattern of results reveals something akin to the classic omitted variable bias problem when consumption and labor supply are not allowed to interact econometrically in marginal utility. Consumption and hours of work are not separable and are direct complements. Given that consumption and property income covary positively, as do consumption and labor supply, omitting consumption imparts a downward (negative) bias on the nonlabor income elasticity of labor supply and an upward bias on the compensated wage elasticity of labor supply. Allowing for nonseparability between consumption and labor supply is important economically. Models that ignore consumption–hours interactions likely provide upper bounds on labor supply elasticities.

To explore the nonseparability issue further, we examined whether a similar pattern emerges in the standard linear labor supply model with and without consumption. We regressed annual hours of work on the log of the real net wage, virtual nonlabor income, and demographics, with and without controls for consumption. The linear labor supply model with consumption is conceptually similar to the conditional demand framework described in Browning and Meghir (1991) where consumption is not formally modeled but simply serves as a conditioning variable for labor supply outcomes. Although the magnitudes of the elasticities are significantly lower in the linear case, which highlights a further potential cost of choosing an inflexible specification of preferences yielding the linear labor supply model, the estimated compensated wage elasticity of labor supply without consumption is 0.024 and with consumption is 0.020. The 20 percent larger linear labor supply wage elasticity without consumption indicates that imposing additivity between consumption and leisure has important consequences for estimates of labor-market behavior.

8.1.4 Summary

Labor supply elasticities are key to understanding the distribution of income as well as the efficiency and equity dimensions of an individual income-based tax. Later sections emphasize the direct relationship between the compensated net wage effect and the efficiency loss, which implies a lower optimal tax rate. Although it has often been the case in policy simulations to use small elasticity values for US men, recent research has re-examined the conclusion that men's elasticities are close to zero. Richer econometric specifications include allowing intertemporal nonseparabilities in the budget constraint (Ziliak and Kniesner 1999), semiparametric forms for the labor supply function (Blomquist, Eklöf, and Newey 2001; Blomquist and Newey 2002), possible social interactions that are labor supply synergies across workers (Grodner and Kniesner 2006a, b), and the joint intertemporal choices of consumption and labor supply that we have focused on here (Ziliak and Kniesner 2005). The additional generality of recent research on male labor supply has yielded larger estimates of the effects of income taxation on labor supply. As the results in table 8.1 show, we find a compensated labor supply elasticity for men of as much as 0.33. The effects of taxes on men is undergoing re-evaluation due to recent econometric advances such that policy intended to minimize deadweight loss and set optimal taxes may require lower tax rates than previously thought based on possibly underestimated effects of income taxes on the labor supply and consumption of US men.

8.2   What We Know about Taxes and Women

The early literature either characterized labor supply via the labor-force participation decision, or via hours of market work with non-workers either discarded or retained but their missing wages imputed by the wages of workers. Each procedure yields biased estimates of the wage elasticity of labor supply, and limiting the scope to the participation decision also makes the research of no use for understanding the consequences of income taxes for the tax base or economic well-being.

Heckman (1974b) modeled participation, wages, and hours of work in a simultaneous equations system using a sample of working and nonworking married women in a way that yields economically and statistically coherent parameter estimates of the labor supply of women. Heckman and MaCurdy (1980, 1982) extended the static model to the life-cycle case. The issues of sample selection bias induced by nonworkers apply to all subgroups, not just married women. Nonparticipation is typically ignored when considering prime-aged male labor supply because most prime-aged men work for pay unless disabled. Despite its importance to labor supply research, the Tobit-type model of Heckman (1974b) imposes a proportionality relationship between the coefficients on the participation and hours-worked margins and does not easily accommodate the presence of fixed costs of work. A more econometrically general approach is to estimate the two labor supply dimensions separately (Heckman 1993; Zabel 1993).

In addition to allowing more flexibility for fixed money and time costs of holding a job, estimating the participation and hours-worked margins separately helps us better understand optimal tax and transfer policy. Saez (2002) demonstrates via simulation that if the bulk of the labor supply response is at the hours-worked margin then the optimal transfer policy is a negative income tax (NIT) with a large guarantee and high phase-out rate. If instead the response is concentrated at the participation margin, and the elasticity is at least 1.0, then the optimal policy is an earned income tax credit (EITC) that has a smaller guarantee coupled with a negative marginal tax rate at low incomes.

There is surprisingly little research providing structural estimates of the wage elasticity of women's labor supply at both the participation and hours worked margins (Kimmel and Kniesner 1998; Heim 2005a, b; Ziliak 2005). Kimmel and Kniesner (1998) use data from the Survey of Income and Program Participation to estimate wage elasticities separately for men and women by marital status, but do not model the tax system because their data are sub-annual. Ziliak (2005) models the labor supply of single mothers in the presence of income taxes and transfers, while Heim (2005a, b) models the labor supply of married women in the presence of income taxation. Hausman (1981), Triest (1990), and Keane and Moffitt (1998) examine women's labor supply in a Tobit-type framework with taxes and the simultaneous choice of hours of work and budget constraint segment (marginal tax rate); consequently, their parameter estimates yield convolutions of extensive and intensive margin elasticities. Meyer and Rosenbaum (2001) did model the tax and transfer system but restricted attention to the participation margin and did not provide a direct estimate of the wage elasticity. Finally, a number of studies have attempted to identify the response of women's labor supply to tax changes from reforms to the EITC (Hotz and Scholz 2003; Eissa and Hoynes 2005). Most of the EITC studies either used reduced form methods or employed difference-in-difference estimators to control for confounding factors so that the estimates do not reveal structural behavioral parameters useful for complex policy evaluation.

8.2.1 Organizing Model

To fix ideas, consider the canonical individualistic static model of labor supply in the presence of nonlinear income taxes as adopted in Ziliak (2005). In any period t the ith woman is assumed to have preferences $U(C_{it}, L_{it})$ over a composite consumption good C_{it} and leisure time L_{it}. She maximizes utility subject to the time constraint $\bar{L} = L_{it} + h_{it}$, where $\bar{L}$ is total time available and h_{it} is hours of market work, in light of the current-period budget constraint $C_{it} = w_{it}h_{it} + N_{it} - T_t(Y_{it})$. As before,

w_{it} is the real before-tax hourly wage rate, N_{it} is real taxable nonlabor income, $I_{it} \equiv w_{it}h_{it} + N_{it}$ is real total taxable income, and $T_t(I_{it})$ is real tax payments. Similarly $\tau_{it} \equiv T'_t(I_{it})$ is the marginal tax rate so that the resulting after-tax wage rate is $\omega_{it} = w_{it}(1 - \tau_{it})$. Although the individualistic framework is most applicable to single women, it is also useful for thinking about married women's labor supply.

We consider only the two labor-market states, employed and not employed, so the decision to work boils down to a comparison of utility in the employed state, $U(C_{it}, L_{it} < \bar{L})$, to utility in the not employed state, $U(C_{it}, L_{it} = \bar{L})$. If we define the net gain from employment as $\Delta_{it} = U(C_{it}, L_{it} < \bar{L}) - U(C_{it}, L_{it} = \bar{L})$, then the indicator variable $e_{it} = 1$ if $\Delta_{it} > 0$ and $e_{it} = 0$ otherwise. If we assume that the stochastic component of the employment decision is distributed normally, then the probability of working is a structural probit model, $P^e_{it} \equiv P(e_{it} = 1) = \Phi(\cdot)$. Because the example woman chooses to work if and only if the offered after-tax market wage ω_{it} exceeds the reservation wage (which is the inverse of the labor supply function when all time is spent in leisure, $L_{it} = \bar{L}$), the structural equation for the probability of employment has the same covariates as the structural hours-worked equation. The same set of variables determines the structural extensive and intensive labor supply choices (Heckman 1974b).

For women choosing labor market work, equilibrium hours worked at the intensive margin is determined similarly to men, where one equates the marginal rate of substitution of market hours for consumption to the real after-tax hourly wage, $-U_{h,t}/U_{C,t} = \omega_t$. When estimating the intensive margin in the presence of nonlinear income taxes, one approach is to specify the complete budget frontier and have the worker simultaneously choose the marginal tax rate segment and hours of work conditional on segment choice (Hausman 1981). A drawback of an econometric model that has the worker choosing both the budget segment and point on the segment is that it effectively imposes global satisfaction of the Slutsky condition at all internal kink points, contrary to much evidence (MaCurdy, Green, and Paarsch 1990). A robust alternative is to linearize the (convex) budget constraint by taking the net wage as given and adding a lump-sum transfer of $\tau_{it}W_{it}h_{it} - T_t(Y_{it})$ to nonlabor income to yield so-called virtual nonlabor income, $\tilde{N}_{it}$, which compensates the worker so that statistically she behaves as if facing a constant marginal tax rate at all income levels.

With linearized budget constraints and virtual income, a common specification for hours worked at the intensive margin is $h_{it} =$

$\alpha + \beta \ln \omega_{it} + \gamma \tilde{N}_{it} + X_{it}\varphi + u_{it}$, where X_{it} is a vector of demographic variables affecting hours choices, and u_{it} is a structural error term (Browning, Deaton, and Irish 1985; Blundell et al. 1998). The intensive-margin wage elasticity of hours worked is then $\hat{\beta}/h_{it}$, which is a declining function of hours worked. Because wages are observed for workers only, and because the marginal tax rate that enters both the net wage and virtual-income variables is a function of hours of work, one treats the net wage and virtual income terms as endogenous while simultaneously controlling for nonrandom self-selection into work. Popular techniques are parametric or semi(non)-parametric control functions such as the Heckman (1979) two-step correction.

Economic theory tells us that the same set of covariates enters both the intensive and extensive margin labor supply decisions so that the corresponding equation for the structural employment-status decision is $P_{it}^e = P(h_{it} > 0) = \Phi(\alpha^e + \beta^e \ln \omega_{it} + \gamma^e \tilde{N}_{it} + X_{it}\varphi^e)$. The superscript e denotes that the coefficients describing the extensive margin need not be the same as the coefficient describing the intensive margin. Under normality, the associated participation elasticity with respect to the net wage is $\hat{\beta}^e[\hat{\phi}_{it}(\cdot)/\hat{\Phi}_{it}(\cdot)]$, where $\hat{\phi}$ and $\hat{\Phi}$ are the probability density function and cumulative distribution function of the normal distribution evaluated at the estimated structural parameters for each sample observation.

Because the wage is not observed for nonworkers, Kimmel and Kniesner (1998) and Ziliak (2005) estimate a structural wage equation for workers only that controls for self-selection into the labor force. Given the selection-corrected wage function parameters, they predict a wage for all women and replace the predicted log wage in the participation equation. Virtual income is likewise treated as endogenous in the structural participation equation.

8.2.2 Issues of Marital Status

Within the canonical model of labor supply the econometric issues surrounding married women's labor supply do not differ much from issues concerning single mothers. Distinguishing between the extensive and intensive margins is crucial for both groups of women given the large percentage of mothers out of the labor force, as is modeling the effects of the age composition of children.

A key difference between single and married mothers in the canonical model is the appropriate marginal tax rate for constructing the after-tax wage. Because single mothers are the sole income earner the marginal tax rate on the first dollar earned is typically zero because of personal exemptions and deductions. For married women the appropriate marginal tax rate on the first dollar earned depends on whether labor supply decisions of the partners are determined jointly or sequentially. The typical assumption is to model married women's labor supply decisions as sequential to the husband's hours choice, so that the marginal tax rate on the woman's first dollar earned is the marginal tax rate facing the husband on his last dollar earned. An alternative approach in the empirical literature has the hours choice jointly determined, the tax filing status jointly determined, and the marginal tax rate as the family's joint tax rate.

Recent research challenges the canonical model of the family on the grounds that the data usually reject income pooling (Lundberg, Pollack, and Wales 1997). The collective model of labor supply is robust to violations of pooling (Chiappori 1992). Indeed evaluating tax policy is a key motivation stated by Chiappori for the structure of his model. The canonical family model of labor supply allows tax policy to affect the distribution of income across families, but not the within-family income distribution. The inter- versus intrafamily difference occurs because the income pooling assumption implies that a dollar in nonlabor income transferred to the wife (e.g., the EITC) has the same effect on household consumption demands as a similar-sized transfer made to the husband. The collective model allows the transfer to affect household spending patterns differentially based on which spouse receives the transfer and the relative bargaining power of that spouse in the family. In the base-case collective model each spouse has egoistic preferences over their own consumption and labor supply choices. After bargaining occurs on how to divide the nonlabor income, the labor supply choice is made independently of the other spouse's decision. Given the ex ante division of nonlabor income in the collective model, the econometric model for married women will then be akin to the model for single mothers.

8.2.3   Estimated Labor Supply Effects

The evidence to date on structural wage elasticities of female labor supply suggest that the elasticity at the extensive margin dominates the elasticity at the intensive margin. Kimmel and Kniesner (1998), using the tri-annual data from the 1984 panel of the SIPP without controls for income taxation, find participation elasticities on the order of 2.4 for single women and 1.85 for married women, and compensated hours-worked elasticities of about 0.7 for both single and married women.

Ziliak (2005) uses 23 years of data on single mothers from the CPS (1980–2002) and tax data from NBER's TAXSIM program to infer income taxes. To identify the after-tax wage elasticities of participation and hours worked, he adopts a scheme similar to that of Blundell et al. (1998), which exploits the fact that the after-tax wage and virtual nonlabor income grew differentially over the sample period. The differential growth in after-tax wages comes from both demand-side factors such as skill-biased technological change and supply side policy reforms such as the ERTA81, TRA86, and expansions in the EITC. The instrumental variables estimator Ziliak uses yields an average participation elasticity of 2.0 and a compensated hours-worked elasticity of 0.15. For single mothers attached to the transfer system, the compensated hours-worked elasticity at the median ranges from 0.4 for women only on the cash welfare program AFDC/TANF to 1.9 for mothers receiving both cash welfare and food stamps. There seems to be substantial heterogeneity in the labor supply response to after-tax wage changes among single mothers.

Heim (2005) uses an econometric model similar to that of Kimmel and Kniesner (1998) and Ziliak (2005), but his research differs in a number of important dimensions. Heim focuses on married women in the CPS over the 25-year period of 1979 to 2003 rather than single mothers, estimates his model year-by-year to yield annual elasticities, defines the after-tax wage rate differently than is typical in the literature, and adopts a different identification scheme. Rather than constructing the after-tax wage rate based on the woman's actual marginal tax rate, Heim uses the NBER TAXSIM program to estimate the marginal tax rate at zero hours of work and at full-time work. For the marginal tax rate applicable to full-time work, Heim imputes a marginal tax rate for each state and year based on the average income of husbands and wives in that state and year. He then applies the imputed state-year tax rate to all working women in each respective state-year cell. The justification is to avoid the endogeneity of the actual marginal tax rate and attendant identification schemes based on exclusion restrictions commonly found in the labor supply literature. Because Heim estimates the elasticities for each year, identification is based strictly on cross-sectional variation. He finds substantially smaller elasticities for married women at both margins compared to Kimmel and Kniesner (1998), with the participation margin elasticity ranging from -0.09 to 0.7 and the hours-worked elasticity ranging from 0 to 0.4. Heim also finds a significant downward trend in both elasticities over the past 25 years.

Several authors estimate structural wage elasticities that are mixtures of the extensive and intensive margins or refer only to the intensive margin (Hausman 1981; Mroz 1987; Triest 1990; Hoynes 1996; Blundell, Duncan, and Meghir 1998; Keane and Moffitt 1998; Kimmel and Kniesner 1998; Kumar 2005). Models that produce mixture elasticities are generally cross-sectional Tobit-type models and estimated via maximum likelihood under the assumption of normally distributed error terms. For example, Hausman (1981), modeling the joint choice of (nonlinear) tax segment and hours of work using data from the 1975 PSID, finds an uncompensated wage elasticity of about 0.9 for married women and about 0.5 for single mothers. In a replication study of Hausman's research, Triest (1990) estimates a range of uncompensated wage elasticities for married women of 0.86 to 1.12, but when he truncates the sample to working women the elasticities fall to between 0.21 and 0.28. Kimmel and Kniesner (1998) supplement their two-step models with Tobit-type estimators and estimate mixture elasticities of 1.67 for single women and 1.82 for married women. Keane and Moffitt (1998), who model the joint choice of work and participation in food stamps, public housing, and AFDC for single mothers in the 1984 SIPP, estimate a net uncompensated wage elasticity of labor supply of about 1.8.

Kumar (2005) estimates Tobit-type models of married women's labor supply, but differs in three respects from other papers in this literature. First, he models labor supply in a so-called life-cycle consistent framework. All aspects of the static model carry forward full force in the life-cycle consistent framework, but the definition of full income includes changes in the family's asset position from one period to the next; that is, full income is defined as $Y_t^F = r_t A_{t-1} + \Delta A_t + B_t - T(l_t, D, E)$, where B_t is non-asset nonlabor income in period t and where ΔA_t controls for the transfer of funds across periods that is absent in the static model. Second, Kumar (2005) supplements standard cross-sectional models with panel-data models to control for unobserved preferences for work. Third, Kumar differs from most in the literature by estimating labor supply using both parametric (Tobit and random effects Tobit) and semiparametric (censored least absolute deviations (CLAD)) estimators, which not only relax restrictive small-sample distributional assumptions but also are more robust to fixed unobserved heterogeneity in nonlinear panel-data models.

Like Heim (2005a, b), Kumar (2005) presents estimated annual elasticities over the period 1982 to 1992 using the PSID and finds a range of uncompensated mixture elasticities between 0.5 and 1.26. Also like Heim, Kumar finds a downward trend in the elasticities over his sample period. Kumar's pooled panel-data uncompensated wage elasticities are 0.4 to 0.7, which are fairly robust across the parametric and semiparametric estimators. Finally, he estimates intensive margin elasticities that are about 0.25, which are about half the size of the mixture elasticities.

Though more dated than the research just described, it is useful to end with Mroz (1987), who uses a two-step estimator for nonrandom selection into the labor force by married women and estimates an uncompensated after-tax hours-worked wage elasticity that is statistically and economically zero. Mroz (1987, p. 795) concludes that "The range of labor supply estimates that we fail to reject suggests that the labor supply behavior of working married women matched the estimated behavior of prime-aged males." Likewise Ziliak (2005) concludes that the labor supply of prime-aged men is similar to that of working single mothers with no attachment to the transfer system (other than the EITC).

8.2.4 Summary

Statistical models of female labor supply, whether in reference to married or unmarried mothers, must account for the large fraction of labor-market nonparticipants and allow the labor-supply response to differ across the participation and hours-worked margins. The few studies to date permitting differential responses across margins suggest that the wage elasticity of labor supply at the extensive margin exceeds the elasticity at the intensive margin, and that the extensive margin elasticity exceeds 1.0, which has implications for the design of optimal tax and transfer programs (Saez 2002). The wage elasticities of hours worked by married and single women with no attachment to the welfare system are small, positive, and not economically or statistically distinguishable from comparable elasticities among prime-age married men. What is still not known is the effect of income taxation on life-cycle decisions of labor supply, marriage, and fertility. Because asset accumulation among single mothers is nearly nonexistent, the static model of labor supply may not be a bad approximation to life-cycle behavior for the population of single mothers (Hurst and Ziliak 2006). However, single status for many women is a transitory state, and how the tax and transfer system affects labor supply and marital decisions across a lifetime is still not known, and is not readily knowable without complex structural models with long panels.

8.3   What We Know about Saving

Much of the early research on the effect of income taxation on saving focused on the effect of the after-tax rate of return to capital on the level of saving—the so called interest elasticity of saving (Boskin 1978; Bernheim 2002). The interest elasticity comes from time-series models of consumption or saving levels as a function of disposable income, the after-tax rate of return, and other factors, with estimates in the range 0 to 0.4. Bernheim (2002) makes the important point that the mode estimate of the interest elasticity is zero. Research on intertemporal consumption by Hall (1978) challenged the basic assumptions of models generating the interest elasticity, such as the exogeneity of disposable income and the net rate of return. Lacking good instrumental variables, empirical research on the interest elasticity using aggregate time-series data on consumption or saving largely disappeared.

Subsequent research sought to infer the saving response to income taxation using household panel data applied to Euler equations governing the growth rate of consumption (Zeldes 1989; Runkle 1991). Under additive separability between consumption and leisure, the typical consumption Euler equation model regresses the log of the change in consumption on the real after-tax rate of return, time effects, and family demographics. In the standard model based on constant relative risk aversion preferences, the coefficient on the after-tax rate of return is the intertemporal substitution elasticity (ISE). Estimates of the ISE, like the interest elasticity, range from 0 in aggregate time-series data (Hall 1988) to over 0.4 in panel data (Runkle 1991). The ISE can reveal how consumption, and thus saving, evolves over the life cycle in response to anticipated changes in the after-tax interest rate. Under the assumption of perfect certainty over prices, interest rates, tax policy, and preferences, it is possible to back out the interest elasticity of saving from the shape of the consumption function. Unfortunately, in the more realistic case of uncertainty and utility preferences other than quadratic, it is not possible to say anything general about the level of saving (Bernheim 2002).

8.3.1 Organizing Model and Estimates

It is informative to policy to back out the saving response to changes in after-tax wage rates and nonlabor (property) income using the model of Ziliak and Kniesner (2005). Note that in any given period t the uses of disposable income are consumption and saving, $I_t = C_t + S_t$, where S_t is after-tax saving. Focusing on the tax on earned income, disposable income is $I_t \equiv \omega_t h_t + N_t$. The total derivative of the uses of disposable income when the tax rate changes is then $h\,d\omega + \omega\,dh + dN = dC + dS$.

To find the uncompensated after-tax wage elasticity of saving, we set $dN = 0$, divide both sides by $d\omega$, and rearrange to yield

$$\varepsilon_\omega^S = (1 + \varepsilon_\omega^h)\frac{\omega h}{S} - \varepsilon_\omega^C \frac{C}{S}, \tag{8.4}$$

where ε_ω^S is the uncompensated wage elasticity of saving, ε_ω^h is the uncompensated wage elasticity of labor supply, and ε_ω^S is the uncompensated wage elasticity of consumption. The average values for the two elasticities on the right-hand side of (4) are -0.49 and 0.23 in Ziliak and Kniesner (2005). In our data the average real after-tax labor earnings of the husband exceed average household saving by a factor of about nine, and average real nondurable household consumption exceeds average household saving by a factor of about 15 (average consumption is about \$48,000 and average saving is about \$3,000). Substituting the values of earnings and consumption relative to saving, along with the wage elasticities of labor supply and consumption into the expression for ε_ω^S, yields an uncompensated wage elasticity of saving of about 0.96. Saving levels are quite responsive to changes in the net of tax real wage rate, and thus saving will respond positively to economically beneficial tax reforms.

8.3.2 Summary

During the late 1980s and through the 1990s there emerged a large and contentious literature on the effects of IRAs on the level of household saving (Bernheim 2002 is a thorough review). With the fiscal strain on public pension-like programs such as Social Security, and the decline in private pension coverage of employees by employers, the role of tax policy in stimulating saving will become increasingly important. More research clearly would seem to be valuable concerning the effects of income taxation on overall personal saving. Our results in Ziliak and Kniesner (2005) refer to within-period decision-making, but how saving responds to wage changes and interest rate changes over the life cycle related to possible unanticipated tax policy is still relatively unknown. Because closed-form solutions are generally not possible with flexible preference structures, the level of saving is often not inferable from life cycle models. However, optimal wealth targets can generally be derived from life cycle models with precautionary and buffer-stock saving (Carroll 1997), and models such as that by Scholz, Seshadri, and Khitatrakun (2006) can be extended to incorporate income taxation more fully.

8.4   What We Know about the Elasticity of Taxable Income

Although the response of labor supply and saving to changes in the after-tax wage rate has been the key behavioral outcomes of interest over the past three decades of research on earned income taxation, related topics include composition of income (taxable vs. nontaxable, cash vs. in-kind), timing of income receipt, composition of portfolios, types of deductions, and the extent of tax avoidance and possibly evasive behavior. Since 1995 there has been much research on the so-called elasticity of taxable income in an effort to quantify the total income response to changes in marginal tax rates (Feldstein 1995; Slemrod 1998; Auten and Carroll 1999; Moffitt and Wilhelm 2000; Gruber and Saez 2002; Saez 2003; Giertz 2004; Kopczuk 2005).

8.4.1   Organizing Model

The taxable income literature reformulates the canonical static labor supply model in the absence of saving. Instead of hours of work, some measure of income (taxable income, I_t, or gross income, $w_t h_t + N$) is used as the dependent variable. Instead of the after-tax wage ω_t, the focal regressor is the after-tax share, or so-called net-of-tax price $(1 - \tau_t)$. The papers in the taxable income literature use panel data to sweep out time-invariant unobserved heterogeneity in income and after-tax shares by first differencing. The first-differenced model of interest is

$$\Delta \ln y_t = \Delta \varphi_t + \theta \Delta \ln(1 - \tau_t) + \Delta d_t \gamma + \Delta \varepsilon_t, \tag{8.5}$$

where y_t is either taxable or gross income (I_t or $w_t h_t + N_t$), φ_t is a vector of time dummies to control for common macroeconomic shocks, d_t is a vector of observed socioeconomic characteristics, and ε_t is a random error term. Because income and after-tax shares are in logarithms, $\hat{\theta}$ is the estimated elasticity of taxable (or gross) income.

8.4.2 Data and Econometric Specification Issues

The debate in the taxable elasticity literature centers on two measurement questions. (1) What is the proper metric of income? (2) What variables should be included in d_t?

Although income can be defined either gross or net of deductions and exemptions, it is usually expressed in constant tax–law terms. Total gross income usually includes wage and salary income, rent, interest, and dividend income, alimony, unemployment insurance, farm income, business income or loss, pension and annuity income, and Schedule E income, but excludes Social Security benefits and capital gains and losses because of their differential tax treatment from ordinary income. Taxable income then nets out deductions and exemptions from gross income. Auten and Carroll (1999) argue that differentiating gross from net income is important because the two measures answer different questions. Gross income yields a total response to tax changes and thus is useful for understanding the implications of tax policy on the before-tax distribution of income, or potential tax base. Taxable income is more relevant if the focus is on the overall behavioral response of taxpayers to tax changes because it includes adjustments and deductions to income, or the actual tax base. Taxable income is relevant for deadweight loss calculations and for optimal tax exercises when one wants to identify the most likely revenue-maximizing tax rate.

The literature has also differed concerning variables to include and how to enter them into the model via control characteristics, d_t. Because they have only two periods of data Auten and Carroll (1999) replace Δd_t with d_0, which is a vector of time-invariant regressors from the initial period. Moffitt and Wilhelm (2000) further suggest that a key variable to include in d_0 is initial income, y_0. The logic is that if a taxpayer has transitorily high or low income in the initial period, which may revert back to normal in the period after the tax change, then failure to control so-called regression to the mean via initial income leads to bias in the estimated tax price elasticity.

Another variable for possible inclusion in a taxable income regression is virtual nonlabor income. Virtual nonlabor income is the adjustment to nonlabor income (N_t) necessary to compensate the worker to act as if he or she faced the same marginal tax rate for all taxable income. Virtual income is $\tilde{N}_t = N_t + \tau_t w_t h_t - T(\cdot)$. Although $\tilde{N}_t$ is a standard regressor in labor supply, Gruber and Saez (2002) were the first to introduce virtual income into the taxable income elasticity literature to separate out income from substitution effects. Their motivation is Feldstein (1995), who argued that because TRA86 was broadly revenue neutral then the taxable elasticity he estimated was a compensated elasticity that readily mapped into deadweight loss calculations. Because TRA86 was not revenue neutral for all income classes, Gruber and Saez (2002) correctly note that Feldstein's interpretation that he estimated a compensated elasticity is incorrect.

8.4.3 Evidence on the Elasticity of Taxable Income

How the researcher defines income and decides what variables to include in Δd_t has a profound effect on the estimated after-tax share elasticity. Estimates range from 0 to 3 overall. Feldstein's (1995) empirical results are from a difference-in-differences regression where the groups are high, medium, and low marginal tax rate payers based on their pre-TRA86 tax status. With the exception of a fixed effect and separation based on pre-reform marginal tax rate there are no additional control covariates in Feldstein's (1995) model. When he defines income as adjusted gross income by netting out deductions such as IRA contributions Feldstein's estimates are 0.75 to 1.3; when he defines income as taxable income Feldstein's estimates are 1.1 to 3.0.

Auten and Carroll (1999) exploited the variation in tax rates from TRA86 just as Feldstein, but instead of using the NBER tax panel for 1985 and 1988, they used the Treasury tax panel for 1985 and 1989. Auten and Carroll also controlled for initial income and additional covariates. Rather than a difference-in-difference estimator, Auten and Carroll used a weighted instrumental variables estimator to control for the possible endogeneity of actual tax price changes with changes in gross income. Their instrument inflates the initial 1985 income to 1989 levels and then constructs a simulated 1989 marginal tax rate based on

1989 tax rules. The instrument Auten and Carroll use is the simulated 1989 after-tax share less the actual 1985 after-tax share. They estimate gross income after-tax share elasticities of 0.45 to 1.13, with a preferred estimate of 0.57, and a similar taxable income elasticity of 0.55.

As did Feldstein, Gruber and Saez (2002) use the NBER tax panel, but their data span multiple tax reforms during the period 1979 to 1990. As did Auten and Carroll, Gruber and Saez control for regression to the mean effects and use an IV estimator with a similarly defined instrument. Gruber and Saez add virtual income as a regressor. Their preferred point estimates are a tax price elasticity for taxable income of 0.4 and a tax price elasticity for gross income of 0.12. Gruber and Saez find that most of the response is driven by taxpayers with gross incomes over $100,000. The gross income elasticity is zero or negative for taxpayers with incomes under $100,000 and ranges from 0.17 to 0.27 for taxpayers with incomes above $100,000. The corresponding estimates for the taxable income elasticity range from zero to about 0.28 for the under $100,000 gross income group and from 0.48 to 0.57 for the over $100,000 gross income group. The differences in taxable income versus gross income tax–price elasticities come from two effects. One effect is mechanical; the gross income definition implies a larger base and thus a smaller potential for response. The other effect is behavioral. Taxable income contains exemptions and deductions which can respond to tax changes. Gruber and Saez (2002) attempt to isolate the two effects and infer that about 40 percent of the difference between the gross income elasticity and taxable income elasticity is due to the mechanical effect and the remaining 60 percent is due to behavioral effects.

Kopczuk (2005) emphasizes that changes in deductions and exemptions may have an independent effect on gross income that had not been adequately addressed in the literature. He notes that changes in the implicit price of deductions can affect behavioral elasticities. Drawing on earlier labor supply research by Triest (1992), Kopczuk (2005) modifies the standard specification by adding an interaction term to Δd_t that permits separating the effects of reforms to the tax base from the effects of reforms to tax rates. The additional variable is $\theta_1 \Delta \psi_t \ln(1 - \tau_t)$, where ψ_t is the share of total gross income that is spent on nontaxable commodities. When gross income is the dependent variable in (5), $\hat{\theta}$ is the gross income tax elasticity if $\psi_t = 0$. That is, when $\psi_t = 0$, the taxpayer has no access to deductions, so $\hat{\theta}$ is the response of gross income induced by substitution away from reported income and toward leisure, fringe benefits, and other forms of income. If $\psi_t \neq 0$, but is time invariant, then the gross income elasticity is $\hat{\theta} + \hat{\theta}_1 \psi$. A straightforward test of the constancy of the tax elasticity is whether $\hat{\theta}_1 = 0$. Kopczuk notes the test is two-tailed because the coefficient on the interaction can be positive or negative depending on whether deductible goods are substitutes or complements with gross income.

Kopczuk (2005) uses the University of Michigan tax panel and marginal tax rates from the NBER *TAXSIM* module, along with an instrumental variables estimator similar to the earlier taxable income elasticity literature. He finds that the estimated direct elasticity $\hat{\theta}$ is close to zero, which is consistent with the small intensive-margin wage elasticity of labor supply also found by Saez (2003). However, the coefficient on the interaction term $\hat{\theta}_1$ is a sizable 0.7 and statistically significant. Kopczuk's results imply that all the taxable income response is driven by taxpayers with access to deductions and exemptions.

It is important to note that the taxable income elasticity literature to date has based its estimates on potentially endogenous samples. Researchers have tended to discard taxpayers with very low base-year gross incomes (less than $10,000 in Gruber and Saez (2002)) or low base-year marginal tax rates (less that 22 percent in Feldstein (1995) and Auten and Carroll (1999)). The argument for choosing tax rate or income-based samples is to remove the undue influence of regression to the mean by taxpayers at the low end of the distribution. Selecting a sample based on tax or income status, which may be an endogenous response to current year tax policy, can produce biased estimates of the behavioral responses of interest. The relevance of sample selection issues was made in the context of labor supply by Blundell, Duncan, and Meghir (1998). They showed that grouping taxpayers based on possibly endogenous tax status yielded different wage and nonlabor income elasticities of labor supply compared to estimates grouped on the basis of attributes likely to be exogenous to current tax policy, such as education attainment and birth cohort. More research on the robustness of the taxable income elasticities to alternative grouping assumptions could be informative to policy considerations.

8.4.4   Taxable Income versus Labor Supply Effects

An important general point raised by Slemrod (1998, 2001) and reiterated by Kopczuk (2005) is that the elasticity of taxable income is not a structural parameter that is simply a function of preferences and technology. Rather, the elasticity of taxable income is a behavioral response that is a function of the tax base and therefore changes when the tax base changes. Slemrod and Kopczuk's point parallels the Lucas Critique for econometric policy evaluation. Exercises such as in Feldstein (1995), where he applied the taxable income elasticities calculated from TRA86 to the 1993 Clinton tax reform, should be viewed warily because the underlying elasticities likely changed with changes in the tax base. Slemrod's critique applies to the difference-in-differences literature in general in that estimates from difference-in-differences models are generally not informative for out-of-sample predictions. The Slemrod criticism does not apply to structural models of labor supply that estimate underlying preference parameters, which should permit statistically informative out-of-sample forecasts (Hausman 1981; Triest 1990; Ziliak and Kniesner 1999, 2005).

Comparing the taxable income elasticities to the structural labor supply elasticities also generally means comparing estimates at the intensive margin. The taxable income elasticity literature has (1) ignored nonworkers' labor force participation responses to changes in the after-tax share and (2) ignored nonrandom sample selection bias potentially in the estimates of the taxable income elasticity based only on workers' responses at the intensive margin. Although they did not focus on the taxable income elasticity per se, Meyer and Rosenbaum (2001) present related results. They present some quasi-structural estimates of the elasticity of employment with respect to the after-tax share for single mothers of about 1.0.

Gruber and Saez (2002) sought to isolate substitution and income effects much like ones found in the structural labor supply literature. They found an income elasticity of about -0.135 for taxable income compared to a substitution elasticity of 0.430. Together the results imply a positive uncompensated wage elasticity, which means that estimated income effects are relatively small. Relatively small income effects is consistent with Ziliak and Kniesner (1999) and earlier papers in much of the literature, but is not in line with what we report in table 8.1 here from Ziliak and Kniesner (2005). Not yet known is whether the difference is an artifact of our functional form versus that used in Gruber and Saez (2002) or of our data versus their data. Finally, the difference between the relative income and substitution effects emerging from the structural labor supply versus taxable income elasticity literatures could also stem from the fact that our estimates are from after-tax wage elasticities and theirs are from after-tax shares, which Slemrod (2001) emphasizes may not be the same if there is endogenous tax avoiding or evading behavior.

8.4.5   Summary

The elasticity of taxable income is important to understanding the roles of tax policy in income inequality as well as for policies related to the capacity of governments to raise revenue in both the short and long runs. The relatively recent empirical literature can be characterized as producing estimates of the elasticity of gross income that lie in the range of 0 to 0.2, and estimates of the elasticity of taxable income that lie in a slightly wider range, 0 to 0.4. What we would like to know more about and could with greater econometric evaluation of model specifications and robustness are the endogenous response at the extensive labor-supply margin, the link between taxation schedule and marital status, or the economic implications for the poor of changes in the net tax price. It is unlikely that we will soon have the data and econometric wherewithal to establish the quantitative links between potential or actual tax base and subtleties of the tax system in the United States such as the role of the AMT, treatment of capital gains, or so-called tax gross-ups among rich tax payers.

8.5   What We Know about the Welfare Effects of Taxation

Inferring how consumer well-being changes in response to taxes has motivated economic analyses of tax reform and labor supply since at least the seminal research of Harberger (1964). Calculations of the efficiency cost of taxation focus either on the total deadweight loss (Harberger 1964; Hausman 1981; Auerbach 1985; Triest 1990; Ziliak and Kniesner 1999) or on the marginal welfare cost of taxation (Wildasin 1984; Browning 1987; Snow and Warren 1996). One measure of total welfare change is a hypothetical payment to the government by the typical worker under the pre–tax-reform wage that would leave welfare unchanged under the post–tax-reform income (Kay 1980). The hypothetical payment, or equivalent variation measure, compares an initial distorted equilibrium with a final distorted equilibrium. The equivalent variation measure fixes utility at its post-reform level and lets wage differences imply a change in worker well being across tax regimes. Another common total deadweight loss measure is of the change in consumers' surplus, called welfare variation, where the wage vector is held at the pre–tax-reform level and utility differs when taxes change (King 1983). The welfare variation measure of moving from one distorted equilibrium to another is the change in consumer utility less the actual revenue extracted. Both the equivalent variation and the welfare variation measures of changes in total welfare give similar ordinal rankings under revenue-neutral tax changes.

8.5.1 Organizing Model

Recent theoretical research considering the efficiency cost of a tax system has focused on the marginal welfare cost of government revenue (*MWC*), which is how much economic welfare changes in response to a change in tax rates and revenue. Within-period utility estimates map straightforwardly into the *MWC*, so the results in Ziliak and Kniesner (2005) are informative to discussions of tax reform. Because the calculations are static they provide a partial picture of the potential behavioral response to a tax change. Other obvious behavioral aspects of interest are intertemporal changes, which may include both anticipated components and the unanticipated components occurring in the case of uncertain tax policy. Still results from the two-stage budgeting formulation we summarize here from Ziliak and Kniesner (2005) use within-period preferences from a life-cycle framework so that the corresponding *MWC* calculations we discuss here are called life-cycle consistent estimates.

The bulk of the econometric estimates of the welfare cost of taxation stemming from models of labor supply and taxes have emphasized tax reforms that are revenue neutral (Hausman 1981; Triest 1994; Ziliak and Kniesner 1999, 2005). Econometric research has largely presented so-called differential tax calculations where there is no balanced-budget spending nor revenue effect so that the *MWC* reflects pure distortions of labor supply (Ballard 1990; Browning 1987). Alternatively, much of the theoretical research on the marginal cost of public funds has focused on balanced-budget tax policy where a marginal dollar of public spending is financed by an additional dollar of tax revenue (Snow and Warren 1996).

An empirically transparent calculation is the marginal welfare cost of government revenue in the event of revenue-neutral reforms (Browning 1987, eq. 10). Browning defines the marginal welfare cost as

$$MWC = \left[\frac{\tau + 0.5d\tau}{1 - \tau}\right]\eta_w^c\frac{d\tau}{d\bar{t}},$$

with τ the marginal tax rate, $d\tau$ the change in the marginal tax rate, η_w^c the compensated wage elasticity of labor supply, $\bar{t}$ the average tax rate, and $d\tau/d\bar{t}$ the change in the progressivity of the tax code in response to the tax reform. The MWC formula highlights that only substitution effects and no income effects matter for revenue-neutral welfare calculations.

8.5.2 Welfare Effect Estimates

For each calculation we set $\tau = 0.323$, which is the sample average marginal tax rate for men, $d\tau = 0.01$, which is a 1 percentage point change in the marginal tax rate, and $d\tau/d\bar{t}$ equal to 1.32, for progressive tax reforms (the ratio of the sample average marginal tax rate to the sample average tax rate) or equal to 1.0 for proportional tax reforms. We consider three specifications for the marginal welfare cost of taxation. In specification (1) we set $\eta_w^c = 0.328$ based on the direct translog MRS elasticities with nondurable consumption; in specification (2) we set $\eta_w^c = 0.092$ for the direct translog MRS elasticities with food consumption; in specification (3) we set $\eta_w^c = 0.652$ for the quadratic direct MRS elasticities with nondurable consumption. There are six calculations, as shown in table 8.2, when we use the three different compensated wage elasticities for the progressive versus proportional changes in the tax code.[2]

In the base-case model with nonseparable preferences in table 8.2 the marginal welfare cost of an additional dollar of taxation ranges from 16 to 21 percent depending on whether the reform is a proportional or a progressive change in the tax structure. The deadweight welfare losses are sizable and suggest possibilities for welfare-improving revenue-neutral tax reforms in the United States. Specification (2) makes clear

Table 8.2
Estimates of the marginal welfare cost of taxation (percent)

	(1)	(2)	(3)
Progressive tax $d\tau/d\bar{t} = 1.32$	20.9	5.9	41.7
	(4.1)	(0.73)	(28.3)
Proportional tax $d\tau/d\bar{t} = 1$	15.9	4.5	31.6
	(3.1)	(0.56)	(21.4)

that how we measure consumption has a large impact on our estimates of welfare loss. With food as our measure the MWC of taxation is a modest 4.5 to 6 percent. Specification (3) pushes the estimated MWC in the opposite direction. Imposing additivity between consumption and leisure yielded a larger estimate of the compensated wage elasticity, which translates into a doubling of the marginal welfare cost of taxation relative to the base case model that relaxes separability. Models with additive preferences between consumption and labor supply likely yield upper-bound estimates of the deadweight loss of taxation.

8.5.3 Summary

There can be improved labor-market efficiency from revenue-neutral tax reforms. Our base-case estimates with nondurable consumption suggest that the marginal welfare cost of taxation is 16–21 percent depending on whether the reform results in a proportional or progressive change in the tax structure. By way of comparison, in Ziliak and Kniesner (1999) we impose separability between consumption and leisure but admit nonseparability in the intertemporal budget constraint stemming from the joint nonlinear taxation of labor and capital income, and estimate that the typical US prime-age married male worker would pay up to 23 percent of his adjusted gross income to eliminate the current progressive income tax (a total welfare loss calculation), and would pay a more modest two percent of adjusted gross income to face an across-the-board cut in income tax rates.

As an additional reference point we note that Hausman's (1981) widely cited estimates of the willingness to pay for removing income taxes are much lower than ours (1/11th). However, our research in Ziliak and Kniesner (2005) highlighted that the functional form of preferences—specifically linearity in the labor-supply response to a wage change or additivity between consumption and leisure—has a significant impact on estimated wage elasticities of labor supply. Separability between consumption and leisure choices, whether in a linear or a nonlinear labor supply model, leads to an upward bias (as much as double) in compensated wage elasticities used in evaluating labor-market and tax policies.

In a recent working paper Feldstein (2006) presented calculations of the marginal welfare cost of taxation with respect to tax revenue that range from 68 to 76 percent, which is considerably higher than what we have emphasized here. Feldstein's estimates are derived from the elasticity of taxable income literature where he relies on a compensated tax price elasticity of 0.4 (the preferred estimate from Gruber and Saez 2002) and an income elasticity of 0.15. As described previously, we would expect his estimates to exceed the estimates reported in Ziliak and Kniesner (2005) because of the additional behavioral margins that adjust in response to marginal tax rate changes. However, Feldstein's (2006) estimates rely on separability of preferences between consumption and leisure (although some forms of deductible consumption are included in his estimates), and as demonstrated in table 8.2 the *MWC* is upwardly biased under the assumption of separability.

Research developing models that combine nonseparable preferences with nonseparable budgets would seem a logical next step in considering more fully the efficiency cost aspects of taxes and pinning down more completely the welfare implications of tax policy.

8.6   What We Know about the Optimal Income Tax

It is not unreasonable to contend that the ultimate objective of research on taxation is to use the estimates in solving for the economically optimal tax structure. The classic issue is that minimizing the excess burden of the tax is constrained by the desire to use tax rates for greater equality of economic well-being. The two goals conflict because economic efficiency is greater with a flatter tax structure while greater equality of outcomes goes with a more progressive tax structure. The trade-off of efficiency against equity becomes more complicated when there are consumption and or leisure externalities to consider in the optimal tax computation (Kooreman and Schoonbeek 2004; Abel 2005; Grodner and Kniesner 2006a).

8.6.1   Organizing Model: An Optimal Tax Considering Efficiency and Equity

A particularly clear development of the numerical links among labor supply wage elasticities, the statistical distribution properties of the tax base, the social planner's objective function, and an optimal income tax appears in Saez (2001, 2002). Saez (2001) uses realistic values for labor supply elasticities with both utilitarian and Rawlsian social welfare weights and finds a general scheme for income tax rates that fall then rise due to phase out of income guarantees as part of equity considerations. This makes for a lower average tax rate and more efficient tax system than one with a single proportional rate that could be 60 percent or more at an optimum.

In the case where both labor supply margins come into play and equity and efficiency trade-off, Saez (2002) shows that the optimal tax bracket scheme has the property that

$$\frac{T_i - T_{i-1}}{c_i - c_{i-1}} = \frac{1}{\zeta_i h_i} \sum_{j=i}^{I} h_j \left[1 - g_j - \eta_j \frac{T_j - T_0}{c_j - c_0} \right],$$

where subscripts index successively higher incomes and taxes, T is total tax, c is taxable income, h measures labor supply, g is a marginal social welfare weight, ζ is the labor force participation elasticity, and η is the hours-worked elasticity. Saez's (2002) formula also clarifies the roles of the labor supply elasticity at the participation versus hours-worked margins to solutions to the basic optimal tax problem. There is general agreement that the labor supply response at the extensive margin exceeds the response at the intensive margin and that, at least for single women, the labor supply elasticity at the extensive margin exceeds 1.0 (Ziliak 2005). The optimal tax and transfer policy in the context of Saez's (2002) model is the following. For low-income populations the optimal tax policy is akin to an EITC program providing a modest guarantee to nonworkers, with tax rates that are negative over a range of low earnings, and tax rates that become positive and high as workers move up the earnings distribution.

8.6.2 Insurance Considerations for an Optimal Tax

Economists have now begun to examine a third dimension of the tax system that need be considered under an optimal tax calculation, the implicit insurance or income and consumption smoothing properties of an income-based tax that supplements the smoothing permitted via private credit and insurance markets. It is important to recognize that even a proportional tax smoothes disposable income by making the variability of net income less than the variability of gross income (Varian 1980). For example, if there is a proportional tax rate τ, so that disposable income is $y^d = (1 - \tau)y$, then $\sigma^2_{y^d} = (1 - \tau)^2 \sigma^2_y < \sigma^2_y$ because $(1 - \tau)^2 < 1.0$. Because of the additional negative covariance term between y and $(1 - \tau)$ a progressive income tax rate such that $\partial \tau / \partial y > 0$ makes the relative variability of disposable income less than under a proportional tax.

In Kniesner and Ziliak (2002b) we show that the US tax system reduces the variability of consumption by about 10 percent compared to what it would be in the absence of income taxes. In Kniesner and Ziliak (2002a) we examine the consumption smoothing issue further by solving explicitly for the welfare benefits to the consumer from the tax-based income insurance that smoothes consumption. We solve explicitly for the proportional increase in consumption needed to make the consumer indifferent to the consumption smoothing benefits of a flatter tax, including a proportional or a lump sum tax. Households confronting the highly graduated pre–ERTA US tax structure would have to be paid up to 2.5 percent of their per capita consumption to switch to a revenue neutral lump-sum tax because of its lack of implicit consumption insurance. Our results in Kniesner and Ziliak (2002a,b) imply that the amount of consumption insurance implicitly in the income-based federal tax system is currently $100 billion to $200 billion, which is similar to the amount US consumers spend on private health or auto insurance.

Anderson and Dognowski (2004) show that even if the individual were somehow able to smooth consumption completely in private credit markets, the individual would still want to smooth leisure. The optimal tax on labor earnings would then be progressive so as to reduce net wage fluctuations. For a logarithmic utility function in consumption and leisure the optimal tax rate that smoothes leisure satisfies the requirement that

$$\frac{1}{(1 - \tau_2)w_2} \frac{\tau_2}{(1 - \tau_2)} = \frac{1}{(1 - \tau_1)w_1} \frac{\tau_1}{(1 - \tau_1)},$$

where the wage rate is unexpectedly higher in state 2. The implication is a procyclical optimal tax rate, although not to the point where the net wage is state independent (Anderson and Dognowski 2004).

8.6.3   Summary

Absent long-run considerations relating to the saving and growth issues that concern many in government, an optimal income tax must consider three dimensions: efficiency, equity, and insurance. A flatter tax creates less deadweight loss but also less after-tax equality of consumption plus more variable consumption and leisure. It is a challenge, perhaps an impossible one, to solve for the structure of income taxes that would maximize a welfare function for society that considered efficiency, equity, and insurance aspects of current income-based taxation.

8.7   What We Know, Could Know, and Probably Will Never Know

As Auerbach (chapter 1 in this volume) notes, the future of tax reform efforts will depend on our empirical knowledge of how taxes affect behavior. There are several aspects of the effects of income taxes on individuals that seem settled, but many more areas are in need of additional research. We now summarize what we know reasonably well.

We know that most of the traditional estimates of the intratemporal uncompensated wage elasticities of labor supply of men and women are positive, but small, with a range of 0 to 0.2. Given the accompanying small negative income effect, the attendant traditional compensated wage elasticities of labor supply are also small. The implication from the mode estimates is that the reduction in the deadweight loss of income taxation is likely to be modest in any given period for most tax proposals. More ambitious reforms could create sizable welfare gains from a lifetime perspective or when labor-supply interactions come into play. Econometrically richer models have enlarged the elasticity estimates somewhat by considering social interactions and less statistically restrictive representations of the budget constraint or the labor-supply function, raising the compensated wage elasticity of labor supply for men to between 0.3 and 0.4.

We also know that the wage response of labor supply at the participation margin exceeds the wage response at the hours-worked margin. The magnitudes at both margins are important for the design of optimal tax and transfer programs (Saez 2002). Although the evidence to date suggests that the extensive margin elasticity exceeds 1.0, most of the work applies to women and thus more research is needed on both margins for men.

The preponderance of evidence to date suggests that the elasticity of taxable income is larger than the uncompensated wage elasticity of labor supply for workers and lies in the 0 to 0.4 range, with more evidence in favor of 0.4. The implication is that taxpayers, notably high-income taxpayers, shift income from nondeductible to deductible income and consumption activities in response to tax reforms.

What we know less well is how taxation affects life-cycle labor supply, consumption, and saving decisions. The evidence to date is consistent with theory, in that intertemporal substitution elasticities exceed their within-period counterparts, with a range of 0.2 to 0.5 for labor supply of men and 0 to 0.5 for consumption—depending on whether one uses aggregate consumption data (0) or micro household panel data (0.5). Perhaps most important, our survey suggests that individual total saving behavior responds to tax policy with an after-tax wage elasticity of as much as 1.0, but much remains unknown and some important behaviors may never be knowable given the difficulty in measuring saving accurately.

Finally, we probably know the least about what some would say is the ultimate objective of research on the personal income tax, the structure of optimal income tax rates. Research has clarified greatly the roles of the sensitivities of consumption and labor supply to tax-related parameters. Particularly valuable has been work on the roles of the labor-supply elasticities at the extensive versus intensive margins in light of the accompanying welfare program transfers and tax credits for the low-income population. The greater participation elasticity of labor supply implies that a traditional welfare program is suboptimal compared to an EITC program. Not to be forgotten is that any income-based tax smoothes disposable income and provides implicit insurance against unwanted fluctuations in consumption and leisure. Recent research suggests that income-based taxes reduce unplanned consumption variability by over 10 percent and that the implicit consumption insurance that income-based taxes provide is of similar aggregate value as health and automobile insurance in the United States. When considering an optimal tax structure comprehensively, one must consider three dimensions: efficiency, equity, and insurance. Although graduated tax rates reduce efficiency, graduated tax rates enhance equity and insurance. It is likely an impossible challenge to derive an optimal tax structure in light of all three margins of policy interest simultaneously.

Discussion

Emmanuel Saez

Kniesner and Ziliak provide a comprehensive summary of the literature on the behavioral responses of labor supply and savings to taxes. Their summary covers not only the positive aspects of the problem—namely the modeling and estimating of such behavioral responses—but also the normative aspects such as the welfare effects of taxation and the derivation of optimal income tax and transfer policy. Obviously this is a very broad topic, and the authors have done an impressive job of organizing and summarizing the key findings and issues in the literature and giving a clear sense of the known, the unknown, and the unknowable in those central tax policy issues.

Because of the breadth of the topic, I will comment primarily on the empirical estimation of the behavioral responses of labor supply and reported income with respect to taxes. I will primarily discuss identification issues. I will also present what I view as solidly known findings in the literature on behavioral responses to taxation. Finally, I will mention some open research questions, whose resolution might have great influence on empirical analysis in this field.

In order to estimate the behavioral effects of tax changes on labor supply or earnings, one would like to be able to compare the behavior of individuals subject to a tax change to the behavior of individuals not subject to such a change. Ideally one would like to carry out a real experiment whereby a given set of individuals are randomly assigned to various tax treatments. If the treatment could be applied different lengths of time (e.g., one year, several years, or as long as a lifetime), and if a number of alternative treatments could be applied (to create pure income effects, pure uncompensated changes, etc.), it would be possible to estimate the key behavioral parameters, such as income effects, uncompensated, compensated and Frisch elasticities, in a very convincing way. Obviously such experiments would be very expensive to carry out both in terms of money (as experimental variation should always be favorable to treatments) and in terms of time and administration. However, if one takes seriously the models of labor supply proposed by economists and summarized by Kniesner and Ziliak, the value of knowing such parameters for designing an optimal tax and transfer policy is very large and would certainly dwarf the costs of experimentation.[3]

Absent such experiments, researchers have had to rely on variations in incentives to work and earn income naturally generated in the real economy. The labor strand of the literature has focused primarily on variation generated by differences in wage rates, while the public finance strand of the literature has tried to use variation generated by taxes to identify behavioral responses. Because variations created by taxes and especially tax reforms comes closer to the idea of the experiment described above, the tax reform literature has tended to adopt reduced form empirical methods without laying out a fully structural model. In contrast, the use of wage rate variation in the labor literature has forced researchers to specify more precisely the sources of wage rate variations (either across or within individuals). Hence they have developed more structural models and put more emphasis on the exact type of behavioral parameters identified.

Each method has advantages and drawbacks. The main advantage of the tax reform analysis approach is that the identifying variation is more transparent, making it easier to assess the validity of the identification assumptions. For example, if one uses the tax increase on high-income individuals enacted in 1993 by the Clinton administration (as recalled in the introduction of the chapter), a natural place to start is to compare the evolution of high incomes (affected by the tax change) to middle incomes (not affected by the tax change). The identifying assumption that, absent the tax change, high and middle incomes would have evolved similarly, can be easily tested using prior data. In practice, this transparency advantage shows in bright light that such identification assumptions are not tenable especially if one wants to estimate the long-run effects of tax changes (e.g., see Saez 2004). As a result the tax reform literature has been successful in demonstrating that taxes matter *in the short run* (particularly around the large changes generated by the Tax Reform Act of 1986). In my view the long-run estimates, which are the most relevant for policy analysis, are still unknown and would require bringing together the evidence from many countries at the same time to become knowable parameters.

There are two disadvantages of the tax reform approach that should be pointed out. First, large and salient tax changes, which provide significant tax variation that tax filers will notice and understand, tend to happen at the higher end of the income distribution. Because high incomes evolve differently than middle incomes for many reasons unrelated to taxation, it is hard to create a good comparison group not affected by the tax change to study the large tax changes affecting high incomes. Obviously the complexity and constantly evolving nature of the US tax code generates myriads of smaller changes, which often affect very specific groups and generate horizontal inequities. Those changes create quasi-experimental variation, but they might not be understood by tax filers.[4] As a result finding no response from such small changes does not necessarily imply that there would be no response from a similar but saliently advertised and well-understood change.[5] Put another way, this suggests that information is an important determinant of the size of behavioral responses especially given the complexity of tax and transfer. The importance of those informational effects is still largely unknown but might be knowable using variation in information generated by advertisement or tax and program outreach campaigns, possibly with a randomized experiment.

Second, reduced form estimation does not immediately identify a well-defined structural parameter. This can lead to misleading welfare consequences derivations. For example, assuming that a large short-run elasticity effect (e.g., the one measured around the Tax Reform Act of 1986) applies in the long run might exaggerate the long-term costs of taxation if the short-run elasticity effect is due to intertemporal substitution.

The advantages and drawbacks of structural estimation are almost the flipside of those of reduced form estimation. The main advantage is that the model is fully specified. Therefore, if the model and identifying assumptions hold, the parameters estimated are well-defined economic parameters. The researcher can then carry out welfare and efficiency analysis in a fully consistent way. Structural estimation uses primarily wage rate variations to identify labor-supply responses. Wage variation has the advantage of being very salient to the individual and hence there are much fewer concerns about lack of information in that context. The main drawbacks of the structural approach are that strong modeling and identifying assumptions are required. The key identifying assumption is that intrinsic taste for work needs to be uncorrelated with the wage rate.[6] There is a presumption that intrinsic taste for work might lead to higher wages through educational choices, intensity of work, or career choices, creating a correlation between the two variables. Related to this point, labor-supply estimation focuses generally on hours of work and hence captures only one dimension of potential responses to taxation and hence might lead to an underestimate of the total efficiency costs of taxation (Feldstein 1999).

On the modeling side, if individuals do not maximize intertemporal utilities according to the standard model with time separable and consistent preferences, then structural estimates might not be meaningful. A number of studies in the field of behavioral economics have cast doubt on the empirical validity of the standard intertemporal model. As a result it seems important to try and analyze how robust the structural estimates of labor supply are to introducing nonstandard intertemporal preferences.

I think that a promising avenue to make progress would be to try and analyze situations where there is plausibly exogenous variation in wages. Such variation could come from demand variations such as in recent studies of taxi-cab drivers (Camerer et al. 1997; Farber 2005) or stadium vendors (Oettinger 1999). Exogenous variation could also come from changes in regulations in industries where compensation is regulated but labor supply is free (e.g., taxi-cab drivers or doctors in many European countries).

In sum, I believe that the analysis of tax-induced behavioral responses is an exciting field where much of what was thought to be known is being revisited, and where new perspectives are pushing the frontier of the unknown.

Discussion

Robin Sickles

Kniesner and Ziliak address a number of issues that are at the heart of the tax policy debate. How does taxation impact labor supply? How does taxation impact consumption? How does taxation impact saving? How does taxation impact preferences? Since there are no a priori theoretical answers, the answers are based instead on empirical evidence. This is not necessarily reassuring, but it does keep empirical researchers in business and provides vested interests with talking points. What is "optimal" tax policy seems to be in the eye of the econometrician. The chapter also explores taxation's impacts in terms of individual and household decision-making under uncertainty. A bottom-line goal is to provide a "clear picture" of what professional economists have discovered about how tax policies impact economic well-being. The authors point out that the savings effects of personal income taxes are poorly understood. Although there appears to be an empirical consensus on the effects of personal incomes on labor supply and the tax base, there does not appear to be an empirical consensus on the design of a comprehensive optimal personal income tax that simultaneously addresses the efficiency costs of tax collection, social equity issues, and consumption smoothing. The chapter provides a survey of econometric public finance studies by all the usual suspects with all the attendant problems. These include strong behavioral assumptions in the form of information, exogeneity, smoothness in decision-making at nonsmooth budget kink points, maximum likelihood estimation versus instrumental variable estimation, and static versus dynamic models. The earlier Ziliak and Kniesner (2005) paper addresses many of these issues. What about women? Ziliak (2005) is the "go to" study. What about taxable income elasticity? Studies are generally panel models using differenced data, where important family and individual specific characteristics impacts are not identified.

Savings? Ziliak and Kniesner (2005). Welfare effects of taxation? Ziliak and Kniesner (2005). Their papers provide a great set of organizing models that frame the issues and focus debate on the fundamentals of modeling and estimation.

Might there be something about preferences that could be tweaked in these analyses? Standard models of consumer choice that provide a framework for specifying models of demand based on a neoclassical theory of the structure of agent preferences are not complete. Extensive experiments from cognitive psychology contradict the neoclassical model of rational choice that underlies economic theories of demand (Tversky and Kahneman 1986). Experiments suggest that preferences are malleable and context-dependent, memory and perceptions are often biased and statistically flawed, and decision tasks are often neglected or misunderstood (McFadden 2005). The endowment effect—consumer aversion to trade from any given status quo—is a good example of behavior that is inconsistent with the neoclassical economic model. Another example is asymmetric loss aversion, wherein the consumer is more sensitive to losses than to gains.

Monte Carlo simulation methods could be used to link these experimental results to the policy simulation exercises that tax reform researchers typically use to assess the impact of new policy initiatives. The methods are distinguished from other simulation methods by being stochastic, that is, nondeterministic in some manner—usually by using random numbers (or more often pseudorandom numbers)—as opposed to deterministic algorithms. A classic use is for the evaluation of definite integrals, particularly multidimensional integrals with complicated boundary conditions.

Simulation of average agent behavior requires calculating expected values, such as

$$E(x) = \int \ldots \int x f(x, z_1, \ldots, z_n) \, dz_1 \ldots dz_n \, dx.$$

More broadly, Monte Carlo methods are useful for modeling phenomena with significant uncertainty in inputs, such as the calculation of risk in business. Monte Carlo simulation methods of the virtual agent could be linked with price, quantity, and other demand information to more accurately model consumer choices. The "black box" of the consumer's preference structure could be opened up through massive simulations based on results of cognitive psychological experiments.

Might public finance economists then be believed by their audience—the policy makers who are their ultimate consumers?

Notes

1. We are grateful for the helpful comments of Emmanuel Saez, Robin Sickles, George Zodrow, and the conference participants.

2. All estimates in table 8.2 are based on Browning (1987, eq. 10) where the marginal welfare cost of taxation is

$$MWC = \left[\frac{\tau + 0.5d\tau}{1 - \tau} \right] \eta_w^c \frac{d\tau}{d\bar{t}},$$

with τ as the marginal tax rate, $d\tau$ the change in the marginal tax rate, η_w^c the compensated wage elasticity of labor supply, $\bar{t}$ the average tax rate, and $d\tau/d\bar{t}$ the change in the progressivity of the tax code in response to the tax reform. For each calculation we set $\tau = 0.323$, $d\tau = 0.01$, and $d\tau/d\bar{t}$ equal to 1.32 for progressive tax reforms (the ratio of the sample average marginal tax rate to the sample average tax rate) or equal to 1.0 for proportional tax reforms. In specification (1) we set $\eta_w^c = 0.328$ based on the direct translog MRS elasticities with nondurable consumption in table 2 of Ziliak and Kniesner (2005), in specification (2) we set $\eta_w^c = 0.092$ for the direct translog MRS elasticities with food consumption in table 3 of Ziliak and Kniesner (2005), and in specification (3) we set $\eta_w^c = 0.652$ for the quadratic direct MRS elasticities with nondurable consumption in table 3 of Ziliak and Kniesner (2005). The standard errors are based on 1,000 bootstrap replications of the MRS and Euler equations.

3. Actually the US government did carry out various such negative income tax experiments in the 1960s and early 1970s when the negative income tax was considered a potential option for tax and transfer reform. The knowledge derived from those experiments was smaller than expected and the costs larger, mostly because of administrative failures (e.g., see Munnell 1986) which could be overcome in newer experiments.

4. For example, Saez (2002) shows that most categories of tax filers do not bunch at the kink points of the tax schedule, as predicted by theory. Interestingly some categories of tax filers such as the self-employed do appear to bunch, suggesting that there is heterogeneity in information or ability to manipulate reported earnings for tax purposes.

5. For example, Duflo et al. (2006) show that the saver's credit provision of the federal income tax which subsidizes retirement savings of some low-income filers generates much smaller behavioral responses than a comparable subsidy saliently presented in the context of a randomized experiment.

6. Structural studies often instrument the current wage rate with lagged wage rates. If tastes for work are relatively stable over time, such a procedure cannot remove the bias created by a correlation between wage rates and tastes for work.

9   Comparing Average and Marginal Tax Rates under the FairTax and the Current System of Federal Taxation

Laurence J. Kotlikoff and
David Rapson

With over 17,000 pages and counting, the US federal tax law is anything but straightforward. Nor is it cheap to use. The annual cost of administering, enforcing, and complying with federal personal and business taxes, according to the GAO (2005), is in the hundreds of billions of dollars. The GAO also estimates that the annual efficiency loss arising from the disincentives of the current tax system range from 2 to 5 percent of GDP. The cost is not simply economic. A small army of well-educated and highly talented lawyers, accountants, and auditors wastes every hour of the working day coping with the US tax code instead of engaging in work of real social and, presumably, psychological value.

With all this effort, one might expect real understanding of how our tax system works. But the system is so complex that no one can claim to fully comprehend its provisions, incentives, or the degree to which it is redistributing income across the population. Indeed the tax code has so befuddled and clogged our brains that we're virtually flying blind when it comes to managing our fiscal affairs.

This is particularly true when it comes to the structure of work and saving incentives. Calculating total effective marginal tax rates on these economic choices is no minor task. Consider, for example, trying to determine the net marginal effective tax rate facing low-income workers on an extra dollar of earnings. Doing so necessitates considering the employer and employee portions of the payroll tax, the federal income tax including the earned income tax credit, the effect of extra current earnings on future Social Security benefits, the extent of future income taxation of future Social Security benefits, the interaction of the payroll tax and the federal income tax, and the procedure for calculating the present value of changes in future Social Security benefits net of changes in future federal income taxes.

Millions of Americans understand the ingredients used to make our tax code sausage and yearn for a wholesale reform that would leave us with a simple, fair, transparent, and easy-to-administer tax system. There are several such candidates, including a value-added tax (VAT), a flat tax, and a federal retail sales tax. Of these the most straightforward is the federal retail sales tax, which taxes purchases of consumption goods and services at a single rate. The VAT and flat taxes would also tax consumption, albeit indirectly and only if they are implemented without special transition rules that exempt from taxation the sale of existing capital goods.

For economists, shifting from our current system, which primarily taxes labor income, to taxing consumption has a number of interesting and important features. First, it broadens the effective tax base from primarily current and future labor income to current and future labor income plus existing wealth. The reason the consumption tax base effectively includes these two components is that current and future consumption purchases are financed by current and future labor earnings plus existing wealth. And taxing these purchases is effectively equivalent to taxing what is used to pay for them.

Second, because it effectively taxes existing wealth, taxing consumption penalizes the rich, potentially enhancing overall tax progressivity. Even if the rich save their existing wealth and bequeath it, plus any accrued capital income, their wealth still ends up getting hit with a tax once their children or other heirs spend these resources. The present value of the taxes paid on the consumption financed by the bequeathed wealth plus the accrued income on that wealth is the same as taxing the wealth immediately (i.e., spending all the wealth immediately and paying consumption taxes right away).

Third, since the elderly have very little labor income and own roughly two-thirds of the nation's wealth, switching to a consumption tax lifts some of the burden of taxation from today's and tomorrow's workers and shifts it onto retirees. While current and future workers are still effectively taxed on their labor earnings when they spend them on consumption, the effective tax rate on those earnings is lower than under the existing system due to the base broadening arising from the switch to consumption taxation, particularly the inclusion of existing wealth in the effective tax base.

Many would think that hitting the poor elderly with a higher tax burden is unfair and immediately discount a consumption tax on that basis. But under our current Social Security system the poor elderly, whose income comes almost exclusively from that source, would be totally unaffected by a consumption tax. The reason is that the system's annual inflation indexation guarantees the real purchasing power of recipients' benefits since any increase in prices associated with the sales tax would lead to equal percentage increases in Social Security benefits.

Fourth, switching our federal tax system in its entirety to consumption taxation would permit reducing effective marginal taxes on labor supply (due to the base broadening) and would eliminate entirely the marginal taxation of saving. Since economic distortions—what economists call the excess burden of taxation—depend in a nonlinear manner on the level of effective marginal tax rates, reducing these tax rates holds the promise of significantly reducing economic inefficiency.

Fifth, a large volume of simulation studies starting with Summers (1981a) and Auerbach and Kotlikoff (1987) show that switching to consumption taxation can dramatically raise a nation's national saving, domestic investment, capital per worker, labor productivity, and real wages. The increase in national saving reflects the elimination of the tax on saving as well as the redistribution away from older spenders to younger savers. As shown in Gokhale, Kotlikoff, and Sabelhaus (1996), America's elderly have much higher propensities to spend, when properly measured, than do the young and, certainly, future generations.

For the United States the predicted increase in domestic investment from switching to consumption taxation occurs whether or not one views the economy as open or closed, at the margin, to international capital flows. If an economy is closed, all national saving is invested at home, so every extra dollar in national saving translates directly into an extra dollar of domestic investment. If an economy is open, domestic investment is determined by how much savers in the United States and abroad want to invest in the country. But if, as in the United States, the wholesale switch to consumption taxation would entail the elimination of a corporate income tax whose marginal effective rate is quite high (the US value is very close to the statutory 35 percent rate), both domestic and foreign savers will find investing in the zero-corporate tax country highly attractive.

The extent to which US tax reform delivers the saving, domestic investment, income, equity, and efficiency gains that appear available in moving to consumption taxation depends, of course, on the degree to which the reform actually taxes consumption. The FairTax, awaiting passage in Congress as HR25, does tax consumption. Indeed, except for imputed rent on existing housing and consumer durables, the Fair-Tax taxes all consumption (including rents on housing, new rental and owner-occupied housing, and new consumer durables) via a federal retail sales tax.

The FairTax would replace the federal personal income tax, the federal corporate income tax, the federal payroll (FICA) tax, the federal estate tax, the federal gift tax, and the federal generation-skipping tax with a federal retail sales tax assessed at a single rate. The FairTax also provides a rebate to each household based on its demographic composition. The rebate is set to ensure that households living at or below the poverty line would pay no net taxes.

In this chapter, we compare average and marginal tax rates on working and saving under the current system with those that would arise under the FairTax. As specified in HR25, the legislation that would implement the reform, the FairTax's tax rate is 23 percent. This tax rate is measured on a tax-inclusive basis, meaning that a dollar's expenditure would yield 77 cents in consumption after payment of the retail sales tax.

Although Gale (2005) questions whether a 23 percent tax-inclusive rate would suffice to maintain real federal spending and also cover the FairTax rebate, a recent analysis by Bachman, Haughton, Kotlikoff, Sanchez-Penalver, and Tuerck (2006) based on CBO 2007 projections indicates that less than a 3 percent scale-back of non–Social Security real federal expenditures would be needed to accommodate a 23 percent FairTax rate. Although such a reduction would be politically difficult, it should be noted that as a share of GDP, these expenditures have risen by over 20 percent since 2000.

In asserting that a real revenue-neutral 23 percent FairTax is feasible, Bachman and colleagues assume that the revenue losses due to evasion and avoidance under the FairTax will be no greater than those already implied by NIPA measures of household consumption. In so doing, they may overstate the FairTax revenue base. On the other hand, they likely understate the revenue base in ignoring the FairTax's general equilibrium, macroeconomic feedback effects. Indeed, as discussed in Kotlikoff (2005), introducing the FairTax would likely raise real wages by 19 percent over the course of the century relative to what technological improvements would otherwise generate. On the other hand, the Kotlikoff paper shows that the aging of society, interacting with our Social Security and government healthcare systems will place significant stresses on the nation's finances. And the ability of the government under a FairTax to maintain the tax system's tax rate at 23 percent or, even lower, will depend critically on reforming these major entitlement programs.

As mentioned, the effective tax base of a consumption tax is existing wealth and current and future labor income. Given its 23 percent rate, the FairTax would effectively tax both existing wealth, other than owner-occupied housing and consumer durables, and current and future labor earnings at a 23 percent rate.

As we show here, current total effective federal marginal tax rates on labor supply appear to be either higher or much higher for almost all American households than they would be under the FairTax. The current system's marginal wage tax rate exceeded the FairTax's 23 percent marginal rate for 38 of the 42 single and married stylized households we consider.

For some low- and middle-income households, the marginal tax on working under our current tax system is more than twice the 23 percent FairTax rate! Take, for example, a married couple earning $35,000 per year with two children. By their federal tax bracket, their loss, at the margin, of the earned income tax credit from earning extra income, and their exposure to marginal FICA taxation, their current marginal tax is 47.6 percent!

Since the FairTax taxes consumption at the same rate no matter when it occurs, it imparts no incentive to consume now as opposed to later, and thus no disincentive to save. In economic terms, the FairTax's marginal effective tax rate on the return saving is zero. In contrast, the existing federal tax system imposes very high marginal effective tax rates on saving. For the 42 households considered here, marginal effective tax rates on saving range from 22.6 to 54.2 percent. This means that when the 42 households we consider reduce their current consumption by $1.00, their future consumption goes up by only 77.4 cents to 45.8 cents, when measured in present value. Under the FairTax, giving up $1.00 of current consumption permits an increase in future consumption equal to the full $1.00, when measured in present value.

In addition to imposing, in almost all cases, much lower marginal taxes on working and, in all cases, dramatically lower marginal taxes on saving, the FairTax imposes much lower average taxes on working-age households than does the current system. The FairTax's reduction in average tax rates on the working-age population reflects the broadening of the tax base from what is now primarily a system of labor income taxation to a system that taxes, albeit indirectly, both labor income and existing wealth. Consider, for example, a single age-30 household earning $50,000. The household's average tax rate under the current system is 21.1 percent and 13.5 percent under the FairTax.

Since the FairTax would preserve the purchasing power of Social Security benefits and also provide a tax rebate, older low-income workers who will live primarily or exclusively on Social Security would be better off. For example, the average remaining lifetime tax rate for an age-60 married couple with $20,000 of earnings falls from its current value of 7.2 percent to −11.0 percent under the FairTax. Compare this with the current 24.0 percent remaining lifetime average tax rate of a 45-year-old married couple with $100,000 in earnings to the 14.7 percent rate that arises under the FairTax.

The current federal fiscal system is highly complex. Understanding its work and saving incentives for any given household requires a very sophisticated analysis that deals with (1) all major provisions of the federal income tax, including the earned income tax credit, the child tax credit, the alternative minimum tax, Social Security benefit taxation, the decision to itemize deductions, the indexation of tax brackets, exemptions, and standard deductions, and the interaction of the federal income tax with each state's personal income tax, (2) the complex determination of Social Security benefits, which include the calculation of primary insurance amounts, early retirement benefit reductions, delayed retirement credits, recomputation of benefits, the earnings test, family benefit maxima, and the scheduled rise in the age of normal retirement, (3) the payroll tax, including its separate employer and employee components, its interaction with federal income taxation, and the projected increase in the covered earnings ceiling, and (4) the reduction in after-tax returns arising from the US corporate income tax. In this chapter, we calculate average and marginal taxes under the existing federal tax system and the FairTax, taking into account all of these factors.[1]

We proceed by first discussing the measurement of effective marginal tax rates on working and saving. We then compare, for a set of stylized households, total effective marginal and average tax rates under the current system with those that would arise under the Fair-Tax. Last we summarize and draw some conclusions. We provide details of our calculations in an appendix.

9.1   Measuring Effective Tax Rates

Economists measure the gain from extra work or saving in terms of consumption. The gain from extra work is typically measured in terms of its *maximum* impact on current consumption. Thus, if a worker earns an extra $100 this year permitting this year's consumption to rise, at most, by $50, we say the worker faces a 50 percent marginal tax of her labor supply.

The gain from extra saving is typically measured in terms of the impact on future consumption of forgoing a fixed amount of current consumption. Consider a two-period (youth and old-age) framework. In the absence of any effective marginal tax on saving, reducing current consumption when young by X would lead to an increase in consumption when old, measured in present value, of exactly X. If consumption when old, measured in present value, rises by only one-half of X, we can say that the saver faces a 50 percent marginal tax on saving. More precisely, we say that the tax on future consumption is 100 percent because the price, measured in present value, of consuming X when old has risen from X to $2X$. We adopt these conventions in measuring effective tax rates on labor earnings and on savings, as described below.

9.1.1   Calculating Effective Marginal Taxes on Labor Earnings

In calculating effective tax rates on working, we assume consumption-smoothing over the life cycle, allowing for variable rates of increase in future consumption. To facilitate the calculation of effective tax rates, we assume that all the net proceeds arising from additional current earnings are spent on current consumption. Net proceeds are defined as the additional current earnings less any increase in current and future taxes plus any increase in current and future Social Security benefits, where changes in future taxes and Social Security benefits are measured in present values.

In calculating effective tax rates on labor earnings, we must specify the maximum amount that can be borrowed to smooth one's living standard (consumption). If a household could not achieve a perfectly smooth living standard without exceeding its borrowing limit, we could calculate the smoothest possible living standard path, one that would involve an n increase at some point over time in the household's living standard. Say a household age 45 earns $50,000 a year, has very

little savings, but expects to inherit $1 million at age 65. If the house-
hold can't borrow against the $1 million, it will have to live with a
lower living standard prior to age 65 and a higher one thereafter. In
this case we could smooth consumption prior to age 65 at the highest
level possible, and then also smooth consumption at a higher level for
all years at and after age 65. However, this would result in a complicated description of effective marginal taxes.

To avoid this problem, we assume that the borrowing limit is high
enough to ensure that the stylized households we consider are able
to smooth their living standard perfectly over their lifetimes. Then, as
noted above, we assume that all the additional spending power from
additional current-year earnings is concentrated solely on current-year
spending, taking into account changes in future Social Security benefits
as well as the taxation of those benefits. The ratio of the change in current year (2005) consumption to the change in 2005 earnings provides
the effective marginal tax rates on labor earnings reported below.

9.1.2 Calculating Effective Marginal Taxes on Saving

Unlike the calculation of effective marginal tax rates on labor supply,
when there is more than one period (more than one future year) in
which to consume, there is no standard definition of the effective tax
rate on saving. One could, for example, consider how much reducing
this year's consumption by, say, $100 will increase the present value of
future consumption spending assuming the additional future spending
power is all allocated to next year's consumption. Alternatively, one
could allocate all the future spending power to consumption 10 years
out, or 20 years out, or in any future year one chooses. One could also
spread the extra spending power uniformly over all future years. Each
such choice will generate a different measure of the effective tax rate.
The reason is that the longer one pushes out the allocation of the extra
spending power, the higher the effective tax rate will be due to the nature of compounding.

To see this more clearly, note that the underlying goods that households are choosing when they make their work and saving decisions
are really how much leisure and consumption to purchase in the current year as well as in each future year. These fundamental goods
have prices in the absence of any taxes, and they have different prices
in the presence of taxes. The difference between the prices of leisure

and consumption with and without taxes determines the tax rate on these underlying goods.

Consider the tax on labor earnings or work. In fact the tax on work is reflected as a change in the price of current leisure. If a worker can earn $20 an hour with no taxes, but only $10 an hour with taxes, the tax system has lowered the price of leisure by a half—from a loss of $20 of consumption per hour of leisure to a loss of only $10 of consumption per hour of leisure. So the tax on work corresponds to a negative tax— a subsidy—on leisure. In this case, the subsidy rate is 50 percent.

Now consider consumption in future years. Take consumption in 2010 as an example. We measure the price of consumption in 2010 in terms of the sacrifice in current (2005) consumption needed to raise future consumption by $1. To make this concrete, let the before-tax rate of return be 5 percent. In this case the price, in the absence of taxes, of consuming $1 more in 2010 is 78.3 cents measured in terms of current consumption. The reason is that one can invest 78.3 cents for five years at 5 percent starting in 2005 and end up with $1.00 in 2010.

If the price of consuming a dollar in five years is that you have to give up 78.3 cents now, what would the price be if you were to face taxes on the return to saving and the after-tax return was not 5 percent but only 3 percent? The answer is 86.3 cents, since investing 86.3 cents for five years at a 3 percent return yields $1.00.

Suppose now, with taxes, that consuming that dollar in five years costs 86.3 cents today but only 78.3 cents in the absence of taxes. The difference in these two numbers indicates the effective tax rate on consumption five years from now. Since 86.3 divided by 78.3 equals 1.10, we can say that the tax system is imposing a 10 percent tax on consuming five years from now.

If we do the same calculations with respect to consuming not five years from now but twenty years from now, the no-tax price of consuming one dollar in twenty years is 37.7 cents but 55.4 cents in the presence of taxes. The ratio of 55.4 to 37.7 indicates that the tax rate on consuming twenty years from now is 46.9 percent. Clearly, which year in the future one considers makes a big difference to one's measure of the size of the incentive to consume now (to dissave) rather than to consume in the future (to save).

The results presented in this chapter calculate the effective tax rate on saving, assuming that the reduction in 2005 spending is allocated uniformly to all future periods. We assume that the living standard in all future periods rises by the same percentage by a discount rate of 7.0 percent, and use the assumed before-tax real rate of return to determine the present value of the change in future consumption measured in 2005 dollars. The 7 percent before-tax rate of return corresponds to the return one would receive before the application of any federal personal or corporate income taxes.

In addition we assume that the effective marginal federal corporate tax rate is the statutory rate of 35 percent. Since 65 percent of 7 percent is 4.55 percent, we assume that the real return to households is 4.55 percent. Coupling this with the assumption of 3.0 percent steady-state inflation rate results in a nominal return of 7.69 percent.[2]

In this and all other calculations in this study, we assume that the stylized households being examined live in a state with no state personal income or corporate income taxes. The reason is that our goal here is to compare total effective federal marginal and average tax rates in our current federal tax regime with the corresponding rates that would arise under the FairTax. Including state income taxes in the analysis would muddy this comparison because of the interaction of state and federal income taxes. Indeed, because of this interaction, it is impossible to clearly distinguish federal from state marginal taxation. To see this, consider a New York household that increases its 2005 earnings by $1,000. This raises the household's federal personal income taxes as well as its New York state income taxes. But the extent to which the federal taxes rise depends on New York state income taxes, since state income taxes are deductible from the federal income tax provided the household itemizes its deductions. One could just as well say that the reduction in federal income taxes arising from the payment of state income taxes reflects a lower federal marginal rate or a lower state marginal rate. Similar problems of distinguishing federal from state marginal taxation of saving arise in the presence of state corporate income taxation.

9.1.3 Calculating Average Remaining Lifetime Tax Rates

In addition to comparing marginal incentives to work and save under the current federal tax system and the FairTax, in this chapter we compare overall fiscal burdens by examining average remaining lifetime net tax rates under the two systems. The term "remaining lifetime" simply refers to the household's remaining years of life—that is, the calculations are prospective, rather than retrospective. Our calculations also consider all future federal tax payments net of Social Security benefits.

We define the average remaining lifetime tax rate as $(A - B)/A$, where A is the present value of spending, defined as consumption and nonfungible spending (college tuition, mortgage and other housing expenses, and life insurance premiums) in the absence of any federal taxation and B is the present value of spending under the tax regime in question. The term spending, as used here, does not include payment of FairTax. Note that in the absence of any federal taxation, A is also equal to the present value of the household's remaining lifetime resources—its current assets plus the present value of its current and future labor earnings and current and future Social Security benefits. So the average tax rates being computed are measured relative to the most comprehensive resource measure available. In forming these present values, we again discount at the before-tax (including before-corporate tax) rate of return of 7.0 percent. In words, this ratio indicates the percentage reduction in the present value of spending arising from the tax in question.

To determine the value of B under the FairTax, we divide the present value of spending in the absence of federal taxes by 1.30, the price of buying a dollar of real consumption under the FairTax inclusive of the sales tax. To see this, note that if the FairTax's retail sales tax rate is set at 30 percent, every dollar of income will yield only 77 cents of consumption since $1.00 divided by $1.30 equals 77 cents. Of course, the fact that the $1.00 of income is only able to purchase 77 cents worth of consumption means that the income is effectively being taxed at a 23 percent rate.

9.2   The Stylized Households

Our stylized households consist of either single individuals or married couples, whose spouses are the same age. We consider households of age 30, 45, and 60. Both the single-headed households and the married households have two children to whom they gave birth at ages 27 and 29. Table 9.1 lists key assumptions about the 7 single and 7 married households we consider. The 7 single households have initial labor earnings ranging from $10,000 to $250,000. For the 7 married couples, the range is double that of the singles, meaning from $20,000 to $500,000. All household heads and spouses retire at age 65 and start

Table 9.1
Profiles of stylized households

Total household income	Assets at age 30	Annual college expense	House value	Mortgage	Monthly mortgage payment	Annual property taxes	Annual home maintenance
Single households							
$10,000	$2,500	$2,500	$20,000	$16,000	$200	$200	$67
$15,000	$3,750	$3,750	$30,000	$24,000	$300	$300	$100
$25,000	$6,250	$5,000	$50,000	$40,000	$500	$500	$167
$35,000	$8,750	$7,000	$70,000	$56,000	$700	$700	$234
$50,000	$12,500	$10,000	$100,000	$80,000	$1,000	$1,000	$333
$100,000	$25,000	$20,000	$200,000	$160,000	$2,000	$2,000	$666
$250,000	$62,500	$20,000	$500,000	$400,000	$5,000	$5,000	$1,667
Married households							
$20,000	$5,000	$5,000	$40,000	$32,000	$400	$400	$133
$30,000	$7,500	$7,500	$60,000	$48,000	$600	$600	$200
$50,000	$12,500	$10,000	$100,000	$80,000	$1,000	$1,000	$333
$70,000	$24,500	$14,000	$140,000	$136,000	$1,400	$1,400	$466
$100,000	$25,000	$20,000	$200,000	$160,000	$2,000	$2,000	$667
$200,000	$50,000	$40,000	$400,000	$320,000	$4,000	$4,000	$1,334
$500,000	$125,000	$40,000	$1,000,000	$800,000	$10,000	$10,000	$3,333

collecting Social Security benefits at age 66. Earnings between the household's current (2005) age and retirement are assumed to remain fixed in real terms.

Each household is assumed to have a home, a mortgage, and non-mortgage housing expenses. The 30-year-old households have initial assets equal to a quarter of a year's earnings. The older households are assumed to have the same assets that the 30-year-olds have accumulated by the age at which we consider the older households. Table 9.1 also shows our assumed annual college tuition and other expenses. The households pay these amounts each year for four years for each child when the child is age 19 to 22.

9.3   Treating Employer-Paid FICA Taxes and Corporate Income Taxes

Since earnings are calculated net of employer-paid FICA taxes, we do not explicitly calculate these taxes. Nor do we explicitly calculate corporate income taxes since expected returns are calculated net of such taxes.

From an economic perspective, employer-paid payroll taxes are no less of a burden or a work disincentive on workers than are those paid directly by employees. There is only one economic difference between employer-paid and employee-paid payroll taxes—employer-paid payroll taxes are excludable from the calculation of adjusted gross income in determining federal personal income tax liability, whereas employee-paid payroll taxes are not.

In calculating marginal effective taxes on labor earnings including the employer FICA tax, we (1) assume a given increase in current earnings, say $500, (2) uniformly adjust the standard of living index values for 2006 and thereafter to ensure that the program's recommended consumption expenditure and standard of living for 2006 and thereafter remain unchanged, even though its recommended consumption and standard of living for 2005 rise, and (3) compare the resulting increase in 2005 consumption spending with the initial earnings increase of $500 plus the additional FICA tax paid on the $500. This sum represents the full before-tax compensation being paid to the household.

We use this same procedure in calculating average remaining lifetime tax rates under the current system; namely we first calculate for each stylized household its present value of spending under the current tax system and compare this present value with the present value of spending that would arise were the household to earn the same amount, grossed up by the employer FICA tax. In determining employer-paid FICA taxes, we incorporate the fact that the OASDI portion of the FICA tax is paid only up to the covered earnings ceiling, while the HI FICA portion is paid on all FICA-eligible earnings.

Like employer-paid payroll taxes, corporate income taxes also reduce the return to input suppliers. But unlike payroll taxes, where the input supply is labor, the input supply relevant to the corporate income tax is household savings. These savings help finance corporations, and when corporations have to pay taxes, they can't pay as high a return to their investors. To capture this discrepancy between the before- and after-corporate tax rates of return, we use the assumed 7.0 percent real return in all the discounting needed to determine marginal effective saving tax rates as well as average remaining lifetime tax rates.

9.4 Findings

9.4.1 Marginal Effective Tax Rates on Working

Tables 9.2 through 9.5 present our findings. Table 9.2 compares the marginal effective tax rates on working under the current tax system with the 23 percent rate that would prevail under the FairTax. Except for single households with extremely low earnings, the marginal tax on work is higher, and often much higher, under the current system than under the FairTax.

Take, as an example, a 45-year-old couple in which each spouse earns $50,000. Each spouse faces a 33.7 percent marginal tax on an extra dollar earned, which is almost 50 percent higher than the 23 percent rate they would face under the FairTax. Since the efficiency cost of the distortion in work and other economic choices rises approximately with the square of the tax levied on the choice, this stylized couple's welfare from the tax-induced distortion of its work-leisure choice is 2.15 times higher under today's tax system than it would be under the FairTax.

As a second example, consider the age-45 single household with $25,000 in earnings. The current marginal work tax is 47.7 percent. This rate is more than twice the FairTax rate and engenders 4.3 times the amount of economic distortion. The reason this rate is so high is the fact that each dollar of earnings lowers the single individual's

Table 9.2
Marginal effective federal tax rates on working

Total household income	Young adult (age 30)		Middle aged (age 45)		Senior (age 60)	
	Current system	FairTax	Current system	FairTax	Current system	FairTax
Single households						
$10,000	−23.1%	23.0%	−23.2%	23.0%	29.8%	23.0%
$15,000	33.3%	23.0%	33.8%	23.0%	22.4%	23.0%
$25,000	34.2%	23.0%	47.7%	23.0%	26.2%	23.0%
$35,000	50.2%	23.0%	28.3%	23.0%	29.0%	23.0%
$50,000	28.2%	23.0%	22.4%	23.0%	36.5%	23.0%
$100,000	27.6%	23.0%	27.5%	23.0%	28.6%	23.0%
$250,000	41.5%	23.0%	37.2%	23.0%	35.5%	23.0%
Married households						
$20,000	33.8%	23.0%	41.4%	23.0%	23.5%	23.0%
$30,000	33.7%	23.0%	47.6%	23.0%	28.2%	23.0%
$50,000	28.0%	23.0%	28.2%	23.0%	28.2%	23.0%
$70,000	28.3%	23.0%	28.2%	23.0%	32.7%	23.0%
$100,000	33.5%	23.0%	33.7%	23.0%	34.3%	23.0%
$200,000	35.3%	23.0%	31.2%	23.0%	37.5%	23.0%
$500,000	38.4%	23.0%	38.4%	23.0%	37.2%	23.0%

earned income tax credit by roughly 22 cents. Adding that to a 10 percent federal tax rate and 15.3 percent payroll tax rate yields the 47.7 percent rate.[3]

The earned income tax credit (EITC) explains the negative effective tax rate on working for single households earning $10,000 or less. By the time the single household reaches age 60, she can no longer receive the credit because her asset income exceeds the eligibility limit. And her marginal tax rate is a positive 29.8 percent.

The striking pattern in table 9.2 is that, under our current tax system, there is no pattern, or at least no monotonic pattern, connecting the size of marginal tax rates on working with the level of earnings. Take 45-year-old married couples. When total household earnings equal $20,000 per year (in today's dollars), the marginal work tax rate is 41.4 percent. This rises to 47.6 percent at $30,000 of earnings, falls to 28.2 percent at $70,000 of earnings, and then rises to 38.4 percent at $500,000 of earnings. There is also no clear pattern by age of these marginal wage tax rates. For some earnings levels, the marginal tax rate rises with age. For other levels, it falls with age.

Table 9.3
Marginal effective federal tax rates on saving

Total household income	Young adult (age 30) Current system	FairTax	Middle aged (age 45) Current system	FairTax	Senior (age 60) Current system	FairTax
Single households						
$10,000	24.6%	0.0%	25.2%	0.0%	24.8%	0.0%
$15,000	24.6%	0.0%	26.2%	0.0%	23.1%	0.0%
$25,000	24.7%	0.0%	27.2%	0.0%	23.2%	0.0%
$35,000	25.2%	0.0%	27.3%	0.0%	26.4%	0.0%
$50,000	25.3%	0.0%	31.3%	0.0%	32.4%	0.0%
$100,000	30.2%	0.0%	34.8%	0.0%	39.2%	0.0%
$250,000	36.0%	0.0%	43.0%	0.0%	37.2%	0.0%
Married households						
$20,000	26.5%	0.0%	27.2%	0.0%	22.6%	0.0%
$30,000	26.6%	0.0%	27.1%	0.0%	23.6%	0.0%
$50,000	29.0%	0.0%	27.5%	0.0%	23.6%	0.0%
$70,000	28.9%	0.0%	30.5%	0.0%	32.2%	0.0%
$100,000	33.4%	0.0%	33.8%	0.0%	36.4%	0.0%
$200,000	37.3%	0.0%	39.4%	0.0%	35.2%	0.0%
$500,000	54.2%	0.0%	50.7%	0.0%	38.2%	0.0%

9.4.2 Marginal Tax Rates on Saving

In addition to generating higher and, often much higher, work disincentives than the FairTax, the current tax system embeds very significant saving disincentives. In contrast, the FairTax generates no saving disincentives whatsoever. As table 9.3 shows, the effective tax rate levied on saving under the current system, as measured here, ranges from a low of 23.1 percent to a high of 43.0 percent for single households and from a low of 22.6 percent to a high of 54.2 percent for married households.

Unlike the wage tax rates of table 9.2, marginal saving tax rates are almost always higher at higher levels of earnings. And they generally decline with age holding the level of earnings fixed. The former pattern simply reflects the fact that higher incomes put households in higher federal income tax brackets. The latter pattern reflects the fact that older households have relatively few years over which to spend their saving and, therefore, relatively few years over which to lose what would otherwise be a much higher real return to saving.

Table 9.4
Marginal effective federal tax rates on saving when return is taxed at capital gains/dividend rate

Total household income	Young adult (age 30)		Middle aged (age 45)		Senior (age 60)	
	Current system	FairTax	Current system	FairTax	Current system	FairTax
Single households						
$10,000	24.6%	0.0%	25.0%	0.0%	21.5%	0.0%
$15,000	24.6%	0.0%	25.1%	0.0%	20.7%	0.0%
$25,000	24.7%	0.0%	26.5%	0.0%	20.1%	0.0%
$35,000	25.2%	0.0%	26.9%	0.0%	24.0%	0.0%
$50,000	25.3%	0.0%	27.8%	0.0%	23.9%	0.0%
$100,000	28.8%	0.0%	33.8%	0.0%	38.1%	0.0%
$250,000	30.4%	0.0%	33.7%	0.0%	26.9%	0.0%
Married households						
$20,000	26.3%	0.0%	25.9%	0.0%	21.3%	0.0%
$30,000	26.9%	0.0%	26.1%	0.0%	21.4%	0.0%
$50,000	27.3%	0.0%	26.5%	0.0%	21.1%	0.0%
$70,000	27.8%	0.0%	27.2%	0.0%	23.7%	0.0%
$100,000	31.9%	0.0%	29.2%	0.0%	27.6%	0.0%
$200,000	32.9%	0.0%	34.1%	0.0%	29.7%	0.0%
$500,000	39.8%	0.0%	38.3%	0.0%	29.8%	0.0%

Table 9.4 examines the marginal saving tax rates of table 9.3 with one change in assumptions, namely that all saving is invested in assets whose return comes either in the form of a capital gain or a dividend. The income from such assets is taxed at most at a 15 percent rate. The ability to pay capital income taxes at a lower rate explains why the saving tax rates under the current system are lower, particularly for upper income earnings, than they are in table 9.3. Nevertheless, there is still a huge saving tax and a huge reduction in the disincentive to save from switching to the FairTax.

9.4.3   Average Remaining Lifetime Tax Rates

Table 9.5 presents our calculation of average remaining lifetime tax rates, both those now prevailing and those that would prevail under the FairTax. To repeat, these tax rates net out Social Security benefits as well as the FairTax rebate. In the case of the FairTax, the Social Security benefits are adjusted upward to maintain the real purchasing power of the benefits.

Table 9.5
Average remaining federal lifetime tax rates: Current system versus FairTax

Total household income	Young adult (age 30)		Middle aged (age 45)		Senior (age 60)	
	Current system	FairTax	Current system	FairTax	Current system	FairTax
Single households						
$10,000	−12.3%	−17.6%	6.2%	−13.5%	6.5%	−27.1%
$15,000	−4.0%	−5.0%	11.3%	−10.0%	9.8%	−28.0%
$25,000	10.2%	5.6%	17.7%	4.7%	14.1%	−6.2%
$35,000	18.5%	10.1%	20.7%	5.4%	16.7%	−5.9%
$50,000	21.1%	13.5%	23.5%	11.4%	21.5%	3.9%
$100,000	27.5%	17.8%	30.3%	14.7%	32.1%	9.2%
$250,000	27.9%	20.8%	33.6%	19.7%	40.8%	18.2%
Married households						
$20,000	3.1%	1.3%	11.0%	1.5%	7.2%	−11.0%
$30,000	12.5%	7.8%	15.3%	3.4%	10.1%	−10.5%
$50,000	19.1%	13.4%	19.6%	11.1%	14.2%	1.4%
$70,000	21.1%	15.6%	21.3%	11.6%	17.0%	2.2%
$100,000	23.2%	17.4%	24.0%	14.7%	22.4%	7.9%
$200,000	27.2%	19.7%	29.0%	17.0%	32.2%	12.3%
$500,000	30.6%	21.6%	35.6%	20.5%	41.5%	19.3%

A glance at the table indicates that the FairTax entails either a significant reduction in the remaining lifetime tax rates for all of our stylized households. For example, the stylized single age-45 household with $35,000 in annual pays, on average, 20.7 percent of its remaining lifetime resources to the government under our current tax system but only 5.4 percent under the FairTax. The same aged married couple in which both spouses earn $35,000 faces a 21.3 percent current average tax rate, but only an 11.6 percent average tax rate under the FairTax.

For older, low-income households, the FairTax generates a major reduction in remaining lifetime taxes. Again, the reason is that under the FairTax the elderly not only continue to receive the same real Social Security benefits but also receive the FairTax rebate. For example, a single 60-year-old earning $15,000 a year experiences a reduction in her average remaining lifetime tax rate from 9.8 percent to −28.0 percent!

The FairTax not only lowers remaining average lifetime net tax rates but also maintains and, indeed, enhances overall progressivity in the tax system. Consider middle-aged married households. The FairTax average lifetime tax rate is very low (only 1.5 percent) for the couple with $20,000 in annual earnings, and much higher (20.5 percent) for the couple with $500,000 in annual earnings. The reduction in the tax rate at low earnings is proportionately much greater at the low end of the earnings distribution than at the high end. In switching to the FairTax, the $20,000-earning couple experiences an 86 percent cut in its average tax rate, whereas the $500,000-earning couple experiences a 42 percent cut.

9.5   Conclusion

Most commentators, including Gale (2005), have considered the Fair-Tax in a vacuum, namely without comparing its marginal and average tax rates with the combined marginal and average tax rates implicit in our current system. Compared with our existing federal tax system, the FairTax, as proposed in HR25, would significantly reduce marginal taxes on work, dramatically reduce marginal taxes on saving, and substantially lower overall tax burdens on current and future workers. Moreover it would do this without limiting tax progressivity. Indeed the FairTax would make our tax system more progressive.

Appendix: Further Details on the Effective Tax Rate Calculations

In performing the calculations of the effective tax rates described in the text, we use dynamic programming techniques to smooth a household's living standard over its life cycle to the extent possible without allowing the household to exceed its borrowing limit. In making these calculations, we take into account the nonfungible nature of housing, bequest plans, economies of shared living, the presence of children under age 19, and the desire of households to make "off-the-top" expenditures on college tuition, weddings, and other special expenses. In addition we simultaneously calculate the amounts of life insurance needed at each age by each spouse to guarantee that potential survivors suffer no decline in their living standards compared with what would otherwise be the case.

We calculate the time-paths of consumption expenditure, taxable saving, and term life insurance holdings in constant (2001) dollars. Consumption in this context is everything the household gets to spend after paying for its "off-the-top" expenditures—its housing expenses, special expenditures, life insurance premiums, special bequests, taxes, and net contributions to tax-favored accounts. Given the household's demographic information, preferences, and borrowing constraints, we calculate the highest sustainable and smoothest possible living standard over time, leaving the household with zero terminal assets apart from the equity in homes that the user has chosen not to sell. The amount of recommended consumption expenditures needed to achieve a given living standard varies from year to year in response to changes in the household's composition. As indicated above, consumption may also rise when the household moves from a situation of being liquidity-constrained to one of being unconstrained. Finally, recommended household consumption can also change to reflect desired changes in living standards over the life cycle.

The computer algorithm used to solve this problem is complicated. But it is easy to check the results to see that given the inputs, preferences, and borrowing constraints, the solution is the highest and smoothest possible living standard that the household can sustain over time.

Since the taxes paid by households depend on their total incomes, which include asset income, how much a household pays in taxes each year depends on how much it has consumed and saved in the past. But how much the household can consume, and therefore how much it will save, depends, in part, on how much it has to pay in taxes. Thus taxes depend on income and assets, which depend on taxes. This simultaneity means that the time paths over the household's life cycle of consumption, saving, life insurance purchases and tax payments must be jointly determined.[4]

The solution method is iterative dynamic programming. The *ESPlanner* computer software program has two dynamic programs that pass data to each other on an iterative basis until they both converge to a single mutually consistent solution to many decimal points of accuracy. The program begins its calculations with initial guesses of taxes, spending, life insurance holdings, and other variables and then updates these variables in successive calculations that smooth the household's living standard through time and find the year-specific life insurance needed to preserve each year's calculated living standard.

Because taxes and Social Security benefits make a critical difference in how much a household should consume, save, and insure, casual calculation of these variables is a prescription for seriously misleading financial recommendations (Gokhale, Kotlikoff, and Warshawsky

2001). As mentioned previously, our calculations include highly detailed depictions of the federal income tax, state income taxes, the Social Security's payroll tax, and Social Security benefits. In particular, the federal and state income tax calculations consider whether the household should itemize its deductions, compute deductions and exemptions, deduct from taxable income contributions to tax-deferred retirement accounts, include in taxable income withdrawals from such accounts as well as the taxable component of Social Security benefits, and calculate total tax liabilities after all applicable refundable and nonrefundable tax credits.

These calculations are made separately for each year that a couple is alive as well as for each year a survivor may be alive. Moreover survivor tax and benefit calculations for surviving wives (husbands) are made separately for each possible date of death of the husband (wife). That is, we consider separately each date the husband (wife) might die and calculate the taxes and benefits a surviving wife (husband) would receive each year thereafter.

Finally, it may be useful to clarify how we index a household's standard of living. The index is fixed at 100 for the current year and can be separately adjusted up or down from 100 for all future years. If, for example, one sets the living standard index to 115 for the years 2020 and beyond, the household's living standard is increased by 15 percent starting in 2020 *relative to the living standard in 2005*. Since the household's resources (assets, income, pensions, etc.) are not changed when one changes the index, we lower the absolute living standard prior to 2020 (and thus its pre-2020 recommended consumption spending) and raise it starting in 2020 (and thus its recommended level of consumption spending in 2020 and thereafter).

As another example, consider setting the living standard index to 95 for all years starting in 2006. The household's living standard is then lowered by 5 percent in each year starting with 2006 *relative to the living standard in 2005*. Again, making this change in the living standard index leaves current and future resources unchanged. So the household's absolute living standard is increased in 2005 (and thus its 2005 recommended consumption spending) and lowered starting in 2006 (and thus its recommended consumption spending for 2006 and beyond).

Now consider changing the household's resources at the same time the living standard index is changed from its default values of 100 for 2005 and all future years. For example, consider uniformly lowering the value of the post-2005 living standard index to 95, and at the same time increasing 2005 earnings by, say, $1,000. In this case the household will still end up with a 2005 living standard that is 5 percent higher than after 2005, but the absolute post-2005 living standard will not necessarily be lower than it was initially because it now has extra resources to spend. If we set just the right values of the post-2005 index, which may be lower or higher than 95, we can keep post-2005 consumption at precisely its initial values and therefore concentrate all additional spending just on 2005.

But if future Social Security benefits are higher, how do we keep future spending from being higher as well? The answer is that we assume the household effectively borrows against those future higher Social Security benefits (net of any changes in taxation of those benefits), leaving it in old age with higher Social Security benefits but also lower assets than would otherwise be the case.

The reason we say that all the additional purchasing power in these calculations is spent on additional 2005 consumption is that the households we consider not only end up consuming the same amounts every year after 2005, but also end up with no remaining assets or liabilities at the end of life. In short, the households die broke. Consequently every penny that can be spent on additional 2005 consumption without altering future consumption and future living standards is indeed being spent. So the change in 2005 consumption takes into account the impact of higher earnings not just on current taxes, but also on future Social Security benefits as well as future taxes of those benefits. And, to repeat, a comparison of the increase in 2005 earnings with the increase in 2005 consumption provides the measure of the effective marginal tax on working.

Discussion

Jane G. Gravelle

The model constructed by Kotlikoff and Rapson to capture true marginal tax rates is an impressive accomplishment. However, the conclusion reached in the chapter, that rates on labor income are lower under the FairTax, is questionable. In addition to addressing this issue, this comment also raises the question of whether comparative marginal tax rates on labor income are an important consideration in evaluating the FairTax.

The authors claim that the FairTax's marginal rate of 23 percent lies below 38 of the 42 calculated tax rates for stylized households. Two problems arise with this comparison. First, to determine the comparison with marginal taxes on labor income under the current system, we need an aggregated tax rate for the current income tax and for some portion of payroll taxes. Second, we need a fair comparison of the two tax bases, which requires adjusting the FairTax for government purchases, evasion, and preferences. The adjustment for government purchases keeps real government purchases constant in the face of a one time price increase related to the imposition of the sales tax. Adjustments for evasion and preferences are needed because comparing the current income tax system with evasion and preferences to the FairTax without evasion and preferences is like comparing apples and oranges. To compare them, one has to lower current income and payroll taxes to account for the preferences and evasion, which involves income effectively taxed at a zero rate, or adjust the FairTax rate upwards to account for untaxed income. I choose the latter approach.

Table 9.6 reports the dollar weighted marginal tax rates on labor income under the current system, for both income and payroll taxes,

The views expressed in this comment do not necessarily reflect those of the Congressional Research Service.

Table 9.6
Dollar-weighted marginal tax rates on labor income: Current tax system

Tax regime	Income taxes	Income and payroll taxes
2005 law	22.52	32.20
No EGTRRA	28.84	35.07

Source: Congressional Budget Office.

estimated by the Congressional Budget Office. Two tax regimes are reported-current law, and the law without the 2001 tax cuts enacted as part of the Economic Growth and Tax Relief Reconciliation Act (EGTRRA), which are currently scheduled to expire in 2010.

Only part of the payroll tax would involve a tax burden as the burden should be offset by the expected value of benefits triggered by the tax. So the combined marginal tax is approximately 32 percent (and approximately 35 percent without the 2001 tax cuts).

Table 9.7 provides adjusted estimates of the FairTax to make it comparable to the current income and payroll tax systems. Regardless of one's views on evasion under a national retail sales tax, it is important to recognize that the current rates in the income and payroll taxes are pushed up somewhat by evasion, and thus overstate the overall tax rate on income compared to the FairTax estimates. A similar argument applies to the existing preferences in the income tax.

Given that adjusting for preferences would significantly increase the tax rate, it would appear that the tax burdens on labor income are likely higher under the FairTax, not lower. This result should not be especially surprising. The tax base is smaller under the FairTax and labor income is more concentrated in lower and moderate income brackets.

Aside from the fact that the marginal tax rates on labor income could be higher under the FairTax, it is not clear that this margin is the only one that matters. While the earned income credit may contribute to higher tax rates in the phase-out range, most studies suggest that it is the participation response (which is positively affected by the credit) and not the hours effect (which may be negatively effected) that is the dominant behavioral effect. But more important, most evidence suggests that the response of labor supply is small, in either a static sense or an intertemporal one.

The marginal tax rate on labor income, however, may not be a very important issue in any case. Clearly, there are some significant effi-

Table 9.7
Estimated tax rates for the FairTax

Adjustments	Tax rates
Basic FairTax base	23.3
FairTax base adjusted for government purchases	26.6
FairTax base adjusted for government purchases and for evasion in current tax	31.3
FairTax adjusted for government purchases, evasion in current tax, and preferences	>31.3

Source: Estimates for the basic rate and the effect of government purchases were prepared by Max Shvedov of the Congressional Research Service. The adjustment for current evasion was based on the tax gap for the income tax.

ciency gains from a consumption tax. Discussion often focuses on gains from eliminating the tax rate on capital income, although the empirical evidence that the intertemporal distortion is large is not particularly compelling. A potentially more important advantage is the elimination of distortions across different types of assets and investments. A series of existing distortions between types of physical assets within a firm, between debt and equity finance, between corporate and noncorporate business, and between business investment and owner-occupied housing would disappear, as would the distortions in payout ratios of corporations due to favorable treatment of capital gains and the lock-in effect of the capital gains tax.

There are also some other issues that may loom as large, or larger, than the effects on labor supply and savings. Many are convinced that evasion would be serious problems with rates as high as those required under the FairTax. It is clear that we have little experience with high rate retail sales taxes, and that it is widely recognized that the reporting mechanisms under a European-style VAT may be the reason these taxes are successful and widely used. These mechanisms would not exist under a retail sales tax.

Also of concern to some are the inevitable distributional effects of flat rate consumption taxes. Even though a demogrant can be used to relieve the burden on lower income individuals, there is no way to prevent the burden from being shifted (at least in the long run) from high-income individuals, who currently have most of the capital income and who are subject to graduated rates, to the middle-income class. A related distributional concern is the significant lump-sum tax on owners of existing capital that arises in a shift from income and wage taxes to consumption taxes. While this lump-sum tax may permit some of the efficiency gains, a basic question of fairness remains.

All of these issues, however, pale into insignificance, in my view, compared to the macroeconomic transition problems for a retail sales tax. This problem is perhaps the most important, and the most overlooked. Most businesses do not have enough profit margin in the short run to pay such a significant tax on gross sales, and can only do so if prices rise or wages fall. Based on the tax inclusive rates reported above, either prices must rise 47 percent or wages fall by 32 percent or some combination of these two effects must occur, to accommodate this tax payment. Given sticky prices and wages, this transition could be quite problematic. Shifting to a retail sales tax creates the specter of a significant inflation, whose effects might reverberate in many ways, or a significant contraction in the economy, if monetary policy does not largely accommodate the price rise. Both seem to me to be extremely serious realistic challenges to adopting the FairTax.

Discussion

Peter Mieszkowski

Summary

Kotlikoff and Rapson compare the average and marginal tax rates on wages and the return to savings imposed by the current system of taxation and the FairTax—a comprehensive national retail sales tax. The authors capture the complexity of the current tax system by using a sophisticated software package, Economic Security Planner, to study the major provisions of the federal tax system, the earned income tax credit, the Social Security system, and various deductions and exemptions. Estimates of average and marginal tax rates under the current system of taxation and the FairTax are presented for single and married households, three age groups, and seven income levels—forty-two household types in all.

The marginal tax rate on work effort under the FairTax is 23 percent for all households. This is considerably lower for most groups than the effective tax rate on work under the current system, which varies between 25 to 40 percent. The difference in the marginal tax rate on savings is even larger. Kotlikoff and Rapson assume a 7 percent real return on capital and a 7 percent discount rate. The current marginal tax rate on corporate profits is assumed to be 35 percent. The authors postulate that the FairTax imposes a zero tax on savings, and they calculate that the current system imposes taxes on savings ranging from 23 to 54 percent depending on the household type. Kotlikoff and Rapson also calculate remaining lifetime tax rates, which are defined as $A - B/A$, where A is the present value of consumption in the absence of tax and B is the present value of consumption under the specific tax regime. These tax calculations net out social security benefits and the FairTax rebate. As expected, the remaining lifetime effective tax rates increase with income for all households. The average tax rates are lower under the FairTax for virtually all groups. The differences in average tax between the current tax system and the FairTax are especially large for the highest income groups who are 60 years old at the time of enactment of the FairTax. These results give the impression that the tax reform will make everybody better off.

To help explain the differences between the current tax system and the FairTax, Kotlikoff and Rapson note the following changes resulting from the adoption of the consumption based system:

1. The tax base will be broadened to include existing wealth.

2. As a consumption tax is based on existing wealth, it penalizes the rich and/or their heirs.

3. Since the elderly have little labor income and about 67 percent of the nation's wealth, the consumption tax will shift the burden from workers to retirees.

4. Indexing Social Security benefits for inflation can protect the poor elderly who live primarily on social security benefits.

5. Due to base-broadening the effective marginal tax rates on labor supply will decrease and the marginal taxation of savings will be eliminated.

6. The tax-induced redistribution away from old spenders to young savers and the zero marginal tax on savings will increase savings and capital per worker.

7. The elimination of the corporate tax will stimulate foreign investment in the United States.

The FairTax is projected to be 23 percent on a tax inclusive basis. In addition to indexing social security benefits, the FairTax provides a rebate or demogrant to each household. The rebate is set so that households living at or below the poverty level will pay zero net taxes.

Some of the results of Kotlikoff and Rapson are easier to understand if I summarize the principal conclusions of a companion paper on the FairTax by Kotlikoff and Jokisch (2005). In this exercise a multigenerational simulation is carried out over a hundred-year period. The substitution of the FairTax for the current federal tax system increases savings and the capital stock significantly, and real wages increase by 19 percent in the long run relative to the base case. The simulations distinguish between three broad income groups, and because of the tax rebate and the indexing of Social Security benefits under the FairTax, the welfare of lowest income group will be increased quite significantly by the tax reform. Those who are "elderly" at the time of reform, persons born between 1920 and 1960 either gain slightly or suffer a loss in welfare if they are middle class or lose if they are well-to-do. These welfare changes are small relative to the gains of the poor and the gains of all income groups born after 1970.

Commentary

The provocative results presented by Kotlikoff and Rapson make a very strong case for the adoption of the FairTax. However, there are well-known reasons for believing that the authors seriously overstate the magnitude of the dynamic effects, which are estimated by simulation and the difference in the effective tax rates under the current system and the FairTax. Also the introduction of the national sales tax is highly problematic on administrative grounds.

Kotlikoff and Rapson maintain that the marginal tax rate on savings under a consumption tax is zero. However, a growing literature beginning with the seminal contribution of Roger Gordon (1985) has called into question the apparent differences between income- and consumption-based tax systems in terms of their effects on savings and investments.

Gordon's fundamental point is that once risk and uncertainty is introduced into the analysis the taxation of corporate income will leave corporate tax investment incentives and individual savings incentives basically unaffected. The government by taxing capital income absorbs a certain proportion of the risk as well as income. Investors earn a lower rate of return but also bear less risk on their investment. Corporate and personal income taxes discourage savings only to the extent that they are paid on a risk free investment. More recently Gentry and Hubbard (1997) and Hubbard (2002) emphasize distributive issues and argue that the standard view that the burden of consumption taxes on wages and old capital is incomplete. Investors who earn risk premium on risky assets or earn intramarginal returns will pay consumption taxes on these high returns. This implies that a substantial portion of the 7 percent rate of return on capital will be taxed under the consumption tax.

More fundamentally, if the taxation of the above normal returns for risk taking has little effect on the equilibrium of the economy the simulation model developed by Kotlikoff and Jokisch on the assumption that the entire return to capital of 7 percent is riskless will significantly overstate the efficiency and growth effects of adopting the FairTax.

Moreover structural changes in the US economy that have occurred over the last twenty years have further blurred the differences between income- and consumption-based tax systems. These changes have been documented in a growing and influential literature (Parente and Prescott 2000; Corrada 2002; and Hand and Lev 2003). Economic growth in the "new economy" no longer depends solely on investments in physical assets but involves intellectual, organizational, institutional, and reputation assets, which together make up intangible assets. The estimated share of intangibles in total corporate assets is as high as 50 percent.

Intangible assets are created by investment expenditures on research and development and in related spending which under the current tax system are expensed at the time the investments are made. As investment in intangibles is currently accorded consumption tax treatment the substitution of the FairTax for the current tax system will have no effect on the incentive to save and invest in intangible assets. Hence the Kotlikoff-Rapson analyses based on a model of tangible capital significantly overstates the efficiency advantages of the FairTax.

A common concern over the adoption of a consumption-based tax system is that the tax burdens on low-income groups and the middle class would increase while the tax burden on more affluent would decrease. Two very different distributional analyses by Mieszkowski and Palumbo (2002) and Altig et al. (2001) confirm that if the current federal tax system is replaced by either a proportional income tax or a proportional consumption tax lower income groups lose and the highest income group gains the most.

The Altig et al. (2001) study is an extension of the Auerbach-Kotlikoff dynamic model and has twelve income groups based on PSID data. The paper by Mieszkowski and Palumbo (2002) is a static analysis, which estimates differential saving behavior at different levels of the income distribution. The main advantage of this study is that it is based on very detailed income and tax data, which includes information on the very rich. However, it is limited to static effects, as it does not allow for behavioral responses and the growth effects of tax reform.

Kotlikoff and Jokisch in their simulation study of the FairTax, consistent with the results presented in other distributional studies, show that it is possible to design a consumption tax system that increases the welfare of low-income groups during the transition and in the long run. Their plan indexes Social Security benefits to inflation and also provides for a demogrant, which eliminates any tax burden on low-income groups, thus overcompensating the poor elderly.

For computational convenience Kotlikoff and Jokisch recognize only three income groups. In the long run, the lowest income group experiences a 26 percent increase in welfare while the highest income group gains only 5 percent. I conjecture that a more disaggregate analysis of the reform, quite independently of any question about the magnitude of the dynamic effect, would be less progressive as the very rich are likely to gain a great deal. I base this conjecture on the static result presented by Mieszkowski and Palumbo (2002) that when a tax rebate is added to the FairTax, then relative to the status quo the tax burden is increased on the middle class with the largest increase for taxpayers with $50,000 to 100,000 in income. The income group with $200,000 to $500,000 in income gains relatively little, but the tax liability for the top bracket group with incomes of one million dollars and above is cut by nearly 50 percent.

A key assumption of the FairTax is that it will be revenue neutral at a tax inclusive rate of 23 percent. This assumption has been vigorously challenged by Gale (1999, 2002, 2005) whose most recent estimate of a revenue neutral tax rate for the FairTax is 31 percent even under the strong assumptions of no avoidance, no evasions, and no legislative erosion of the private and public consumption tax base. Kotlikoff and Rapson acknowledge that 23 percent rate will require a 20 percent cut in federal purchases and non–Social Security transfer payments. If these cuts are impossible they estimate the FairTax could be enacted at a tax inclusive rate of 27 percent.

While the difference in estimated rates has narrowed it remains large. However, the most difficult administrative issue facing the successful introduction of the FairTax is the potential for evasion. A rate of evasion of 15 percent, which is equal to the current rate of evasion under the income tax, seems a likely lower bound. This would increase the tax exclusive tax rate of the FairTax to close to 50 percent. There is no experience with a sales tax rate of this magnitude, which is more than triple the rate at which most experts believe evasion under a sales tax will be a serious problem.

Yet the proponents of the FairTax who are outspoken critics of the Internal Revenue Service propose to abolish this agency and rely on states to collect the FairTax for the federal government. This seems unrealistic and counterproductive as enforcement and compliance under the FairTax would be greatly improved if cross reporting and withholding are retained. For administrative and compliance reasons it will be necessary to modify the single-stage sales tax under which only households are taxed exclusively at the retail level.

These are two possible ways in which this might be done. One approach is to adopt a hybrid sales tax where withholding of sales tax would occur at pre-retail stages of production and distribution. The second more radical departure from a sales tax is to introduce a multi-stage value added tax. A VAT is equivalent to a sales tax in terms of its economic effects.

My comments on the Kotlikoff-Rapson chapter on marginal and average tax rates extends to the simulation work on the FairTax. I agree with the authors that the current system is extremely complicated and in need of reform. However, as the differences between the current tax system and a consumption based tax are smaller than their simple characterizations suggest, the long-run gains of adopting the FairTax are unquestionably significantly smaller than those they calculate.

Finally, if a consumption based tax is to be adopted, then on grounds of enforcement and compliance a cash-flow tax such as a flat tax or a VAT are both superior to the FairTax.

Notes

We thank FairTax for research support and John Diamond, Jane Gravelle, and Peter Mieszkowski for very helpful discussions and suggestions.

1. We perform these calculations using a sophisticated personal financial planning computer software program called *ESPlannerTM* (Economic Security Planner™) developed by Kotlikoff and Dr. Jagadeesh Gokhale. This program smoothes households' consumption to the maximum extent possible without violating the households' borrowing limits, taking into account all the aforementioned tax and benefit provisions as well as a host of others. Because it focuses on lifetime planning, the program considers how current work and saving decisions affect not just current taxes and Social Security benefits, but also all future taxes and Social Security benefits. This life-cycle/dynamic element is vital to understanding the size of effective marginal taxes, since earning or saving another dollar this year alters not only this year's taxes and, potentially, Social Security benefits but also, potentially, all future taxes and Social Security benefits; all of these future tax and benefit changes must be considered to accurately measure the gain from extra work or saving.

2. Note that the nominal interest rate equals 1 plus the inflation rate times 1 plus the real rate minus 1.

3. One cannot strictly add these rates together because the employer's FICA contribution is an exclusion from the federal personal tax because earning more at age 45 affects future

Social Security benefits as well as taxation of those benefits, and because there are a variety of features in the personal income tax (tax credits, the alternative minimum tax, and the claw back of itemized deductions at high levels of adjusted gross income, etc.) that influence a tax payer's effective tax bracket.

4. We not only calculate the appropriate levels of life insurance at each age for each spouse when both are alive, but also how much life insurance each surviving spouse needs to purchase.

10 Behavioral Economics and Fundamental Tax Reform

Edward J. McCaffery

I come not to praise behavioral economics and its relation to fundamental tax reform, but to bury it. To be more precise, I mean to bury
the most commonly and particularly suggested application of behavioral economics to fundamental tax reform: using the insights of
behavioralism to support proposals to promote individual savings
through ad hoc, tax-favored vehicles. This may come as a bit of surprise because I have long advocated the relevance of behavioral economics or its intellectual parent, cognitive psychology, to the field of
tax (McCaffery 1994a), most recently in a co-edited volume attempting
to give birth to the field of "behavioral public finance" (McCaffery and
Slemrod 2006; and see generally McCaffery and Baron 2006). Yet while
I do think that it is critically important to apply the insights of behavioral economics to fundamental tax reform, I also believe that it is critically important to get the terms of the marriage down right, preferably
in advance of producing any (more) offspring.

The typical but, I will argue, wrongheaded view of the possible marriage of the two subject areas is that reformers should consider substituting an irrational ("behavioral") model of human behavior for a
rational one such as the long-term dynamic optimization protocol at
the core of the life-cycle hypothesis (LCH) for savings behavior first
advanced by Modigliani and Brumberg (1954). The LCH holds that
taxpayers use savings and other capital market transactions to spread
out consumption over their lifetimes, maximizing utility by allocating
the "right" amounts of their lifetime wealth to each time period. Of
course, there are rational reasons to deviate from an LCH, such as having a bequest motive; a seminal paper by Kotlikoff and Summers (1981)
found that as much as 80 percent of all savings gets transmitted inter-
generationally. Others have questioned both the magnitude of this
effect and its interpretation (Modigliani 1988; Gale and Scholz 1994)—

after all, one reason for intergenerational transmissions can be imperfect implementation of an LCH strategy, perhaps because of the failure of private annuities markets (see generally Kotlikoff and Spivak 1981). But deeper and more persistent criticisms of the LCH have come from the realm of common sense, amplified and supported by behavioral economics. Challenges to the realism of the LCH and its demanding cognitive tasks are indeed compelling. Most notably, Shefrin and Thaler (1988) advocated a behavioral life-cycle hypothesis (BLCH) to supplant the earlier rational model (see also Thaler 1994). The BLCH holds that, for reasons relating to myopia, problems of self-control, and "mental accounting"—the cognitive tendency to ignore the fungibility of money/value, as in spending windfall gains (e.g., lottery winnings) on consumption binges not within one's "normal" budget set or utility function)—ordinary persons fail to adhere to the strict predictions of the LCH.

Since savings and the varying tax treatments of savings are at the core of the income-versus-consumption debate, and hence of all discussions of fundamental tax reform (McCaffery 2002, 2005a), tax policy theorists are left to consider whether a BLCH model of individual savings behavior should lead to different tax reform options than the LCH model would—specifically, whether behavioral models suggest the use of ad hoc tax-favored savings vehicles rather than more fundamental reform (e.g., see Bernheim 2002, and Auerbach's chapter 1 of this volume, both discussing the possibilities of such an approach without specifically endorsing it).

So goes the traditional logic, which I intend, like a rebellious child, to fight at every turn. Let me clarify my perspective from the outset. I am a tax lawyer, trained in economics but not an econometrician, who has also toiled in the terrain of behavioralism for some time now, with some impressive guides. Mine is not an empirical project, weighing in on the too-much-or-too-little-or-just-right savings debate. Moomau (in her comment in this volume) surveys some of this debate, then backs off to note the "general consensus that there is not enough savings in the US economy." Rather mine is a project rooted in common sense, on the one hand, and a sound analytic understanding of the structure of our current tax laws, on the other. Simply put, if all people are indeed rational LCH savers, then there is no reason for ad hoc, tax-favored savings vehicles—comprehensive tax reform will get things just right. And if people—some or all or most people—are not rational LCH savers, then there is *also* no good reason to think that ad hoc tax-favored savings vehicles will get things right, and it is more likely than not that these vehicles will get things wrong, precisely for the "behaviorally challenged" persons for whom they are meant to help. (I will address the possible counterexample on this point suggested by Strnad (in his comment in this volume) in due course). And since these ad hoc tax-favored savings vehicles are in any event complex, confusing, and costly, we ought to get rid of them in the name of doing something structural and fundamental. While my comments here are limited to the particular case of tax-favored savings vehicles, I humbly suggest that the lesson is more general: complex tax law provisions, sometimes justified in the perceived light of "behavioral economics," are rarely worth the candle.

I will continue my rebel's ride with a consideration of the state of play in fundamental tax reform today.

10.1   Tax Reform Today: Groundhog Day, All over Again

In Harold Ramis's 1993 film, *Groundhog Day*, Phil Connors, a big city weatherman played by Bill Murray, finds himself stuck inside of Punxsutawney, Pennsylvania (the "weather capital of the world") where he had ventured in the midst of an horrific snow storm to report on whether "Punxsutawney Phil," the famous groundhog, would see his shadow, in which case there would be six more weeks of winter. Each morning Connors awakes to discover that it is still February 2, Groundhog Day. Everyone around him is stuck in a perpetual present, endlessly repeating the same old actions and conversations, while he alone has knowledge of the movement of time.

Longtime followers of tax policy and the call for fundamental tax reform can easily empathize with Connors' plight. The fundamental things continue to apply as time goes by. There is by now a no longer surprising consensus in favor of certain basically well-known (or easily knowable) principles: that the current tax system is too complicated and in need of some fundamental overhaul (President's Advisory Panel on Federal Tax Reform, 2005); that any move should somehow be in the direction of consumption taxation, lowering if not eliminating the taxation of capital (Weisbach 2006; Auerbach's chapter 1 in this volume); that responsible tax policy means paying attention to incentive effects and maintaining low marginal tax rates (Diamond and Mirrlees 1971; Bankman and Griffith 1987) and minimizing transaction costs (Slemrod 1990a; Weisbach 2000). These are discussions that have been going on for decades and by some measures centuries. The case for consumption taxation, after all, can be traced back to Thomas Hobbes (1660), Adam Smith (1776), and John Stuart Mill (1848), and has found currency among contemporary political philosophers such as John Rawls (1971) and Roberto Unger (2000). Proposals for broad-based cash-flow taxation, as in the failed Nunn-Domenici USA Tax of the mid-1990s (Seidman 1995; on current proposals, see McCaffery 2002, ch. 3) can be traced back at least to Nicholas Kaldor's work on expenditure taxation (1955), which was in turn brought into the American tax policy mainstream by William Andrews (1972, 1974). David Bradford and his colleagues at the US Treasury (1977) laid out the two great fault lines in comprehensive tax reform in the landmark *Blueprints* study—perfect or improve the income tax by broadening its base and lowering its rates (ideas that can be traced back at least as far as Stanley Surrey, if not Henry Simons himself; see Surrey 1973; Surrey and McDaniel 1985; and also Simons 1938), or abandon the attempt to tax capital directly altogether and move to a systematic consumption tax along "postpaid" or cash-flow lines, as sketched out by Kaldor and Andrews. The basic analytic insight that prepaid (yield-exempt, wage-based) and postpaid (cash-flow, qualified account, sales-based) consumption taxes are equivalent under certain assumptions, mainly constant tax rates and rates of return (Andrews 1974; Warren 1975, 1980, 1996; McCaffery 1992, 2005a) led predictably enough to "flat tax" proposals (Hall and Rabushka 1983), essentially prepaid consumption or wage taxes. Add on progressivity and get an X-tax (Bradford 1986 and 1996a), and most of the options now floating about—a national retail sales tax, a value-added tax (VAT), a "flat" tax without any capital taxation, a consistent cash-flow consumption tax—have lain before us for decades.

Proving perhaps that the less things change, the more they stay the same (with apologies to the wittier French subtitle of Auerbach, Gale, and Orszag 2006), the recent President's Advisory Panel on Federal Tax Reform's report (2005) basically tread in these same trenches, coming out, in the end, with an "expand the base/lower the rates" approach, along with a nod toward a consumption tax, that could easily have been written, but for a few specific details here and there, two or three decades ago. The chapters in this volume, once again but for some admittedly important updating here and there—certainly the *titles* of the chapters in this volume—could have featured in any of several tax policy conferences in the 1970s and 1980s, as reflected, for example, in several well-known Brookings' Institution publications (Pechman 1980, 1984; Aaron and Galper 1985; Aaron, Galper, and Pechman 1988).

All this consensus, and so little action; water, water everywhere, but not a drop to drink. The tax system is still a complex mess; the people are still unhappy; scholars are still debating and writing about the tax base (income versus consumption), transitions, implementation, and so forth, on and on. Yet little really changes: it is still Groundhog Day. In hindsight, it seems clear that the then epochal Tax Reform Act of 1986 chose the wrong fork in the road (McCaffery 2005a) when it opted for nonfundamental, incremental reform under the existing "income" tax rather than anything more radical. In the subsequent two decades, the pace of tax law changes has dramatically accelerated (Doernberg and McChesney 1987; Steuerle 2005). The President's Advisory Panel on Federal Tax Reform (2005) noted that there have been 15,000 changes to the tax code—two per day—since the 1986 act. The income tax is more detailed than ever, with features such as the capital gains preference, briefly eliminated by the 1986 act, back in full force. The people clamor for something—anything?—different, and yet practical politicians cannot see clear to recommend anything fundamental. Once again, the President's Advisory Panel—badly handicapped by its marching orders, which included maintaining revenue and rough distributional neutrality, implementing a "fix" to the alternative minimum tax (AMT), and which also assumed the permanent extension of all recent tax cuts—serves as Exhibit A. While repealing the AMT and the deduction for state and local taxes (Internal Revenue Code Section 164), and substituting some low-rate credits for deductions may be good incremental ideas to clean up the income tax, they will hardly sate anyone's appetite for fundamental reform.

What's up? As Representative Rahm Emmanuel (D-Ill) (2004) said on the House floor, in regard to tort reform legislation, "We take up legislation that we have taken up before that is going nowhere and going nowhere fast. It is Groundhog Day here in this Congress" (quoted in McCaffery and Cohen 2006, p. 170). So too, it seems, with fundamental tax reform, for the tax policy community. Before this essay is through, I will return to address this question, speculating that part of the problem lies in our—the tax policy community's—thinking about the problem. As Einstein once said (more or less), we cannot solve a problem by the same kind of thinking that led to the problem in the first place. Perfecting our economic and econometric models about labor and capital supply elasticities under alternative tax regimes, or sorting out the most nettlesome questions of transition from one hypothetical ideal tax system to another, are not what is needed to move on from the perpetual present of Groundhog Day. We need a sound, careful rethinking of the analytics of tax. The insights of behavioral economics, I will argue, can be—and must be—enormously helpful in explaining and enacting fundamental tax reform. But first we have to escape from the clutches of "ad hocery" where, I fear, behavioralism—as it exists in the service of tax policy and reform—is now situated.

10.2   The Usual Thought

Back to where we are, as a practical matter: we do not have a pure income or a pure consumption tax, but rather a hybrid income-consumption tax (Andrews 1974; Aaron, Pechman and Galper 1988; McCaffery 1992). This is largely because of the realization requirement occasioned by the 1920 Supreme Court case of *Eisner v. Macomber*. Although more particular hybrid features abound, the realization requirement alone, combined with the analytic fact that borrowing is not "income" under a pure income tax (because the positive consumption or savings represented by the use of the proceeds is offset by the liability representing the dissavings; in other words, there is no "net accession to wealth" when one borrows; see McCaffery 2002, 2005a), means that a significant amount of economic income, in the form of capital appreciation, escapes the tax base, even if the value is put to use as consumption. The "stepped-up basis" for assets passing on death, Internal Revenue Code (IRC) Section 1014, adds a critical third element in the death of the income tax as a comprehensive ideal tax on all forms of material enhancement. The realization requirement, the non-taxation of debt, and the stepped-up basis rule lead to what I have called Tax Planning 101: the advice to buy/borrow/die (McCaffery 2002, 2005a). By buying assets that appreciate without producing taxable cash flows, borrowing against the appreciation to finance present consumption (and/or wealth transfers to others), and dying with debt and appreciated assets in tow, the propertied classes can avoid all federal taxes.[1]

Now whether self-consciously reflecting in the milieu of the hybrid income-consumption tax, or considering the matter as if we had a pure, ideal income tax, a familiar thought comes to tax policy theorists. Savings is, of course, central to the intellectual task of fundamental

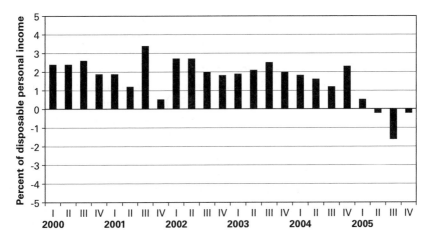

Figure 10.1
Personal savings rate, 2000 to 2005 (source: http://www.bea.gov/briefrm/saving/htm)

tax reform because the varying tax treatment of savings marks the distinctions between and among the major tax reform options, which all consist of income, prepaid or postpaid consumption taxes, or some combination thereof (McCaffery 2005b). Thus the topic of savings is featured in many of the chapters in this volume. And savings or, rather, the lack of savings, is an enormous problem in the United States today; as figure 10.1, based on data from the Bureau of Economic Advisors, shows, the personal savings rate (as a percent of disposable income), long drifting downward, went into negative territory in 2005. Even with considerable questions about how to measure national savings, there seems little doubt that Americans save too little (Bernheim 2002, Moomau's discussion in this volume).[2] Since an income tax is designed, in theory, to double tax savings (Mill 1848), the perceived need for more savings is generally thought to imply the need for a systematic, fundamental conversion to a consumption tax (Bernheim 2002, Auerbach's chapter 1 in this volume).

This first-best scenario typically assumes that individuals are rational life-cycle savers, who use their savings to solve a dynamic optimization problem, maximizing their utility across their lifespan by saving in order to smooth out consumption in each period. In this fully informed, "rational" setting there seem to be few good reasons for ad hoc savings vehicles under the income tax—mechanisms of single taxation, superimposed on the income tax's double-tax frame.

Let me explain. Consider that it is a standard analytic result in the tax policy literature that under the usual assumptions—mainly of constant tax rates and rates of return—"prepaid" consumption or wage taxes, where the single tax is levied upfront, and never again (e.g., the Roth IRAs of current IRC Section 408A), and "postpaid" or cash-flow consumption taxes, where the single tax is imposed later, on ultimate consumption or private preclusive use (e.g., sales taxes, VATs, and "traditional" IRAs under current IRC Section 408), lead to the same result (McCaffery 2005b). Yet analytically there is *no* reason why a particular tax-favored vehicle using either mechanism should work to effect new savings under an ideal income or the existing income-with-realization tax, again assuming that the LCH holds.

Prepaid accounts cannot prevent the movement of existing capital into the tax-favored accounts, simply giving a windfall bonus to existing accumulation while imposing transaction costs and theoretically reducing the need to save (on account of the windfall gain) (Bernheim 2002). Such accounts also afford little solace to mid-life wage earners, struggling to meet their household expenses from paycheck to paycheck, because they afford no cash-flow relief to help save (McCaffery 2005c). Further, now looking to the actual income-plus-realization tax, it is hard to see where prepaid savings accounts are much needed, given the ease with which capital investments can avoid further taxation under rather basic tax planning such as buy/borrow/die (McCaffery 2002); the prepaid accounts simply seem to substitute one set of transactions costs (e.g., the rules for penalties on early withdrawal) for another set (e.g., the tendency to remain in noninterest or non–dividend-bearing securities, and the associated lack of diversification in a buy/borrow/die portfolio).

Meanwhile, postpaid accounts cannot promise any net new savings at all, given the ease with which taxpayers can arbitrage out of them, simply by dissaving, or borrowing, at the same time as investing in the tax-favored accounts, thus generating a present deduction with no net savings (McCaffery 2005a, b). Note that this arbitrage operation is possible with or without an interest deduction for the debt (compare Auerbach, this volume), which deduction was curtailed by the Tax Reform Act of 1986 in IRC Section 163 (see especially IRC Section 163d); the arbitrage comes about because the borrowing of the *principal* is not income, and yet its use in funding the tax-favored account triggers an immediate deduction. Interest deductibility, where it obtains, only sweetens the deal for the taxpayer. More on this, anon.

Under these analytic facts, there is no reason why a rational life-cycle saver—who, *by definition*, would be optimizing her savings under the existing tax structure—should increase her savings in the presence of tax-favored vehicles. Such vehicles at best only increase the rate of return to savings by reducing the effective taxation of the yield to capital, leading most likely to *less* savings under the dynamic optimization model (ignoring here possible effects on labor supply); or they do little at all because the taxpayer is already (rationally, by stipulation) not saving; or, on yet another hand, for those taxpayers saving without bearing any effective tax on their savings (as by taking advantage of buy/borrow/die), the tax-favored vehicles do little, such as making it less transaction-costly to avoid the income tax's double-tax sting, or nothing at all. If all taxpayers were fully rational life-cycle savers, in other words, the case for ad hoc tax-favored savings vehicles would be very weak indeed—these provisions would impose complexity and transaction costs without evident gain—and policy theorists could return to the more global, welfare economic analysis of general consumption versus income taxation: fundamental, not ad hoc, tax reform (e.g., see Bernheim 2002).

Given these analytics and a continued unwillingness of tax reform—in the Tax Reform Act of 1986 or otherwise—to address any of the basic planks in the buy/borrow/die tax advice (McCaffery 2005a), the case for ad hoc, targeted savings vehicles *must* therefore turn on a rejection of the LCH in favor of a BLCH or some other behavioral alternative. And so, in theory, advocates of these particular pro-savings provisions point to the possibility that myopic individuals, lacking self control, might focus on the tax-favored savings vehicles to increase their savings (Bernheim 2002 and Auerbach's chapter 1 in this volume, each noting the approach without specifically endorsing it). This then leads to the possibility—a possibility lacking if a strict version of the LCH were to hold—that the tax-favored provisions are "working," that is, that they are increasing savings. Applied public finance theorists have rushed in to analyze the data to settled the perceived debate.

Unfortunately, perhaps, the econometric challenges involved in ascertaining whether or not ad hoc tax-favored savings vehicles "work" have been formidable, and the results, best understood, have been inconclusive. Studying the comparative statics of the introduction of IRAs in 1974, for example, Feenberg and Skinner (1989) and Venti and Wise (1986, 1992) found that IRAs did indeed lead to new savings, sometimes significantly so. But other research has looked at different numbers and reached different conclusions. Engen and Gale (1997) find, for example, that any increases in savings under 401(k) plans, largely a creature of the 1980s, were offset by higher mortgage borrowing and correspondingly lower home equity, a result that suggests a simple arbitrage operation was taking place, although Bernheim (1997) questions this result. What seems unquestionable is that the plethora of tax-favored provisions in the tax code is costly, under a static revenue analysis, and that our national savings is low and falling, notwithstanding decades of these creatures being out and about in the tax code. A recent Urban Institute study found—just to drive the point home—that the annual revenue loss from tax-favored savings provisions was greater in 2004 than the annual aggregate increase in private savings in that year (Bell, Carrasso, and Steuerle 2004), suggesting, in a crude nutshell, that the Treasury is *subsidizing taxpayers to consume more today by means of tax-favored savings vehicles.*

I suspect that the econometrics will never yield decisive answers, although we could put the whole question of the efficacy of ad hoc tax-favored savings accounts in the "unknown but knowable" category. The real world is a messy laboratory, and the mechanisms for dissaving and moving around old savings are subtle and complex to track. Yet there are good analytic reasons to believe, as the next section presses, that the utility of ad hoc savings provisions is very limited—reasons that do not rest on accepting the LCH and rejecting a BLCH, in toto. Far from it: the lessons of behavioral economics, best understood, suggest that ad hoc tax-favored savings vehicles should *not* work. But none of this has stopped actual tax policy from piling on one tax-favored savings provision after another. Tax-favored pension plans started in the 1940s; traditional IRAs were added in the 1970s; 401(k) plans were enacted in 1978 and began to take off in popularity in 1981; "Roth" IRAs were added in the 1990s; today we have Roth 401(k)s, medical savings accounts, Section 529 Qualified Tuition plans, and more. It is a little bit odd, and disconcerting, that while behavioralism still has to fight fierce battles to justify its very relevance inside the academy (compare Rabin 2002 with Epstein 2006a, b; Glaeser 2006), practical politicians and applied public finance theorists have been off and running with reforms that can *only* be justified if a particularly simplistic and naïve version of behavioralism were pervasively and specifically true. It is not.

10.3   Critique of the Usual Approach

10.3.1   The Known and the Knowable

From these basic principles, and drawing on what is known, we can construct a critique of the typical approach to engrafting behavioral economics onto fundamental tax reform. First, from the world of tax and economics, as traditionally practiced, abetted by common sense, here is what we know:

• Americans by and large do not save.

• An income tax is designed to tax savings, and thus favors present over deferred consumption.

• Since the 1940s the United States tax system has engrafted pro-savings vehicles onto its income tax system, hoping to facilitate and even encourage savings, a trend that has accelerated dramatically in the last two to three decades, to where we now have a panoply of tax-favored savings vehicles in the Internal Revenue Code, including retirement, educational, lifetime savings, and health accounts.

• These pro-savings vehicles within the Code are built on one of the two basic models for consumption taxation, namely the postpaid (no tax now, tax later) or prepaid (tax now, no tax later) approaches.

• Analytically there is no reason for postpaid accounts to lead to enduring new savings because it is trivial to arbitrage against the savings by "saving" with one hand and dissaving, or borrowing, with the other.

• Analytically, there is also no reason for the prepaid savings accounts to lead to new savings, either, because these vehicles offer no alleviation from the cash-flow stresses of the working classes, since they give no present tax (or other economic) benefit, and they also have no enforceable mechanisms to prevent old savings from simply being transferred into the new skins. Further, fairly basic tax planning under the current, income-with-realization tax can lead to this same prepaid consumption tax treatment (McCaffery 2002). And prepaid accounts have no mechanisms to prevent or deter dissaving, or spending down accumulated wealth.

What does behavioral economics—also enlightened common sense—add to this knowledge?

• Most people, most of the time, are myopic, paying greater attention to the present and lacking the self-control to behave consistently with the solution to a dynamic, long-run optimization problem (Thaler and Sheffrin 1981; Thaler 1994).

• People can focus on certain salient clues, are loss averse, and generally resistant to change (Tversky and Kahneman 1986; Kahneman, Knetsch, and Thaler 1991; McCaffery and Baron 2006).

From these facts the usual approach gets constructed. The two behavioral biases are set against each other. Let us make savings plans salient in the income tax, the thinking goes, to get people to act in their long-range self-interest by saving more, notwithstanding their myopia, and then hope that inertia (the "status quo bias") will take hold, leading to enduring individual savings. This is a happy tale, to be sure. But a mere modicum of deeper, more careful thinking reveals it to be little more than a "just so" story, extremely unlikely to hold in the real world—and certain to lead to incremental, unhelpful, complexifying, and likely counterproductive tax reform.

10.3.2   Why Care about Savings?

We ought first to pause and reflect over just why, exactly, "we" want more savings. There are two broad sets of reasons. One we can call "micro," looking to behavior at the individual level: people do not save enough, on their own lights, to maximize their own utilities; that is, they are not rational life-cycle savers. The other we can call "macro," looking to the collective: our aggregate capital stock is too small to maximize collective social welfare. It is common among at least some traditional welfare economists to assert that only the micro question has normative force: that, by definition, the optimal capital stock is what rational individuals on their own would choose, summed up. Under this view, the only way we can have "too little" savings—the only way for that concept to have meaning—is if some people are irrational, or "behavioral," that is, wrong on their own lights. The macro is the micro summed, no more and no less.

This is puzzling. For one thing, the aggregate capital stock clearly has features of a classic public good: the total capital of society, which affects interest rates and the returns to labor, and so forth, is nonrivalrous and nonexclusive. Under plausible conceptions of the social production function, labor—that is, workers, who, by and large, the non-savers are—would benefit from more social savings. It is a quite sensible social policy to help the poor and lower economic classes, not by tricking them into saving more, but rather by allowing the *not-poor* to save more, more easily (McCaffery 2002). Social theorists (e.g., Sen 1961; Rawls 1971) have long recognized, too, that the capital stock affects third parties not present at the micro-level decisions, such as the unborn: another reason why the problem of savings may not easily reduce to the sum of all micro problems. Certainly the curiously non-parallel literature on the government's budget deficit seems to presume that the macro-level capital stock is the problem, if there is a problem. Indeed, in a strict or "hyper rational" model, government deficits would not matter because rational self-interested agents would counteract any deficit in their own private savings decisions (Barro 1974), and since these individuals would be rational savers, too, there would be no problem at all. But that possibility has not stopped policy makers and applied public finance theorists from endlessly analyzing the government's dissavings "problem," in a story for another Groundhog's Day.

Even if there were indeed nothing to talk about except the micro foundations for the optimal social capital stock, in an ideal or first-best setting, the current status quo is far from ideal, with tax and other social economic policies distorting individual decisions. I will give some more content to this thought below. For now, note that it is a heroic leap to conclude that there is no problem with savings at all, except for the myopia of some (many?) such that, if only we can get individuals to be better utility-maximizers on their own lights, we would have the "right" level of aggregate capital accumulation. And, finally, even if this were true—that the only "problem" lies in the irrationality of some (many? most?)—then, unless we had some confidence that we could cure the myopia of *all*, the social planner might still have to look to the aggregate capital stock: we would need the "over savings" (by stipulation) of some to compensate for the "under savings" of others (most?).

All of this suggests that there are indeed reasons for tax and fiscal policy to look to the macro level as well as the micro foundations of savings. The good news is that both views might lead to the same place—a place different from where we are heading, full speed forward, now.

10.3.3   Some Ground Rules

The rush toward ad hoc tax-favored savings plans has been furthered along by an ad hoc adoption of ad hoc findings from behavioral economics. Too much ad hocery, all in all. In general, I share Matthew Rabin's (2002, p. 659) thought that: "As a rule, it is bad to spend time on 'methodological' and broad-stroke issues rather than the nitty gritty of the phenomenon being studied. The goal of this research program [of psychology and economics] is that it become 'normal science,' and, as such, the nitty gritty is the point." But rules have exceptions, and it is clear that the hoped-for marriage at the core of this essay—of behavioral economics and fundamental tax reform—is stumbling on the usual thing that marriages stumble over, a failure of communication and to fully understand each other. It rewards practical policy analysts to step back and reflect on some core analytic principles of behavioral economics. As at least a fellow-traveler with many fine behavioralists, I offer four ground rules of relevance to the task at hand, foundations for a possible happy and long-term marriage.

One, theory matters. There is nothing in behavioralism to suggest any rejection of any facts of the matter (Rabin 2002). The analytics of the tax system discussed above are the facts of the matter. It is possible, given the fungibility of money/value, to move old savings into new prepaid tax-favored savings accounts. It is possible to arbitrage against postpaid tax-favored savings accounts by dissaving, that is, running up debts, or by not saving as much as one otherwise would but for the tax-favored account, and so on. These facts of the matter must be taken into account in any sound analysis of tax reform, incremental or fundamental. They do not somehow disappear or lose their status as facts of the matter because individuals make systematic mistakes in their thinking about them or anything else.

Two, not all people are the same. It is a very large conceit of much social scientific policy writing—perhaps a vestige of the representative agent models common in graduate school training—that all people are identical (McCaffery 1994b, 2000). Much of the literature on the LCH and BLCH has an all-or-nothing quality, as if people must either be rational dynamic optimizers or hopelessly lacking in self-control; it reminds one of the futile reductionism of the pre-Socratics, debating whether there are one, two, three or four primal substances from which all else follows (e.g., earth, water, air, and fire). Clearly, people are different. Savings have multiple and mixed motives both within and across individuals. Some people save for life-cycle reasons, some for precautionary purposes; some of these are rational, some of these are irrational, as in being excessively risk averse and failing to take advantage of financial market vehicles such as annuities and insurance products. Some people save to make bequests; others make bequests only because they failed to annuitize their wealth. Some people save because they make more than they can think to spend; some people save because they think it is moral or right or just to do so. In thinking about fundamental tax reform—and whether we care about just the micro- or the macro-level capital questions—we have to think through the significance of this heterogeneity of people and savings behaviors. Similar conceits are that people act with single utility functions, and that theories must be all-right or all-wrong. There are no such meta-rules, certainly not coming out of "behavioralism" per se.

Three, the widespread prevalence of cognitive heuristics and biases, central to behavioral economics, does not mean that people are stupid and helpless, or that behavioralists think that they are, or that "paternalism" in one or another of its dreaded garbs is warranted. It is always best, I believe, to treat people with respect. Ordinary citizens are busy, struggling to make do and juggle competing tasks and demands in a complex world. There is plenty of evidence that all of us mortals make "mistakes" in judgment and decision-making; there is very little evidence that these mistakes are devastating in their impacts, or keep us from living happy, meaningful, even flourishing lives. The various rules of thumb that we employ are often, perhaps even usually, right. These heuristics can sometimes lead us astray, but our failure to counteract the biases does not mean that we are simply stupid and helpless. Further not all actions that *can* be explained by "irrational" explanations are, in fact, irrational. Good social policy theory should always begin and end with good—careful and respectful—thinking about the people to be affected by any policy.

Take savings behavior. The usual thought about the subject before us relies on a simple syllogism:

People should save, for their own good.

People do not save.

Therefore people are irrational.

But this does not follow, logically. There are *reasons* that people might not save, having to do with the general structure of society and its

institutions, and having nothing to do with irrationality—there is, or
can be, "rational myopia," as it were. For example, it may not be a rational strategy for a lower income worker—and lower income workers
are especially unlikely to save, as figure 10.2 illustrates—to save small
sums of money over an extended period of time in order to build up a
modest nest egg. For example, $50 a month saved for ten years at even
a 6 percent interest (high for a real rate of return), compounded monthly, yields an amount considerably less than $10,000 by the end of the
decade. Does it help to have $8,000 in the bank? Such a relatively mea-
ger accumulation might only make one disqualified for financial or
government aid programs, such as educational or medical benefits,
as well as making one vulnerable to the wants or demands of
family and other potential claimants. It is hard to afford good financial advice at such low wealth levels. In this social and institutional
setting, I have argued (McCaffery 1994b) that it can be fully rational
to play the lottery—as the vast majority of US citizens in fact do—
notwithstanding the fact that lotteries are a wildly unfair actuarial bet.
Whether we conceptualize this as "episodic risk preference" or whatever, the fact of the matter is that having a small nest egg may not
mean much, and may even impose costs, such that the lower classes
"invest" in a chance at a transformative wealth event: there is a kink in
the social utility function, as it were. Yet another rational reason not to
save, even under an LCH, is the thought or hope that things will get
better tomorrow: a better job, a higher earning spouse or partner or
child, more generous public benefits. These hopes may get dashed,
more often than not, but they are not irrational—and they may even
be, instrumentally, vitally important to have, for a host of reasons
relating to health and well-being. (Compare Loewenstein, Small, and
Strnad 2006, discussing the instrumental value of the "identifiable vic-
tim bias" in public policy.)

   This is not the same as the parlor game of converting all irrational
behavior into a rational explanation by playing with semantics. To the
contrary, it is first considering, and ruling out, rational explanations
before considering irrational ones, looking to the people with respect.
To me and most behavioralists I know, "irrationality" has a precise
meaning, involving the violation of one of the basic axioms of rationality, such as consistency, reflexivity, or transitivity (continuity is a bit
more complex) (McCaffery and Baron 2006). If a person likes her glass
half-full but rejects it half-empty, or if another person uses cash to
avoid a penalty on credit cards but uses credit cards and forswears a

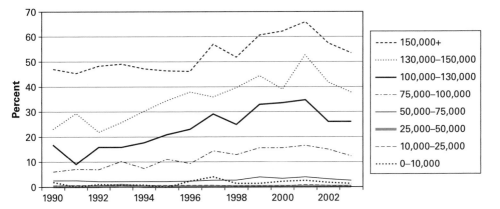

Figure 10.2
Percentage of workers contributing maximum to 401(k) plans by earnings, constant 2004 dollars (source: Kawachi, Smith, and Toder 2006).

As is shown, few eligible employees at any earnings level take full advantage of the tax-favored treatment of IRC Section 401(k) plans. The lines, covering a twelve-year period (1990–2002), follow earnings levels rather precisely. Only in the top four categories, for earnings above $75,000 (well above the median income), do as many as 10 percent of workers "max out" in their 401(k) plans. Even at the highest wage level, above $150,000, typically only about half of the workers take full advantage of the plans. For all workers earning less than $75,000, almost none maximize their contributions—and this despite the fact that 401(k) plans operate as a percentage of earnings such that the absolute dollar amounts for low earners are small. (It is also typically the case that low earners are in low tax rate brackets, meaning that the benefit of a tax deduction is also low.) The figure suggests two points about the policy of ad hoc tax-favored savings programs. One, since so few workers are taking full advantage of existing plans, the case for increasing such plans, or adding new ones to the law, is weak, although this case is being made constantly inside the Beltway. Two, whether because of the low rate of savings or the minor inducement offered by an income tax deduction, tax-favored savings vehicles are especially little used among the middle and lower income classes.

bonus for using cash, something is up. But in the subject matter before us—savings—it is not obvious that "myopia," or present-bias, which is easy to elicit in experimental settings, is what is up. And even if it is so for some people, it need not be so for all, as Ground Rule Two had held. For a good many Americans, savings is simply not a viable option, and it would be best for social policy theorists to understand and accept this, as I will discuss further in the next section. And note, finally, that this "rational" set of explanations *fits* with the data—that we have and have had for decades pro-savings policies, but our savings rate is low and declining—in a way that the easy "behavioral" explanations do *not*.

Four, it is important to distinguish, in thinking about cognitive errors, between the cognitive and the experiential "spaces" of human endeavor. Danny Kahneman (2000) has of late been using a distinction between "decision utility," or the weights people put on matters in forming a judgment or decision, and "experienced utility," which is how people feel about the experience that their decision led to, during or after the decision. Because there is a gap, Kahneman has been recommending paternalism of one sort or another. This is not exactly what I have in mind. The decisions that we care about lead to actions. But the time and distance of the action from the decision, and the duration of the action's effects, can vary. Sometimes, the decision alone is almost performative, as in voting, or forming an opinion to express to a public opinion pollster: the thought *is* the action. Other times, the thought leads to an action that will or can endure for a long time, out in the world. Of course, savings is a paradigm example of the latter: an action, or set of actions that, by definition, has consequences that endure through time. And so we ought to distinguish, as social policy theorists, between how we *think* about savings, and how we in fact, over time, *save*.

The reason for laying out and stressing this ground rule relates to another reason why widespread cognitive errors have limited real-world harms, most of the time (the first was that these heuristics or rules of thumb were often correct, or adequate to the tasks at hand). The real world of experiences is set up in the presence of people's ordinary cognitive skills and shortcomings. Very often, in private financial markets, institutions arbitrage against and effectively "cure" the cognitive errors (McCaffery and Baron 2006). Thus competition and the market assure marginal cost pricing, even if few if any of us are capable of discerning what anything really costs. We can all venture into the supermarket and act as if we were fully rational agents. But this is not always so. The careful theorist should pay attention to society's institutional structures to see when these counteract—and when they exacerbate—persistent, individual-level cognitive bias. I will have more to say on this point soon enough.

10.3.4   What's Wrong with the Usual Approach

Putting the ground rules together with the facts of the matter leads to a deep critique of the trend in tax policy over the last several decades, toward ad hoc tax-favored savings vehicles. In essence, there is almost no reason why anyone should think that vehicles would "work," which is why no one ought to be surprised that the macro-level data typically suggest that they are not in fact working.

Consider, first, the micro-level policy objective, to get individuals to save more, on their own lights, for their own good. Let us accept that some, perhaps many, even most, individuals are myopic, lacking in self-control. Since we are only talking about savings, this means that they do not save enough for their own good. Now let us look at the two broad policy options for ad hoc tax-favored savings vehicles.

Consider first prepaid accounts, which have been the dominant recent trend in tax policy (McCaffery 2005a). These accounts offer no solace to the myopic, cash-flow-constrained individual because they offer no immediate benefit for savings. Indeed the *reasoning* for putting money into these accounts must be somewhat—perhaps even foolishly—far-sighted: one has to think ahead to whether or not the tax advantages of the Roth-style accounts outweigh their disadvantages. One ought even to reflect on whether or not Congress will renew or extend the tax-favored treatment; Section 529 qualified tuition plans, for example, are set to expire, with no automatic "grandfathering" of existing accounts on the books. Should one transfer wealth into a 529 plan, and should Congress decide not to renew or extend the "favorable" tax treatment, the investor will be (double) taxed, having given up an opportunity, afforded by present law, to avoid that second tax on one's own. There is nothing very helpful to the myopic, here.

It is no surprise, then, that most commentators going down the path of considering tax-favored accounts as a cure for rampant myopia are thinking of postpaid accounts (Thaler 1994; Bernheim 2002; Auerbach's chapter 1 in this volume). But the tale is no better here. For one thing, for the fully "rational" myopic, postpaid accounts create a mechanism for more *consumption* today by greater *dissaving*, the simple arbitrage operation mentioned above. Imagine a taxpayer, Jill, in the 35 percent marginal tax bracket. Jill can borrow $2,000 on a credit card on April 15, and open a tax-deductible, traditional IRA. There is no net savings here, the $2,000 IRA account being offset by the $2,000 debt (which must be repaid, perhaps at a very high rate with nondeductible interest). But Jill has, immediately, gained $700 more to consume, *today*, by lowering her taxes, due by the stroke of midnight. (And it is curious, if perhaps coincidental, that contributing to an IRA is one of the few financial actions that can reduce one's taxes well after the taxable year has concluded.) A more prevalent problem may come from the "naively" myopic individual, Jack. Because of a persistent money illusion (Shafir, Diamond, and Tversky 1997) or whatever, Jack simply forgets that taxes must be paid out of his traditional IRA or 401(k) plan. So the balance Jack sees in his monthly or quarterly statement leads him to a false sense of security, and he consumes even more, running up credit card or home equity debt, and so on, and saving less than he "should."

Here is the deep, dark problem in all this: these "arbitrage" operations do not depend on exquisite calculations or the solving of complex, long-term dynamic optimization problems. They depend, rather, on ... myopia! That is, the *very same cognitive or behavioral tendency on which the ad hoc "patch" is justified is the tendency that can or will undo the efficacy of the patch*. The theory of postpaid tax-favored savings accounts within an income tax structure, in other words, is like the strategy of pouring water on a drowning man.

Now in the face of this critique, Professor Strnad, drawing on the work of Bernheim and Rangel (2005a, b), suggests a counterpossibility. Perhaps some individuals are generally "rational" but suffer from "hot flashes," so to speak, during which they temporarily lose control and would, if they could, spend everything they had. Such "episodic myopics" as we might call them, would be benefited by tax-favored savings accounts with built-in liquidity constraints. Now I have little doubt, consistent with my general theme that not all people are the same, that there are indeed people like this: some of my best friends are, as the saying goes. But so what? It cannot be the right approach to public policy to put in place a byzantine system and then, ex post, construct a personality profile for whom the system maximizes individual welfare. In any event the solution to the Strnad-Bernheim-Rangel "problem" is to create savings vehicles with liquidity constraints, with or without tax preferences: Christmas Clubs, for example, would do the trick perfectly well. The tax system need not be constructing Ulysses's mast for him.

Further, because savings take place in the real world of experiences, and, by definition, must endure over and through time, the actual institutions of society will interface with the individual decisions (Ground Rule Four). This fact just makes things worse. Contrary to the general tendency of private markets to arbitrage against individual heuristics and biases and effect better, more efficient results, such as marginal cost pricing (McCaffery and Baron 2006), the institutions of society are perfectly content to *encourage* individual myopia in the case at hand. Financiers will not cease to send out invitations for new credit cards, and retailers will not cease to offer "no money down" financing, simply because Congress has decided to engraft ad hoc tax-favored savings vehicles onto an income tax structure. On the other hand, there is no reason to doubt that private markets would generate the kind of self-imposed liquidity constraints that would solve the Strnad-Bernheim-Rangel problem of *episodic* myopia, discussed above, as they have in fact done.

Consider next the macro-level concern, about the aggregate capital stock. Here again the ad hoc approach scores poorly. Looking first to prepaid savings accounts, these not only give no reason for any new savings, they also eliminate almost all barriers to *dissaving*. The wealthy, having initially benefited from the windfall gain to existing capital (and thereby perhaps reducing their savings, under the LCH), now face no barrier whatsoever to spend away, tax free. Note that they need not even wait until they turn 59.5 years of age, or whatever the statutory minimum age is for tax-free withdrawal, because they can borrow today, tax free, and wait to pay off the debt until they hit the magic number. Since myopic individuals, who do not now save, are given no new reason or ability to save, and since the present savers, who are (almost by definition) less myopic, are given a windfall, a reason to save less, and an easier path to dissavings, there is little reason to expect greater social capital under prevalent ad hoc prepaid savings accounts.

Postpaid accounts fare no better. These offer no strong reason to save, as we have seen, and even encourage, both on account of rational myopia, and irrational money illusion, greater dissavings today. Once again, the myopic nonsaver today may see her present bias worsen. Another, and potentially very large problem with the postpaid savings account technique, is that it compels the withdrawal of funds from the account, both by minimum distribution rules and by the potentially extreme taxation of the accounts on death (because they are subject to both "income tax in respect of decedent" rules, IRC Section 691, and the estate tax, a potential taxation of 75 percent or more of their principal balance). But if most savings comes from rational or even irrational long-term, intergenerational savers (Kotlikoff and Summers 1981), these tax-favored accounts can have a perverse effect on the aggregate capital stock. By essentially forcing people into a "life-cycle" model, postpaid tax-favored savings accounts may be encouraging the dissipation of America's best, most stable, and longest term pools of private capital.

10.3.5 Summing Up: The Known and Knowable, Redux

A brief word from the author: My initial professional training is as a tax lawyer. While I added an economics degree after commencing my position as a legal academic, I lack the skills or resources to perform an in-depth, data-intensive, econometric analysis of the efficacy of tax-favored savings vehicles. But perhaps this is a blessing in disguise. Rather than "crunch the numbers" myself, I have studied the work of others, and I have reflected on what I do know. I now know much about behavioral economics, and I have long been toiling in the terrain of fundamental tax policy, on a legal and analytic level. I have also tried, against all temptations to the contrary, to maintain a modicum of common sense. Here, then, is what I consider to be known and/or knowable about the present state of affairs:

One, Americans do not save. And we have not saved any more since the 1940s, when a policy of hybridization to encourage savings was born in the income tax, with tax-favored pension plans. Nor has the situation improved since the 1970s, when we added IRAs to the IRC; or the 1980s, when 401(k) plans took off; or the 1990s, when we added Roth IRAs; or the present decade, when we have seen the birth of medical and educational and lifetime savings accounts and Roth 401(k)s, and on and on.

Two, these savings provisions in fact cost more in forgone tax revenue than we observe in new savings each year (Bell, Carraso, and Steuerle 2005).

Three, there is no reason, with or without the insights of behavioral economics, that this should be anything but as it appears.

10.4   A New Marriage: Escape from Groundhog Day

The cause of fundamental tax reform seems stuck in a perpetual present, endlessly debating the same old, same old questions of income versus consumption taxation, implementation, transitional rules, and so on. Savings behavior—and Americans' lack of it, by and large—features prominently in this debate. Because, in a certain limiting case, it is hard to see any problem, by definition, if all people are fully rational life-cycle savers, tax policy theorists have looked to forge a marriage with behavioral economics, taking off-the-shelf findings that people are myopic and lack self-control but can be tricked into changing their behavior—and thus, one hopes, saving—by salient vehicles. Hence tax policy has recommended engrafting ad hoc tax-favored savings vehicles onto the income tax. Like a football coach running the same play over and over until it no longer works, one thing has led to another, and we now have dozens of pro-savings vehicles in the tax code, with more on various drawing boards inside the beltway. Only, unlike the football coach, there is precious little evidence that the vehicles *do* work, and no reason, in theory, to think that they *should*. And so we see the past is what is keeping us in the present: we repeat the same techniques, and go down the same intellectual paths, while the law gets more and more complex and the people seethe with anger and frustration for reform. It's Groundhog Day, forever.

In this penultimate section, I sketch out the outlines of a happier marriage, one that can get us out of the rut of the present, toward a better, more principled, future.

10.4.1   Fundamental Tax Reform

The analysis to this point leads to the surprisingly simple thought that fundamental tax reform should be fundamental. Reviewing the ground rules, recall that theory matters; ordinary people are not all the same but they are not generally stupid, foolish, or helpless; and life plays itself out in the realm of experiences, where institutions interact with individual behaviors. The problem with ad hoc tax-favored savings vehicles, seen in this light, is that these can *only* work if all or most people are (1) the same, (2) myopic but easily distractable by salient cues to act in their self-interest, (3) persistently short-sighted enough not to learn the techniques of arbitrage, so as to unravel the effects of the myopia-curing actions, and if (4) institutions in society do not in fact rise up to counteract the effects of the salient myopia cures by teaching the people how to arbitrage (or just doing it for them). There is good reason to conclude that none of these four conditions obtain; certainly it is hard to conclude that all of them do. We can look to the real world and see, on the one hand, the plethora of tax-favored savings vehicles and, on the other hand, much evidence of low and declining personal savings rates.

In the face of this dire state of the world, there is an obvious strategy to try. We could tighten up the tax-favored savings accounts themselves, layering them with rules making them nonfungible, preventing easy arbitrage: keep them out of bankruptcy, do not allow them to be pledged as security for loans, have mandatory anti-withdrawal rules backed by penalties, and so on. But there are reasons to think that such techniques, like "spendthrift" or anti-alienation clauses in trusts, simply drive up the costs of any countervailing arbitrage mechanism. Certainly such rules, in themselves, do not change the fact of the matter that myopic individuals will want to arbitrage, or that social institutions, such as credit and retail markets, have every incentive to try to get individuals so to arbitrage. Patching up a Maginot Line is not far-sighted social policy.

This then leads to the thought of a Copernican revolution, in which we invert our gaze, and look not to the tax-favored savings vehicles themselves, but to the residual, default tax system. If we were to convert that system to a consistent, postpaid, or cash-flow consumption tax, arbitrage would not be possible (McCaffery 2005c). Savings would not be taxable, but debt used to consume would trigger tax (Seidman, 1995; McCaffery 2002, 2005a, c). Hence there would be no reason to save, on the one hand, and borrow or dissave, on the other: this would not generate any additional funds for immediate consumption. There would now be no *tax-centric* reason for particular, ad hoc tax-favored savings accounts, but of course that is true today, under the status quo, as discussed above. (Note, however, that it is a mistake to think that there are no reasons for special savings accounts given comprehensive cash-flow consumption taxation; I pick up this theme in the following section). Finally, a consistent, comprehensive conversion to postpaid consumption taxation—and I believe this ought to be done without a separate, freestanding gift and estate tax (McCaffery 2002, ch. 4)—would do something more: it would make it easier for savers to save, for as much and as long as they want. None of this is to say that fundamental tax reform will be easy or seamless: transitions are

hard, economically and politically; implementation details can be dev-
ilish; and opportunities for evasion arise under any tax system.[3]

These recommendations follow from bearing in mind that theory
matters, and that people are different. Tricking myopic non-savers into
savings in a world in which there is no rational reason for the tricks
to work is not a sensible blueprint for reform. Changing the world to
make the rules systematically pro-savings (or not anti-savings) does
make sense. And it lays a better foundation for addressing the "problem" of savings, on both micro and macro levels.

10.4.2   Savings

The insights of behavioral economics do not suggest or justify the use
of ad hoc tax-favored savings within a basic income tax structure to
address the problem of savings. Far from it: there is good reason, even
and maybe especially accepting that many and perhaps most of us are
myopic, to suspect that such vehicles will not work. And while it may
not yet be quite "known," it seems pretty close to being "knowable"
that this strategy has not worked. It is better to pay attention to the
lessons of theory, and implement, probably sooner rather than later, a
consistent, comprehensive consumption tax. What then to do about
the problem of savings?

First, on a macro level, the analysis above has suggested that most
Americans do not and will not save. But some Americans clearly save
a lot. There is much to be said for letting them do so. This is not to
agree with the point made by Strnad (this volume) about a "barbell"
shaped distribution, with some oversavers, some undersavers, and a
vast middle. I have no reason to believe that the distribution will not
be continuous, and some reason to hope that a sensible tax policy will
inculcate—and encourage the private market to develop mechanisms
to inculcate—"better" approaches to savings. But I am certainly
skeptical that existing tax policy can be any kind of simple, fair, or efficient mechanism to prop up undersaving, with its ill-thought-through
mechanism for the myopic, or to clamp down on oversaving, with its
equally ad hoc mandatory distribution rules and so forth. A consistent,
progressive, postpaid consumption-without-estate tax is an attractive vehicle for just such ends. This tax system allows and even encourages people to build up large stores of nominally "private" wealth.
These tax-favored accounts can be monitored or regulated, however
loosely, much as IRAs, 401(k)s, pension plans, and other large pools of

"private" savings (e.g., the endowments of nonprofits) are today. Any withdrawal from the accounts to finance private preclusive use will bear the brunt of progressive tax rates. Nor will this system let second and third generation heirs off the social hook, as the current, porous, income-with-realization-with-estate tax all too often does. To the contrary, the heirs will bear a tax when and as they withdraw "their" savings to consume. The system works like a global carryover basis regime, where the basis of all savings and investments is zero. Strnad (this volume) is right to fret that some future government might view the tax-favored accounts as an object of confiscation, but this is no more true for generally tax-favored savings accounts than for the ad hoc tax-favored savings accounts we have to day. Whatever America's failings, we seem to have found a way to remain credibly committed to not simply taking the private wealth of the most privileged few.

On the micro level, such fundamental reform will let life-cycle savers be life-cycle savers and, as just suggested, will facilitate if not encourage bequest and precautionary savings. What of the myopic masses? Here, another mistake of the flawed early marriage of behavioral economics and fundamental tax reform is the conclusion that if we adopt fundamental tax reform in lieu of ad hoc tax-favored savings vehicles, there is no remaining role for the lessons of behavioral economics. This is wrong. There is no reason why the ideas of Thaler and Bernatzi (2004), in their Save More Tomorrow™ plan, or of Choi et al. (2006), in their idea that the default should be set for workers to be "in" their employer-provided pension plans, should not take hold in a world of comprehensive postpaid consumption taxation. To the contrary, the argument above has led to the conclusion that these ideas can *only* work, in any enduring fashion, in such a world where arbitrage against them bears a tax price. It is another characteristic of our biases as a tax policy community that we can only think of tax-based inducements, as if a man with a hammer could only use nails. Employers can still give matching funds, and the government can, too, to encourage private savings in a world fundamentally set up not to discourage it. Let a thousand flowers bloom, and let the market try to create "focal" and salient savings plans in a setting where theory supports the potential practical efficacy of just such ideas.

The facts also suggest another approach to savings. I strongly suspect, at least given current cultural attitudes and mores, and the structures of our capitalist, consumerist marketplace, that whatever the government does via fiscal policy, most Americans will not save, period. We can and ought to look at the full range of social policies—not just tax—that have led to this being the case. What is unknown and almost certainly unknowable is what kind of people we would be today if we had not gone down the path we did in the first place. But there is in any event much to be said for accepting the facts as the facts. Letting those people so inclined to "oversave" do so seems one perfectly sensible response to this brute fact of the matter. Creating and providing nonfungible and secure government benefits, such as Medicare, old age and disability insurance, and education, seems another. Of course, getting the government to save more, or dissave less, may be part of the answer, too, but let us leave that one for another Groundhog Day.

10.4.3   Behavioral Economics, Redux

I promised pages ago that I would come back and discuss how it is that fundamental tax reform and behavioral economics might have a stable, long-term, productive marriage. Banishing ad-hocery from the union is an important first step. I have argued to replace the ever-growing panoply of ad hoc tax-favored savings vehicles in an income tax structure with a consistent, fundamental conversion to a postpaid consumption tax, allowing the market or even the government to use salient savings vehicles within such a consistent theoretical structure. This advice follows from—it does not contradict—the lessons of behavioral economics and common sense. So, too, with the advice that a better, less fungible social safety net, wherein the society provides in-kind goods to those suffering from want of private funds, makes more sense than trying to trick people into savings in a world generally set up both to discourage (because of the tax system) and to require (because of the absence of more generous in-kind support) private savings.

There is another domain in which behavioral economics is relevant to fundamental tax reform. The topic to this point, of individual savings, has concerned a set of actions that by definition endure through time. Thus we have the possibility—I have suggested the likelihood—of individuals coming to arbitrage against the tax-favored savings accounts, with an institutional, market-driven economy set up to help them do just that. But recall the ground rule about some actions staying pretty close to the decisional bone. Sometimes what is important is precisely what the people think about something. So it is, I believe, and have worked extensively to test and prove experimentally (see generally McCaffery and Baron 2006), with fundamental tax reform. It is a platitude that fundamental tax reform cannot occur without broad popular support and understanding, typically coalesced by presidential "leadership." But how can the people, preoccupied by the demands of daily life, understand the lessons of public finance, such as optimal taxation and corporate tax incidence? And why should they try? The benefits to greater knowledge are miniscule, the costs significant. And yet it is far from clear that politicians have a properly aligned incentive here to maximize welfare: think of a single politician suggesting abolition of the corporate tax, as an example. In private markets, arbitrage against behavioral anomalies is a private good; in public markets, it is a public good, predictably undersupplied (McCaffery and Baron 2006).

Behavioral economics can and I believe should teach those of us interested in fundamental tax reform how and why ordinary citizens think the way that they do about matters of public finance. Behavioral insights can also help us think of mechanisms that might tend toward the adoption and widespread support for policies "we" know, from our expert vantage points, to be good for us all. These are important roles for a discipline to play, more enduring than helping to craft ad hoc and counterproductive savings plans.

10.5   Closing Thoughts

We need fundamental tax reform. And fundamental tax reform must begin with fundamental—clear, good, rigorous—thinking and theory. It must also begin, I believe, with a respect for the people. Viewing the masses of citizenry as confused and helpless souls, on their own lights, who need to be tricked by sleight of hand into doing what is in their own self-interests to do, will not lead to success. Rather we theorists and policy makers should treat ordinary people as noble and thoughtful yet busy, overworked, and overtired workers, who have neither the time nor the reasons to discern the lessons of optimal public finance. We should not use the insights of behavioral economics in an ad hoc way, for ad hoc reform that builds irrational mechanisms onto a system in the hope that two or more wrongs can make a right. Rather, we should identify objectives and move toward them with coherent strategies, predicated on our understanding of how people actually behave—which, after all, is the point of behavioral economics.

Let's return to Punxsutawney, PA, on Groundhog Day. Phil Connors explores every angle he can to manipulate the situation of his endlessly repeating the same day. But he cannot do what he really wants to do: get the girl, of course, here named Rita (played by Andie MacDowell). Phil learns Rita's secrets; he teaches himself great skills such as piano playing and French; he even amasses wealth and baubles and beads. None of this works to woo Rita. What he must do, to escape from the perpetual present, is to learn to look within, to change his internal self, and to come up with a more respectful view of others, especially the object of his desires. Then at last Phil can move on, to February 3.

It is high time for fundamental tax reformers to turn within, too. The ultimate lesson is about how we think. Like Phil Connors, tax policy theorists seem trapped in a perpetual present, unable to learn the lessons of the past to paint a better future. Our tax system, or at least the part of it (the income tax) that we endlessly discuss, is designed to tax (i.e. discourage) productive work and to double-tax savings. This made sense once, when the tax was small in breadth and depth, and meant to exert a toll on East Coast financiers (McCaffery 2005a). But as the tax grew in scale and scope, its anti-savings bias became a problem. We tried to patch things up, here and there, but we never went back to first principles. We got addicted to the quick fix, and started to pile on more and more ad hoc tax-favored savings vehicles into the code. This made little or no sense, in theory, and so we needed an irrational model of behavior to justify what we were doing. We turned to behavioral economics, which most theorists neither well understood nor generally accepted, and picked findings, ad hoc, off the shelf—people were myopic, but they could be tricked by salient cues. The floodgates opened. As the tax system grew more and more complex, we debated the "data," wondering against all reason if the policies we had advocated "worked," comfortable in the knowledge, or hope, that we had a theory to make sense of it all. But we did not. If we had thought through the theory again, we could have come up with better answers. We could have fundamental tax reform, a more coherent tax policy, and a more sensible global approach to the problem of undersavings on the micro and macro levels. We do not have any of that, today, and have not had any of it, for decades. It is time to move on, beyond Groundhog Day.

It is not, however, too late. It is still Groundhog Day. But that cannot last forever.

Discussion

Pamela H. Moomau

Economists' case for fundamental tax reform is generally founded on the basis of predicted responses to tax reform by perfectly rational, utility-maximizing economic decision makers. Reform that reduces or eliminates taxes on savings is expected to remove disincentives to save, thus increasing total savings, investment, and thus labor productivity and economic output. The behavioral economics literature, in contrast, focuses on economic behaviors that are not consistent with the predictions of these standard economic models. Particularly with respect to savings behavior, behavioral economics finds that many people do not tend to save as much as the life-cycle consumption hypothesis (LCH) would predict, and they therefore may not respond to changes in after-tax returns to savings as LCH models would predict.

One difficulty in bringing lessons from behavioral economics to bear on the best approach to tax reform is that as Slemrod and McCaffery state, "the field self-consciously lacks a general 'field theory' of human behavior" (McCaffery and Slemrod, 2004, p. 4). The behavioral economics literature comprises a number of empirical and experimental studies that paint a relatively consistent picture of individuals not making savings choices according to the LCH, rational actor model, and it includes some attempts at modeling certain types of non-LCH choices in an internally consistent manner. (See Bernheim and Rangel 2005 for a description of some of these models.) But an underlying model of individual choice that would be consistent with all the observations of seemingly "irrational" choices in the behavioral economics literature remains "unknown," and is possibly "unknowable." Yet, tax reform is a "general field" type of public policy endeavor.

The views expressed are solely those of the author, and not the members or staff of the Joint Committee on Taxation.

McCaffery notes that many observers look to the discipline of behavioral economics to prescribe an approach that relies on "ad hoc tax-favored savings vehicles" over "more fundamental reform" to promote more savings. But he adamantly resists this conclusion, declaring at the beginning of his chapter: "I mean to bury the most commonly ... suggested application of behavioral economics to fundamental tax reform: using the insights of behavioralism to support proposals to promote individual savings through ad hoc, tax-favored vehicles." He suggests that, given what he views as failed efforts at incremental tax reform such as the Tax Reform Act of 1986, the discipline of behavioral economics can best inform the debate only when it has "escape[d] the clutches of 'ad hocery'"—that the lesson from behavioral economics is that only fundamental tax reform will achieve an increase in savings.

This viewpoint seems to owe to an emphasis on a subset of the findings of behavioral economics with respect to individuals' savings behavior, and may be unduly pessimistic with respect to the public policy potential for carefully implemented tax-favored savings vehicles.

McCaffery's argument focuses, in particular, on two types of observations about the findings with respect to savings in behavioral economics. The first would seem to be a rejection of the underpinnings of behavioral economics, in that he contends that many people are behaving rationally when they choose not to save. What may appear under a simple LCH model to be suboptimal savings for many individuals is in fact optimal, given the full set of personal and institutional constraints and public policy incentives faced by those individuals. For example, it may not be optimal for some individuals with limited long-run earnings opportunities to save, given that the availability of some government transfer payment programs declines with wealth accumulation. In addition some forms of "investment," such as expenditures on education for oneself or one's children, may look like consumption when in fact they are likely for many families to yield a higher rate of return than conventionally measured savings and investment.

This line of argument is quite appealing to conventional economics, affirming as it does the validity of the well-behaved rational actor model of economic behavior. And the notion that individuals are in fact saving more optimally than it would appear has some support in the literature. For example, Scholz, Seshadri, and Khitatrakun (2006) find, in a recent paper using data from the University of Michigan

Health and Retirement Survey, that when expected social security benefits, defined benefit pensions, and other forms of wealth accrual are taken into account, households who were between the ages of 51 and 61 in 1992 have been saving optimally, or under certain parameterizations, more than optimally. They, of course, caution that this finding may not be generalizable to other cohorts over different time periods.

McCaffery offers as a "known" statistic the observation that personal savings rates as measured by the Bureau of Economic Analysis (BEA) have been drifting downward for decades, reaching negative territory in 2005. According to the most recent BEA release as of this writing, they have continued into even more negative territory in the first quarter of 2006 (National Income and Product Accounts, tab. 2.1, updated May 25, 2006). However, this apparent "fact" of grossly inadequate savings rates may more properly fall into the category of "unknown, but knowable," because BEA personal savings statistics do not take into account changes in wealth due to unrealized appreciation of individuals' stock of assets. Thus these figures may be misleading with respect to how inadequate personal savings really are.

If we were to stop right here, the conclusion might be that individuals do in fact respond to savings incentives in an LCH manner when incentives and savings amounts are properly measured, that personal savings may be larger than we at first might think, and that special tax-subsidized savings vehicles are therefore not necessary or desirable. Of course, this observation could also lead to the conclusion that there is no need for any form of consumption tax reform to promote savings, as savings are apparently already at "optimal levels" based on the evidence of individual choices. Setting aside the fact that (the observations above notwithstanding) there is a general consensus that there is not enough savings in the US economy, this conclusion would not be in the spirit of analyzing the prospects of growth-promoting fundamental consumption tax reform. And it is not in the spirit of analyzing what behavioral economics brings to the table regarding tax policy and saving. Thus we turn to the second set of observations from behavioral economics that McCaffery deploys to discredit the utility of ad hoc tax-preferred savings vehicles.

One of the main findings in behavioral economics is that many individuals appear to have "time-inconsistent" consumption preferences, making consumption choices that imply they value consumption in the current period much more highly than consumption in the future but see little distinction in the value of consumption at different points in the future. Some behavioral economists have shown that in theory people with such quasi-hyperbolic discounting in their utility functions may be induced to save more if offered a savings subsidy such as those provided in certain tax-preferred savings vehicles. (See Bernheim and Rangel 2005 for a summary of some of this literature.) These individuals, recognizing their time-inconsistent preferences as a form of lack of self control, would use, particularly, postpaid savings vehicles to bolster their future self-control by precommitting themselves to save.

However, McCaffery contends that through various borrowing and arbitrage arrangements, both rational life-cycle savers and hyperbolic discounters can essentially extract some or all of the tax subsidies provided for in postpaid vehicles without actually increasing their amount of savings. And, he points out, prepaid vehicles offer no apparent incentives to non-LCH savers (to whom he refers as BLCH savers for behavioral life-cycle consumption hypothesis) because prepaid vehicles do not offer any up-front benefits to entice the BLCH savers into precommitting to increased savings.

McCaffery observes that despite a proliferation of tax-preferred savings vehicles in the United States since the 1940s, there has been no apparent increase in savings. By itself this fact does not mean the savings vehicles have been ineffective, as it does not address the question of how much savings there might have been without these vehicles. However, empirical investigations of the effects of some of the more recent such vehicles, Internal Revenue Code Section 401(k) plans and individual retirement arrangements (IRAs) on savings have yielded mixed results. While savings within these accounts have clearly grown and contracted in predictable directions, depending on the restrictions placed on their use, the empirical challenge is disentangling how much of this flow of savings into and out of these accounts represents substitution with other forms of savings, as opposed to changes in savings. Thus McCaffery argues that the effect of such savings vehicles on personal savings remains in the unknown category. See Poterba, Venti, and Wise (1996) and Engen, Gale, and Scholz (1996) for two opposing interpretations of this literature. Each set of authors claims to know the effects of these vehicles on savings; since the former know that they increase savings, and the latter that they do not, it seems McCaffery's evaluation on the state of knowledge with respect to this issue stands.

Early analysis of usage of a more recent tax subsidy for savings for low- and moderate-income individuals, the saver's credit, indicates a continuing pattern of light usage of such incentives. Enacted in 2001, the saver's credit provides a tax credit for up to 50 percent of an individual's elective deferrals or voluntary contributions to the following types of savings plans: 401(k), 403(b), 457(b), simplified employee pension–IRA (Sep-IRA), savings incentive match plans for employees (SIMPLE), and traditional or Roth IRAs. The maximum matched amount is $2,000, and the maximum match rate phases out from 50 percent for joint filers with incomes of $30,000 or less to 10 percent for joint filers with incomes up to $50,000. Koenig and Harvey (2005) found that usage of the credit in 2002 and 2003 increased with income (thus decreasing with the amount of the subsidy) but did not go above 19 percent for any income group in either year. On average, usage of the credit by eligible taxpayers was about 14 percent in 2002 and 15 percent in 2003.

Because this credit is subject to a fairly complex set of rules, it might be expected that information costs could be affecting usage. In 2002 fully one-third of taxpayer who were eligible for the saver's credit *and who made contributions or deferrals that were eligible for the credit* failed to claim the credit on their tax returns. Encouragingly, information costs apparently diminish with tax filing assistance. While only 44 percent of eligible taxpayers who made qualifying contributions and prepared their own tax return claimed the credit, 76 percent of those with qualifying contributions who used a tax preparer or tax software claimed the credit.

The role of information, framing, and default options in determining peoples' savings choices is an area of behavioral economics that McCaffery fails to bring into his discussion of tax-preferred savings vehicles. Perhaps the most promising result in terms of increasing participation of individuals in tax-preferred savings plans has been the observation, in a number of studies in recent years, that people can be induced to participate more and contribute more to tax-preferred savings vehicles by changing the default choice from electing out to electing into participation. Gale, Iwry, and Orszag (2005) provide a summary of this literature. This result is consistent with the behavioral economics finding that people tend to express a preference for the status quo, and to exhibit hyperbolic discounting in the evaluation of the costs of information gathering about savings options as well as with respect to consumption. One objection that has been raised to relying on a default "opt-in" option for 410(k) participation is that in the presence of heterogeneous optimal savings paths, the default "opt-in" option may still result in a substantial amount of nonoptimal savings decision-making. Choi et al. (2005) find that increased 401(k) savings relative to the "opt in" default can be achieved by making "active choice" (requiring employees to make a choice regarding participation) the default option, while preserving savers' ability to make optimal choices.

A recent experiment on the incentive effects of providing matches at different rates (of 0, 20, and 50 percent) for contributions to IRAs was conducted by Duflo et al. (2006) in conjunction with H&R Block. This was a simpler program than the saver's credit, as the match amount was not linked to income or to the availability of different types of employer-sponsored savings plans. Matching amounts for contributions to H&R Block "X-IRAs" (which are available to all taxpayers) were randomly assigned to all filers in 60 H&R Block offices in St. Louis between March 5 and April 5, 2005. Consistent with conventional economic theory about savings, contributions to IRAs increased with the match rate, and increased with the income of the taxpayers.

Of particular interest from a behavioral economics standpoint, contribution rates were higher for taxpayers working with certain preparers, suggesting that the way the information about the X-IRA and the match was framed influenced taxpayers' choices. Further indication of the importance of information in taxpayer usage of these incentives comes from the observed interactions between the saver's credit and the H&R Block X-IRA. On one hand, the higher match rate afforded by joint eligibility for the saver's credit and the X-IRA did result in a higher take-up rate of the X-IRA by saver's credit users. However, some taxpayers whose income was just over the eligibility cliff for the saver's credit could have increased their tax refund by contributing to the X-IRA, and thus qualifying for the saver's credit, but they failed to do so. Most taxpayers eligible for the saver's credit failed to contribute enough to maximize their match.

Since these X-IRA accounts stayed with H&R Block there is also some information about the extent of "arbitrage" type activity conducted by participants. Participants could have made the contribution to receive the match, and then withdrawn the contribution without penalty, and retained the credit. Very few individuals followed that procedure. Duflo et al. speculate that this failure to "game" the system was most likely due to lack of information about the gaming possibilities. This finding casts some doubt on the likelihood of widespread arbitraging of such vehicles, thus providing, perhaps, more hope than

McCaffery holds out for the efficacy of tax-preferred savings vehicles in actually increasing savings.

These experiments indicate that such behavioral economics—informed tactics as changing the default option for 401(k)s and providing both promotional information and matches for IRA contributions can provide some additional incentives for participation in tax-preferred savings plans. Perhaps some of the non–time-inconsistency-related insights from behavioral economics can provide guidance for more successful ad hoc savings policy initiatives in the future. However, persistently low take-up rates even within these experiments would seem to confirm McCaffery's general pessimism about the efficacy of "ad hocery" in promoting large increases the rate of savings by BLCH savers.

McCaffery concludes that fundamental tax reform, in the form of switching from a tax system that is primarily income-based to one that is consumption-based is the only way to effectively increase savings. Noting the failure of several past attempts to effect such a wholesale policy shift, he suggests that what behavioral economics can contribute to this effort is a lesson in the importance of "framing" in bringing about such fundamental tax reform. This is an interesting transformation in the application of behavioral economics—from analyzing how individuals respond to incentives and cues in making economic decisions to drawing implications about influencing political choices made by policy makers. However, it seems likely that policy makers are ahead, rather than behind behavioral economists, with respect to understanding the importance of framing an issue in the policy-making process.

Discussion

Jeff Strnad

Ed McCaffery's central goal in his chapter is to attack the use of behavioral insights "to support proposals to promote individual savings through ad hoc, tax-favored vehicles" (hereinafter, AHTFVs). The main arguments are that AHTFVs are extraneous or counterproductive for rational "life-cycle hypothesis" savers under the current system, AHTFVs do not help individuals who undersave because they are myopic, and a better approach would be to adopt a consistent postpaid (cash-flow) consumption tax (hereinafter, CFCT) with no estate tax.

The chapter includes many interesting and cogent points. The most important are that heterogeneity among individuals matters in considering policy; optimal second-best schemes do not necessarily involve each individual saving optimally—instead oversaving by some might offset undersaving by others; it is important to keep in mind that social institutions (e.g., markets) may mitigate or circumvent cognitive errors on the part of individuals; and each individual may mix mistakes with rationality—the "mixture" point.

This comment picks up on these points, especially heterogeneity and the mixture point to make four critiques: (1) AHTFVs can help some of the "myopic" if we consider a range of cognitive functioning, (2) the discussion of the CFCT proposal downplays heterogeneity in ways that both understate the power of the proposal and hide some of its weaknesses, (3) concentrating saving and wealth may have major effects that undermine the benefits of the proposal, and (4) the relative power of non–tax-tightening moves as an adjunct to current AHTFVs is dismissed too quickly.

Helping the Myopic

McCaffery makes it quite clear that AHTFVs will not help if a person is a naive hyperbolic discounter since that person wants to and will attempt to overconsume currently. Prepaid AHTFVs will have no effect, and the naive hyperbolic discounter will use the up front deduction feature of postpaid AHTFVs to consume more presently, offsetting the investment in the AHTFV by fresh borrowing. McCaffery's conclusion is very sensible when restricted to this type of individual: it is not smart policy to go to great lengths to try to force people to do something they do not want to do.

Nonetheless, AHTFVs may help if we consider departures from rational life-cycle hypothesis saving other than naive hyperbolic discounting. For instance, Bernheim and Rangel (2005a) propose a model of savings with cue-triggered mistakes. In any given period, individuals behave rationally with high probability. At random times, however, the individuals make mistakes in the form of consumption binges. When not in the binge state, individuals will attempt to blunt anticipated future binges by imposing restrictions on credit (e.g., by destroying credit cards) and by exploiting the restrictions on AHTFVs to build up illiquid savings accounts. This model is very much in the spirit of McCaffery's mixture point—people mix rationality and "mistakes," but McCaffery adopts a more rigid view similar to naive hyperbolic discounting when discussing the impact of AHTFVs.

More generally, behavioral economics phenomena can be subtle, with various shades of the same phenomenon calling for quite different policy responses. As pointed out in Bernheim and Rangel (2005b), an excellent survey, researchers have only explored some of the possible behavioral channels that might affect saving, and there is a dearth of empirical evidence comparing the alternative behavioral models that have been developed. An illustration that is internal to the chapters of this volume involves "mental accounting," the tendency for individuals to view different accounts or types of resources in isolation when making saving and consumption decisions. Alan Auerbach (chapter 1 in this volume) discusses some positive effects that may arise from AHTFVs due to mental accounting: people may exercise self-control by isolating savings in specialized accounts. A related argument is that the existence of AHTFVs has a salience effect—inducing individuals to focus on their savings decisions when confronted with issues such as how much to invest in their 401(k) plans. On the other hand, as pointed out by McCaffery, mental accounting may lead to the problem that the left hand does not know what the right hand is doing. For example, substantial IRA balances might make an individual feel secure as a "saver," even though the individual has simultaneously run up offsetting high-interest credit card balances. Each view has a following and a literature.

It would be very valuable if behavioral economics researchers spent more time detailing the alternative implications of different behavioral models and the relative salience of the models. We need a "thicker" view of the behavioral situation both across individuals, and consistent with McCaffery's mixture point, within each individual.

Heterogeneity and the CFCT Proposal

In discussing the CFTC proposal, it seems that McCaffery unintentionally downplays important heterogeneity considerations. Thus he says, "most Americans will not save, period," and "letting those people so inclined to 'oversave' to do so seems one perfectly sensible response to the brute fact of the matter." This language conjures up the image of a barbell-shaped distribution where at one end a mass of people save nothing, while at the other there is a mass of oversavers. But is there no mass of people in the middle who are elastic with respect to schemes to increase savings? The literature seems to suggest that there is such a mass. McCaffery himself refers to the consistent finding that default options matter—if the default option under a 401(k) or other AHTFV is to save, then many will do so who would not if the default was no saving. There is much additional evidence that points in the same direction. For instance, Bernheim, Garret, and Maki (2001) find that high school students exposed to mandated financial education accumulate more assets as adults.

Downplaying a potential mass of people in the "middle" who are elastic to saving incentives, including AHTFVs, results in underemphasis of one of the strongest arguments in favor of the CFCT proposal. In particular, if one buys the assumption that a CFCT would shut off the arbitrage routes that exist currently, then, as McCaffery notes, behavioral based schemes to increase savings will work under the CFTC that do not work under the current system. In the absence of the ability to do low cost offsetting borrowing, savings induced by behaviorally centered schemes, including some forms of AHTFVs, will "stick," and there may be a virtuous cycle as individuals see the results as assets accumulate. If there is a large mass of elastic people in the "middle," this feature of the CFTC will have tremendous value. In the fourth section below, I discuss some reasons that go beyond individual saving for inducing saving behavior in this "middle" group.

496 Jeff Strnad

On the negative side, the CFCT's savings effects may be less than expected if one considers heterogeneous savings motivations. If the CFTC is progressive enough, life-cycle savers aiming at very high consumption during retirement will be discouraged. On the other hand, steep progressivity will have less impact on dynastic savers and no impact at all on "empire builders" such as Andrew Carnegie. Carnegie in fact may be taken as the hero of various McCaffery sagas—Carnegie being a man who was not motivated to make bequests or to consume but strictly by the desire to enhance production, building an efficient, dynamic steel industry. Given that dynasty savers and empire builders already can avoid being taxed on savings (for reasons pointed out in the chapter), adopting a CFTC might even have a net negative effect on all current savers as a group. Those motivated to save in order to enjoy high consumption at some later date will save less and no other major group of savers will save more.

Possible Side Effects of Concentrated Saving and Wealth

Some of the language in the chapter suggests that we should give up on inducing the masses to save and focus on bulking up saving by "oversavers." The idea is that aggregate saving will reach a desirable level and that transfer programs will shift an acceptable level of resources in the future to the large group of people who do not save. Suppose that under this program we end up with 10 percent of the population saving huge amounts of money while 90 percent are wards of the state, drawing their retirement resources from the social safety net. This 90 percent group is likely to lack any kind of saving ethic along with any savings, and individuals in the group very well might become myopic about aggregate saving as well as their own saving.

This later point raises an important question: Is this policy time consistent or will the wards of the state vote for policies that confiscate wealth in ways that lower welfare? Will they confiscate Carnegie's steel empire before he finishes building it up to its fullest height of production efficiency? It is possible that general equilibrium effects of the savers' accumulations such as higher wages would flow out consistently enough that the ninety percent group would not resort to inefficient confiscations. Nonetheless, there is a serious issue of political dynamics here.

Adding AHTFVs (or non–tax-based ad hoc vehicles) to encourage saving by a broader set of people under a CFTC might be a good way to address this issue. The target would be the "middle" group who are not big savers but who are not hopelessly myopic either. If one buys the argument that the CFTC makes saving stick more easily, these measures would tend to be effective. An "ownership society" effect might follow. A large group of people would become politically defensive about their savings accounts, however modest, and, at the same time, would become less myopic socially as well as individually—perhaps even becoming activists on issues such as government deficits. It is worth noting that substantial "ownership society" benefits could flow from AHTFV devices even if they induced relatively little "new saving." Their real purpose would be to create time consistency and make the world safe for future Andrew Carnegies to drive economic progress.

Tightening Moves—The CFCT versus the Current System

The chapter assumes "arbitrage would not be possible" under its CFCT proposal because debt used to consume would trigger tax. In contrast, measures to tighten up AHTFVs under current law to avoid arbitrage via offsetting borrowing would amount to "patching up a Maginot Line." Individuals would still want to arbitrage. The costs to do so would be higher, but retail and credit market institutions would help lower these costs. In the face of these conclusions, McCaffery avoids comparing the proposed CFCT to alternative tightening moves using AHTFVs in the current system. I believe the situation is not nearly as clear-cut.

First, the CFCT, in practice, would have holes that allow arbitrage or similar maneuvers. One big problem is that the lines between consumption, borrowing, and investment often are not very clear. The possibility that taxpayers would exploit these ambiguities to engage in tax-free consumption is a major potential weakness of the CFCT.

Individuals facing a CFCT might even be able to construct schemes very similar to the buy/borrow/die strategy under current law emphasized by McCaffery. Suppose, for example, that the taxpayer pays $X for ongoing consumption under a "rental contract" that effectively provides for payment with interest far in the future. The contract specifies a nominal (very small) "rent" per period and allows the buyer to take "full possession" of the consumption by paying a fixed amount. The phrasing deliberately casts the situation as if the buyer were purchasing a durable asset. Upon the buyer's death the "purchase option" is triggered automatically and the seller is paid with interest out of a specified "postpaid" savings account where the buyer deposited the full purchase price initially and in which interest has been accruing at the compound market rate. "Consumption" occurs in the final period of the buyer's life as a result of the payment, but if the buyer dies insolvent, there will be no money to pay taxes to the government. The end result would be that the taxpayer has consumed tax free, paying X rather than $X/(1 - \tau)$, where τ is the applicable tax rate. The scheme works by using disguised borrowing. One would expect that retail and credit markets would devise appropriate strategies and standard approaches to make the disguise effective and low cost. Of course, one would expect that the government would attempt to block such schemes just as it has attempted to address buy/borrow/die arbitrage under current law. The point is that there are problems and holes under the CFCT. In comparing approaches, it is not appropriate to assume these problems away.

Second, there are imaginable tightening moves under the current system that might be very effective. To take an extreme example, suppose that at age 59 or older, the law provides a simple process that makes all debt excusable to the extent that individual net wealth falls below some fixed amount such as $2,000,000. "All debt" would include secured debt such as home mortgages. The likely credit market response would be to make it hard or impossible for individuals without substantial savings to hold debt when nearing retirement and during retirement. This system would guarantee that amounts saved in IRAs and other AHTFVs as well as Social Security wealth will be fully available as savings to individuals who have failed to accumulate substantial assets by the beginning of retirement. This scheme has obvious drawbacks. It would lead to a drop in welfare for rational individuals who would borrow at 59 and later if unconstrained. The politics may be tricky—how would politicians react to the elderly losing homes because they cannot refinance their mortgages at 59? Finally, this scheme would not be immune from evasion possibilities. For example, children of elderly parents might buy the parents' home when they reach 59, mortgage it, and then charge the parents a nominal amount of rent. It is interesting to note that at least the first two drawbacks might be less serious than they seem. If individuals have present bias but also "foresight" in the sense of being aware of the bias, they may favor drastic public measures that commit them to save. Malin (2005) discusses savings floor policies (i.e., requiring a particular level of net savings) in a general equilibrium setting where individuals are hyperbolic discounters with foresight but vary in the severity of their present bias. In the model, individuals exhibit "extreme preferences": favoring either no savings floor at all or a savings floor so high that it precludes borrowing and lending. The savings floor functions as a "public commitment" device which may lead to a net increase in welfare as well as sufficient political support for enactment.

Regardless of what one thinks of any of these schemes, there is a general point. The CFCT is not self-executing and would require "tightening" measures to shore up various weak points. On the other hand, there are ways to make AHTFVs more effective in the current environment. It would be useful for future work to compare tightening the current system to a real-world CFTC that would require its own tightening measures.

Concluding Thoughts

The theme of this volume is to speculate on what is "known, unknown, and unknowable" about various aspects of tax reform. I find it most comfortable to adopt a Bayesian view of this task. Under this view the three categories blend into a continuum. The "known" consists of features for which we have sharply concentrated posterior probabilities at present, meaning there may be a current professional consensus that certain crucial elasticities or other parameters lie in a particular narrow range with high probability. The "unknowable" typically involves some feature for which our beliefs are more diffuse and for which there are apparent impediments to sharpening our knowledge. In my opinion two aspects characterize our knowledge about behavioral economics as applied to tax reform. First, it is not very clear which models of behavior are most relevant to key issues such as the connection between savings and various tax policies or even if any of the current models is suitable. Second, despite uncertainty about the behavioral models, there is a good chance that behavioral phenomena play an important, if not decisive, role for many tax policy issues. There is much work to be done to clarify the uncertainties, and this work may have a major impact on the way in which we assess potential reforms.

Notes

I thank James Alm, Alan Auerbach, Colin Camerer, Bill Gale, James R. Hines Jr., and George Zodrow for helpful conversations and editorial assistance; Pamela Moomau and Jeff Strnad for their thoughtful commentaries; and Ted Dillman for excellent research assistance.

1. Once again, mine is an analytic claim about possibilities, not an empirical claim about the extent to which the "buy/borrow/die" strategy is in fact implemented. But certainly the fully "rational" investor/saver would be aware of the possibilities; there is ample evidence that rich investors are; and the mere possibilities of the strategy constrain important elements of tax system design. I discuss all this at much greater length in McCaffery (2002, 2005a).

2. Note that even if many or most Americans are indeed saving enough (see Scholz, Seshadri, and Khitatrakum 2006 for an argument that they are or might be), this chapter's basic conclusions obtain, as these "optimal" savers could continue to do so under a general consumption tax structure.

3. I do not share the skepticism of Strnad (discussion in this volume) on this point, though, if that is what it is. Strnad, in his fourth section, lists a possible "arbitrage" mechanism under a consistent cash-flow consumption tax, in which, as I understand it, an individual borrows to consume today, as by purchasing a long-lived asset, and defers repayment until after his death, when the government is left holding the bag. But it is hard to ascertain who such a lender would be, and I do not understand why the government would give him, her or it priority over its own claims to whatever monies were left in the estate.

Bibliography

Aaron, Henry J., and Harvey Galper. 1985. *Assessing Tax Reform*. Washington: Brookings Institution.

Aaron, Henry J., and William G. Gale, eds. 1996. *Economic Effects of Fundamental Tax Reform*. Washington: Brookings Institution Press.

Aaron, Henry J., Harvey Galper, and Joseph Pechman, eds. 1988. *Uneasy Compromise: Problems of a Hybrid Income-Consumption Tax*. Washington: Brookings Institution.

Abel, Andrew B. 2005. Optimal taxation when consumers have endogenous benchmark levels of consumption. *Review of Economic Studies* 72: 21–42.

Abel, Andrew B., and Janice C. Eberly. 2002. Investment and q with fixed costs: An empirical analysis. Working paper. Wharton School, University of Pennsylvania.

Abel, Andrew B., and Janice C. Eberly. 2004. Q theory without adjustment costs and cash flow effects without financing constraints. Working paper. Wharton School, University of Pennsylvania.

Abel, Andrew B., and Janice C. Eberly. 2005. Investment, valuation, and growth options. Working paper. Wharton School, University of Pennsylvania.

Acga, Senay, and Abon Mozumdar. 2005. The impact of capital market imperfections on investment–cash flow sensitivity. Working paper. George Washington University.

Ackerman, Jonathan Z., and Rosanne Altshuler. 2006. Constrained tax reform: How political and economic constraints affect the formation of tax policy proposals. *National Tax Journal* 59: 165–87.

Alesina, Alberto, Edward Glaeser, and Bruce Sacerdote. 2005. Work and leisure in the U.S. and Europe: Why so different. Working paper 11278. National Bureau of Economic Research, Cambridge, MA.

Allayannis, George, and Abon Mozumdar. 2004. The impact of negative cash flow and influential observations on investment–cash flow sensitivity estimates. *Journal of Banking and Finance* 28: 901–30.

Alti, Aydogan. 2003. How sensitive is investment to cash flow when financing is frictionless? *Journal of Finance* 58: 707–22.

Altig, David, Alan J. Auerbach, Lawrence J. Kotlikoff, Ken A. Smetters, and Jan Walliser. 2001. Simulating fundamental tax reform in the United States. *American Economic Review* 91: 574–95.

Altonji, Joseph G., Fumio Hayashi, and Laurence J. Kotlikoff. 1997. Parental altruism and inter vivos transfers: Theory and evidence. *Journal of Political Economy* 105(6): 1121–66.

Altshuler, Rosanne, and Harry Grubert. 2001. Where will they go if we go territorial? Dividend exemption and the foreign location decisions of U.S. multinational corporations. *National Tax Journal* 54: 787–809.

Altshuler, Rosanne, and Harry Grubert. 2002. Repatriation taxes, repatriation strategies, and multinational financial policy. *Journal of Public Economics* 87: 73–107.

Altshuler, Rosanne, and Harry Grubert. 2004. Taxpayer responses to competitive tax policies and tax policy responses to competitive taxpayers: Recent evidence. *Tax Notes International* 34: 1349–62.

Altshuler, Rosanne, and Harry Grubert. 2006. The three parties in the race to the bottom: Host governments, home governments and multinational corporations. *Tax Notes* 110: 979–92.

Altshuler, Rosanne, and R. Glenn Hubbard. 2002. The effect of the Tax Reform Act of 1986 on the location of assets in financial services firms. *Journal of Public Economics* 87: 109–27.

Altshuler, Rosanne, Harry Grubert, and T. Scott Newlon. 2001. Has U.S. investment abroad become more sensitive to tax rates? In James R. Hines Jr., ed., *International Taxation and Multinational Activity*. Chicago: University of Chicago Press.

Amromin, Gene, Paul Harrison, and Steve Sharpe. 2005. How did the 2003 dividend tax cut affect stock prices? Finance and economics discussion paper series 61. Board of Governors of the Federal Reserve System, Washington, DC.

Anderson, Torben M., and Robert R. Dogonowski. 2004. What should optimal income taxes smooth? *Journal of Public Economic Theory* 6: 491–507.

Andrews, Edmund L., and David D. Kirkpatrick. 2004. GOP constituencies split on tax change. *New York Times*, November 21, p. C-1.

Andrews, William D. 1972. Personal deductions in an ideal income tax. *Harvard Law Review* 86: 309–85.

Andrews, William D. 1974. A consumption-type or cash flow personal income tax. *Harvard Law Review* 87: 1113–88.

Antos, Joseph R. 2006. Is there a right way to promote health insurance through the tax system. *National Tax Journal* 59: 477–90.

Atkinson, Anthony B., and Joseph E. Stiglitz. 1976. The design of tax structure: Direct versus indirect taxation. *Journal of Public Economics* 6: 55–75.

Auerbach, Alan J. 1979. Wealth maximization and the cost of capital. *Quarterly Journal of Economics* 93: 433–46.

Auerbach, Alan J. 1983a. Corporate taxation in the United States. *Brookings Papers on Economic Activity* 14: 1451–1505.

Auerbach, Alan J. 1983b. Taxation, corporate financial policy, and the cost of capital. *Journal of Economic Literature* 21: 905–40.

Auerbach, Alan J. 1985. The theory of excess burden and optimal taxation. In Alan Auerbach and Martin Feldstein, eds., *Handbook of Public Economics*, vol. 1. Amsterdam: Elsevier Science, North-Holland.

Auerbach, Alan J. 1989a. Tax reform and adjustment costs: The impact on investment and market value. *International Economic Review* 30: 939–62.

Auerbach, Alan J. 1989b. The deadweight loss from "Nonneutral" capital income taxation. *Journal of Public Economics* 40: 1–36.

Auerbach, Alan J. 1991. Retrospective capital gains taxation. *American Economic Review* 81: 167–78.

Auerbach, Alan J. 1996. Tax reform, capital allocation, efficiency and growth. In Henry Aaron and William Gale, eds., *Economic Effects of Fundamental Tax Reform*. Washington: Brookings Institution.

Auerbach, Alan J. 1997. The future of fundamental tax reform. *American Economic Review* 87: 143–46.

Auerbach, Alan J. 2002. Taxation and corporate financial policy. In Alan Auerbach and Martin Feldstein, eds., *Handbook of Public Economics*, vol. 3. Amsterdam: Elsevier Science, North-Holland.

Auerbach, Alan J. 2005. Who bears the corporate tax? A review of what we know. In James Poterba, ed., *Tax Policy and the Economy*, vol. 19. Cambridge: MIT Press.

Auerbach, Alan J. 2006. The choice between income and consumption taxes: A primer. Working paper 12307. National Bureau of Economic Research, Cambridge, MA.

Auerbach, Alan J., and Dale W. Jorgenson. 1980. Inflation-proof depreciation of assets. *Harvard Business Review* 58: 113–18.

Auerbach, Alan J., and Daniel Feenberg. 2000. The significance of federal taxes as automatic stabilizers. *Journal of Economic Perspectives* 14: 37–56.

Auerbach, Alan J., and Joel Slemrod. 1997. The economic effects of the Tax Reform Act of 1986. *Journal of Economic Literature* 35: 589–632.

Auerbach, Alan J., and Kevin A. Hassett. 1991. Recent U.S. investment behavior and the Tax Reform Act of 1986: A disaggregate view. *Carnegie-Rochester Conference Series on Public Policy* 35: 185–215.

Auerbach, Alan J., and Kevin A. Hassett. 2003. On the marginal source of investment funds. *Journal of Public Economics* 87: 205–32.

Auerbach, Alan J., and Kevin A. Hassett. 2005a. Conclusion. In Alan J. Auerbach and Kevin A. Hassett, eds., *Toward Fundamental Tax Reform*. Washington: AEI Press.

Auerbach, Alan J., and Kevin A. Hassett. 2005b. The 2003 dividend tax cuts and the value of the firm: An event study. Working paper 11449. National Bureau of Economic Research, Cambridge, MA.

Auerbach, Alan J., and Kevin A. Hassett. 2007. Dividend taxes and firm valuation: New evidence. *American Economic Review*, forthcoming.

Auerbach, Alan J., and Laurence J. Kotlikoff. 1987. *Dynamic Fiscal Policy*. Cambridge: Cambridge University Press.

Auerbach, Alan J., William G. Gale, and Peter R. Orszag. 2006. The budget: Plus ça change, plus c'est la même chose. *Tax Notes* 111: 349–70.

Auten, Gerald, and Robert Carroll. 1999. The effect of income taxes on household income. *Review of Economics and Statistics* 81: 681–93.

Bachman, Paul, Jonathan Haughton, Laurence J. Kotlikoff, Alfonso Sanchez-Penalver, and David G. Tuerck. 2006. Taxing sales under the FairTax—What rate works? Manuscript. Beacon Hill Associates of Suffolk University.

Baicker, Katherine, William Dow, and Jonathan Wolfson. 2006. Health savings accounts: Implications for health spending. *National Tax Journal* 59: 463–76.

Ballard, Charles. 1990. Marginal efficiency cost calculations: Differential analysis vs. balanced-budget analysis. *Journal of Public Economics* 41: 263–76.

Ballentine, J. Gregory. 1986. Three failures in economic analysis of tax reforms. *Proceedings of the Annual Conference on Taxation*. Columbus OH: National Tax Association–Tax Institute of America.

Bankman, Joseph, and Michael Schler. 2005. Tax planning under the flat tax/X tax. Paper presented at the American Tax Policy Institute Conference on Taxing Capital Income, September.

Bankman, Joseph, and Thomas Griffith. 1987. Social welfare and the rate structure: A new look at progressive taxation. *California Law Review* 75: 1905–67.

Barnett, Steven A., and Plutarchos Sakellaris. 1998. Nonlinear response of firm investment to Q: Testing a model of convex and non-convex adjustment costs. *Journal of Monetary Economics* 42: 261–88.

Barnett, Steven A., and Plutarchos Sakellaris. 1999. A new look at firm market value, investment, and adjustment costs. *Review of Economics and Statistics* 81: 250–60.

Barro, Robert J. 1974. Are government bonds net wealth? *Journal of Political Economy* 82: 1095–1117.

Bartelsman, Eric J., and Roel M. W. J. Beetsma. 2003. Why pay more? Corporate tax avoidance through transfer pricing in OECD countries. *Journal of Public Economics* 87: 2225–52.

Bell, Elizabeth, Adam Carasso, and C. Eugene Steuerle. 2004. Retirement savings incentives and personal savings. *Tax Notes* 105: 1689.

Bernanke, Benjamin, Henning Bohn, and Peter Riess. 1988. Alternative nonnested specification tests of time-series investment models. *Journal of Econometrics* 37: 293–326.

Bernheim, B. Douglas. 1997. Rethinking saving incentives. In Alan J. Auerbach, ed., *Fiscal Policy: Lessons from Economic Research*. Cambridge: MIT Press.

Bernheim, B. Douglas. 2002. Taxation and saving. In Alan Auerbach and Martin Feldstein, eds., *Handbook of Public Economic*, vol. 3. Amsterdam: Elsevier Science, North-Holland.

Bernheim, B. Douglas, and Antonio Rangel. 2005a. Savings and cue-triggered decision processes. Working paper. Stanford University.

Bernheim, B. Douglas, and Antonio Rangel. 2005b. Behavioral public economics: Welfare and policy analysis with non-standard decision makers. Working paper 11518. National Bureau of Economic Research, Cambridge, MA.

Bernheim, B. Douglas, Daniel M. Garret, and Dean M. Maki. 2001. Education and saving: The long-term effects of high school financial curriculum mandates. *Journal of Public Economics* 80: 435–65.

Bird, Richard. 2002. Why tax corporations? *Bulletin of International Fiscal Documentation* 56: 194–203.

Birnbaum, Jeffrey, and Alan Murray. 1987. *Showdown at Gucci Gulch: Lawmakers, Lobbyists, and the Unlikely Triumph of Tax Reform*. New York: Random House.

Blomquist, N. Soren. 1985. Labor supply in a two-period model: The effect of a nonlinear progressive income tax. *Review of Economic Studies* 52: 515–24.

Blomquist, N. Soren, and Whitney Newey. 2002. Nonparametric estimation with nonlinear budget sets. *Econometrica* 70: 2455–80.

Blomquist, Soren, Matias Eklöf, and Whitney Newey. 2001. Tax reform evaluation using non-parametric methods: Sweden 1980–1991. *Journal of Public Economics* 79: 543–68.

Blouin, Jennifer L., Jana Smith Raedy, and Douglas A. Shackelford. 2004. Did dividends increase immediately after the 2003 reduction in tax rates? Working paper 10301. National Bureau of Economic Research, Cambridge, MA.

Blundell, Richard, and Thomas MaCurdy. 1999. Labor supply: A review of alternative approaches. In Orley Ashenfelter and David Card, eds., *Handbook of Labor Economics*, vol. 3A. Amsterdam: North-Holland.

Blundell, Richard, Alan Duncan, and Costas Meghir. 1998. Estimating labor supply responses using tax reforms. *Econometrica* 66: 827–61.

Blundell, Richard, Costas Meghir, Elizabeth Symons, and Ian Walker. 1988. Labour supply specification and the evaluation of tax reforms. *Journal of Public Economics* 36: 23–52.

Blundell, Richard, Martin Browning, and Costas Meghir. 1994. Consumer demand and the life-cycle allocation of household expenditures. *Review of Economic Studies* 61: 57–80.

Bond, Stephen, and Jason Cummins. 2001. Noisy share prices and the Q model of investment. Working paper WP01/22. Institute for Fiscal Studies, London.

Bond, Stephen, Alexander Klemm, Rain Newton-Smith, and Gertjan Vlieghe. 2004. The roles of expected profitability, Tobin's Q and cash flow in econometric models of company investment. Working paper WP04/12. Institute for Fiscal Studies, London.

Boskin, Michael. 1978. Taxation, saving, and the rate of interest. *Journal of Political Economy* 86: S3–S27.

Boskin, Michael J. 1996. *Frontiers of Tax Reform*. Palo Alto, CA: Hoover Institution Press.

Boyle, Glenn W., and Graeme A. Guthrie. 2003. Investment, uncertainty, and liquidity. *Journal of Finance* 58: 2143–66.

Bradford, David F. 1981. The incidence and allocation effects of a tax on corporate distributions. *Journal of Public Economics* 15: 1–22.

Bradford, David F. 1986. *Untangling the Income Tax*. Cambridge: Harvard University Press.

Bradford, David F. 1995. Fixing realization accounting: Symmetry, consistency and correctness in the taxation of financial instruments. *Tax Law Review* 50: 731–85.

Bradford, David F. 1996a. *Fundamental Issues in Consumption Taxation*. Washington: AEI Press.

Bradford, David F. 1996b. Consumption taxes: Some fundamental transition issues. In Michael J. Boskin, ed., *Frontiers of Tax Reform*. Stanford: Hoover Institution Press.

Bradford, David F. 1996c. Treatment of financial services under income and consumption taxes. In Henry J. Aaron and William G. Gale, eds., *Economic Effects of Fundamental Tax Reform*. Washington: Brookings Institution Press.

Bradford, David F. 1998a. Tax reform: Waiting for a new consensus of the experts. *Tax Notes* 79: 899–901.

Bradford, David F. 1998b. Transition to and tax rate flexibility in a cash-flow type tax. In James M. Poterba, ed., *Tax Policy and the Economy*, vol. 12. Cambridge: MIT Press.

Bradford, David F. 2000. *Taxation, Wealth, and Saving*. Cambridge: MIT Press.

Bradford, David F. 2004. *The X-Tax in the World Economy*. Washington: AEI Press.

Bradford, David F. 2005. A tax system for the twenty-first century. In Alan J. Auerbach and Kevin A. Hassett, eds., *Toward Fundamental Tax Reform*. Washington: AEI Press.

Bradford, David F., and U.S. Treasury Tax Policy Staff. 1984. *Blueprints for Basic Tax Reform*, 2nd ed. Arlington, VA: Tax Analysts.

Brander, James A., and Barbara J. Spencer. 1985. Export subsidies and international market share. *Journal of International Economics* 16: 18–100.

Brinner, Roger, Mark Lansky, and David Wyss. 1995. Market impacts of flat tax legislation. *DRI/McGraw-Hill U.S. Review*, June.

Brown, Jeffrey R., Nellie Liang, and Scott Weisbenner. 2004. Executive financial incentives and payout policy: Firm responses to the 2003 dividend tax cut. Working paper 11002. National Bureau of Economic Research, Cambridge, MA.

Browning, Edgar. 1987. On the marginal welfare cost of taxation. *American Economic Review* 77: 11–23.

Browning, Martin. 2005. A working paper from April 1985: Which demand elasticities do we know and which do we need to know for policy analysis? *Research in Economics* 59: 293–320.

Browning, Martin, and Costas Meghir. 1991. The effects of male and female labor supply on commodity demands. *Econometrica* 59: 925–51.

Bruce, Donald, and Douglas Holtz-Eakin. 1999. Fundamental tax reform and residential housing. *Journal of Housing Economics* 8: 249–71.

Bruce, Donald, and Douglas Holtz-Eakin. 2001. Will a consumption tax kill the housing market? In Kevin A. Hassett and R. Glenn Hubbard, eds., *Transition Costs of Fundamental Tax Reform*. Washington: AEI Press.

Burman, Leonard E., and David Weiner. 2004. Suppose they took the AM out of the AMT? *Proceedings of the 97th Annual Conference on Taxation*. Washington: National Tax Association.

Burman, Leonard E., and William G. Gale. 2005. A preliminary evaluation of the Tax Reform Panel's report. *Tax Notes* 109: 1349–68.

Burtless, Gary, and Jerry Hausman. 1978. The effect of taxation on labor supply: Evaluating the Gary negative income tax experiment. *Journal of Political Economy* 86: 1103–30.

Caballero, Ricardo J., Eduardo M. R. A. Engel, and John C. Haltiwanger. 1995. Plant-level adjustment and aggregate investment dynamics. *Brookings Papers on Economic Activity* 2: 1–54.

Camerer, Colin, Linda Babcock, George Loewenstein, and Richard Thaler. 1997. Labor supply of New York City cabdrivers: One day at a time. *Quarterly Journal of Economics* 112: 407–41.

Capozza, Dennis R., Richard K. Green, and Patric H. Hendershott. 1996. Taxes, mortgage borrowing, and residential land prices. In Henry J. Aaron and William G. Gale, eds., *Economic Effects of Fundamental Tax Reform*. Washington: Brookings Institution.

Cappozza, Dennis R., Richard K. Green, and Patric H. Hendershott. 1998. Tax reform and house prices: Large or small effects. *Proceedings of the 91st Annual Conference on Taxation*. Washington: National Tax Association.

Carlson, George N., Gary C. Hufbauer, and Melvin B. Krauss. 1976. Destination principle border tax adjustments for the corporate income and Social Security taxes. Office of Tax Analysis Paper 20. US Department of the Treasury, Washington.

Carroll, Christopher. 1997. Buffer-stock saving and the life-cycle/permanent income hypothesis. *Quarterly Journal of Economics* 111: 1–57.

Carroll, Christopher, and Lawrence Summers. 1991. Consumption growth parallels income growth: Some new evidence. In B. Douglas Bernheim and John Shoven, eds., *National Saving and Economic Performance*. Chicago: University of Chicago Press.

Carroll, Robert, Douglas Holtz-Eakin, Mark Rider, and Harvey S. Rosen. 2000. Income Taxes and Entrepreneurs' Use of Labor. *Journal of Labor Economics* 18: 324–51.

Carroll, Robert, Douglas Holtz-Eakin, Mark Rider, and Harvey S. Rosen. 2001. Personal income taxes and the growth of small firms. In James M. Poterba, ed., *Tax Policy and the Economy*, vol. 15. Cambridge: MIT Press.

Carroll, Robert, Kevin A. Hassett, and James B. Mackie III. 2003. The effect of dividend tax relief on investment incentives. *National Tax Journal* 56: 629–51.

Chamley, Christophe. 1986. Optimal taxation of capital income in general equilibrium with infinite lives. *Econometrica* 54: 607–22.

Chetty, Raj, and Emmanuel Saez. 2005. Dividend taxes and corporate behavior: Evidence from the 2003 dividend tax cut. *Quarterly Journal of Economics* 120: 791–833.

Chetty, Raj, and Emmanuel Saez. 2007. The effect of the 2003 dividend tax cut on corporate behavior: Interpreting the evidence. *American Economic Review*, forthcoming.

Chiappori, Pierre-Andre. 1992. Collective labor supply and welfare. *Journal of Political Economy* 100: 437–67.

Chirinko, Robert S. 1987. The ineffectiveness of effective tax rates on business investment: A critique of Feldstein's Fischer-Schultz lecture. *Journal of Public Economics* 32: 369–87.

Chirinko, Robert S. 2002. Corporate taxation, capital formation, and the substitution elasticity between labor and capital. *National Tax Journal* 55: 339–55.

Chirinko, Robert S., and Huntley Schaller. 1995. Why does liquidity matter in investment equations? *Journal of Money, Credit, and Banking* 27: 527–48.

Chirinko, Robert S., and Huntley Schaller. 2001. The irreversibility premium. Working paper. Emory University.

Chirinko, Robert S., and Huntley Schaller. 2004. A revealed preference approach to understanding corporate governance problems: Evidence from Canada. *Journal of Financial Economics* 74: 181–206.

Chirinko, Robert S., and Robert Eisner. 1983. Tax policy and investment in major U.S. macroeconomic econometric models. *Journal of Public Economics* 20: 139–66.

Chirinko, Robert S., Steven M. Fazzari, and Andrew P. Meyer. 2007. A new approach to estimating production function parameters: The elusive capital–labor substitution elasticity. University of Illinois at Chicago and Washington University.

Chirinko, Robert S., Steven M. Fazzari, and Andrew P. Meyer. 1999. How responsive is business capital formation to its user cost? An exploration with micro data. *Journal of Public Economics* 74: 53–80.

Choi, James J., David Laibson, Brigitte C. Madrian, and Andrew Metrick. 2005. Optimal defaults and active decisions. Working paper 11074. National Bureau of Economic Research, Cambridge, MA.

Christensen, Kevin, Robert Cline, and Tom Neubig. 2001. Total corporate taxation: "Hidden," above-the-line, non-income taxes. *National Tax Journal* 54: 495–506.

Christian, Ernest S., and Gary A. Robbins. 2002. Stealth approach to tax reform. *Washington Times*, November 1, p. A-21.

Clausing, Kimberly A. 2003. Tax-motivated transfer pricing and U.S. intrafirm trade prices. *Journal of Public Economics* 87: 2207–23.

Clausing, Kimberly A. 2007. The role of U.S. tax policy in offshoring. In Susan Collins and Lael Brainard, eds., *Brookings Trade Forum 2005*. Washington: Brookings Institution, forthcoming.

Cleary, Sean. 1999. The relationship between firm investment and financial status. *Journal of Finance* 54: 673–92.

Cline, Robert, John Mikesell, Tom Neubig, and Andrew Phillips. 2005. Sales taxation of business inputs: Existing tax distortions and the consequences of Extending the Sales Tax to Business Services. *State Tax Notes* 35 (February 14): 457–70.

Cline, Robert, Tom Neubig, and Andrew Phillips. 2006. Total state and local business taxes: Nationally 1980–2005, by state 2002–2005, and by industry 2005. *State Tax Notes* 40 (May 1): 373–90.

Cline, Robert, William Fox, Tom Neubig, and Andrew Phillips. 2003. A closer examination of the total state and local business tax burden. *State Tax Notes* 27 (January 27): 295–304.

Cogan, John E., R. Glenn Hubbard, and Daniel Kessler. 2004. Brilliant deduction. *Wall Street Journal*, December 8.

Congressional Budget Office. 2005. *Taxing Capital Income: Effective Rates and Approaches to Reform*. Washington: Congressional Budget Office.

Congressional Budget Office. 2006. *The Budget and Economic Outlook: Fiscal Years 2007 to 2016*. Washington: Congressional Budget Office.

Conlan, Timothy J., Margaret T. Wrightson, and David R. Beam. 1990. *Taxing Choices: The Politics of Tax Reform*. Washington: Congressional Quarterly.

Cooper, Russell, and Joao Ejarque. 2001. Exhuming Q: Market power vs. capital market imperfections. Working paper 8182. National Bureau of Economic Research, Cambridge, MA.

Cooper, Russell, and Joao Ejarque. 2003. Financial frictions and investment: Requiem in Q. *Review of Economic Dynamics* 6: 710–28.

Cooper, Russell W., and John C. Haltiwanger. 2000. On the nature of capital adjustment costs. Working paper 7925. National Bureau of Economic Research, Cambridge, MA.

Cooper, Russell W., and John C. Haltiwanger. 2006. On the nature of capital adjustment costs. *Review of Economic Studies* 73: 611–33.

Corrada, Carol A., John Haltiwanger, and Daniel Sichel. eds. 2005. *Measuring Capital in the New Economy*. Studies in Income and Wealth, vol. 65. Chicago: University of Chicago Press and National Bureau of Economic Research.

Corrado, Carol A., Charles R. Hulten, and Daniel E. Sichel. 2006. Intangible capital and economic growth. Working paper 11948. National Bureau of Economic Research, Cambridge, MA.

Cullen, Julie Berry, and Roger H. Gordon. 2002. Taxes and entrepreneurial activity: Theory and evidence for the U.S. Working paper 9015. National Bureau of Economic Research, Cambridge, MA.

Cummins, Jason G., Kevin A. Hassett, and R. Glenn Hubbard. 1994. A reconsideration of investment behavior using tax reforms as natural experiments. *Brookings Papers on Economic Activity* 2: 1–60.

Cummins, Jason G., Kevin A. Hassett, and Stephen D. Oliner. 2006. Investment behavior, observable expectations, and internal funds. *American Economic Review* 96: 796–810.

Cutler, David. 1988. Tax reform and the stock market: An asset price approach. *American Economic Review* 78: 1107–17.

Davis, Steven J., and Magnus Henrekson. 2004. Tax effects on work activity, industry mix and shadow economy size: Evidence from rich country comparisons. Working paper 10509. National Bureau of Economic Research, Cambridge MA.

De Mooij, Ruud A., and Sjef Ederveen. 2003. Taxation and foreign direct investment: A synthesis of empirical research. *International Tax and Public Finance* 10: 673–93.

Deaton, Angus. 1991. Saving and liquidity constraints. *Econometrica* 59: 1121–42.

Desai, Mihir A., and Austan D. Goolsbee. 2004. Investment, overhang, and tax policy. *Brookings Papers on Economic Activity* 2: 285–338.

Desai, Mihir A., and James R. Hines. 2003. Evaluating international tax reform. *National Tax Journal* 56: 487–502.

Desai, Mihir A., C. Fritz Foley, and James R. Hines Jr. 2001. Repatriation taxes and dividend distortions. *National Tax Journal* 54: 829–51.

Desai, Mihir A., C. Fritz Foley, and James R. Hines Jr. 2002. Chains of ownership, regional tax competition, and foreign direct investment. Working paper 9224. National Bureau of Economic Research, Cambridge, MA.

Desai, Mihir A., C. Fritz Foley, and James R. Hines Jr. 2004. Foreign direct investment in a world of multiple taxes. *Journal of Public Economics* 88: 2727–44.

Devereux, Michael P., Ben Lockwood, and Michela Redoano. 2004. Do countries compete over corporate tax rates? Working paper. University of Warwick.

Diamond, John, and George R. Zodrow. 1998. Housing and intergenerational redistributions under a consumption tax reform. *National Tax Association Proceedings of the 91st Annual Conference on Taxation*. Washington: National Tax Association.

Diamond, John, and George R. Zodrow. 2005. Description of the tax policy advisers general equilibrium model. Manuscript. Rice University.

Diamond, John, and George R. Zodrow. 2006. Reflections on the use of life-cycle computable general equilibrium models in analyzing the effects of tax reform. *NTA Network*. Washington: National Tax Association.

Diamond, Peter A., and James A. Mirrlees. 1971. Optimal taxation and public production I: Production efficiency. *American Economic Review* 61: 8–27.

Dietz, Robert D., and Donald Haurin. 2003. The social and private micro-level consequences of homeownership. *Journal of Urban Economics* 54: 401–50.

Doernberg, Richard L., and Fred S. McChesney. 1987. On the accelerating rate and decreasing durability of tax reform. *Minnesota Law Review* 71: 913–62.

Domar, Evsey D., and Richard A. Musgrave. 1944. Proportional income taxation and risk-taking. *Quarterly Journal of Economics* 58: 388–422.

Duflo, Esther, William G. Gale, Jeffrey Liebman, Peter R. Orszag, and Emmanuel Saez. 2006. Saving incentives for low- and middle-income families: Evidence from a field experiment with H&R block. Working Paper. February.

Ebrill, Liam, Michael Keen, Jean-Paul Bodin, and Victoria Summers. 2001. *The Modern VAT*. Washington: International Monetary Fund.

Eissa, Nada. 1996. Labor supply and the Economic Recovery Tax Act of 1981. In Martin Feldstein and James M. Poterba, eds., *Empirical Foundations of Household Taxation*. Chicago: University of Chicago Press.

Eissa, Nada, and Hilary Hoynes. 2005. Behavioral responses to taxes: Lessons from the EITC and labor supply. Working paper 11729. National Bureau of Economic Research, Cambridge, MA.

Engen, Eric, and William G. Gale. 1996. The effects of fundamental tax reform on saving. In Henry J. Aaron and William G. Gale, eds., *Economic Effects of Fundamental Tax Reform*. Washington: Brookings Institution.

Engen, Eric M., and Kevin A. Hassett. 2002. Does the U.S. corporate tax have a future? *Tax Notes*. 30th Anniversary Issue, pp. 15–27.

Engen, Eric M., and William G. Gale. 1997. Debt, taxes, and the effects of 401(k) plans on household wealth accumulation. Manuscript. Brookings Institution. Available at SSRN: ⟨http://ssrn.com/abstract=40180 or DOI: 10.2139/ssrn.40180⟩.

Engen, Eric M., William G. Gale, and John Karl Scholz. 1996. The illusory effects of savings incentives on saving. *Journal of Economic Perspectives* 10: 113–38.

Engen, Eric, Jane Gravelle, and Kent Smetters. 1997. Dynamic tax models: Why they do the things they do. *National Tax Journal* 50: 657–82.

Epstein, Richard A. 2006a. Second order rationality. In Edward J. McCaffery and Joel C. Slemrod, eds., *Behavioral Public Finance*. New York: Russell Sage.

Epstein, Richard A. 2006b. Behavioral economics: Human errors and market corrections. *University of Chicago Law Review* 73: 111–32.

Erickson, Timothy, and Toni M. Whited. 2000. Measurement error and the relationship between investment and *q*. *Journal of Political Economy* 108: 1027–57.

Erickson, Timothy, and Toni M. Whited. 2002. Investment-cash flow sensitivity and proxy quality thresholds. Working paper. University of Wisconsin.

Erickson, Timothy, and Toni M. Whited. 2007. On the accuracy of different measures of *Q*. *Financial Management*, forthcoming.

Erosa, Andres, and Martin Gervais. 2002. Optimal taxation in life-cycle economies. *Journal of Economic Theory* 105: 338–69.

Farber, Henry. 2005. Is tomorrow another day? The labor supply of New York City cab drivers. *Journal of Political Economy* 113: 46–82.

Fazzari, Steven. M., R. Glenn Hubbard, and Bruce C. Petersen. 1988. Financing constraints and corporate investment. *Brookings Papers on Economic Activity* 1: 141–95.

Fazzari, Steven. M., R. Glenn Hubbard, and Bruce C. Petersen. 2000. Investment-cash flow sensitivities are useful: A comment on Kaplan and Zingales. *Quarterly Journal of Economics* 115: 695–705.

Feenberg, Daniel R., and Jonathan Skinner. 1989. Sources of IRA saving. In Lawrence Summers, ed., *Tax Policy and the Economy*, vol. 3. Cambridge: MIT Press.

Feldstein, Martin. 1978. The welfare cost of capital income taxation. *Journal of Political Economy* 86: S29–S51.

Feldstein, Martin. 1993. Tax rates and human behavior. *Wall Street Journal*, May 7, p. A14.

Feldstein, Martin. 1995. The effect of marginal tax rates on taxable income: A panel study of the 1986 Tax Reform Act. *Journal of Political Economy* 103: 551–72.

Feldstein, Martin. 2006. The effect of taxes on efficiency and growth. Working paper 12201. National Bureau of Economic Research, Cambridge, MA.

Feldstein, Martin, and Charles Horioka. 1980. Domestic savings and capital flows. *Economic Journal* 90: 314–29.

Feldstein, Martin, and Gilbert E. Metcalf. 1987. The effect of federal tax deductibility on state and local taxes and spending. *Journal of Political Economy* 95: 710–36.

Feldstein, Martin, Louis Dicks-Mireaux, and James Poterba. 1983. The effective tax rate and the pretax rate of return. *Journal of Public Economics* 21: 129–58.

Felipe, Jesus, and Franklin M. Fisher. 2003. Aggregation in production functions: What applied economists should know. *Metroeconomica* 54: 208–62.

Fullerton, Don, and Diane Lim Rogers. 1993. *Who Bears the Lifetime Tax Burden?* Washington: Brookings Institution.

Furman, Jason. 2006. Two wrongs do not make a right. *National Tax Journal* 59: 491–508.

Gale, William G. 1999. The required tax rate in a national sales tax. *National Tax Journal* 52: 443–57.

Gale, William G. 2005. The national retail sales tax: What would the rate have to be? *Tax Notes* (May 16): 889–911.

Gale, William G., and Janet Holtzblatt. 2002. The role of administrative issues in tax reforms: Simplicity, compliance, and administration. In George R. Zodrow and Peter Mieszkowski, eds., *United States Tax Reform in the 21st Century*. Cambridge: Cambridge University Press.

Gale, William G., and John K. Scholz. 1994. Intergenerational transfers and the accumulation of wealth. *Journal of Economic Perspectives* 8: 145–60.

Gale, William G., and Peter R. Orszag. 2005. Deficits, interest rates, and the user cost of capital: A reconsideration of the effects of tax policy on investment. *National Tax Journal* 58: 409–26.

Gale, William G., J. Mark Iwry, and Peter R. Orszag. 2005. The automatic 401(k): A simple way to strengthen retirement savings. *Tax Notes* 106: 1207–14.

Gale, William G., Scott Houser, and John K. Scholz. 1996. Distributional effects of fundamental tax reform. In Henry J. Aaron and William G. Gale, eds., *Economic Effects of Fundamental Tax Reform*. Washington: Brookings Institution.

Gentry, William M., and R. Glenn Hubbard. 1997. Distributional implications of introducing a broad-based consumption tax. In James M. Poterba, ed., *Tax Policy and the Economy*. Cambridge: National Bureau of Economic Research.

Gentry, William M., and R. Glenn Hubbard. 2004. "Success taxes," entrepreneurial entry, and innovation. Working paper 10551. National Bureau of Economic Research, Cambridge, MA.

Gentry, William M., Deen Kemsley, and Christopher J. Mayer. 2003. Dividend taxes and share prices: Evidence from real estate investment trusts. *Journal of Finance* 58: 261–82.

Giertz, Seth H. 2004. Recent literature on taxable-income elasticities. *Congressional Budget Office Technical Paper 2004-16*. Washington: Congressional Budget Office.

Gillis, Malcolm, Peter Mieszkowski, and George Zodrow. 1996. Indirect consumption taxes: Common issues and differences among the alternative approaches. *Tax Law Review* 51: 725–44.

Ginsburg, Martin D. 1995. Life under a personal consumption tax: Some thoughts on working, saving, and consuming in Nunn-Domenici's tax world. *National Tax Journal* 48: 585–602.

Glaeser, Edward L. 2006. Paternalism and psychology. *University of Chicago Law Review* 73: 133–56.

Gokhale, Jagadeesh, Laurence J. Kotlikoff, and Alexi Sluchynsky. 2002. Does it pay to work? Working paper 9095. National Bureau of Economic Research, Cambridge MA.

Gokhale, Jagadeesh, Laurence J. Kotlikoff, and John Sabelhaus. 1996. Understanding the postwar decline in U.S. saving. *Brookings Papers on Economic Activity* 1: 315–407.

Gokhale, Jagadeesh, Laurence J. Kotlikoff, and Mark Warshawsky. 2001. Comparing the economic and conventional approaches to financial planning. In Laurence J. Kotlikoff, ed., *Essays on Saving, Bequests, Altruism, and Life-cycle Planning*. Chicago: University of Chicago Press.

Golosov, Mikhail, Narayana Kocherlakota, and Aleh Tsyvinski. 2003. Optimal indirect and capital taxation. *Review of Economic Studies* 70: 569–87.

Gomes, Joao F. 2001. Financing investment. *American Economic Review* 91: 1263–85.

Goolsbee, Austan. 1997. What happens when you tax the rich? Evidence from executive compensation. Working paper 6333. National Bureau of Economic Research, Cambridge, MA.

Goolsbee, Austan. 1998. Investment tax incentives and the price of capital goods. *Quarterly Journal of Economics* 113: 121–48.

Gordon, Roger H. 1985. Taxation of corporate capital income: Tax revenues versus tax distortions. *Quarterly Journal of Economics* 100: 1–27.

Gordon, Roger H., and James R. Hines Jr. 2002. International taxation. In Alan J. Auerbach and Martin Feldstein, eds., *Handbook of Public Economics*, vol. 4. North-Holland: Elsevier Science.

Gordon, Roger H., and Joosung Jun. 1993. Taxes and the form of ownership of foreign corporate equity. In Alberto Giovannini, R. Glenn Hubbard, and Joel Slemrod, eds., *Studies in International Taxation*. Chicago: University of Chicago Press.

Goulder, Lawrence H. 1989. Tax policy, housing prices, and housing investment. Working paper 2814. National Bureau of Economic Research, Cambridge MA.

Goulder, Lawrence H., and Lawrence H. Summers. 1989. Tax policy, asset prices, and growth. *Journal of Public Economics* 38: 265–96.

Graetz, Michael J. 2002. 100 million unnecessary returns: A fresh start for the U.S. tax system. *Yale Law Journal* 112: 261–310.

Graetz, Michael J., and Paul W. Oosterhuis. 2002. Stucturing an exemption system for foreign income of U.S. corporations. *National Tax Journal* 54: 771–86.

Gravelle, Jane G. 1994. *The Economic Effects of Taxing Capital Income*. Cambridge: MIT Press.

Gravelle, Jane G. 1995. The flat tax and other proposals: Who will bear the tax burden? Congressional Research Service Report for Congress 95-1141E. Washington: Government Printing Office.

Gravelle, Jane G. 1996. The flat tax and other proposals: Effects on housing. Congressional Research Service Report for Congress 96-379E. Washington: Government Printing Office.

Gravelle, Jane G. 2006. Feasible but hard-to-believe models: Computable general equilibrium intertemporal models. *NTA Network*. National Tax Association (January): 3–4.

Gravelle, Jane G., and Kent A. Smetters. 2001. Who bears the burden of the corporate tax in the open economy? Working paper 8280. National Bureau of Economic Research, Cambridge MA.

Gravelle, Jane G., and Kent A. Smetters. 2006. Does the open economy assumption really mean that labor bears the burden of the corporate tax? *Advances in Economic Analysis and Policy* 6: 1–42. Available at BE Journals, ⟨http://www.bepress.com/bejeap/⟩.

Greenstein, Robert, and Iris Lav. 2005. The Graetz tax reform plan and the treatment of low-income households. Washington: Center on Budget and Policy Priorities.

Grodner, Andrew, and Thomas J. Kniesner. 2006a. Social interactions in labor supply. *Journal of the European Economic Association* 4, forthcoming.

Grodner, Andrew, and Thomas J. Kniesner. 2006b. An empirical model of labor supply with social interactions: Econometric issues and tax policy implications. Working paper 69. Center for Policy Research, Syracuse University.

Gruber, Jonathan, and Emmanuel Saez. 2002. The elasticity of taxable income: Evidence and implications. *Journal of Public Economics* 84: 1–32.

Grubert, Harry. 1998. Taxes and the division of foreign operating income among royalties, interest, dividends and retained earnings. *Journal of Public Economics* 68: 269–90.

Grubert, Harry. 2001. Enacting dividend exemption and tax revenue. *National Tax Journal* 54: 811–27.

Grubert, Harry. 2003. Intangible income, intercompany transactions, income shifting, and the choice of location. *National Tax Journal* 56: 211–42.

Grubert, Harry. 2004. The tax burden on cross-border investment: Company strategies and country responses. In Peter Birch Sorensen, ed., *Measuring the Tax Burden on Labor and Capital*. Cambridge: Cambridge University Press.

Grubert, Harry, and Joel Slemrod. 1998. The effect of taxes on investing and income shifting to Puerto Rico. *Review of Economics and Statistics* 80: 365–73.

Grubert, Harry, and John Mutti. 1991. Taxes, tariffs and transfer pricing in multinational corporation decision making. *Review of Economics and Statistics* 33: 285–93.

Grubert, Harry, and John Mutti. 1995. Taxing multinationals in a world with portfolio flows and R&D: Is capital export neutrality obsolete? *International Tax and Public Finance* 2: 439–57.

Grubert, Harry, and John Mutti. 2001. *Taxing International Business Income: Dividend Exemption Versus the Current System.* Washington: AEI Press.

Grubert, Harry, and Scott Newlon. 1995. The international implications of consumption tax proposals. *National Tax Journal* 48: 619–47.

Hall, Robert E. 1978. Stochastic implications of the life cycle–permanent income hypothesis: Theory and evidence. *Journal of Political Economy* 86: 971–87.

Hall, Robert E. 1988. Intertemporal substitution in consumption. *Journal of Political Economy* 96: 339–57.

Hall, Robert E. 1996. The effect of tax reform on prices and asset values. In James Poterba, ed., *Tax Policy and the Economy*, vol. 10. Cambridge: MIT Press.

Hall, Robert E. 1997. The effects of tax reform on prices and asset values. In James M. Poterba, ed., *Tax Policy and the Economy*. Cambridge: MIT Press.

Hall, Robert E. 2004. Measuring factor adjustment costs. *Quarterly Journal of Economics* 119: 889–927.

Hall, Robert E., and Alvin Rabushka. 1983. *Low Tax, Simple Tax, Flat Tax.* New York: McGraw-Hill.

Hall, Robert E., and Alvin Rabushka. 1985. *The Flat Tax.* Stanford: Hoover Institution Press. (Second edition, 1995.)

Hall, Robert E., and Alvin Rabushka. 1995. *The Flat Tax,* 2nd ed. Stanford: Hoover Institution Press.

Hall, Robert E., and Dale W. Jorgenson. 1967. Tax policy and investment behavior. *American Economic Review* 57: 391–414.

Hall, Robert E., and Dale W. Jorgenson. 1971. Application of the theory of optimum capital accumulation. In Gary Fromm, ed., *Tax Incentives and Capital Spending.* Washington: Brookings Institution.

Hall, Robert E., and Fredric Mishkin. 1982. The sensitivity of consumption to transitory income: Estimates from panel data on households. *Econometrica* 50: 461–81.

Hand, John R. M., and Baruch Lev, eds. 2003. *Intangible Assets.* Oxford: Oxford University Press.

Harberger, Arnold C. 1962. The incidence of the corporate income tax. *Journal of Political Economy* 70: 251–40.

Harberger, Arnold C. 1964. Taxation, resource allocation and welfare. In John Due, ed., *The Role of Direct and Indirect Taxes in the Federal Reserve System.* Washington: Brookings Institution.

Harberger, Arnold C. 1980. Vignettes on the world capital market. *American Economic Review* 70: 331–39.

Harberger Arnold C. 1995. The ABCs of corporation tax incidence: Insights into the open-economy case. In American Council for Capital Formation, *Tax Policy and Economic Growth.* Washington: American Council for Capital Formation, pp. 51–73.

Hassett, Kevin A. 2004. Comment on "Investment, Overhang, and Tax Policy." *Brookings Papers on Economic Activity* 2: 339–45.

Hassett, Kevin A., and Aparna Mathur. 2006. Taxes and wages. Working paper. American Enterprise Institute.

Hassett, Kevin A., and R. Glenn Hubbard. 1998. Are investment incentives blunted by changes in prices of capital goods? *International Finance* 1: 103–25.

Hassett, Kevin A., and R. Glenn Hubbard. 2002. Tax policy and business investment. In Alan J. Auerbach and Martin Feldstein, eds., *Handbook of Public Economics,* vol. 3. Amsterdam: North-Holland.

Hausman, Jerry. 1981a. Labor supply. In Henry Aaron and Joseph Pechman, eds., *How Taxes Affect Economic Behavior.* Washington: Brookings Institution.

Hausman, Jerry. 1981b. Income and payroll tax policy and labor supply. In Lawrence H. Meyer, ed., *The Supply Side Effects of Economic Policy.* Boston: Kluwer Academic.

Hausman, Jerry, and Paul Ruud. 1984. Family labor supply with taxes. *American Economic Review Papers and Proceedings* 74: 242–48.

Hayashi, Fumio. 1982. Tobin's marginal q and average q: A neoclassical interpretation. *Econometrica* 50: 213–24.

Heckman, James. 1974a. Life cycle consumption and labor supply: An explanation of the relationship between income and consumption over the life cycle. *American Economic Review* 64: 188–94.

Heckman, James. 1974b. Shadow prices, market wages, and labor supply. *Econometrica* 42: 679–94.

Heckman, James. 1979. Sample selection bias as specification error. *Econometrica* 47: 153–61.

Heckman, James. 1993. What has been learned about labor supply in the past twenty years? *American Economic Review Papers and Proceedings* 83: 116–21.

Heckman, James, and Thomas MaCurdy. 1980. A life cycle model of female labour supply. *Review of Economic Studies* 47: 47–74.

Heckman, James, and Thomas MaCurdy. 1982. Corrigendum on a life cycle model of female labour supply. *Review of Economic Studies* 49: 659–60.

Heim, Bradley. 2005a. The impact of the earned income tax credit on the labor supply of married couples: Structural estimation and business cycle interactions. Manuscript. Duke University.

Heim, Bradley. 2005b. The incredible shrinking elasticities: Married female labor supply, 1979–2003. Manuscript. Duke University.

Hendershott, Patric H., and Sheng Cheng Hu. 1981. Inflation and extraordinary returns on owner-occupied housing: Some implications for capital allocation and productivity growth. *Journal of Macroeconomics* 3: 177–203.

Hennessy, Christopher A. 2004. Tobin's Q, debt overhang, and investment. *Journal of Finance* 59: 1717–42.

Hennessy, Christopher A., and Toni M. Whited. 2007. How costly is external financing? Evidence from a structural estimation. *Journal of Finance*, forthcoming.

Hines, James R., Jr. 1995. Taxes, technology transfer, and the R&D activity of multinational firms. In Martin Feldstein, James Hines Jr., and R. Glenn Hubbard, eds., *The Effects of Taxation on Multinational Corporations*. Chicago: University of Chicago Press.

Hines, James R., Jr. 1996. Fundamental tax reform in an international setting. In Henry Aaron and William G. Gale, eds., *Economic Effects of Fundamental Tax Reform*. Washington: Brookings Institution Press.

Hines, James R., Jr. 1997. Tax policy and the activities of multinational corporations. In Alan J. Auerbach, ed., *Fiscal policy: Lessons from Economic Research*. Cambridge: MIT Press.

Hines, James R., Jr. 1999. Lessons from behavioral responses to international taxation. *National Tax Journal* 52: 305–22.

Hines, James R., Jr. 2004. Do tax havens flourish? Working paper 10936. National Bureau of Economic Research, Cambridge, MA.

Hines, James R., Jr., and Eric Rice. 1994. Fiscal paradise: Foreign tax havens and American business. *Quarterly Journal of Economics* 109: 149–82.

Hobbes, Thomas. [1660] 1996. *Leviathan*. Reprint, J. C. A. Gaskin, ed. New York: Oxford University Press.

Holtz-Eakin, Douglas. 1996. Comment. In Henry J. Aaron and William G. Gale, eds., *Economic Effects of Fundamental Tax Reform*. Washington: Brookings Institution.

Hotz, V. Joseph, and John Karl Scholz. 2003. The earned income tax credit. In Robert Moffitt, ed., *Means-Tested Transfers in the U.S.* Chicago: University of Chicago Press.

Hotz, V. Joseph, Finn E. Kydland, and Guilerme L. Sedlacek. 1988. Inter-temporal preferences and labor supply. *Econometrica* 56: 35–60.

House, Christopher L., and Matthew D. Shapiro. 2006. Temporary tax incentives: Theory with evidence from bonus depreciation. Working paper 12514. National Bureau of Economic Research, Cambridge, MA.

Hoynes, Hilary W. 1996. Welfare transfers in two-parent families: Labor supply and welfare participation under AFDC-UP. *Econometrica* 64: 295–332.

Hubbard, R. Glenn. 1997. How different are income and consumption taxes? *American Economic Review* 87: 138–42.

Hubbard, R. Glenn. 1998. Capital-market imperfections and investment. *Journal of Economic Literature* 36: 193–225.

Hubbard, R. Glenn. 2002. Capital income taxation in tax reform: Implications for analysis of distribution and efficiency. In George R. Zodrow and Peter Mieszkowski, eds., *United States Tax Reform in the 21st Century*. Cambridge: Cambridge University Press.

Hurst, Erik, and James P. Ziliak. 2006. Do welfare asset limits affect household saving? Evidence from welfare reform. *Journal of Human Resources* 41: 46–71.

Imai, Susumu, and Michael P. Keane. 2004. Intertemporal labor supply and human capital accumulation. *International Economic Review* 45: 601–41.

Institute for Fiscal Studies. 1978. *The Structure and Reform of Direct Taxation*. London: Allen and Unwin.

Jensen, Michael C. 1986. Agency costs of free cash flow, corporate finance, and takeovers. *American Economic Review* 76: 323–29.

Johnston, David Cay. 2006a. Many utilities collect for taxes they never pay. *New York Times*, March 15.

Johnston, David Cay. 2006b. Special Tax Cost Investors Tax Breaks, Report Shows. *New York Times*, May 10, p. D-2.

Joint Committee on Taxation. 2005a. *Options to Improve Tax Compliance and Reform Tax Expenditures*. JCS-2-50. Washington: Government Printing Office.

Joint Committee on Taxation. 2005b. *Present Law and Background Relating to the Individual Alternative Minimum Tax*. Washington: Government Printing Office.

Joint Committee on Taxation. 2006. *Estimates of Federal Tax Expenditures for Fiscal Years 2006–2010*. Washington: Congressional Printing Office.

Jorgenson, Dale W. 1996. Capital theory and investment behavior. *American Economic Review* 53 (May 1963): 247–59. Reprinted in Dale W. Jorgenson, *Investment. Volume 1: Capital Theory and Investment Behavior*. Cambridge: MIT Press.

Jorgenson, Dale W., and Kun-Young Yun. 2001. *Investment. Volume 3: Lifting the Burden: Tax Reform, the Cost of Capital, and U.S. Economic Growth*. Cambridge: MIT Press.

Judd, Kenneth L. 1985. Redistributive taxation in a simple perfect foresight model. *Journal of Public Economics* 28: 59–83.

Judd, Kenneth L. 1997. The optimal tax rate for capital income is negative. Working paper 6004. National Bureau of Economic Research, Cambridge, MA.

Julio, Brandon, and David Ikenberry. 2004. Reappearing dividends. *Journal of Applied Corporate Finance* 16: 89–100.

Kahneman, Daniel. 2000. Experienced utility and objective happiness: A moment-based approach. In Daniel Kahneman and Amos Tversky, eds., *Choices, Values, and Frames*. Cambridge: Cambridge University Press.

Kahneman, Daniel, Jack Knetsch, and Richard Thaler. 1991. Anomalies: The endowment effect, loss aversion, and status quo bias. *Journal of Economic Perspectives* 5: 193–206.

Kaldor, Nicholas. 1958. *An Expenditure Tax*. London: Allen and Unwin.

Kaplan, Steven N., and Luigi Zingales. 1997. Do investment–cash flow sensitivities provide useful measures of financing constraints? *Quarterly Journal of Economics* 112: 169–215.

Kaplan, Steven N., and Luigi Zingales. 2000. Investment–cash flow sensitivities are not valid measures of financing constraints. *Quarterly Journal of Economics* 115: 707–12.

Kaplow, Louis. 1994. Taxation and risk taking: A general equilibrium perspective. *National Tax Journal* 47: 789–98.

Kawachi, Jannette, Karen E. Smith, and Eric Toder. 2006. *Making Maximum Use of Tax-Deferred Retirement Accounts*. Washington: Urban Institute.

Kay, John A. 1980. The deadweight loss of a tax system. *Journal of Public Economics* 13: 111–19.

Keane, Michael, and Robert Moffitt. 1998. A structural model of multiple welfare program participation and labor supply. *International Economic Review* 39, 553–89.

Killingsworth, Mark. 1983. *Labor Supply*. Cambridge: Cambridge University Press.

Kimmel, Jean, and Thomas J. Kniesner. 1999. New evidence on labor supply: Employment versus hours elasticities by sex and marital status. *Journal of Monetary Economics* 42: 289–301.

King, Mervyn A. 1983. Welfare analysis of tax reforms using household data. *Journal of Public Economics* 21: 183–214.

King, Mervyn A. 1977. *Public Policy and the Corporation*. London: Chapman and Hall.

King, Mervyn A., and Don Fullerton, eds. 1984. *The Taxation of Income from Capital*. Chicago: University of Chicago Press and National Bureau of Economic Research.

Kleinbard, Edward. 2006. Designing an income tax on capital. Paper presented at the American Tax Policy Institute conference on Taxing Capital Income, September.

Kleinbard, Edward. 2005. The business enterprise tax: A prospectus. *Tax Notes*, vol. 106.

Klump, Rainer, and Chris Papageorgiou, eds. forthcoming. *A Bright Future at the Age of 50—The CES Production Function in the Theory and Emprics of Economic Growth.* Conference proceedings to appear in special issue of *Journal of Macroeconomics.*

Kniesner, Thomas J., and James P. Ziliak. 2002a. Tax reform and automatic stabilization. *American Economic Review* 92: 590–612.

Kniesner, Thomas J., and James P. Ziliak. 2002b. Explicit versus implicit income insurance. *Journal of Risk and Uncertainty* 25: 5–20.

Koenig, Gary, and Robert Harvey. 2005. Utilization of the saver's credit: An analysis of the first year. *National Tax Journal* 58: 787–806.

Kooreman, Peter L., and L. Schoonbeek. 2004. Characterizing Pareto improvements in an interdependent demand system. *Journal of Public Economic Theory* 6: 427–43.

Kopczuk, Wojciech. 2005. Tax bases, tax rates, and the elasticity of reported income. *Journal of Public Economics* 89: 2093–2119.

Kotlikoff, Laurence, and Scott Burns. 2004. *The Coming Generational Storm.* Cambridge: MIT Press.

Kotlikoff, Laurence J. 1998. The A-K model: Its past, present and future. Working paper 6684. National Bureau of Economic Research, Cambridge, MA.

Kotlikoff, Laurence J. 2005. Simulating the dynamic micro and macroeconomic effects of the FairTax. Working paper W11858. National Bureau of Economic Research, Cambridge, MA.

Kotlikoff, Lawrence J., and Avia Spivak. 1981. The family as an incomplete annuities market. *Journal of Political Economy* 89: 372–91.

Kotlikoff, Lawrence J., and Lawrence Summers. 1981. The role of intergenerational transfers in aggregate capital accumulation. *Journal of Political Economy* 89: 706–32.

Kotlikoff, Lawrence J., and Sabin JoKisch. 2005. Simulating the dynamic macroeconomic and microeconomic effects of the Fair Tax. Working paper 11858. National Bureau of Economic Research, Cambridge, MA.

Kueschnigg, Christian. 1990. Corporate taxation and growth: Dynamic general equilibrium simulation study. In Johann Brunner and Hans-Georg Petersen, eds., *Simulation Models in Tax and Transfer Policy.* Berlin: Campus Verlag.

Kumar, Anil. 2005. Lifecycle consistent estimation of effect of taxes on female labor supply in the U.S: Evidence from panel data. Manuscript. Federal Reserve Bank of Dallas.

Laibson, David. 1997. Golden eggs and hyperbolic discounting. *Quarterly Journal of Economics* 112: 443–77.

Lazear, Edward P., and James M. Poterba. 2005. Reforming taxes to promote economic growth. *Economists' Voice* 3 (December 13).

Loewenstein, George, Deborah A. Small, and Jeff Strnad. 2006. Statistical, identifiable, and iconic victims. In Edward J. McCaffery and Joel C. Slemrod, eds., *Behavioral Public Finance.* New York: Russell Sage.

Low, Hamish, and Daniel Maldoom. 2004. Optimal taxation, prudence, and risk sharing. *Journal of Public Economics* 88: 443–64.

Lundberg, Shelly, Robert Pollak, and Terrence Wales. 1997. Do husbands and wives pool resources? Evidence from the UK child benefit. *Journal of Human Resources* 32: 463–80.

Lyon, Andrew B., and Peter R. Merrill. 2001. Asset price effects of fundamental tax reform. In Kevin A. Hassett and Glenn R. Hubbard, eds., *Transition Costs of Fundamental Tax Reform*. Washington: AEI Press.

MaCurdy, Thomas. 1981. An empirical model of labor supply in a life-cycle setting. *Journal of Political Economy* 89: 1059–85.

MaCurdy, Thomas. 1983. A simple scheme for estimating an inter-temporal model of labor supply and consumption in the presence of taxes and uncertainty. *International Economic Review* 24: 265–89.

MaCurdy, Thomas, David Green, and Harry Paarsch. 1990. Assessing empirical approaches for analyzing taxes and labor supply. *Journal of Human Resources* 25: 415–89.

Madrian, Brigitte, and Dennis Shea. 2001. The power of suggestion: Inertia in 401(k) participation and savings behavior. *Quarterly Journal of Economics* 116: 1149–87.

Malin, Benjamin A. 2005. Hyperbolic discounting and uniform savings floors. Discussion paper 04-34. Stanford Institute for Economic Policy Research, Stanford, CA.

Mankiw, N. Gregory, and Matthew Weinzierl. 2006. Dynamic scoring: A back-of-the-envelope guide. *Journal of Public Economics*, forthcoming.

Martin, Cathie Jo. 1991. *Shifting the Burden: The Struggle over Growth and Corporate Taxation*. Chicago: University of Chicago Press.

McCaffery, Edward J. 1992. Tax policy under a hybrid income-consumption tax. *Texas Law Review* 70: 1145–1218.

McCaffery, Edward J. 1994a. Cognitive theory and tax. *UCLA Law Review* 41: 1861–1947.

McCaffery, Edward J. 1994b. Why people play lotteries, and why it matters. *Wisconsin Law Review* 1994: 71–122.

McCaffery, Edward J. 2000. The tyranny of money. *Michigan Law Review* 98: 2126–53.

McCaffery, Edward J. 2002. *Fair Not Flat: How to Make the Tax System Better and Simpler*. Chicago: University of Chicago Press.

McCaffery, Edward J. 2005a. A new understanding of tax. *Michigan Law Review* 103: 807–938.

McCaffery, Edward J. 2005b. Three views of tax. *Canadian Journal of Law and Jurisprudence* 18: 153–64.

McCaffery, Edward J. 2005c. Good hybrids/bad hybrids. *Tax Notes* (June 27): 1699–705.

McCaffery, Edward J., and Jon Baron. 2006. Thinking about tax. *Psychology, Public Policy and Law* 12: 106–35.

McCaffery, Edward J., and Linda R. Cohen. 2006. Shakedown at Gucci gulch: The new logic of collective action. *University of North Carolina Law Review* 84: 101–94.

McCaffery, Edward J., and Joel Slemrod. 2004. Introduction. In *Toward an Agenda for Behavioral Public Finance*. Draft, April 19, 2004.

McCaffery, Edward J., and Joel Slemrod, eds. 2006. *Behavioral Public Finance*. New York: Russell Sage.

McFadden, Daniel. 2005. The new science of pleasure: Consumer behavior and the measurement of well-being. Frisch lecture. Econometric Society World Congress.

McLure, Charles E., Jr. 1988. The 1986 Act: Tax reform's finest hour or death throes of the income tax? *National Tax Journal* 41: 303–15.

McLure, Charles E., Jr., and George R. Zodrow. 1987. Treasury I and the Tax Reform Act of 1986: The economics and politics of tax reform. *Journal of Economic Perspectives* 1: 37–58.

McLure, Charles E., Jr., and George R. Zodrow. 1996. A hybrid approach to the direct taxation of consumption. In Michael J. Boskin, ed., *Frontiers of Tax Reform*. Stanford: Hoover Institution Press, pp. 70–90.

Merrill, Peter R., and Harold Adrion. 1995. Treatment of financial services under consumption-based tax systems. *Tax Notes* 68: 1496–1500.

Meyer, Bruce, and Dan Rosenbaum. 2001. Welfare, the earned income tax credit, and the labor supply of single mothers. *Quarterly Journal of Economics* 116: 1063–1114.

Mieszkowski, Peter, and Michael G. Palumbo. 2002. Distributive analysis of fundamental tax reform. In George R. Zodrow and Peter Mieszkowski, eds., *United States Tax Reform in the 21st Century*. Cambridge: Cambridge University Press.

Mill, John Stuart. [1848] 1994. *Principles of Political Economy*. Reprint Jonathan Riley, ed. New York: Oxford University Press.

Miller, Merton. 1977. Debt and taxes. *Journal of Finance* 32: 261–75.

Mills, Lillian, Edward Maydew, and Merle Erickson. 1998. Investments in tax planning. *Journal of the American Taxation Association* 20: 1–19.

Modigliani, Francisco. 1988. The role of intergenerational transfers and life cycle saving in the accumulation of wealth. *Journal of Economic Perspectives* 2: 15–40.

Modigliani, Francisco, and Richard Brumberg. 1954. Utility analysis and the consumption function: An interpretation of cross-section data. In Kenneth K. Kurihara, ed., *Post-Keynesian Economics*. New Brunswick: Rutgers University Press.

Modigliani, Franco, and Merton Miller. 1961. Corporate income taxes and the cost of capital. *American Economic Review* 53: 433–43.

Moffitt, Robert, and Mark Wilhelm. 2000. Taxation and the labor supply decisions of the affluent. In Joel Slemrod, ed., *Does Atlas Shrug? The Economic Consequences of Taxing the Rich*. New York: Russell Sage.

Moyen, Nathalie. 2004. Investment–cash flow sensitivities: Constrained versus unconstrained firms. *Journal of Finance* 59: 2061–92.

Mroz, Thomas. 1987. The sensitivity of an empirical model of married women's hours of work to economic and statistical assumptions. *Econometrica* 55: 765–99.

Muthitacharoen, Athiphat, and George R. Zodrow. 2006. State and local taxation of business property: A small open economy perspective. *Proceedings of the Ninety-Eighth Annual Conference on Taxation.* Washington: National Tax Association, pp. 434–40.

Mutti, John. 2003. *Foreign Direct Investment and Tax Competition.* Washington: IIE Press.

Mutti, John, and Harry Grubert. 2006. New developments in the effect of taxes on royalties and the migration of intangible assets abroad. Paper presented at the CRIW conference on International Services Flow, April.

Nelson, Robert H. 2006. An accidental tax boon. *Washington Post,* June 1, p. A-19.

Neubig, Tom. 2006. Where's the applause? Why most corporations prefer a lower rate. *Tax Notes* (April 24): 483–86.

Norquist, Grover. 2002. Five easy steps to tax reform. *American Enterprise Magazine,* December, p. 18.

Oettinger, Gerald S. 1999. An empirical analysis of the daily labor supply of stadium vendors. *Journal of Political Economy* 107: 360–92.

Office of Tax Analysis, US Department of the Treasury. 2006. A dynamic analysis of permanent extension of the president's tax relief. Office of Tax Analysis, US Department of the Treasury.

Parente, Stephen L., and Edward C. Prescott. 2000. *Barriers to Riches.* Cambridge: MIT Press.

Pechman, Joseph A., ed. 1980. *What Should Be Taxed, Income or Expenditure?* Washington: Brookings Institution Press.

Pechman, Joseph A., ed. 1984. *Options for Tax Reform.* Washington: Brookings Institution Press.

Pencavel, John. 1986. Labor supply of men. In Orley Ashenfelter and Richard Layard, eds., *Handbook of Labor Economics,* vol. 1. Amsterdam: North-Holland.

Poterba, James M., Steven F. Venti, and David A. Wise. 1996. How retirement saving programs increase saving. *Journal of Economic Perspectives* 10: 91–112.

Poterba, James M. 1992. Taxation and housing: Old questions, new answers. *American Economic Review* 82: 237–42.

Poterba, James M. 1994. State responses to fiscal crises: The effects of budgetary institutions and politics. *Journal of Political Economy* 102: 799–821.

Poterba, James M. 2004a. Taxation and corporate payout policy. *American Economic Review* 94: 171–75.

Poterba, James M. 2004b. Valuing assets in retirement saving accounts. *National Tax Journal* 75: 489–512.

Poterba, James M., and Lawrence H. Summers. 1985. The economic effects of dividend taxation. In Edward I. Ahman and Marti G. Subrahmanyan, eds., *Recent Advances in Corporate Finance.* Homewood: Irwin.

Prescott, Edward C. 2004. Why do Americans work so much more than Europeans? *Federal Reserve Bank of Minneapolis Quarterly Review* 28: 2–13.

Prescott, Edward C. 2005. The elasticity of labor supply and the consequences for tax policy. In Alan J. Auerbach and Kevin A. Hassett, eds., *Toward Fundamental Tax Reform*. Washington: AEI Press.

President's Advisory Panel on Federal Tax Reform. 2005. *Simple, Fair, and Pro-Growth: Proposals to Fix America's Tax System*. Washington: Government Printing Office.

Price Waterhouse. 2002. *Corporate Taxes—A Worldwide Summary*. Washington: Price-Waterhouse.

Rabin, Matthew. 2002. A perspective on psychology and economics. Alfred Marshall lecture. *European Economic Review* 46: 657–85.

Randolph, William. 2005. *Corporate Income Tax Rates: International Comparisons*. Washington: Congressional Budget Office.

Rauch, Jonathan. 2006. A bad tax with good timing. *National Journal*, March 18, p. 16.

Rawls, John. 1971. *A Theory of Justice*. Cambridge: Harvard University Press.

Razin, Assaf, and Efraim Sadka. 2006. Vying for foreign direct investment: A EU-type model of tax competition. Working paper 11991. National Bureau of Economic Research, Cambridge, MA.

Razin, Assaf, Yona Rubinstein, and Efraim Sadka. 2004. Fixed costs and FDI: The conflicting effects of productivity shocks. Working paper 10864. National Bureau of Economic Research, Cambridge, MA.

Razin, Assaf, Yona Rubinstein, and Efraim Sadka. 2005. Corporate taxation and bilateral FDI with threshold barriers. Working paper 11196. National Bureau of Economic Research, Cambridge, MA.

Richman, Peggy B. 1963. *Taxation of Foreign Investment Income: An Economic Analysis*. Baltimore: Johns Hopkins University Press.

Ring, Raymond R., Jr. 1999. Consumer's and producer's share of the general sales tax. *National Tax Journal* 52: 79–90.

Rosen, Harvey S. 1985. Housing subsidies: Effects on housing decisions, efficiency, and equity. In Alan J. Auerbach and Martin Feldstein, eds., *Handbook of Public Economics*, vol. 1. Amsterdam: North-Holland: Elsevier Science.

Runkle, David E. 1991. Liquidity constraints and the permanent-income hypothesis: Evidence from panel data. *Journal of Monetary Economics* 27: 73–98.

Saez, Emmanuel. 2001. Using elasticities to derive optimal income tax rates. *Review of Economic Studies* 68: 205–29.

Saez, Emmanuel. 2002. Optimal income transfer programs: Intensive versus extensive labor supply responses. *Quarterly Journal of Economics* 117: 1039–73.

Saez, Emmanuel. 2003. The effect of marginal tax rates on income: A panel study of "bracket creep." *Journal of Public Economics* 87: 1231–58.

Sah, Raaj Kumar. 1983. How much redistribution is possible through commodity taxes? *Journal of Public Economics* 20: 89–101.

Scholz, John Karl, Ananth Seshadri, and Surachai Khitatrakun. 2006. Are Americans saving "optimally" for retirement? *Journal of Political Economy* 114: 607–43.

Seidman, Laurence. 1995. *The USA Tax.* Cambridge: MIT Press.

Sen, Amartya K. 1961. On optimising the rate of saving. *Economic Journal* 71: 479–96.

Shafir, Eldar, Peter Diamond, and Amos Tversky. 1997. Money illusion. *Quarterly Journal of Economics* 112: 341–74.

Shakow, David. 1986. Taxation without realization: A proposal for accrual taxation. *University of Pennsylvania Law Review* 134: 1111–1205.

Shapiro, Matthew D. 1986. The dynamic demand for capital and labor. *Quarterly Journal of Economics* 101: 513–42.

Shaviro, Daniel. 1989. Selective limitations on tax benefits. *University of Chicago Law Review* 56: 1189–1260.

Shaviro, Daniel. 1990. Beyond public choice and public interest: A study of the legislative process as illustrated by tax legislation in the 1980s. *University of Pennsylvania Law Review* 139: 1–123.

Shaviro, Daniel. 2000. *When Rules Change: An Economic and Political Analysis of Transition Relief and Retroactivity.* Chicago: University of Chicago Press.

Shaviro, Daniel. 2004. Replacing the income tax with a progressive consumption tax, *Tax Notes* 103: 91–161.

Shaviro, Daniel. 2005. A blueprint for tax reform? Evaluating Reform Panel's report. *Tax Notes* (November 7): 827–35.

Shaviro, Daniel. 2006. *Taxes, Spending, and the U.S. Government's March Towards Bankruptcy.* New York: Cambridge University Press.

Shaw, Kathryn. 1989. Life-cycle labor supply with human capital accumulation. *International Economic Review* 30: 431–56.

Shefrin, Hersh M., and Richard H. Thaler. 1988. The behavioral life-cycle hypothesis. *Economic Inquiry* 26: 609–43.

Shiller, Robert J. 1989. *Market Volatility.* Cambridge: MIT Press.

Shiller, Robert J. 2000. *Irrational Exuberance in the Media.* Princeton: Princeton University Press.

Shleifer, Andrei, and Robert W. Vishny. 1997. A survey of corporate governance. *Journal of Finance* 52: 737–83.

Sialm, Clemens. 2005. Tax changes and asset pricing: Time-series evidence. Working paper 11756. National Bureau of Economic Research, Cambridge, MA.

Sieg, Holger. 2000. Estimating a dynamic model of household choices in the presence of income taxation. *International Economic Review* 41: 637–68.

Simons, Henry C. 1938. *Personal Income Taxation: The Definition of Income as a Problem of Fiscal Policy.* Chicago: University of Chicago Press.

Slemrod, Joel. 1990a. Optimal tax and optimal tax systems. *Journal of Economic Perspectives* 4: 157–78.

Slemrod, Joel. 1990b. The economic impact of tax reform. In Joel Slemrod, ed., *Do Taxes Matter? The Impact of the Tax Reform Act of 1986.* Cambridge: MIT Press, pp. 1–12.

Slemrod, Joel. 1998. Methodological issues in measuring and interpreting taxable income elasticities. *National Tax Journal* 51: 773–88.

Slemrod, Joel. 2001. A general model of the behavioral response to taxation. *International Tax and Public Finance* 8: 119–28.

Slemrod, Joel, and Marsha Blumenthal. 1996. The income tax compliance cost of big business. *Public Finance Quarterly* 24: 411–38.

Slemrod, Joel, and Varsha Venkatesh. 2002. *The Income Tax Compliance Costs of Large and Mid-Sized Businesses*. Report to the Internal Revenue Service Large and Mid-Size Business Division, Washington, DC, September.

Smith, Adam. [1776] 2003. *The Wealth of Nations*. Reprint, Alan B. Krueger (Introduction). New York: Bantam.

Snow, Arthur, and Ronald Warren. 1996. The marginal welfare cost of public funds: Theory and estimates. *Journal of Public Economics* 61: 289–305.

Stamper, Dustin. 2005. House taxwriter gives Democratic tax reform efforts a boost. *Tax Notes* 109: 1499–1503.

Steuerle, Eugene. 1985. *Taxes, Loans, and Inflation*. Washington: Brookings Institution.

Steuerle, Gene. 2005. *Contemporary U.S. Tax Policy*. Washington: Urban Institute Press.

Stiglitz, Joseph E. 1973. Taxation, corporate financial policy, and the cost of capital. *Journal of Public Economics* 2: 1–34.

Strawczynski, Michel. 1998. Social insurance and the optimum piecewise linear income tax. *Journal of Public Economics* 69: 371–88.

Sullivan, Martin A. 2004a. U.S. multinationals move more profits to tax havens. *Tax Notes* 102: 690–93.

Sullivan, Martin A. 2004b. Data show dramatic shift of profits to tax havens. *Tax Notes* 104: 1190–94.

Summers, Lawrence H. 1981a. Capital taxation and accumulation in a life-cycle model. *American Economic Review* 71: 533–44.

Summers, Lawrence H. 1981b. Taxation and corporate investment: A q-theory approach. *Brookings Papers on Economic Activity* 1: 67–127.

Surrey, Stanley S. 1973. *Pathways to Tax Reform: The Concept of Tax Expenditures*. Cambridge: Harvard University Press.

Surrey, Stanley S., and Paul McDaniel. 1985. *Tax Expenditures*. Cambridge: Harvard University Press.

Swenson, Deborah L. 2001. Tax reforms and evidence of transfer pricing. *National Tax Journal* 54: 7–26.

Thaler, Richard H. 1994. Psychology and savings policies. *American Economic Review* 84: 186–92.

Thaler, Richard H., and Hersh M. Shefrin. 1981. An economic theory of self-control. *Journal of Political Economy* 89: 392–406.

Triest, Robert K. 1990. The effect of income taxation on labor supply in the United States. *Journal of Human Resources* 25: 491–516.

Triest, Robert K. 1992. The effect of income taxation on labor supply when deductions are endogenous. *Review of Economics and Statistics* 25: 91–99.

Triest, Robert K. 1994. The efficiency cost of increased progressivity. In Joel Slemrod, ed., *Tax Progressivity and Income Inequality*. Cambridge: Cambridge University Press.

Tversky, Amos, and Daniel Kahneman. 1986. Rational choice and the framing of decisions. *Journal of Business* 59: 5251–78.

US Bureau of Economic Analysis. 2004. National income and product accounts. *Survey of Current Business*, vol. 84, 11.

US Bureau of Economic Analysis. 2005. National income and product accounts. *Survey of Current Business*, vol. 85, 7.

US Department of the Treasury. 1977. *Blueprints for Basic Tax Reform*. Washington: Government Printing Office.

US Department of the Treasury. 1992. *Integration of the Individual and Corporate Tax Systems: Taxing Business Income Once*. Washington: Government Printing Office.

US Department of the Treasury. 2003. *General Explanations of the Administration's Fiscal Year 2004 Revenue Proposals*. Washington: Government Printing Office.

US General Accounting Office. 1988. *IRS' Tax Gap Studies*. GAO/GGD-88-66BR. Washington: General Accounting Office.

US Government Accountability Office. 2005. Summary of estimates of the costs of the federal tax system. Washington: General Accounting Office.

US Internal Revenue Service. 2004. *Interactive Tax Gap Map*. Washington: National Headquarters Office of Research, March.

Unger, Roberto Mangabiera. 2000. *Democracy Realized: The Progressive Alternative*. New York: Verso.

Van Soest, Arthur. 1995. Structural models of family labor supply: A discrete choice approach. *Journal of Human Resources* 30: 63–88.

Varian, Hal. 1980. Redistributive taxation as social insurance. *Journal of Public Economics* 14: 49–68.

Venti, Stephen F., and David A. Wise. 1986. Tax-deferred accounts, constrained choice, and the estimation of individual saving. *Review of Economic Studies* 53: 579–601.

Venti, Stephen F., and David A. Wise. 1992. Government policy and personal retirement saving. In Lawrence Summers, ed., *Tax Policy and the Economy*, Cambridge, MA: MIT Press.

Viard, Alan D. 2006. The alternative minimum tax: A better system? *Tax Policy Outlook* 1: 1–6.

Warren, Alvin C., Jr. 1975. Fairness and a consumption-type or cash-flow personal income tax. *Harvard Law Review* 88: 931–46.

Warren, Alvin C., Jr. 1980. Would a consumption tax be fairer than an income tax? *Yale Law Journal* 89: 1081–1124.

Warren, Alvin C., Jr. 1996. How much capital income taxed under an income tax would be exempt under a cash-flow tax? *Tax Law Review* 52: 1–16.

Weisbach, David A. 2000. Ironing out the flat tax. *Stanford Law Review* 52: 599–664.

Weisbach, David A. 2003. Does the X-tax mark the spot? *SMU Law Review* 56: 201–38.

Weisbach, David A. 2004. The (non)taxation of risk. *Tax Law Review* 58: 1–57.

Weisbach, David A. 2006. The case for a consumption tax. *Tax Notes* 110: 1357–59.

Westin, Richard. 1997. Addressing tax revolutions that lack empirical validity. *Tax Notes* 76: 259–69.

Wildasin, David. 1984. On public good provision with distortionary taxation. *Economic Inquiry* 22: 227–43.

Zeldes, Stephen P. 1989. Consumption and liquidity constraints: An empirical investigation. *Journal of Political Economy* 97: 305–46.

Zhou, Chunsheng. 2000. Time-to-build and investment. *Review of Economics and Statistics* 82: 273–82.

Ziliak, James P. 2005. Taxes, transfers, and the labor supply of single mothers. Manuscript. University of Kentucky.

Ziliak, James P., and Thomas J. Kniesner. 1999. Estimating life-cycle labor-supply tax effects. *Journal of Political Economy* 107: 326–59.

Ziliak, James P., and Thomas J. Kniesner. 2005. The effect of income taxation on consumption and labor supply. *Journal of Labor Economics* 23: 769–96.

Zodrow, George R. 1988. The windfall recapture tax: Issues of theory and design. *Public Finance Quarterly* 16: 387–424.

Zodrow, George R. 2002. Transitional issues in the implementation of a flat tax or a national retail sales tax. In George R. Zodrow and Peter Mieszkowski, eds., *United States Tax Reform in the 21st Century*. Cambridge: Cambridge University Press.

Zodrow, George R. 2005. Should capital income be subject to consumption-based taxation? Paper presented at the American Tax Policy Institute conference on Taxing Capital Income, September.

Zodrow, George R., and Peter Mieszkowski. 1989. Taxation and the tiebout model: The differential effects of head taxes, taxes on land rents and property taxes. *Journal of Economic Literature* 27: 1098–1146.

Zodrow, George R., and Peter Mieszkowski. 2002a. The fundamental question of fundamental tax reform. In George R. Zodrow and Peter Mieszkowski, eds., *United States Tax Reform in the 21st Century*. Cambridge: Cambridge University Press.

Zodrow, George R., and Peter Mieszkowski. 2002b. *United States Tax Reform in the 21st Century*. Cambridge: Cambridge University Press.

Index